INTERNATIONAL TRADE AND BUSINESS LAW ANNUAL

Information For Contributors

International Trade and Business Law Annual is the official publication of the Australian Institute of Foreign and Comparative Law of The University of Queensland, Australia. The Annual acknowledges the financial support of Mayer, Brown & Platt, Lawyers, Chicago. The Annual is published by Cavendish (Australia) Pty Ltd.

International Trade and Business Law Annual publishes articles, comments and book reviews dealing with international commercial law, foreign law and comparative law. This issue of the Annual may be referred to as (2002) 7 ITBLA.

International Trade and Business Law Annual welcomes the submission of manuscripts for consideration by the editors with a view to publication. Manuscripts should be sent to:

The Editors
International Trade and Business Law Annual
The Australian Institute of Foreign and Comparative Law
TC Beirne School of Law
The University of Queensland
St Lucia, Qld 4072
Australia

Telephone: 61 07 3365 3053
Facsimile: 61 07 3365 1466
Email: g.moens@mailbox.uq.edu.au

International Trade and Business Law Annual is a fully refereed publication. At present, the Annual is published once a year. Contributors are requested to comply with the style guide, a copy of which is available on request from the editors. A manuscript should not normally exceed 10,000 words and should be an unpublished work or a work over which the contributor has copyright. The manuscript should be typed, double spaced, on one side only of A4 paper. Footnotes should be numbered consecutively through the article and should appear at the end of each page. Contributors are required to submit a hard copy and a copy on a 3½ inch disk (Word 7).

INTERNATIONAL TRADE AND BUSINESS LAW ANNUAL

First published 2002 by Cavendish Publishing (Australia) Pty Limited, 3/303 Barrenjoey Road, Newport, New South Wales 2106

Telephone: (02) 9999 2777 Facsimile: (02) 9999 3688

Email: info@cavendishpublishing.com.au

Cavendish Publishing Limited, The Glass House, Wharton Street, London WC1X 9PX, United Kingdom

Telephone: +44 (0)20 7278 8000 Facsimile: +44 (0)20 7278 8080

Email: info@cavendishpublishing.com

Website: www.cavendishpublishing.com

ISBN 1 876213 40 X

Printed and bound in Great Britain

INTERNATIONAL TRADE AND BUSINESS LAW ANNUAL
VOLUME 7 2002

Tang Thanh Trai Le, Emeritus Professor of Law, University of Notre Dame, Indiana

Hans Van Houtte, Professor of Law, University of Leuven, Belgium

Geoffrey de Q Walker, Emeritus Professor of Law, Formerly Dean and Head, TC Beirne School of Law, The University of Queensland

Contributors

Phuong-Trinh Nguyen, Vietnamese Lawyer

Jacqueline Mowbray, Solicitor, Freehills, Melbourne

Tim Sherman, Solicitor, Mallesons Stephen Jaques, Melbourne

David Morrison, Senior Lecturer in Law, TC Beirne School of Law, The University of Queensland

Jeffrey Weeks, Australian Aviation Lawyer

Steve Williams, Senior Lecturer in Management, The University of Queensland

GL Davies, Judge, Court of Appeals, Brisbane

Annelies Moens, Compliance Officer, Federal Privacy Commissioner, Australia

Andrew Stumer, Judge's Associate, Supreme Court, Queensland

JA Tarr, Senior Lecturer in Law, TC Beirne School of Law, The University of Queensland

John Trone, Australian Lawyer

Bruno Zeller, Lecturer in Law, Victoria University of Technology

Acknowledgments

The editors would like to thank the following attorneys and summer associates at the Law Firm of Mayer, Brown & Platt for their invaluable assistance with the editing of the articles in this issue:

Attorneys

Gary S Colton, Jr

Gayle L Elsner

Neville S Hedley

John Hildy

Matthew C Houchens

Neil B Posner

Wladek Rzycki

Stuart E Thiel

Russell R Young

Summer Associates

Tiffany P Cunningham

Dana S Douglas

Kristen R Seeger

Technology. In 1991, the tax controversy group tried a significant case for Westreco before the US Tax Court. This transfer pricing case involved the allocation of income between Nestlé SA and Westreco, a US research and development subsidiary of Nestlé SA. Additionally, the group has represented several clients, including the Hitachi companies and Commodore International Ltd, in successfully defending against Internal Revenue Service summons enforcement cases in federal district courts.

CONTENTS

Book Reviews

BOOK NOTICE

The Taiwanese Semiconductor Industry's Experience with US Antidumping Law: a View from the Defense

Kok-Choo Chen

Introduction

When the Taiwanese semiconductor industry found itself a defendant in multiple antidumping actions that threatened to block its access to the US market, industry management faced the unenviable task of educating itself on the complex, and somewhat arcane, US antidumping law and devising an effective strategy for defending its interests. This article recounts the experience of the Taiwanese industry in this ordeal in the hope that it might benefit other exporters similarly targeted in the future. The lessons learned from the experience of Taiwan's semiconductor industry apply to all sectors potentially subject to US antidumping litigation. This article first explores the history of antidumping proceedings in the semiconductor sector. It then provides a brief overview of the antidumping process, and finally discusses Taiwan's efforts to mount a successful defense.

I A pattern revealed in the history of antidumping proceedings in the semiconductor sector

Trade in semiconductors in the US market, particularly memory semiconductors, such as dynamic random access memory devices (DRAMs) and static random access memory devices (SRAMs) devices, has been remarkably acrimonious and litigious. A review of the unique trade pattern for these devices explains why it gives rise to such tension.

In the 1980s, with the advent of the personal computer (PC) revolution, trade in memory semiconductors, which were a critical input to PCs, mushroomed. Production of these devices required manufacturing prowess as constant expansion of computing capacity impelled a race to develop new 'denser' generations of chips, 'shrinking' ever more transistors onto a single memory chip. This, in turn, required increased capital investment because production of new generations of chips required new production lines comprising highly sophisticated and expensive technology and equipment.[1]

---

1 Each generation of DRAM devices normally constitutes a fourfold increase in density from the previous generation. Thus, the 1 megabit DRAM (1 million transistors on one chip) gave way to the 4 megabit DRAM, which was supplanted by the 16 megabit DRAM.

Like other goods dependent on mass production, these memory devices are commodity products. Yet they have a unique market cycle driven by two critical factors. First, in the production of each new generation of memory semiconductors, prices and unit costs are initially high, but fall rapidly after manufacturing bugs are resolved and high volume production is stepped up. Second, the market for memory devices is infamously volatile because producers plan investment and production decisions based on fallible projections for future world-wide demand for memory, which is largely dependent on projections of world-wide demand for PCs. When projections overestimate demand, there is oversupply, prices decline, and producers who have made substantial investments suffer losses. Conversely, when projections underestimate demand, prices soar and producers make handsome profits. These cyclical swings generally have occurred every 3–5 years.

The classic 'boom and bust' nature of the memory industry, caused by this unique combination of global market forces is virtually taken for granted. One must say 'virtually' because the US memory industry, largely represented by a single company, Micron Technology, Inc, has added a different spin. The US PC industry has a sizable share of the global PC market, and memory imports are drawn to the US as supply follows demand. When US demand has decreased and prices have fallen, Micron has blamed imports. Micron has manifested this blame by filing antidumping complaints with the US government. A dumping complaint alleges that imports of 'unfairly' priced products are materially injuring US producers, and demands that duties be imposed on these imports to offset the 'unfair' pricing.

In the past 15 years, these complaints have followed each major market downturn, and have targeted whoever was the new market entrant of the moment. A review of the period bears out this tactic, as first Japan, then Korea, and finally Taiwan were marked for attack.

A Japan as a target

In the mid 1980s, when the global memory industry was still in its early years, the target was Japan. Japan was emerging as a highly skilled manufacturer of memory devices during a period of trade friction between the US and Japan. The market tailed-off into a serious decline largely because of global mis-forecasts of demand, and consequent over investment and oversupply. Many producers suffered significant losses, and some in the US opted out of the volatile memory market entirely and into more lucrative areas such as logic products.

Faced with pressure from the US memory industry, the US government initiated an antidumping action against Japanese DRAMs in 1985.[2] US

2 Dynamic Random Access Memory Semiconductors (DRAMs) of 256k and above from Japan, 50 Fed Reg 51,450 (Dec 17, 1985).

producers filed an antidumping case against another type of Japanese memory product in the same year.[3] Because the cases were filed when prices were in a severe down-cycle, and given the inherent bias in the antidumping law against exporters, the US authorities initially ruled that Japanese memory devices were injuring the US industry, and were being sold at 'dumped' prices.[4]

Eventually the main Japanese exporters entered into agreements with the Department of Commerce (DOC) 'suspending' the investigations. Under these agreements, they committed to sell in the US at a pre-approved minimum price, which would be higher than their full cost of production.[5] These government-enforced arrangements arguably had the effect of helping the Japanese exporters by enforcing a minimum, highly profitable US price for all Japanese exports, which the suppliers themselves were banned from enforcing because of US antitrust laws. Like most protectionist measures, they also hurt the immediate US consumer, the PC industry, which had to pay higher prices for critical inputs. These cumbersome, closely supervised agreements were revised in 1991 to reduce the US government's oversight role, although the Japanese companies continued to be obligated to sell above their full cost of production.[6]

---

3 Intel Corp AMD, Inc and National Semiconductor Corp filed an antidumping petition against erasable programmable read only memories (EPROMs, in response to which, the US Department of Commerce initiated an investigation: Erasable Programmable Read Only Memories (EPROMs) from Japan, 50 Fed Reg 43,603 (Oct 21, 1985)

4 EPROMs from Japan, 50 Fed Reg 47,852 (Nov 20, 1985) (ITC injury); 51 Fed Reg 39,680 (Oct 30, 1986) (DOC dumping); DRAMs from Japan, 51 Fed Reg 4,661 (Jan 22, 1986) (ITC injury); 51 Fed Reg 9,457 (Mar 19, 1986) (DOC dumping).

5 DRAMs from Japan, 51 Fed Reg 28,396 (Aug 7, 1986); EPROMs from Japan, 51 Fed Reg 28,253 (Aug 6, 1986). The major Japanese exporters entered the Agreement with the Commerce Department. Under the Agreement, each was required to obtain prior approval from Commerce for prices of memory products to be sold in the United States each quarter, to file with Commerce voluminous price and cost data each quarter, and to submit to on-site audits of prices and production costs each quarter.

6 The EPROM Suspension Agreement was revised in 1991 to reflect a standard price undertaking under US law. Signatory exporters were obligated to collect and maintain the previous four quarter's price and production cost data, and to have this information ready to submit to the US government on a 'fast track' basis (ie, within 14 days). The Agreement did not require quarterly submission to the US government, or pre-approval of US prices. 56 Fed Reg 37,523 (Aug 7, 1991).

The DRAM Agreement was terminated (51 Fed Reg 37,522), and was replaced by a looser, government-to-government understanding called the 'Semiconductor Arrangement'. See Exchange of Letters between the United States Trade Representative and the Embassy of Japan, June 19, 1991. Under this unusual and controversial Arrangement, the Japanese government agreed to encourage the Japanese semiconductor producers to maintain and collect cost and price data (in a manner similar to EPROMs above) for six types of semiconductors, including DRAMs, and to submit the data on a 'fast-track' basis in the event that a dumping case was initiated against the product.

The Arrangement also called for both governments to monitor the share of Japan's semiconductor market accounted for by 'foreign' suppliers, and to seek a foreign share of 20%. This latter provision resulted in controversy about US efforts to force managed trade, and to force Japanese buyers to discriminate in favor of US suppliers at the expense of other foreign suppliers. It also led to disagreements between Japan and the United States as to how to measure foreign market share, with each government issuing its own quarterly statistics.

When these revised agreements expired five years later in 1996, the Japanese government and industry, using the growing market share of US semiconductor producers in Japan as leverage, objected to continued government involvement in overseeing data collection and market penetration. The resulting compromise, which favored Japan, was a voluntary agreement between the US and Japanese private industry associations to collect cost and sales data on a 'fast-track' basis, with the interesting twist that the US side, namely Micron, was also committed to collecting data.[7] As part of the compromise, the two industry groups also agreed to create what was to become the World Semiconductor Council (WSC), with membership open, at US insistence, only to industry groups from countries that had eliminated all semiconductor tariffs or had committed to do so.[8] The European producers, although disappointed they were not included at the outset, joined the WSC shortly thereafter, and the Council eventually welcomed Korea and Taiwan. The governmental role was limited to a loose, information-sharing counterpart of the WSC known as the Global Government Forum, open to all countries.[9] The Forum had no mandate to oversee market share or antidumping data collection. In 1999, the WSC was renewed by the relevant industry associations.[10]

Japan was determined to defend itself against US antidumping actions and its efforts were not without success. Japan has not been the target of a US antidumping investigation in over ten years, and its early defense resulted in the creation of institutions and the development of procedures that remain relevant today.

It is worth noting that European memory producers, observing the effectiveness of the antidumping initiative of the US industry, emulated this strategy. In 1986, European producers filed an antidumping complaint against Japanese exporters of certain memory products.[11] In 1987, the European

---

7 See, Electronic Industries Association of Japan ('EIAJ')/ US Semiconductor Industry Association ('SIA') Statement Regarding Effective and Expeditious Antidumping Measures. Dec 19, 1996.

8 See, The Agreement Between the EIAJ and SIA on International Cooperation Regarding Semiconductors, Aug 2, 1996, known as the 'Vancouver Agreement.' The Agreement was renewed in 1999.

The WSC is a cooperative information sharing arrangement covering such issues as environment, technology and industry promotion. It does not cover fast-track submission of data for antidumping purposes, which is limited to the United States and Japan.

9 Agreement Establishing A New World Semiconductor Council, April 1999, between charter members the EIAJ, SIA, European Electric Component Manufacturers Assoc. (EECA) and the Korean Semiconductor Industry Association (KSIA). The Governments agreed to continue their general meetings on semiconductor issues through a Global Consultative mechanism. See, Joint Statement Concerning Semiconductors by the Governments of the United States, Japan, Korea, and the European Communities and Their Member States (Apr 1999).

10 Joint Statement by the Government of Japan and the Government of the United States Concerning Semiconductors, Aug 2, 1999.

11 The European Electronic Component Manufacturers Association ('EECA') and SGS-Thomson filed an antidumping complaint against seven Japanese manufacturers of EPROMs in 1986.

industry filed an antidumping complaint against Japanese DRAM exporters.[12] Like the US government, the EC Commission first determined that the Japanese exporters were dumping, and then entered a settlement arrangement, which called for the quarterly submission of prices and costs to the EU Commission by the Japanese exporters.[13] Later, as in the US, the Japanese producers successfully pressed for the elimination of the government from the settlement process. As a result, the EC cases were terminated, and antidumping compliance measures were undertaken pursuant to a private industry arrangement between the Japanese and European industries, entered in December of 1997.[14]

B Korea as a target

After the downcycle in 1985–1986, which gave rise to the antidumping cases against Japan, the next global decline in memory semiconductor prices took place in 1992–1993. Although less severe than in 1985, it provided an opportunity to target a relatively new entrant to the memory semiconductor market – Korea – which was blamed for the price declines at the time.

In 1992, Micron filed an antidumping complaint against Korean DRAM imports, and the US government initiated an investigation.[15] After a lengthy antidumping investigation, the US government found injurious dumping by two of the three major Korean exporters and imposed duties on their products.[16] During the investigation, the Korean exporters and the Korean government sought to settle the case via a suspension agreement or price undertaking similar to the one forged by the Japanese. The US complainant, Micron Technology Inc, vehemently opposed settlement, although the US government was reluctant to settle the case over the objection of the domestic industry.[17]

These exporters later obtained zero or *de minimis* antidumping rates as a result of the administrative review process, and the DOC reinstated these rates

12 In February of 1987, EECA, SGS-Thomson, Siemens and Motorola UK filed a complaint against nine Japanese manufacturers of DRAMs.

13 The antidumping case on DRAMs was settled pursuant to a price undertaking in August 1989, which resulted in the suspension of the antidumping investigation. The EC Commission provisionally agreed to commence the price undertaking with regard to eleven Japanese DRAM manufactures in January of 1990. The EPROM case was suspended pursuant to a similar price undertaking in March of 1991.

14 See EIAJ/EECA Statement Regarding Effective and Expeditious Antidumping Measurers Concerning DRAMs and EPROMs, Dec 10, 1997.

15 Dynamic Random Access Memory Semiconductors (DRAMs) of One Megabit and Above From the Republic of Korea, 57 Fed Reg 21,231 (May 19, 1992).

16 58 Fed Reg 27,520 (May 10, 1993) (final determination); the US government initially imposed duties on all three Korean exporters. However, after a court appeal, the dumping order for one producer, Samsung, was revoked. 61 Fed Reg 4,765 (Feb 8, 1996).

17 58 Fed Reg 15,467 (Mar 23, 1996).

in three consecutive reviews.[18] The exporters then requested revocation of the order, pursuant to US regulations[19] and provisions of the World Trade Organization (WTO) Antidumping Agreement.[20] The Korean requests were supported by the US PC industry, including DEC, Compaq, and Dell. However, the DOC insisted on a fourth review, reasoning that the prior three years' rates had been achieved in an 'upcycle' market (1993–1995) and that the exporters must be prepared to prove they would not dump in a declining market (1996–1997).[21]

Korea challenged the US decision not to terminate the case before a WTO panel pursuant to the dispute resolution provisions of the WTO Antidumping Agreement.[22] In the fourth review, which took place during the start of a decline in the global DRAMs market, the Department of Commerce determined that the Korean exporters were selling at dumped prices.[23] In subsequent reviews during the downcycle, the DOC continued to find that the Korean exporters were selling at dumped prices.

The recovery of the DRAMs market in 1999 came at an opportune time for the Korean exporters, as in 2000 the US government commenced a five year 'sunset' review of the antidumping order on Korean DRAMs to analyze whether the order continued to be necessary.[24] It appeared clear that the Korean exporters were going to follow in the footsteps of the Taiwanese industry, which was successful in defending itself against antidumping claims, as discussed below. The US industry thus decided to settle the DRAMs

---

18 Oct 29, 1992-Apr 30, 1994, 61 Fed Reg 20,216 (Oct 2, 1996); May 1, 1994-Apr 30, 1995, 62 Fed Reg 965 (Jan 7, 1997); May 1, 1995-Apr 30, 1996, 62 Fed Reg 39,809 (July 24, 1997)

19 See 19 CFR § 353.222. The US normally revokes an antidumping order after three consecutive reviews result in a determination of zero or *de minimis* margins, so long as there is a determination that dumping is not likely to recur.

20 See WTO Antidumping Agreement, Article 11.

21 63 Fed Reg 37,328 (Sept 23, 1998).

22 See Article 17 of the WTO Antidumping Agreement, which sets forth a special standard of review for antidumping cases, within the context of the Understanding On Rules And Procedures Governing The Settlement Of Disputes of the WTO Agreement.

The WTO panel accepted the argument of the Korean government that the US government applied the incorrect standard in deciding not to revoke the antidumping duty on Korean DRAMs. According to the panel, the Administering Agency, the US Department of Commerce, should have revoked the duty unless it found that dumping was likely to recur, rather than if it found dumping was not likely to recur, a more difficult standard. US - Antidumping Duty on DRAMs of One Megabit or Above from Korea, Report of the Panel, WT/DS99/R (Jan 29, 1999). The US government revised its regulation in response to this panel, but in a manner that did not change the outcome of its determination not to revoke the Korean DRAM order. The Korean government then challenged the US government implementation of the panel decision. This challenge ultimately was dropped pursuant to the general settlement agreement.

23 63 Fed Reg 50,867 (Sept 23, 1998); Id. at 56,906 (Oct 23, 1998).

24 65 Fed Reg 7890 (Feb 16, 2000); Id. at 16,632 (Mar 29, 2000). The sunset review provisions require the administering authority to revoke an antidumping order after five years from its imposition unless the authorities determine that revocation of the antidumping duty would be likely to lead to a continuation or recurrence of dumping and injury. This requirement is mandated by the WTO Antidumping Agreement at Article 11.3, and is embodied in US law at 19 USC § 1675a.

litigation, advocating termination of the entire antidumping case[25] in exchange for an agreement from the Korean producers to enter a voluntary data collection agreement similar to the one between the Japanese and US industry groups, and the Korean Government's agreement to drop its WTO challenge. There was some irony here, given that Micron had earlier refused to settle the case.

It is worth noting that, like its US counterparts, the EU DRAMs industry also targeted Korean exporters in an antidumping complaint when the market declined in 1992–1993. This antidumping litigation was eventually terminated in favor of private industry data collection arrangements, similar to those executed in the US between the US and Japanese industries.[26]

C Taiwan as a target

In 1996, the world memory semiconductor market began to slide into a severe downturn that lasted until late 1999. In this atmosphere, the US company Micron Technology, on February 25, 1997, filed an antidumping complaint against SRAMs from Korea and, for the first time, Taiwan.[27] Although the timing of the case was predictable, it was unclear why Micron brought a case concerning SRAMs, a memory product of which Micron was not a significant supplier.[28] It appeared that Micron was issuing a 'warning shot' or exploratory attack in anticipation of a future case on its main product, DRAMs.

As the market continued to slide into an historic low, Micron threw its second punch, aimed only at Taiwan. On October 22, 1998, Micron filed an antidumping petition against DRAMs from Taiwan. Although the world market was in a pronounced decline, Micron's action was a surprise because Micron had grown stronger during this time.[29]

In both cases, Micron's actions raised questions about why it would commit significant resources to target Taiwan, a comparatively small and less sophisticated supplier of memory semiconductors. Indeed, in both product

25 65 Fed Reg 59,391 (Oct 5, 2000). In response to Micron's statement of no further interest in the case, the US Department of Commerce effectively terminated the Korean DRAMs case effective Jan 1, 2000, the date on which an unfavorable ruling in the sunset review would have taken effect.

26 See EECA/KSIA Agreement Regarding a Data Collection and Maintenance System ('DCMS') (Sept. 9, 1997.)

27 The US government initiated the antidumping investigation on Mar 21, 1997.

28 Micron's petition was supported by a majority of the domestic industry at the time the petition was filed, although these companies would not join as petitioners. However, Micron's petition was also opposed by significant elements of the US SRAMs industry.

29 Micron had been able to buy out its only major domestic competitor, Texas Instruments, and to attract a _ billion dollar investment from Intel, which sought to ensure that the PC industry that would purchase its microprocessors would have a ready supply of DRAMs, a necessary corollary in the computing process. Micron thereby become the largest and most sophisticated DRAMs producer in the world.

areas, Taiwan accounted for only a small percentage of total imports - slightly above the negligible standard of 3%[30] – and an even lower share of the US domestic market.[31] The answer is that Micron viewed Taiwan as a future competitor, and was attempting to blame the new competitor for declining prices and profits during a market downturn, thereby blocking indefinitely the competitor's future access to the US market with antidumping duties. This strategy had proved highly effective in the past, allowing Micron to grow into a technologically dominant and highly profitable memory producer.

Taiwan's emergence as a semiconductor source did not follow the traditional pattern. Historically, semiconductor producers have been large, vertically integrated companies. That is, major Japanese, Korean and US manufacturers conduct design and manufacturing research in-house, fabricate the silicon wafer (the most sophisticated 'front-end' part of the manufacturing process), and then undertake the 'back-end' assembly process in which the individual semiconductor chips are encapsulated and tested prior to sale.

The Taiwanese industry departed from this pattern and took a revolutionary 'non-integrated' approach to semiconductor manufacture. Under the Taiwanese model, separate, unaffiliated companies focused on each of the three production processes - design, fabrication and assembly. By focusing on a single area of core competence, Taiwanese semiconductor companies were able to achieve novel efficiencies, and offer customers unique services. In addition, they were nimble and adaptable, a special virtue in the volatile memory field.[32] Thus, certain companies (called 'design houses') focused only on semiconductor design, other companies (called 'foundries') focused on the fabrication of semiconductors, and others dedicated themselves to assembly or testing of semiconductor chips.

Interestingly, the Taiwanese foundries serviced many US producers looking for reliable, high-quality second sources of supply. The availability of foundries in Taiwan, which did not exist in the US, led to the emergence of a new sector in US economy – a large and growing group consisting of independent US-based design-houses.[33] These US design-houses, which contributed high value-added jobs to the US economy, were directly threatened by Micron's actions as it potentially impaired their access to the Taiwanese foundries. Given Taiwan's novel approach to semi-conductor manufacturing, it is perhaps unsurprising that Micron saw the Taiwanese

30 See DRAMs of One Megabit and Above from Taiwan, USITC Pub 3256, Inv No 731-TA-811 (Dec 1999) at 20.

31 See, *Taiwan Semiconductor Industry v United States*, slip op No 00-113, (Ct Int'l Trade Aug 29, 2000). No 00-113, slip op (Ct Int'l Trade Aug 29, 2000).

32 See Far Eastern Economic Review, Oct 14, 1999, at 10. While some Taiwanese semiconductor producers adhered to the traditional integrated approach, most followed the novel, non-integrated structure.

33 See, the website of the Fabless Semiconductor Association. [www.fsa.org]

industry as a future competitor, and thus sought to snuff it out via the antidumping laws.

Before discussing how the Taiwanese industry grappled with the double antidumping assault, for the purposes of reference, this article will briefly review the fundamentals of the antidumping process.

II The antidumping process

A A powerful weapon

The Uruguay Round Agreements eliminated most import protection mechanisms, leaving antidumping measures as the most viable basis for imposing or preserving protective duties.[34] In this post-Uruguay Round era, antidumping complaints have emerged as a profoundly effective weapon. In the US, the number of antidumping investigations increased from 99 cases during the period for July 1989–July 1990, to 314 for July 1998–July 1999.

Often, the mere filing of an antidumping complaint has a marked effect on competition, affecting price levels and import volume. The complex and discretionary antidumping rules, and the burdens an antidumping investigation imposes, often place exporters and importers at a severe disadvantage. For instance, the US Department of Commerce, which is responsible for investigating whether exporters are dumping in the US, has a dumping 'conviction rate' of over 96%.[35]

B Company-specific measurement of dumping

An antidumping investigation commences after the national authority accepts a petition from a complainant in the domestic industry alleging that a designated type of merchandise imported from one or more countries is being sold in the national market at dumped (ie, 'unfairly' low) prices.[36] As noted above, the DOC is the national authority responsible for the 'dumping' phase of investigations in the US. The DOC selects for investigation the exporters of the subject product from the targeted country[37] and then issues to such companies a questionnaire requesting sales and cost information for the

---

34 See Corr, 'Trade Protection in the New Millennium: The Ascendancy of Antidumping Measures' (1997) 18 Northwestern Journal of International Law & Business: 49.

35 Ibid; Import Trade Administration website at [http://www.ita.doc.gov/import_admin/ records/stats], showing that only 3.9% of active cases from January 1, 1980 to July 31, 1997 resulted in a 'negative' dumping determination (ie, a finding that exporters were not dumping). The International Trade Commission ('ITC'), the US entity responsible for assessing whether a domestic industry is materially injured by dumped imports (the other phase of an antidumping investigation), makes affirmative findings in over 60% of the cases brought before it, a less certain but still troubling scenario for exporters and importers faced with an antidumping action.

36 See 19 USC § 1673; Antidumping Agreement art 5.

37 19 USC § 1677f-1c(c)(i); Antidumping Agreement art 6.10.

investigation period, generally the year preceding initiation of the complaint. After the questionnaire responses are submitted, the DOC usually sends auditors to conduct an on-site visit to the exporting company to verify the accuracy of the data.[38]

1 Comparison of export price to 'normal value'

The DOC determines whether dumping is occurring by comparing the export price of subject merchandise with the 'normal value' of the merchandise.[39] The export price is the targeted exporting company's price to an unaffiliated customer for consumption in the domestic market of the importing country.[40] 'Normal value' can be calculated in several manners. The first approach is to select comparable sales in the exporting companies' domestic or 'home' market. The home market will be used, however, only when there are sufficient sales (ie, at least five percent of the amount sold to the importing country)[41] of comparable or 'like' merchandise (ie, identical or similar models).[42] The DOC may also investigate whether home market sales are made below the cost of producing the product.[43] Sales made below cost and in substantial quantities may be rejected as a basis for comparison.[44] If home market sales cannot serve as a basis for comparison, the DOC will elect either to use export sales to third countries or, alternatively, to calculate a 'constructed value' of the exported merchandise.

The determination of 'constructed value' is based on the cost of production of the merchandise sold to the importing country plus the profit earned in selling the merchandise.[45] Cost of production is the total of the manufacturing cost (the 'actual' cost of materials, labor and overhead incurred in producing and packaging the merchandise sold in the comparison market) as well as selling, general and administrative expenses.[46] When 'constructing' the cost of production, the DOC can grant a 'start-up' adjustment to account for the distorted costs associated with the use of a new production facility or a new product line requiring substantial additional investment.[47] The adjustment is of significant importance in the semiconductor sector, but the DOC has not been liberal in granting this adjustment.

Because normal value can be based on home market price or constructed value, the exporter must bear in mind that it can still be found guilty of dumping even if its export price is (i) above home market price, and (ii) is above production cost.

38 19 USC § 1677m(h)(i); Antidumping Agreement art 6.7.
39 19 USC § 1677b; Antidumping Agreement art 2.2.
40 19 USC § 1677a; Antidumping Agreement art 2.3.
41 19 USC § 1677b(a)(1)(B)(ii)(II); Antidumping Agreement art 2.2 n 2.
42 19 USC§§ 1677(10), 1677(16); Antidumping Agreement art 2.6.
43 19 USC § 167b(b); Antidumping Agreement art 2.2.1.
44 19 USC § 167b(b); Antidumping Agreement art 2.2.1.
45 19 USC § 1677b(e); Antidumping Agreement art 2.2.2.
46 19 USC §§ 1677b(a)(1)(C), 1677b(a)(3); Antidumping Agreement art 2.2.1.
47 19 USC § 1677b(f)(1)(C); Antidumping Agreement art 2.2.1.1.

2 *The antidumping margin calculation*

After the DOC has determined the appropriate normal value and has derived the adjusted ex-factory unit prices, it will calculate the dumping margin. To do so, the Department compares export to normal value on an average or a transaction-specific basis.[48]

Average unit export prices are generally subtracted from average unit normal value, on a product-by-product basis, to measure the dumping amount. When the net export price for a product is higher than the normal value, the margin amount for the product is normally set to zero (ie, the exporter is not given credit for a 'negative' margin). When the net export price is less than normal value, a quantity-weighted dumping margin is calculated.[49] The margins for sales of all product types are tallied to derive a total dumping margin.

The WTO Antidumping Agreement requires that separate margin rates be derived for each exporting company where possible, but the administering authority has discretion to sample selected exporters when it cannot examine them all.[50] For those exporters in the targeted country that were not specifically investigated, an 'all others' duty based on the average of the rates for sampled exporters is applied.[51]

III Injury analysis of country-wide imports

In addition to the dumping determination, the US International Trade Commission ('ITC') must investigate whether the US domestic industry has been materially injured or threatened with injury by reason of the targeted merchandise.[52] The ITC is comprised of a panel of six Commissioners and issues affirmative injury determinations when either a simple majority of Commissioners find injury or the Commissioner panel is divided equally. This means that an equal division is resolved in favor of a finding of injury to the domestic industry.[53]

---

48 19 USC § 1677f-1(d); Antidumping Agreement art 2.4.2.

49 This methodology essentially ignores the effect of negative margins, which unfairly inflates the margin. India recently challenged the European Union practice of 'zeroing' negative margins at the WTO. This challenge may require a change in US as well as EU practice. See European Communities – Anti-Dumping Duties on Imports of Cotton-Type Bed-Linen from India, WT/DS141.

50 19 USC § 1677f-1(c); Antidumping Agreement arts 6.10, 9.2.

51 19 USC § 1677f-1(c)(2); Antidumping Agreement art 9.4.

52 19 USC § 1673; Antidumping Agreement art 3.

53 19 USC § 1677(ii).

A Injury standard

The ITC must assess the impact of dumping on the domestic industry by examining both the volume of subject imports deemed to have been dumped, and the effect of these imports on domestic prices and producers.[54] The ITC must examine the absolute and relative volume of subject imports as compared to domestic production or consumption. In analyzing price effects, the ITC must consider a number of factors, including price undercutting and price depression by dumped imports. The factors considered in determining the effect of dumped imports on domestic producers include trends in sales, market share, capacity utilization and profits, as well as employment and investment levels.[55]

Exporting countries with less than a three percent share of imports subject to a particular investigation (negligible countries) are excluded from the investigation and from the imposition of antidumping duties, unless the cumulative share of imports from such negligible countries is greater than 7%.[56]

Under the Antidumping Agreement, the ITC must conduct the investigation of injury on as narrow a product range as possible.[57] However the Antidumping Agreement explicitly permits the national authority to 'cumulate' the effect of dumped imports from more than one country under investigation.[58]

After assessing these factors, the national authority must determine whether the domestic industry is: (i) materially injured, (ii) threatened with material injury, or (iii) materially retarded in its establishment.[59]

B Causation

Before making an affirmative injury determination, the ITC must demonstrate the causal relationship between the dumped imports and the injury to the domestic industry.[60] The Antidumping Agreement also requires the national authority to examine 'any known factors other than the dumped imports' which might also cause the injury, such as non-dumped import volumes and contraction of demand.[61] The ITC must not attribute these causes to dumped imports.

---

54 19 USC § 1677(7)(c); Antidumping Agreement art 3.

55 19 USC § 1677(7)(c)(iii); Antidumping Agreement art 3.4.

56 19 USC § 1677(24); Antidumping Agreement art 5.8

57 Antidumping Agreement art 3.6.

58 19 USC § 1677(7)G); Antidumping Agreement art 3.3.

59 19 USC § 1673; Antidumping Agreement 3 n 9.

60 19 USC § 1673; Antidumping Agreement art 3.5.

61 Antidumping Agreement art 3.5.

If both the dumping and injury investigations result in an affirmative determination, the DOC may impose a definitive antidumping duty.

IV Mounting a successful defense: Taiwan's experience

A Initial reaction and strategy

1 Resolve to fight

The institution of antidumping cases against SRAMs and DRAMs threatened severe harm to a vital segment of the Taiwan semiconductor industry which was still in start-up mode. More broadly, it threatened the plans of Taiwan to foster the growth of a high tech sector to balance Taiwan's traditional economy and enhance its economic independence. The initial reactions from various components of the industry varied between dejection, disillusionment, disbelief and denial. It was difficult to accept that the industry was in for a multi-year ordeal, facing a biased legal process that threatened to block one of Taiwan's key export markets.

Unfortunately, once the antidumping proceedings were initiated, the targeted Taiwanese industries had little time for reflection - the preliminary determination of whether Taiwanese exports were causing injury to the US industry would be issued within forty-five days of commencement. It was therefore imperative that the Taiwanese industry rally to defend itself.

The first step involved meetings among the industry to share information regarding the antidumping action. As all members of the industry were not aware of the ramifications of the antidumping proceeding and the measures necessary for defense, a certain amount of self-education was in order. The most critical initial step was to reach a consensus among the industry that Taiwan was determined to defend itself. Failure to do so, via a token or inept effort at defense, would only encourage future law suits. It is perhaps inevitable and ironic that the more one is targeted by litigation, the better one becomes at organizing a defense. Thus, in the case of Taiwan, the industry was more prepared in the DRAM antidumping case to organize a defense, having already experienced the growing pains of organizing a defense in the case against SRAMs.

2 Empowerment of the Industry Association

In the analysis of injury, an antidumping investigation examines the collective effect of the targeted country's exports. It is therefore critical to undertake a cohesive and coordinated defense on behalf of as many producers and exporters as possible. This proved a more difficult task for Taiwan, given its non-integrated structure, than for the Korean industry, which is comprised of only two or three very large integrated manufacturers. Accordingly, the various elements of the Taiwanese industry needed an impartial facilitator that could disseminate information, encourage coordination and cooperation, and provide a forum for meetings and the exchange of ideas. Generally, the role of facilitator must be shouldered by the industry association. In the case of Taiwan, the Taiwan Semi-Conductor Industry Association (TSIA) ably filled this role. Although it had represented the Taiwanese industry on a host of technical and environmental issues prior to the SRAMs case, it had not previously played such a critical role in litigation. It rose to the task admirably, forging consensus among disparate groups.

3 Selection of the appropriate law firm

One of the fundamental first steps that an industry must take in forging a consensus is to accept that US litigation is expensive and prolonged, but that the alternatives to a vigorous defense are unacceptable. Given that the US antidumping process is highly legalistic, specialized and somewhat arcane, it is imperative to select an appropriate law firm. This selection must come early in the process so that the industry can meaningfully participate in the preliminary phases of the case, when critical threshold decisions are made. Many law firms will offer their services, touting various levels of experience, and quoting a broad array of fees. Selecting counsel based primarily on cost is dangerous because in procuring legal services, like other goods and services, you often 'get what you pay for.' The experience of the law firm is paramount, and should be closely examined to ensure that the firm was lead counsel in the cases that it cites as experience. The Taiwanese industry closely examined the number of experienced partners and associates, as well as other specialists that the various law firms had to offer. Ultimately, in both the SRAMs and DRAMs cases, the Taiwanese industry chose counsel that had experience in Taiwan on the semiconductor sector, and also had a proven track record of success.

Exercising vigorous due diligence in the selection of the law firm at the outset will pay dividends later on and should lead to a strong attorney-client relationship characterized by trust, cooperation and efficiency. In the case of Taiwan, the attorney-client bond that developed during the SRAMs investigation served Taiwan's interest in the subsequent DRAMs investigation, and in later court appeals.

B Procedural and long-term strategy

1 Defense at the ITC

As discussed above, the defense at the International Trade Commission (ITC), the administering agency which conducts the injury investigation, must be advanced on a country-wide basis. Because the proceedings of the Department of Commerce concerning the measurement of 'dumping' are heavily biased against the exporter, it is the ITC investigation that normally affords the best opportunity for a successful defense. It is therefore crucial that the industry join together to devise both a procedural and a substantive strategy.

In terms of procedure, the industry must reach a consensus on the selection of counsel and other consultants. Next, in consultation with counsel, the industry must choose expert advisers to play a lead role in devising substantive strategy and to serve as expert witnesses at the ITC hearing. Finally, the members of the industry must cooperate in reaching out to allies in the US, such as the consumer industry and other industries likely to be adversely affected by the antidumping order. While the public at large must ultimately pay the bill for antidumping duties as costs are passed along to the ultimate consumer, public awareness of the adverse effect of antidumping duties is not yet high enough to have any weight in the discussion.[62]

The various members of the industry must also agree upon the substantive arguments to be made at the ITC. Counsel will play a lead role in devising the strategy based on the regulations and precedent of the ITC. The defense ultimately must be based on facts, most of which are collected confidentially via the issuance of questionnaires to producers, importers and US purchasers.[63] The industry nevertheless plays an important role because it has knowledge of the actual conditions of competition in the market, channels of distribution and trade flow, which are vital to an effective defense.

The key issues that must be addressed in the arguments to the ITC regarding injury are: (1) the volume of imports into the US during the investigation period;[64] (2) the conditions of competition in the market at the time; (3) the price effect of the subject imports; and (4) the effect of subject imports on the domestic industry.[65] The defense must also address whether foreign production capacity, trade patterns and inventories represent an imminent threat of injury.

The industry must be prepared to act swiftly. The ITC's preliminary determination is issued 45 days after initiation of the proceeding; within that time, the ITC must issue questionnaires, collect data, hold a hearing and solicit comments from interested parties.[66] The final determination, which is issued at the end of the antidumping investigation, gives the exporters significant additional time to focus on strategy.[67] Given the country-wide nature of the

62 The WTO Agreement for the first time called for an opportunity for consumer industries to make their views known. See WTO Antidumping Agreement Article 6.12: 'The authorities shall provide opportunities for industrial users of the product under investigation and for representative consumer organizations in cases where the product is commonly sold at the retail level, to provide information which is relevant to the investigation regarding dumping, injury and causality.' These requirements are implemented in US law in 19 USC § 1677f(h) although, in practice, it is unclear how much weight, if any, the administering authorities give to such third parties.

63 Only counsel with access under administrative protective orders have access to this information, and this limits to some extent the role of the industry associations and the details of the argument.

64 The ITC typically considers a three-year investigation period, reaching backward from the time of the investigation.

65 19 USC § 1677(7).

66 19 USC § 1673b(a).

67 *Ibid*, at 1673d(b).

defense at the ITC and the need for consensus and coordination, the industry association plays a vital role. In both the SRAMs and DRAMs investigations, the TSIA served a critical function, not only facilitating and coordinating the defense, but also sending its head to serve as the chief industry witness on behalf of the exporters.

2 *Defense at the department of commerce*

In the DOC phase of the antidumping proceeding involving the measurement of 'dumping', a separate rate is determined for each investigated company based on that company's sales and cost information. Typically, each company selects its own counsel, although, depending on the circumstances, there may be some benefit in different companies selecting common counsel, even if those companies are unaffiliated.

Where there are numerous producers and exporters, as in the case of Taiwan, the DOC will select only a few to sample during the investigation.[68] Although a number of companies sought to participate in the investigation and thus to control their fate, the DOC refused these requests and ultimately selected only four respondents in both the SRAMs and DRAMs cases. For those companies not investigated, the DOC imposes an antidumping duty rate that is a weighted average of the rates calculated for the investigated companies.[69]

Despite the focus on individual companies in the dumping phase of the investigation, it is still necessary for the industry to coordinate its defense and assist the investigated companies on common issues. In each semiconductor investigation, for example, there were issues common to all Taiwanese companies that called for a strong, unified response. As discussed below, the DOC's adverse treatment of Taiwan's generally accepted profit-sharing and research and development methodologies, as well as its treatment of foundries, had repercussions across the Taiwanese industry.

Moreover, the effect of an antidumping duty calculated for a single company may reverberate well beyond that company. Given that the DOC metes out dumping rates in almost all cases due to its biased procedures, it is important that at least some companies obtain a dumping rate that is low or manageable, so that some portion of the industry can continue to sell in the export market. Further, because the many non-investigated companies are subject to an average dumping duty rate, the rate for each investigated company has a bearing on the future of these non-investigated companies, as well as start-ups that have yet to commence exporting. For instance, in the SRAMs investigation, while three of the investigated companies received very

68 See 19 CFR § 351.204. Unlike the case of Korea, for example, where there were only two or three exporters who could be included in the investigation, the Taiwanese industry is composed of numerous producers, exporters and design houses. For instance, in the Taiwanese DRAMs case, the DOC initially canvassed over 20 potential respondents.

69 See 19 CFR § 351.107.

high antidumping rates, one respondent, Integrated Silicon Solutions, Inc, obtained a relatively low rate and was allowed to continue serving the US market. This also had a significant effect in lowering the 'all others' average rate applicable to non-investigated companies.[70]

3 Possible settlement

Depending on the circumstances of the case, the industry may wish to propose settlement of the case through a suspension agreement similar to the one entered into by the Japanese exporters.[71] A suspension agreement normally covers at least 85 percent of subject imports.[72] A decision on whether to propose a suspension agreement must be made early in the investigation process, ie, within 15 days after issuance of the DOC's preliminary determination.[73] Thus the industry must reach a consensus on whether to go forward before that time. Again, the role of the industry association is vital, particularly in Taiwan where there are many industry members with potentially divergent views.

The main advantage of a suspension agreement is that it allows targeted companies to deliver subject imports into the US free of any dumping duty deposit requirements or any concerns with regard to future antidumping liability. The exporters would likely have the certainty of US government-approved minimum prices without the need for price monitoring.

However, there are significant disadvantages as well. A suspension agreement typically imposes inflated cost-based constraints on the prices that exporters may charge in the US. In some cases the price can be prohibitive. Further, the exporters and producers are forced to collect a substantial amount of sales and cost data and are subject to regular audits by the US government.

Even if the industry decides to propose a suspension agreement, it is unlikely that one will be accepted. Notwithstanding the agreement involving the Japanese exporters, the US government generally does not favor suspension agreements due to the administrative burdens it imposes. Moreover, when the US domestic industry opposes settlement via a suspension agreement, the DOC will not normally override this view. For example, during the Korean DRAMs investigation in 1992, the Korean

---

70 See 63 Fed Reg 18,883 (Apr 16, 1998), wherein three investigated companies, Alliance Semiconductor Corp, UMC, and Windbond Electronics Corp received rates of 50.15%, 93.71% and 101.53% respectively. ISSI, on the other hand, received a rate of 7.56%. The 'all others' rate applicable to non-investigated companies was 41.75%, not acceptable, but nevertheless much lower due to the rate achieved by ISSI.

71 In particular, the suspension agreement would require the covered exporters to submit quarterly price and cost information. Based on this information, the DOC would issue quarterly minimum US prices.

72 19 CFR § 351.208.

73 *Ibid.*

semiconductor industry unsuccessfully sought a suspension agreement. Despite the support of US semiconductor users, particularly the PC industry, and a visit by high-level Korean officials, the DOC refused to enter into any agreement to suspend the investigation as a result of opposition from Micron.[74]

In the Taiwan DRAMs case, before a consensus could be reached on whether to proceed with a settlement proposal, Micron indicated that it would strongly oppose one. Thus, the matter did not proceed further.

4 *Continuing the challenge by appeal*

As part of a commitment to defend itself vigorously, the industry must be willing to appeal adverse decisions to appropriate authorities. One possible avenue of appeal is the US court system. Final decisions by the ITC or the DOC that are adverse to the exporters or importers of subject products may be appealed to the Court of International Trade.[75] Thus, as explained below, although Taiwan at first received adverse determinations from the agency in the SRAMs case, its commitment to challenge adverse determinations in the Court resulted in an ultimate reversal in Taiwan's favor.[76] The industry also must be willing to join an action to defend favorable decisions. For example, in the DRAMs case, the TSIA intervened in Micron's challenge to the ITC final determination.

A new remedial forum for exporters is the World Trade Organisation dispute settlement process. Decisions by US administering authorities that are inconsistent with US obligations under the WTO Antidumping Agreement may be challenged at the WTO through a request for a dispute settlement panel. However, these appeals must be made by the government, rather than by industry. Moreover, even when a favorable ruling is issued, the US government will typically implement the decision by making changes that have only a prospective effect, which may not benefit the exporter complaining of improper prior determinations.[77] In any event, a WTO challenge was not an option for Taiwan which had not yet acceded to the WTO.

5 *Other forms of defense*

Taiwan has a significant domestic memory market, driven by its large domestic PC and motherboard industry. The same worldwide conditions affecting the memory market in the US also had an impact in Taiwan. Faced with the potential loss of their US export market, it was important for the Taiwanese producers to ensure that dumping by Micron did not threaten their

74 58 Fed Reg 15,467 (Mar 23, 1992).

75 28 USC § 1581(c).

76 In the SRAMs case, ISIA lost in the original preliminary and final determinations of the US International Trade Commission, and again on remand. In the DRAMs case, TSIA lost in the International Trade Commission preliminary determination.

77 19 CFR § 3583(a).

home market. In 1998, Taiwanese producers therefore requested antidumping relief from imports of US DRAMs. The Taiwanese industry successfully established that it was being injured by reason of US DRAMs in the preliminary determination.[78] In the dumping phase of the investigation, Micron did not respond to the Taiwanese government's questionnaires.[79] The Taiwanese government ultimately terminated the case after a final determination that there was no injury.[80]

Finally, faced with the uncertainty of potential antidumping duties applying indefinitely, exporters must implement internal compliance programs to limit future dumping.[81] In subsequent reviews, the exporters can then, in theory, obtain lower duty rates and receive refunds of deposits paid. Many exporters faced with prolonged antidumping duties, such as Korean DRAMs exporters, have survived and thrived in this manner. Many Taiwanese companies have also instituted dumping compliance programs, which have resulted in lower dumping expenses.[82]

C Integration of local action

1 Role of government

During the course of an antidumping investigation, the primary role of the government is to ensure that all relevant members of the industry are informed about the filing of the case, as well as the gravity of the potential consequences and the need for quick and determined defensive action. The government must be served by the initiating foreign government with notice of the antidumping complaint and initiation of the investigation. The government must then ensure that this information is passed along to the relevant industry members at the outset of the investigation. The government also plays a high profile role in supporting the industry at a time of potential economic crisis, and encouraging all members of the industry to cooperate with one another for the common good. Further, given the vital role played by the industry association, the government must ensure that the industry association is appropriately funded and staffed so that it may carry out its role.

In the US, an antidumping investigation normally proceeds along distinct, legalistic tracks, and is not susceptible to influence from government lobbying. Nevertheless, it is appropriate for the government, through its trade

---

78 See, Preliminary Determination of the Taiwan International Trade Commission, DRAMs from the United States, May 29, 1999.

79 See Final Determination of the Taiwan Ministry of Finance, DRAMs from the United States, Jan 3, 2000.

80 See, Final Determination of the Taiwan International Trade Commission, DRAMs from the United States, which resulted in termination of the case on Apr 13, 2000.

81 See Corr, *supra*, note 34, for a discussion of dumping compliance programs.

82 *Ibid.*

ministry and its Washington representatives, to monitor the case closely and to ensure that its US counterparts are informed of the government's interest in the case.

Perhaps the most important and potentially influential role of government in the antidumping process is through the WTO. As noted above, only a government member of the WTO may challenge another member's antidumping action on the ground that it is adverse to its national exporters or producers. The WTO dispute settlement process provides for binding dispute resolution, and as such is a potent weapon against arbitrary and unfair use of the antidumping law by WTO member states.[83] This important role will be available to Taiwan's government upon its accession to the WTO.

2 *Role of the Industry Association*

As the unified voice and spokesperson for the targeted industry, the industry association plays perhaps the most crucial role. In the ITC investigation, which requires an industry-wide defense, the industry association's role as representative, strategy formulator, and disseminator of information is predominant and vital. A weak industry association that is unable to organize a procedural and substantive consensus among exporters and producers and to ensure an adequate budget for the defense increases the risk of defeat.

The industry association must be adroit at hammering out a consensus on important defense positions and 'bringing the troops into line' after a period of reasonable debate. It is also the representative in discussions with allies such as consumer industries and others adversely affected by the antidumping case. In addition, the industry association plays an important role in proposing any settlement agreement, with support from the government.

Finally, the industry association must assist in coordinating any court appeals, including facilitating decisions on whether to appeal, selection of the appropriate counsel and the budget for the appeal.

3 *Individual companies*

The targeted exporters and producers of the subject goods are the ones most directly threatened by antidumping litigation. Their commitment to support the industry association during the injury phase of the proceeding, and to defend their individual interests vigorously in the DOC phase of the proceeding, will determine the fate of the industry.

The individual companies must also bear the costs of litigation and must find an agreeable way to share the costs for the common defense, particularly at the ITC. Furthermore, individual companies must be prepared to defend their company-specific issues in court, including the appeal of adverse determinations made by the DOC in the dumping phase of the case.

---

83 For instance, Korea challenged the DOC determination not to revoke the antidumping duty in the Korean DRAMs case. WT/DS99/R (Jan 29, 1999).

The government, the industry association and the individual producers and exporters each play important roles in the defense, and when operating in harmony, achieve important synergies.

D Prevailing in the end

In the Taiwanese SRAMs and DRAMs antidumping investigations, the government, the TSIA and the individual exporters and producers pulled together in a time of crisis, and doggedly resisted the attacks by Micron. Their combined, concerted efforts helped Taiwan prevail in both cases.

1 Taiwan SRAMs

As discussed above, the antidumping law is biased against defendant exporters. The Taiwanese industry encountered these biases in both the dumping and injury phases of the SRAMs antidumping investigation. By holding to a strategy of persistent resistance, Taiwan ultimately held out against the allegations.

(a) The dumping phase

In measuring whether 'dumping' exists, the DOC has a roughly 96 percent 'conviction' rate, a daunting track record for new respondents. In the DRAMs and SRAMs cases, the DOC made numerous findings and adjustments which had an adverse effect on the ultimate antidumping margin rates calculated.[84] A number of issues relating to the unique structure of the Taiwanese industry were overlooked by the DOC, which ruled against Taiwan.

First, the DOC insisted that Taiwanese producers' profit-sharing with their employees must be included in the SRAMs production cost, thereby inflating the antidumping margin. The DOC arbitrarily disregarded the audited books and records of the Taiwanese producers, as well as Taiwan's Generally Accepted Accounting Principles, neither of which treated profit-sharing as a production cost.[85]

Second, the DOC determined that the Taiwanese foundries were not entitled to status as 'producers' in the investigation, a counter-intuitive finding since the foundries were responsible for the highest value-added and most complex phase of manufacturing – the 'production' of the fabricated wafer.[86] This led to the illogical designation of the US design houses as 'producers' even though they had nothing to do with the fabrication of the product in

84 63 Fed Reg 18,883 (Apr 16, 1998). See *supra*, note 70, for per-company antidumping margin rates for each investigated company.

85 63 Fed Reg 8,921–23 (Feb 23, 1998).

86 *Ibid* at 8,915–8,918. The DOC ruled that the foundries were mere sub-contractors, thereby ignoring its own regulations that provide that sub-contractors have status as 'producers' when they own the subject merchandise or control the sale of the merchandise. See 19 CFR § 351.401(h). In this case, foundries purchased all raw materials and owned subject merchandise until they sold it to an unaffiliated customer.

Taiwan. This decision has been appealed to the US Court of International Trade.[87]

Third, the Taiwan producers all recorded research and development expenses by product line, and thus research costs for the subject SRAMs were easily identified. The DOC, however, again ignored the audited accounting record of the Taiwanese respondent, and insisted that production include all research and development costs, including research for disparate products such as logic semiconductors and non-volatile memory devices.[88]

(b) The injury phase

The ITC determined that Taiwanese SRAMs were the cause of material injury to the domestic industry, even though the evidence demonstrated that Taiwanese imports had no real effect on the domestic market.[89] Taiwanese import levels were barely above the 'negligible' level that would have required termination of the case. Moreover, the record indicated that the prices of the Taiwanese imports had no effect on US price levels.[90]

The unusual manner in which the ITC's determination was reached may explain this unfair result. As noted above, the ITC is normally comprised of six sitting Commissioners but at the time of the Taiwanese SRAMs proceedings, three Commissioners had left the ITC and had not been replaced. Moreover, one of the remaining Commissioners recused herself from participation in the case. Therefore, only two Commissioners remained to vote on the Taiwanese SRAMs case, and they disagreed. That is, one Commissioner voted that Taiwanese SRAMs imports were causing injury, and the other voted that they were not. Unfortunately, a tie vote is interpreted against the exporter and this unusual one-to-one tie vote was deemed to be an affirmative determination by the entire ITC that Taiwanese SRAM imports were injuring the US industry.

The Taiwanese SRAM exporters were disappointed with the decision and were adversely affected by the application of the antidumping duty. The TSIA therefore rallied the industry, which resolved to appeal the ITC determination. The history of Taiwan's SRAM appeal stands as a testament that when challenging an antidumping determination exporters must take a long-term view and must not give up.

---

87 At the time of this article, that appeal was pending.

88 63 Fed Reg 8,921–8923 (Feb 23, 1998)

89 Statistic Random Access Memory Semiconductors from the Republic of Korea and Taiwan, USITC Pub. 3,098, Inv. No. 731-TA-762 (Apr 1998).

90 Indeed, when Taiwan prices were higher than US prices, the industry was not doing well, but when Taiwan prices were below US prices, the industry was performing strongly. See Taiwan Semiconductor Industry Association *et al*, the United States *et al*, No. 00-113, slip op (Ct Int'l Trade, Aug 29, 2000).

The appeals process in that case commenced in May 1998, when the TSIA and certain Taiwanese producers and exporters appealed the ITC affirmative final determination. Roughly one year later, after vigorous litigation, the Court of International Trade ruled that the ITC had made significant errors in its final determination and remanded the case back to the ITC for further consideration.[91] On remand, the ITC held its ground and continued to find in the affirmative.[92] Notwithstanding this setback, the TSIA once again challenged the ITC's remand determination in Court. After additional litigation, the Court once again determined that the ITC had made errors in issuing its first remand determination.[93] Following further argument and fact-finding at the ITC, the TSIA's efforts were finally vindicated when the ITC reversed its earlier decisions and ruled that Taiwan SRAMs imports were not injuring or threatening material injury to the domestic industry.[94] However, determination was then challenged by Micron, the petitioner. After more litigation, and more than two years after the filing of the initial appeal, the Court affirmed the TSIA's resounding victory, entering a final judgment approving the ITC reversal.[95] Micron appealed this decision to the Court of Appeals for the Federal Circuit.

2 *Taiwanese DRAMs*

Having gained experience of litigation in the SRAMs case, the Taiwanese industry was girded for the DRAMs case which followed thereafter. The Taiwanese industry rallied quickly to the call of the TSIA, mustering the human and monetary resources necessary to defend itself vigorously.

In the dumping phase of the case, the DOC's biased approach, and its adverse findings on the same issues as those considered in the context of the SRAMs case, virtually assured a determination of 'dumping'. However, the Taiwanese producers and exporters who were investigated obtained results more favorable than those obtained in the SRAMs proceeding, which reflects the growing familiarity in Taiwan with the US antidumping law.[96]

---

91 See *Taiwan Semiconductor Industry Association v United States*, 23 CIT, 59 F Supp 2d N 2314 (June 30, 1999).

92 See Commissions Determination on Remand, SRAMs from Taiwan (Aug 30, 1999). Although there were five sitting Commissioners at the time of the remand, only one, the Commissioner who originally voted affirmative, participated in the remand proceeding.

93 See *Taiwan Semiconductor Association v United States*, 93 F Supp 2d 1283 (Ct Int'l Trade Apr 11, 2000). In this decision, the court made it known that it expected the full Commission to participate in the second remand proceeding, not only one Commissioner.

94 See Commission's Second Determination on Remand (June 26, 2000). The ITC voted 4-to-1 in the negative with one Commissioner abstaining.

95 See *Taiwan Semiconductor Industry Association v United States*, Slip Op 00-113 (Aug 29, 2000).

96 64 Fed Reg 56,308 (Oct 19, 1999). The final margins for the Taiwan DRAM producers were as follows – Vanguard International Semiconductor, Corp (8.21%), Nan Ya Technology Corp (14.18%), Mosel Vitelic, Inc (35.58%), and Etron Technology, Inc (69%). The weighted average 'all others' rate was 21.35% which, although high, was less than half the 'all others' rate in the SRAMs case.

Taiwan found its advantage in the injury phase of the investigation. Micron's classic strategy of blaming foreign exporters for the adverse effects of a world-wide memory market downturn was finally revealed in this injury proceeding. While the world memory market was in an historic slump in 1998 when the complaint was filed, the market was beginning a dramatic recovery in late 1999 at the time of the ITC final investigation. It appeared Micron had miscalculated in seeking to file the complaint at the bottom of the world-wide slump, because the market recovered before it could convince the ITC that the downturn was the fault of targeted foreign exporters.

Before the full Commission, the TSIA presented extensive evidence of an improving market, a domestic industry that had grown more dominant during the downturn, and a lack of any effect by Taiwanese DRAMs on the relevant market. As a result, the ITC voted overwhelmingly that Taiwanese DRAMs imports were not causing or threatening material injury to the domestic industry.[97] After a bruising battle of almost three years, this determination was a welcome and well-earned victory.

IV Conclusion

In view of the bias against exporters inherent in the antidumping law, there can be no guarantee that undertaking a vigorous, coordinated defense will result in a swift victory for respondents. Nevertheless, given the stakes and consequences, targeted exporters and producers are well advised to defend their interests and their market share. A strong resolve to defend the targeted industry's interests over the long term, and committed working relationship among the government, industry associations and private companies are of paramount importance. The Taiwanese semiconductor sector's recent experience in multiple antidumping cases suggests that despite the odds against targeted exporters, determined defensive efforts can result in ultimate victory.

97 See Dynamic Random Access Memory Semiconductors of One Megabit and Above from Taiwan, USITC Pub 3256, Inv No 731-TA-811 (Dec 1999). The ITC voted 3 to 1 in the negative, with two Commissioners abstaining.

Vietnam's Emerging Stock Market and the Enterprise Law

Phuong-Trinh Nguyen

Introduction

The long-awaited stock market in Vietnam launched its first transaction on 28 July 2000. This event was a significant landmark for the economic renovation program in Vietnam, known as *Doi Moi*.[1] The introduction of the stock market confirms the intention of the Vietnamese Government to establish a market driven economy with a socialist orientation.[2] At the time, First Deputy Prime Minister Nguyen Tan Dung stated that financing of enterprises had been a deep concern of the Vietnamese Communist Party and that capital mobilization was a key factor for the development of the national economy.[3] This was an affirmation that the development of a market economy requires the existence of a stock market and a securities industry as vehicles for corporate fund raising.[4]

A prerequisite for this type of reform is the development of legislation governing the issuance of shares and the operation of the stock market. While some countries include the provisions on share issuance and the operation of stock market in general company legislation, others regulate these issues through securities regulations.[5] For example, Australia has constructed a comprehensive Corporations Law that encompasses stock market issues whereas Vietnam and China have placed stock market regulations in separate legislation. Regardless of the manner in which securities issues are governed, the securities industry can only be established and developed in the presence of a comprehensive legislative system for corporations. Therefore, it is not surprising that the securities market has not emerged until very recently since

1 This program was initiated by the resolution of the 6th Communist Party Congress. *Doi Moi* means 'transform' or simply 'changes'.

2 See Ha Thang, 'Exchange Evidence of New *Doi Moi* Era' Vietnam Investment Review No 458, 24-30 July 2000. [www.vir-vietnam.com]

3 *Ibid.*

4 This point of view was confirmed by First Deputy Prime Minister Nguyen Tan Dung in an interview with the Vietnam Investment Review. See Ha Thang, 'Stock Market Now Ready for July Initiation' Vietnam Investment Review No 448, 15–21 May 2000. [www.vir.vietnam.com]

5 This significance of this distinction is discussed in OECD General Principles of Company Law for Transition Economies, at 7. [www.oecd.org]

Vietnamese corporations legislation was only significantly elaborated with the promulgation of the Enterprise Law in 1999.[6]

The Enterprise Law contains basic provisions on share-holding companies and fund raising by issuance of shares as well as basic principles for management. There are links between the Enterprise Law and provisions in the legislation governing the securities industry. Therefore, the operation of the stock market cannot be examined in isolation from the influence of the Enterprise Law. In turn, the emerging stock market will test the feasibility of the Enterprise Law.

To understand the emergent Vietnamese stock market, one must also master the unique characteristics of the Vietnamese legal system, which reflects a socialist orientation on the political front and a market orientation on the economic front. As Vietnam commits to economic revitalization and aims at constructing a market driven economy,[7] some degree of change in the socialist legal framework is inevitable. However, communist countries stress the possibility of integrating Marxism into the new situation and 'stretching' Marxism to accommodate the practice of socialist legality.[8] This flexible approach has been promoted by Deng Xiao Ping, the architect of Chinese reform, who argues: 'It doesn't matter the colour the cat so long as it catches mice.'[9] In the Vietnamese context, the pursuit of economic growth for the purpose of increasing national strength and individual wealth can only be achieved by economic reforms such as a stock market. Once introduced, the stock market further requires a legal framework that allows for the autonomy of enterprises and legal equality between state and private sectors.

In the process of integration with the world economy, which includes the preparation of the legal framework for the stock market, Vietnam has examined various models from around the world and transplanted some Western and Chinese legal ideology into its drafting. However, given the socialist orientation of Vietnam, the application of Western models had to be adjusted to suit the Vietnamese context.

This paper examines the application and variation of foreign corporate principles and securities rules in the Vietnamese context. Where necessary, Chinese and Australian law will be contrasted with Vietnamese legislation on corporations and the stock market. The paper comprises three main parts, each of which stresses the impact of Vietnam's socialist orientation on corporate life and the operation of the stock market. Part A discusses the development of

---

6 The Enterprise Law replaced the Law on Companies and the Law on Private Enterprises, which governed limited liability companies, shareholding companies, and private enterprises.

7 See M Scown, 'As the Embargo Crumbles, Vietnam Prepares for US Investors' (1993) 4 Journal of International Taxation: 12, at 12.

8 See Chih-Yu Shih, 'China's Socialist Law Under Reform: The Class Nature Reconsidered' (1996) 44 American Journal of Comparative Law: 627.

9 See Anna Han, 'China's Company Laws: Practicing Capitalism in a Transitional Economy' (1996) 5 Pacific Rim Law & Policy Journal: 457, at 468.

corporate law and the legal and economic context in which the stock market has emerged. It also provides an overview of law-making mechanisms in Vietnam. Part B examines the issuance of shares and the relationship between shareholders and management under the Enterprise Law. Part C examines the characteristics of the emerging stock market and the legal foundation for its establishment. In Part C, securities legislation will be examined to highlight core issues such state management in the operation of the stock market and protection of investors.

A: Overview of laws governing corporations and the formation of the stock market

I: Background on the law making system in Vietnam and recent legal reform

(1) The law making system in Vietnam

In 1996, the Law on Promulgation of Legislation was passed in order to create a legislative hierarchy, by defining the competency of each State Agency and the procedure and format of legislation issued by each Agency. This Law has helped to resolve some of the previous confusion in the law-making process.[10]

Vietnamese laws are usually drafted in general terms and therefore they are not enforced until the guidelines for implementation are issued by the Government or by the relevant Ministry. Both the Government and its ministries participate in the process by issuing implementing legislation in the form of Decrees, Circulars and Directives. The government thus takes a primary role not only in the law-making process but also in the implementation and interpretation of the laws. This is in addition to the interpretive function fulfilled by the courts and other relevant authorities.[11] The overlapping jurisdiction of the Government and the courts to interpret the law raises concerns about consistency and fairness for individuals.

Commentators have observed that new laws may not be properly implemented after they come into force in the absence of implementing legislation to act as a guideline.[12] For instance, there is confusion in implementation of the Enterprise Law, which was passed in 1999 and came into force in January 2000. Though the fundamentals of the Enterprise Law were implemented by Government Decrees, there are still no answers to questions such as what licences need to be obtained. The lack of answers to these questions hinders the proper implementation of the Enterprise Law.

10 J Gillespie, 'Vietnam: The Emergence of a Law-based State' in Alice Tay (ed), *East Asia: Human Rights, Nation Building, Trade*, 1999, Baden-Baden: Nomos Verlagsgesellschaft, at 355.

11 Article 52 of the Law on Promulgation of Legislation.

12 Timothy Reinold, 'Implementing the Law in Vietnam' Newsletter of British Business Group in Hanoi.

Many ministries and State bodies have resisted issuing clarifying Directives in their sectors. The British Business Group in Vietnam concluded that difficulties in the implementation of the Enterprise Law resulted from the following factors: different regional interpretations; vagueness of some of the language used in legislation or poor drafting; an inability to adapt to change; an unwillingness to cede 'sovereignty' over an issue; and inability or unwillingness to allow one ministry to be in charge of and to co-ordinate the necessary legislation on behalf of all the ministries involved.[13]

In Vietnam, legislation continues to be valid until it is denounced or repealed by other legislation issued by the same authority or by a higher authority. Any implementing legislation will also be invalidated once a new law is passed dealing comprehensively with the same subject matter. In practice, there are situations in which provisions of the implementing legislation for repealed laws, which are not contrary to the new law, may temporarily be used, pending the issuance of new implementing legislation. To legalise the continuing use of old implementing legislation, the Government will issue a notice sanctioning interim use. It is questionable whether this Government notice, which has lower legislative authority, can determine the validity of higher ranked legislation.

(2) Recent legal reform: country renovation

The Constitution of the Socialist Republic of Vietnam, passed in 1992, has paved the way for the renovation of the country. Article 15 of the Constitution provides that the State will promote a multi-component, commodity-based economy functioning in accordance with market mechanisms. One of the main ideas of the renovation program is to recognise the existence of economic sectors other than the State sector. Nevertheless, the intention to retain a socialist orientation is clearly expressed in Article 15, which re-affirms the leading role of the state economic sector. While private ownership is recognised as valid, ownership by the entire people and by collectives constitutes the foundation of the State economy.[14] Accordingly, the Vietnamese Constitution is designed to achieve socialist goals on the political front and at the same time to develop a market-driven economy.

The 1992 Constitution has without doubt marked a fundamental change in the economic system of Vietnam. Since 1992, Vietnam has no longer pursued a solely planned economy and the economic system has shifted towards a market orientation. The Vietnamese Communist Party, whose role as the leader of society is confirmed in the 1992 Constitution,[15] argues that the development of socialism goes through stages and that Vietnam is presently in a transition to a brand of socialism in which different forms of ownership co-

---

13 *Ibid.*

14 Article 15 of the 1992 Constitution.

15 Article 4 of the 1992 Constitution.

exist.[16] This phasing theory is also adopted by Chinese Marxist scholars who argue that at the primary stage of socialism the acceptance and acknowledgement of multiple economic sectors is essential and thus 'socialist legality in a transitional period is not necessarily aimed at eliminating the capitalist phenomenon'.[17]

Traditional Marxist theory postulates that the 'infrastructure' of the economic system will be reflected in the 'superstructure', which includes the legal system. In its relationship with the economy, the legal system will therefore be designed to reflect changes in the economic environment. The revised concepts developed by some Chinese Marxist theorists regarding a parallel relation between infrastructure and superstructure[18] may explain the co-existence of a socialist political system and a market-driven economy.

By stressing the difference between the capitalist market economy and a socialist-oriented market economy, Vietnamese Marxists attempt to explain the unique nature of socialist legality in a transition period. They stress that although different forms of ownership co-exist, as occurs in the capitalist market economy, state ownership will remain in its dominant role in the socialist-oriented market economy.[19] In practical terms, this leads to the maintenance of incentives and advantages for the State sector.

On the other hand, by acknowledging the existence of non-state sectors, the Vietnamese Government is committed to creating a legal environment for them to operate in and fairly compete with each other.[20] By initiating economic reform, recognising the importance of the private sector and introducing a stock market, Vietnam has committed itself to creating a legal environment which suits market mechanisms. The old legal system, which was designed to serve a purely planned economy, will not work in the new environment. The non-state sectors, including the foreign investment sector, require a legal framework that ensures their autonomy and comparable treatment with the State sector. In this respect, the Vietnamese situation is very similar to the reform process in China. To provide a platform for all sectors to flourish in a market-oriented economy, the country is required to ensure legal equality among the sectors. Further, as observed by practitioners and

---

16 Some fundamental points of the draft political report to be made to the 9th National Party Congress, delivered by Nguyen Phu Trong, Politburo Member, Standing Member of the Document Subcommittee of the 9th National Party Congress presented at the rapporteur Conference held by the Party Central Commission for Culture and Ideology on 17 July 2000 at Hanoi. [http://www.cpv.org.vn/hotnews/nguyenphutrong_fundamentalpoints.htm]

17 Chih-Yu Shih, 'China's Socialist Law Under Reform: The Class Nature Reconsidered' (1996) 44 American Journal of Comparative Law: 627, at 641.

18 *Ibid.* Some Chinese Marxists scholars believe that the legal system as superstructure does not have to exclusively reflect either the political or the economic systemic because there is a parallel relation between the understructure and superstructure.

19 *Ibid.*

20 Nguyen Phu Trong, *supra*, note 16.

commentators, the Chinese Government has had to relinquish a portion of its control to achieve the market dynamics demanded by companies.[21]

(3) *The response of the legal system to a dual task: establishing a market economy while maintaining a socialist orientation*

(a) The dual tasks of the legal system

It has been observed that legislators in communist countries and former communist countries that are undergoing reform have faced challenges in creating a predictable legal system which will safeguard property sufficiently to encourage enterprise investment and which at the same time will maintain the 'social order and social lubrication'.[22] The 1992 Vietnamese Constitution emphasises the task of the State in constructing a multi-sector economy while maintaining a socialist orientation. Fundamental legal concepts such as private ownership and property rights, which are necessary in a market economy, must be introduced to the legal system of Vietnam under the renovation programme. Equivalence of juridical subjects before the law is another fundamental legal issue confronting legislators in Communist countries. Pashukanis, a Marxist legal theorist, expounded the principle that all legal subjects must be equal before the law. This principle is stated in the Vietnamese Constitution:

> Production and trading enterprises belonging to all components of the economy must fulfil all their obligations to the State; they are equal before the law; their capital and lawful property shall receive State protection.[23]

In communist countries under reform, including Vietnam, there is recognition of a multi-sector economy and protection of legitimate private ownership. However, State ownership still retains its central position. As noted above, Article 15 of the Constitution paves the way for the construction of legislation in favour of State owned enterprises, which are purportedly subject to the ownership of the entire people. The distinction between different types of ownership and the existence of different laws for different types of companies has been criticized by practitioners and business communities as a failure to create a level playing field across all sectors.[24]

(b) The legal response to the dual tasks

The legal system in Vietnam is being required to serve simultaneously as a means of market liberalization and as a continuing tool to maintain the

21 Anna Han, 'China's Company Laws: Practicing Capitalism in a Transitional Economy' (1996) 5 Pacific Rim Law & Policy Journal: 457, at 467.

22 E Kamenka and A Tay, 'Legal Entities, Property and the Collapse of Communism' (1993) 19(1) India Socio-Legal Journal: 157.

23 Article 22 of the 1992 Constitution.

24 This issue has been a topic of informal discussion among the business community and has been addressed in some articles including: 'Positive Proposals: Equal Treatment to All Businesses' *Saigon Times Weekly* No 13'-00 (442) 25 March, 2000. [www.saigontimesweekly.saigonnet.vn]

political authority of the Vietnamese Communist Party.[25] One response to these dual tasks is to amend legislation piece by piece in order to meet economic demands without altering the basic underlying principles of a socialist country.

For example, by a licensing and reporting mechanism, the State is empowered to oversee the business activities of companies. Prior to the enactment of the Enterprise Law, the incorporation of a domestic company or foreign investment enterprise was subject to a time-consuming procedure conducted by the assessment departments of local governments.[26] A company was incorporated once a licence was granted by and registered with the relevant authority. The State would intervene in the business by defining the objectives within which the company could operate. The incorporation process is simplified under the Enterprise Law. In the normal situation, a company can be incorporated by registration without the need to apply for a business licence.

However, the licensing system continues to apply to the establishment of a company, which operates a conditional business. In such a case, the company promoters must apply to the relevant authority for a business licence. By the approval process and licence issuing procedure, the State can maintain its control over selected business areas in pursuit of its socialist objectives.

In addition, a company that intends to issue shares is required to apply for a licence from the State Securities Commission (SSC). Furthermore, in order to be listed on the stock exchange, an issuer must obtain another licence from the Stock Trading Centre, which is a subordinate of the SSC. During the investment period, increases of capital, changes in business objectives and transfers of interest will not take effect until approval is obtained from the relevant authority.

Another solution to the dual tasks is to word legislation broadly so that local institutions are allowed the flexibility necessary to implement economic reform, while retaining social and political security. This approach is modelled after the example of China. Chinese laws tend to be vaguely and broadly drafted, giving maximum room for Government officials to interpret the laws in accordance with changes in policy.[27] As the laws are drafted in broad terms, Chinese legislators are able to control interpretation by issuing implementing legislation to restrict activities which are deemed to be contrary to the socialist orientation.[28] Likewise, in Vietnam, the obligation of interpreting laws rests

25 Mark Sidel, 'Vietnam: The Complex Transition from Soviet Models in Legal Scholarship and Training' (1993) 11 UCLA Pacific Basin Law Journal: 221.

26 Kerkvliet, 'Diological Law Making and Implementation in Vietnam' in Alice Tay (ed), *East Asia: Human Rights, Nation Building, Trade*, 1999, Baden-Baden: Nomos Verlagsgesellschaft, at 419.

27 Anna Han, 'China's Company Laws: Practicing Capitalism in a Transitional Economy' (1996) 5 Pacific Rim Law & Policy Journal: 457, at 466.

28 *Ibid.*

on officials whose exposition is subjective and varies depending on individual ability. As a result, the efficiency of a new law in Vietnam is subject to the ability of Government officials to interpret laws in the correct manner.

This potential for inconsistency does not satisfy the need for a legal system that creates a platform for the private sector to expand. The market economy requires a united legal system and common principles equally applicable throughout the country. The law-making mechanism in Vietnam, and the dual tasks imposed on the legal system by the requirements of socialism, impact upon the corporate life of Vietnam and consequently affect the operation of the new stock market.

II General features of the development of corporate law in Vietnam

(1) Lack of uniform laws for corporations

Unlike in Australia where a uniform corporations law applies to all companies regardless of their source of capital, Vietnamese companies are classified by their ownership. Companies in Vietnam will thus be governed by one of three different laws: the State Owned Enterprise Law,[29] the Foreign Investment Law,[30] and the Enterprise Law.[31]

Companies owned by the State are separately governed by the State-Owned Enterprise Law while companies with foreign capital are subject to the Foreign Investment Law. Companies with non-State domestic capital are incorporated under the Enterprise Law. Two main corporate forms are introduced in the Enterprise Law: (1) Limited liability companies (which are similar to companies limited by guarantee) and (2) Shareholding companies (which are equivalent to Australian public companies). Both types of companies bear limited liability, however, only shareholding companies are able to raise funds through public share offerings.

Among the three laws, the Enterprise Law is the most general and comprehensive and the other two laws regulate certain areas by reference to it. For instance, a foreign investment enterprise, which is established under the Foreign Investment Law, is regarded as a Vietnamese entity bearing limited liability as defined in the Enterprise Laws.[32]

Under the Foreign Investment Law, foreign investment enterprises are not allowed to be incorporated in the form of shareholding companies and

29 The State Owned Enterprise Law was passed in 1996.

30 The Foreign Investment Law, originally introduced in 1987, was amended for the fourth time in July 2000.

31 The Enterprise Law was passed in 1999 and came into effect in January 2000. The Enterprise Law is a unification of the Law on Companies and the Law on Private Enterprises, which respectively governed limited liability companies, shareholding companies and private enterprises.

32 Articles 6 and 15 of the Foreign Investment Law, which took effect in July 2000.

therefore their shares are not freely transferable.[33] The reason for this restriction will be discussed in Part C, which deals with foreign participation in the stock market.

Under Vietnamese laws, a State-owned enterprise (SOE) is a company that is wholly-subsidized by the State. Similar to Chinese State companies, Vietnamese SOEs are not formed through the approval and registration mechanism but rather by administrative decision. SOEs are separately governed by the State Owned Enterprise Law, which contains incentives reflecting the recognition of the priority of State owned enterprises. Accordingly, the operation or winding-up of an SOE is not governed by the same laws that apply to other kinds of companies.

However, a State owned enterprise can be privatized and converted into a shareholding company governed by the Enterprise Law,[34] following which it will be able to issue shares subject to the applicable conditions under the Enterprise Law. Shares in equitized companies of this nature dominate the Vietnamese corporate securities market.

Constructing a uniform legal system which disciplines corporate life in Vietnam has been a contentious topic. The State's efforts to create a common platform for all sectors have been reflected through the promulgation of the Enterprise Law, which prepares the legal ground for the transformation of State-owned enterprises into shareholding companies.

(2) Foreign and Vietnamese characteristics of the enterprise law

During its law reform program, Vietnam received legal drafting assistance from foreign countries. As a result of this assistance, foreign legal ideology has been transplanted into the Vietnamese legal system. However, the transplantation of foreign legal ideology into the Vietnamese legal system is inconsistent and at times inappropriate because western advisers failed to take into account local economic and social factors.[35] Moreover, as commentators have observed, 'big-bang' reforms whereby the existing socialist legal system is replaced with western ideology are not suitable in Vietnam.[36] The Russian experience with high levels of social instability as a result wholesale transplantation of Western legal ideas demonstrates that western legal ideology must be implemented with great attention to the prevailing social conditions.[37]

33 A draft amendment to the Foreign Investment Law proposed that foreign investors have the right to form shareholding companies that would be entitled to raise funds through share issuance. However, this amendment was rejected by the National Assembly.

34 State Bank Circular 07/1998/TT-NHH1 dated 28 September 2000 provides for a transition period during which an equitised company continues to enjoy incentives in bank loans as they did prior to privatisation.

35 J Gillespie, 'Vietnam: The Emergence of a Law-based State' in Alice Tay (ed), *East Asia: Human Rights, Nation Building, Trade*, 1999, Baden-Baden: Nomos Verlagsgesellschaft, at 356.

36 *Ibid*, at 357.

37 *Ibid*.

In accordance with the 1992 Constitution, Vietnam has persistently maintained a socialist orientation while constructing a market-driven economy. This feature of the economy is very similar to Chinese law, which introduces and promotes the new concept of a 'socialist market'.[38] Chinese legislation has therefore had significant influence on Vietnamese legislation governing corporate life. However, Vietnamese legislators have learned from Chinese mistakes and have modified the principles of company law in areas such as powers of shareholders and classification of shares owned by foreign investors. While sharing common socialist principles, Vietnamese society is not at the same stage of development as China and cannot adopt all aspects of the Chinese model. This observation accords with OECD guidelines for transition economies which recommend that legal systems should not be copied either from the law of mature markets or even from the law of other countries at a similar stage of development.[39]

In the opening Statement of General Principles, the Enterprise Law emphasises economic renovation, and recognises equality between all economic sectors. Furthermore, the Enterprise Law applies Western legal corporate principles to ensure investor confidence. Like the Australian Corporations Law, the Enterprise Law seeks to protect the legitimate rights and interests of investors. However, the adoption of western legal ideology is tailored to suit Vietnam's socialist policies. The Enterprise Law explicitly states its aim of strengthening the effectiveness of State management over business activities. A socialist orientation is reflected in the presence of the Supervisory Board and in the distribution of powers and obligations among the shareholders and the Board of Management. The Enterprise Law is similar to the Chinese Company Law in its efforts to allow business autonomy and maximum operating efficiency while giving up the minimum amount of political control.[40]

B: Share issuance and the shareholder-management relationship under the enterprise law

I: Share issuance under the Enterprise Law

(1) Conditions for an initial share offering

A company wishing to issue shares must satisfy the conditions for an initial share offering, which cannot be launched until a licence is obtained from the State Securities Commission.

38 See Anna Han, 'China's Company Laws: Practicing Capitalism in a Transitional Economy' (1996) 5 Pacific Rim Law & Policy Journal: 457.

39 OECD General Principles of Company Law for Transition Companies. [www.oecd.org]

40 See Anna Han, 'China's Company Laws: Practicing Capitalism in a Transitional Economy' (1996) 5 Pacific Rim Law & Policy Journal: 457.

The first requirement is that the promoters must hold at least 20% of ordinary shares within the first 3 years from the date the business registration certificate is obtained.[41] The second requirement for an initial issuance of shares is a minimum level of authorized capital of 10 billion dongs.[42] China has a similar requirement regarding level of capital. Both China and Vietnam have experienced a poor supply of shares offered in the stock exchange partly as a result of this rigid capital requirement.[43] The Vietnamese Government has attempted to justify this condition on the basis that it will ensure quality shares for the emerging stock market and win the confidence of investors.[44] However, there is no necessary correlation between the size of a company and its profitability.

The third requirement is that at least 15% of shares must be issued to one hundred investors other than the promoters.[45] By this requirement, the Government seeks to avoid domination of a company by a small number of investors. This appears to be an application of the theory of distributing wealth to the public at large in order to provide opportunities for common people. Whether it is possible to impose this socialist ideology on the stock market is questionable. The main reason for a company to issue shares is to raise funds for development and whether the funds come from many or few people is irrelevant. Furthermore, from a practical point of view, it is unlikely that an issuer will know, at the time of applying for an issuing licence, the number of investors likely to be interested in purchasing shares. This requirement also fails to take account of increased involvement in the stock market by institutional investors. Modern individual shareholders tend to invest through fund management schemes or other institutions with professional staff trained to obtain relevant investment information and reduce the element of risk.

(2) Classes of shares and dividends

The Australian Corporations Law restricts the right of companies to create preference shares, however Vietnamese companies are free from such restrictions. In accordance with s 254A(2) of the Corporations Law, a company is not entitled to issue preference shares unless the company Constitution or a special resolution expressly sets out the right to issue preference shares. By contrast, under the Enterprise Law, in addition to ordinary shares, a shareholding company may issue two types of preferential shares.[46] The first type, voting preferential shares, allow for a greater number

41 Article 58 of the Enterprise Law.

42 Article 6 of Decree 48/CP dated 11 July 1998.

43 Alison Chan, 'East Meets West: A Discussion of China's Company Law from an Australian Perspective' (1999) 10 Australian Journal of Corporate Law: 290.

44 *Saigon Times* interview with Mr Vu Bang, Vice Chairman of the State Securities Commission and Director of the HCMC Stock Exchange. [www.stockmarket.vnn.vn]

45 The minimum level is 20% if the issued capital exceeds 100 billion dongs.

46 Article 52 of the Enterprise Law.

of votes than ordinary shares. The numbers of votes allocated to voting-preferential shareholders will be determined in the constitution of the issuing company.[47] The second type, dividend-preferential shares, have a higher rate of dividend but without rights to participate and vote at the Shareholders' General Assembly.[48]

Voting preferential shares cannot be issued to the public at large but only to organizations authorized by the Government and the promoters.[49] The Enterprise Law requires that entities eligible to purchase preference shares must be specified in the company's constitution.[50] This requirement appears to be imposed for the purpose of increasing the involvement and influence of governmental shareholders and promoters.

Voting preferential shares will automatically be converted into ordinary shares after three years from the issue of a business registration certificate. By their nature, preferential shares are not transferable[51] but may be converted into ordinary shares at any time subject to the approval of the General Shareholders' Assembly. Ordinary shares cannot be converted into preferential shares.

Dividend preferential shares are comparable to non-participating preference shares in Australia. The holders of dividend preferential shares are entitled to a higher and more stable rate of dividend. In this respect the Enterprise Law is more specific than its Australian counterpart, providing that the dividend of a dividend preferential shareholder will comprise: (1) a fixed rate which is not dependent on the company's operating result; and (2) a bonus dividend.[52] In return dividend-preferential shareholders are entitled neither to vote nor to attend the General Shareholders' Assembly nor to nominate the Board of Directors.[53]

In addition to these two classes of shares, redeemable preference shares may be offered by an issuing company. In common with the Australian Corporations Laws, the Enterprise Law restricts share-buy backs by the company. However, companies are entitled to issue preference shares which the company will redeem at any time as requested by the relevant owner, or on the conditions stated in the redeemable-preferential share certificate. Both the Corporations Law and the Enterprise Law provide comparable treatment to the holders of redeemable preference shares and creditors. Article 56(2) of the Enterprise Law confirms the priority of redeemable shareholders to be fully repaid the capital contribution. This priority is ranked as high as the priority of

47 Article 55 of the Enterprise Law.

48 Article 56 of the Enterprise Law.

49 Article 52(3) of the Enterprise Law.

50 Article 52(4) of the Enterprise Law.

51 Article 55 of the Enterprise Law.

52 Article 56(1) of the Enterprise Law.

53 Article 56(3) of the Enterprise Law.

creditors. While the Australian Corporations Law covers issues such as the redemption process and the procedure for cancellation of shares after redemption,[54] the Enterprise Law is silent on these issues. Vietnamese issuers and shareholders will experience difficulties in implementing redemption provisions until a specific process for redemption is provided in the implementing legislation.

As analyzed above, in both Australia and Vietnam, redeemable preference shareholders are exposed to the same risk as creditors since they can recall their capital at their own discretion or after a certain period. From the issuer's perspective, the issue of redeemable preference shares has advantages and disadvantages in comparison with obtaining loans. By issuing redeemable preference shares, the issuer can call for the capital needed without entering into mortgage or guarantee procedures, which are time-consuming. Moreover, in Vietnam, loans from a foreign lenders are subject to the approval of the State Bank of Vietnam. However, redeemable preference shares are disadvantageous in terms of tax consequences for the issuer. While interest paid to lenders will be tax deductible, the payment of a fixed dividend to redeemable shareholders is not.[55]

III: Shareholder-management relations

(1) The distribution of power between shareholders and the board of management

The General Assembly of Shareholders is the highest authority within the corporation. The Assembly is a meeting of shareholders held at least once a year to approve important matters such as contracts with a value of more than 20% of the assets of the company,[56] share buy-backs greater than 10% and restructuring of the company.[57] The Shareholders' Assembly will also, upon the recommendation of the Board of Management, determine the type and quantity of shares to be offered as well as the dividend from issued shares.

Vietnam has learnt from China's experience in the overlap and conflict of powers between the Shareholders' Assembly and the Board of Management.[58] The Enterprise Law distributes powers so that the Board of Management is

54 See discussion in HAJ Ford, RP Austin and IM Ramsay, *Ford's Principles of Corporations Law*, 9th edn, 1999, Melbourne. Butterworths: at [24.610].

55 See P Lipton and A Herzberg, *Understanding Company Law*, 1999, Sydney: LBC Information Services, at 164.

56 Article 87 of the Enterprise Law.

57 Article 70 of the Enterprise Law.

58 Alison Chan, 'East Meets West: A Discussion of China's Company Law from an Australian Perspective' (1999) 10 Australian Journal of Corporate Law: 290, at 297. Article 38(1) of the Chinese Company Law empowers the shareholders meeting to determine the business operation of investment plans of the company while Article 46 imposes on the directors the responsibility to decide the business and investment plan of the company.

responsible for producing a development strategy and investment plan, however, the medium and long term business plan prepared by the Board of Management is subject to the approval of the Shareholders' Assembly.[59] This distinction, however, is not clear enough to resolve potential conflicts between the powers of the Board of Management and the interests of shareholders.

Though the Shareholders' Assembly appears to hold the supreme power in corporate life, the Board of Management is able to influence the Shareholders' Assembly by recommending the matters for the Assembly to consider. This is because the Board of Management is authorized to approve the agenda of the Shareholders' Assembly.[60] In addition, the limited rights of Vietnamese shareholders are revealed in relation to the authority to request a general meeting, which is more limited than that of shareholders in Australia. A shareholder or a group of shareholders will have the authority to request a general meeting only where they hold 10% of the company shares for six consecutive months or a lesser percentage as specified in the company's charter,[61] and where the board of management commits serious breaches of their obligations.[62] Subject to these conditions, Vietnamese shareholders are authorised to 'request' a general meeting while their Australian counterparts have authority directly to convene a general meeting.[63] Australian shareholders are permitted to call a general meeting if they hold 5% of issued shares.[64]

(2) *No separation of ownership and management*

Vietnamese corporate laws do not address fundamental corporate principles such as separation of ownership and management, corporate governance and directors' duties. In the same way as China's Company Law,[65] the Vietnamese Enterprise Law gives the shareholders supreme power in theory but limits the authority of shareholders in practice. To some extent, shareholders under the Enterprise Law are able to influence the business decision-making process. For example, the Shareholders' Assembly is required to approve contracts the value of which exceeds 20% of the assets of the company.[66] As the

59 Articles 70 and 80 of Enterprise Law.

60 Article 80 of the Enterprise Law.

61 Article 53(2)(b) of the Enterprise Law.

62 Article 86 of the Enterprise Law sets out serious breaches by the Board of Management which would give rise to the authority of a shareholder or group of shareholders holding 10% of shares to call for a general meeting. These breaches include (1) the failure to exercise rights and duties allocated in a truthful and dedicated manner; (2) the failure to comply with the notification obligations towards creditors when the company cannot pay its debts; (3) the failure to make recommendations on how to deal with financial difficulties (4) the use of assets of the company to gain benefits for themselves and other people.

63 Section 249F of the Corporations Law.

64 *Ibid.*

65 Alison Chan, 'East Meets West: A Discussion of China's Company Law from an Australian Perspective' (1999) 10 Australian Journal of Corporate Law: 290, at 297.

66 Article 87 of the Enterprise Law.

Shareholders' Assembly usually meets only once a year, this requirement for approval of contracts before the Board of Management can sign may slow down business transactions. This power enables the shareholders to influence management decisions causing difficulties for efficient business operation.

The motivation behind the legal requirement for approval of large contracts is related to the democratic principles of a socialist country as well as to the philosophy of investor protection. However, this extent of democratic involvement may not be workable in the dynamic context of a market-driven economy where fierce competition requires quick and accurate reactions from the Board of Management. The balance between the powers of the Board of Management and the interests of investors would be solved with the introduction of a corporate governance culture into Vietnamese corporations legislation.

(3) Lack of explicit provisions on directors' duties of care

Unlike the Australian Corporation Laws under which Directors' duties of care are heavily regulated, Article 86 of the Vietnamese Enterprise Law only touches briefly upon the obligations of management staff by requiring them to 'exercise rights and duties allocated in a truthful and dedicated manner in the interests of the company and share-holders of the company'.[67] The Enterprise Law does not specify the sanctions against the violation of a director's duty of care and duty to act with good faith. In the absence of a specific sanction against the violation of the directors' duty of care, the efficiency of Article 86 is questionable.

Rather than providing specific measures to handle breaches of the duty of care, the Enterprise Law sets forth a general provision on the handling of breaches in Article 121. By this provision, the Enterprise Law characterises the directors' duty of care in the same manner as the general duties, making directors liable to pay compensation in damages. However, Article 121 of the Enterprise Law only provides a general remedy for breaches:

> Where a breach has caused damage to the interests of an enterprise, its owner, members, shareholders, creditors, or other persons, the violator must compensate for damage in accordance with the law.

This provision is, on the one hand, broad enough to include general breaches affecting the interests of a company and its shareholders, but on the other hand, is not specific enough to enforce the directors' duty of acting in good faith. The wording of Article 121 focuses on the consequences of the violation and in cases where the breach causes 'damage' the violators will be required to compensate. In this context, the injured shareholders must prove the causal connection between the violation and the damage. However, neither the definition of damage nor the form of compensation is explicitly set out in the

67 Article 86 of the Enterprise Law.

Enterprise Law. These issues will require either considerable judicial consideration or illuminating implementing legislation.

Similar rules can be found in the Chinese counterpart to the Enterprise Law. The Chinese Company Law does not expressly impose a duty of care upon Directors.[68] However, China considers the duties of care and good faith to be implied duties 'which are in fact more onerous than the implied duties of directors in Australian companies'.[69] The incompetence or negligence of the directors in managing a company may constitute a breach of these general duties.[70]

(4) Disclosure through the reporting mechanism

Disclosure obligations, which are extremely crucial in making the stock market operate smoothly, are discussed in the new Enterprise Law and in Decree 48/1998/ND-CP (Decree 48) in the form of reporting requirements. Decree 48 and State Security Commission Decision 04/1999/TT-UBCK[71] stress the importance of the reporting regime for the purposes of state management[72] and do not elaborate on how information is to be made available and accessible to the public and to investors. The principle ways of informing the public are publication in newspapers and availability of prospectuses at the State Security Commission and the Securities Trading Centre.

C: The stock market

I: Conditions prior to the establishment of the stock market

(1) The need for a stock market

As Vietnam has been persistent in its socialist orientation, the laws on companies are tailored to emphasise the importance of companies under State ownership. Only after the launch of the economic renovation program in 1986 was the private sector officially recognized. At the time, the Law on Companies, a predecessor to the Enterprise Law, was passed to govern companies with private-owned capital. The formation of joint-stock companies was first allowed under the Law on Companies. The Enterprise Law further elaborates the management of joint-stock companies as well as the corporate finance issues of joint-stock companies.

---

68 Alison Chan, 'East Meets West: A Discussion of China's Company Law from an Australian Perspective' (1999) 10 Australian Journal of Corporate Law: 290, at 301.

69 *Ibid.*

70 *Ibid.*

71 State Security Commission Decision 04/1999/TT-UBCK on Regulations on Members, Listing, Publication of Information and Securities Trading.

72 See Article 18 of Decree 48/1998/ND-CP dated 11 July 1998 and Article 5.2 of Decision 04/1999/TT-UBCK dated 27 March 1999, specifying a detailed report regime to the State Security Commission.

Nevertheless, in the absence of a stock market, fund raising in Vietnam was very restricted. This restriction prompted the Government to establish a stock market in Vietnam. The Government started to discuss the establishment of a stock market in 1993, however, its formation was delayed considerably.[73] State leaders explained that the reason for the lengthy establishment process was the careful implementation of the stock market including the creation of a legal system dealing with establishment and operation of a securities industry.[74]

This process began with the introduction of the comprehensive Enterprise Law in 1998, which introduced more detailed provisions on corporate finance, and formed the foundation for the operation of a stock market. Following this was the issue of a series of legislation on the stock market, including Decree 48/CP which played the key role in regulating the operation of the stock market.

(2) Challenges for the emergent stock market

Despite the initial excitement produced by the new investment form of the stock market, concern was expressed over the limited number of trading opportunities. It was reported that the first transactions traded shares issued from only five companies.[75] Accordingly, except for Government bonds, products traded in the Stock Exchange are limited to the shares offered from five equitised companies. The reasons for such deficiency of stock for trading can be traced back to the characteristics of corporate law in Vietnam. Not until the Enterprise Law was passed did the concept of shareholding companies become popular in the corporate life of Vietnam. The total number of shareholding companies established under the Law on Companies, the predecessor to the Enterprise Law, was only 300. With the introduction of the Enterprise Law, however, the number of shareholding companies had doubled by May 2000.

(3) Privatization program and first public share offerings in the stock exchange

Privatization is the process whereby State ownership in a government enterprise is shifted to the private sector.[76] There are three basic models which enable a shift of ownership from the government sector to the private sector: (1) conversion into a shareholding company; (2) transfer of the undertaking to a government owned company; and (3) direct transfer to the purchaser.[77] In

73 AFP, 'Trial Bourse to Open on Time Despite Scepticism' Vietnam Investment Review No 452, 12–19 June 2000. [www.vir.vietnam.com]

74 Ha Thang, 'Stock market Now Ready for July Initiation' Vietnam Investment Review No 448, 15–21 May 2000. [www.vir.vietnam.com]

75 Source: www.stockmarket.vnn.vn

76 B Collier and S Pitkin (eds), *Corporatisation and Privatisation in Australia: A Collection of Papers Examining Legal, Economic and Policy Issues*, 1999, North Ryde: CCH Australia, at xv.

77 'Legal techniques in Privatization – Using the Law to Facilitate the Sale Process' in B Collier and S Pitkin (eds), *Corporatisation and Privatisation in Australia: A Collection of Papers Examining Legal, Economic and Policy Issues*, 1999, North Ryde: CCH Australia.

Vietnam, this process occurs by way of conversion of a state enterprise into a shareholding company in accordance with the Enterprise Law and Decree 44/CP of 28 June 1998 (Decree 44).

Scholars have observed that the privatization trend 'has swept the world'.[78] Vietnam is no exception to this world trend. In Vietnam, the process of transforming state enterprises into shareholding companies is referred to as 'equitisation' rather than 'privatization'. Foreign commentators have criticised the replacement of the term 'privatisation' with the term 'equitisation', interpreting it as a sign that the term 'privatization' remains 'taboo' in Vietnam.[79] However, equitization is an appropriate term to refer to the process of dividing capital of a State owned enterprise into equal share portions which will then be sold to the employees and the public. The term 'equitization' has the implication of 'equity' and 'equality'[80] in sharing and distributing the interests of companies throughout society.

The process of equitisation will convert State owned enterprises into shareholding companies whose shares will be distributed to non-state sectors. However, in some equitised companies, the State still holds a large quantity of shares. Moreover, the State retains its controlling rights by obtaining voting preferential shares, which carry more votes than ordinary shares. As a result, State shareholders can still dominate the voting and decision-making procedures in an equitised company.

One defining characteristic of the Vietnamese stock market, apart from the high presence of Government bonds, is that the first transactions at the Stock exchanges all involved listed shares from equitized companies. However, out of 420 State owned enterprises converting into shareholding companies, only 50 met the requirements for listing of their shares.[81] The slow implementation of equitization has been heavily criticised.[82] One explanation for the slow progress of equitization is the lack of policies regulating the equitisation process. For instance, a Decree on equitisation was issued but specific guidelines from relevant Ministries and authorities are still unavailable.[83] A second explanation is the difficulty in assessing the value of assets in

78 'Privatisation Policy in the 1990s' in B Collier and S Pitkin (eds), *Corporatisation and Privatisation in Australia: A Collection of Papers Examining Legal, Economic and Policy Issues*, 199, North Ryde: CCH Australia, at 3.

79 Kevin Bubel, 'Equitisation of Enterprises in Vietnam' Market Report, 1 September 1998.

80 David Lempert, 'Interpreting Vietnam: Ideology and "Newspeak"' (2000) 24 Legal Studies Forum 175.

81 Source: www.stockmarket.vnn.vn

82 'SOEs Under Close Inspection: A Discussion with the Central Committee for State-owned Enterprises Reform' *Saigon Times Weekly* No 21-'00 (450), 20 May 2000. [www.saigontimesweekly.saigonnet.vn]

83 *Ibid.*

State-owned enterprises, a problem exacerbated by insufficient legal guidance.[84]

In response to the need for guidance in determination of asset value, Decree 44 sets out principles to determine the value of enterprises. According to Decree 44, the actual value of an equitised enterprise shall be determined based on current quality and technical unity and shall be subject to agreement between the enterprise and share purchasers. Decree 44 allows an equitised company to include in its value business advantages derived from its geographical location and product prestige. However, most of the business advantages of a State-owned enterprise result from preferential treatment by the State. Therefore, it is hard to evaluate business advantages in accordance with the criteria provided by Decree 44, such as geographical location and product prestige. This confusion in determining the actual assets of an equitised company will not only slow down the equitisation process but will also affect the accuracy of share prices.

In addition, directors and employees of State-owned enterprises contribute to the delay in equitisation. Foreign critics observe that neither directors nor employees of State-owned enterprises are enthusiastic about the program. The directors of State-owned enterprises are concerned that without the State acting as an umbrella, they will be subject to the whims of the shareholders.[85] Directors' concerns are also grounded in the change of status brought to State-owned enterprises upon equitisation. Once converted under the equitisation program, a shareholding company will be governed by the Enterprise Law and will no longer be entitled to preferential treatment under the State-Owned Enterprise Law.

To allay such concerns, Vietnamese legislators grant taxation and banking incentives for equitised companies. In addition to the incentives under Article 13 of Decree 44, which provides a tax deduction of 50% for the first two successive years after transformation into a shareholding company, equitised companies are entitled to retain incentives in banking granted to their predecessors. Interests rate and incentives in obtaining loans from credit institutions remain unchanged for equitised companies. They are also entitled to the preferential loan mechanism available to State-Owned Enterprises.[86]

It is presumed that equitised companies will continue to enjoy banking incentives for the entire life of the company since the Vietnamese State Bank does not specify any time limitation for these entitlements. This system perpetuates the practice of unequal treatment among companies of the same

84 See 'Progress of Implementation of Equitisation is Still Slow' Saigon Liberation 25 August 1997.

85 See Cindy Nguyen, 'The Vietnamese Stock Market: Viability in Southeast Asia and Appeal Around the World' (1998) 21 Loyola of Los Angeles International & Comparative Law Journal: 607. Nguyen cites Jonathon Birchall, 'Making Haste Slowly', Vietnam Economic Times, August 1997.

86 Article 1 of Circular 07/1998/TT-NHNN1 dated 28 September 1998.

type. As a result of slow equitisation and the limited number of shareholding companies that meet rigid the requirements for listing, the Vietnamese stock market has experienced serious imbalances between demand and supply of shares. In the three trading sessions of September 13, 15 and 18, there were 648,700 buy orders but only 128,900 were met. In other words, share demand was almost six times larger than supply.[87]

II: New laws governing the stock market

(1) Legal framework for the operation of the stock market

The Vietnamese stock market was in operation before a comprehensive securities law was passed. Deputy Prime Minister Nguyen Tan Dung stated that 'the securities market is a new idea in Vietnam' and a 'very sensitive factor of the market economy', thus, 'careful implementation will be the highest priority in Vietnam's consideration'.[88] It may be inferred from the 'careful implementation' of the Vietnamese Government that it wishes to operate the stock market on an experimental basis and to draw experience from reality. This assumption might also be supported by the fact that the securities law in Vietnam was issued in the form of a Government Decree, which is easily amended to accord with changes in Government policy.[89]

Vietnam chose to activate the securities industry with the legal basis of a Government Decree (Decree 48/CP) and a series of implementing legislation mainly issued by the State Securities Commission (SSC), a body in charge of monitoring and supervising the stock market.[90] This legal framework, based on a Government Decree, will give rise to more potential for flexibility at the discretion of the Government. In the legislative hierarchy, a Government Decree can easily be amended or repealed by another Decree issued by the Government or by new legislation. However, from the investors' point of view, this creates instability, and could affect the investment flow in the stock market.

The legal foundation for the securities market must be read closely with the Enterprise Law, which governs the operation and management of shareholding companies. The Enterprise Law contains basic provisions on

87 'Fledgling Stock Market Hampered by Serious Imbalances' Vietnam Investment Review No 467, 25 September – 1 October 2000. [www.vir.vietnam.com]

88 Ha Thang, 'Stock market Now Ready for July Initiation' Vietnam Investment Review No 448, 15-21 May 2000. [www.vir.vietnam.com]

89 Though the National Assembly Standing Committee drafted an Ordinance on Securities, the legislation was eventually issued in the form of a Government Decree rather than in the form of a Law or Ordinance.

90 Though the stock market was first introduced in July 2000, the SSC was formed under a Government Decision in 1996 with the main function of drafting legislation in preparation for the establishment of the stock market. Since the introduction of the stock market, the SSC has exercised State management over the securities industry while continuing its function of drafting legislation governing the industry.

Initial Public Offering ('IPO'), internal management, and the rights and obligations of the shareholders and Boards of Management. Further requirements for a shareholding company can be found in Decree 48/CP and its subordinate legislation. The Enterprise Law, however, only applies to companies under private ownership. Therefore, only companies with capital generated from the domestic private sector can be incorporated in the form of shareholding companies. The investment vehicle for foreign investors is restricted to the limited liability company.[91]

(2) *State management of the securities industry and the role of State Securities Commission*

(a) ***State management mechanism***

The Vietnamese securities industries is centrally organised under the uniform state management of the State Securities Commission (SSC), which was established pursuant to Decree 75/CP dated 28 November 1996. The SSC is an agency attached to the Government with the responsibility of coordinating with Ministries and industries for the organization, establishment and realization of the securities market in Vietnam.[92] The People's Committee and relevant industries are granted subordinate roles in the management of the stock market in Vietnam.[93]

The principal role of the SSC in performing uniform State management of the securities market is confirmed in Decree 48. Article 76 of Decree 48 provides that State management activities shall include: (1) Promulgation of legislation on securities and the securities market; (2) Formulating strategies, policies and plans for development of the securities market; (3) Granting or withdrawing various licences in relation to securities issue, business and services; (4) Organising and regulating the Centralised Exchange Market; (5) Inspecting and examining breaches of laws on securities and the securities market; (6) Providing professional training and disseminating knowledge on securities and the securities market; and (7) International co-operation in relation to securities and the securities market. The SSC began to perform its tasks by compiling the legislation governing the stock market.[94] The SSC is also responsible for the implementation of the legislation.

(b) ***The lack of a supervisory role***

Since a lack of corporate transparency can cause losses for investors, the assurance of proper disclosure is vital for the success of any stock market. For

---

91 Limited Liability Company in defined in Article 26 of the Enterprise Law as a company in which the members are responsible for the enterprise's liabilities and other property obligations to the extent of the capital proportion committed to be contributed into the enterprise. The members of a Vietnamese limited liability company will not exceed 50. A limited liability company is not entitled to issue shares.

92 Articles 1 and 2 of Decree 75 dated 28 November 1996.

93 Article 75.2 of Decree 48 states that the State Securities Commission shall be a body that exerts State management over the securities market.

94 Article 2 of Decree 75/CP dated 28 November 1996.

this reason, securing investor's interests has become the most important task of the securities commission in most countries with a stock market. Decree 48 does not place significant emphasis on the role of the SSC in protecting investors. The provisions setting out the role of the SSC in both Decree 75/CP and Decree 48/CP do not expressly address the role of supervising and enforcing the disclosure of information, though the disclosure of information falls within the scope of authority of the SSC.[95] It is critical that Decree 48 does not provide a supervision mechanism for the disclosure of information and does not specify the circumstances under which the disclosure of information is subject to inspection.

The Australian counterpart to the SSC, the Australian Securities and Investments Commission (ASIC) has a clear commitment 'to promote the confident and informed participation of investors and consumers in the financial system' and to ensure that information is available as soon as practicable for access by the public.[96] This approach reflects ASIC's due consideration for the importance of access to information by the public and potential investors.

Likewise, the Chinese State Securities Commission also makes a commitment to promoting information transparency and the confidence of investors. These efforts result from the Chinese experiences with declining investor confidence in the stock market caused by market fraud. The Chinese securities law places importance on the inspection role of The State Securities Commission in relation to disclosure of information connected to issuing and trading of securities.[97] In order to meet international standards, the Vietnamese SSC should take a greater role in supervising information disclosure procedures.

III: Market operation rules

(1) Securities trading centres and conditions for being listed on the stock exchange

Having obtained a license to issue shares, an issuer,[98] will not automatically be listed on the stock exchange but must first register to become listed.[99] An issuer wishing to list its shares on the stock exchange must submit a number of documents to a Securities Trading Centre (STC). For the time being

95 Article 78.2 of Decree 48/C dated 11 July 1998.

96 Section 1(2) of the Australian Securities and Investments Commission Act 1989 (Cth).

97 Roman Tomasic and Jian Fu, 'The Securities Law of the People's Republic China: An Overview' (1999) 10 Australian Journal of Corporate Law: 268, at 271.

98 An issuer is the term officially used in Decree 48/CP to refer to a legal entity permitted to issue securities to the public in accordance with the provisions of the Decree.

99 Article 16 of Decision 04/1999/TT-UBCK of SSC dated 27 March 1999.

Vietnam has only one Securities Trading Centre in Ho Chi Minh City where the first transaction took place in July 2000. Unlike the Australian Stock Exchange, the Vietnamese Securities Trading Centre is subordinate to the SSC and wholly subsidised by the State budget although the STC is a legal entity with its own seal, office and bank account.[100] The chairman of the SSC, as authorised by the Prime Minister, will appoint the directors of STCs and promulgate regulations for the organization and operation of STCs. This process allows the State to maintain control over the stock market.

Securities of an issuing organisation will be listed at the STC five (5) working days from the date on which the STC completely receives the application for registration. A company that registers to be listed at the STC but fails to list its shares within one year from the registration date, will be required to submit audited financial statements for two successive years together with the reasons for not listing the shares. This application must then be considered by the STC within 45 days.[101]

The listing requirement is even more rigid in China. Listing of shares on the Stock Exchange is subject to an approval, which is separate from the approval for issuance of shares. Registered companies are required to submit to the Stock Exchange certain documents, which are made available to the public along with the listing announcement published by the exchange, if and when the listing is approved.[102]

(2) Requirement for a prospectus

(a) Definition of a prospectus

An issuer of shares is obliged to prepare and submit a prospectus,[103] which is a written document representing its financial standing, business performance and plans for using capital obtained by issuing of shares.[104] According to Decree 48/CP, a prospectus is prepared by an issuer to provide the public with sufficient information to make a decision on purchasing shares.[105] In Vietnam, a prospectus forms an integral part of the application dossier for the issuing of a license.[106] It is not clear if the file lodged with the SSC as the application for issuing of a license must be disclosed to the public.

The information contained in the prospectus must comply with a 'check-list' provided in Decree 48 and its implementing legislation. In addition to

100 Article 21 of Decree 48/CP.

101 *Ibid.*

102 Jay Zhe Zhang, 'Securities Markets and Securities Regulation in China' (1997) 22 North Carolina Journal of International Law & Commercial Regulation: 557, at 597.

103 Article 50 of Decree 48/CP requires that the application for the issuing licence must include a prospectus.

104 Article 2 of Decree 48/CP.

105 *Ibid.*

106 Article 9 of Decree 48/CP dated 11 July 1998.

basic details of the company such as name, address, management structures, apportionment of shares and profiles of the Board of Management, the prospectus must contain an analysis of financial activities and the plan for issuing shares. A prospectus must also clearly state the rights attached to the shares.[107] Chinese law also sets out detailed lists of information that a prospectus must contain, including risk assessments, important contracts and pending lawsuits. This essential information is not expressly required in a prospectus under Vietnamese law. However, a listed company is obliged to make publication in central or local newspapers within 24 hours from the occurrence of any of a number of specified events.[108]

Vietnamese securities legislation does not expressly state that the listing of shares on an STC or Stock Exchange is compulsory and there is no requirement of information disclosure and publication for unlisted issuers. Accordingly, unlisted issuers may not be obliged to keep investors informed of the lawsuits and important matters relating to the issuer's business.

Instead of using a checklist for the information required in a prospectus, Australia adopts a general disclosure test. Section 1022 of the Corporations Law requires a prospectus to contain all information that investors and their professional advisers would reasonably expect to find in the prospectus.

(b) Making a prospectus known to the public

An issuer is not only obliged to prepare a prospectus but also to make some aspects of the prospectus known to the public. The concept of 'making known to the public' is critical to the disclosure process. As a means of ensuring publication, the obligation to publicize is imposed not only on the share issuer, but also upon the Stock Exchange.[109] In Vietnam an issuer is required to publicise a brief prospectus, which contains core information and specifies the share prices as stated in the prospectus submitted to the SSC. This information must be made available at branches of issuing agencies or public locations to which investors have convenient.[110] It is unclear what locations are deemed to be accessible. For example, it is difficult to determine whether the launch of a brief prospectus on a company web-site will satisfy the publicity requirement.

(3) Advertising prior to share issue

Prospectus advertising and securities hawking have concerned stock market regulators because investors can be misled by pre-issuance advertising. In an attempt to protect investors against advertising campaigns of issuers which may affect investment decisions, legislators regulate advertising prior to the issue of shares. The scope of regulation, however, varies from country to

107 Part III and Part IV of Circular 01/98/TT-UBCK dated 13 October 1998.

108 See below, note 142 and accompanying text.

109 Article 31 of Circular 04/1999/TT/UBCK dated 27 March 1999.

110 Part VI 4.5 Circular 01/1998/TT-UBCK dated 13 October 1998.

country. The Australian Corporations Law does not permit the advertising of share issue prior to the publication of a prospectus.[111] Under s 1025 of the Australia Corporations Law, share-holding companies are prohibited from publishing a notice offering unissued securities for subscription. The definition of 'publish' and 'notice' under s 9 of the Corporations Law can be broadly interpreted to include any statement that was circulated or distributed by means of broadcasting or televising or by publication in a newspaper.

In China, a prospectus must not be disclosed prior to approval for the issuance of shares. However, there is no prohibition on offering shares before the issuing license is granted. Consequently, investors can potentially purchase shares without adequate information about the company, placing their investments at risk.

Learning from China's experience, Vietnam tightened the rules on advertising or offering of shares prior to the grant of a licence. Hence, in Vietnam, even after a prospectus is submitted to the State Securities Commission in the form of an application for the issuance of shares, the issuer is not permitted to advertise or offer the shares in any form until the approval for issuance is granted. If a company proposes to conduct market research prior to approval it must be based on the information contained in the submitted prospectus.[112] There is a prohibition on the use of mass media to conduct market research prior to the grant of a licence.[113]

(4) Foreign participation as share issuers, purchasers or brokers

Foreign participation in the stock market is permissible under Vietnamese laws subject to certain restrictions. Foreign participation in the Vietnamese stock market is a highly complex issue. While acknowledging that foreign involvement in the stock market will contribute to its durability, the State Securities Commission holds the view that the degree of foreign involvement in the stock market should be controlled to avoid excessive reliance on foreign financial resources.[114]

(a) Foreign participation as share issuers

In Vietnam, foreign enterprises are not permitted to issue shares. A draft amendment to the Foreign Investment Law proposed that foreign enterprises be allowed to issue shares. The vehicle for the change was to be a new type of investment involving joint foreign-domestic investment companies. Under the Draft, existing foreign investment enterprises, which were formed as limited

111 Sections 995 and 1025 of the Corporations Law. See discussion in HAJ Ford, RP Austin and IM Ramsay, *Ford's Principles of Corporations Law* 9th edn, 1999, Melbourne: Butterworths, at [22.240].

112 Article 12 of Decree 48/CP dated 11 July 1998.

113 Article 71.2 of Decree 48/CP dated 11 July 1998.

114 Ha Thang, 'Foreign Firms Take Stock as Bourse nears Opening' Vietnam Investment Review No 353, 23-26 July 1998. [www.vietnamonline.net]

liability companies, were to be permitted to convert into public share-holding companies. However, these provisions were not eventually included in the Foreign Investment Law passed in 2000. The reluctance of the Vietnamese Government to allow participation by foreign investment enterprises appears to result from fear of foreign domination of the stock market.[115] Vietnam has been made cautious by the experience of neighbouring countries where foreign investors pulled out of the countries by selling their shares.[116]

(b) Foreign participation as purchasers

Foreign investors are, however, allowed to participate in the stock market as purchasers, subject to certain conditions. China deals with foreign purchasers on the stock market by classifying shares into many classes and only permitting foreign investors to hold a specific type of shares known as 'B' shares.[117] Foreign investors are not allowed to purchases 'A' shares, which are denominated and paid in Chinese currency-RMB.[118] Therefore, 'A' shares can only be purchased and traded by domestic investors while 'B' shares are only traded among foreign investors.[119]

Rather than limiting the types of shares that can be purchased and traded by foreign investors, Vietnam applies a percentage limit to foreign shareholders in a company. In 1993, the Governor of the State Bank issued Decision 228/QDNH5 which permitted foreigners, on a case-by-case basis, to invest in Vietnam by purchasing interests in a Vietnamese joint-stock bank. The total share owned by foreign investors could not exceed 30% of the total shares of the company while individual foreign investor could own a maximum of 10% of the shares of the company.

Decree 48 ensured the rights of foreigners to purchase and sell securities in the Vietnamese stock market.[120] However, it was not until the issue of Prime Minister's Decision 145/1999/QD-TTg dated 28 June 1999 (Decision 145), that the acquisition of shares by foreign investors became a reality. Under Decision 145, foreign individuals and organisations are entitled to acquire up to 30% of the shares in a shareholding company or an equitised State Owned Enterprise.[121] The restrictions on foreign ownership in a shareholding company contained in Decision 145 differ from those imposed on foreign

---

115 Duc Hung, 'Foreign Equity Option Put on Backburner' Vietnam Investment Review No 447, 8–14 May 2000. [www.vir.vietnam.com]

116 *Ibid.* See also Ha Thang, 'Stock market Now Ready for July Initiation' Vietnam Investment Review No 448, 15–21 May 2000. [www.vir.vietnam.com]

117 IA Tokley and T Ravn, *Company and Securities Law in China, Hong Kong*: 1998, Sweet & Maxwell Asia, at 71.

118 *Ibid.*

119 *Ibid.*

120 Article 67 of Decree 48/CP.

121 Prior to Decision 145 foreign purchasers were not allowed to hold more than 20% of shares currently circulated by an issuer and each foreign organisation or individual was permitted to own no more than 7% and 3% respectively: Decision 139/CP.

shareholders of a joint-stock bank contained in Decision 228, which was issued prior to the existence of Decree 48 and its implementing legislation. It is still unclear whether a joint-stock bank will be classified as a company under the Enterprise Law and whether the general restriction contained in securities legislation is applicable to the acquisition of shares by foreign investors in a joint-stock-bank.

(c) Foreign participation as brokers and securities traders

The Vietnamese Government imposes restrictions on foreign brokers and securities traders who it is feared would foster instability in the newly established stock market.[122] A foreign organization, however, is entitled to participate in the Vietnamese stock market as a broker subject to the following conditions: (1) It must establish a joint-venture with a Vietnamese organisation in which the foreign organisation holds no more than 30% of the joint-venture capital;[123] (2) It is licensed to trade securities in its home country.[124]

IV: Protection of shareholders

Shareholder protection is a central issue in every stock market. The OECD recommends its inclusion as a general principle in the securities law of all transition economies.[125] In the context of communist countries, the assurance of ownership recognition and protection releases investors from the fear that their shares will be nationalised. In theory, Vietnam has provided constitutional recognition and protection to the ownership rights of shareholders.

(1) Constitutional protection: recognition of ownership rights

The 1992 Constitution of the Socialist Republic of Vietnam grants protection to capital and lawful property located in Vietnamese territory whether it is owned by Vietnamese nationals or foreign individuals and organisations. This property will not be nationalised.[126] In cases where there is a forcible purchase or requisition for the purposes of national defence or national interest, compensation must be given.[127] By these provisions, the lawful rights of domestic and foreign shareholders are protected at the constitutional level.

---

122 Kevin Bubel, 'Equitisation of Enterprises in Vietnam' Market Report, 1 September 1998.

123 *Ibid.*

124 SSC Decision 04/1998/QD-UBCK3 dated 13 October 1998.

125 OECD Principles of Company Law for Transition Economies. [www.oecd.org]

126 Articles 22 and 25 of the 1992 Constitution.

127 Article 22 of the 1992 Constitution.

(2) *Protection provided by the Enterprise Law and Securities Regulations*

(a) ***Recognition ad protection of lawful ownership***

The lawful ownership of shareholders of their interest in enterprises is affirmed in the Enterprise Law. Article 4(2) that: 'The State acknowledges and protects property ownership rights, investment capital, income and other lawful rights and interests of an enterprise and its owner.'

(b) ***Accountability of information***

Mandatory auditing,[128] which is expressly spelled out in the Enterprise Law may help to allay investors' concerns regarding the accuracy of company financial statements.[129] However, prudent investors will be concerned about the reputability of the auditor and the accounting regime that will be used for the audit. So far Vietnam has several licensed international auditing companies, including Price Waterhouse Coopers, KPMG and other reputable accounting firms. However, given that Vietnam aims to extend its securities industry to the international stock market, the compulsory Vietnamese accounting standards[130] used in all Vietnamese enterprises will constitute an obstacle for foreign investors in the future. Foreign accounting standards will not be applicable until permission is obtained from the Ministry of Finance.[131]

(c) ***Transparency and accessibility of corporate information***

Information disclosure and transparency are two of the most important factors that help to foster market discipline,[132] and therefore the Enterprise Law provides for public access to the data-base of the SSC.[133] This is the first time that Vietnamese legislation has explicitly provided for a public search of this type of information and it must be viewed as a positive step towards a transparent and fair market in Vietnam. The information package available to the public includes annual reports and other basic information on the business submitted at the time of registration.

(d) ***Disclosure requirements as a measure to protect interests of investors***

The opportunity to access information regarding the activities of share issuers is essential in order for investors to make prudent decisions. Investments made on the basis of insufficient or unreliable information are extremely risky.

---

128 Article 92 of the Enterprise Law provides that annual reports of shareholding companies must be certified by an independent auditing company.

129 According to statistics released by the Ministry of Finance in 1996, only 5% of Vietnamese companies have been audited. See Le Dang Doanh, 'Economic Reform in Vietnam: Legal and Social Aspects and Impacts' (1996) 6 Australian Journal of Corporate Law: 289, at 294.

130 Decision No 1141/TC/QD/CDKT dated 1 November 1995 to issue enterprises accounting system.

131 *Ibid.*

132 See Cyndy Nguyen, 'The Vietnamese Stock Market: Viability in Southeast Asia and Appeal Around the World' (1999) 21 Loyola Los Angeles International & Comparative Law Journal: 607.

133 Article 93 of the Enterprise Law.

Therefore, as a fundamental principle, most stock markets impose upon share issuers and the Stock Exchange an obligation to disclose appropriate information.

In accordance with this, an issuer wishing to list its shares at the Securities Trading Centre (SCT) must abide by the publication regulations of the SCT. A listed organization is required to disclose to information to the public either through the STC or through the mass media. The appointment by share issuers of staff in charge of publishing information is a mandatory requirement and these appointments must be registered with the STC.[134]

A listed organization is required to release its annual reports together with financial statements of subsidiary companies in which the listed organization held 50% of the shares within a period of ninety days from the end of the financial year. The annual report must include: (1) account balance statements; (2) statements of business operations; (3) explanations of financial statements in accordance with the forms currently in force; (4) the report of an independent auditor); and (5) general reports.[135]

A listed organization is required to release its annual reports together with financial statements of subsidiary companies in which the listed organization held 50% of the shares within a period of ninety days from the of the financial year. The annual report must include: (1) account balance statements; (2) statements of business operations; (3) explanations of financial statements in accordance with the forms currently in force; (4) the report of an independent auditor; and (5) general reports.[136]

An issuer is required to report to the State Securities Commission in a timely manner and disclose any information that may affect its share price.[137]

---

134 Article 31 of Decision 04/1999/TT UBCK dated 27 March 1999.

135 Article 32 of Circular 04/1999TT-UBCK dated 27 March 1999.

136 Article 32 of Circular 04/1999TT-UBCK dated 27 March 1999.

137 Article 18 of Decree 48/CP dated 11 July 1998:

(a) Suspension or blockage of bank accounts or the cancellation of suspension of bank accounts;

(b) Becoming bankrupt or making a decision on dissolution;

(c) Making a decision on merger, incorporation, division or split;

(d) Cessation of business activities for more than three (3) months; suspension of business; or suspension from distribution of main products;

(e) The business registration certificate or the operating licence is withdrawn;

(f) Suffering from a loss of more than ten per cent (10%) of the value of share capital;

(g) Being brought to court for matters relating to the listed organisation;

(h) Making a decision on payment of dividends;

(i) Making a decision on modification of business objectives;

(j) Making a decision to invest in business and production expansion worth more than 10% of the total share capital of the listed organisation;

(k) Making a decision to application of new technology or transfer of technology; purchase or sale of fixed assets worth more than ten per cent (10%) of the total share capital; ... [cont]

However, the relevant Decree does not provide for any ground to determine which events will be deemed to affect the share price. In addition to periodic publication, an issuer is required to make instant publication upon the occurrence of any of the events listed in Articles 33 and 34 of Circular 04/1999/TT-UBCK. Among other things, a pending lawsuit involving an issuer must be published within 24 hours while a court judgment affecting the business must be published within three days.[138]

Furthermore, at the request of the State Securities Commission or the Securities Trading Centre an issuer must publish information when: 'There are rumours about the listed organisation which affect the securities price and such rumours need to be clarified and the price and quantity of the listed securities vary abnormally.'[139]

In theory, information disclosure will enable the public to make wise investment decisions based on adequate information. However, the OECD has observed that by imposing public disclosure obligations on issuers with a small number of shareholders the company is exposed to the risk of bad faith access by other companies, including competitors. It is recommended by the OECD that in transition economies a company with a small number of shareholders should not be required to disclose its financial statements in public.[140] The OECD guideline suggests an issuer ought not to be obliged to disclose its financial statement unless the number of its shareholders exceeds a threshold of 50. The relevant threshold, however, should be determined based on the situation of each country.[141]

---

137 [cont]

(l) Making a decision on investment in shares of another organisation worth more than ten per cent (10%) of the total share capital of the listed organisation;

(m) Making a decision on split, reverse split, increase or decrease in shares licensed to be circulated; having a decision on issues of bonds associated with the right to purchase shares or issue convertible bonds;

(n) The tax office investigates any breaches of the tax laws; or a judgment of court is made relating to the business operations of the company;

(o) Signing a loan contract or issuing bonds worth more than thirty per cent (30%) of the total share capital;

(p) Issuing reward shares or issuing shares in order to pay dividends worth more than ten per cent (10%) of the total share capital;

(q) Convening of a general meeting of shareholders (including annual or extraordinary general meetings);

(r) Lodging an application for cancellation of listing;

(s) The occurrence of other events which might affect the price of shares or the interests of investors.

138 Article 32 of Circular 04 dated 27 March 1999.

139 General Principles of Company Law for Transition Economies at p 48, available at www.oecd.org.

140 General Principles of Company Law for Transition Economies at p 48, available at www.oecd.org.

141 'The Exchange of Experiences by Vietnam and China will Promote and Accelerate Socialist Construction in Both Countries' Vietnam News, 12 November 2000. [http://www.cpv.org.vn/hotnews/exchange_experience_vnchina.htm]

However, in the Vietnamese context, in order to gain public confidence and to attract investors, transparency of corporate information has been prioritised over the protection of companies against bad faith access from competitors. There is no distinction between the public disclosure obligations of companies with more shareholders and those with less shareholders.

Conclusion

The introduction of the stock market in Vietnam is an integral step in the country's move toward a market economy. The stock market will operate as a tool for capital mobilisation and also as a barometer for measuring the performance of issuing companies. It would be premature to make a judgment at this early stage on the extent to which the stock market in Vietnam will be successful. However, a crucial factor will be the ability of the Vietnamese Government to balance its socialist orientation with the economic imperatives of capitalism. The Vietnamese Communist Party has stated that the experience of China should be used as a reference point for economic and legal reform in Vietnam.[142] Nevertheless, it will take some time before Vietnam's legal framework can be adjusted to ensure the smooth functioning of the stock market.[143]

The changes currently required to both the Enterprise Law and the stock market regulations involve matters of internal company management and the external relations between share-holding companies, investors and creditors. The most pressing need for internal reform is the extension of the powers of the Board of Management to allow efficient business decision-making. This can be achieved by introducing a corporate governance culture into Vietnamese legislation. In relation to the external factors, reform is required in the disclosure laws so that investor confidence will be boosted. Furthermore, the role of the State Securities Commission should be expanded so that it is able to assist shareholders and potential shareholders, rather than simply facilitating state management through administration.

Constructing a legal framework that will provide equal opportunities for all sectors to participate in the stock market ought to be the next goal of Vietnamese legislators. At present, Vietnam draws a distinction between state companies and private companies and regulates each type of company under a different law. Vietnamese legislators ought to unify the legislation governing

142 Deng Xiao Ping, one of the architects of Chinese reform, believed that: 'Good policy makers make their way across the river by feeling the stones with their toes.' Quoted in N Makgetla, A Seidman and R Seidman, 'Macro-economic Changes from Centralized to Market Economies: Big Bang v Gradual Change: Big Bangs and Decision-making: What Went Wrong?' (1995) 13 Boston University International Law Journal: 435.

143 The same point has been made in relation to the fledgling Nepalese security market. B Pyakuryal and K Uperty, 'Nepal: The Emerging Security Market (Legal and Policy Aspects)' (1996) 9 Transnational Lawyer: 421, at 436.

corporations since division in the corporate legal system hinders fair competition between the state and private sectors. The policy behind this legislative distinction is reflected in the predominance on the stock market of shares from former state owned enterprises that have undergone 'equitisation'.

It is inevitable that, in the initial stages, the Vietnamese stock market will be dominated by equitised companies, and hence the success of the equitisation program will contribute to the success of the share market. However, in the long term, excessive reliance on shares produced by the equitisation program will hinder the functioning of the stock market. At present, the equitisation program is proceeding in a slow manner and thus the supply of shares is insufficient to meet demand. The supply and demand of shares plays a crucial role in the proper functioning of the stock market since an imbalance will cause volatility in share prices.[144] Furthermore, the limitation of investment opportunities to shares in equitised companies reduces the attractiveness of the Vietnamese stock market in the eyes of investors. To resolve this problem, the law ought to be amended as soon as practicable to allow foreign investment enterprises to issue shares on the stock market. In addition, if the participation of foreign investment enterprises is encouraged these companies will be able to raise capital to expend on projects in Vietnam.

Vietnamese legislators have attempted to transplant the principles of market economics into a socialist legal and political system. In an endeavour to avoid the social instability experienced in other countries undergoing major reform, Vietnam has made gradual adjustments to the existing legal system to accommodate the requirements of the new stock market. It may be some time before substantial changes are made that will allow the stock market to function alongside socialism. Since Vietnam has approached the construction of economic laws on an experimental basis, subsequent supplementation and amendments will be necessary to make the Enterprise Law and securities legislation more comprehensive.

---

144 The same point has been made in relation to the fledgling Nepalese security market. B Pyakuryal and K Uperty, 'Nepal: The Emerging Security Market (Legal and Policy Aspects)' (1996) 9 Transnational Lawyer: 421, at 436.

Australia's International Tax Treaties: a Critical Appraisal

Jacqueline Mowbray and Tim Sherman

Introduction

Since the end of the World War II, Australia's approach to regulating international tax issues has been to conclude a series of bilateral treaties, largely based on the OECD Model Double Taxation Convention on Income and on Capital ('the Model Treaty'). To a large extent, this approach has been a great success. However, as the effects of globalisation increase the volume of transactions with international tax implications at an exponential rate, it is important to examine whether the current system meets Australia's needs. This paper critically examines Australia's current approach to international tax issues by examining problems with the current system and then analysing possible solutions to those problems. It begins by asking the fundamental question of whether a series of bilateral tax treaties is in fact the best approach to Australia's international tax issues. It then identifies specific problems with Australia's current treaties, focusing on five areas:

1 Implications of source tax reductions;

2 Categorisation of income;

3 Problems arising from the development of e-commerce;

4 Problems associated with the 'separate entity' principle; and

5 Treaty shopping issues.

Problems with the existing bilateral treaty framework

The current international tax system is characterised by a network of over 1,500[1] separate bilateral treaties, which have developed from the OECD Model Treaty. This bilateral approach arose as a result of the diversity of domestic tax systems around the world. It was not seen as feasible for countries to cede national tax sovereignty and adopt a multilateral approach to international tax issues. The focus was therefore to reconcile differences between tax systems at the interface of those tax systems, that is, by means of bilateral treaties.

---

1 OECD, http://www.oecd.org/daf/fa/treaties/treaty.htm at 16 January 2001.

In spite of the fact that the bilateral treaty network is considered a great success, the question is increasingly being asked whether international tax issues would not better be dealt with in some sort of multilateral context, rather than by an extensive and complex network of bilateral tax treaties.

Problems with the bilateral framework

1 Inconsistency

Although most bilateral treaties are based on the OECD Model, often only with fairly minor variations, the fact remains that the treaties are different and often inconsistent. The bilateral system was intended to develop in this way. However, in an increasingly global world, it has to be asked whether this inconsistent, 'ad hoc' approach to international tax law is still appropriate.

Problems arise not only as a result of inconsistencies between the treaties themselves, but also as a result of inconsistent interpretations of the same, or similar, treaty provisions by courts in different treaty countries. As national courts are not bound by the decisions of courts in other countries, a particular provision could be interpreted in quite different ways by different national courts. This results in inconsistency and uncertainty in the international tax system.

2 Inability to respond to change

A major problem with the bilateral treaty network is its inflexibility and inability to respond to changing patterns of international business. The large number of bilateral treaties means that, in a practical sense, the treaties cannot be changed because there are so many of them. This means that the treaty network is unable to respond adequately to emerging tax issues. The OECD seeks to overcome this problem by amending the Commentary to the Model Treaty, which is used as a guide to interpreting treaty provisions. However, at least in an Australian context, it is doubtful whether this is effective.

3 'Lock in'[2]

Many bilateral tax treaties are accompanied by 'most favoured nation' protocols under which the treaty country undertakes not to grant more favourable terms to any other country without also granting the more favourable terms to the treaty partner in question. Protocols of this type mean that Australia is 'locked in' to minimum ceiling tax rates of 15% for dividends, 10% for interest and 10% for royalties. The effect is that, although the bilateral treaty system developed in response to nations' need for flexibility in negotiating tax agreements, the system in fact restricts their freedom to negotiate beneficial treaties with other countries.

---

2 Richard Vann, 'A Model Tax Treaty for the Asian-Pacific Region?' (Pt 1) (March 1991) Bulletin of International Fiscal Documentation 99, 110; Richard Vann, 'A Model Tax Treaty for the Asian-Pacific Region?' (Pt 2) (April 1991) Bulletin of International Fiscal Documentation 151.

4 *Lack of stability*

The stability and integrity of the international tax system is threatened by the fact that the bilateral treaty framework does not provide significant protection for smaller countries in the event that larger countries choose to disregard their treaty obligations. On their own, smaller countries are unlikely to have the power to influence larger countries to comply with their treaty obligations. They also lack the power to take effective retaliatory action in the event of treaty violations by the larger country. The problem with the bilateral treaty system is that it does leave smaller countries 'on their own'. Whereas a breach of a multilateral treaty is of concern to all the treaty partners, action for a breach of a bilateral treaty is effectively only taken by the relevant treaty partner.[3] Given the tendency of larger countries to find ways to ignore their treaty obligations,[4] this can be a significant problem. As a relatively small player on the international political scene, this issue is of particular concern to Australia.

5 *Effect on internal law*

The network of bilateral treaties leads only to more treaties. The bilateral network is now so firmly established that a series of bilateral treaties is the only real alternative for a country seeking to deal with other countries in relation to international tax issues. The effect of this is that countries have a perverse incentive to adopt totally unreasonable provisions of internal tax law, particularly in relation to the taxation of non-residents. This is because, when negotiating treaties, the country in question will then be able to make 'concessions' from this unreasonable position, and in return demand concessions from its treaty partner. There is therefore no incentive for states to adopt more sensible internal laws, which may lead to greater harmonisation of tax laws, reduce the need for treaties, and produce a more consistent and workable international tax system.[5]

Possible solution: a multilateral treaty

The multilateral tax treaty has often been proposed as an alternative to the bilateral tax treaty network. In fact, the 1963 OECD Draft Model Treaty was a draft for both multilateral and bilateral agreements, and the resolution adopting the 1977 Model encouraged groups of countries to use it as the basis of multilateral negotiations.[6]

---

3 Although a larger country may violate several of its treaties in the same way, the treaties may not all be in the same terms, and so united resistance from the treaty partners in respect of the violations is unlikely.

4 For example, in 1986 the United States introduced anti-treaty shopping provisions into its domestic law to override many of its treaties: Internal Revenue Code of 1986, s 884 (e). Similarly, the United States ignored aspects of its treaty obligations in its Foreign Investment in Real Property Act 1980.

5 John Avery Jones, 'Are Tax Treaties Necessary?' 53 Tax L Rev 1, 3–4.

6 Vann, above n 2 (Pt 2) 151.

There would appear to be two main barriers to the implementation of a multilateral tax treaty:

1 The diversity of tax systems;

2 The perception that it would compromise national sovereignty/national interests too greatly.

Diversity of tax systems

The diversity of tax systems is a significant barrier to the negotiation of one multilateral treaty. As Vann puts it:

> It is possible bilaterally to solve most of the conflicts between two tax systems; it is generally considered impossible to secure agreement multilaterally on the many specifics arising from tax systems' diversity that are raised in tax treaty negotiations.[7]

Further, as Slemrod[8] has indicated, countries differ in their revenue requirements, capacity to raise taxes and general attitude towards the purpose of taxation (for example, the need to use tax policy to affect economic activity).

One of the significant advantages of a multilateral treaty is that it provides for uniform definitions of key concepts. However, it is precisely in the area of important definitions that it is hardest to achieve consensus.

Harmonisation

One possible way around the problem is to move towards greater uniformity of tax laws before attempting to negotiate a multilateral treaty. As indicated above, the present bilateral system does not encourage harmonisation of tax laws. However, the general role played by the OECD in the field of international tax could encourage countries to develop greater uniformity of tax laws. OECD Reports and Studies on particular aspects of international tax law, and the OECD Commentary to the Model Treaty, are important and influential documents, not just to member countries of the OECD but to all countries. Further, the OECD produces reports on tax law issues outside the scope of international law. The effect of this sharing of information and discussion is likely to be greater uniformity of tax laws, as consensus in particular areas is gradually built up within the international community.[9]

However, achieving greater uniformity of tax laws could still be a very long and difficult process. In the EU, for example, income tax has proven to be one of the most difficult areas to harmonise. And uniformity among the tax systems of member states of the EU could be expected to be significantly

7 Vann, above n 2 (Pt 2) 153.

8 Joel Slemrod, 'Tax Principles in an International Economy', in *World Tax Reform: Case Studies of Developed and Developing Countries*.

9 Vann, above n 2 (Pt 2) 153.

higher than among countries globally. Harmonisation of tax laws at a global level could therefore be just as difficult to achieve as consensus on a multilateral treaty.

Harmonisation on a regional level may be easier to achieve, particularly in the context of trade blocs, such as the EU. Trade blocs aim to remove all tariff and non-tariff barriers to trade within the bloc. To the extent that differences in tax laws may constitute non-tariff barriers to trade, trade blocs may seek to harmonise tax laws.[10] Even in regions which do not constitute formal trade blocs, however, it could be expected that there would be greater uniformity of tax laws amongst the countries in the region than exists at the global level.

Regional multilateral treaties?

In view of the greater potential for regional harmonisation of tax laws, the establishment of regional multilateral treaties has been suggested as a more viable alternative to the global multilateral treaty.[11] However, it is interesting to note that although the resolution adopting the OECD Model Treaty encouraged groups of countries to use the Model as a basis for multilateral agreements, there are to date only two multilateral tax treaties in existence: the Nordic treaty, between various Scandinavian countries, and the Andean Treaty, between various Central and South American countries.[12] This suggests that regional multilateral treaties may not be so easy to negotiate and operate.

A major barrier to the development of regional multilateral treaties is the fact that the existing bilateral network would continue outside the area of operation of the multilateral treaty. Any multilateral treaty would have to be compatible with the treaty countries' existing bilateral obligations. In particular, 'most favoured nation' protocols may lock each country in to particular positions, making a uniform multilateral position impossible to achieve.

A further problem with the development of regional multilateral treaties is that they may in fact make it more difficult to negotiate a global multilateral treaty at some time in the future. As Vann states:

> The difficult and delicate political process of achieving an agreed position within a trade bloc may create the same kind of lock-in effect produced by the bilateral tax treaty network, that is, the members of the trade bloc having resolved an issue among themselves after protracted negotiation will be unwilling for it to be re-opened.[13]

---

10 Considerable harmonisation of tax laws has been effected by the EU, although it should be noted that harmonisation has focused on VAT and not on income tax.

11 See, for example, Vann, above n 2.

12 Vann, above n 2 (Pt 2) 151.

13 Vann, above n 2 (Pt 2) 155.

The global multilateral treaty

It therefore seems that a global multilateral treaty may, after all, be the best option. There is already considerable multilateralism in the international system through the consistent use of the Model Treaty. The existing bilateral treaties virtually all consist of the Model Treaty with only minor variations. Further, the international community has already concluded a multilateral convention in the tax area in the form of the Convention on Mutual Administrative Assistance in Tax Matters. It has therefore already been possible to achieve a large degree of consensus and cooperation on international tax issues.

Significantly, one of the two existing multilateral tax treaties, the Nordic treaty, is in fact a series of bilateral treaties put together. It contains separate double taxation relief provisions for each country, and also deals with additional bilateral problems. If this multilateral treaty is really just existing bilateral treaties put together, it does not seem such a big step for the current bilateral treaties, which are based on the Model Treaty and largely consistent, to be combined to form a global multilateral treaty.

Form of the global multilateral treaty system

Given the key role played by the OECD in the international tax arena, evolution to a multilateral treaty would most easily be effected if the OECD were to become the body overseeing the treaty. In view of this, a possible model for the multilateral tax system could be the multilateral trade system, as overseen by the World Trade Organisation (WTO).[14] The WTO is responsible for administering several multilateral instruments in the area of international trade (the WTO agreements), which include the General Agreement on Trade and Tariffs (GATT) and the General Agreement on Trade in Services (GATS). The WTO also reviews the development of international trade law and national trade policies, acts as a forum for international trade negotiations and resolves disputes between its members as to the operation of the WTO agreements. As the WTO plays a central role overseeing the operation of the WTO agreements, it is possible for the agreements themselves, and undertakings made by member countries, to be more flexible. Countries make the undertakings they feel they are able to make with respect to decreasing tariff barriers, and there are numerous side agreements which countries may or may not enter into.

Similarly, under a multilateral tax system, the OECD could have responsibility for developing international tax on a world basis. It could administer the treaty and determine disputes between parties to the treaty. If the OECD were to take on this institutional role, it would be possible to have a multilateral treaty although not all countries agreed on all provisions, in the

14 This approach has been suggested by several commentators. See, for example, Slemrod, above n 8 and Vann, above n 2.

same way that there is flexibility in the WTO system. Further, it would be possible to introduce general rules into the multilateral treaty, such as a general rule against double taxation, as these rules would be able to be consistently interpreted by the OECD. Through such interpretation, the OECD could build up a body of jurisprudence as to the meaning of these rules. The advantage of such general rules is that they could be applied in novel situations and situations not currently addressed by the very specific rules in the Model Treaty.

Such a multilateral system would address most of the problems with the current bilateral system outlined earlier in this paper:

- uniform treaty provisions, consistently interpreted by the OECD, would create a more consistent, certain international tax system;
- a multilateral treaty would be easier to amend in response to changing circumstances;
- the system could allow for greater flexibility in terms of the undertakings countries are required to make;
- the OECD as a whole could take decisive action in the event of treaty violations, which would result in greater stability and integrity of the international tax system;
- the integrated approach to international tax issues could encourage countries to develop more sensible and harmonised internal laws. Harmonisation could also be pursued by the OECD, as the body administering the international tax system.

National interests

A further and more significant barrier to the creation of a multilateral tax treaty is the perception that such a treaty would compromise national sovereignty too greatly. Countries do not wish to cede authority with respect to tax policy to an international institution or agreement. National revenue is simply too important. As a result, calls for an international multilateral treaty have received fairly luke warm responses.[15]

As Slemrod has indicated, this is likely to be an almost insuperable barrier to the development of a multilateral treaty. Further, at the end of the day, the success of a such a treaty will depend upon the attitude of the US and EU, and at this stage neither seems to be committed to developing a multilateral treaty framework in the near future.

Conclusion

In view of all the difficulties involved, the inevitable conclusion is that while a multilateral treaty framework may be ideal, it is unlikely to become a reality in

15 This has been noted by various commentators, including Vann, above n 2 and Slemrod, above n 8.

the immediate future. Australia's focus now should therefore be on improving its existing system of bilateral treaties.

Negotiating source state taxation

Australia generally seeks to follow 'established international principles' when negotiating its tax treaties.[16] These 'established international principles' generally[17] include the reduction of source state taxation[18] on income earned from transactions which have a weak nexus with the source state. Such income would generally include income earned by businesses with insignificant connections to the source state and passive income paid from the source state to the resident state.

The negotiation of reduced source state taxation is understandable. Under Australia's foreign tax credit regime, lower source state taxation means that a taxpayer has fewer foreign tax credits to offset the taxpayer's resident taxation obligations. Accordingly, the taxpayer has a higher Australian tax liability than it otherwise would. These source tax reductions are usually reciprocated by Australia's treaty partners. This means that, providing the investment flows between Australia and the particular treaty partner are balanced, the increase in Australian resident taxation should be offset by the decrease in Australian source taxation.

The theory is therefore that Australian revenue authorities are compensated for the reduction in source state taxation by an increase in resident state taxation. However, as suggested by Roin,[19] the strength of this theory is dependent, in part, upon the nature of the concessions provided by Australia and its treaty partner for foreign tax paid.

Australia's foreign tax credit regime,[20] in broad terms, seeks to provide Australian taxpayers with a credit ('foreign tax credit') for foreign tax paid in respect of foreign income. The quantum of the foreign tax credit is limited to the Australian tax which would be levied on that foreign income. Australia calculates this limitation on a 'worldwide' basis. This means that Australian taxpayers can combine their foreign income (derived from all foreign jurisdictions) for the purposes of determining the extent to which a foreign tax credit will be available. Typically, the 'relief from double taxation' Article in

16 See, for a recent example, The Australian Taxation Office, Australia-Russia Double Taxation Agreement, Press Release 8 September 2000, 10 December 2000 http://www.ato.gov.au/content.asp?doc=/content/Businesses/russiaagr.htm.

17 See David Rosenbloom, 'Tax Treaty Abuse' (1983) 15 Law & Policy International Business 763, 776 (discussing the US treaty policies).

18 'Source state taxation' refers to the taxation of income by the state of the 'source' of the income. 'Resident state taxation' refers to the taxation of income by the state of residence of the taxpayer.

19 Julie Roin, 'Rethinking Tax Treaties in a Strategic World with Disparate Tax Systems' (October 1995) 81 Virginia Law Review 1753.

20 Set out in section 160AF of the Income Tax Assessment Act 1936 ('1936 Act').

Australia's tax treaties extends the operation of the foreign tax credit regime to the treaties.[21] This foreign tax credit regime produces a number of anomalous consequences.

1 Treaty partners are encouraged to impose taxes at rates at least equal to the Australian rates

If our treaty partners reduce their tax rates below Australia's tax rates, this will decrease their revenue collections without providing Australian investors with an incentive to invest in their jurisdiction (because the Australian investors will remain subject to higher resident taxation in Australia). There is therefore no incentive for treaty partners to reduce their tax rates below Australian levels.

2 Australian outbound investors are discouraged from minimising foreign tax

Since Australian outbound investors can claim a credit for foreign tax paid, there is no incentive for them to reduce their foreign tax below the level of Australian tax payable.

This has a detrimental effect on the Australian revenue without conferring on Australian outbound investors any economic competitive advantage (that is, Australian outbound investors remain liable in any case for the Australian tax payable).

In the same way, an increase in the tax rates of a foreign jurisdiction (up to the Australian level) is borne by the Australian revenue.

3 Foreign investors may be encouraged to minimise Australian tax

The absence of an incentive for Australian outbound investors to reduce their foreign tax could be balanced by foreign investors experiencing the absence of an incentive to reduce their Australian tax. However, where foreign investors are residents of countries which use an exemption system, this balance is unlikely to exist.

Such an exemption system will exclude Australian income from taxation in the resident state. Consequently, the foreign investor will only be liable for the tax imposed by Australia. As a result, the foreign investor's rate of return will be increased by any reduction in Australian taxation. This provides these foreign investors with an incentive to decrease their Australian tax.

4 Australian outbound investors benefit from source tax reductions not the Australian revenue.

The existence of a relatively low Australian corporate tax rate means that there are more taxpayers with surplus foreign tax credits (which are 'wasted' because they cannot be utilised). These taxpayers, and not the Australian revenue, benefit from a foreign tax rate reduction to the level of the Australian corporate tax rate.

21 See, for example, Article 22 of the Australia/US Treaty.

Further, Australian outbound investors obtain foreign tax credits based on their 'worldwide' foreign income. As a result, even where a foreign tax rate is reduced below the Australian rate, this will not necessarily benefit the Australian revenue. This is because Australian investors can 'blend' low-taxed and high-taxed foreign income.[22] In other words, a taxpayer may have surplus foreign tax credits from a high tax country which can be 'offset' against the reduction in tax payable in the low tax country.

Possible solutions

These anomalous consequences can theoretically be avoided. However, practically, Australia is unlikely to convince treaty partners they should replace their exemption system with a foreign tax credit regime or convince Australian outbound investors they should minimise their foreign tax .

It may, however, be possible to increase the benefit to the Australian revenue of source state tax reductions within the confines of the existing tax treaties and the broad framework of the foreign tax credit regime. Currently, foreign tax credits are granted in respect of classes of income with a separate limitation on foreign tax credits for each class of income.

As the benefits of the source tax reductions are most often conferred on income in the 'passive' class, it would be possible to ensure that the benefits of such source tax reductions were not obtained by taxpayers at the expense of the Australian revenue by preventing income derived in high-taxed foreign jurisdictions from being 'blended' within this class. This would require the inclusion of a provision in Australia's foreign tax credit regime which prevented income from a high-taxed foreign jurisdiction from being included in the 'passive income' class.

The US has introduced such a provision into its foreign tax credit regime. Under Internal Revenue Code 904(d)(2)(A)(iii), passive income earned in a non-treaty country and subjected to a high source tax is included in the general income basket. Income included in the general income basket is more likely to have been subjected to high source tax. As Roin[23] concludes, instead of being able to credit the full amount of foreign taxes paid on the highly-taxed passive income by combining it for foreign tax credit purposes, with low-taxed passive income, the highly-taxed passive income is likely to create excess (and unusable) credits in the general income basket.[24] The introduction of such a

22 Roin, above n 19, 1772. Roin draws this conclusion in the context of the US foreign tax credit provisions.

23 Roin, above n 19, 1773.

24 Roin, above n 19, 1773. Roin relies on recent Treasury studies that show that about 75% of foreign source income is included in the general income category, and about 50% of that is associated with multinational corporations that are in an excess credit position. See US Department of Treasury, 'International Tax Reform: An Interim Report' 57–58 (Jan 15, 1993), reprinted in Daily Tax Rep Jan 22, 1993, at L-1, L-24.

provision into Australia's foreign tax credit regime would benefit the Australian revenue.

Schedular structure and categorisation of income

One of the major problems with the international treaty network, which has been identified by numerous commentators,[25] is that the treaties are structured on a schedular basis. That is, they have different rules for different categories of income. There are different treaty Articles dealing with royalties, interest, business profits, dividends etc. So, for example, in Australia's treaty with Germany, dividends are dealt with in Article 10 and are taxed at 15%, whereas interest is dealt with in Article 11 and is taxed at 10%.

There are two basic problems with this approach. Firstly, it can be difficult to distinguish between different types of income. As Avery Jones states:

> We are concerned with whether payments for software are for services or a royalty, with thin capitalisation (in other words, whether a payment is interest or a dividend), and whether futures contracts come under the business profits, capital gains, or other income articles. And that was before derivatives demonstrated that there was no real distinction between types of income so far as financial products are concerned.[26]

The second problem, which flows from the first, is that the system encourages taxpayers to manipulate their income so that it falls into certain categories. For example, if a treaty provides that business profits are to be fully taxed in the source country but that royalties are not, then a non-resident parent corporation with a subsidiary in the source country is encouraged to reduce the business income of the subsidiary by payment of royalties to the parent.[27] As Vann points out, these problems are particularly acute in the case of corporate groups as 'recharacterization is much easier to achieve since it is a matter of indifference from a commercial view how funds are shunted around groups'.[28]

Several methods have been suggested to overcome this problem.

1 Use of residence-based taxation only

This would involve taxation of a resident's global income by the country of residence and abolition of withholding taxes, thus removing the problem of source taxation being levied at different rates on different types of income. Avery Jones supports such an approach on the grounds that it:

25 See, for example, Vann, above n 2 and Avery Jones, above n 5.

26 Avery Jones, above n 5, 17.

27 See Vann, above n 2 (Pt 1) 103.

28 Vann, above n 2 (Pt 1) 103.

> ... will recognize the reality of not being able to tax capital income, remove the problems of not being able to define different types of income, and remove the distortions on direct investment at the same time.[29]

2 *Making withholding taxes more consistent*

This would involve ensuring that withholding taxes are levied only within a certain narrow band of rates, and that the rates are the same for different types of income.

3 *Abolishing withholding taxes on monies paid from subsidiary to parent companies*

This would address the worst effects of the schedular structure, that is, the way in which it is manipulated by corporate groups. In the EU, withholding tax has already been abolished on dividends paid by subsidiaries to parents.

4 *Consolidation of corporate group accounts for tax purposes*

This approach, suggested by Vann, requires a substantial shift in the way in which corporate groups are taxed at the international level. It essentially involves a formulary apportionment system, under which the international tax base of the group is divided by a formulary method between the various countries with taxing rights in relation to the group. According to Vann:

> In the case of recharacterization of income, the effectiveness of this activity within the group is eliminated by consolidation and outside the group by the division of the tax base through an appropriate formula and application of a single source country tax rate.[30]

All these approaches require a substantial reworking of the international treaty network, and are therefore unlikely to be achieved in the near future, if at all. Total abolition of withholding taxes, in particular, will not be welcomed by countries such as Australia which are net capital importers and will not want to lose source income. It therefore seems likely that, in spite of its problems, the schedular structure is a feature of the international tax system, which, for the moment at least, will have to be accepted.

Taxing e-commerce business profits

The e-commerce problem

The Australian Taxation Office ('ATO') recognises e-commerce as an important consideration in planning for the future. In the Discussion Report of the ATO Electronic Commerce Project[31], the ATO recognised that 'the global

29 Avery Jones, above n 5, 17.

30 Above n 2 (Pt 2) 158.

31 Australian Taxation Office, 'Tax and the Internet: Discussion Report of the Australian Taxation Office Electronic Commerce Project' ('ATO Internet Report') (1997) (1 November 2000) <http://www.ato.gov.au/content.asp?doc=/content/Businesses/ecommerce_Ecp.htm>

nature of the Internet creates challenges for tax jurisdictions and the current source, residency, permanent establishment and allocative rules'.[32] The ATO believes that:[33]

> It is likely that the existing international rules will need to be substantially revised in light of electronic commerce. There are also concerns about the increased scope for tax planning, especially using tax havens, and for increased accidental non-compliance, as small to medium businesses engage in international trade and become subject to international taxation obligations with which they may not be familiar.

E-commerce challenges Australia's current international tax regime because e-commerce transactions do not fit within the 'normal' business structures on which the current system was based. So, for example, the intangible nature of e-commerce transactions means there may be no physical 'supply' of goods. And the goods may be 'supplied' by a computer. Can the computer constitute a permanent establishment? Must we distinguish between computer equipment and the data and software which is used by that equipment, such that a web site will not constitute a permanent establishment, but the server on which the web site is stored will? Can the business of an enterprise be said to be wholly or partly carried on at the location where the enterprise has equipment such as a server?[34] E-commerce challenges the international tax regime in ways which have never been considered before.[35]

E-commerce is expected to generate hundreds of billions of dollars in revenue within the next few years. It is therefore vitally important to address the inability of the current international tax regime to deal with issues such as income characterisation, permanent establishment and transfer pricing.[36] In the absence of certainty, Australia's treaty partners will naturally seek to widen their taxation base to include 'borderline' e-commerce transactions. This can result in either double taxation or an unfair allocation of tax between Australia and the foreign jurisdiction.

---

32 ATO Internet Report, above n 31, 7.

33 ATO Internet Report, above n 31, 7.

34 OECD, 'Clarification on the application of the permanent establishment definition in e-commerce: Changes to the Commentary on Article 5' 22 December 2000.

35 For this reason, the argument that e-commerce transactions are analogous to mail-order transactions and do not demand amendment of Australia's tax treaties (see, for example, James Cigler and Susan Stinnett, 'Treasury Seeks Cybertax Answers with Electronic Commerce Discussion Paper' 8 (1997) Journal of International Taxation 56, 63), seems flawed.

36 Arthur Cockfield, 'Balancing National Interests in the Taxation of Electronic Commerce Business Profits' 74 Tul L Rev 133, 168.

Possible solutions[37]

1 Focus on residency based taxation

In an e-commerce environment it can be almost impossible to link an item of revenue with a specific geographical source. The US Treasury Department has therefore suggested that e-commerce be taxed on a residency basis.[38] Under this approach, source states would be unable to tax the profits generated by e-commerce transactions even if a permanent establishment in the source state arguably existed under traditional treaty or national law principles.[39]

From Australia's perspective, there are three problems with this approach:

(1) *It relies on the integrity of a taxpayer's residency*

The residency of a taxpayer is, in broad terms, a function of the taxpayer's place of incorporation or place of central management and control. However, a taxpayer's place of incorporation can be manipulated, and technology such as video-conferencing has strained the 'place of central management and control' test to the extent that its integrity cannot be left unquestioned.[40]

As a result, two or more countries could assert the right to tax earnings on the basis of residency. In such a case, 'tie-breaker' provisions are needed to determine which country will have taxing rights. However, tie-breaker provisions tend to encounter the same problems as the 'place of central management and control' test because they generally rely on the place where the effective management is located.[41] It can therefore be difficult to determine which country is the taxpayer's true country of residence.

(2) *Companies are encouraged to relocate e-commerce operations to countries with lower tax rates than Australia.*

(3) *Net importers of e-commerce services are disadvantaged*

Not surprisingly, the United States, as a major exporter of e-commerce goods and services, is likely to be the greatest beneficiary of a residency

---

37 This analysis is based largely on that of Cockfield, above n 36.

38 Cockfield, above n 36, 169, citing Office of Tax Policy, US Dept of the Treasury, Selected Policy Implications of Global Electronic Commerce ('Treasury Report') 7.1.5, at 18–19 (1996) (October 1, 1999) <http://www.fedworld.gov/pub/tel/internet.txt> The Treasury Report makes it clear that it does not represent US legal or policy views.

39 Cockfield, above n 36, 169 citing Ine Lejeune *et al*, 'Does Cyber-Commerce Necessitate a Revision of International Tax Concepts?' (1998) 38 Eur Taxation 50, 50–55.

40 ATO Internet Report, above n 31.

41 See, for example, Article 3(3) of the Australia/UK Treaty.

based taxation system.[42] Australia, however, as a net importer of e-commerce goods and services, would suffer significant revenue loss as a result of the abolition of source state taxation.

2 *Formula approach*

Under this approach, the e-commerce income tax base would be divided amongst foreign jurisdictions on the basis of a pre-agreed formula. This would result in e-commerce income being apportioned using factors that match industry specific requirements.

The problem with this approach is that it would result in transactions which are similar in substance being taxed differently. For example, hard-cover newspapers would be taxed differently to on-line newspapers. This is clearly undesirable and contrary to the principle of fiscal neutrality.

Further, on a practical level, Australia would have difficulties introducing a formula approach into its treaties, as the OECD,[43] a number of European tax experts,[44] and the United States Treasury Department[45] have all rejected a global formula approach.

3 *Expanded concept of 'permanent establishment'*

Under this approach, profits related to e-commerce transactions would be attributable to a fictional permanent establishment, such as a 'website that is briefly stored within a consumer's hard drive when it is accessed within a source country', provided some threshold amount is reached, for example, gross sales to consumers are greater than $100,000.[46] This income could then be taxed in the source state.[47]

A potential problem with such an approach is that it undermines the existing international principles which require temporal permanence and a significant geographical connection with source countries before source state tax can be levied.[48] Further, it creates different regimes for the taxation of e-

---

42 Cockfield, above n 36, 172 citing OECD, The Economic and Social Impacts of Electronic Commerce: Preliminary Findings and Research Agenda 27 (1999) (January 20, 2001) <http://www.oecd.org/subject/e_commerce/summary.htm> ('OECD Electronic Commerce Report') [29] (indicating the US accounts for 80% of the global total of e-commerce).

43 OECD, 'Transfer Pricing Guidelines for Multinational Enterprises and Tax Administrations' 65–68 (1994).

44 Commission of the European Communities, 'Report of the Committee of Independent Experts on Company Taxation' (1992).

45 Cockfield, above n 36, 174.

46 Cockfield, above n 36, 175.

47 Australia's tax treaties already use provisions that permit the source state to assess income derived from activities that would otherwise escape source taxation. See, for example, the 'Shipping and Air Transport' Article (Article 8 of the Australia/US Treaty, for example) which taxes these businesses only where the place of effective management is located.

48 Cockfield, above n 36, 176.

commerce transactions and traditional forms of commerce, which is contrary to the principle of fiscal neutrality.

4 *Development of destination based rules*

Under this approach, income in respect of the supply of goods or services would be taxable in the country where the supply is made.[49]

Professor Avi-Yonah[50] has developed a model on this basis, which includes the imposition of withholding tax on the e-commerce income based on the destination of the e-commerce goods and services. The imposition of such a withholding tax would require a review of Australia's foreign tax credit regime, given that such a tax may not readily fall within the definition of foreign tax[51] because of its relationship to consumption.

The difficulty with this approach is identifying the consumer and the location of the supply. As e-commerce transactions often eliminate the link between the activity and its source, particularly in the case of direct e-commerce transactions (where goods and services are provided in electronic form to the consumer's computer), it may remain difficult to determine where the supply occurs.

5 *The 'Cockfield approach'*

In his article, 'Balancing National Interests in the Taxation of Electronic Commerce Business Profits',[52] Cockfield proposes his own solution to the challenges presented by e-commerce, which involves balancing residence-based taxation of e-commerce with an expansion of the tax base of the source country. His proposal has three elements:

1 a residence-based taxation regime for international e-commerce transactions;
2 source state withholding tax on all e-commerce payments above a specified threshold;
3 'permanent establishment protection'.

---

49 The application is similar to that of the Australian goods and services tax, which is dependent upon the 'taxable supply' having the necessary connection with Australia.

50 Reuven Avi-Yonah, 'International Taxation of Electronic Commerce' (1997) 52 Tax L Rev 507, 532–41.

51 Refer to the definition of foreign tax in section 6AB(2) of the 1936 Act: 'tax imposed by a law of a foreign country, being:

(i) tax upon income; or
(ii) tax upon profits or gains, whether of an income or capital nature; or
(iii) tax deemed by section 160AFC to have been paid in respect of a dividend; or
(iv) any other tax, being a tax that is subject to an agreement having the force of law under the International Tax Agreements Act 1953.'

52 Cockfield, above n 36.

(1) *Residence-based taxation*

Under Cockfield's residence-based taxation regime, computer servers, computer networks, telecommunications equipment, related hardware and software equipment, web pages, web sites and other related e-commerce 'spaces' (collectively, 'e-commerce spaces') are not treated as permanent establishments. (If they were, it would present a multitude of tax planning opportunities because e-commerce spaces can be located anywhere in the world, can transfer their programs instantaneously to other jurisdictions, do not require any connection with income-producing activities, and do not require maintenance by employees of the company.)

Since e-commerce spaces are not permanent establishments, the burden of assessing e-commerce income will fall on the resident state. Of course, it can be difficult to identify the country of residence of an e-business. Cockfield acknowledges this, citing the fact that when the ATO attempted to identify the 'real world' identity of Australian enterprises operating websites, it could only do so in 85% of cases.[53] To address this issue, Cockfield proposes self-regulation of websites through a central register, on which businesses can record their location to encourage 'customer trust and loyalty'.

The situation could still arise, however, in which two or more countries claimed to be the resident country. Cockfield therefore proposes that the tie-breaker rules for determining residency be improved. In particular, he suggests that the 'place of effective management' test require examination of the residence of the directors of a company at the time decisions are made. This would take into account the effects of technology such as video-conferencing.[54]

(2) *Withholding tax on international e-commerce payments*

Cockfield suggests different taxation treatment for e-commerce income depending upon whether it exceeds a threshold amount of $1 million.

For those e-commerce transactions under the threshold, it is suggested that the treaties include a clause which deems[55] all international e-commerce income to be business profits of the enterprise. Accordingly, in the absence of a permanent establishment, such income will only be subject to taxation in the resident state.

Those sales above the threshold would be deemed to generate 'e-commerce royalty income' which would be subject to source state

53 ATO Internet Report, above n 31, paragraph 7.3.2.

54 Cockfield, above n 36, 193.

55 Cockfield, above n 36, 193 suggests a clause which deems 'all cross-border transfers of e-commerce goods, services, and capital that generate active business income to generate income from sales proceeds within the source country'. The deeming of such income to be business profits of the enterprise effectively prohibits the source state from taxing royalties, services, sales and rents in relation to the transfer of e-commerce goods, services and capital, providing there does not exist a permanent establishment within the source state.

withholding tax (which could be separately negotiated with individual treaty states). Professor Richard Doernberg,[56] who has also suggested an e-commerce withholding tax, believes that a 10% rate would be reasonable. Cockfield believes a 5% rate would be better so as not to impede e-commerce flows.[57]

(3) Permanent establishment protection

As e-commerce income is subject to concessional taxation treatment in those states where the enterprise does not have a permanent establishment (that is, no taxation where the e-commerce income does not exceed the threshold and only withholding tax where it does exceed the threshold) states may be concerned that enterprises may seek to relocate all their e-commerce income to states where the enterprise does not have a permanent establishment. Enterprises could achieve this by simply relocating the base for Internet sales to their existing customer network to another state.

It is therefore important to protect the tax base of existing permanent establishments. This could be done by deeming goods sold to customers in the state of the permanent establishment to be sold through the permanent establishment. This would mean that profits derived from goods sold from another state to customers in the state of the permanent establishment would be attributed to the permanent establishment.

The intention of such a provision would be to restrict permanent establishments from relocating their sales offshore. Accordingly, the provision would only apply to goods of a similar nature to those sold 'onshore' through the permanent establishment.

A provision such as that proposed in the United Nations Model Treaty could be used:[58]

> The profits of an enterprise of a Contracting State shall be taxable only in that State unless the enterprise carries on business in the other Contracting State through a permanent establishment situated therein. If the enterprise carries on business as aforesaid, the profits of the enterprise may be taxed in the other State but only so much of them as is attributable to (a) that permanent establishment; (b) sales in that other State of goods or merchandise of the same or similar kind as those sold through that permanent establishment; or (c) other business activities carried on in that other State of the same or similar kind as those effected through that permanent establishment.

56 Richard Doernberg, 'Electronic Commerce and International Tax Sharing' 16 Tax Notes International 1013.

57 Cockfield, above n 36, 203.

58 United Nations Model Double Taxation Convention Between Developed and Developing Countries, Jan 1, 1980, Tax Treaties (CCH) p 206, Article 7(1).

Conclusion

The 'Cockfield approach' is consistent with the ATO Internet Report and fairly represents the interests of both taxpayers and the Australian revenue authorities. Accordingly, the inclusion of such an approach in Australia's tax treaties is recommended.

The 'separate entity' principle

The existence of different tax rates between countries creates incentives for shifting income and deductions in order to minimise the overall taxation burden. In the absence of an objective standard, the movement of income and deductions throughout a corporate group would be effortless. Australia's tax treaties use arm's length separate accounting to prevent related enterprises and different parts of the same enterprise from shifting income and deductions to obtain tax benefits.

Under arm's length separate accounting, the existence of a transaction between related corporations is usually accepted, but an arm's length price is substituted where the actual price is different. The arm's length separate accounting principle is developed further under the Model Treaty so that an enterprise is divided into separate parts where it has a permanent establishment in a state which is not the resident state of the enterprise.[59] In such cases, it is necessary to construct notional transactions between the head office and the permanent establishment and to apply the arm's length separate accounting principle as if the permanent establishment were a separate entity.

The merits of the arm's length separate accounting principle have long been debated. Vann argues that the arm's length separate accounting principle was developed at a time when commerce mainly involved transactions relating to tangible goods[60] and that it has been unable to recreate itself as a methodology to deal with increased transactions relating to intangibles. However, the competing formulary apportionment system, while capable of correcting some of these imperfections, requires international agreement on a range of issues. Given the practical difficulty in reaching consensus on issues including the definition of a worldwide tax base, this paper does not set out to restate the arguments for and against arm's length separate accounting and formulary apportionment. Instead, this paper reviews the application of the arm's length separate accounting principle to transactions between a head office and its permanent establishment, by specifically considering the 'separate entity' principle.

59 Vann, above n 2 (Pt 1) 105.

60 Vann, above n 2 (Pt 1) 105.

Basis of the 'separate entity' principle

The Model Treaty provides the basis for analysis of arm's length separate accounting between the head office and permanent establishments of a corporation. Australia's tax treaties do not use identical provisions to those set out in the Model Treaty. Where this is relevant, reference will be made to the specific provisions. All other references are to the terms of the Model Treaty.

The Model Treaty does not generally allow source state taxation for business profits of a non-resident enterprise. Rather, it allows source state taxation only if the non-resident enterprise has a permanent establishment in the source state. And then, only so much of the business profits as are attributable to that permanent establishment may be taxed in the source state.[61]

The Model Treaty provides guidelines for determining the business profits attributable to the permanent establishment. These guidelines are based on the application of the separate entity principle. The separate entity principle requires, in broad terms, that taxable income of permanent establishments be based on the income and expenses actually incurred by those permanent establishments, including income and expenses resulting from arm's length dealings with other permanent establishments of the foreign corporation.

The Model Treaty is in the following terms:

> Article 7(2): Subject to the provisions of paragraph 3, where an enterprise of a Contracting State carries on business in the other Contracting State through a permanent establishment situated therein, there shall in each Contracting State be attributed to that permanent establishment the profits which it might be expected to make if it were a distinct and separate enterprise engaged in the same or similar activities under the same or similar conditions and dealing wholly independently with the enterprise of which it is a permanent establishment.

> Article 7(3): In determining the profits of a permanent establishment, there shall be allowed as deductions expenses which are incurred for the purposes of the permanent establishment, including executive and general administrative expenses so incurred, whether in the State in which the permanent establishment is situated or elsewhere.

Applying the 'separate entity' principle

The 'separate entity' principle is deceptively simple. In practice, its application gives rise to a number of difficulties.[62] This creates a level of uncertainty in calculating the profits attributable to a permanent establishment which is helpful neither to taxpayers nor the ATO.

---

61 See, for example, Article 7(1) of the Australia/US Treaty.

62 TW Magney, 'Australia's Double Taxation Agreements: A critical appraisal of key issues' *Legal Books Intelligence Reports International Business Communications*, Sydney, 1994, 27.

Meaning of 'profits attributable to' the permanent establishment

As we have seen, when transactions occur between head office and permanent establishments, so much of the profits as are attributable to the permanent establishment may be taxed in the source state.[63] However, there are two possible approaches to determining the profits attributable to the permanent establishment.

The first, which has been termed the 'overall profit approach',[64] requires so much of the profits of the *enterprise* as are attributable to the permanent establishment to be taxed. This approach requires the enterprise to make an overall profit before profit is attributed to the permanent establishment.[65] Vogel[66] argues that this approach is justified under Article 7(1), which states that profits of the enterprise shall only be taxable in the resident state unless the enterprise carries on business through a permanent establishment. This, according to Vogel, imposes a threshold test, that is, there must be profits of the enterprise.

The second approach, which has been termed the 'independent entity approach',[67] attributes profits to the permanent establishment as if it were a distinct and separate enterprise. This would require profits to be attributed to the permanent establishment even where the enterprise has not made an overall profit.[68]

The existence of these two competing approaches creates uncertainty for both the ATO and for taxpayers, which is clearly undesirable. Unlike the overall profit approach, the independent entity approach provides equivalent treatment for an enterprise investing in a non-resident state through either a permanent establishment or a subsidiary. It is therefore consistent with the key concept of fiscal neutrality. It would also tend to increase source state revenue and would therefore be more favourable for Australia. Accordingly, Australia should clarify that the independent entity approach should be adopted. This could be done by adding an additional sentence to the equivalent of Article 7(2) in Australia's treaties:

> The absence of profits of an enterprise will not prevent profits being attributed to the permanent establishment.

---

63 Articles 7(1) and 7(2) of the OECD Model Treaty.

64 Magney, above n 62.

65 This approach was followed in *Commissioner of Taxation (NSW) v Hillsdon Watts Ltd* (1937) 1 AITR 42. That case involved consideration of section 28(1) of the Income Tax (Management) Act 1938. Refer to Magney, above n 62, 29 for commentary.

66 Klaus Vogel, *Vogel on Double Taxation Conventions*, Kluwer.

67 Magney, above n 62.

68 Magney, above n 62, 31 indicates that it has been suggested that support for this approach may be found in *Sharkey v Wernher* (1955) 36 TC 275.

Calculation of profits

There are three possible methods for calculating the profits attributable to the permanent establishment, as Magney has stated:[69]

1 *the independent dealer price method*, under which profits are calculated as a function of the 'list price' to end consumers;

2 *the commission method*, under which profits are calculated as a function of the gross revenue received less incidental costs of the permanent establishment; and

3 *the constructed factory price method*, under which profits are calculated as a function of the gross revenue received less the cost of manufacture for the head office.

Each of these methods results in a different amount of profits being attributed to the permanent establishment. The absence of a clear statement as to which is the correct approach therefore introduces an undesirable element of uncertainty into Australia's international tax law. It is therefore important for Australia to clarify which method should be applied when calculating the profits attributable to a permanent establishment.

The constructed factory price method is consistent with the independent entity approach outlined above, and with the methodologies sanctioned by the ATO in Taxation Ruling TR 1999/1 ('TR 1999/1').[70] Accordingly, this would be the best method for Australia to adopt.

In the absence of third parties acquiring goods from the head office on the same terms as the permanent establishment, the constructed factory price method requires a complete system of cost accounting to compute the price at which head office would be willing to sell the goods to independent dealers. Such a cost system must take into account the cost of materials, the cost of converting them to finished goods, overheads and a return on investment. Accordingly, Australia could insert the following into the equivalent of Article 7(2) of its treaties:

> In calculating the profits attributable to the permanent establishment, regard will be had to the costs incurred by the enterprise and an appropriate mark up in light of the functions performed and the market conditions.

Deductions

Article 7(3) of the Model Treaty provides that in determining profits of a permanent establishment, there shall be allowed as deductions expenses which

69 Magney, above n 62, 31 acknowledges that the consideration of these three methods is based on a paper by Ralph C Jones entitled 'Allocation Accounting for Taxable Income of Industrial Enterprises' published by the League of Nations in Volume V of Taxation of Foreign and National Enterprises in 1933 and a paper by Mitchell Carroll also published in 1933 which was used as the basis for the draft Convention for the Allocation of Business Income.

70 Taxation Ruling TR 1999/1 seeks to follow the international consensus on the arm's length principle and its application among OECD countries expressed in Transfer Pricing Guidelines for Multinational Enterprises and Tax Administrations, published in July 1995 ('the 1995 OECD Report').

are incurred for the purposes of the permanent establishment (including executive and general administrative expenses) irrespective of where the expenses are incurred.

This allows deductions for expenses which may not otherwise be deductible in the state in which the permanent establishment is situated. Australia has attempted to prevent this by inserting in a number of its treaties a restriction in respect of expenses which would not otherwise be deductible in the source state:

> However, no deduction is allowable in respect of expenses which are not deductible under the law of the Contracting State in which the permanent establishment is situated.[71]

However, in view of recent judicial interpretation of the 'separate entity' principle, this may not be sufficient to protect the Australian revenue base.

In *National Westminster Bank plc v USA*,[72] the US Court of Federal Claims held that the separate entity principle requires that profits of a US branch of a UK banking corporation should be determined by taking into account intra-enterprise loans. Specifically, the court held that Treasury Regulation section 1.882-5 was inconsistent with the separate entity principle because of two factors.[73] Firstly, the Regulation, in the computation of the interest expense deduction, disregarded all interbranch transactions. Secondly, the interest deduction granted under the Regulation was determined on the basis of worldwide assets and liabilities of the entire foreign enterprise, rather than determining the interest deduction on the basis of the separate and independent operations of the branch. The court held that this was clearly inconsistent with the 'separate entity' principle contained in Article 7 of the treaty.

In *Cudd Pressure Control Inc v Her Majesty The Queen*,[74] McDonald JA indicated that:

> ... in an appropriate case, an amount for notional rent may be deducted by a corporation incorporated outside Canada in computing the industrial and commercial profits attributable to its permanent establishment in Canada, notwithstanding that a resident of Canada can not benefit from a similar deduction.[75]

At paragraph 29, McDonald JA went on to expand the operation of the 'separate entity' principle, by concluding that, in the case at hand, an

---

71 See, for example, Schedule 4 to the Tax Agreements Act 1953, 'Agreement between the Government of Australia and the Government of New Zealand for the avoidance of Double Taxation and the prevention of fiscal evasion with respect to taxes on Income' Article 7(3).

72 7 July 1999, Tax Analysts Document Number 1999-23444 in section III.

73 7 July 1999, Tax Analysts Document Number 1999-23444 in section IX.

74 [1998] CTC 2382.

75 This case concerned Article I of the Canada-United States Reciprocal Convention (1942) which provides that: 'An enterprise of one of the contracting states is not subject to taxation by the other contracting state in respect of its industrial and commercial profits except in respect of such profits allowable in accordance with the articles of this Convention to its permanent establishment.'

independent third party would not have entered into the relevant transaction at all, given the 'nature of the business and the type of equipment at issue'.

These cases do not directly concern Australia's tax treaties. However, the reasoning suggests that Australia's inclusion of a restriction on deductions which would not otherwise be deductible under the law of Australia may be contrary to the 'separate entity' principle and therefore ineffective. This is a matter which Australia would be well advised to consider.

Application of the 'separate entity' principle to Australia's proposed thin capitalisation rules

The Ralph Report[76] has recently recommended amending Australia's 'thin capitalisation' rules.[77] Specifically, the Ralph Report recommends restricting the interest deductions available to permanent establishments located in Australia by reference to an arm's length test based on the gearing level which could have been borne by an independent party.[78] In determining whether the gearing level could have been borne by an independent party, the Ralph Report recommends that regard will be had to, amongst other things, the worldwide gearing level of the associated group.

This restriction of interest deductions using the 'presumed' debt and the 'presumed' equity of the permanent establishment (calculated by reference to the worldwide gearing of the group) appears inconsistent with the 'separate entity' principle. This is because it ignores the fiction of the permanent establishment as a separate entity. Rather, it treats the permanent establishment as a subsidiary forming part of a corporate group and then imputes the characteristics of the corporate group to the permanent establishment.

Incorporation of the Ralph proposal in Australia's domestic legislation will remain subject to Australia's tax treaties.[79] Accordingly, if the proposed thin capitalisation rules are inconsistent with the 'separate entity' principle embodied in Australia's tax treaties, they will not be available to limit the

76 Review of Business Taxation, 'A Tax System Redesigned' (July 1999) 659.

77 Presently set out in Division 16F of Part III of the 1936 Act.

78 Subject to the application of a fixed safe harbour gearing ratio.

79 Australia's tax treaties are incorporated into domestic law as schedules to the International Tax Agreements Act 1953 ('Tax Agreements Act'). Accordingly, the 'separate entity' principle as it appears in Australia's tax treaties needs to be read in the context of the Tax Agreements Act. Section 3(2) of the Tax Agreements Act provides that for the purposes of that Act and the 1936 Act and the Income Tax Assessment Act 1997 ('1997 Act'), a reference in Australia's tax treaties to profit of an activity or business, shall, in relation to Australian tax, be read, where the context so permits, as a reference to taxable income derived from that activity or business. This means the taxable income of the enterprise is initially determined in accordance with the provisions of the 1936 Act and 1997 Act. However, if such a calculation is inconsistent with Article 7(2) and Article 7(3), the operation of section 4(2) of the Tax Agreements Act would result in Article 7 overriding the inconsistent provisions.

interest deductions of a permanent establishment. It will therefore be necessary for Australia to consider modification of the 'separate entity' principle in its tax treaties if it wishes to apply its domestic law universally. This could perhaps be done by restricting the fiction of the permanent establishment constituting a 'separate entity'. This could be achieved by amending Article 7(2) as follows:

> Subject to the provisions of paragraph 3, where an enterprise of a Contracting State carries on business in the other Contracting State through a permanent establishment situated therein, there shall in each Contracting State be attributed to that permanent establishment the profits which it might be expected to make if it were a distinct and separate enterprise *incorporated in the other Contracting State, owned wholly by the enterprise of which it is a permanent establishment*, engaged in the same or similar activities under the same or similar conditions and dealing wholly independently with the enterprise of which it is a permanent establishment.

Treaty shopping

Treaty shopping occurs where taxpayers invest in a country indirectly in order to secure benefits under treaties which would not otherwise be available to them.[80] Generally the treaty shopper creates a corporation in a country that has a favourable tax treaty with the source country and then reroutes the income from the source through this conduit entity.[81] The practice has arisen as a result of the variation in benefits available under different bilateral treaties,[82] and the absence of treaties between certain countries, the effect of which is that the tax treatment of non-residents' income differs depending on the country of residence of the investor.

Potential effects

Treaty shopping undermines the principle of reciprocity. By taking advantage of treaties which would not normally apply to them, the residents of a third country are able to take advantage of the benefits of that treaty, while the source country's residents are not necessarily able to obtain similar benefits

80 See, for example, the discussion in the UN Ad Hoc Group of Experts on Tax Treaties between the Developed and Developing Countries guideline on abuse of tax treaties, 'UN Department of International Economic and Social Affairs, Contribution to International Co-Operation on Tax Matters'. Also, Rigby, 'A Critique of Double Tax Treaties as a Jurisdictional Coordination Mechanism' (1991) 8 Australian Tax Forum 301, 417.

81 In this context treaty shopping has been described as having three elements:(i) a reduction of source country taxation; (ii) a low or zero effective tax rate in the payee country; and (iii) a low or zero rate of tax on payments from the payee country to the taxpayer: Gordon, Tax Havens and their Use by United States Taxpayers an Overview (1981) US Treasury Department, 158.

82 For example, US treaties reduce the interest withholding tax rate from the statutory 30% (in the absence of a treaty) to 15% (under the treaty with Canada), 10% (under the treaty with Australia), 5% (under the treaty with Switzerland) and zero (under the treaty with the UK).

from the third country. This can affect both the source country's government and its resident investors.

Further, treaty shopping has the potential to significantly distort investment flows. For example, in 1988, 42% of foreign investment on the Madrid stock exchange came from the UK, in contrast to 5% from the US. This has been attributed to the fact that at that time there was no tax treaty between the US and Spain, and therefore investment flows from the US were routed through the UK to take advantage of the treaty between the UK and Spain.[83]

All this results in significant revenue losses for individual countries. Haug, in her article on the US anti-treaty shopping provisions,[84] cites the fact that in 1981, 68% of US source income was paid to persons residing in five US treaty countries, three of which were considered tax havens. She concludes from this that many third country investors took advantage of existing treaties for their investments in the US, and that the US consequently lost a substantial amount of revenue.

Since treaty shopping essentially reduces the tax which can be levied by the source country, revenue loss from treaty shopping is much greater in the case of countries which are net capital importers rather than net capital exporters.[85] Australia is a net capital importer and therefore stands to suffer significant revenue losses as a result of treaty shopping practices. Accordingly, Australia needs to protect its right to tax source income by preventing treaty shopping.

It is true that any restriction on treaty shopping has an impact on the cost of capital for Australian resident companies. If those investing in Australia are to be subject to higher withholding tax, then they will seek to recoup those losses by demanding higher rates of return from the Australian companies in which they are investing.[86] However, the potential loss of revenue from treaty shopping outweighs any benefit in terms of lower cost of capital for Australian companies. It is therefore important for Australia to be protected against treaty shopping.

---

83 Simone Haug, 'The United States Policy of Stringent Anti-Treaty Shopping Provisions: A Comparative Analysis' (March 1996) 29 Vanderbilt Journal of Transnational Law 191, 214.

84 Haug, above n 83.

85 For this reason, Avery Jones believes that the United Kingdom (a net capital exporter) does not need anti-treaty shopping provisions, as these would mainly have the effect of protecting the treaty partner's withholding taxes: John Avery Jones, 'Anti-treaty Shopping Articles – A United Kingdom View' (1989) Intertax 331.

86 Such an impact was acknowledged in the case of United States' multinational companies using Netherlands Antilles international finance subsidiaries. These subsidiaries were only used to obtain tax treaty benefits which would not otherwise be available and, accordingly, constituted treaty shopping. Convinced of the impact on the cost of capital for US resident companies, US Treasury attempted to convince Congress to enact legislation eliminating US withholding tax on portfolio bond interest paid to foreign persons. In the meantime, however the US Treasury and the IRS tacitly condoned the use of Antilles finance subsidiaries to achieve the same result (Letter of July 30, 1980 from H. David Rosenbloom, International Tax Counsel of the Treasury Department, to Rep Sam M Gibbons, question 18, 11 Tax Notes 251, at 259 (11 August 1980)).

Does Australia currently have adequate protection against treaty shopping?

Treaty provisions

Limitation on residence status test (OECD Model Art 4)

Only residents of treaty partners are entitled to treaty benefits. Several of Australia's treaties exclude from the definition 'resident of a contracting state' any person who is liable to tax in that state in respect only of income from sources in that state or capital situated therein.[87] According to the OECD Commentary, this sort of limitation could operate to exclude foreign-held companies exempted from tax in the intermediary country on their foreign income. However, it could also be interpreted so broadly as to exclude all residents of countries which apply a territorial principle to their taxation. As a result, the provision is likely to be interpreted restrictively, and its effectiveness is therefore limited.[88]

Beneficial ownership test (OECD Model Arts 10, 11 and 12)

Under Australia's treaties, reduced rates of withholding tax are applicable only to interest, dividends and royalties to which a resident of a contracting state is 'beneficially entitled'. This could be seen to prevent the beneficial owner from obtaining the benefit of treaties to which he or she would not otherwise be entitled by using conduit entities in another country. In practice, however, a corporation will be found to be beneficially entitled to income unless it is clearly a sham corporation whose function is limited to that of a nominee or agent.[89]

Specific anti-treaty shopping provisions

Both the OECD and a number of its Member countries have recognised that the two tests set out above, which are based on provisions of the OECD Model, are of limited application. Paragraphs 11 to 21 of the OECD Commentary on Article 1 of the Model suggest specific anti-treaty shopping provisions which could be included in bilateral treaties. A number of Member countries have introduced these and other provisions into their tax treaties. The United States, for example, has included anti-shopping clauses in its treaties since as early as the 1970s.[90] The United Kingdom also has anti-shopping provisions in its treaties with countries including the Netherlands, Luxembourg and Switzerland.

---

87 See, for example, Art 4 Australia/Netherlands Treaty.

88 The UN Ad Hoc Group of Experts reached a similar conclusion in relation to the equivalent article of the UN Model Treaty: UN Department of International Economics and Social Affairs, Contribution to International Co-operation in Tax Matters, UN Doc ST/EA/203, UN Sales No E.88.XVI 9 (1988).

89 See, Haug, above n 83, 224–25.

90 Gzell, 'Treaty-Shopping' 27 Australian Tax Review 65, 70.

Australia does not have specific anti-shopping provisions in its treaties.[91] Further, the Australian courts have been reluctant to find a general principle against abusive treaty-shopping in international law, which could be applied when interpreting treaties in light of their 'purpose'. For example, in *FCT v Lamesa Holdings BV*,[92] the Commissioner argued that it was inconsistent with the purpose of the Australia/Netherlands treaty for it to operate such that Australia did not have taxing power in circumstances where Dutch law did not impose tax and the sole reason the taxpayer engineered the application of the Australia/Netherlands treaty was to avoid taxation. The Court rejected this argument and found that the operation complained of by the Commissioner was consistent with the policy underlying the treaty.

Domestic law

Part IVA of the Income Tax Assessment Act 1936 was intended to protect Australia from the harmful effects of treaty shopping. The Explanatory Memorandum to the Income Tax Laws Amendment Bill (No 2) 1981 stated that:

> ... the anti-avoidance operation of Pt IVA is not to be limited by anything else in the general income tax law, whether in the Principal Act or in a double taxation agreement with another country.

However, as Gzell points out in his article 'Treaty-Shopping',[93] Part IVA only operates if there is a tax benefit as defined.[94] A tax benefit under Part IVA only arises where an amount is not included in a taxpayer's assessable income which, but for the scheme, might reasonably be expected to have been so included.[95] The way in which a treaty will normally provide a 'tax benefit' is by excluding the right of Australia to tax. Gzell therefore considers that the effect of the treaty is not to exclude an amount from the taxpayer's assessable income, but to exclude Australia's right to tax that assessable income. Accordingly, Part IVA can have no application. If this view is correct, then Australia has little effective protection against treaty shopping.

Conclusion

Australia's current anti-treaty shopping provisions do not provide adequate protection against the harmful effects of treaty shopping. Australia should therefore take specific measures to prevent treaty shopping practices. This could be achieved either by introducing anti-treaty shopping provisions into Australia's tax treaties, or by making appropriate amendments to domestic law.

---

91 Gzell, above n 90, 78.

92 97 ATC 4752.

93 Gzell, above n 90, 73–74.

94 1936 Act, sections 177C(1) and 177CA.

95 1936 Act, section 177(1)(a).

Potential anti-treaty shopping measures

Treaty provisions

As discussed earlier, the OECD Commentary provides examples[96] of specific measures which could be introduced into tax treaties to prevent treaty shopping. In addition, the limitation of benefits articles used more recently by the US provide refined illustrations of specific anti-treaty shopping provisions.

There are four general types of anti-treaty shopping clause.[97]

1 Ownership or look-through clauses

Under these clauses, companies are not entitled to treaty benefits unless they are owned by residents of one of the contracting states. The suggested OECD wording of such a clause is as follows:

> A company which is a resident of a Contracting State shall not be entitled to relief from taxation under this Convention with respect to any item of income, gains or profits unless it is neither owned nor controlled directly or through one or more companies, wherever resident, by persons who are not residents of a Contracting State.

The OECD Commentary indicates that individual contracting states should determine the criteria according to which a company will be considered as owned by non-residents. One possibility is to require at least 50% of the company's shares to be held by residents who are individuals, companies in whose shares there is substantial and regular trading on a recognised stock exchange, or not-for-profit tax exempt organisations.[98]

The problem with these clauses is that they can be circumvented through the use of corporations with a small equity capital held by genuine residents, but which are essentially funded by debt, the interest on which flows to non-residents.

2 Base-erosion clauses

Under base erosion rules, companies are not entitled to treaty benefits if more than a certain percentage (usually 50%) of their gross income is used to meet liabilities to persons not entitled to benefits under the treaty,[99] that is, where income is used to pay interest or royalties to non-residents. This approach prevents the situation discussed above, where companies are essentially funded by debt, the interest on which is paid to non-residents.

The suggested OECD base-erosion clause is as follows:

---

96 Refer to paragraphs 11–21 to the OECD Commentary on Article 1.

97 The following analysis is based on the detailed discussion of anti-treaty shopping clauses by Haug, n 83.

98 US/Germany Treaty, Article 28(1)(e)(aa).

99 *Ibid*, Article 28(1)(e)(bb).

> Where income arising in a Contracting State is received by a company which is a resident of the other Contracting State and one or more persons who are not resident of that other Contracting State (a) have directly or indirectly or through one or more companies, wherever resident, a substantial interest in such company, in the form of a participation or otherwise, and (b) exercise directly or indirectly, alone or together, the management or control of such company, any provision of this Convention conferring an exemption from, or a reduction of, tax shall not apply if more than 50 percent of such income is used to satisfy claims by such persons (including interest, royalties, development, advertising, initial and travel expenses, depreciation of any kind of business assets including those on immaterial goods, processes, etc).

3 Exclusion provisions

These provisions deny treaty benefits to companies that are subject to a special tax regime in their country of residence, such that they are tax-exempt or nearly tax-exempt. The purpose of an exclusion provision is to prevent such privileges being used in connection with the benefits offered by a tax treaty. The suggested OECD wording for such a clause is as follows:

> No provision of the Convention conferring an exemption from, or reduction of, tax shall apply to income received or paid by a company as defined under [the relevant provision of domestic legislation conferring special tax regimes on companies], or under any similar provision enacted ... after the signature of the Convention.

Such provisions are of limited application, however, and have little impact on conduit companies which carry on *bona fide* business.

4 Subject-to-tax clauses

Subject-to-tax clauses allow tax relief in the source country only if the income will be subject to tax in the recipient's country of residence. The OECD does not recommend such provisions, however, as they are difficult to administer, may adversely affect deserving exempt entities such as charities, and will not address the situation discussed above of companies funded by debt, the interest on which is paid to non-residents.

Overall, it would seem that incorporating an ownership rule and a base-erosion rule into Australia's tax treaties would address the major forms of treaty-shopping likely to adversely affect Australia.[100] It should be noted, however, that such rules do not necessarily distinguish between third country entities used for treaty shopping purposes and those that are not. And as Rigby points out, it is important to ensure that anti-treaty shopping provisions do not hinder international capital flows, cross border mergers and acquisitions and direct investment by multinational companies.[101] It may therefore be

---

100 Such a combination of an ownership rule and base erosion rule is the approach favoured by the US, see for example, US/Germany Treaty Article 28.

101 Rigby, 'A Critique of Double Tax Treaties as a Jurisdictional Coordination Mechanism' (1991) 8 Australian Tax Forum 301, 419.

appropriate to include provisions guaranteeing treaty benefits in *bona fide* situations.[102] The following approaches are suggested by the OECD:[103]

1 *Stock exchange test*

This test grants relief to companies traded on a recognised stock exchange, on the basis that such companies are unlikely to be set up for the purpose of tax treaty abuse. The OECD recommended wording for such a clause is as follows:

> The foregoing provisions shall not apply to a company which is a resident of a Contracting State if the principal class of its shares is registered on an approved stock exchange in a Contracting State or if such a company is wholly owned – directly or through one or more companies each of which is a resident of the first-mentioned State – by a company which is a resident of the first-mentioned State and the principal class of whose shares is so registered.

2 *Active trade or business test*

This test provides relief to companies engaged in substantive business operations and genuine commercial activity, on the basis that such companies are 'genuine' residents of a contracting state. The OECD suggests the following clause:

> The foregoing provision shall not apply where the company is engaged in substantive business operations in the Contracting State of which it is a resident and the relief from taxation claimed from the other Contracting State is with respect to income which is connected with such operations.

It is, of course, difficult to define what constitutes substantive business operations, but such a provision is still useful as it provides a general ground on which relief can be granted to *bona fide* companies.

3 *Motive test*

This test provides that a company can be granted relief if it can demonstrate that its structure and the conduct of its business is motivated by ordinary commercial considerations and not by the desire to obtain tax relief. It is essentially a subjective version of the objective 'active trade or business' test. The suggested wording is:

> The foregoing provision shall not apply where the company establishes that the principal purpose of the company, the conduct of its business and the acquisition or maintenance by it of the shareholding or other property from which the income in question is derived, are motivated by sound business reasons and thus do not have as a primary purpose the obtaining of any benefits under this Convention.

---

102 The United States, for example incorporates active business exceptions and a discretion to allow treaty benefits to persons which would otherwise not be entitled to those benefits because of the limitation of benefits article, in their treaties. See, for example, Art 28(2) US/Germany Treaty.

103 OECD Commentary to Article 1, para 19.

As the application of the provision depends on the subjective purpose of the taxpayer, this test can be difficult to apply. Nonetheless, it is useful to supplement the application of the 'active trade or business' test.

4 *Alternative relief test*

This test essentially asks whether, by interposing an entity in a third country, the taxpayer has obtained any treaty benefits additional to those he or she would obtain by investing directly in the source country. If not, then the taxpayer is to be granted relief, as this suggests that the taxpayer's purpose in interposing the entity in the third country was not to obtain tax benefits. In effect, this is a specific form of the motive test.

The OECD suggests that this test be incorporated into treaties by providing that the term 'non-residents of a Contracting State':

> shall not be deemed to include residents of third states that have income tax conventions in force with the Contracting State from which relief from taxation is claimed and such conventions provide relief from taxation not less than the relief from taxation claimed under this Convention.

The incorporation of some or all of these tests into Australia's tax treaties would provide a relatively effective safeguard against the use of anti-treaty shopping provisions to deny benefits to third country entities which are in fact used for legitimate purposes.

Domestic legislation

There has been a recent international trend towards the introduction of specific anti-treaty shopping provisions in domestic legislation. For example, in August 1997, section 894 was introduced to the US Internal Revenue Code, to deny foreign persons the reduced rates of withholding tax under treaties with the US on income derived through a fiscally transparent entity.

As Gzell[104] points out, 'such unilateral action may breach the Vienna Convention[105] and give rise to threats of repercussion by ... treaty partners'. However, perhaps Australia could achieve a similar result without so blatantly breaching the Vienna Convention through the use of general domestic anti-avoidance provisions.[106] All that would be required would be to amend the definition of 'tax benefit' in Part IVA of the Income Tax Assessment Act 1936 to clarify that it includes the situation where income is not taxable by Australia as a result of the operation of a treaty.

Such general anti-avoidance provisions do not, of course, offer the same protection as specific anti-treaty shopping provisions inserted in the treaties, as, to a large extent, their application depends on the way in which they are

104 Gzell, n 90, 70.

105 Vienna Convention on Treaties under which member states are under an obligation not to pass domestic legislation inconsistent with treaty obligations.

106 As Gzell, n 90, 77 notes there has been a trend towards the use of such general anti-avoidance provisions, for example, section 245(2) of the Canadian Income Tax Act, introduced in 1988.

interpreted by the Australian courts. Nonetheless, general anti-avoidance rules could provide a useful supplement to specific treaty provisions, and would provide some protection in the context of treaties which do not contain specific anti-shopping clauses.

Conclusion

While Australia's tax treaties are largely a success story, there are some areas in which problems may arise. It must be recognised, however, that while there may be 'ideal' solutions to these problems, in a practical sense, such solutions may not be able to be implemented, at least in the near future. Accordingly, this paper suggests the implementation of practical solutions to the problems arising in relation to:

1 Negotiation of source state taxation;

2 The development of e-commerce;

3 The 'separate entity' principle; and

4 Treaty shopping.

31 January 2001

This paper was awarded the Commissioner's 2000 Prize for Research in Taxation, by the Australian Commissioner of Taxation.

An Historical and Economic Overview of the Insolvent Trading Provision in the Corporations Law

David Morrison

1.0 Introduction

The purpose of this paper is to provide an outline of the development of the law with respect to insolvent trading, in particular the prohibition upon directors allowing companies to trade while insolvent. It is important to consider the historical context because the development of the law provides an opportunity to understand the reasons for the introduction of insolvent trading provisions and the reasons for the subsequent amendment of those provisions. This allows an insight into the operation of the current law of insolvent trading in Australia. The historical context also creates a base against which to critique the current insolvent trading provisions, so as to examine the efficacy of such provisions, and acts as important background information that will facilitate suggestions for further reform in the area.

This paper does not attempt to provide a comprehensive account of all changes to the insolvent trading legislation. Rather, the paper seeks to provide an historical context and reasons for the changes that have occurred to the insolvent trading provisions. It is important to provide such a context in order to gain an insight into the stated reasons for increased legislative protection given to company creditors by the evolution of the insolvent trading provisions.

1.1 Insolvent trading – English background

1.1.1 Introduction

Division 3 of Part 5.7B of the Corporations Law titled 'Director's duty to prevent insolvent trading' has its origins in the amendments made to the Companies Act 1900 (UK) (the Companies Act) in England in 1907. Before these amendments, there were no provisions dealing with creditor protection mechanisms.

The English Companies Act 1862 allowed for the creation of a company[1] and, as noted by Lord Macnaghten in *Salomon v Salomon*,[2] at the time the

1 Section 6 provides for seven or more persons, subscribing their names to a memorandum of association, for a lawful purpose to form a company with limited or unlimited liability.

2 [1897] AC 22, at 51.

main reasons to form a company were to avoid the risk of personal bankruptcy via the mechanism of limited liability and to allow for the raising of money by debenture issue.

In *Salomon*, the primary shareholder, Mr Salomon, held a floating charge over the assets of the company. The floating charge had been created at the time Mr Salomon sold his business into the company. Upon the liquidation of the insolvent company, Mr Salomon's floating charge ranked ahead of the unsecured creditors claims on the company. The unsecured creditors claimed that they should be given priority over Mr Salomon's floating charge security. The possibility of a company being used as a means of defrauding creditors was discussed[3] however the House of Lords decided that, notwithstanding a slightly unrealistic selling price by Mr Salomon, there was no fraud generally[4] or upon the creditors.[5] Lord Macnaghten stated that:

> For such a catastrophe as has occurred in this case some would blame the law that allows the creation of a floating charge. But a floating charge is too convenient a form of security to be lightly abolished ... ordinary trade creditors of a trading company ought to have a preferential claim on the assets in liquidation in respect of debts incurred within a certain limited time before the winding-up. But that is not the law at present. Everybody knows that when there is a winding up debenture holders generally step in and sweep off everything; and a great scandal it is.[6]

If 'everyone knows' that debenture holders take priority over unsecured creditors in the event of company insolvency, then 'everyone' presumably includes unsecured creditors. Thus unsecured creditors have a responsibility to protect themselves, perhaps in the absence of fraud (or at least with a remedy in the event of fraud), against prior interests claimable against the company.[7] Indeed, knowing that there is a risk of such exposure might well prompt a prudent unsecured creditor to make such an inquiry. Lord Watson opined that unsecured creditors should protect their interests by informing themselves of the debtor company's arrangements and status. Lord Watson felt that the Companies Act imposed a duty upon unsecured creditors to make such inquiry stating that:

> Whatever may be the moral duty of a limited company and its shareholders, when the trade of the company is not thriving, the law does not lay any obligation upon them to warn those members of the public who deal with them on credit that they run the risk of not being paid.[8]

---

3 [1892] AC 22, at 39–40 *per* Lord Watson, at 52–53 *per* Lord Macnaghten.

4 [1892] AC 22, at 57 *per* Lord Davey.

5 [1892] AC 22, at 33–34 *per* Lord Halsbury, at 39 *per* Lord Watson, at 47 *per* Lord Herschell, at 52 *per* Lord Macnaghten.

6 [1897] AC 22, at 53 *per* Lord Macnaghten.

7 [1897] AC 22, at 40 *per* Lord Watson, 'The unpaid creditors of the company ... if they had thought to avail themselves of the means of protecting their interests ... could have informed themselves'.

8 [1897] AC 22, at 40.

Noting the view of Lord Macnaghten that the creditors ought to be protected in some way,[9] Lord Watson stated that a creditor's apathy and indeed negligence in protecting themselves did not give the right to assert fraud against the company.[10] The decision in this case is generally regarded as the high water mark for the separate legal entity principle.

1.1.2 Loreburn Committee Report

Prior to the Loreburn Committee Report[11] neither the legislature nor the reports of inquiries questioned the need to protect creditors. The Loreburn Committee's attention was directed, *inter alia*, towards '(a) the growing practice of issuing companies without a prospectus'.[12] The Loreburn Committee considered that the consequence of the Companies Acts, 1862-1900 was to encourage commercial enterprise, such that the adoption of the company form in order to conduct such enterprise was becoming increasingly popular.[13] Indeed the Loreburn Committee was prompted to report that the range of persons affected by such company enterprise was 'legion' encompassing 'shareholders, debenture holders, stockholders, customers, creditors, and employees'.[14] Notwithstanding the increasing quantum of funds in the economy being passed through the company business enterprise structure, nor the number and range of people involved in and affected by the company system, the Loreburn Committee felt that 'the majority of these companies are honestly formed and conducted' and furthermore that the introduction of legislation affecting the range of people involved should be introduced most cautiously. The Loreburn Committee felt that this was necessary because 'whilst it is desirable by all reasonable means to repress fraud, the utmost care should be taken not unduly to curtail the facilities and advantages under which honest enterprise has for so many years flourished and still flourishes'.[15] The Loreburn Committee report gives an early historical view of the risks that unsecured creditors faced in dealing with companies, recognising that the risks of insolvency arising from the incidents of trade and commerce are diminished by the use of the limited company. Where the limited company was caused to trade into insolvency, then the company's fortunes as well as its creditors suffered loss, and for a significant number, insolvency, whether as a result of commercial misfortune or by the insolvent company's misconduct. In such circumstances, the Loreburn Committee took the view that 'the legislature cannot insure against such

9 [1897] AC 22, at 53.

10 [1897] AC 22, at 40.

11 Report of the Company Law Amendment Committee, Cd 3052, London, HMSO, February 1905, (Loreburn Committee Report).

12 *Ibid*, at 1.

13 *Ibid*, at 2.

14 *Ibid*, at 2.

15 *Ibid*, at 2.

losses', stating that 'those who choose to deal with limited companies must take the risk of doing so, must make their own inquiries, and act on their own judgment'.[16]

This clear enunciation by early law reformers that the unsecured creditor would not be afforded protection by the legislature was on the basis that their responsibilities as transacting creditors were in no way diminished because they were dealing with a limited company. Indeed, the Loreburn Committee felt that it was the creditor's responsibility to take advantage of the existing opportunity to conduct searches of the publicly available company records to inform themselves of the various relevant matters, including the contents of the company's constitution and the extent to which the company's capital was mortgaged or charged. The Loreburn Committee did however support further disclosure by recommending that creditors be able to obtain from the public record an annually issued and audited balance sheet of the company they were proposing to deal with. The balance sheet was required to contain a summary of the company's capital, 'its liabilities and assets, and how the values at which the fixed assets stand are arrived at'.[17] It is interesting to note that this enhanced information was not accompanied by a recommendation to include a profit and loss statement.[18] Further, the Loreburn Committee was urged to consider exempting private companies from disclosing their balance sheet information on the basis that private companies did not appeal to the public for funding. The Loreburn Committee recommended the balance sheet disclosure for all companies, public and private, on the basis of adequate disclosure for those unsecured creditors acting cautiously in their dealings with companies.[19] The subsequent legislation did, however, exempt private companies.

The minority comprising three of the members of the Loreburn Committee, in a separate submission, expressed the view that floating charges were open to abuse and as a consequence, companies ought not to have greater power or wider opportunity to borrow funds than that of individual unsecured creditors.[20] This proposal, if adopted, would have limited the company to unsecured borrowings or fixed charge borrowings as for individual creditors. The interesting aspect of the submissions for the purposes here is the extremely small number of 'very grave scandals'[21] that the minority members of the Loreburn Committee refer to in order to justify significant change

16 Report of the Company Law Amendment Committee, Cd 3052, London, HMSO, February 1905, at 12.

17 *Ibid*, at 13. The Loreburn Committee further recommended that company annual meetings be held every 12 months and not later than 15 months from the previous annual meeting, thus adding to the amount of disclosure of information by the company for the benefit of unsecured creditors, at 22.

18 A comparison of successive balance sheets though, could easily enable a calculation of change in net worth to be made with the shortcoming of a lack of detail as to precisely how that change was made.

19 *Ibid*, at 17.

20 *Ibid*, at 27–29.

21 *Ibid*, at 29.

affecting a much greater number of other participants. This is an important insight because it is direct evidence that the justification for the legislative change is grounded in assertion rather than empirical proof. This is an issue that goes to the heart of commercial morality, especially since the latter is itself a normative proposition.

Another difficulty for unsecured creditors noted by the Loreburn Committee was the committee's inability to determine from the publicly available information, the extent to which company assets were mortgaged for certain types of charges. Indeed, the Loreburn Committee noted the 'extraordinary popularity' of the floating charge, the difficulty for unsecured creditors being in the isolated cases where 'a floating charge is framed and utilised for the purpose of entrapping unsecured creditors'.[22] In such circumstances, the Loreburn Committee reported that the mischief was usually a person, not at arms length with the company, taking a floating charge security and exercising the option to appoint a receiver the moment an unsecured creditor took steps to enforce payment of the company's obligation to the unsecured creditor.[23] The Loreburn Committee accordingly recommended that the inconsistencies in the existing register of mortgages and charges be remedied to ensure a comprehensive reporting of such instruments[24] and their availability to unsecured creditors by public inspection.[25] The Loreburn Committee did not seek to otherwise limit the use of the floating charge on the basis that to do so would cause detriment to the greater majority of lawfully operating companies.[26]

A further Loreburn Committee recommendation of some historic significance to creditors was that arrangements and reconstructions of companies be allowed prior to the winding up procedure in circumstances of financial difficulty. Such arrangements and reconstructions would provide for an alternative to the winding up of a company where the creditors and shareholders were willing to try such an alternative.[27] This was accompanied by a further recommendation that the company be allowed to 'reorganise its capital without liquidation'.[28]

---

22 Report of the Company Law Amendment Committee, Cd 3052, London, HMSO, February 1905, at 15.

23 *Re London Pressed Hinge Company Limited* [1905] Ch 576.

24 Including that a person obtaining an order for the appointment of a receiver or manager, give notice. Report of the Company Law Amendment Committee, Cd 3052, London, HMSO, February 1905, at 24.

25 *Ibid*, at 13–14.

26 Although note that recommendations were made to challenge the validity of charges registered within three months of company insolvency to secure a past debt. *Ibid*, at 15–16.

27 *Ibid*, at 19.

28 *Ibid*, at 20. Arrangements and reconstructions were originally provided for by the Companies Act 1862 (UK) that allowed for the liquidator to make shareholder or creditor compromises. See now Part 5.1 of the Corporations Law. Ultimately, the development of the voluntary administration procedure now contained in Part 5.3A of the Corporations Law altered the rights of unsecured creditors and the incidence of insolvent trading cases.

The Loreburn Committee's recommendations for unsecured creditors were significant because they reflected the prevailing commercial morality of the time. The Loreburn Committee found that, in the main, most company business was conducted lawfully and that legislative amendments affecting their operations should be made cautiously.[29] In the context of this prevailing view of the general conduct of companies, the Loreburn Committee recommended changes based on the principle of enhanced disclosure with the balance of responsibility resting upon unsecured creditors to be sure of their bargain with the company.[30] Indeed the Loreburn Committee stated that 'if these amendments were made in the law, traders and others would be far better able to inform themselves as to the financial position of a company with which they might have, or propose to have, dealings'.[31]

The Loreburn Committee Report minority views with respect to floating charges[32] demonstrate the inevitable mix of conflicting opinions and views that underlie the recommendations of any law reform committee. This raises the important consideration of whether the collective views of the population are adequately represented by the membership of such committees and whether there is one optimal basis upon which to evaluate the amendments to the law made as a result of such deliberations. The Loreburn Committee was comfortable with its individual committee members having different views of what constituted acceptable commercial behaviour. Provided however, that they were satisfied that most creditors were adequately protected, there was no need for major change to the companies legislation to protect creditors from limited liability.

1.1.3 Greene Committee Report

The Greene Committee Report[33] was the first general review of the Companies Acts since the Loreburn Committee Report. The Greene Report articulated that the existing companies law was 'highly satisfactory' and 'should not be altered in any matter of principle except where alteration is imperatively demanded' noting that private and public companies were 'honestly and conscientiously managed'.[34] Interestingly the Greene Committee noted that a number of the submissions made to it were grounded in the belief that any mischief occurring in the commercial conduct of companies might be readily resolved by 'the simple expedient of a [statutory] prohibition'.[35] In this context the Greene Committee expressed the view that

29 Report of the Company Law Amendment Committee, Cd 3052, London, HMSO, February 1905, at 2.

30 *Ibid*, at 12.

31 *Ibid*, at 14.

32 *Ibid*, at 27–29.

33 Company Law Amendment Committee Report 1925–26, Cmd 2657, London, HMSO, 1926 (Greene Committee Report).

34 *Ibid*, at 4.

35 *Ibid*, at 4.

the impact of company law upon the business community made it desirable that the company law retain 'a certain amount of elasticity' if it was to work.[36]

Notwithstanding the Greene Committee's lucid articulation of both the existing law's satisfactory function and its reluctance to impinge on the elasticity of the existing company law, the Greene Committee changed the law to allow for increased creditor protection. While the Loreburn Committee had clearly stated that it was reluctant to over-regulate[37] and the Greene Committee appeared to agree, opining that the system of company law was 'well understood' and 'highly satisfactory' in meeting both the needs of the commercial community and the community at large, the Greene Committee expressed the view that the system of company law had stood the test of time and 'should not be altered in any matter of principle except where alteration [was] imperatively demanded.'[38] The Greene Committee seemed to embrace the Loreburn Committee's sentiment regarding business honesty and fraud stating:[39]

> The evidence satisfies us that the great majority of limited companies both public and private are honestly and conscientiously managed. Cases in which fraud or lesser forms of dishonesty or improper dealing are comparatively few, and the public interest which such cases naturally arouse tends to divert attention from the vast number of honestly conducted concerns and to create an exaggerated idea of the evils connected with limited companies and their activities. We are further satisfied that the abnormal conditions prevailing during and since the war have been largely responsible for some of the matters which have given rise to unfavourable public comment, and we are of the opinion that the return to more normal conditions will tend to eliminate certain unsatisfactory features which have shown themselves in recent years. Many of the suggestions made to us show that the idea that fraud and lesser malpractices can be stopped by the simple expedient of a prohibition in an Act of Parliament, dies hard. Other witnesses ... have advocated the imposition of statutory regulations ... but [they] place quite intolerable fetters upon honest business. It is often forgotten that in dealing with a matter such as company law, which affects so closely the whole business life of the nation, a certain amount of elasticity is essential, if the system is to work in practice. Impressed by these considerations we have refrained from recommending any important change which was not, in our view, quite clearly demanded and justified by the evidence before us.

---

36 Company Law Amendment Committee Report 1925–26, Cmd 2657, London, HMSO, 1926, at 4.

37 'Applying the information furnished to us from the personal experience of some members of the Committee and that afforded by the statements received from Chambers of Commerce throughout the country, we are satisfied that the great majority of these companies are honestly formed and conducted. Convinced therefore of the beneficial operation of the present company system we have felt that legislation affecting interests of such magnitude demands great caution, and that whilst it is desirable by all reasonable means to repress fraud, the utmost care should be taken not unduly to curtail the facilities and advantages under which honest enterprise has for so many years flourished and still flourishes.'

38 Company Law Amendment Committee Report 1925–26, Cmd 2657, London, HMSO, 1926, at 4.

39 *Ibid*, at 4.

> We realise that the system of limited liability leaves opportunities for abuse. Some of these we consider to be part of the price which the community has to pay for the adoption of a system so beneficial to its trade and industry. It appears to us, as a matter of general principle, most undesirable, in order to defeat an occasional wrongdoer, to impose restrictions which would seriously hamper the activities of honest men and would inevitably re-act upon the commerce and prosperity of the country. A number of suggestions have also been made to us, the object of which was to remove certain of the restrictions imposed by the present law upon limited companies and those concerned in their formation and management. Here again, we have not felt justified in making any recommendations except such as appeared to us to be called for by a strong body of business opinion and as to which we have satisfied ourselves that no undesirable consequences are likely to follow. In dealing with an instrument so nicely balanced as the existing law relating to limited companies there is always the danger that some alteration, apparently desirable in itself, may have unexpected repercussions throughout the whole mechanism.

Notwithstanding the Greene Committee's desire to keep the law fluid for the benefit of the majority, the Greene Committee 'unanimously agreed'[40] to change the law to enhance creditor protection.

In particular, the Greene Committee referred to the circumstances noted by the Loreburn Committee where a person in control of the (usually private) company 'holds a floating charge and, while knowing that the company is on the verge of liquidation, 'fills up' his security by means of goods obtained on credit and then appoints a receiver'.[41] The Greene Committee felt that such behaviour was fraudulent and named it 'fraudulent trading', considering that the solution to such activity did not rest with altering the law relating to floating charges. Rather the Greene Committee was of the view that the fraudulent director so acting be subjected to unlimited personal liability and that his security interest be charged with the liability. Finally, the Greene Committee recommended that such behaviour be grounds for disqualification of directorship and be a criminal offence.[42] Indeed s 270 of the Companies Act, introduced as a result of the Committee's report, allowed an official receiver to apply to the Court for an order that the errant director be publicly examined, however this was only allowed where the company was in the process of a winding up.

The further difficulty of this recommendation was the requirement of finding fraud on the part of the errant director. The subsequently amended provision (s 332) required a fraudulent intent on the part of the director. The requirement of finding fraudulent intent raises a stricter test for the aggrieved creditor, than the simpler requirement of intent *per se*.

---

40 Company Law Amendment Committee Report 1925-1926, Cmd 2657, London, HMSO, 1926, at 5.

41 *Ibid*, at 28.

42 *Ibid*, at 28–29.

The Greene Committee also recommended that it be compulsory for a company to keep proper books of account noting that the arrangements put in place by the Loreburn Committee regarding access to the company's accounts were insufficient.[43] The Greene Committee recommended that the last audited balance sheet of the company be the financial record registered for public access[44] and that private companies continue to enjoy their exemption from so filing.[45]

These Greene Committee recommendations are interesting because up to this point, the real mischiefs are identified as being fraudulent directors in the context of public company fundraising rather than the company itself practising a mischief or indeed the idea that a private company might have creditors and mistreat them.

The difficulty with the increased disclosure of audited financial statements as recommended by the Greene Committee, is that it does not really assist the inquiring creditor. This is because, at best, the information in the accounts will only be slightly out of date and therefore the position of the balance sheet, though accurate, is no longer relevant. In any event, the Greene Committee recognised that the balance sheet is not the perfect means of understanding the company's financial position in relation to paid-up capital.[46]

In commenting on the position of holding companies, the Greene Committee stated that 'undue interference by the legislature is to be avoided, even if some risk of hardship in individual cases is involved'.[47] As a general principle, this is indeed a reflection of the Loreburn Committee's approach. However, by virtue of the Greene Committee making further recommendations, such a statement can hardly be taken at face value. For example, various recommendations as to the contents and further detail of the company balance sheet were made by the Greene Committee.[48] However such recommendations ignore the general principle that if upon searching two company records, a creditor in determining whether or not s/he ought to deal with one company or another, finds on the one hand a fully detailed set of accounts with more than adequate disclosure and on the other discovers questionable information, then this indeed conveys important relative information about the conduct of the two companies. It is suggested that the statutory requirement that companies present uniform accounts was in itself just as misleading, because a legislative requirement to attain uniformity conceals important information that would otherwise have been conveyed to

43 Company Law Amendment Committee Report 1925–26, Cmd 2657, London, HMSO, 1926, at 32–33.

44 *Ibid*, at 33.

45 *Ibid* at 33, 45.

46 *Ibid*, at 38.

47 *Ibid*, at 34.

48 *Ibid*, at 34-37.

creditors and other interested parties conducting searches of the relevant company's affairs. Further whilst both the Loreburn Committee and the Greene Committee identified the misuse of the floating charge as being a threat to creditors and made recommendations for increased financial disclosure, the Greene Committee in recommending enhanced disclosure, did not first inquire as to the extent to which creditors had previously accessed and utilised the publicly available information about companies with whom they were dealing. Nor indeed was information sought as to the composition of those making inquiry, for example determining the proportion of creditors, shareholders and other interest groups seeking further information about the company's operations. The absence of such information, when recommending significant legislative change seeking to address a mischief, makes it difficult (admittedly in hindsight) to understand how the Greene Committee formed the view that such change would prevent corporate malpractice. It seems clear that the absence of information about the use of the company's published financial reports would make it very difficult to mount an argument for the efficacy of increased disclosure.

The Greene Committee also made observations and recommendations regarding private companies. They were 'satisfied that the great majority of private companies on the register' were conducted honestly and that 'much of the criticism in question is directed to cases of fraudulent trading by undischarged bankrupts[49] and others through the medium of a private company and cases of directors holding debentures which they enforce at a time convenient to themselves'.[50] Because the Greene Committee continued the exemption of private company account filing, they were forced to consider an interesting development that had occurred with the advent of the distinction; namely 'the practice of public companies to form or acquire private companies' avoiding the disclosure requirements placed upon public companies.[51] The Greene Committee recommended that holding companies account[52] for information and continued to recommend the exemption for private companies.

The Greene Committee's recommendations to assist creditors against being defrauded by errant directors or fraudulent companies were enshrined into s 275 of the Companies Act 1929 (UK). With respect to the intent to defraud creditors, the section was interpreted by Maugham J in *Re William C Leitch Brothers Limited*[53] as meaning 'that if a company continues to carry on

49 A further and somewhat related difficulty reported by the Greene Committee was the incidence of undischarged bankrupts acting as directors of a company to the detriment of creditors trading with the company.

50 Company Law Amendment Committee Report 1925–26, Cmd 2657, London, HMSO, 1926, at 45.

51 *Ibid*, at 45.

52 *Ibid*, at 32–37.

53 [1932] 2 Ch 71, at 77.

business and to incur debts at a time when there is to the knowledge of the directors no reasonable prospect of the creditors ever receiving payment of those debts, it is, in general, a proper inference that the company is carrying on business with intent to defraud'. In this case the director was held to be personally liable, thus s 275 was held to be in the nature of a punitive provision.[54]

In *Leitch*, a company was incorporated in 1927 to acquire the various businesses of Mr Leitch (the respondent). In exchange for those businesses, the company paid the respondent £5,000 in the form of 1,000 £1 fully paid ordinary shares in the company and a debenture, for £4,000 secured by floating charge against the company's undertaking. After the sale of the business, some of the property to be transferred to the company remained vested in the respondent. By 1930 the company experienced severe financial difficulty and had, to the knowledge of the respondent, no means of paying for goods purchased. In his capacity as a debenture holder, the respondent then appointed a receiver on the basis that he (the respondent) had not been paid the interest due on the debenture. The respondent in this case had also engaged in some misfeasance.

In *Re William C Leitch Brothers Limited (No 2)*,[55] Eve J outlined the circumstances where s 275 could apply noting that it could 'only be brought into operation in the course of a winding-up and in cases where there is *prima facie* evidence of the company's business having been carried on for fraudulent purposes ... It is directed solely to the particular offence of fraudulent trading and to attaching personal responsibility ... to directors who knowingly have been parties thereto. It imposes a liability, but it does not purport to create any new rights for the creditors'.[56]

Section 275 was later adopted by the various Australian states into their companies acts. Thus the Greene Committee Report recommendation provided the impetus for the first Australian company legislation to protect creditors.

1.1.4 Summary of the English view of creditor protection

The Loreburn Committee report gave an early indication that outsiders, proposing to be involved with the company in a matter of commerce, were taking a risk, and with all the risks, would need either to insure against the possible unwanted consequence of the risk or to take the risk on. The Loreburn Committee made it clear that it was not the function of the legislature to insure outsiders, including creditors, for the various risks they might encounter when engaging in commercial enterprise.

54 [1932] 2 Ch 71, at 79.

55 [1933] 1 Ch 261.

56 [1933] 1 Ch 261, at 266.

Notwithstanding the Loreburn Committee's view of legislative protection, the committee was nonetheless prepared to regulate in favour of increased disclosure. This was a mild form of protection available for those creditors willing to take some responsibility in determining more about company debtors before advancing them credit. The Greene Committee Report increased disclosure of information about the company for the use of outsiders and properly established the regulatory trend towards the protection of creditors dealing with companies engaging in insolvent trading.

The Greene Committee made the first recommendation for the prohibition of fraudulent trading and those provisions were the precursor to the Australian insolvent trading provisions now in place. Section 275 of the Companies Act 1929 (UK) made company directors personally liable where those directors caused the company to defraud creditors. Whilst this provision was based upon fraudulent behaviour, as distinct from an insolvent trading prohibition *per se*, it saw the commencement of the legislature's interest in regulating company arrangements with creditors. That interest developed over time to the provisions now in place in Australia, namely s 588G of the Corporations Law.

1.2 Insolvent trading – Australian background

1.2.1 Introduction

The origins of the Australian insolvent trading provisions are grounded in English law.[57] The various Australian states followed s 275 of the Companies Act 1929 (UK).[58]

Section 284 of the Companies Act 1931 (Qld) was the first fraudulent trading provision introduced in Australia. The Queensland provision sought to regulate 'fraudulent' company directors in a manner similar to the English provisions (s 275). The remaining Australian states followed the Queensland legislation.[59] Section 284 specifically provided for the intent to defraud creditors. Where it could be shown that a director had knowingly carried on such conduct, the section allowed for personal liability for the debts of the company. The section also provided for imprisonment of up to one year[60] and for disqualification from office for a period of up to five years.[61] The requirement of the section that the company's business was carried on for a fraudulent purpose or with the intent to defraud creditors encompassed a fairly

---

57 McQueen R, 'An Examination of Australian Corporate Law and Regulation 1901–1961' (1992) 15 University of New South Wales Law Journal 1.

58 Section 275 being the enactment designed to overcome the deficiencies in the law allowing fraudulent behaviour to prejudice the interests of unsecured creditors as identified by the Greene Committee Report.

59 Followed by s 290 Companies Act 1934 (SA), s 307 Companies Act 1936 (NSW), s 226 Companies Act 1938 (Vic), s 281 Companies Act 1943 (WA), s 237 Companies Act 1962 (Tas).

60 Section 284(3).

61 Section 284(4).

narrow range of conduct and did not contemplate the later developed nature of 'insolvent trading' *per se*. The Queensland provision closely followed s 275 of the 1929 English act using terminology that required an actual dishonesty averse to the objective standards of 'fair trading among commercial men'.[62] Thus, up until this stage of the legislative development for the protection of creditors, protections for non-payment were limited to director fraud. Indeed in *re Patrick and Lyon Limited*,[63] Maugham J noted that whilst 'it is not high-minded for a person who is forming a company to form it with a very small share capital and to cause the company to purchase his stock in trade by an issue of debentures to himself; [such conduct] has never yet been held to be fraud'.[64] Thus in the early stages of the development of the law for protection of creditors, at least the notion of director reasonableness regarding the company's ability to pay its debts was starting to evolve. Protection for company creditors from insolvent trading by directors became enshrined in Australian legislation by s 303 of the Uniform Companies Act 1961–62.

1.2.2 The Uniform Companies Act

The introduction of s 303 of the Uniform Companies Act 1961–62 represented the next development of insolvent trading law within Australia.

Section 303(3) provided for up to three months imprisonment or a fine where a company officer incurred a debt without reasonable grounds of the company being able to pay the debt. However the section was limited to prosecution of this event in the course of winding up the company.[65]

Section 303(3) provided '(3) If in the course of the winding up of a company it appears that an officer of the company who was knowingly a party to the contracting of a debt proved in the winding up had, at the time the debt was contracted, no reasonable or probable ground of expectation, after taking into consideration the other liabilities, if any, of the company at the time, of the company being able to pay the debt, the officer shall be guilty of an offence against this Act. Penalty: Imprisonment for three months or two hundred dollars'.

Section 303(3) specifically provided for the occurrence of the event of insolvent trading as distinct from the mischief of fraudulent trading that the previous provisions were seeking to address. Section 303(3) required that the person who incurred the debt knew that they were so acting and knew that there was no reasonable prospect of the company being able to pay for the debt. Because the offence provided for by s 303(3) was criminal, conviction of

62 *Re Patrick and Lyon Limited* [1933] Ch 786, at 790, *per* Maugham J.

63 [1933] Ch 786.

64 [1933] Ch 786, at 792.

65 In 1961, the Uniform Companies Act, by s 303, created criminal liability (triggered by winding up) for 'the contracting of a debt provable in the winding-up'. Section 291 defined such debts in wide terms, including 'all debts payable on a contingency' *per* Baxt R, 'Guarantees and Section 592, Corporations Law: the Dynamics of Debt' (1992) 21 Australian Business Law Review 212, at 213.

an errant director did not assist the financial position of the company's creditor. This was because there was no means for the creditor to recover funds from the director. Section 304(1) however gave the court power to recover funds from the director for the creditor's benefit when it could be shown that the director had acted with the intent to defraud creditors.

Interim English developments

In the meantime, a further review of English company law was taking place. The Jenkins Committee Report[66] reviewed the English companies legislation including company formation and powers,[67] directors' duties,[68] investor protection,[69] further recommendations for the registration of loan capital,[70] accounting requirements,[71] including recommendations for the preparation of a profit and loss account[72] and the appointment of a suitably qualified auditor.[73]

The Jenkins Committee continued the movement towards greater control in company law matters, whilst at the same time recommending greater disclosure. It was not the view of the Committee that the two were mutually exclusive. The Jenkins Committee, like the Greene Committee before it, stated its concern about the prolix nature of the legislation and the 'undesirability of imposing restrictions which would seriously hamper the activities of honest men in order to defeat an occasional wrongdoer, and the importance of not placing unreasonable fetters upon business which is conducted in an efficient and honest manner'.[74] At the same time the Jenkins Committee recommended a raft of changes to the Companies Act 1929 (UK) including:

- s 270 should be extended to empower the Court in England to order the public examination of all or any of the directors or other officers of an insolvent company where there is some *prima facie* case of culpability, or of such impropriety, recklessness or incompetence as might lead to disqualification of the person or persons concerned under s 188;[75]
- s 332(1) should be extended to make directors and others, who have carried on the business of the company in a reckless manner, personally

66 Report of the Company Law Committee, Cmnd 1749, London, HMSO, June 1962 (Jenkins Committee Report).

67 *Ibid*, at 21–54.

68 *Ibid*, at 86–99.

69 *Ibid*, at 219–52.

70 *Ibid*, at 295–306.

71 *Ibid*, at 330–423.

72 *Ibid*, at 381–97.

73 *Ibid*, at 424–35.

74 *Ibid*, at 3.

75 Note that the Cohen Committee, (Report of the Committee on Company Law Amendment, Cmnd 6659, London, HMSO, June 1945), had previously made recommendations to widen the powers of the Board of Trade, in investigating the affairs of companies, at 98–104.

responsible without limitation of liability, for all or any of the debts or other liabilities of the company, if the Court so declares on the application of the Official Receiver or the liquidator or any creditor or contributory of the company. The criminal penalty provided in s 332(3) should not, however, extend to reckless trading;

- it should be made clear that s 332(3) provides a penalty for fraudulent trading where the facts are discovered in other circumstances than in the course of winding up;
- s 333(1) should be amended by substituting for 'breach of trust in relation to the company' a reference to any breach of duty in relation to the company which would involve civil liability at the suit of the company. The effect of this change would be to bring actionable negligence of directors and others within the scope of the section. Section 333(1) should also be amended to bring a receiver of any property of the company within its scope.[76]

The Jenkins Committee also stated that:

> Accordingly, in our consideration of proposals to impose further statutory restrictions and requirements on companies or their directors, we have asked ourselves whether the new restriction or duty proposed would, if it was made law, improve to an extent worthy of legislation the position of the investors or creditors it was designed to protect; and if so whether its implementation would to any significant extent hamper or impede the company in the efficient conduct of its legitimate business, thus perhaps operating to the detriment of those very persons.[77]

A further recommendation made by the Jenkins Committee was that the Companies Act include a general statement outlining the fiduciary duties owed by a director to his company. The Committee found fault with the principle enunciated by *Percival v Wright*[78] 'that no fiduciary duty is owed by a director to individual members of his company, but only to the company itself, and *a fortiori* that none is owed to a person who is not a member'.[79]

Further, the Jenkins Committee recommended that the Companies Act provide for the director to owe a general duty of good faith to the company[80] and not to take improper advantage of information or opportunity that belongs to the company.[81] Further recommendations were made regarding a company's acquisition of its own shares, the basis of which included the possible need to protect creditors' interests.[82]

76 Report of the Company Law Committee, Cmnd 1749, London, HMSO, June 1962, at 195.

77 *Ibid*, at 3.

78 *Ibid*, at 31.

79 *Ibid*, at 31.

80 *Ibid*, at 34.

81 *Ibid*, at 35.

82 *Ibid*, at 65.

The Jenkins Committee made recommendations that the disqualification provisions of the existing law[83] be amended to include the disqualification of directors where those directors have been convicted (or indicted) of an offence involving fraud or dishonesty whether or not in connection with a company. Further, that directors who have acted in an 'improper, reckless or incompetent manner in relation to the companies affairs' be also disqualified.[84]

The Act does not at present provide a sufficient deterrent to dissuade directors from continuing the business of a company which they know to be hopelessly insolvent ... it has been pointed out that while the Act provides criminal penalties for fraudulent trading if the facts are discovered in the course of a winding up, the section does not extend to fraudulent trading discovered in other circumstances, for example, as the result of an inspection by an inspector appointed by the Board of Trade.[85]

The Jenkins Committee also reported concerns that these additional recommended powers would not of themselves result in greater standards of director behaviour unless the Board of Trade[86] was 'prepared to invoke them by applying in proper cases for court action against fraudulent reckless and incompetent company directors'.[87]

Further, the Committee was of the view that prosecution was not necessarily always the most appropriate means of enforcing the act and that other sanctions, such as s 353, that allowed a company to be struck off the register for failing to file a return were more effective and perhaps might be made more readily available to encompass other circumstances.[88] Accordingly, the Jenkins Committee recommended that upon the recommendation of the Registrar, the Court be empowered to wind up a company in persistent breach of its statutory duties or if being carried on for an unlawful purpose.[89]

Whilst the Jenkins Committee recognised that the purpose of the prohibition against insolvent trading was to prevent the defrauding of company creditors, its recommendations to widen the offence to include reckless or incompetent director behaviour were not made law. These

83 Section 188 of the Companies Act allowed the Court to order the disqualification of a company director convicted of fraud or breach of directors' duties. The Jenkins Committee further recommended that the ambit of s 188 be extended to also include disqualification of receivers, managers and liquidators in such circumstances. Report of the Company Law Committee, Cmnd 1749, London, HMSO, June 1962, at 196.

84 *Ibid*, at 29.

85 *Ibid*, at 194.

86 The Board of Trade being the Department charged with the responsibility of enforcement of the duties owed by officers pursuant to the Companies Act.

87 *Ibid*, at 194.

88 *Ibid*, at 199.

89 *Ibid*, at 201.

recommendations were not examined until the Cork Committee Report in 1982.[90]

1.2.3 Civil liability

In New South Wales s 304(1A) was introduced[91] into the Uniform Companies Act in 1964.[92] Section 304(1A) overcame the deficiency of s 303(3) which did not make directors responsible for irresponsible trading decisions that impacted on the company creditor's ability to be paid.[93]

Section 304(1A) provided:

> Where a person has been convicted of an offence under subsection (3) of section three hundred and three in relation to the contracting of such a debt as is referred to in that subsection the Court, on the application of the liquidator or any creditor or contributory of the company, may, if it thinks proper to do so, declare that the person shall be personally responsible without any limitation of liability for the payment of the whole or any part of that debt.

The introduction of this provision caused much interest in Parliament because there was confusion as to how the provision would apply and further affect the operation of companies.[94]

The first case to fully consider the legislative relationship between directors of companies and their creditors was *Shapowloff v Dunn*.[95] This case was important because it provided some insight into the operation of the then insolvent trading provisions. Unfortunately, the insight is limited because of the confusion surrounding the interpretation of the provisions during this period of time.[96]

The appellant was a director of a company (Stirling Henry Ltd) which gave instructions to its broker (Donovan & Co) to purchase on behalf of the company shares to be paid for upon delivery of the scrip by the various vendors to the company's broker. The appellant was a director of the company at the time the company became insolvent. The broker remained unpaid for certain amounts owing as a result of the share transactions.

---

90 Report of the Review Committee – Insolvency Law and Practice, Cmnd 8558, London HMSO, June 1982 (Cork Committee Report).

91 Companies (Amendment) Act (1964) (NSW), section 5(a).

92 Section 5 Companies (Amendment) Act (1964) (NSW).

93 In 1964 civil liability was introduced and in 1971, while the concept of 'the contracting of a debt' was retained, liability was triggered not only by winding up, but also by official management, inspectorship or receivership. This necessarily broke the nexus with debts provable in a winding up', *per* Baxt R, 'Guarantees and Section 592, Corporations Law: the Dynamics of Debt' (1992) 21 Australian Business Law Review 212, at 213.

94 For details of the Parliamentary discussion see Coburn NF, *Insolvent Trading: A Practical Guide*, 1998, Sydney: John Libbey, at 10–11.

95 (1981) 148 CLR 72; ([1973] 2 NSWLR 468 at first instance).

96 *Op cit*, n 94, at 13.

A summons was issued against the appellant who made application to the Court of Appeal on the basis that the circumstances were sufficiently unusual to require the Court to make a declaration on the construction of s 303(3). In particular, he sought a ruling on the application of the section in circumstances where a series of contracts were made for the purpose of acquiring shares – whether each liability was a debt and when each liability arose. Because in the circumstances of the case, some monies owing to the broker had been repaid by the company, the issue for determination was whether the balance owing was the same thing as a debt referred to by s 303(3).[97]

The court concluded that the company's balance due on its account to the broker was not a debt provable in the winding up stating that s 303(3) was best interpreted generally. The 'debt' referred to meant the incurring of a liability and, in circumstances similar to the instant case, where there are:

> A series of contracts ... made from time to time which result in a liability on behalf of the company to pay in respect of each of them, then each such liability constitutes a debt; and the time when each such debt is contracted is the time when each respective liability arises, and not the time or times when the balance is declared or computed.[98]

The High Court upheld the Court of Appeal's decision finding that the meaning of 'debt' in s 303(3) referred to the date of the execution of the contract to buy the particular parcel of shares as between the company and its broker.[99] In this case, there were a number of distinct transactions to purchase shares that did not alter the basis of the liability between the parties.[100] This date was therefore the date that the debt was contracted rather than the time when the balance of an account was calculated. Wilson J considered the meaning of the words 'having no reasonable or probable ground of expectation ... of the company being able to pay the debt' in the context of the similar wording contained in the bankruptcy legislation:[101]

> Against the background provided by the history of the phrase in the bankruptcy legislation, it seems to me that the meaning of the relevant words of s 303(3) is clear. The prosecution must prove beyond reasonable doubt that at the time of contracting the debt the defendant himself had no expectation, reasonably grounded in the whole

97 *Shapowloff v Dunn* [1973] 2 NSWLR 468, at 471 *per* Jacobs P; 'The question which arises is whether for the purposes of s303(3) of the Companies Act, where a series of contracts are made from time to time which result in a liability on the part of the company to pay in respect of each of them, then each such liability constitutes a debt, and whether the time when each such debt is contracted is the time when each respective liability arises and not the time or times when any balance is declared or computed.'

98 *Shapowloff v Dunn* [1973] 2 NSWLR 468, at 473.

99 *Shapowloff v Dunn* (1981) 148 CLR 72, at 78 *per* Stephen J; 'On that day the broker began and completed the execution of the company's buying order and the company became liable to indemnify the broker for the purchase price of the shares. That liability was contingent... [upon] the delivery of the scrip by the selling broker. But such a contingent liability falls within s 303(3) and is enough to constitute a debt falling within that section.'

100 *Shapowloff v Dunn* (1981) 148 CLR 72, at 79 *per* Stephen J; 'The basis of the debt between company and broker was the giving of the order by the company, involving a concomitant promise to pay.'

101 Section 233 Bankruptcy Act 1849 (UK).

> of the circumstances then existent as he knew them, of being able to pay the debt. It will be seen that the test involves a blending of subjective and objective considerations. The test of reason imports an objective standard, but it is to be applied to the facts as known to the defendant.[102]

Thus, s 303(3) was inherently flawed and did not increase assistance for creditors, to any significant extent, to recover against directors in insolvent trading circumstances. In hindsight, the difficulty with the legislation was that it did not specifically assist an individual creditor in making a claim against an errant director. Instead the legislation was couched as a means of making good a director's behaviour towards the creditor. Section 303(3) only allowed for the criminal conviction of a director and was of no benefit to the individual creditor. Further, when s 304(1A) was introduced in 1964, allowing for civil proceedings by creditors against directors, the section still relied upon the director having been successfully convicted pursuant to s 303(3). The Harmer Committee Report[103] subsequently noted that, 'Creditors thus had to rely on the relevant authority to prosecute the criminal offence and satisfy a criminal standard of proof before there was any prospect of civil recovery ... Even if a conviction and subsequent recovery were obtained, the procedure was lengthy'.[104]

The prevailing attitude of the courts in Australia towards company directors was that company directors could not be responsible for all errors that they made in the running of the business. This rearticulation of the age-old principle permeated various aspects of scrutiny of director conduct[105] including the provisions seeking to prevent insolvent trading.

Thus, insofar as insolvent trading was concerned, it was necessary to obtain a conviction for an offence as provided for by the legislation. After this conviction had been secured, then the court might declare the convicted person personally responsible for the payment (wholly or in part) of the debt upon which the conviction was made. The payment would be made to the company and, usually as a result of the liquidation process, would then be available to all of the company's creditors. This meant that the creditor who had taken the trouble to secure the conviction had no exclusive right to share in the successful proceedings against the director.

---

102 *Shapowloff v Dunn* (1981) 148 CLR 72, at 85.

103 The Law Reform Commission, Report No 45, General Insolvency Inquiry ALRC 45, AGPS, Canberra, 1988 (Harmer Committee Report).

104 The Law Reform Commission, Report No 45, General Insolvency Inquiry ALRC 45, AGPS, Canberra, 1988, at 124.

105 *Harlowe's Nominees Pty Ltd v Woodside Oil Co* NL (1968) 121 CLR 483–84, at 493 *per* Barwick CJ, McTiernan J, Kitto J: 'Directors in whom are vested the right and the duty of deciding where of the company's interests lie and how they are to be served may be concerned with a wide range of practical considerations, and their judgment, if exercised in good faith and not for irrelevant purposes, is not open to review in the courts. Thus... the present case is not a matter for judicial concern ... [unless] the allotment [of shares was] an abuse of the fiduciary power.'

1.2.4 The national companies scheme

In December 1978, the Australian government formed an agreement with the State governments and the Australian Capital Territory that there be a regime of nationally uniform companies legislation.[106] The primary legislation emanating from these arrangements was the making of the Companies Code of each State uniform, adopted by each State and referred to as the Companies Act 1981 (Cth).[107] At this time, various amendments were made to the companies legislation including amendments to the insolvent trading provisions.[108]

Section 556(1) of the 1981 Act provided that:

> If a company incurred… a debt… and immediately before the time when the debt is incurred there are reasonable grounds to expect that the company will not be able to pay all its debts as and when they become due; or there are reasonable grounds to expect that, if the company incurs the debt, it will not be able to pay all its debts as and when they become due; and the company is, at the time when the debt is incurred, or becomes at a later time, a company to which this section applies, [then] any person who was a director of the company, or took part in the management of the company, at the time when the debt was incurred is guilty of an offence and the company and that person or, if there are 2 more such persons, those persons are jointly and severally liable for the payment of the debt. Penalty: $5000 or imprisonment for 1 year, or both.

Section 557(1) of the 1981 Act provided that:

> Where a person has been convicted of an offence under subsection 556(1) in respect of the incurring of a debt, the Court, on the application of the Commission or the person to whom the debt is payable may, if it thinks it proper to do so, declare that the first-mentioned person shall be personally responsible without any limitation of liability for the payment to the person to whom the debt is payable of an amount equal to the whole of the debt or such part of it as the Court thinks proper.

Sections 556 and 557 of the Companies Act 1981 (Cth) were considered by Rogers J in the Supreme Court of New South Wales in *3M Australia Pty Ltd v Watt*.[109] His Honour took the view that the right to bring proceedings against directors was not restricted to the circumstances of liquidation of the debtor

---

106 *Hawkins v Bank of China* (1992) 26 NSWLR 562, at 574, *per* Kirby P, 'The principal purpose of the development of a national approach to company law in Australia has been to recognise the vital importance of corporations to the economic well-being of the whole country; the typical organisation of many corporations today on a national basis; and the inefficiency and uncertainty caused by differing constructions of the same law in different parts of Australia'.

107 The Northern Territory joined in 1986.

108 Paragraph 1219 of the Explanatory Memorandum, circulated upon the introduction of the Bill to enact the 1981 Companies Act/Code, referred to the clause that ultimately became s 556. Paragraph 1219 stated that the provision had been 'restructured to place greater responsibility on persons who are directors or managers of the company at the time that unreasonable debts are incurred by the company and to provide that such persons, and the company, are liable to creditors for repayment of any debts incurred'. The section, also, introduced 'the phrase "incurs a debt" rather than "contracting of a debt"', *per* Baxt, R, 'Guarantees and Section 592, Corporations Law: The Dynamics of Debt' (1992) 21 Australian Business Law Review 212, at 213.

109 (1984) 9 ACLR 203.

company. Further s 556 existed to allow a debtor to take action against the directors of the creditor company for a breach of their statutory duty towards the company.[110] Rogers J further noted important interpretation characteristics and difficulties with the 1981 Act stating:

> I think that it should be acknowledged that the mini code constituted by ss 556, 557 and 558 exhibits difficulties. Perhaps insufficient attention was paid by the draftsman to the fact that s 556 creates a civil liability on the part of directors and others to pay the amount of the debt while s 374C of the 1961 Act which it replaces provided only for the criminal offence included in s 556. Section 557 replaces s 374D of the former Act. It is structured the same way as its predecessor in making a conviction under s 556 a condition precedent to jurisdiction to make, *inter alia*, a director liable for the whole or part of a debt. In framing s 557, the change effected by s 556 appears not to have been fully taken into account. It is also somewhat odd that s 556(1) establishes both a criminal and civil liability where a debt is incurred without reasonable grounds for repayment while the much more serious offence of fraudulent trading provided for by sub-s (5) does not automatically attract a civil liability. That is a function left to s 557(2) as was the case under the former Act.

Notwithstanding the 'mini-code', the 'link between conviction of the criminal offence and the imposition of civil liability'[111] unnecessarily duplicated creditors proceedings for insolvent trading and lengthened the process considerably, although 'the break in the link between prosecution for the criminal offence and the imposition of civil liability' was a 'welcome amendment to the law'.[112] Rogers J also opined that the 'mini-code' might, contrary to the intention of Parliament, expose a director for liability more than once for the same debt stating: 'Again, s 557 deals with an obligation to pay the company. Is this additional to the obligation imposed on say a director by s 556 to make payment direct to the creditor? Is one payment a discharge of the other obligation?'[113] Nonetheless Rogers J opined 's 556 is available as a cause of action to a creditor who can make out the facts required to be proved to enliven the section'.[114] The Full Court approved the reasoning of Rogers J.[115]

In the subsequent case of *Hawkins v Bank of China*[116] Kirby P reinforced the view of Rogers J, in considering the nature of the operation of s 556, being that the purpose of s 556 'was to discourage officers of corporations from improvidently committing the corporation to obligations to pay money as a

110 (1984) 9 ACLR 203, at 207.

111 Herzberg A, 'Insolvent trading' (1991) 9 Company and Securities Law Journal 285, at 286.

112 *Ibid.*

113 (1984) 9 ACLR 203, at 207.

114 (1984) 9 ACLR 203, at 207.

115 (1985) 3 ACLR 324.

116 (1992) 26 NSWLR 562.

debt when they have reasonable grounds for supposing that their corporation is (or will, upon incurring the debt in question) become insolvent'.[117]

Nonetheless the application of the 1981 provisions resulted in a series of uneven interpretations of the legislation in the cases considering the provisions. Rogers J was to repeat his discomfort with the drafting of the provisions in *NEC Home Electronics Aust Pty Ltd v White*.[118] In the Court of Appeal in *Watt v 3M Australia Pty Ltd*,[119] Priestley JA stated the need to consider amendment to the legislation to overcome the confusion arising from the 'apparently conflicting provisions of ss 556 and 557'.[120] In *Ross McConnel Kitchen & Co Pty Ltd v Ross*,[121] Young J was sympathetic to the reasoning of Rogers J in *3M Australia Pty Ltd v Watt*.[122] Apart from the articulated concerns the judiciary had about the drafting of the legislation, its interpretation was treated cautiously because s 556 was a criminal provision and, consistent with the view of Isaacs J in *Scott v Cawsey*,[123] an unduly wide interpretation of which might be unjust.[124] In short, the particular points of statutory interpretation of concern in the s 556 cases were the meaning and ambit of paying 'all its debts as and when they became due', 'reasonable grounds to expect', and when the debt was incurred. Associated issues[125] were the standard of reasonableness, the facts to be taken into account and the standard of proof.[126]

---

117 (1992) 26 NSWLR 562, at 577.

118 (1984) 9 ACLR 203, at 207.

119 (1985) 3 ACLC 324.

120 (1985) 3 ACLC 324, at 326; 'There are parts of those two sections which appear to be marching in quite different directions. In the administration of some liquidations this could quite seriously hamper those concerned with the affairs of the company, both creditors and liquidators, in their efforts to sort out the respective rights of unsecured creditors.'

121 (1985) 3 ACLC 326. Note further that 'despite the obvious merits of collective action the cases … assert that s 592 does not give a liquidator standing at all', *per* Herzberg A, 'Insolvent Trading', (1991) 9 Company and Securities Law Journal 285, at 288.

122 (1985) 3 ACLC 326, at 329.

123 (1907) 5 CLR 132, at 154–55.

124 *Metal Manufacturers v Lewis* (1986) 4 ACLC 739, at 747 *per* Hodgson J; *Group Four Industries Pty Ltd v Brosnan and Anor* (1992) 8 ACSR 463, at 470 *per* Matheson J; *Standard Chartered Bank Ltd v Antico* (1995) 38 NSWLR 290, at 313 *per* Hodgson J. Notwithstanding the clarity of the section that civil proceedings only required the balance of probabilities to establish liability, 'the construction of s 592 … has, in some cases, been coloured by the fact that it is also a penal provision … if the section is capable of differing interpretations the approach which will be adopted by the courts in civil proceedings will be the one which favours the defendant … [further] the strict construction approach particularly in relation to the…defences, confronts a creditor with an almost impossible task of proving a case against a director who was not actively involved inn incurring the debts', *per* Herzberg A, 'Insolvent Trading' (1991) 9 Company and Securities Law Journal 285, at 287.

125 For a summary of the relevant issues see Herzberg A, 'Contracting unpayable debts' (1985) 3 Company and Securities Law Journal 202.

126 *Standard Chartered Bank Ltd v Antico* (1995) 38 NSWLR 290 gives a concise summary of these issues.

Interpretation of the defences to the section also proved difficult. Section 556(2) provided that the defendant would escape the operation of sub-s (1) if s/he could prove:

(a) that the debt was incurred without his express or implied authority or consent; or

(b) that at the time when the debt was incurred, he did not have reasonable cause to expect–

(i) that the company would not be able to pay all its debts as and when they became due; or

(ii) that, if the company incurred that debt, it would not be able to pay all its debts as and when they became due.

In the case of *Metal Manufacturers Ltd v Lewis*[127] the second defendant director of the debtor-company was a director in name only. She had only agreed to become a director of the company at the request of her husband, (the other director of the company). She successfully relied on the defences provided for by the section. Wilson J in *Shapowloff v Dunn*[128] had declared 'the prosecution must prove beyond reasonable doubt that at the time of contracting the debt the defendant himself had no expectation, reasonably grounded in the whole of the circumstances then existent as he then knew them, of being able to pay the debt. It will be seen that the test involves a blending of subjective and objective considerations. The test of reason imports an objective standard, but it is to be applied to the facts as known to the defendant',[129] Hodgson J felt that s 303(3) required the prosecution 'to negative a reasonable ground to expect that the company would be able to pay the debt in question' whereas in s 556(2) the onus rested with 'the defendant to negative a reasonable cause to expect that the company would not be able to pay all its debts'.[130] His Honour felt that this question was to be addressed as a single inquiry so as not to place too great a burden upon the defendant.[131]

Further, Hodgson J felt that the test in s 303(3) was limited to the actual knowledge of the defendant. On the other hand His Honour felt that s 556(2) encompassed both facts and knowledge actually known to the defendant as well as 'facts and circumstances which the defendant ought to know, having regard to the defendant's position in the company and the duties associated with that position'.[132] In deciding the case Hodgson J felt the crucial factor was that 'a defendant who is not an actual participant in the incurring of a debt does not give actual authority or consent to it'[133] and accordingly decided that

127 (1986) 4 ACLC 739.

128 (1981) 148 CLR 72.

129 (1981) 148 CLR 72, at 85.

130 (1986) 4 ACLC 739, at 748.

131 (1986) 4 ACLC 739, at 750.

132 (1986) 4 ACLC 739, at 749.

133 (1986) 4 ACLC 739, at 752.

the second defendant did not give her husband (the first defendant) her authority or consent in incurring the debt in question.[134]

On appeal, the majority of the court agreed with the lower court's finding and held that the second defendant did not, by merely acquiescing to the first defendant's wishes, give her express or implied authority or consent to the incurring of the debt in question. Mahoney JA commented upon the difficulties of interpreting the section thus:

> But to see the key to the meaning of a section in the policy or purpose of the legislation is, in my opinion, to take a less than sophisticated view of the art of the parliamentary draftsman. In many cases, the interpretation of a provision is difficult, not because the policy or purpose of the legislation is not clear, but because the section is directed, not simply to effecting that policy or purpose, but to achieving a compromise between it and other considerations. In the present case, the evil and the remedy are clear. The draftsman sought to prevent the improper incurring of debts and to do so by criminal and civil liability on relevant directors. The difficulty that arises in the interpretation of s 556(2) arises because, having the mischief and the remedy clear, the draftsman had to determine the 'true reason' of the remedy chosen, that is, how far he should apply it without infringing the rights of otherwise innocent directors. I do not think that policy or purpose are of assistance in determining whether a director should be responsible for all debts incurred by his managing director or only for those to which he has given a particular authority or consent.[135]

On a similar set of circumstances, the Victorian Supreme Court came to a different conclusion about the operation of s 556(2) in *Statewide Tobacco Services v Morley*[136] where the defendant had merely served as the required second director in a company that her husband controlled until just prior to his death. After his death, the defendant's son although not properly appointed as managing director acted as such and assumed his father's responsibilities. The defendant was otherwise not involved in the running of the business except for the signing of company returns. The court held that she was liable under s 556(1) because the act of conferring authority on her son to run the business amounted to authorisation of incurring the debts that accrued.[137] In any event,

134 Hodgson J also believed that the decision in *Shapowloff v Dunn* (1981) 148 CLR 72 was not a satisfactory basis in determining the meaning of s 556(2) and whilst agreeing with Foster J in *3M Australia Pty Ltd v Kemish* (1986) 10 ACLR 371, at 376–77 disagreed with other decisions considering the application of the provision, including *Pioneer Concrete Pty Ltd v Ellston* (1985) 10 ACLR 289; *John Graham Reprographics Pty Ltd v Steffens* (1987) 12 ACLR 779 and *Grimm v Roy Galvin & Co Pty Ltd* (1988) 13 ACLR 745. In any event s 303(3) required that the director was knowingly a party to the contracting of the relevant debt and this was clearly not the case in interpreting s 556 *per* Murphy J in *EL Bell Packaging Pty Ltd v Allied Seafoods Ltd & Ors* (1990) 4 ACSR 85, at 93.

135 [1988] 13 NSWLR 315, at 326.

136 [1990] 2 ACSR 405.

137 This decision, together with *Metal Manufacturers v Lewis* (1986) 4 ACLC 739 demonstrate the difficulties that the insolvent trading prohibition had with sleeping directors. Different variations of the same problem arose in *Commonwealth Bank of Australia v Friedrich and Ors* (1991) 5 ACLR 115, where the chairman of the company had failed to properly read and understand the accounts of the company and was held liable because the court would not make the distinction between the duties owed by a full-time and the duties owed by a part-time company director.

her failure to inquire about the state of the company's affairs did not entitle her to plead the s 556(2) defence that she had no reasonable cause to believe that the company was insolvent.[138] The Full Court dismissed the appeal[139] agreeing with the observations of Ormiston J regarding the statutory construction of the defence contained in s 556(2).[140] The working status of a company's director (executive vs non-executive) was subsequently determined to be a factor in determining the availability of the defence provided for in s 556(2).[141]

A further concern relating to the differences between the *Lewis* case and the *Morley* case was noted in an article by Young J where he stated that: 'Although it is difficult to compare case with case because small differences of fact may make a vast difference in the result, New South Wales appears to have taken an attitude to the housewife director which is both more technical and more protective than have Victoria and South Australia ... These deviations from a common policy must be resolved. One of the problems in having eight different courts administering the same Act is that the doctrine of precedent appears to have broken down, at least in respect of the old custom of treating as almost binding the decision of a Full Supreme Court of another State and treating as persuasive the considered judgment of a Judge of a Supreme Court of another State.'[142]

A most useful synthesis of the interpretation of the s 556 insolvent trading provision and an attempt to resolve the ambiguity presented by it was offered by Kirby P in *Hawkins & Ors v Bank of China.*[143] The particular legal ambiguity to be resolved was the interpretation of the phrase 'incurs a debt',[144] however Kirby P made some insightful comments about the operation of the insolvent trading provisions. First, he noted that there was ambiguity in the legislation and that it was the function of the court to resolve it. He stated that resolution of the purpose of the legislation being 'ascertained only within the words used by Parliament'.[145] Second, Kirby P noted that in interpreting the legislation to determine the types of 'debt' included, the cases

138 Ormiston J spends a considerable portion of the judgment interpreting the key words of s 556. Were the section adequately drafted and clear in its intent, such analysis might not have been necessary.

139 [1993] 1 VR 423.

140 Similar issues arose in the interpretation of s 556(2) with respect to sleeping directors in *Commonwealth Bank of Australia v Friedrich & Ors* (1991) 5 ACLR 115 and *Group Four Industries Pty Ltd v Brosnan & Anor* (1992) 8 ACSR 463. See also Baxt, R, 'Sleeping directors get a second chance' (1992) 20 Australian Business Law Review 78.

141 *Commonwealth Bank of Australia v Friedrich* (1991) 5 ACSR 115, at 124, *per* Tadgell J. For commentary on the operation of the defence and the decisions in Morley and Lewis see Herzberg A, 'Insolvent Trading' (1991) 9 Company and Securities Law Journal 285, at 298–306.

142 Young J, 'Uniformity in the Corporations Law' (1992) 66 The Australian Law Journal 402, at 403–04.

143 (1992) 26 NSWLR 562.

144 (1992) 26 NSWLR 562, at 576.

145 (1992) 26 NSWLR 562, at 576.

from *Dunn v Shapowloff*[146] forward, clearly included contingent debts within the ambit of the insolvent trading provision.[147] Further, His Honour opined that it was not the function of the court to frustrate the purpose of the legislature.[148]

Kirby P noted that:

> By the amendments of the Uniform Companies Act in 1971, the circumstances in which the personal obligations of the officers would arise were expanded... When the Act was replaced by the Code in 1982 it was clearly the intention of those presenting the Code to Parliament that s 556 would increase, and not reduce or limit, the obligations imposed upon officers of the corporation. It is apparent that, so far at least as the purpose of the legislation was concerned, nothing was done to reverse the interpretation that Mahoney JA had offered in *Dunn v Shapowloff* concerning contingent debts. On the contrary, the legislature, after *Dunn v Shapowloff*, followed a consistent line of expanding the personal liabilities of officers.[149]

Further, Kirby P added reasons of policy for preferring this construction of s 556 stating that:

> It would be absurd if an officer of an insolvent corporation could, with impunity, cause the corporation to enter into a guarantee of a liability which could immediately thereafter mature into an absolute obligation as a debt. The whole purpose or object of s 556 of the Code was to discourage officers of corporations from improvidently committing the corporation to obligations to pay money as a debt when they have reasonable grounds for supposing that their corporation is (or will, upon incurring the debt in question) become insolvent.[150]

Kirby P felt that a contrary finding would frustrate the 'legislature's purpose'[151] citing the Explanatory Memorandum accompanying the 1981 Bill:

> This is a new provision... designed to protect a person who either does not authorise incurring the relevant debt or does not realise that the company will not be able to pay its debts.[152]

In terms of the general operation of the s 556 insolvent trading provision, notwithstanding the difficulties in construction of the legislation, others opined that perhaps s 556 was capable of a clear interpretation.[153] However the

146 [1978] 2 NSWLR 235.

147 (1992) 26 NSWLR 562, at 576.

148 (1992) 26 NSWLR 562, at 577.

149 (1992) 26 NSWLR 562, at 577.

150 (1992) 26 NSWLR 562, at 577.

151 (1992) 26 NSWLR 562, at 577.

152 (1992) 26 NSWLR 562, at 577.

153 *Re New World Alliance Pty Ltd* (1994) 122 ALR 531, at 540 *per* Gummow J, 'Any conflict between the authorities may be more illusory than real and factual rather than legal. I would not consider such an issue to be a question of law to be decided by the application of a rigid rule. Rather, the statute appears to focus attention upon what it is reasonable to expect in a given set of circumstances, such a consideration necessarily being made by someone operating in a practical business environment.'

interpretation offered by Kirby P did not seem to stem the difficulty in the judicial interpretation of the provision.[154]

The case of *Standard Chartered Bank Ltd v Antico*[155] gave a thorough review of s 556 (over 120 pages) and whilst only a single judge decision it is significant in two respects. First, the circumstances of the case were outside those previously contemplated by case law, and, second, the case considered the possible breach of s 556 in the wider context of ss 52 and 75B of the Trade Practices Act 1974 (Cth).[156] The Bank claimed against three directors of a company, Giant Resources Ltd (Giant). The Bank also claimed that Pioneer International Ltd (Pioneer) had taken part in the management of Giant and that it was, in fact, a director of Giant under the extended definition of director.[157] These claims arose out of certain transactions entered into between the Bank and Giant. In October 1988 the Bank had agreed to make available to Giant a bill acceptance and discount facility of $30 million.

During 1989, there was a deterioration of the financial position of Giant. In order to satisfy other bankers, some assets were sold in the period February to March 1989. Pioneer agreed to make up to $10 million available on certain conditions. Subsequently, Pioneer decided to advance a further $5 million and to seek security. Pioneer also sought to have Giant restructure its operations. By the end of June 1989, Giant had given Pioneer a second charge and some of its assets were given to Pioneer. This was not disclosed to the Bank during negotiations over the refinancing of its loans. Eventually payments on the facility were not made and Giant was ordered to be wound up.

Amongst the findings of Hodgson J were the following:[158]

1 Giant did not incur a debt when it rolled over the bills of exchange or the acceptance facility where the principal remained outstanding. In accordance with the requirements of s 556, Giant did incur a debt on 25 July 1989 in respect of the interest in respect of the new agreement entered into at that time.

2 At that time Pioneer was a director of Giant. This did not arise merely because of nominee directors on the board of Giant. However, a number of other factors led Hodgson J to the conclusion that Pioneer was a director within the extended definition of s 5. Amongst the factors which were considered significant were:

---

154 See Baxt R, 'Guarantees and Section 592, Corporations Law: The Dynamics of Debt' (1992) 21 Australian Business Law Review 212.

155 (1995) 38 NSWLR 290.

156 The following details are drawn from Anderson CJ and Morrison DS, '*Standard Chartered Bank of Australia Ltd v Antico*: Towards a New Understanding of Insolvent Trading' (1996) 4 Current Commercial Law 1.

157 There was also a claim by the Bank against Pioneer on the basis of negligent advice concerning the financial position of Giant.

158 (1995) 38 NSWLR 290, at 374–76.

- Pioneer had a 42% shareholding in a situation were there were no other significant shareholders;
- Pioneer imposed financial reporting requirements on Giant;
- Pioneer exercised controls in relation to the board of Giant; and
- Pioneer had substantial influence in relation to significant decisions of Giant.

3 When the debt was incurred there were reasonable grounds to expect that Giant would not be able to pay its debts. There were no grounds to expect that the bank would extend the credit in the absence of the failure by Giant to disclose the true position of that company. Further, there were no grounds for believing that Pioneer would give any further assistance to Giant.

4 As regards the defences available under s 556(2), Hodgson J concluded:

> (4) None of these defendants has discharged the onus under s 556(2) of proving that the debt was incurred without his (or its) authority or consent, or that he (or it) did not have reasonable cause to expect that Giant would be unable to pay its debts as and when they became due. The debt was one which Pioneer (and its directors, Antico, Quirk and Gardiner) knew or had reasonable cause to suspect Giant would incur, and each of them encouraged, and did nothing to prevent, its being incurred. None of the defendants discharged the onus under s 556(2)(b)(ii). And each of them had reasonable cause to believe that the SCBAL [the Bank] debt had fallen due on 30 June 1989, and would continue to be due, except in so far as proper negotiations for and/or grant of an extension might mean otherwise; that failure to disclose to SCBAL the Pioneer security over Curragh and the debt it secured was likely to induce SCBAL to negotiate for and grant such an extension; and that Giant was contractually obliged to make this disclosure. I am not satisfied that any of them did not have reasonable cause to believe that the disclosure had been made. In these circumstances, I am not satisfied that any of them did not have reasonable cause to believe and expect that the SCBAL debt was due as at 25 July and thereafter, that Giant could not pay it, and that Pioneer would not pay it except as a last resort.[159]

5 As regards the misleading and deceptive conduct, it was concluded by Hodgson J that there had been misleading conduct on two occasions but that the conduct was not known by the three directors in question and further that the knowledge of the misleading conduct should not be inferred to Pioneer.

The implications of the case were the expanded view of the term 'director', the interest on the debt and the meaning of 'a debt incurred', the objective question of reasonable grounds and the consideration of the application of misleading and deceptive conduct legislation.

159 (1995) 38 NSWLR 290, at 374–75.

Although s 556(1) placed liability on directors or on any person who took part in management, Hodgson J chose to analyse the position by seeking to answer the question whether Pioneer was undertaking a director-like role. He adopted the reasoning of *Holpitt Pty Ltd v Swaab*[160] where Burchett J said:

> The only direct guidance, apart from these considerations arising out of the subject matter of the section, is the use of the word 'director'. An application of the maxim *noscitur a sociis* would suggest that the other persons embraced by the section are persons whose management role may be likened to that of a director.[161]

Hodgson J thus came to the conclusion that Pioneer was a director of Giant at least from March 4 1989. This represents one of the few cases where an artificial person has been deemed to have been a director. In so doing Hodgson J seems to have relied upon the decision in *Kuwait Asia Bank v National Mutual Life Nominees Ltd.*[162] In that case the bank had two nominees on the board of National Mutual Life Nominees Ltd and in a claim against the bank it was alleged that the bank was a director. This issue however, was a relatively minor argument in the context of what was at issue. The Privy Council's judgment in relation to the argument merely said:

> (4) Finally the plaintiff relied on section 2 of the Companies Act 1955 in which a 'director' is defined as
>
> > A person in accordance with whose directions or instructions the persons occupying the position of directors of a company are accustomed to act.
>
> In the present case House and August were two out of five directors, the other three being appointees of Kumutoto. And there is no allegation (and it is also inherently unlikely) that the directors in these circumstances were accustomed to act on the direction or instruction of the bank.[163]

Although it may be that 'the Privy Council appears to have accepted that in a proper case, the New Zealand equivalent of s 60 could have application in the context of a corporate group, to cause the parent to become a shadow director of a subsidiary'[164] it is hardly strong support for the proposition. Although there were clearly other factors influencing the decision by Hodgson J in this regard, the board of Giant from February 1989 comprised of nine directors, only three of which were representing Pioneer. Hodgson J does not refer to Australian cases that have dealt with the issue of whether a person is acting like a director. The leading case is probably *Harris v S*[165] followed in *Bluecorp Pty Ltd (in liq) formerly Lloyds Ships Holdings Pty Ltd (in liq) v*

160 (1992) 105 ALR 421.

161 (1992) 105 ALR 421, at 424.

162 [1991] 1 AC 187.

163 [1991] 1 AC 187, at 223.

164 Ford HAJ, Austin RP and Ramsay IM, *Ford's Principles of Corporations Law*, 9th edn, 1999, Butterworths, Sydney, at 285.

165 (1976) 2 ACLR 51.

ANZ Executors and Trustee Co Pty Ltd.[166] In *Harris v S*, speaking of a similar provision in the Companies Act 1962–72 (SA), Wells J commented:

> In my opinion, the extension has effect only where there are directors who are fulfilling their role and function as directors, but who carry out that role and function in accordance with directions or instructions given by someone dehors the directorate such as the governing director of a holding company who directs and instructs the directors of the subsidiary what to do. For this provision to apply it must appear first that although the outside person calls the tune it is the directors who dance in their capacity as directors; and, second, that the directors perform positive acts not simply forebear to act or desist from acting.[167]

Further elaboration of the concept of the deemed director is given in the same case by Sangster J. In discussing the position there of a managing director who was taking instructions from an advisory committee where a scheme of arrangement was being undertaken, he said:

> In my opinion the other directors did not 'act' upon the respondents' directions or instructions – they simply did not act at all ... In my opinion for any person to be a 'director' (as defined by the Act) by virtue of his control of the directors, it must be shown ... that it is his will, and not the independent will of the appointed directors which determined the resolutions of the board of directors. So, too, in my opinion, for a person ... to control the acts of a managing director, not in relation to his functions as a member of the board of directors but only in relation to his functions as a working executive ... is of no moment in an inquiry whether he controls the acts of 'the directors'.[168]

It is not clear that Hodgson J has clearly considered these matters. He does state that 'in my view, the conditions imposed following the decision to fund Giant in March 1989 show a willingness and ability to exercise control and an actuality of control, over the management and financial affairs of Giant'.[169] However, as the judgments in *Harris v S* make clear, what is important is that 'the directors' (the board as a whole) were being controlled by the alleged de facto director. This distinction is also brought out to some extent in *Dairy Containers Ltd v NZI Bank Ltd*[170] where Thomas J of the New Zealand High Court dealt with a similar provision in the New Zealand Act. There he said:

> They were as directors of DCL [the subsidiary], standing (or sitting) in the shoes of NZDB [the holding company] at the board table, but they had not and did not receive directions or instructions from their employer. Even when a firm instruction from NZDB was made, it was directed at the company not at the directors.[171]

---

166 (1994) 13 ACSR 386.

167 (1976) 2 ACLR 51, at 63–64.

168 (1976) 2 ACLR 51, at 71–72.

169 (1995) 38 NSWLR 290, at 327–28.

170 (1995) 13 ACLC 3211.

171 (1995) 13 ACLC 3211, at 3238.

Therefore, with due respect to Hodgson J, it does not seem entirely clear whether there was evidence of control over the board. Indeed, Hodgson J does seem to concentrate as a whole on the activities of the nominees of Pioneer and the decisions of Pioneer rather than focus on the control of the Giant board.

A further issue arose as to the interest on the debt, since it was the only debt incurred when rolling over the loan facility. Hodgson J spent much of his judgment considering the true nature of whether the interest on the debt constituted 'a debt incurred'. His Honour stated that:

> (1) A debt for the principal of a loan (or each part thereof) is incurred when the principal (or such part) is first received by the borrower: generally, no debt for the principal is incurred either by non-repayment of the principal, or by entry into a new agreement to repay the principal.
>
> (2) Where the loan is for a fixed term, a debt for the interest (at the prompt payment rate, if any) for the term of the loan is incurred when the agreement is made or the loan is received; at least unless it is possible to escape from interest by early repayment of principal, and early repayment is a realistic option, in which case interest may be incurred from day to day by the borrower choosing not to repay.
>
> (3) Where the loan is not for a fixed term, or a fixed term has expired, in relation to periods where repayment is a real option for the borrower, the borrower generally incurs interest from day to day by choosing not to repay. However, in relation to periods where repayment is not a real option for the borrower, it may be reasonable to say that the debt for interest was incurred either when the loan was taken, or when the borrower last chose not to make a repayment which it could have made.
>
> (4) Where a borrower enters into a new agreement to pay interest on a loan which is due or overdue for repayment, it generally incurs a debt for interest to the same extent as when it made the original agreement and took the loan.[172]

Perhaps the following assists us in understanding these situations in practice:

(i) Section 556 is couched in terms of lifting the corporate veil to make company directors liable where they cause the company to incur debts which it cannot pay. The section further provides that this will occur when the company is either already insolvent or *ex post* the transaction insolvent;

(ii) It follows that s 556 does not catch a transaction for an advance of funds where the company is solvent both before and after the transaction;

The difficulty highlighted by this case occurs in circumstances where an advance of funds is made to a solvent company that remains solvent immediately after the advance but where the nature of the advance facility allows for ongoing financing. In such circumstances, the court in the instant

172 (1995) 38 NSWLR 290, at 317.

case, was faced with the consideration of the question of whether the continuation of the advance loan facility, beyond the date of the initial advance, amounted to the company incurring a debt at the time of renegotiation.

The following appears clear:

(a) That a refinancing of that debt principal does not amount to the incurring of a new debt and is therefore not within the ambit of s 556;

(b) That the interest which will accrue as a result of the refinancing will amount to the incurring of a new debt.

At the time of a refinancing it seems reasonable to require directors to examine the company's financial position (as indeed they are duty bound to do on a regular basis) to determine the company's financial status and capacity to repay the debt. It does however seem awkward to treat interest payable on a loan facility in the same manner as a debt incurred for a single sum on a single item, for example the purchase of an item of capital equipment with the amount due being payable in 30 days. Where debt for longer periods is incurred, it seems that the equating of total interest debt with solvency becomes less easy because of unforeseen future events.

The test of whether a reasonable director would have cause to expect insolvency is a requirement of the insolvent trading provisions. In this case Hodgson J considered the ability of the directors to predict insolvency. In this respect it is important to remember that Antico *et al* were not proprietary company directors, but rather business people recognised for their considerable abilities and skill. Previous cases have established an objective standard in this regard.

In the case of *Rema Industries & Services Pty Ltd v Coad*[173] Lockhart J stated that:

> In my opinion when sub-section (1) of s 592 refers to 'reasonable grounds' it requires the establishment of grounds which are reasonable according to the standards of directors or officers of companies of reasonable ability. Reasonable ability is a relative concept designed to be applied with some flexibility. The test is objective and is not measured by or subject to considerations personal to the defendant.[174]

Lockhart J considered the test of reasonableness stating that:

> the test of reasonable cause' in the context in which the expression appears imports an objective standard, but it must be implied to the facts and circumstances known to the Defendant and facts and circumstances which, by reason of the Defendant's duties as a director or officer of the company, ought have been known to him. It would be absurd for a Defendant to be able to establish a defence simply on the basis

173 (1992) 107 ALR 374.

174 (1992) 107 ALR 374, at 382.

> of what he in fact knew. This would reward the incompetent director who ought to have known a great deal more than he in fact knew.[175]

In this case, these considerations were relevant to Hodgson J. His Honour firstly recognised the relevance of the character of each of the directors stating that:

> Antico, Quirk and Gardiner were all ostensibly successful and capable businessmen; and they say in effect that they conscientiously attended to their duties, and that at material times, they believed that Giant would be able to pay its debts as they fell due. If I accept them as honest and reliable witnesses, then I believe this evidence carries weight as to what a director of appropriate ability and prudence ought to have expected, on the facts known to them; and in my view this has some relevance to the objective question of reasonable grounds under s 556(1) as well as being clearly relevant to the question of reasonable cause under s 556(2).[176]

His Honour secondly found as to character as follows:

> I reach these conclusions ... notwithstanding evidence by Antico, Quirk and Gardiner that each of them believed, as at 25 July 1989, that Giant was able to pay all its debts as they fell due, and notwithstanding my view that each of them is a conscientious and capable businessman who is more qualified than I am to make judgments in business matters I feel able to come to a different opinion on this matter because I believe that, at critical times, they were actually having regard to Pioneer's interests rather than the interests of Giant and its creditors ...[177]

Thus in *Antico*, Hodgson J did to a certain extent discount the opinion of the directors as presented in their oral evidence. It says something of the test required in s 556 that Hodgson J admits that the directors were 'conscientious and capable' and 'more qualified than I am to make judgments in business matters'. In the particular facts of this case Hodgson J adopted an interesting interpretation of what was required under s 556(1):

> Suppose that the debt being incurred is for a loan which will enable other debts to be paid out, and which gives the company time in which to acquire resources to pay out the particular loan: in that case, the reasonable director would not have the expectation in para (ii) [of s 556(1)(b)]. However, if (as a reasonable director would have known) that particular loan transaction itself is vitiated by some action of the company, then in my view, the directors cannot rely on the existence of that transaction to escape the effect of para (i). The reasonable grounds to expect that the company would not be able to pay its debts as they fell due, under para (i) would not be negatived by the expectation of this particular transaction because (as a reasonable director would have known) it was only obtained by misleading conduct.[178]

---

175 (1992) 107 ALR 374, at 382.

176 (1995) 18 ACSR 1, at 39, not quoted in the NSWLR version.

177 (1995) 38 NSWLR 290, at 338.

178 (1995) 38 NSWLR 290, at 336.

Ultimately the situation described above was found to exist in the case at hand. If the test applied by Hodgson J says no more than that in testing reasonable grounds to expect insolvency, the director must take into account the true value of assets available, there can be little objection to what is raised. However, it appears that the test takes directors' obligations somewhat further. It appears that it means that a director is obliged to establish the legal position with respect to each transaction. In other words certain assumptions are being made as to the ability of a reasonable director to evaluate whether a contract or agreement will be vitiated because of some action of the company.

The test of reasonableness established earlier is evaluated according to the 'standards of directors or officers of companies of a reasonable standard'.[179] If the test in s 556 can be reasonably applied, it is because it is a commercial test whereby the director is required to assess the ability of a company to pay its debts as they fall due. Whilst there is implicit in this a judgment of the legal basis for both the liabilities and the assets it seems that to have to disregard certain sources of funds on the basis that they may be later set aside,[180] establishes a higher and perhaps unrealistic standard of behaviour required from directors.

To some extent this is illustrated by the *Antico* case itself. On the facts, Hodgson J admitted to the fact that these directors were 'conscientious and capable'. Further, in dealing with the question of whether a director could rely upon the fact that a creditor does not seek a winding up to show that the company was able to pay its debts, His Honour said:

> Section 556 of the Code does not proceed on the basis that a debt is only due when a creditor moves to wind up the debtor or even to enforce the debt in other ways: A debt is due when the relevant contract says it is due, subject to any relevant practices or agreements or other commercial considerations which make it reasonable to regard the debt as not being due.[181]

Thus it would seem that for certain purposes, a director has regard to the contractual position only; yet in other respects, a director must look beyond the contract to evaluate further legal issues involved in the transaction. Finally, there is the fact that in assessing the trade practices claim, Hodgson J had little difficulty in deciding that each of the directors of Giant, including the deemed director (Pioneer), did not know of the misleading conduct as required by the Trade Practices Act 1974 (Cth).[182]

Thus for the purposes of s 556 Hodgson J seems to require directors to establish that the contracts will not be set aside for some possible reason

179 *Rema Industries & Services Pty Ltd v Coad* (1992) 107 ALR 374, at 382.

180 For example, where there is a reasonable probability that a value enhancing contract with the company will be set aside.

181 (1995) 38 NSWLR 290, at 357.

182 Section 75B, Trade Practices Act 1974 (Cth); (1995) 38 NSWLR 290, at 371.

before they can establish whether the company is able to pay its debts, and that a reasonable director ought to have been aware of these factors.

One of the novel aspects of the case was the claim that Giant and the directors had engaged in misleading and deceptive conduct by failing to disclose the position of the company when applying to refinance the loan. Misleading conduct by Giant was found because it failed to disclose certain defaults in the loan agreements with the bank. However it was not established that the directors were knowingly concerned in, or a party to, that conduct. Further, Pioneer was not aware of the misleading conduct and was therefore not liable.

This is significant because the use of such an action in conjunction with conduct prohibited under s 556 represents a new direction in such cases. This is because the mischief behind the insolvent trading provisions is probably that the creditors have been mislead by the directors as to the true financial state of the company. Misleading and deceptive conduct may provide a more effective basis for imposing liability upon directors. The next significant event affecting the regulation of insolvent trading in Australia was the Commonwealth government's unilateral attempt to comprehensively legislate for the creation and conduct of Australian companies.

1.2.5 The Corporations Law

In 1990 after a constitutional challenge[183] the Commonwealth government and the States negotiated a means for the Commonwealth to have jurisdiction to regulate the incorporation and operation of companies. The agreement[184] allowed the Commonwealth to use the Corporations Act 1989 (Cth) to make ACT legislation governing the operation of companies, pursuant to s 122 of the Commonwealth Constitution, thus obviating the need to rely upon the 'incomplete' corporations power pursuant to s 51(xx) of the Constitution. The other State jurisdictions (and the Northern Territory) then adopted the Act and the Corporations Law (being the substantive companies legislation) applied from 1 January 1991.

The introduction of the Corporations Law resulted in the renumbering of the provisions therein. Accordingly, s 592 replaced the s 556 insolvent trading provision. The case law decided pursuant to s 592 continued to apply the broad interpretation given to s 556, and this consistency was not surprising since s 592 was 'in identical terms in all material respects'[185] to s 556.

Thus s 592 was interpreted as comprising two classes of offences, being the insolvent trading prohibition and the intent to defraud. The section provided for a civil penalty in the event of insolvent trading. Section 592 required determination and satisfaction that the company had incurred a debt

183 *NSW v Commonwealth* (1990) 169 CLR 482.

184 The Alice Springs Agreement, June 1990.

185 *Rema Industries and Services Pty Ltd v Coad* (1992) 10 ACLC 530, at 535 *per* Lockhart J.

and this carried with it the need to determine the company's solvency at that time and when the debt was incurred.[186] The section's reference to 'reasonable' was held to require 'the establishment of grounds which are reasonable according to the standards of directors or officers of companies of reasonable ability. Reasonable ability is a relative concept designed to be applied with some flexibility. The test is objective and is not measured by subjective considerations personal to the defendant'.[187] Similarly, 'reasonable' in the defence offered by s 592 was a test that imported 'an objective standard ... applied to the facts and circumstances known to the defendant and facts and circumstances which, by reason of the defendant's duties as a director or officer of the company, ought to have been known to him'.[188]

1.2.6 Harmer Committee Report

The Harmer Committee was the first comprehensive review of the insolvent trading provisions in Australia.[189] The Harmer Committee noted that there 'was a clear need for further reform'[190] of the insolvent trading provisions to address the primary concern associated with insolvent trading. The Committee felt that a clearly drafted provision imposing a positive duty on the director would assist the recovery of monies owing to creditors stating that:

> Former and existing legislation has centred upon the incurring of a particular debt or debts and subjecting a director to notional joint responsibility for the debt or debts. This produces a series of isolated examinations of each instance of the incurring of a debt. Yet the real abuse is permitting the company to trade after a point where, on an objectively considered basis, the company is unable to pay all its debts.[191]

Thus the recommendation was to totally restructure the insolvent trading provision so that it was 'clear, rational and readily enforceable in a manner which permits all creditors to share equally in the sums recovered'[192] thus promoting the equal sharing in insolvency principle currently provided for in s 555.

The Harmer Committee provided an historical background to the Australian insolvent trading provisions,[193] noting that when the Uniform Companies Act was passed in 1961 it:

---

186 *Rema Industries and Services Pty Ltd v Coad* (1992) 10 ACLC 530, at 536.

187 *Rema Industries and Services Pty Ltd v Coad* (1992) 10 ACLC 530, at 536.

188 *Rema Industries and Services Pty Ltd v Coad* (1992) 10 ACLC 530, at 537.

189 The Cooney Committee Report, (Senate Standing Committee on Legal and Constitutional Affairs, Company Directors' Duties; Report on the Social and Fiduciary Duties and Obligations of Company Directors, November 1989, AGPS), also considered the operation of the general fiduciary duties of directors in the context of the operation of s 556.

190 The Law Reform Commission, Report No 45, General Insolvency Inquiry ALRC 45, AGPS, Canberra, 1988, at 125.

191 *Ibid.*

192 *Ibid.*

193 *Ibid*, at 123–24.

> adopted a new *criminal offence* where it appeared, in the course of winding up, that an officer of a company was *party to the incurring of a debt* by the company *without a reasonable expectation that the debt could be paid.*

The report also noted that when the Companies Code was passed in 1981, there was no necessity for a prior conviction. However the recovery was by individual creditors not by the liquidator. The Harmer Report went on to outline the deficiencies in the various approaches to insolvent trading in Australia[194] since 1961:

> At no stage since its introduction in 1961 has the liability of a director for incurring debts without a reasonable prospect of payment been in a form appropriate for giving creditors (considered as a class) a suitable remedy.
>
> - The liability contained in the 1961 uniform legislation was criminal only. Even if a conviction was obtained (which was difficult, since the offence related to incurring a debt without reasonable prospect of paying *that debt*) it was of no benefit to the creditors as a whole and of no benefit to the individual creditor involved in the transaction.
> - When civil liability was introduced in 1964, it was dependent upon a prior conviction for the offence. Creditors thus had to rely on the relevant authority to prosecute the criminal offence and satisfy a criminal standard of proof before there was any prospect of civil recovery. There were few successful prosecutions and even fewer instances of successful civil recovery.
> - Even if a conviction and subsequent recovery were obtained, the procedure was lengthy. In one case, a summons against a director for the criminal offence was issued in September 1982 in connection with a company which was wound up in January 1980. A conviction was recorded in August 1984 and the director fined $500. The declaration under a 374D was made in November 1984, almost five years after the winding up.
> - The 1981 provisions contain a curious mixture of civil and criminal sanctions but have at least taken the positive step of providing a civil remedy which is independent of any criminal conviction for the errant behaviour (as mentioned, this was argued for as far back as 1962). However, although the nexus between civil and criminal liability has been broken, the legislation:
>   - continues to combine civil and criminal aspects in the one legislative provision;
>   - gives any benefit of the civil liability to the creditor taking action and thus is only of advantage to a creditor with the resources to take such action;
>   - fails to provide a liquidator with standing to bring an action for the benefit of all creditors;

194 In England the Cork Committee similarly found that previous reviews of insolvency provisions 'were piecemeal and limited in their ambit', *Report of the Review Committee – Insolvency Law and Practice*, Cmnd 8558, London HMSO, June 1982.

- contains a number of technical deficiencies; and
- requires a multiplicity of actions if all creditors who have been affected by the behaviour of the directors are to be compensated, with the possible result that the first creditors to take action may exhaust the assets of the errant directors.[195]

There was broad support for the Harmer Committee view that the insolvent trading provisions providing for director liability be totally restructured.[196] As with the previous committees of inquiry, the recommendations for reform proposed by the Harmer Committee were justified on the basis of submissions made to the committee and upon the 'desirability' and perceived working of the current provisions.[197] Further, whilst the Harmer Committee report comprehensively outlined the historical operation of the insolvent trading provision and made recommendations for its future operation, no measure or means of evaluation of the new provision was provided.[198] Thus, neither at the time of the recommended legislative change nor at any time later, was there proposed to be some means of ensuring that the legislative mechanism might consider the effectiveness of the provision on an ongoing basis. Hence the Harmer Committee continued the age-old legal tradition of tampering with the legislation without full consideration of maintaining the operating legislation.

The Harmer Committee's insolvent trading reform recommendations were consistent with the philosophy behind s 555,[199] insofar as the proposed insolvent trading provision suggested a change in philosophy to 'promote the principle of equal sharing in an insolvency'.[200]

On 23 June 1993, Parts 4 and 5 of the Corporate Law Reform Act 1992 (Cth) commenced operation. The 'flawed'[201] s 592 of the Corporations Law

---

195 The Law Reform Commission, Report No 45, General Insolvency Inquiry ALRC 45, AGPS, Canberra, 1988, at 124–25.

196 *Ibid*, at 126.

197 *Ibid*, at 125, 'Need for reform. Despite the 1981 legislation, there is still a clear need for further reform. The responsibility of a director with regard to insolvent trading has not, thus far, been expressed as a positive duty owed to the company to prevent the company from engaging in that activity'.

198 This lack of 'measurement' is in the context of there being no attempt made to analyse the implications for directors of bearing the additional responsibility / risk nor the effect that such responsibility might have upon the investment decisions of the company.

199 Report of the Review Committee – Insolvency Law and Practice, Cmnd 8558, London HMSO, June 1982, at 62, 'Adequate measures must exist to ensure that the assets available for the general body of creditors are not unreasonably depleted prior to the insolvency proceedings so as to put beyond their reach. Secondly, if the proceedings are to be recognised as truly collective in their nature, they should be capable of embracing as many as possible of the legitimate and valid claims against the insolvent, irrespective of such matters as the precise legal origin of any particular claim or the residence or place of business of the claimant'. See Keay AR, McPherson The Law of Company Liquidation, 4th edition, LBC Information Services, Sydney, 1999, at 376.

200 The Law Reform Commission, Report No 45, General Insolvency Inquiry ALRC 45, AGPS, Canberra, 1988, at 125.

201 Herzberg A, 'Insolvent trading' (1991) 9 Company and Securities Law Journal 285, at 286.

was replaced by s 588G (within Part 5.7B) as a result of recommendations made by the Harmer Committee.[202]

Interestingly the Cork Committee expressed a sentiment similar to the Harmer Committee in relation to the Committee's review of equivalent English wrongful trading offence:

> … a director or officer of a failed company who has been a party to wrongful trading may be subjected to personal liability for some or all of the debts of the company. An alteration to the law in this respect will mean that a director who, when judged by the current standards of commercial morality, is found to have abused the privilege of limited liability will forfeit that privilege. His position in such a case will be to all intents and purposes the same as if he had been trading on his own account and at his own risk; he will be guaranteeing, out of his own pocket, the debts incurred by the company while under his direction to creditors who are left unpaid.[203]

1.3 Conclusion

This paper has provided an historical insight and understanding of the development of the law of insolvent trading in Australia. This examination of historical influences to the insolvent trading provision is important because it provides both the reasons for the introduction of this form of creditor protection and the reasons for its amendment in the context of changing attitudes towards creditor protection in both England and Australia. The stated reasons for the legislative change to the legislation have been identified as have the criticisms of the law by subsequent inquiries, the judiciary and legal commentators. Comparative insight has been provided in order to demonstrate that Australia is not unique in either its incidence of insolvent trading or in having difficulty with effective regulation of the offence. With the evolution of a more sophisticated insolvent trading provision there has been an erosion of the limited liability status of the company director. This contextual analysis is important and useful because it provides a background to the most recent changes made to insolvent trading laws in Australia.

202 The Law Reform Commission, Report No 45, General Insolvency Inquiry ALRC 45, AGPS, Canberra, 1988.

203 Report of the Review Committee – Insolvency Law and Practice, Cmnd 8558, London HMSO, June 1982, at 407.

The Future of the Rome Convention on Damage Caused by Aircraft to Third Parties on the Surface: Will All Roads Lead Away from Rome?

Jeffrey Weeks

Introduction

On 25 July 2000, Air France Concorde flight 4590 crashed in a fiery explosion into a hotel shortly after take-off from Charles de Gaulle airport. All 109 passengers and crew on board were killed instantly while four people on the ground, employees of the hotel, also lost their lives. Two weeks after the disaster, Mr Phillippe Calavia, Deputy Managing Director of Air France, announced that the relatives of all 113 victims would be compensated.[1] Mr Calavia explained that, while insurance companies were bound to compensate relatives of those on board the Concorde, it had not been clear about the compensation owed to victims on the ground. 'Even though it is not spelt out in the texts', he said, 'Air France will also compensate the families of victims who were on the ground'.[2]

This recent example illustrates the doubt and confusion that surrounds the question as to the legal ramifications of death, injury or damage by aircraft to third parties on the surface. Unlike the aircraft passenger, who is likely to receive compensation wherever in the world they may be injured or killed,[3] the bystander on the ground is subject to the compassion (or perhaps, more realistically, the fear of bad publicity) of the airline company and national legislation for compensation for their damage or injuries suffered. In the Netherlands, for example, which did not have specific liability legislation relating to damage by aircraft to third parties on the surface, claims arising out of the 1992 El Al crash in the Bijlmer neighbourhood of Amsterdam, in which 43 people on the ground were killed, are still awaiting settlement.[4]

---

1 'Air France to Compensate Concorde Crash Relatives', 8 August 2000, CNN.com, <http://www.cnn.com/2000/WORLD/europe/08/08/concorde.insurance.reut/index.html>. Visited 9 August 2000.

2 See CNN n 1.

3 Airline passengers are always likely to be covered by, at a minimum, the Convention for the Unification of Certain Rules Relating to International Carriage by Air, Warsaw, 2 October 1929 (Warsaw Convention). They may also, by virtue of Article 22 of the Warsaw Convention, be covered by special contracts between the carrier and the passenger fixing higher limits of liability such as provided for in the European Council Regulation No 2027/97 of 9 October 1997 on Air Carrier Liability in the Event of Accidents. This regulation also mandates advance payments to the relatives of deceased passengers to the level of 15 000 SDR: Article 5 EC Regulation No 2027/97.

4 Damage by Aircraft Bill (Cth) 1999 (Explanatory Memorandum), as accessed via 'BillsNet' Parliament of Australia Parliamentary Library <http://www.aph.gov.au/parlinfo/billsnet/main.htm>. Visited 15 November 2000.

In the 1930s, attempts were made to create an international scheme to enable third parties on the ground to recover automatically for damage caused to them by foreign aircraft.[5] These attempts resulted in the 1933 Rome Convention,[6] which was later modified and replaced by the 1952 Rome Convention.[7] However these conventions failed to achieve the uniformity they sought and consequently they were ratified by relatively few nations. Australia, which was one of the few nations that did ratify the 1952 Rome Convention, formally denounced it on the passing of the new Damage by Aircraft Act 1999, which came into force on 8 November 2000.

This paper looks at the question of whether the Rome Convention has a future. Could a modified, updated Rome Convention encourage more nations to ratify it, or would it take a totally new, redrafted, renegotiated international multilateral treaty on damage to third parties on the ground to gain support from nations? Or is there even really a need for an 'international' convention on damage to third parties on the ground? What purposes are served by having an international scheme or do national laws in the form of general principles of negligence or legislation suffice to protect the 'innocent bystander' on the ground?

Part I of this paper looks at the situation of the common law and general principles of negligence relating to damage on the surface caused by aircraft. This part discusses the early confusion as to whether the flight of an aircraft over land was actionable in trespass, nuisance, negligence or combinations of these. Finally, Part I discusses the debate as to whether liability arising from damage by aircraft required proof of negligence or was based on strict liability.

Part II will discuss national approaches to damage by aircraft to the surface. The nations looked at are the Netherlands, which does not have specific legislation to deal with damage by aircraft and continues to use general principles of negligence, Great Britain, Germany and China, which have legislated for strict liability, and finally the United States, which has a mixture of reliance on the common law, legislation imposing strict liability and legislation stating that the law applicable to torts on land shall determine liability.

Part III considers the attempt in the 1952 Rome Convention to create international uniformity for damage by aircraft to third parties on the surface. This part looks at the birth of the Rome Convention and why it was thought beneficial to have a uniform international scheme to cover the area. This part

5 See the discussion in Part III for the reasons why it was thought necessary to follow the example of the Warsaw Convention and create an international scheme.

6 International Convention for the Unification of Certain Rules Relating to Damage Caused by Aircraft to Third Parties on the Surface, Rome, 29 May 1933 (1933 Rome Convention).

7 Convention on Damage Caused by Foreign Aircraft to Third Parties on the Surface, Rome, 7 October 1952 (1952 Rome Convention). See Appendix I.

will also discuss the main points of contention during negotiations of the Convention, the main features of the Convention, and finally, why it failed in its objective of achieving international uniformity.

Part IV will look at the position of Australia and Australian states and territories in relation to damage by aircraft. This involves looking at the implementation of the Rome Convention into Australian law by the Civil Aviation (Damage by Aircraft) Act 1958. This part also discusses why Australia decided to denounce the Rome Convention and compares the new regime, the Damage by Aircraft Act 1999, with the Rome Convention.

Finally, Part V looks at the recent 'rediscovery' of the Rome Convention. Although the Rome Convention has been described as 'moribund', a new interest has suddenly awoken to modernise the Convention and change some of the perceived deficiencies, including the introduction of environmental damage issues. This final part will discuss the prospects of success for a new, born-again Convention.

Part I: The common law and general principles of negligence approach

1.1 A swift but confused response

It is nothing short of astonishing to consider that, at this time a century ago, flight in machines heavier than air was still but a dream.[8] The Great War of 1914 and events such as Charles Lindbergh's historic crossing of the Atlantic in 1927 would prove that air transportation was here to stay. While the law may often be criticised for its inability to keep up with the pace of human change and development, aviation law proved that the law often can (when it must) adapt quickly. As stated by Diederiks-Verschoor: 'air law offers a striking example of how existing legal rules can be swiftly adapted to the impressive technological progress achieved …'[9]

Common law judges and legislatures had little choice but to 'swiftly adapt' to the reality of air transportation. The courts of the common law used the established causes of action of trespass, nuisance and negligence to spell out the rights and obligations of pilots and owners of aircraft in order to adequately protect the general public. There was however initial confusion as to when these actions applied and their scope.

8 The first flight by the Wright Brothers took place on 17 December 1903 at Kitty Hawk, North Carolina.

9 Diederiks-Verschoor, IPH, *An Introduction to Air Law*, 6th edn, 1997, The Hague: Kluwer Law International, at 1.

1.2 Rights over airspace: trespass or nuisance?

When courts first began to contend with the legal issues surrounding aircraft there was confusion relating to the rights of a landowner to the airspace above the land. The traditional starting point for the courts on the issue of aircraft liability, and the source of much of the confusion, was Lord Coke's statement:[10]

> And lastly, the earth hath in law a great extent upwards, not only of water, as hath been said, but ayre and all other things, even up to heaven; for *cujus est solum, ejus est usque ad coelum* as is holden ...

The origin of the maxim, *cujus est solum, ejus est usque ad coelum* (translated as 'whose is the soil is also the heavens'), has been accredited to Accursius, a Bolognese glossator of the 13th century.[11] This maxim was the basis for a claim in trespass, and the advantage of framing an action in trespass is that, unlike for an action in nuisance or negligence, one does not have to prove actual damage occurred. In fact, *cujus est solum, ejus est usque ad coelum* was held to apply in cases concerning overhanging buildings,[12] advertising signposts[13] and telephone wires.[14]

In *Kelsen v Imperial Tobacco Co (of Great Britain and Ireland) Ltd*,[15] a mandatory injunction was granted to prevent the invasion of an advertising signpost from intruding four inches over the land of the plaintiff. Mr Justice McNair stated that because there was no actual damage or inconvenience to the plaintiff by the intrusion, an action in nuisance was not available.[16] However he concluded that, 'a trespass and not a mere nuisance was created by the invasion of the plaintiff's airspace by this sign'.[17]

This can be distinguished from cases involving bullets shot across the land of another. In the case of *Clifton v Viscount Bury*,[18] bullets that did not fall onto the plaintiff's land but rather passed 75 feet over it, were held not to be a

10 As quoted in Keenan PB, Lester A and Martin P, *Shawcross and Beaumont on Air Law*, 3rd edn, 1966, London: Butterworths, at 533.

11 *Bernstein of Leigh (Baron) v Skyviews & General Ltd* [1978] QB 479 at 485. See also Kerr MRE and Evans AHM, *McNair's Law of the Air*, 3rd edn, 1964, London: Stevens & Sons, at 393 for an interesting discussion on the origin and history of the maxim *cujus est solum, ejus est usque ad coelum.*

12 *Baten's* case (1610) 9 Rep 53b, as cited in Kerr, n 11, at 32.

13 *Kelsen v Imperial Tobacco Co (of Great Britain and Ireland) Ltd* [1957] 2 QB 334.

14 *Wandsworth Board of Works v United Telephone Co* (1884) 13 QBD 904, where the Court of Appeal held that although there was no trespass in this case because of the legislative definition of 'street', it had no doubt that 'the wire would have amounted to trespass against an ordinary proprietor of land': see Kerr, n 11, at 38.

15 [1957] 2 QB 334.

16 *Kelsen v Imperial Tobacco Co (of Great Britain and Ireland) Ltd* [1957] 2 QB 334, at 343.

17 *Kelsen v Imperial Tobacco Co (of Great Britain and Ireland) Ltd* [1957] 2 QB 334, at 345.

18 (1887) 4 TLR 8 as cited in Kerr, n 11, at 40.

trespass. However, because this affected the plaintiff's quiet enjoyment of the land, the judge found an action lay in nuisance.

Therefore, there was confusion for a number of years as to the scope of trespass and nuisance in the common law for intrusion into airspace. Courts had held *cujus est solum, ejus est usque ad coelum* applied for trespass for stationary objects above the land, but for flying bullets, *in vacuo* above the land, the cause of action appeared to lie in nuisance (if a person's right to the quiet enjoyment of the land was interfered with), or negligence (if damage could be proven). Furthermore, although trespass is an absolute right, not requiring actual damage to be proven, there must be a degree of reasonableness as to what may be properly described as 'damage'. Just as it would be absurd to hold that there was a battery or trespass to the person if two people met in a narrow passage and one touched the other lightly, so too would it be absurd to hold a plane flying at great height above land was trespassing or creating a nuisance.

This is the position that Mr Justice Griffiths took in the case of *Bernstein of Leigh (Baron) v Skyviews & General Ltd.*[19] In this case the defendant had flown over the plaintiff's land to take photos of his property. Mr Justice Griffiths stated that there could be no trespass and that a landowner has rights to the airspace above, 'to such height as is necessary for ordinary use and enjoyment of his land and the structures upon it … above that height he has no greater rights in the airspace than any other member of the public'.[20]

1.3 Strict liability or proof of negligence

The discussion above focused on the rights of a landowner to the airspace above their land, without any actual contact with the surface. In the event of an air crash or something falling from a plane while in flight and damaging a third party on the surface, negligence is the action of choice. To succeed in an action for negligence a plaintiff must 'show that the defendant was under a legal duty to him to take reasonable care, and that he has suffered damage as a result of the defendant's breach of such duty'.[21]

Pilots and owners of aircraft are obviously 'neighbours'[22] to the people below them, establishing the duty of care. Similarly, it is generally easy for the plaintiff to prove that damage has occurred. The contentious issue centres on the question of the defendant's breach of the duty and whether, in the event of a crash, a plaintiff had to prove negligence of the pilot or owner of the aircraft or whether the plaintiff could invoke strict liability and recover after merely proving that damage had occurred to them.

19 [1978] QB 479.

20 [1978] QB 479, at 488.

21 Kerr, n 11, at 72.

22 *Donoghue v Stevenson* [1932] AC 562.

Despite a few decisions to the contrary such as *Rochester Gas & Elec Comp v Dunlop*[23] and attempts to bring damage by aircraft to third parties on the surface within the scope of the rule in *Rylands v Fletcher*,[24] it is generally accepted that the common law requires the plaintiff to establish proof of negligence. This has not however stopped the academic debate on the subject. There are four main arguments as to why strict liability should apply to damage by aircraft to third parties on the surface.

1.4 Arguments in favour of strict liability

First, there is the 'one-sidedness' of the activity in regards to the receipt of benefits to one party and the creation of risks to the other.[25] As stated succinctly by Vold:[26]

> Airplanes crash down on their victims by force of gravity. Victims below do not fly up and strike the planes. Aviation operators get the benefits, create the risks to those below, and do the damage to those below. In this regard, their victims below endanger nobody overhead. They get no benefits. Yet they suffer damage. Here the one-sidedness is glaring.

Second, there is the argument that flying an aircraft is an extra-hazardous activity. As will be stated below, this can no longer be seriously argued and there is no reason why air transportation be regarded as less safe than road transport, for which the proof of negligence is required in a tort case.

The third argument is that the aviation industry is so large and wealthy that it can distribute the loss from damage to third parties through insurance or simply as part of its costs of business.[27]

Finally, it is argued that, on a practical note, there should be strict liability for it is impossible for the injured party to prove what has caused the accident. As stated by Newman in 1929, 'when an airplane out of control falls it will often be completely demolished; its pilot and occupants may be killed and there will rarely be an observer competent to testify as to the cause of the crash'.[28]

---

23 266 NY Supp 469 (County Ct 1933).

24 (1868) LR 3 HL 330. The rule in *Rylands v Fletcher* involves the imposition of strict liability on occupiers of land when a thing they bring on the land escapes and causes damage. As pointed out by Keenan, n 10, at 549, there is a real conceptual difficulty with the idea of aircraft 'escaping' from the owners land. Nor can it be seriously argued any more today, that aircraft can be regarded as a 'dangerous thing' to which strict liability attaches.

25 Vold L, 'Strict Liability for Aircraft Crashes and Forced Landings on Ground Victims outside of Established Landing Areas' (1953) 5 Hastings Law Journal 1. See also the dissenting judgment of Justice Brachtenbach in *Crosby v Cox Aircraft* 746 P.2d 1198 (Wash 1987), at 1203 where he states, 'it is apparent that fairness and common sense suggest that the loss should not be allocated to the innocent bystander'.

26 Vold, n 25, at 17.

27 See Vold, n 25, at 20 for further discussion on this point.

28 'Damage Liability in Aircraft Cases' (1929) 29 Columbia Law Review 1039, at 1042.

1.5 Arguments against strict liability

On the other hand, there are four main arguments that favour the use of the ordinary rules of negligence and require the plaintiff to prove negligence.

First, it is argued that the airplane is not a dangerous instrument, or in any event, can no longer be regarded as any more dangerous than an automobile, train or ship, so why then should torts of the land not apply also to aircraft? This was the main argument of the majority (5:4) judgment of Justice Callow in the Washington State case of *Crosby v Cox Aircraft Company of Washington*.[29] The case involved the crash of a DeHavilland DHC-3 Otter aircraft. The aircraft met Federal Aviation Administration standards, but unfortunately, after the replacement of a piston-driven engine with a turbine engine, ran out of fuel in mid-flight, and crashed into a garage in West Seattle.

Justice Callow looked at the Restatement (Second) of Torts.[30] Paragraph 519 sets out the general principle, that if one carries on an 'abnormally dangerous activity', they are subject to strict liability, even after exercising the utmost care to prevent harm.

Paragraph 520 of the Restatement states that in determining whether an activity is 'abnormally dangerous' one considers the following factors:

(a) existence of a high degree of risk of some harm to the person, land or chattels of others;

(b) likelihood that the harm that results from it will be great;

(c) inability to eliminate the risk by the exercise of reasonable care;

(d) extent to which the activity is not a matter of common usage;

(e) inappropriateness of the activity to the place where it is carried on; and

(f) extent to which its value to the community is outweighed by its dangerous attributes.

Paragraph 520A states that ground damage from aircraft is of 'special application' and requires strict liability to be found.

Justice Callow found however that the flying of an aircraft could no longer be regarded as an 'ultra-hazardous activity'.[31] He pointed out that only six American States imposed strict liability and that several had legislated to provide that ordinary negligence apply to aviation accidents.[32] He also stated that statistics now showed air transportation to be safer than automobile transport, and that 'extensive governmental regulation of transport and the continuing technological improvements in aircraft manufacture, maintenance and operation reduced the overall risk of serious injury.[33]

29 746 P.2d 1198 (Wash 1987).

30 Restatement (Second) of Torts (1977) (Restatement).

31 *Crosby v Cox Aircraft* 746 P 2d 1198 (Wash 1987), at 1200.

32 *Crosby v Cox Aircraft* 746 P 2d 1198 (Wash 1987), at 1200.

33 *Crosby v Cox Aircraft* 746 P 2d 1198 (Wash 1987), at 1201.

However, as alluded to by Mr Justice Brachtenbach in his powerful dissenting judgement in *Crosby v Cox Aircraft*, notwithstanding the fact that aircraft flight is no longer 'abnormally dangerous' as it was in the past, there are still strong policy reasons (such as the ones mentioned above), for imposing strict liability.[34]

Second, it is argued that absolute or strict liability would discourage flying. While this may have been an appropriate argument when the airline industry was at its infancy and there was a real need for pilots to experiment with aircraft, this can no longer be regarded as the case. Further, where strict liability was imposed by legislation in England by s 9 of the Air Navigation Act 1920 (UK) and most of Western Europe, the aviation industry continued to flourish.

Third, there is the argument that that the burden placed on a plaintiff needing to prove negligence is not so onerous for they could employ the doctrine of *res ipsa loquitur* to assist them. *Res ipsa loquitur* is a rule of evidence that is justified for two reasons. First on the basis that 'things do not normally fall out of the sky'[35] and therefore the 'accident must be one which would almost be impossible or at least extremely unlikely to happen in the absence of negligence.[36] Second, *res ipsa loquitur* may be justified as a 'device to prevent the injustice of denying recovery to a probably meritorious plaintiff because the ability to prove the cause of his injury rests exclusively with his opponent'.[37]

However, it is submitted that the maxim of *res ipsa loquitur* would not be of much use to a plaintiff in many instances. While the maxim may be of use when a plane crashes on a fine, sunny day, when there should be no reason for the accident, when there is evidence that 'acts of God' in the form of bad weather may be involved, *res ipsa loquitur* can be of little assistance to the plaintiff.

Finally, there is the argument that passengers of aircraft involved in accidents must prove negligence and that, 'the likelihood of serious injury to a passenger is at least as great as is the case with persons or property on the ground'.[38] With all due respect, this argument fails to recognise that an important difference between the passenger and the innocent bystander on the ground is that the passenger has assumed the risk of air travel. The victim however is 'powerless to guard against airplane crashes and aircraft debris'.[39]

34 *Crosby v Cox Aircraft* 746 P.2d 1198 (Wash 1987), at 1203.

35 Kerr, n 11, at 78.

36 Bohlen FH, 'Aviation under the Common Law', (1935) 6 Air Law Review 155, at 164.

37 Bohlen, n 36, at 165.

38 Justice Callow (majority judgment) in *Crosby v Cox Aircraft* 746 P 2d 1198 (Wash 1987), at 1202.

39 Jones W, 'Strict Liability for Hazardous Enterprise' (1992) 92 Columbia Law Review 1705, at 1748.

1.6 Public policy and fairness favour strict liability

In conclusion, the common law requires that the plaintiff prove negligence on the part of the defendant. However, there are powerful public policy and fairness arguments that support the imposition of strict liability for any damage by aircraft to third parties on the ground. As stated by Justice Brachtenbach in his dissenting judgement in *Crosby v Cox Aircraft*:[40]

> What a peculiar, aberrant twist of tort law is created by the majority … almost a decade ago we held that when a wineglass shatters in the hands of a wine drinker, the seller of the wine, who merely supplied the glass, is strictly liable. The law demanded and gave compensation without proof of fault. Today the majority tells the wholly innocent, inactive home owner into whose house an airplane suddenly crashes 'you must prove by a preponderance of the evidence that someone was at fault; never mind that you had no part in this damage, go forth and prove negligence and if you cannot, the loss is all yours'. How can that be?

It is submitted, that reliance on the common law or on general principles of negligence does not adequately protect the innocent bystander on the ground. Any national legislation or international convention on damage by aircraft to the surface should provide that the pilot or owner of the aircraft be strictly liable for damage caused.

Part II: The national approach

2.1 National legislative schemes

With the courts coming down in favour of the plaintiff being required to prove negligence in the event of damage by aircraft, it was for the legislature either to allow the normal rules of negligence to apply, or to legislate their own national scheme to deal with the problem, or to implement into their national laws the international scheme of the Rome Convention. This Part considers the national laws for damage by aircraft to third parties on the surface of the Netherlands, the United Kingdom, Germany, China and the United States.

2.2 The Netherlands

The Netherlands provides the perfect example of the problems that arise when a country does not have specific rules relating to damage by aircraft to third parties on the surface. In October of 1992, an Israeli El Al Boeing 747 cargo plane crashed into an apartment block in the Bijlmer neighbourhood of Amsterdam. 43 people were killed and there was considerable immediate surface damage to the entire region. In the 1999 Dutch Parliamentary Inquiry,

40 746 P 2d 1198 (Wash 1987), at 1202.

(named the Commission Meijer after its chairman) it was found that there was a total of 282 kilograms of depleted uranium in the plane's tail wing, which it is feared, may cause sickness in the future to the rescuers and to those who lived in the area at the time of the crash.[41] Although at the time of the crash the Netherlands had a new Civil Code for negligence, which contained a number of strict liabilities for defective objects, aircraft had been specifically excluded and therefore general principles of negligence applied.[42] As Stolker pointed out:[43]

> The Netherlands now have the somewhat strange situation that someone who causes damage to an apartment window with a remote-controlled toy airplane will be held to a strict liability standard, whereas when a fully-loaded Boeing 747 crashes into an apartment building, the operator is liable only if the victim can prove negligence.

As a result of the Bijlmer disaster, the new Dutch Transportation Act will have specific regulations ensuring there is strict liability for damage by aircraft.[44]

2.3 United Kingdom

By 1920, the United Kingdom had enacted the Air Navigation Act 1920 (UK). Even at this early stage, the act provided for strict liability for damage to the surface by aircraft.[45] Contrary to the fears of some that strict liability would discourage flying for the infant industry, the enactment of the Air Navigation Act did not have any 'untoward effect on [England's] aviation industry'.[46]

The current provisions relating to damage to the surface by aircraft are found in the Civil Aviation Act 1982 (UK). Section 76(1) provides that no action may now lie in trespass or nuisance so long as the flight is at a reasonable height above the ground, taking into consideration the wind and weather conditions and as long as there is no 'dangerous flying'[47] and all Air Navigation orders are complied with. This section mirrors the rule in Bernstein of *Leigh (Baron) v Skyviews & General Ltd.*[48]

Section 76(2) states:

> where material loss or damage is caused to any person or property on land or water by, or by a person in, or an article, animal or person falling from, an aircraft while in flight, taking off or landing, then unless the loss or damage was caused or

41 Van der Keur H, 'Uranium Pollution from the Amsterdam 1992 Plane Crash', May 1999, Laka Foundation, <http://www.antenna.nl/wise/uranium/dhap997.html>. Visited 15 November 2000.

42 Stolker C and Levine D, 'Compensation for Damage to Parties on the Ground as a Result of Aviation Accidents' (1997) XXII Air and Space Law 60, at 61.

43 Stolker, n 42, at 61.

44 Diederiks-Verschoor, n 9, at 132.

45 Section 9 Air Navigation Act 1920 (UK).

46 Newman, n 28, at 1044.

47 'Dangerous flying' is defined in s 81 of the Civil Aviation Act.

48 [1978] QB 479. See discussion above on the rights over airspace.

> contributed to by the negligence of the person by whom it was suffered, damages in respect of the loss or damage shall be recoverable without proof of negligence or intention or other cause of action, as of the loss or damage had been caused by the wilful act, neglect or default of the owner of the aircraft.

This section ensures that in a case of an aircraft crash in the United Kingdom, regardless of whether that aircraft be on a domestic or international flight, liability is strict and unlimited.

2.4 Germany

In Germany, the second part of the *Luftverkehrgesetz*, paragraphs 33 to 43, contains the rules for the 'Haftung für Personen und Sachen, die nicht im Luftfahrzeug befördert werden': liability of damage by aircraft to third parties that are not being transported (my translation).[49] Paragraph 33(1) states that if someone is killed, injured or suffers property damage, the owner of the aircraft must compensate the victims and replace what is damaged. Paragraph 34 provides that any contributory negligence is to be taken into account when calculating the damages owed. Paragraph 35(1) states that damages for death of the person on the surface are unlimited and include the costs of medical aid, as well as lost earnings of the victim. Paragraph 35(2) provides that dependents of the victim may claim the future lost earning potential of the victim, calculated on the basis that the victim had not been killed.

Paragraph 36 relates to the compensation available for temporary injury to third parties on the ground. By virtue of §37(2) this is limited to 500,000 German marks (hereafter 'DM'). Paragraph 37 provides for limited liability in the case of damage to property. The limits are calculated on the basis of weight of the aircraft.[50] These cover model planes weighing up to 20 kilograms (limit of 2,5 million DM) to aircraft weighing more than 14,000 kilograms (limit of 100 million DM).

These laws provide for strict liability, but the most striking feature of the German *Luftverkehrgesetz* are the differing limits of liability. For the death of a person liability is unlimited, but for temporary injury and damage to property there is limited liability. As will be discussed below, one of the main reasons for the 'rejection' of the Rome Convention has been the fact that it imposes limited liability in all cases, except when damage is caused by a deliberate act or omission of the operator, his servants or agent, in which case liability is unlimited.[51] This German approach of differentiating between death, injury and damage to property and applying unlimited liability only in

49 *Das deutsche Luftverkehrgesetz*, as accessed via 'Luftrecht-Online', <http://www.luftrecht-online.de>. Visited 7 November 2000.

50 This is also the basis for calculations of all damage suffered under Article 11 of the Rome Convention.

51 Article 12 of the Rome Convention.

the event of death, may be a possible compromise in any renegotiation of the Rome Convention.[52]

2.5 The People's Republic of China

The Civil Aviation Act of the People's Republic of China was adopted at the 16th Meeting of the Standing Committee of the Eighth National People's Congress on 30 October 1995, promulgated by Order No 56 of the President of the People's Republic of China on 30 October 1995 and came into effect on 1 March 1996.[53]

The Act deals with all aspects of aviation law. Chapter XII is dedicated to the liability of damage to third parties on the surface. Article 157 provides that:

> any person on the surface ... who suffers death or personal injury or damage to property caused by a civil aircraft in flight or by any person or thing falling therefrom shall be entitled to compensation. Nevertheless, the person suffering damage shall have no right to compensation if the damage is not a direct consequence of the incident giving rise thereto, or if the damage results from the mere fact of passage of the civil aircraft through the airspace in conformity with air traffic regulations concerned of the State.

The first part of Article 157 is in similar terms to s 76 Civil Aviation Act (UK) and implements strict liability while the second part mirrors the second sentence of Article 1 of the 1952 Rome Convention.

2.6 United States of America

All the states of the United States have jurisdiction to deal with the issues raised by damage by aircraft to third parties on the surface of their own state. Originally 23 states were party to the Uniform Aeronautics Act 1922 which provided for strict liability for any damage to third parties. However in the past 20 years that number has diminished significantly and now there are only six states party to that act.[54] These states include Hawaii, New Jersey, Delaware, Minnesota, and Vermont. The Restatement (Second) of Torts (1977), which carries considerable persuasive authority, also provides for strict liability.[55]

However, the trend in American law has been to move away from strict liability and to treat damage by aircraft in the same way as any other tort on

52 This will be further discussed in Part V.

53 Paglee CD, 'PRC Civil Aviation Law' 29 April 1998, Chinalaw Web <http://www.qis.net/chinalaw/prclaw89.htm>.

54 Jones, n 39, at 1747.

55 Paragraph 520A. However as seen in the discussion above, at 1.5, the majority in the case of *Crosby v Cox Aircraft* 746 P.2d 1198 (Wash 1987) expressed doubt as to the accuracy of this authority.

the ground. This has been done in two ways. First, some states have no state legislation, leaving case law and the common law to deal with the issue. This, as we have seen, requires proof of negligence to be found.[56] States such as Florida and Texas have taken that course. Second, the majority of states have specifically legislated that ordinary tort law applies to aviation accidents. A typical example is the state of Wisconsin. Section 114.05 of the Wisconsin statute reads:[57]

> DAMAGES BY AIRCRAFT. The liability of the owner, lessee and pilot of every aircraft operating over the lands or waters of this state for injuries or damage to persons or property on the land or water beneath, caused by the ascent, descent or flight of such aircraft, or the dropping or falling of the aircraft or of any object or material therefrom, shall be determined by the law applicable to torts on land, except that there shall be a presumption of liability on the part of the owner, lessee or pilot, as the case may be, where injury or damage is caused by the dropping or falling of the aircraft or of any object or material therefrom, which presumption may be rebutted by proof that the injury or damage was not caused by negligence on the part of the owner, lessee or pilot and the burden of proof in such case shall be upon such owner, lessee or pilot to show absence of negligence on his part.

Although the onus is on the defendant to prove that they were not negligent, in effect, this requirement is merely a restatement of *res ipsa loquitur*. The defendant is not strictly liable for damage caused by aircraft to the surface. This trend away from strict liability appears to be a uniquely American phenomenon, and has been justified on the basis that flying is no longer an ultra-hazardous activity.[58]

Part III: The international approach – the Rome Convention

3.1 Road to Rome: a need for an international approach?

When aircraft first caught the attention of legal academics, most discussion focused on potential damage to third parties on the surface. The possibility of aircraft passengers was still beyond imagination, and most concern was for the innocent bystander on the ground. By the 1920s, however, with passenger flight a reality, the Warsaw Convention on International Air Carriage 1929 was negotiated. Since that time, liability in relation to passengers has created the most discussion and remains most relevant for any study in Aviation Law. The main reason attention has focused on the passenger is because the frequency of deaths to passengers compared to third parties on the surface is

56 See discussion in Part I, at 1.3.

57 See s 222 of the 1993 Wisconsin Act 492 as accessed via Lexis, <http://www.lexis.com>. Visited 16 November 2000.

58 See Stolker, n 42, at 62 and discussion at 1.5 of this Chapter.

much higher. From 1970 to 1999 over 40,000 passengers have been killed in aircraft, while in the same period approximately 700 people on the surface have been killed by aircraft crashes.[59] It is extremely rare for a plane to crash and kill innocent bystanders on the ground, so there is little urgency encouraging nations to negotiate an international scheme.

Further, damage by aircraft to third parties on the surface does not involve the same conflict of laws issues and complexities as that of injury to passengers on board the aircraft. When an Australian citizen, domiciled in France is killed travelling from Jakarta to Los Angeles in a Singaporean airline, what jurisdiction should the case be heard in and what law should be applied? When a German tourist is killed in Australia by a crashing plane, regardless of where the action is heard, Australian law applies.[60] The need for uniform international legislation to deal with conflict of laws involved in damage by aircraft to the surface is far less than for passengers in an aircraft.[61]

Nevertheless, shortly after the Warsaw Convention was negotiated, most nations acknowledged 'the utility of regulating in a uniform manner liability for damage caused by aircraft to third parties on the surface'.[62] Thus in 1933 the first Rome Convention was signed.

The 1933 Rome Convention was eventually only ratified by five countries: Belgium, Brazil, Guatemala, Rumania and Spain. In 1948 the Legal Committee of the International Civil Aviation Organisation (ICAO), a specialised agency of the United Nations, decided to redraft a new convention to improve and supersede the 1933 Rome Convention.[63] In 1952, the new Rome Convention was opened for signature and, among other things, it more clearly defined a number of important terms such as when the plane was 'in-flight',[64] and 'operator';[65] improved on the details of rules of procedure[66] set out more detailed formulae for ascertaining the limits of liability based on weight;[67] and provided that an aircraft above the high seas was regarded as part of the territory of the State in which it was registered.[68]

59 'Accident Rates by Year', Airdisaster.com, <http://www.airdisaster.com/statistics/yearly.html>. Visited 15 November 2000.

60 In the case of *Murray v Pan Am World Airways,* 16 F.3d 513 (1994) concerning the 549 Lockerbie residents that sued Pan Am, Judge McLaughin, at 517 made it clear that regardless of where the case was heard, the law of the cause was British.

61 The Warsaw Convention has had little success in resolving conflicts of laws issues: see Bechky, PS, 'Mismanagement and Misinterpretation: US Judicial Implementation of the Warsaw Convention in Air Disaster Litigation' (1995) 60 Journal of Air Law and Commerce 455.

62 Keenan n 10, at 518.

63 Diederiks-Verschoor, n 9, at 131.

64 Article 1(2) of the 1952 Rome Convention.

65 Article 2 of the 1952 Rome Convention.

66 Article 20 of the 1952 Rome Convention.

67 Article 6 of the 1952 Rome Convention.

68 Article 23(2) of the 1952 Rome Convention.

3.2 Main features of the Rome Convention

The first main feature of the Convention is that strict liability is imposed on the defendant: Article 1. This was solidly supported by a majority of states with only the United States voting for proof of negligence to apply.[69] The second sentence of Article 1 reinforces the notion that there can be no trespass resulting from the mere passage of an aircraft though airspace, nor does a nuisance arise from a factor such as noise, provided the aircraft passing through the airspace conforms with air traffic regulations.

A second feature of the Convention is that actions may be brought only before the courts of the Contracting State where the damage occurred: Article 20. This issue has been described as 'the most controversial issue at Rome',[70] and 'constitutional issues [regarding Article 20] were probably the major deterrent to United States ratification'.[71]

Articles 15 and 16 establish a regime to provide security for operator liability. These Articles were extremely important to the Convention and were one of the main reasons it was felt there was a need for an international scheme for damage by aircraft to third parties. Finally, the main reason now given for dissatisfaction with the Rome Convention is that by virtue of Article 11 there is only limited liability for damage by aircraft and these levels of liability are perceived as too low.[72]

3.3 Limited or unlimited liability?

Article 11 of the Convention describes the extent of liability for damages. The calculation is based on the maximum weight with which an aircraft is certified to take-off: Article 11(3). The calculation is in francs with the minimum amount of 500,000 francs for aircraft weighing 1,000 kilograms or less, and the maximum amount of 10,500,000 francs for aircraft weighing over 50,000 kilograms.

The first argument in support of limited liability was that the airline industry was an infant industry, in need of protection so that people would be encouraged to fly. While this may have been a valid argument in the past, it can no longer be said that the airline industry is still in its 'infancy'. For the aviation industries of many developing nations, this argument could still be

69 Rinck G, 'Damage Caused by Foreign Aircraft to Third Parties' (1963) 28 Journal of Air Law and Commerce 405, at 406.

70 Rinck, n 69, at 411.

71 Brown EG, 'The Rome Conventions of 1933 and 1952: Do They Point a Moral?' (1961–63) 28 Journal of Air Law and Commerce 418, at 437.

72 There is only unlimited liability if the person suffering the damage can prove damage was caused by a deliberate act or omission by the defendant done with an intent to cause harm: Article 12 of the Rome Convention.

raised, but it is submitted, that in issues of public safety there can be no excuse for anything but the highest standards, regardless of where the airline flies.

Second, if insurance companies know what the limit of liability is, they are better able to keep premiums low and this in turn means the price of a plane ticket for the consumer does not have to be inflated. Yet while the passenger assumes the risk when flying, and is gaining a service out of the flight, the innocent bystander on the ground gains no benefit at all and is potentially left with very little once claims are distributed among the victims. The user should pay and the innocent bystander on the ground should not have to sacrifice full compensation only because the passenger wishes to pay lower airfares.

Finally, it is submitted that the most persuasive argument for limits of liability is the fact that limited liability can potentially create a balance between fair compensation for injuries caused by aircraft and swift receipt of that compensation. Some law firms boast of 'record settlements' for the families of victims of air disasters.[73] However, one must often question whether exorbitant compensation is in fact necessary and what percentage of it is actually received by the relatives of the victim. Further, the court process can often take a long time to proceed. Pan Am's litigation against the passengers and third parties on the ground in the Lockerbie disaster lead to Pan Am's bankruptcy and the litigation dragged out for over a decade.[74]

The aim of a limited liability regime should be to find a balance between fair and timely receipt of compensation. Unfortunately, many countries believe that the Rome Convention has not achieved the appropriate balance. Low amounts of liability were cited by Australia as a reason for its denunciation of the Rome Convention.[75] A scheme such as the one in the German *Luftverkehrgesetz* whereby there is limited liability for property damage and temporary disability but unlimited liability in instances of death, may be considered as a fair compromise to the victims and ensure quick yet fair amounts of compensation.

3.4 Why the Rome Convention did not achieve international uniformity

One of the reasons the Rome Convention did not achieve international uniformity was the perception that liability limits were too low and many nations felt, in any case, that unlimited liability was more appropriate.

---

73 See for instance the claim of Clifford Law Offices that they received a 'record $110 million settlement with American Airlines' for the victims of a crash while boasting that they won a personal injury verdict of $28.2 million for a 70 year-old woman injured in an Iowa crash: 'Aviation Liability', Clifford Law Offices, <http://www.cliffordlaw.com/cliffordlaw/aviation/aviation.html>.

74 Bechky, n 61, at 457.

75 Damage by Aircraft Bill (Cth) 1999 (Explanatory Memorandum), as accessed via 'Bills Net' Parliament of Australia Parliamentary Library <http://www.aph.gov.au/parlinfo/billsnet/main.htm>. Visited 15 November 2000.

Another explanation for the failure of the Rome Convention to achieve international uniformity is the fact that no widely accepted uniform system was created due to the small number of ratifications. By virtue of Article 23, the Convention only applies to damage caused in a Contracting State by an aircraft registered in the territory of another Contracting State. As a result, had more nations ratified the Rome Convention and had uniformity been achieved, a consistent status quo between the nations would have been established. However, because there were not as many ratifications as were hoped for, the Contracting States were faced with the situation of having one system of liability for the aircraft registered in a Contracting State and another system of liability for aircraft not registered in a Contracting State. This was the situation in Australia and created an incredibly confusing national scheme of liability.

Also, as stated above, since there are so few incidents of aircraft crashing into apartment blocks and school-yards, governments do not feel it necessary to ratify an international scheme of damage by aircraft to the surface. This leads to another reason for lack of support for the Rome Convention – namely, that there are no great conflict of laws issues that require an international approach. As we have seen, many nations have appropriate national legislation that protects their citizens in the case of damage by aircraft. For these nations, the Rome Convention added little to their national approaches.

Part IV: The Australian approach: the Damage by Aircraft Act 1999

4.1 Australia and Rome: the Civil Aviation (Damage by Aircraft) Act

Australia ratified the 1952 Rome Convention on 10 November 1958. The Convention became effective with the passing of the Civil Aviation (Damage by Aircraft) Act 1958 (the Act). The scope of Federal coverage was extended by this Act to include, not only damage by international aircraft registered in Contracting States under the Rome Convention,[76] but also other damage, not included in the Rome Convention.[77] In effect, this created a two-class system of coverage: aircraft registered in a Contracting State which gained full coverage by Rome, and aircraft registered in non-Contracting States, which were partly covered by Rome and partly by special provisions in the Act.

4.2 Part II of the Act: Damage to which the Rome Convention Applies

Part II of the Act governed the damage to which the Rome Convention would apply. By virtue of Article 23 (which was incorporated as a Schedule to the Act), the Convention applied to damage caused in the territory of a

76 Part II, ss 8–15 Civil Aviation (Damage by Aircraft) Act.

77 Part III, ss 16–19 Civil Aviation (Damage by Aircraft) Act.

Contracting state by aircraft registered in the territory of another Contracting State. This meant that if Qantas were to cause damage to the surface in Belgium, a Contracting State, the damage caused would be covered by the Rome Convention. Qantas would be liable to strict, but limited liability. However, had Qantas caused damage to the surface in Great Britain, it would have been liable under British legislation in the form of s 76(2) of the Civil Aviation Act 1982 (UK). Alternatively, if Alitalia or Sabena (airlines registered in Italy and Belgium, both of which are Contracting States) were to crash and cause damage to the surface in Australia, the Rome Convention would apply with the consequence of strict but limited liability.

This illustrates the very narrow scope of the Rome Convention. Full coverage is only extended to international flights of aircraft registered with Contracting States. Only 44 States are parties to the Convention and, furthermore, only seven of these 44 countries have aircraft that are licensed to operate over Australian territory.[78]

4.3 Part III of the Act: other damage to which the Act applies

Part III of the Act governed types of damage to which the Rome Convention would not ordinarily apply. By virtue of s 16(1), aircraft registered in Australia being used in the course of trade and commerce, and aircraft flying between a place in Australia and a place outside Australia, came within the scope of the Act. Section 16(2) provided that the Act would apply to aircraft not registered in Australia or a Contracting State, which were being used for trade and commerce between Australia and another country.

Section 17 then stated that the Rome Convention applies to aircraft of this description with the exception of Chapter III (security given for operator's liability), Article 20 (Court procedure involved for claims under the Convention), Articles 23, 27, 28 and 29 (general provisions relating solely to the implementation of the Convention) and Chapter VI (final provisions).

Furthermore, for aircraft described in s 16(2) of the Act, that is international aircraft from countries not party to the Rome Convention, important provisions of Chapter II (on the limits of liability) and Articles 18 and 21 (on limitation periods), do not apply. Thus, international aircraft registered in countries not party to the Rome Convention were still subject to strict liability, but were not protected by the limitation of liability provisions of Chapter II.

78 Damage by Aircraft Bill (Cth) 1999 (Explanatory Memorandum), as accessed via 'BillsNet' Parliament of Australia Parliamentary Library <http://www.aph.gov.au/parlinfo/billsnet/main.htm>. Visited 15 November 2000. See also Appendix II for a table of the Contracting States.

4.4 The denunciation of Rome

By virtue of Article 35 of the Rome Convention, a Contracting State may denounce the Convention by notification of denunciation to the International Civil Aviation Authority. Canada was the first nation to take advantage of Article 35, denouncing the Convention on 29 June 1976.[79]

Australia presented its notification of denunciation with ICAO on 8 May 2000, and this took effect on 8 November 2000. One of the main reasons for the denunciation was the fact that airline companies registered in Contracting States were subject only to limited liability. The Explanatory Memorandum to the Damage by Aircraft Bill 1999 states that, notwithstanding confusion as to the actual interpretation of the gold conversion mechanism allowed under the Convention, even the most favourable calculations put the total liability limit for a Boeing 747 at about $A36 million.

Furthermore, the Explanatory Memorandum states that because there are two different types of liability schemes, one for aircraft registered in a Contracting State and one for aircraft registered in a non-Contracting State,[80] various regimes impose differing burdens of proof and differing compensation outcomes are created. This lack of national uniformity in a regime for the protection of the public is unsatisfactory.

The explanatory memorandum also states that most of the foreign international carriers such as the United States, Japan, China and the United Kingdom are not subject to the Rome Convention and that aircraft from only seven countries that operate in Australia are subject to it. The fact that the Rome Convention failed to achieve the international uniformity it sought, was seen as another reason for denunciation.

4.5 The new Damage by Aircraft Act 1999

It was decided that 'only legislation can establish a new regime with strict and unlimited liability that will provide the courts with the power to settle disputed cases quickly and adequately to the benefit of the plaintiff'.[81] The Damage by Aircraft Act 1999 came into force on 8 November 2000.

Section 10 of the Act describes the type of damages for which the defendant is liable and involves the situation where a person or property (on land or water) suffers personal injury, loss of life, material loss, or damage or destruction from the impact of an aircraft or part of an aircraft. Section 10 also covers the situation when a person, animal or thing, dropped from an aircraft

79 Explanatory Memorandum to the Damage by Aircraft Bill (Cth) 1999, n 78.

80 See discussion above, at 4.1–4.3 of this Chapter.

81 Explanatory Memorandum to the Damage by Aircraft Bill (Cth) 1999, n 78.

while in flight, causes damage to the surface (thereby providing for the case of suicide or a failed parachuting).

By virtue of s 10 the recovery for this kind of damage does not require proof of intent of negligence, and there is no limit to the amount of damage recoverable.

This Act now covers all Australian territories and external territories. It extends to Commonwealth aircraft, all international aircraft, air navigation between the States engaged in trade and commerce, air navigation conducted by a foreign corporation or a trading or financial corporation and aircraft that take off and land from a place acquired by the Commonwealth for public purposes: s 9 of the Act. State legislation covers aircraft that fly intrastate and all States except South Australia and Queensland have legislation that invokes strict and unlimited liability.[82] In South Australia and Queensland, damage by aircraft to third parties on the surface remains subject to the common law, meaning there needs to be proof of negligence by the pilot or the owner of the aircraft in any claim. South Australia and Queensland plan to draft legislation similar to that in the other States in 2001.

Part V: A revised or new international approach?

5.1 Conclusion: a future for Rome?

ICAO and the international community have reached the conclusion that the Rome Convention in its current form has little future. Not only has the Convention failed in achieving its purpose of international uniformity, but countries such as Canada and Australia have denounced it and reverted back to their own national schemes.

A feature of the Rome Convention that need not change is strict liability since this feature is supported Canada, China, Great Britain, Australia and most European nations. The main problem with the Rome Convention and the element which most nations found unacceptable was the limited liability scheme. In 1978, an attempt was made to increase these limits of liability in the Montreal Protocol.[83] Only six countries have ratified this Protocol. This suggests that merely increasing the limits of liability will not be enough to save the Rome Convention.

However, all is not lost for the Rome Convention. In a surprise move at the 31st Session of the Legal Committee of ICAO (held from 28 August to 8 September 2000), Sweden, supported by two other delegations, proposed

82 Section 2(2) Damage by Aircraft Act 1952 (NSW); s 4(1) Damage by Aircraft Act 1963 (TAS); s 31(1) Wrongs Act 1958 (VIC); s 5(1) Damage by Aircraft Act 1964 (WA).

83 Protocol to Amend the Convention on Damage Caused by Foreign Aircraft to third Parties on the Surface signed at Rome on 7 October 1978 (Montreal Protocol).

modernisation of the Rome Convention to reflect recent developments, including liability limits and environmental damage on the ground caused by aircraft.[84] One delegation felt that it would be 'premature to decide to modernise the Rome Convention before an extensive deliberation on the issue was undertaken'.[85] The proposal was thereby amended to read 'Consideration of the Modernisation of the Convention on Damage Caused by Foreign Aircraft to Third Parties on the Surface, signed at Rome on 7 October 1952' and the Legal Committee recommended the item be assigned priority No 4.

While it is not suggested that the modernisation of the Rome Convention is a high priority for nations or for ICAO, this Swedish proposal indicates that there is still some support for an international approach to the issues. Nations can legislate for their own territorial jurisdiction and have sovereignty over their airspace. Any aircraft that flies over a country is subject to the laws of that nation and any entry into that country's airspace is contingent on submission to the national jurisdiction. As such, some nations may believe that an international approach to damage to third parties on the surface is not of great value. However, for nations that do not have adequate means to implement and enforce laws on damage by aircraft, a modernised, updated Rome-like Convention that could act as a framework for such nations is still worthy of debate, discussion and serious contemplation.

With the Empire of Rome in decline and with many nations presently well served by their national schemes, it is unlikely that any minor modifications to the Rome Convention will be useful. However, a total reconsideration and reworking of the Rome Convention may provide the impetus for another attempt to create an international approach. This would involve retaining strict liability, perhaps compromising and following a German-like solution to the issue of unlimited liability and including environmental issues. Despite the limitations of the existing Convention, it is submitted that a unified international regime will ensure that even for those nations without appropriate legislation there is at least a minimum level of protection in the event of damage by aircraft to third persons on the surface.

---

84 Koukharskaia T (Treaty Clerk of the Legal Bureau, ICAO), 'Re: Rome Convention', 15 November 2000, Personal email (16 November 2000).

85 See Koukharskaia, n 84.

APPENDIX I

CONVENTION ON DAMAGE CAUSED BY FOREIGN AIRCRAFT TO THIRD PARTIES ON THE SURFACE, SIGNED AT ROME, ON 7 OCTOBER 1952 (ROME CONVENTION 1952)

THE STATES SIGNATORY to this Convention

MOVED by a desire to ensure adequate compensation for persons who suffer damage caused on the surface by foreign aircraft, while limiting in a reasonable manner the extent of the liabilities incurred for such damage in order not to hinder the development of international civil air transport, and also

CONVINCED of the need for unifying to the greatest extent possible, through an international convention, the rules applying in the various countries of the world to the liabilities incurred for such damage,

HAVE APPOINTED to such effect the undersigned Plenipotentiaries who, duly authorised, HAVE AGREED AS FOLLOWS:

CHAPTER I PRINCIPLES OF LIABILITY

Article 1

1 Any person who suffers damage on the surface shall, upon proof only that the damage was caused by an aircraft in flight or by any person or thing falling therefrom, be entitled to compensation as provided by this Convention. Nevertheless there shall be no right to compensation if the damage is not a direct consequence of the incident giving rise thereto, or if the damage results from the mere fact of passage of the aircraft through the airspace in conformity with existing air traffic regulations.

2 For the purpose of this Convention, an aircraft is considered to be in flight from the moment when power is applied for the purpose of actual take-off until the moment when the landing run ends. In the case of an aircraft lighter than air, the expression 'in flight' relates to the period from the moment when it becomes detached from the surface until it becomes again attached thereto.

Article 2

1 The liability for compensation contemplated by Article 1 of this Convention shall attach to the operator of the aircraft.

2 (a) For the purposes of this Convention the term 'operator' shall mean the person who was making use of the aircraft at the time the damage was caused, provided that if control of the navigation of the aircraft was retained by the person from whom the right to make use of the aircraft was derived, whether directly or indirectly, that person shall be considered the operator.

(b) A person shall be considered to be making use of an aircraft when he is using it personally or when his servants or agents are using the aircraft in the course of their employment, whether or not within the scope of their authority.

3 The registered owner of the aircraft shall be presumed to be the operator and shall be liable as such unless, in the proceedings for the determination of his liability, he proves that some other person was the operator and, in so far as legal procedures permit, takes appropriate measures to make that other person a party in the proceedings.

Article 3

If the person who was the operator at the time the damage was caused had not the exclusive right to use the aircraft for a period of more than fourteen days, dating from the moment when the right to use commenced, the person from whom such right was derived shall be liable jointly and severally with the operator, each of them being bound under the provisions and within the limits of liability of this Convention.

Article 4

If a person makes use of an aircraft without the consent of the person entitled to its navigational control, the latter, unless he proves that he has exercised due care to prevent such use, shall be jointly and severally liable with the unlawful user for damage giving a right to compensation under Article 1, each of them being bound under the provisions and within the limits of liability of this Convention.

Article 5

Any person who would otherwise be liable under the provisions of this Convention shall not be liable if the damage is the direct consequence of armed conflict or civil disturbance, or if such person has been deprived of the use of the aircraft by act of public authority.

Article 6

1 Any person who would otherwise be liable under the provisions of this Convention shall not be liable for damage if he proves that the damage was caused solely through the negligence or other wrongful act or omission of the person who suffers the damage or of the latter's servants or agents. If the person liable proves that the damage was contributed to by the negligence or other wrongful act or omission of the person who suffers the damage, or of his servants or agents, the compensation shall be reduced to the extent to which such negligence or wrongful act or omission contributed to the damage. Nevertheless there shall be no such exoneration or reduction if, in the case of the negligence or other wrongful act or omission of a servant or agent, the person who suffers the damage proves that his servant or agent was acting outside the scope of his authority.

2 When an action is brought by one person to recover damages arising from the death or injury of another person, the negligence or other wrongful act or omission of such other person, or of his servants or agents, shall also have the effect provided in the preceding paragraph.

Article 7

When two or more aircraft have collided or interfered with each other in flight and damage for which a right to compensation as contemplated in Article 1 results, or when two or more aircraft have jointly caused such damage, each of the aircraft concerned shall be considered to have caused the damage and the operator of each aircraft shall be liable, each of them being bound under the provisions and within the limits of liability of this Convention.

Article 8

The persons referred to in paragraph 3 of Article 2 and in Articles 3 and 4 shall be entitled to all defences which are available to an operator under the provisions of this Convention.

Article 9

Neither the operator, the owner, any person liable under Article 3 or Article 4, nor their respective servants or agents, shall be liable for damage on the surface caused by an aircraft in flight or any person or thing falling therefrom otherwise than as expressly provided in this Convention. This rule shall not apply to any such person who is guilty of a deliberate act or omission done with intent to cause damage.

Article 10

Nothing in this Convention shall prejudice the question whether a person liable for damage in accordance with its provisions has a right of recourse against any other person.

CHAPTER II

EXTENT OF LIABILITY

Article 11

1 Subject to the provisions of Article 12, the liability for damage giving a right to compensation under Article 1, for each aircraft and incident, in respect of all persons liable under this Convention, shall not exceed:

(a) 500 000 francs for aircraft weighing 1000 kilogrammes or less;

(b) 500 000 francs plus 400 francs per kilogramme over 1000 kilogrammes for aircraft weighing more than 1000 but not exceeding 6000 kilogrammes;

(c) 2 500 000 francs plus 250 francs per kilogramme over 6000 kilogrammes for aircraft weighing more than 6000 but not exceeding 20 000 kilogrammes;

(d) 6 000 000 francs plus 150 francs per kilogramme over 20 000 kilogrammes for aircraft weighing more than 20 000 but not exceeding 50 000 kilogrammes;

(e) 10 500 000 francs plus 100 francs per kilogramme over 50 000 kilogrammes for aircraft weighing more than 50 000 kilogrammes.

2 The liability in respect of loss of life or personal injury shall not exceed 500 000 francs per person killed or injured.

3 'Weight' means the maximum weight of the aircraft authorised by the certificate of airworthiness for take-off, excluding the effect of lifting gas when used.

4 The sums mentioned in francs in this Article refer to a currency unit consisting of 65 _ milligrammes of gold of millesimal fineness 900.

These sums may be converted into national currencies in round figures. Conversion of the sums into national currencies other than gold shall, in case of judicial proceedings, be made according to the gold value of such currencies at the date of the judgment, or, in cases covered by Article 14, at the date of the allocation.

Article 12

1 If the person who suffers damage proves that it was caused by a deliberate act or omission of the operator, his servants or agents, done with intent to cause damage, the liability of the operator shall be unlimited; provided that in the case of such act or omission of such servant or agent, it is also proved that he was acting in the course of his employment and within the scope of his authority.

2 If a person wrongfully takes and makes use of an aircraft without the consent of the person entitled to use it, his liability shall be unlimited.

Article 13

1 Whenever, under the provisions of Article 3 or Article 4, two or more persons are liable for damage, or a registered owner who was not the operator is made liable as such as provided in paragraph 3 of Article 2, the persons who suffer damage shall not be entitled to total compensation greater than the highest indemnity which may be awarded under the provisions of this Convention against any one of the persons liable.

2 When the provisions of Article 7 are applicable, the person who suffers the damage shall be entitled to be compensated up to the aggregate of the limits applicable with respect to each of the aircraft involved, but no operator shall be liable for a sum in excess of the limit applicable to his aircraft unless his liability is unlimited under the terms of Article 12.

Article 14

If the total amount of the claims established exceeds the limit of liability applicable under the provisions of this Convention, the following rules shall apply, taking into account the provisions of paragraph 2 of Article 11:

(a) If the claims are exclusively in respect of loss of life or personal injury or exclusively in respect of damage to property, such claims shall be reduced in proportion to their respective amounts.

(b) If the claims are both in respect of loss of life or personal injury and in respect of damage to property, one half of the total sum distributable shall be appropriated preferentially to meet claims in respect of loss of life and personal injury and, if insufficient, shall be distributed proportionately between the claims concerned. The remainder of the total sum distributable shall be distributed proportionately among the claims in respect of damage to property and the portion not already covered of the claims in respect of loss of life and personal injury.

CHAPTER III

SECURITY FOR OPERATOR'S LIABILITY

Article 15

1 Any Contracting State may require that the operator of an aircraft registered in another Contracting State shall be insured in respect of his liability for damage sustained in its territory for which a right to compensation exists under Article 1 by means of insurance up to the limits applicable according to the provisions of Article 11.

2 (a) The insurance shall be accepted as satisfactory if it conforms to the provisions of this Convention and has been effected by an insurer authorised to effect such insurance under the laws of the State where the aircraft is registered or of the State where the insurer has his residence or principal place of business, and whose financial responsibility has been verified by either of those States.

(b) If insurance has been required by any State under paragraph 1 of this Article, and a final judgment in that State is not satisfied by payment in the currency of that State, any Contracting State may refuse to accept the insurer as financially responsible until such payment, if demanded, has been made.

3 Notwithstanding the last preceding paragraph the State overflown may refuse to accept as satisfactory insurance effected by an insurer who is not authorised for that purpose in a contracting State.

4 Instead of insurance, any of the following securities shall be deemed satisfactory if the security conforms to Article 17:

(a) a cash deposit in a depository maintained by the Contracting State where the aircraft is registered or with a bank authorised to act as a depository by that State;

(b) a guarantee given by a bank authorised to do so by the Contracting State where the aircraft is registered, and whose financial responsibility has been verified by that State;

(c) a guarantee given by the contracting State where the aircraft is registered, if that State undertakes that it will not claim immunity from suit in respect of that guarantee.

5 Subject to paragraph 6 of this Article, the State overflown may also require that the aircraft shall carry a certificate issued by the insurer certifying that insurance has been effected in accordance with the provisions of this Convention, and specifying the person or persons whose liability is secured thereby, together with a certificate or endorsement issued by the appropriate authority in the State where the aircraft is registered or in the State where the insurer has his residence or principal place of business certifying the financial responsibility of the insurer. If other security is furnished in accordance with the provisions of paragraph 4 of this Article, a certificate to that effect shall be issued by the appropriate authority in the State where the aircraft is registered.

6 The certificate referred to in paragraph 5 of this Article need not be carried in the aircraft if a certified copy has been filed with the appropriate authority designated by the State overflown or, if the International Civil Aviation Organization agrees, with that Organization, which shall furnish a copy of the certificate to each contracting State.

7 (a) Where the State overflown has reasonable grounds for doubting the financial responsibility of the insurer, or of the bank which issues a guarantee under paragraph 4 of this Article, that State may request additional evidence of financial responsibility, and if any question arises as to the adequacy of that evidence the dispute affecting the States concerned shall, at the request of one of those States, be submitted to an arbitral tribunal which shall be either the Council of the International Civil Aviation Organization or a person or body mutually agreed by the parties.

(b) Until this tribunal has given its decision the insurance or guarantee shall be considered provisionally valid by the State overflown.

8 Any requirements imposed in accordance with this Article shall be notified to the Secretary General of the International Civil Aviation Organization who shall inform each contracting State thereof.

9 For the purpose of this Article, the term 'insurer' includes a group of insurers, and for the purpose of paragraph 5 of this Article, the phrase 'appropriate authority in a State' includes the appropriate authority in the highest political subdivision thereof which regulates the conduct of business by the insurer.

Article 16

1 The insurer or other person providing security required under Article 15 for the liability of the operator may, in addition to the defences available to the operator, and the defence of forgery, set up only the following defences against claims based on the application of this Convention:

(a) that the damage occurred after the security ceased to be effective. However, if the security expires during a flight, it shall be continued in force until the next landing specified in the flight plan, but no longer than twenty-four hours; and if the security ceases to be effective for any reason other than the expiration of its term, or a change of operator, it shall be continued until fifteen days after notification to the appropriate authority of the State which certifies the financial responsibility of the insurer or the guarantor that the security has ceased to be effective, or until effective withdrawal of the certificate of the insurer or the certificate of guarantee if such a certificate has been required under paragraph 5 of Article 15, whichever is the earlier;

(b) that the damage occurred outside the territorial limits provided for by the security, unless flight outside of such limits was caused by *force majeure*, assistance justified by the circumstances, or an error in piloting, operation or navigation.

2 The State which has issued or endorsed a certificate pursuant to paragraph 5 of Article 15 shall notify the termination or cessation, otherwise than by the expiration of its term, of the insurance or other security to the interested contracting States as soon as possible.

3 Where a certificate of insurance or other security is required under paragraph 5 of Article 15 and the operator is changed during the period of the validity of the security, the security shall apply to the liability under this Convention of the new operator, unless he is an unlawful user, but not beyond fifteen days from the time when the insurer or guarantor notifies the appropriate authority of the State where the certificate was issued that the security has become ineffective or until the effective withdrawal of the certificate of the insurer if such a certificate has been required under paragraph 5 of Article 15, whichever is the shorter period.

4 The continuation in force of the security under the provisions of paragraph 1 of this Article shall apply only for the benefit of the person suffering damage.

5 Without prejudice to any right of direct action which he may have under the law governing the contract of insurance or guarantee, the person suffering damage may bring a direct action against the insurer or guarantor only in the following cases:

(a) where the security is continued in force under the provisions of paragraph 1(a) and (b) of this Article;

(b) the bankruptcy of the operator.

6 Excepting the defences specified in paragraph 1 of this Article, the insurer or other person providing security may not, with respect to direct actions brought by the person suffering damage based upon application of this Convention, avail himself of any grounds of nullity or any right of retroactive cancellation.

7 The provisions of this Article shall not prejudice the question whether the insurer guarantor has a right of recourse against any other person.

Article 17

1 If security is furnished in accordance with paragraph 4 of Article 15, it shall be specifically and preferentially assigned to payment of claims under the provisions of this Convention.

2 The security shall be deemed sufficient if, in the case of an operator of one aircraft, it is for an amount equal to the limit applicable according to the provisions of Article 11, and in the case of an operator of several aircraft, if it is for an amount not less than the aggregate of the limits of liability applicable to the two aircraft subject to the highest limits.

3 As soon as notice of a claim has been given to the operator, the amount of the security shall be increased up to a total sum equivalent to the aggregate of:

(a) the amount of the security then required by paragraph 2 of this Article, and

(b) the amount of the claim not exceeding the applicable limit of liability.

This increased security shall be maintained until every claim has been disposed of.

Article 18

Any sums due to an operator from an insurer shall be exempt from seizure and execution by creditors of the operator until claims of third parties under this Convention have been satisfied.

CHAPTER IV

RULES OF PROCEDURE AND LIMITATION OF ACTIONS

Article 19

If a claimant has not brought an action to enforce his claim or if notification of such claim has not been given to the operator within a period of six months from the date of the incident which gave rise to the damage, the claimant shall only be entitled to compensation out of the amount for which the operator remains liable after all claims made within that period have been met in full.

Article 20

1 Actions under the provisions of this Convention may be brought only before the courts of the Contracting State where the damage occurred. Nevertheless, by agreement between any one or more claimants and any one or more defendants, such claimants may take action before the courts of any other Contracting State, but no such proceedings shall have the effect of prejudicing in any way the rights of persons who bring actions in the State where the damage occurred. The parties may also agree to submit disputes to arbitration in any Contracting State.

2 Each Contracting State shall take all necessary measures to ensure that the defendant and all other parties interested are notified of any proceedings concerning them and have a fair and adequate opportunity to defend their interests.

3 Each Contracting State shall so far as possible ensure that all actions arising from a single incident and brought in accordance with paragraph 1 of this Article are consolidated for disposal in a single proceeding before the same court.

4 Where any final judgment, including a judgment by default, is pronounced by a court competent in conformity with this Convention, on which execution can be issued according to the procedural law of that court, the judgment shall be enforceable upon compliance with the formalities prescribed by the laws of the Contracting State, or of any territory, State or province thereof, where execution is applied for:

(a) in the Contracting State where the judgment debtor has his residence or principal place of business or,

(b) if the assets available in that State and in the State where the judgment was pronounced are insufficient to satisfy the judgment, in any other Contracting State where the judgment debtor has assets.

5 Notwithstanding the provisions of paragraph 4 of this Article, the court to which application is made for execution may refuse to issue execution if it is proved that any of the following circumstances exist:

(a) the judgment was given by default and the defendant did not acquire knowledge of the proceedings in sufficient time to act upon it;

(b) the defendant was not given a fair and adequate opportunity to defend his interests;

(c) the judgment is in respect of a cause of action which had already, as between the same parties, formed the subject of a judgment or an arbitral award which, under the law of the State where execution is sought, is recognized as final and conclusive;

(d) the judgment has been obtained by fraud of any of the parties;

(e) the right to enforce the judgment is not vested in the person by whom the application for execution is made.

6 The merits of the case may not be reopened in proceedings for execution under paragraph 4 of this Article.

7 The court to which application for execution is made may also refuse to issue execution if the judgment concerned is contrary to the public policy of the State in which execution is requested.

8 If, in proceedings brought according to paragraph 4 of this Article, execution of any judgment is refused on any of the grounds referred to in subparagraphs (a), (b) or (d) of paragraph 5 or paragraph 7 of this Article, the claimant shall be entitled to bring a new action before the courts of the State where execution has been refused. The judgment rendered in such new action may not result in the total compensation awarded exceeding the limits applicable under the provisions

of this Convention. In such new action the previous judgment shall be a defence only to the extent to which it has been satisfied. The previous judgment shall cease to be enforceable as soon as the new action has been started

The right to bring a new action under this paragraph shall, notwithstanding the provisions of Article 21, be subject to a period of limitation of one year from the date on which the claimant has received notification of the refusal to execute the judgment.

9 Notwithstanding the provisions of paragraph 4 of this Article, the court to which application for execution is made shall refuse execution of any judgment rendered by a court of a State other than that in which the damage occurred until all the judgments rendered in that State have been satisfied.

The court applied to shall also refuse to issue execution until final judgment has been given on all actions filed in the State where the damage occurred by those persons who have complied with the time limit referred to in Article 19, if the judgment debtor proves that the total amount of compensation which might be awarded by such judgments might exceed the applicable limit of liability under the provisions of this Convention.

Similarly such court shall not grant execution when, in the case of actions brought in the State where the damage occurred by those persons who have complied with the time limit referred to in Article 19, the aggregate of the judgments exceeds the applicable limit of liability, until such judgments have been reduced in accordance with Article 14.

10 Where a judgment is rendered enforceable under this Article, payment of costs recoverable under the judgment shall also be enforceable. Nevertheless the court applied to for execution may, on the application of the judgment debtor, limit the amount of such costs to a sum equal to ten per centum of the amount for which the judgment is rendered enforceable. The limits of liability prescribed by this Convention shall be exclusive of costs.

11 Interest not exceeding four per centum per annum may be allowed on the judgment debt from the date of the judgment in respect of which execution is granted.

12 An application for execution of a judgment to which paragraph 4 of this Article applies must be made within five years from the date when such judgment became final.

Article 21

1 Actions under this Convention shall be subject to a period of limitation of two years from the date of the incident which caused the damage.

2 The grounds for suspension or interruption of the period referred to in paragraph 1 of this Article shall be determined by the law of the court trying the action; but in any case the right to institute an action shall be extinguished on the expiration of three years from the date of the incident which caused the damage.

Article 22

In the event of the death of the person liable, an action in respect of liability under the provisions of this Convention shall lie against those legally responsible for his obligations.

CHAPTER V

APPLICATION OF THE CONVENTION AND GENERAL PROVISIONS

Article 23

1 This Convention applies to damage contemplated in Article 1 caused in the territory of a Contracting State by an aircraft registered in the territory of another Contracting State.

2 For the purpose of this Convention a ship or aircraft on the high seas shall be regarded as part of the territory of the State in which it is registered.

Article 24

This Convention shall not apply to damage caused to an aircraft in flight, or to persons or goods on board such aircraft.

Article 25

This Convention shall not apply to damage on the surface if liability for such damage is regulated either by a contract between the person who suffers such damage and the operator or the person entitled to use the aircraft at the time the damage occurred, or by the law relating to work-men's compensation applicable to a contract of employment between such persons.

Article 26

This Convention shall not apply to damage caused by military, customs or police aircraft.

Article 27

Contracting States will, as far as possible, facilitate payment of compensation under the provisions of this Convention in the currency of the State where the damage occurred.

Article 28

If legislative measures are necessary in any Contracting State to give effect to this Convention, the Secretary General of the International Civil Aviation Organization shall be informed forthwith of the measures so taken.

Article 29

As between Contracting States which have also ratified the International Convention for the Unification of Certain Rules relating to Damage caused by Aircraft to Third Parties on the Surface opened for signature at Rome on the 29 May 1933, the present Convention upon its entry into force shall supersede the said Convention of Rome.

Article 30

For the purposes of this Convention:

'Person' means any natural or legal person, including a State.

'Contracting State' means any State which has ratified or adhered to this Convention and whose denunciation thereof has not become effective.

'Territory of a State' means the metropolitan territory of a State and all territories for the foreign relations of which that State is responsible, subject to the provisions of Article 36.

CHAPTER VI

FINAL PROVISIONS

Article 31

This Convention shall remain open for signature on behalf of any State until it comes into force in accordance with the provisions of Article 33.

Article 32

1 This Convention shall be subject to ratification by the signatory States.

2 The instruments of ratification shall be deposited with the International Civil Aviation Organization.

Article 33

1 As soon as five of the signatory States have deposited their instruments of ratification of this Convention, it shall come into force between them on the ninetieth day after the date of the deposit of the fifth instrument of ratification. It shall come into force, for each State which deposits its instrument of ratification after that date, on the ninetieth day after the deposit of its instrument of ratification.

2 As soon as this Convention comes into force, it shall be registered with the United Nations by the Secretary General of the International Civil Aviation Organization.

Article 34

1 This Convention shall, after it has come into force, be open for adherence by any non-signatory State.

2 The adherence of a State shall be effected by the deposit of an instrument of adherence with the International Civil Aviation Organization and shall take effect as from the ninetieth day after the date of the deposit.

Article 35

1 Any Contracting State may denounce this Convention by notification of denunciation to the International Civil Aviation Organization.

2 Denunciation shall take effect six months after the date of receipt by the International Civil Aviation Organization of the notification of denunciation; nevertheless, in respect of damage contemplated in Article 1 arising from an incident which occurred before the expiration of the six months period, the Convention shall continue to apply as if the denunciation had not been made.

Article 36

1 This Convention shall apply to all territories for the foreign relations of which a Contracting State is responsible, with the exception of territories in respect of which a declaration has been made in accordance with paragraph 2 of this Article or paragraph 3 of Article 37.

2 Any State may at the time of deposit of its instrument of ratification or adherence, declare that its acceptance of this Convention does not apply to any one or more of the territories for the foreign relations of which such State is responsible.

3 Any Contracting State may subsequently, by notification to the International Civil Aviation Organization, extend the application of this Convention to any or all of the territories regarding which it has made a declaration in accordance with paragraph 2 of this Article or paragraph 3 of Article 37. The notification shall take effect as from the ninetieth day after its receipt by the Organization.

4 Any Contracting State may denounce this Convention, in accordance with the provisions of Article 35, separately for any or all of the territories for the foreign relations of which such State is responsible.

Article 37

1 When the whole or part of the territory of a Contracting State is transferred to a non-contracting State, this Convention shall cease to apply to the territory so transferred, as from the date of the transfer.

2 When part of the territory of a Contracting State becomes an independent State responsible for its own foreign relations, this Convention shall cease to apply to the territory which becomes an independent State, as from the date on which it becomes independent.

3 When the whole or part of the territory of another State is transferred to a Contracting State, the Convention shall apply to the territory so transferred as from the date of the transfer; provided that, if the territory transferred does not become part of the metropolitan territory of the Contracting State concerned, that Contracting State may, before or at the time of the transfer, declare by notification to the International Civil Aviation Organization that the Convention shall not apply to the territory transferred unless a notification is made under paragraph 3 of Article 36.

Article 38

The Secretary General of the International Civil Aviation Organization shall give notice to all signatory and adhering States and to all States members of the Organization or of the United Nations:

(a) of the deposit of any instrument of ratification or adherence and the date thereof, within thirty days from the date of the deposit, and

(b) of the receipt of any denunciation or of any declaration or notification made under Article 36 or 37 and the date thereof, within thirty days from the date of the receipt.

The Secretary General of the Organization shall also notify these States of the date on which the Convention comes into force in accordance with paragraph 1 of Article 33.

Article 39

No reservations may be made to this Convention.

IN WITNESS WHEREOF the undersigned Plenipotentiaries, having been duly authorised, have signed this Convention.

DONE at Rome on the seventh day of the month of October of the year One Thousand Nine Hundred and Fifty Two in the English, French and Spanish languages, each text being of equal authenticity.

This Convention shall be deposited with the International Civil Aviation Organization where, in accordance with Article 31, it shall remain open for signature, and the Secretary General of the Organization shall send certified copies thereof to all signatory and adhering States and to all States members of the Organization or the United Nations.

APPENDIX II

CONVENTION

ON DAMAGE CAUSED BY FOREIGN AIRCRAFT TO THIRD PARTIES ON THE SURFACE

SIGNED AT ROME ON 7 OCTOBER 1952

(Status as of 21 June 2000)

Entry into force: **The Convention came into force on 4 February 1958.**

Status: **26 signatories, 45 contracting States**

State	**Date of signature**	**Date of deposit of Instrument of Ratification or Adherence**	**Effective date**
Algeria		13 April 1964	12 July 1964
Angola		24 February 1998	25 May 1998
Argentina	7 October 1952	26 September 1972	25 December 1972
Australia (4)	20 October 1953	10 November 1958	8 February 1959
Azerbaijan		23 March 2000	21 June 2000
Bahrain		3 March 1997	1 June 1997
Belgium	7 October 1952	11 August 1966	9 November 1966
Bolivia		9 July 1998	7 October 1998
Brazil	7 October 1952	19 December 1962	19 March 1963
Cameroon		23 July 1969	21 October 1969
Cuba		8 September 1965	7 December 1965
Denmark	7 October 1952		
Dominican Republic	7 October 1952		
Ecuador		12 May 1958	10 August 1958
Egypt	7 October 1952	23 February 1954	4 February 1958
El Salvador		13 February 1980	13 May 1980
France	7 October 1952		
Gabon		14 January 1970	14 April 1970
Gambia		20 June 2000	18 September 2000

Greece	5 April 1955	10 May 1983	8 August 1983
Guatemala			
Guinea		28 May 1990	26 August 1990
Haiti		24 March 1961	22 June 1961
Honduras		5 October 1960	3 January 1961
India	2 August 1955		
Iraq		19 July 1972	17 October 1972
Israel	7 October 1952		
Italy	7 October 1952	10 October 1963	8 January 1964
Kenya		5 July 1999	3 October 1999
Kuwait (1)		27 November 1979	25 February 1980
Liberia	7 October 1952		
Libyan Arab Jamahiriya	11 August 1954		
Luxembourg	7 October 1952	19 February 1957	4 February 1958
Maldives		5 September 1995	4 December 1995
Mali		28 December 1961	28 March 1962
Mauritania		23 July 1962	21 October 1962
Mexico	7 October 1952		
Morocco		31 March 1964	29 June 1964
Netherlands	7 October 1952		
Niger		27 December 1962	27 March 1963
Nigeria		6 March 1970	4 June 1970
Norway	10 December 1954		
Pakistan	25 February 1957	6 November 1957	4 February 1958
Papua New Guinea (2)		15 December 1975	16 September 1975
Paraguay		26 May 1969	24 August 1969
Philippines	7 October 1952		
Portugal	7 October 1952		
Russian Federation (3)		21 April 1982	20 July 1982

Rwanda		17 May 1971	15 August 1971
Seychelles		15 September 1980	14 December 1980
Spain	7 October 1952	1 March 1957	4 February 1958
Sri Lanka		31 March 1959	29 June 1959
Sweden	11 August 1954		
Switzerland	7 October 1952		
Thailand	7 October 1952		
Togo		2 July 1980	30 September 1980
Tunisia		16 September 1963	15 December 1963
United Arab Emirates		12 February 1990	13 May 1990
United Kingdom	23 April 1953		
Uruguay		8 November 1978	6 February 1979
Vanuatu		15 January 1982	15 April 1982
Yemen		26 September 1986	25 December 1986

Note: Canada signed the Convention on 26 May 1954 and ratified it on 16 January 1956. On 29 June 1976, a notification of denunciation of the Convention by the Government of Canada was received by the International Civil Aviation Organization, which took effect on 29 December 1976.

(1) It is understood that the adherence to the Convention on Damage Caused by Foreign Aircraft to Third Parties on the Surface done in Rome, 1952, does not mean in any way recognition of Israel by the State of Kuwait. Furthermore, no treaty relation will arise between the State of Kuwait and Israel.

(2) On 15 December 1975, a declaration dated 6 November 1975 was deposited with the International Civil Aviation Organization by the Government of Papua New Guinea indicating that Papua New Guinea desired to be treated as a party in its own right to the Rome Convention, which had entered into force for Australia on 8 February 1959 and had applied to the Territory of Papua and Trust Territory of New Guinea. Papua New Guinea attained independence on 16 September 1975.

(3) Declaration dated 22 February 1982 by the Government of the Union of Soviet Socialist Republics (now the Russian Federation) that 'the provisions of Articles 30, 36 and 37 of the Convention on Damage Caused by Foreign Aircraft to Third Parties on the Surface, dated 7 October 1952, which have the effect of extending the applicability of the Convention to territories for the foreign relations of which a contracting State is responsible, are obsolete and in

conflict with the Declaration of the United Nations General Assembly on the Granting of Independence to Colonial Countries and Peoples (Resolution 1514/XV of 14 December 1960)'.

(4) On 8 May 2000, a notification of denunciation of the Convention by the Government of Australia was received by the International Civil Aviation Organization, which will take effect on 8 November 2000.

(5) This information and table was obtained via the Legal Bureau, ICAO, <http://www.icoa.org.int/icao/en/leb/rome1952.htm>. Visited 15 November 2000.

Legal Strategies of Queensland Food Export Firms: a Case Study

Steve C Williams

Introduction

Exporters today face increasing uncertainty in the world's economic, political, and social situations. As well as the usual hurdles of different currencies, tariff rates, exchange rates, and trade policies, exporters have to cope with rapid changes in consumer tastes and preferences, and changing requirements in legislation, both domestic and foreign. In order to remain competitive, exporters have to develop marketing and other strategies that will give them real advantages in their target markets, and give them the returns they need to remain in business and to grow.

As export trading has increased, there has been growth in publication of textbooks and articles on the topic. Such texts usually define what exporting is, and go on to describe various export strategies. For example, Piercy[1] defined exporting as the whole managerial process of selling and distributing goods overseas, including such factors as the financial arrangements, the documentation and office procedures, and the organisational structures. Export marketing was defined as the marketing decisions necessary to direct the flow of goods and communications overseas, while export strategy was defined as the selection of export markets, and the design of a program of marketing strategies to achieve the objectives set in terms of profit, volume and liquidity, together with all the organisational, administrative, and financial implications of exporting.

Cavusgil and Zhu[2] suggest that export performance is influenced by the choice of export marketing strategy, and that strategy choice is influenced by internal characteristics, that is, the firm and its product, as well as external characteristics such as conditions in the local industry and in export markets. Export marketing strategies include pricing, promotion, mode of entry, seeking the best 'spot' price, risk reduction, 'holding' while awaiting a better price, vertical integration, market development, and new product development. External factors include the political, social and legal environments impacting on the firm.

---

1 N Piercy, Export Strategy – Markets and Competition, 1982, New York: Allan and Unwin.

2 ST Cavusgil and S Zhu, 'Marketing Strategy / Performance Relationship: An Investigation of the Empirical Link in Export Market Ventures' (1994) 58 Journal of Marketing: 1–21.

Surprisingly, while most texts on exporting mention the legal environment as an external factor, little mention is made of legal strategy.[3] Legal strategies for exporting seem to be the province of more specialised texts. These more specialised texts[4] suggest that a detailed knowledge of relevant legal environments allows development of sophisticated legal strategies for exporting, and that the export contract plays a vital part in the legal strategy. Fox notes that a legal strategy is in every sense as important as a marketing strategy, and that in many cases a successful marketing strategy depends on the choice of a legal strategy.[5]

The contract is a particularly useful vehicle for strategy as the parties to a contract are generally free to frame whatever agreement they choose. Through the twin processes of planning and negotiation, a company can build a strategic legal position into its contract that will provide it with distinct marketing and competitive advantages. All export marketing strategies, whether product-related, price-related or distribution-related, have legal aspects that can be considered in the strategy formation phase.

At another level, the extent to which the exporting firm can achieve its export marketing objectives depends on how well, and how creatively it can deal with the various laws affecting export operations applied by the home country, the target country, and international organisations like the World Trade Organisation (WTO).[6] Australia, for example, has more than twenty major pieces of legislation affecting food exports. To these must be added all legislation applying in the target country as well as all relevant international laws.

For example, an Australian exporter sending products to the United Kingdom is subject to the Unfair Contract Terms Act and also the Consumer Protection Act, to name but a few. The Consumer Protection Act imposes obligations on exporters to the UK by requiring that certain safety regulations are complied with. If the regulations are not complied with, an injured party can bring an action for breach of a statutory duty. The Commission of Customs can seize any imported goods and detain them to see if they comply with the safety provisions.

If the Australian exporter has established a place of business in the UK, it comes under UK jurisdiction and actions can be brought in UK Courts. The Courts can also serve the exporter in Australia with a claim if contractual or tortious damage was sustained within the UK, even if the exporter has no UK office.

---

3 K Yalpaala, 'Strategy and Planning in Global Product Distribution – Beyond the Distribution Contract' (1994) 25 Law and Policy in International Business: 839–944 at 846.

4 For example, WF Fox, *International Commercial Agreements*, 2nd edn, 1998, Boston: Kluwer.

5 *Ibid.*

6 K Yalpaala, 'Strategy and Planning in Global Product Distribution – Beyond the Distribution Contract' (1994) 25 Law and Policy in International Business: 839–944.

The exporter has to make many decisions on aspects such as mode of entry, channels of distribution, and other elements of the marketing mix. This will often involve a host of contracts with different players including distributors, agents and advertising executives, all of which should rest on a sound legal strategy.

The aim of this paper is to examine recommended 'best practice' for legal strategy in exporting and compare this with the findings from a survey of Queensland export firms.

The use of legal strategy

Mintzberg[7] broadly defined strategy as a pattern of organized activities directed towards the achievement of an objective. A legal strategy in exporting can then be defined as a pattern of organized legal activities directed towards the achievement of export objectives.

The firm may have objectives that extend far beyond the particular transaction in question. For example, the firm may envisage the first export transaction as the start of a short, medium, or long-term association with a particular partner, or a plan that begins with simple exporting may result in the company establishing its own operations in a range of other countries.

These objectives will affect how particular transactions are carried out. For example, if the transaction is small, and one-off, the firm may negotiate briefly at arm's length with its partner and focus its legal attention in contracting on speed, security, the use of standard contractual terms and clauses, and limited communication with its partner. If the value of the one-off transaction is large, the firm may focus particularly in its contract on security and also on the tax implications.

On the other hand, if the firm plans a long-term relationship with a particular partner, it may focus extensively in its contract on friendly negotiation, conciliatory terms, custom-made clauses, extensive communication, and so on. The firm may or may not make extensive use of legal counsel, depending on the sensibilities and customary business practices of the other side. The firm may even choose to deliberately put itself in a weaker position (eg, accede to a request not to use a letter of credit) in order to demonstrate its sincerity and trust, if this is required to secure the business. It may remove particular 'standard' clauses it commonly uses in order not to give any offence to the other side through 'excessive' legalese.

Companies in unequal, dominant positions in transactions can often dictate terms in contractual negotiations with smaller buyers or suppliers. They have sufficient 'negotiation leverage' to extract concessions from the other side

7 Q Mintzberg, 'Crafting strategy', in Mintzberg, H and Quinn, JB, *The Strategy Process – Concepts, Contexts, Cases*, 1991, New York: Prentice, 105–14.

with respect to key strategic positions in contract such as the choice of law clause and the choice of legal forum for disputes. They can exert influence on the wording of variation and modification clauses, price escalation clauses and tax clauses, as well as review or renegotiation clauses that allow the contract to be renegotiated at a future date.[8]

Entry strategy such as the location of processing facilities is often governed by opportunities to take advantage of favourable tax laws. Companies established in offshore tax havens can be used by exporters to minimise tax payable in the home country.[9] A firm can purposely negotiate its contract to minimise tax, to delay payment of tax, to take advantage of government incentives, and to comply with wider objectives with respect to transfer pricing, business structure, and ownership. Even issues such as working conditions of employees, safety, and compliance can be addressed.

The firm can also use the contract as part of a wider strategy with respect to positioning itself in a market as an important 'player', or for purposes of corporate citizenship and networking. For example, by becoming a regular supplier to a prestigious firm, an exporter may find it has access to new circles of contacts associated with the prestigious firm. It can also build into its contracts a broad strategy of corporate risk management. Once the level of risk exposure that is acceptable is determined, the firm can seek the contractual terms that will provide the required level of protection against losses.

Decisions such as choice of trading partner, choice of product (eg, unprocessed versus processed), choice of distribution channel (eg, direct or via intermediaries), and choice of promotion can all be governed by legal considerations. Yalpaala states that: 'Deliberate use of the law to develop and select the distribution method within a broader corporate strategy will tend to protect the … enterprise in the long run.'[10]

For example, the target market and type of distribution may be chosen in terms of favourable laws governing product liability. Similarly, the choice whether or not to standardize a product may be based primarily on the legal implications.

It is clear that inclusion of a legal strategy in an export operation has many advantages. For example, a strategy to establish a wholly-owned subsidiary overseas gives a number of important legal benefits. As a 'local' corporation, the firm may be entitled to legal protection both within and outside that country market. It will receive the same benefits accorded to purely domestic

8 In contracts with European buyers exporters ought to tread carefully when negotiating terms as the European Commission has promulgated a Directive on Unfair Contract Terms: OJ L 95/29 21.4.93. This came into effect in 1995.

9 These companies are used as intermediaries in the export operation so that most of the profit is derived in the tax haven.

10 K Yalpaala, 'Strategy and Planning in Global Product Distribution – Beyond the Distribution Contract' (1994) 25 Law and Policy in International Business: 839–944 at 847.

firms. For example, an Australian firm based in the USA is entitled to the protection of US Laws governing investment outside the USA, trademarks and intellectual property and competition from parallel imports. This protection may well outweigh any negative aspect of coming under USA jurisdiction, such as enforcement of embargos against third countries like Cuba.

The Queensland food export industry

The Queensland food industry covers a very wide range of products – live, processed and unprocessed. Food exports from Queensland exceeded A$4 billion in 1998[11] with Japan the largest trading partner in addition to other markets world-wide. A significant factor that characterises the Queensland industry is that most firms are relatively small. A firm that employs more than 20 people is regarded as a large firm. Most are located in the south east of the state. Most food products are exported by sea, but in recent years, more use is being made of air transport, especially to markets in South East Asia. In a study of export strategies of the Queensland seafood export industry in 1997, Williams found that few exporters had any knowledge of the legal environments that applied to their export operations.[12] It was decided to expand this study to Queensland food exporters generally.

The study

The extended study, funded by the Australian Research Committee, was completed in 1998, and included the following hypotheses relating directly to legal strategy:

H1: Legally sophisticated exporters (those with some legal training or who use legal counsel) are more likely to focus on contract formation and content (in terms of having detailed written contracts, and a wide range of terms) than legally unsophisticated firms

H2: Legally sophisticated exporters will have fewer problems (eg disputes with trading partners, customs etc) than legally unsophisticated firms.

H3: Large firms are more likely to focus on contract formation and content than small firms.

H4: Firms with extensive experience in exporting ('old hands') are more likely to focus on contract formation and content than firms new to exporting.

The survey instrument was a mail survey of all firms in Queensland advertising themselves as 'food exporters' in the various food categories (eg,

11 Australian Bureau of Statistics, Foreign Trade (unpublished data).

12 SC Williams, 'Legal Aspects of Queensland Seafood Exports', in *Proceedings of 5th International Trade Law Conference*, TC Beirne School of Law, Brisbane, July 1997.

dairy products, nuts, fruit and vegetables) listed in the 1997–1998 Queensland yellow pages for all districts. An exploratory study was conducted by personal interview with five food-exporting firms in South East Queensland to refine the content of the survey and to test the proposed questions in a situation where direct feedback could be obtained. The companies personally interviewed ranged in size from large (> 20 employees) to small (2–4 employees). The main survey instrument was a detailed questionnaire (25 questions) applied by mail. It was designed to be able to be completed in less than 15 minutes. The questions were derived from the international legal and business literature and from discussions with leading international law firms in Brisbane. Questions included the extent to which legal services were used, research done into legal environments, legal problems experienced in export operations, and the nature and details of contracts used.

The sample for the study was 107 firms listed as being food exporters. The survey began in May 1998 and a reminder notice was sent out three weeks later. There were 47 responses (43.9%) and 20 survey forms (18.7%) were returned unopened as undeliverable. Of the 47 responses, 12 (11.2%) reported that the company was no longer exporting. This left 35 useable responses, representing 32.7% of the original sample. This was a sufficiently representative sample for the study, especially since all firms surveyed were involved in exporting food, and is comparable with other studies done on exporting.[13]

The findings

The findings in general were surprising. Only two exporters reported that they had a legal strategy of any kind, or specifically made use of their contracts as a vehicle for achieving some strategic objective.

Seventy-one percent of firms surveyed used a written contract, and the remainder relied on verbal contracts only. Most contracts that were written were very abbreviated as to content. For example, while 75% of firms specified basic terms such as price, quality and delivery date, less than 25% specified terms often considered essential by international business law texts, such as warranties, liabilities, choice of law, and dispute resolution clauses. Only 25% of respondents said that they were concerned that they had a legally enforceable contract.

13 KA Kau and JS Tan, 'A Study of Small and Large Manufacturing Exporters in Singapore, in Roberts, G (ed), *Proceedings of the 31st World Conference, International Council of Small Business*, 1986: 67–74; GR Harrison, Internationalization and the Problems of International Business for New Zealand Firms. Master of Commerce Thesis, University of Otago, 1990; DL Dean, B Mengue, and CP Meyers, 'The Ongoing Debate over Export Performance: An Investigation of New Zealand Small Industrial Firms' Commerce Division Discussion Paper, No 57 Canterbury, Lincoln University, 1998.

Firms were asked whether they had experienced disputes of any kind in their trading operations and 57% responded positively. Most of these disputes (65%) were related to specifications, with the next major categories identified as non-payment (15%), damage (5.7%), delivery dates (2.85%) and fraud (2.8%). Of these disputes, 63% were resolved by personal negotiation, 10.5% by litigation, and 5% by mediation.

Most firms (88.5%) reported that they had never had any problems with customs or anti-dumping authorities overseas.

To test the hypotheses, firms were divided into three paired groups: 'legally sophisticated' versus 'unsophisticated'; large versus small; and 'old hands' versus 'new'.

Because the overall sample was small, a simple but robust nonparametric test (z-test for a significant difference between two proportions) was used to test the null hypotheses posed (ie that there was no difference between the two groups tested in each case). Again, the results were surprising.

H1: Legally sophisticated firms were no more likely to place emphasis on contract formation and content than unsophisticated firms. The null hypothesis (that there was no significant difference between the two groups) was not able to be rejected. [z = + 1.923, sd = .0936] The z value must be more than 1.96 to reject the null hypothesis at the .05% confidence level.

H2: There was no apparent difference in response between legally sophisticated firms and unsophisticated firms with respect to the number of problems experienced. [z = +.3879, sd = .1654] This again was not sufficient to reject the null hypothesis at the .05% confidence level.

H3: Large firms appeared no more likely to focus on contract formation and content than small firms. [z =+1.386, sd = .101]

H4: 'Old hands' appeared no more likely to focus on contract formation and content than firms new to exporting. [z =+ 1.598, sd =.0782]

Discussion

These findings suggest that there is a considerable gap between recommendations in international business law textbooks in relation to knowledge of the legal environments and development of a legal strategy, and the current practice of Queensland food export firms. The majority of the firms surveyed are engaging in international trade, apparently successfully, without a legal strategy, and most are not particularly concerned about legal issues. They do not customise their contracts according to the particular transaction, and they do not use the contract as a vehicle for specific or wider legal strategies. They do not particularly care whether the contract is legally enforceable or not. The question that arises is how can these exporters successfully engage in international transactions without paying attention to legal strategy?

Piercy states that: 'Most prescriptive theory … rests on the assumption that individuals and organizations make "rational" decisions usually in the sense of seeking acceptable goals and evaluating alternative ways of achieving them, before making decisions on courses of action.'[14] The results of the survey suggest that many food exporters are not making 'rational' decisions with respect to their contracts. They are not taking steps to reduce legal risks, and they are not taking advantage of the opportunities a legal knowledge of their trading environments might bring. Other considerations must be taking precedence.

If one considers the prospects for reducing risks, it is clear that, in international trade, substantial amounts of risk can be absorbed from transactions via non-legal avenues – in other words, most of the law may not needed by most of the people involved.[15] Kaspar states that:

> International trade has always operated in frameworks of internal institutions that traders and middlemen developed and typically enforce informally. Thanks to these effective internal rules of the trading community, international trade now takes place at surprisingly low transaction costs. Business partners in different countries rely on self-enforcing mechanisms to obtain contract compliance, for example, by tit for tat, reliance on good reputation, shunning, and middlemen networks (whose contract breaches would mean exclusion from the network).[16]

He noted that while a limited number of disputes do occur, most are settled privately between the principals. Where a dispute cannot be resolved directly by the parties concerned, it is more likely to be resolved by private arbitration as opposed to litigation, and few of the arbitrated settlements are challenged in court.

Given the current trend of communication becoming more accessible and at lower costs, most firms are now able to maintain daily personal contact with their trading partners. This tends to lower the occurrence of disputes and the risks faced by exporters. Potential problems can quickly be identified and resolved. For many firms in the survey, the relationship with many overseas customers had matured over time to one of ease and informality. Most respondents reported that business was regular, and most was done by telephone call.

---

14 N Piercy, *Export Strategy – Markets and Competition*, 1982, New York: Allan and Unwin, 9.

15 W Kaspar, *Ignorance, Discovery and Choice: A Critique of Economic Rationalism*, Paper presented at the Joint Conference of the Australian Society of Legal Philosophy and The Centre for the Legal and Economic Study of Institutions, Law, Economics, and the Problem of Knowledge: Prospects for an Institutional Approach, The University of Queensland. 19 September, 1997.

16 W Kaspar, 'International Competition and the Production of Institutional Capital', in *Proceedings of the Australia and New Zealand International Business Academy Conference – The Challenge of Globalization*, Melbourne, 13–14 November 1998: 197–205.

Other factors that reduce risk are the use of letters of credit, which guarantee both delivery and payment, and the existence of a 'business code' which permeates all trading, domestic and international, and which has unwritten rules of conduct for honest dealing and trading. In addition, increasing competition at all levels of international trade means that there are substantial competitive advantages in being as free and as flexible as possible in trading operations. Several respondents reported that to do business with some countries (eg, the USA) the insistence on a detailed contract and the use of letters of credit meant a loss of business.

One respondent noted that business in some areas is now too fast-moving for the textbook ideal of pre-contractual research, planning and negotiation, and elaborate written contracts designed to achieve some strategic advantage. More and more business is being done using standard contracts as recommended by the various international trade organizations, and there has been a rapid acceptance of common international trading rules and standards.[17] The emphasis now, according to the respondent, is on becoming a recognized and accepted 'player' as quickly as possible. This is done by doing the deals, taking the risks, wearing the losses, and staying in the game.

This does not mean, however, that there is no role at all for the law. Much legal risk still remains. While some companies can withstand substantial losses from inadvertently breaking a law or from an extended and expensive legal dispute, many cannot. Small firms are especially at risk. The fact that 57% of firms reported that they had experienced problems in their exporting operations means that both industry and government have no cause for complacency. There is still much room for legal input at the corporate and operational level. For example, the legal specialist can ensure the firm complies with all relevant laws, and provide advice as to the most appropriate strategy for contracting, choice of market, mode of market entry, distribution, risk management, and taxation.

Conclusion

Government, industry groups and the public are vitally interested in ensuring that an industry such as food exporting operates on the highest possible revenue curve. This means that the product is put into the highest-value use at the lowest possible cost.[18] An exporter with a good legal strategy can achieve both aims.

17 A prominent example of standard terms are the International Chamber of Commerce International Commercial Trade Terms, 2000 (ICC INCOTERMS 2000).

18 LM Van Mier, 'A Study of Policy Considerations in Managing the Georges Bank Haddock Fishery, 1965', in Bell, FW and Hazleton JE (eds), *Recent Developments and Research in Fisheries Economics,* 1967, New York, Oceania Publications, 72.

Governments are especially interested in encouraging 'rational' exporter behaviour, which promotes Australia's image as a worthy trading partner and discourages exporters who, through their slipshod international transactions, produce negative spillover effects to Australian exporters generally. Running foul of international or foreign market law is one such example.

Many export studies[19] have found that exporter use of government export assistance can contribute to successful exporting efforts. The survey showed that many firms had little legal knowledge, and many had experienced disputes with trading partners. Governments can readily provide assistance in this area.

Such assistance might involve discreet indirect pressure being applied at a government-to-government level in order to resolve disputes quickly. In could involve more direct forms of assistance such as the provision of step-by-step procedural materials on legal aspects of exporting and wide dissemination of materials relating to the legal obligations of exporters. This has already been done by some government departments in Australia, such as the Commonwealth Quarantine Service. Similarly, useful information could be disseminated on current international law such as the Vienna Convention,[20] the UNIDROIT Principles[21] and INCOTERMS,[22] as well as general advice on exporting. At the moment, such information is not always readily available from government or from the relevant industry bodies.

There is also a role for the legal profession, in that it was clear from the survey that few exporters would consider input from a lawyer except when a major problem emerged. Yalpaala notes that: 'Some managers may view a lawyer doing anything more than drafting the … contract as interfering with the client's operations.'[23] There is clearly an opportunity here for the legal profession to demonstrate to exporters the advantages of legal input at the contractual and corporate strategy levels.

---

19 For example O Singer and MR Czinkota, 'Factors Associated with Effective Use of Export Assistance' (1994) 2(1) Journal of International Marketing: 53–71.

20 United Nations Convention on Contracts for the International Sale of Goods (CISG).

21 The UNIDROIT Principles of International Commercial Contracts, UNIDROIT 1994. These principles can be incorporated into contracts as the governing law and the terms of the contract.

22 International Chamber of Commerce International Commercial Trade Terms, 2000 (ICC INCOTERMS 2000).

23 K Yalpaala, 'Strategy and Planning in Global Product Distribution – Beyond the Distribution Contract' (1994) 25 Law and Policy in International Business: 839–944 at 916.

Justice in the 21st Century[1]

GL Davies[2]

1 Introduction

In a lecture given at Cambridge University in 1998 entitled 'The Future of the Common Law',[3] Lord Bingham, then Lord Chief Justice, noted that his was the second lecture of that title delivered at that University in a little over a year. His Lordship likened his position to that of PG Wodehouse who, in the preface to his novel '*Summer Lightning*' acknowledged that there was already in circulation a work by another author bearing the same title. Undeterred, Wodehouse expressed the hope that his own book might be included in any future list of the 100 best books called '*Summer Lightning*'.

I don't feel optimistic enough to express a similar hope about what I say today. For when Justice Buckley asked me to speak on the topic Justice in the 21st Century, I had only recently read a learned and very comprehensive book of that title by the Honourable Russell Fox QC and I was aware that I could never hope to emulate that feat, let alone in 40 minutes or so. Moreover the title is such a catchy one and we are so early in the century that there are bound to be many others who will speak or write on it also.

I had two additional problems in speaking to you on this topic. The first is, as you are no doubt all aware, I know very little about Family Law and the kind of law which I deal with daily is not of direct interest to you. So although, no doubt, we have a common view of justice in a philosophical sense we try to give effect to justice according to law in different contexts and in different ways.

My second difficulty is that I think, as no doubt many of you do also, that the greatest changes to the way in which each of us will give effect to justice according to law will be the result of advances in information and communication technology. And I acknowledge at the outset that though what I propose to say to you will touch on these advances from time to time I am by no means an expert on such questions. Indeed I have no doubt that there are many of you who know more about those things than I.

---

1 A paper delivered at the Family Court of Australia Judges' Annual Conference 'Challenges for the 21st Century', Sydney, 7 July 2000.

2 Judge of Appeal, Court of Appeal, Queensland.

3 (1999) 18 CJQ 203.

I shall therefore eschew the impossible task of trying to be comprehensive on this topic or of venturing too deeply into the field of technology. Instead I would like to discuss two related trends which are already emerging, both of which will accelerate during the course of this century and both of which will, I believe, have a considerable influence on all of us.

The first of these is the convergence of legal systems and the decline of orality. The legal systems to which I refer are of course the two great world systems of law, the common law system and the civil law system, the concept of orality being traditionally of the essence of the common law system.

The second is the increased public perception of the choices which judges make. One aspect of this has received considerable publicity in recent years. This is the perception of judicial creativity by the High Court in controversial areas both of common law (*Mabo* and *Wik* being examples of that) and constitutional law especially in the implication of rights in the Constitution. But the question is much broader than of perceptions of judicial creativity and its consequences are substantial, as I shall endeavour to show. I turn first to the convergence of legal systems.

2 The convergence of legal systems and the decline of orality

(a) Convergence[4]

Over the past few decades, common law systems have grown, almost imperceptibly, to look more like civil law systems (and more like one another). An examination of the causes of that will, I think, explain why it will continue. At the same time civil law systems have come to look more like common law systems. Those trends will, I think, continue at an accelerating pace. Convergence is occurring, arguably, in at least four areas: in the sources of law and judicial method; in substantive law; in procedural law; and, at least possibly, but by no means certainly, in the constitutional position of the judiciary which I shall call judicial structure. I shall say something briefly about each of those. A decline in orality is, in part, a consequence of this movement although it has, as I shall attempt to show, other causes as well.

The sources of law and the judicial method

Traditionally the essence of the common law system is judge made law; the importance accorded to the decisions of judges, and in particular appellate judges, as sources of law. A consequence of this is a process of reasoning

4 This is not a new topic. See, for example, J Merryman, 'On the Convergence (and Divergence) of the Civil Law and the Common Law' in M Cappelletti (ed), *New Perspectives for a Common Law of Europe*, 1978, European University Institute, Florence.

which is substantially inductive or analogical.[5] That system may generally be contrasted with civil systems which are traditionally codified systems owing their inspiration to the principles of the Code Napoleon. And a characteristic of such codified systems is, traditionally, that they tend to state principles and obligations in broad terms, leaving it to the courts to decide their specific application; there being no doctrine of precedent; with the consequence that the process of reasoning is substantially deductive or institutional.

But much of this has already changed, at least from our point of view. In the first place over the past half century the extent to which legislation has been a source of law has increased substantially and continues to do so, particularly in areas such as health, social security, industrial safety, accident compensation, unfair competition, consumer protection, environment protection and anti-discrimination safeguards. Secondly there has been a substantial increase in codification. And thirdly more statutes are cast in broader terms, using concepts such as reasonableness,[6] fairness,[7] good faith,[8] justice[9] and conscionableness.[10]

Of course there are areas in which the common law is still dominant; torts is an obvious example.[11] But commercial law is increasingly governed by statutes and many areas of law such as your own, corporations law, industrial law and most areas of property law have now long been the subject of codification.

Of course also, there have long been areas of statute law under which judges were given choices; contributory negligence, testator's family provision, maintenance and custody are obvious examples. But in more recent times the extent of this has increased substantially and, even in areas of law involving commercial relationships, where it was formerly thought that certainty was the primary consideration, recent statutes have conferred broad choices on judges.

5 See *Sutherland Shire Council v Heyman* (1985) 157 CLR 424 at 481 *per* Brennan J; *Murphy v Brentwood District Council* [1991] 1 AC 398 at 461; and, more recently, *Perre v Apand Ltd* (1999) 73 ALJR 1190 at 1206, 1256.

6 Trade Practices Act 1974, s 68A.

7 *Ibid*; Anti-Discrimination Act 1991 (Qld), s 175; Commercial Arbitration Act 1990 (Qld), s 22 and analogues elsewhere; Corporations Act, s 256A; Workplace Relations Act 1996, s 143.

8 Insurance Contracts Act 1984, s 13; Trade Practices Act 1974, s 51AC; Anti-Discrimination Act *supra* s 147(2).

9 Contracts Review Act 1980 (NSW), ss 7, 8, 10; Credit Act 1987 (Qld), Part 9 and analogues elsewhere; Family Law Act 1975, s 79; Property Law Act 1974 (Qld), s 286 and analogues elsewhere.

10 Trade Practices Act 1974, ss 51AB, 51AC.

11 See however comprehensive accident compensation in New Zealand and various occupier's liability and defamation statutes. The adoption of strict liability compensation schemes, at least in relation to workplace injuries, is becoming more common in both common law and civil systems. NB recent suggestions by Small Business Minister J Hockey to adopt a similar system in Australia.

The task of interpreting statutes imposing obligations in broad terms has been accentuated in England where for some time now judges have been confronted with interpreting broadly stated European Community Directives[12] and are now confronted with interpreting and applying European Human Rights Law.[13]

The increase in statute law, in codification and in statutes stating broad principles has changed not only the primary sources of law in our system but also the way in which judges reason. Our process of reasoning is now much more deductive than it once was. Those changes have been complemented, in many areas of the common law, by judges stating broader unifying principles.

At the same time there has been an increased tendency by courts in at least some civil law countries to follow judicial precedent. In theory they are not obliged to but pragmatically and in practice they do and that practice is enforced by appellate courts.[14] There has also been an increase, in civil law countries, in more specific, detailed legislation.

Convergence of substantive law

Over much the same period there has been an increasing movement towards globalization of law. The technical advances which I mentioned at the outset are rapidly shrinking the commercial world. So are the removal of trade barriers and the adoption of international conventions. The apparent emergence in common law jurisdictions of concepts of good faith in the performance and enforcement of contracts,[15] and perhaps even in their formation,[16] and of proportionality in administrative law,[17] concepts which are traditionally part of European civil law,[18] are evidence of that.[19] It seems

---

12 See T Rensen, 'British Statutory Interpretation in the Light of Community and Other International Obligations' (1993) 14 Stat LR 186.

13 Human Rights Act 1998 (UK).

14 M Morin, '*Portalis v Bentham*? The Objective Ascribed to Codification of the Civil Law and the Criminal Law in France, England and Canada' (1999) www.lcc.gc.ca/en/papers/rapport/ldi.1999.pdf; B Markesinis, 'Learning from Europe and Learning in Europe', in *The Gradual Convergence: Foreign Ideas, Foreign Influences and English Law on the Eve of the 21st Century*, 1994, Oxford: Clarendon Press, 30; D Coester-Waltjen and AAS Zuckerman, 'The Role of Lawyers in German Civil Litigation' (1999) 18 CJQ 291 at 294.

15 *Alcatel Australia v Scarcella* (1998) 44 NSWLR 349; United States Uniform Commercial Code, s 1-203.

16 *Interfoto Picture Library Ltd v Stiletto Visual Programmes Ltd* [1989] QB 433 at 445; *Sabemo Pty Ltd v North Sydney Municipal Council* [1977] 2 NSWLR 880 at 902–03; and see generally Sir Anthony Mason, 'Good Faith and Equitable Standards' (2000) 116 LQR 66.

17 Although care must be taken in comparing these concepts in civil and the common law for they are not identical.

18 As to the first, see now the EC Directive on Unfair Terms in Consumer Contracts and UK Regulations implementing it. It uses the concept of good faith. This and other civil law concepts, such as significant imbalance, are likely to have an increasing influence on UK commercial law. As to the second, see J Jowell and A Lester 'Proportionality: Neither Novel Nor Dangerous', in Jowell and Oliver, eds, *New Directions in Judicial Review*, London, Stevens, 1988.

19 So, too, at least in part, is the increase in statutes imposing broad standards: see fn 4 to fn 8.

almost inevitable that other branches of law will increasingly benefit from the cross-fertilization which increased commercial and cultural intercourse brings and, particularly in the areas of protection of the environment[20] and of human rights,[21] from the recognition and implementation by domestic courts of international treaties. Economic and cultural convergence brings legal convergence. This movement is accentuated in the countries of the European Community, including Great Britain, because of the obligation of their courts to give effect domestically to decisions of the European Court[22] and European Community Directives.

Convergence of procedures

Procedurally too, our system is moving closer to those in civil law countries. Of course it was never correct to speak of adversarial and inquisitorial[23] systems as if they were mutually exclusive opposites. The reality was never like that. But it could once have been said that on an adversarial/inquisitorial scale, our system was towards the adversarial end and some others, such as the French, were towards the inquisitorial end. A number of changes to our procedural system have moved it and will continue to move it more toward the middle of that scale.

The adversarial model was premised on the assumption that civil litigation was essentially a private matter. The parties were left to conduct proceedings as they saw fit and according to their own timetable. The judge assumed a passive role, intervening like an umpire only if a non-delinquent party sought the imposition of sanctions. The responsibility was upon the parties alone to identify the issues in dispute, and it was for the party making an assertion to prove it, without assistance from his or her opponent. The judge, being the impartial arbiter, was left with the job of determining the contest according to what was presented to her or him. The judge could not transgress beyond the issues and evidence presented by the parties. All steps in the action were intended to lead up to a climactic trial. It was the trial to which all attention was directed. Orality was an essential characteristic.

To state the elements of the adversarial model in that way shows immediately how far we have already departed from it. Case management systems, in various forms, and a greater assumption by judges of responsibility for the speed at which and the form in which disputes are conducted, and even for the issues upon which they will be conducted, have changed much of that. With some limited exceptions, of which the Family

20 As in the *Tasmanian Dam* case (1983) 158 CLR 1.

21 For example *Minister for Immigration v Teoh* (1995) 183 CLR 273; *Dietrich v The Queen* (1992) 177 CLR 292; *Mabo v Queensland (No 2)* (1992) 175 CLR 1 at 42; and see fn 11.

22 See, for example, European Communities Act 1972 (UK).

23 The term 'inquisitorial' is itself an inappropriate one to describe the procedure in civil law systems except possibly in their criminal jurisdiction. Nevertheless I use it here, as others have, to describe the model referred to below.

Court is one, however, there is still a tendency on the part of many litigating lawyers and judges to look towards an ultimate single trial as the main event.

To me this seems curious, given the legal and practical advantages, in many cases, in deciding issues separately. The single climactic trial was, of course, dictated by the jury system. It would have been at least inconvenient and costly, and sometimes impossible, to conduct a trial over several hearings whilst the civil jury system was retained. But that is now, of course, almost extinct in civil litigation and consequently the only need for a single climactic trial has gone. I mention this, not to complain about the failure of most courts to move away from the concept of a single trial more quickly and in more cases but to point to the inevitability of future increase in the resolution of issues separately.[24]

The trend towards increased judicial control of litigation, which commenced with control of processes leading up to a hearing, has, of course, now extended to greater control of hearings; of the form which evidence and submissions will take, of the number of witnesses who may be called on any issue and of time limits for oral evidence and submissions. In both of these respects that trend will continue and information technology will enable it to become increasingly sophisticated, efficient and economical.

But there is one other respect in which our procedural system has not yet emulated the civil law systems. That is in not ensuring, as best it can, that the evidence of witnesses other than the parties is as objective and consequently as reliable as it possibly can be by requiring them to be proofed and called by the court. The increased cost to government of such a requirement makes it unlikely that that will even occur with respect to witnesses of fact. That may not matter a great deal because of the likely increased reliability of fact evidence, referred to below. But that will still leave the problems of adversarial bias in and cost of multiple opinion evidence. As some of you may know I have in the past, on a number of occasions, expressed the view that in this respect we should emulate the practice in civil systems of court appointed experts.[25] I shall not repeat my reasons for that view. But it seems to me that there is at least one reason which will make that inevitable in many, if not most cases. That is an increasing difficulty in understanding and therefore of judging scientific opinion.

That increasing difficulty is a necessary consequence of advances in science and of its increasing complexity. If a judge cannot understand what competing experts are saying, how can she or he decide between their competing views? Of course a system of court-appointed experts is not a complete answer to the problem of the increasing complexity of science and

---

24 The exception to this is, of course, the United States where civil jury trials remain the norm.

25 For example in 'Judicial Reform: A Personal Perspective' (1997) 15 Aust Bar Rev 109 at 112.

consequently of scientific evidence.[26] The expectation of a client is not the only source of bias; the source of a scientist's research funding may be a factor as may disharmony between different schools of thought. A system of court-appointed experts may not reveal such biases and may even conceal them; and it may reduce the capacity of a court to determine whether an opinion expressed is within the expertise of the witness expressing it. But as is so often demonstrated by litigation in the United States and sometimes in this country, adversarial bias is the greatest threat to reliability of expert evidence, and a system of court appointment eliminates that risk. It also increases the capacity of the judge to understand and assess the opinions given.

The inquisitorial model was premised on judicial conduct of the processes of evidence gathering and presentation, the parties' powers being extremely limited in both respects. The pace of litigation was also controlled by the court which would ordinarily conduct a number of hearings at which it would make both procedural and substantive decisions. Oral evidence and submissions were of less importance than in the adversarial tradition.

The reality, however, is rather different. In countries like France the sheer volume of litigation, or insufficiency of numbers of judges, has meant that much of the control of litigation has been left to the parties.[27] In others like Germany the system has always been closer to ours,[28] the most substantial difference being judicial conduct of evidence gathering and presentation; but the choice of witnesses is left to the parties. And a number of civil systems are moving towards 'concentration' of the trial; that is, fewer hearings with, wherever possible, one substantial final hearing.[29] Moreover in one respect, in having no procedure for compelling mutual disclosure, most civil law systems are more adversarial than their common law counterparts.

Consequently, the procedural differences are not as great now as might at first sight appear or as once they were. Moreover they are diminishing with increased judicial control of proceedings in our system.

Of course we can no longer assume that disputes will be resolved within established structures. Both domestically and internationally an increasing proportion of disputes are resolved outside existing courts. Alternative dispute resolution has become an important part of both common law and civil systems. Moreover, at least in the commercial area, standard form contracts including standard form provisions for resolution of disputes and,

26 And, unless it is carefully implemented, it could give rise to problems under Chapter III of the Constitution.

27 See, for example, D Lariviere, 'Overview of the Problems of French Civil Procedure' (1997) 45 Amer J Comp L 737 at 745; L Cadiet, 'Civil Justice Reform: Access, Cost and Delay - The French Perspective', in *Civil Justice in Crisis*, 1999, Oxford: OUP, at 308–09.

28 See, for example, D Coester-Waltjen and AAS Zuckerman, 'The Role of Lawyers in German Civil Litigation' (1999) 18 CJQ 291.

29 See J Merryman, *The Civil Law Tradition, an Introduction to the Legal Systems of Western Europe and Latin America*, 2nd edn, 1985, Stanford University Press, at 112–13.

internationally, increasing adoption of the Vienna Sales Convention as the relevant substantive law have had a substantial unifying effect.

Convergence of judicial structures

There is one important respect in which our system will not and should not emulate civil ones. More than ever, as executive governments and government instrumentalities increasingly become involved in litigation, judicial independence is of primary importance. And in the wake of scandals involving investigating magistrates, first in Belgium and more recently in France, plainly attributable to their lack of independence from executive government, many in civil law countries are tending to agree. There is some prospect that, in the wake of these scandals, some changes will be made. We will have to wait and see how extensive they are. But I think that this is one respect in which we cannot expect rapid substantial change.

Convergence generally

In substantive law, in the manner in which laws are made, in methods of reasoning and in procedures for dispute resolution, convergence is already occurring and will continue. That is not to say that there will not remain differences in law; indeed pluralism in societies is likely to become more evident. But that is not inconsistent with the convergence which is occurring.

(b) The decline of orality

As mentioned earlier an essential characteristic of the adversarial system has been its oral tradition; evidence given orally and submissions made orally by the parties or their lawyers. Face to face contact with full cross-examination of the witnesses and competing addresses by counsel has traditionally been thought to be the best way of achieving a fair result. But much of this has already changed, the main driving forces being time and cost, the first necessarily affecting the second. Most of the changes, for these reasons, have been implemented by judges, concerned not only about the cost to the parties of the resolution of their disputes, but also about the best use by the public of the scarce resources of courts. An additional cause of these changes has been an increased appreciation, by common law judges, of some of the efficiencies, with no apparent diminution in fairness, of some civil systems in which orality has never been of as much importance as it has in ours.

The result has been a substantial increase in the production of evidence in statement or affidavit form and in written submissions, in both cases generally supplemented orally. Two factors, so far insufficiently appreciated, will, I think accelerate the decline of orality. The first is technology; the second is an increasing appreciation of the unreliability of oral evidence and of the difficulty in assessing it.

The effect of technology

Technology has revolutionized both the recording of information and communication. Not only has it substantially changed the way in which we do both; it has also substantially changed the extent to which we do both. Because the recording of information, including of communications, is easy and cheap, and will become even easier and cheaper, we will continue to record more of what we do including our communications with others. And because we will continue to record more of what we do and say, in both our business and our domestic affairs, we will have less need to try to recall events months or even years later. More importantly for the purposes of litigation, these recordings will be much more reliable evidence of what we did and said than our later reconstructions. Moreover in many cases in which participants in an event which later gives rise to litigation do not record what they did or said there will increasingly be others who will have done so, often for some other purpose. In short, increased use of technology will result in a massive increase in reliable contemporaneous evidence of events later giving rise to litigation.

The unreliability of oral evidence

Most people involved in the law have long known how unreliable oral evidence can be. Many of us have seen demonstrations of the unreliability of eye witness evidence of a fleeting event and we know how we ourselves tend to reconstruct past events in a way in which we would prefer to recollect them. The truth is that most judges accept oral evidence of past events only because there is no other evidence.

However, I do think that some of us indulge in a little self-deception when it comes to deciding between competing oral versions of an event. I accept that there are many occasions now in which a judge has no choice but to decide between two such competing versions without the benefit of any more reliable evidence. But it seems to be a piece of common human self-deception, endorsed by appellate courts, that to see and hear witnesses giving competing oral versions enables a trier of fact to decide which of them is true or at least substantially improves the prospect of doing so. Experiments over more than 30 years have shown this to be false; that we would be at least as well off if we heard but did not see the witnesses giving evidence and possibly even if we neither saw nor heard them but simply read a transcript of their evidence.[30]

30 O Wellborn, 'Demeanor' (1991) 76 Cornell Law Review 1075; J Blumenthal, 'A Wipe of the Hands, a Lick of the Lips: the Validity of Demeanor Evidence in Assessing Witness Credibility' (1993) 72 Nebraska Law Review 1175; see also C Fife-Schaw, 'The Influence of Witness Appearance and Demeanour on Witness Credibility: A Theoretical Framework' (1995) 35 Medicine, Science and the Law 107; Kapardis, *Psychology and Law*, 1997, Cambridge: Cambridge Law Press 211–15.

There are, I think, two reasons why the unreliability of oral evidence and the difficulty in assessing its credibility are rarely discussed. One is a pragmatic one; in many cases judges have no option but to decide a case on oral evidence, sometimes competing oral evidence and they have to do the best they can. The other is the element of self-deception to which I referred; a belief that oral evidence is more reliable than in fact it is and that some of us have the capacity, from seeing and hearing a witness, to tell whether she or he is telling the truth. Both of these factors will diminish in the foreseeable future. The practical necessity to which I referred will arise less frequently because of the rapid increase in the use of technology and the self-deception will dissipate or at least diminish as the unreliability of oral evidence and the inability of people to assess the veracity of witnesses is more widely demonstrated.

3 An increased public perception of the choices which judges make and some consequences for the judiciary

(a) Some causes of the increased perception

There are, I think, three main causes. The first is an increased frankness of judges, mainly about the fact that we make choices but also, up to a point, about the extent of those choices. The second is a trend in substantive law towards broader principles. I have already mentioned the increasing prevalence of concepts such as reasonableness, fairness and conscionability in statute law. But the same trend is evident in judge made law. And the third cause, which unlike the others is beyond our control, is an increasing trend by others, especially academic lawyers, to find underlying personal values in our judgments. I shall say something briefly about each of those.

Greater frankness by judges

The nature of our system has been such that judges have always made choices at two levels. They have always necessarily made choices in finding facts, in categorizing facts in legal terms and in deciding legal issues which involve the weighing of factual considerations. For example, the exercise of judicial choice could mean the difference between a finding of negligence and no negligence; the imposition of a custodial sentence or a non-custodial one; the granting or withholding of an injunction; and the granting of custody of children of a dissolved union to their mother or their father. And at a higher, generally appellate level judges have always made choices in the development of the common law to meet changing circumstances and values and, more recently, in finding implied rights in our Constitution.

Most judges have long recognized the existence of choices which they make and occasionally some have spoken of them openly.[31] Lord Reid's famous 'Aladdin's Cave' speech,[32] for example, was nearly 30 years ago. On the whole, we remain reluctant to admit and perhaps even contemplate the extent of those choices and, particularly, the possibility that they may be influenced by idiosyncratic predilections. However the extent to which these questions are being discussed is increasing.

Broader legal principles

In the areas of torts, contract and personal relationships, concepts of reasonableness, fairness and conscionableness have already unified and expanded areas of the common law[33] and that trend will continue. A similar trend by legislatures[34] has conferred increased discretionary powers on judges and that will also continue. The statement of the law in broader unifying principles both broadens the choices and reveals them more clearly.

There has been a recent tendency, by some politicians and journalists, unfamiliar with the way in which judges develop the common law, to exaggerate the extent of those choices, and the frequency with which the opportunity to make them arises, particularly in the area commonly called judicial lawmaking. As judges know, there are important limitations upon judicial lawmaking, some self-imposed, others not. The most important of these is the need to maintain certainty and an internal consistency in the law.[35] For that reason, when judges develop the law, they generally do so incrementally and by analogy;[36] they endeavour to do so by reference to enduring community values,[37] not passing attitudes or prejudices or their own predilections; and many of these values already inhere in the legal system.[38]

More analyses of judges' underlying values

There is a third factor, beyond our control, which may result in a further increase in this public perception and in its further distortion. That is an increase in the empirical analysis by academic writers of judgments of courts with a view, amongst other things, to ascertaining the underlying values of

---

31 For example, the Hon Sir Anthony Mason, 'The Judge as Law-maker' (1996) 3 JCULR 1 at 12–14; Justice W Rehnquist, 'Remarks on the Process of Judging' (1992) 49 Washington and Lee L Rev 263; Justice Kirby, 'Judging: Reflections on the Moment of Decision' (1999) 18(1) Aust Bar Rev 4 at 19, 21.

32 Lord Reid, 'The Judge as Law Maker' (1972) 12 J Soc Pub T L 22.

33 Hon M McHugh, 'The Judicial Method' (1999) 73 ALJ 37 at 41; Hon Sir Anthony Mason, 'The Judge as Law-Maker' (1996) 3 JCULR 1 at 3, 'Contract, Good Faith and Equitable Standards in Fair Dealing' (2000) 116 LQR 66 at 94.

34 See fn 4–fn 8.

35 *Dietrich v The Queen* (1992) 177 CLR 292 at 320; *Breen v Williams* (1996) 186 CLR 71 at 115.

36 See fn 3.

37 *Dietrich v The Queen, supra* fn 21 at 319; *Mabo v Queensland (No 2) supra* fn 21.

38 Hon M McHugh 'The Judicial Method' (1999) 73 ALJ 37 at 46.

judges which influence those judgments. That has not occurred, at least to any substantial degree, in Australia. As long ago as 1972, Professor Blackshield conducted such an analysis of the High Court of Australia between 1964 and 1969.[39] It was a very thorough and revealing analysis of judgments of the then members of the High Court. But there has been very little here since then.[40]

However in the United States this is now a fertile field of study, called Jurimetrics,[41] and the sophistication of modern computer assisted statistics on this topic can be seen from recent studies.[42] Moreover the extent of literature on this topic in the United States has grown substantially in recent years.[43] Of course United States courts, particularly the United States Supreme Court, lend themselves to such analyses for three reasons. The first is that United States judges, when appointed, are generally openly either Democrat or Republican and although not all have been true to those values in their judgments, most have. Secondly the United States Supreme Court sits all nine judges in almost all cases and maintains a fairly stable membership over long periods, thereby providing an adequate sample. And thirdly that court sits in a high proportion of human rights cases where the exercise of value judgment may less readily be.[44]

Notwithstanding the difference between the United States and Australian courts in the first and third of these respects I think an increase in analyses of this kind is inevitable. It has occurred recently in England where one might have least expected it.[45] Moreover advances in information technology are making such analyses easier to do and more reliable. They can perform a useful purpose. There is, however, a risk of exaggeration of what such studies do in fact show.

(b) Some of its consequences

I turn now to three consequences for the judiciary of this increased public perception. The first is an increased need to publicly explain our role. The

39 A Blackshield, 'Quantitative Analysis: The High Court of Australia, 1964–1969' (1972) 3 Lawasia 1.

40 See, however, G Lehmann, 'Income Tax Judgments of the Barwick Court' (1983) 9 Mon LR 115 at 149.

41 There is, for example, a programme on the subject at Michigan State University titled 'The Program for Law and Judicial Politics'.

42 See, for example, (1999) 113 Harv L Rev 400ff.

43 See, for example, Revesz, 'Environmental Regulations, Ideology and the DC Circuit' 83 VAL Rev 1717 (1992); Cross and Tiller, 'Judicial Partisanship and Obedience to Legal Doctrine: Whistleblowing on the Federal Courts of Appeals' 107 Yale LJ 2155 (1998); Sisk, Heise and Morriss, 'Charting the Influences on the Judicial Mind: An Empirical Study of Judicial Reasoning' 73 NYU L Rev 1377 (1998). See also Sisk, 'Judges are Human, Too' (2000) 83 Judicature 178.

44 The first two of these factors were referred to by Professor Blackshield in his article.

45 D Robertson, 'Chapter 2 – A Statistical Analysis of Judicial Discretion', in *Judicial Discretion in the House of Lords,* Oxford, 1998; and see the review of this by Lord Justice Sedley in (1999) 58 Cambridge LJ 627.

second is the need to reduce the risk of idiosyncratic views influencing judgments. And the third is the need to reduce, if possible, an increased risk of political appointments being made because of this perception.

The need to publicly explain our role

Both the Australian Institute of Judicial Administration and the Judicial Conference of Australia have taken some steps to achieve this.[46] But much more needs to be done. In particular the public need to be better informed of the way in which judges arrive at decisions; of the choices which judges make in arriving at decisions and, in particular, of the limitations upon those choices. And the public should be informed of the extent to which, by the public nature of the judicial process and the obligation to give reasons, judges are accountable for their decisions. As some of you may know, I have spoken on this topic at some length previously[47] and I shall not repeat myself here.

The need to eliminate or at least substantially reduce personal views in our judgments

It is easy to exaggerate the extent to which our judgments may be influenced by idiosyncratic views. But we must accept that, on occasions, there is a risk that judges will mistake their own moral predilections, affected as they must be by their sex, race, religion, socio-economic background, and sometimes even political views, for the 'moral imperatives which, by broad consensus, enjoy recognition and compliance'.[48] Those occasions and the breadth of choice are both increased by the trend, referred to earlier, towards stating legal standards in broader terms. There are, it seems to me, at least two things which can be done to reduce that risk.

The first is for judges to be more explicit about the real reasons for their decisions. Judicial reasons must be and be seen to be a public justification for a decision. This means that the real reasons for decision must be given in terms which are reasonably intelligible to non-lawyers. Judges must remember that judgments are not written primarily for the legal education of their peers and others but to explain why they reached one result rather than another. And if that involves making a choice then that choice should be stated and the reasons given for making it one way rather than another.

That is not an easy task for most judges. In the first place we often remain reluctant to admit to the choices which we make even when we advert to them. And secondly our training in the 'strict and complete legalism'[49] of Sir Owen Dixon has tended to diminish our own capacity to perceive the choices

46 See, in particular, S Parker, B Petrie-Rapar, 'Judicial Independence in Australia – Briefing Materials for the Community' <www.law.monash.edu.au/JCA/com.html>.

47 'Judicial Reticence' (1998) 8 JJA 88 at 93ff.

48 Sir Gerard Brennan, 'Commercial Law and Morality' (1989) 17 Melb Univ L Rev 100 at 101–02.

49 Swearing in of Sir Owen Dixon as Chief Justice (1952) 85 CLR xiv; Concerning Judicial Method (1956) 29 ALJ 468.

which we make. This then brings me to the second thing which I think can be done to reduce that risk.

We must be able to devise ways which will increase our own perception of the choices we make and why we make them. And we must be able to be made aware of the extent to which those choices are motivated by idiosyncratic moral predilections rather than by moral imperatives which, by broad consensus, enjoy recognition and compliance. To the extent that we can be made aware of these we are better able to guard against their influence.

I do not mean to suggest by this that there will always be some uniformly correct answer in every legal case. In many there will be room for legitimate differences. In the end we must all, as judges, make up our own minds for we have all sworn to do justice according to law to the best of our ability. But we cannot rationally do that if we do not consider and understand views other than our own and why we hold a view contrary to or different from those.

I have already mentioned analyses by others of our judgments. These we may find both intrusive and embarrassing. But they may reveal to us predilections which we did not know we had or had not fully adverted to; or at least enable us better to reassess our own values and how they affect our judgments.

In the United States the National Judicial College runs courses aimed at teaching judges how their personalities and environments affect their decisions.[50] We should investigate the possibility of running similar courses here.

Each of these consequences of the greater public perception of the choices which judges make arises within the judicial process itself and is, plainly, one which the judiciary must itself address. The third consequence, however, arises from outside that process and what, if anything, we as judges should do about it is a matter on which minds will plainly differ. It is the increased likelihood of judicial appointments being made on the basis of sex, race, perceived political allegiance or on some other extraneous basis rather than on merit.

The danger of judicial appointments on some basis other than merit

There is no doubt that such appointments have been made throughout our judicial history. Fortunately they have been rare. However they have been increasing lately and I believe that the risk of their being made is increasing. One reason for this increase is, I believe, an exaggerated perception of the choices which judges make. That exaggerated perception gives rise to a number of misconceptions. One of the most common of these is that benches should be more representative.

---

50 Arrendondo & Ors, 'To Make a Good Decision' (1988) 27 Judges Jo 23. See also J Kennedy Jr, 'Personality Type and Judicial Decision Making' (1998) 37 Judges Jo 5.

That is one reason why it is so important for us as judges to educate the public, and, in particular, those elements among the media and politicians who call for a more 'representative' judiciary, about what our role is and what it is not. It is not to decide cases in accordance with our own idiosyncratic notions of justice; it is to decide them according to law, that is, by reference to legal principle and doctrine; and in all but a few cases that involves very little choice. In order to achieve that judges should not be or be seen to be representing any particular interest, whether of sex, ethnicity, religion or politics. Impartial justice is the antithesis of representative justice.[51] On the contrary it requires the best legal minds capable of applying correct legal principles to the facts as found. A failure to understand all of this may explain why 'merit' is often used by politicians and the media but never defined by them. It means character, temperament, legal ability and relevant experience; and 'appointment on merit' means the appointment of the person, out of all possible candidates, who best has those qualities.

Appointments made on a more representative basis, rather than on merit alone, will result, not in a broader based and consequently better judiciary, but in a mediocre one. And a mediocre judiciary is, of course, a weak one.

That is not to say that, ideally, the judiciary should not be more broadly based than it is now. There is undoubted merit, in my opinion, in the view that it is undesirable that the judiciary should be comprised, as it is at present, mainly of middle-aged to old males of British or Irish descent.

Unfortunately, however, that is an almost inevitable result of the times in which we have lived. Almost all law graduates in my Year were males of British or Irish descent. That continued to be so for at least two decades. The result is that the vast majority of lawyers in this country of sufficient ability and experience for appointment to the Bench fall into that category. Of course that is changing. For example, there are now at least as many women graduating in law from our universities as there are men. And no-one of intelligence could doubt that, ideally, the judiciary should be comprised of women and men in approximately equal numbers, no doubt varying in proportions in accordance with the appointment of the best candidate at all times. Relative intelligence or aptitude of the sexes is simply not an issue. But relevant experience is. And the question is: is it worth sacrificing the quality of the judiciary in order to accelerate what I believe will occur inevitably over the next few decades?

More generally, however, political appointments are a problem we must confront. The question is whether we ought to do something about them. We can, I think, reduce the risk of them being made. But we can only do that if we are prepared to go public when they are made and that is something which we

51 The Hon JJ Doyle 'The Eighth Robert Harris Oration: The Judiciary and the Community' (1999) 18 Aust Bar Rev 95 at 100; The Rt Hon Sir Harry Gibbs, Inaugural Oration on the opening of the Supreme Court Library Rare Books Room, Brisbane, 11 February 2000.

have so far resisted doing, at least partly out of deference to the feelings of the appointee.

I should preface my remarks about what can be done by saying that I believe that the right to appoint judges should remain in the executive government. I doubt the wisdom of judicial commissions making rather than merely recommending judicial appointments.[52] But I think that two simple steps would at least reduce the risk of appointments being made otherwise than on merit; in other words political appointments.

The first is the formation of a committee of persons, in respect of each court, who are best able to judge the relevant character, temperament, ability and experience of possible candidates for appointment to that court. A possible composition of such committee might be the Chief Justice of the court and if the appointment is to a specialist division, the head of that division, the President of the Bar Association (if not a candidate for appointment), the President of the Law Society (if not a candidate for appointment) and an appointee from the Deans of the local law schools (also if not a candidate for appointment).[53] That committee should, when a vacancy occurs in the court, recommend to the government a panel of names, perhaps of five or seven, or even more, of possible candidates whom the committee would recommend for appointment to the court and the order in which they would recommend them.

The second step involves advising the government that if it chooses an appointee from outside the list of recommended candidates the committee may choose to publish that fact. As is, perhaps, self-evident, this step is designed to keep governments honest; to avoid the appointment of candidates who are insufficiently qualified for appointment, but politically acceptable. It should never be necessary to publish the names of those whom the committee recommended. It should be sufficient in the event of an inappropriate appointment to publish the fact that the committee recommended five or seven sufficiently qualified persons, as the case may be, and that the government chose to go outside those recommended names.

4 Conclusion

Predicting the future is fraught with danger. I have attempted to avoid or at least reduce that danger by taking two current trends, albeit not fully

52 There are, however, many who favour appointment by an independent commission of judges and lawyers; see, for example the International Bar Association's Code of Minimum Standards of Judicial Independence, par 3a.

53 There is talk, from time to time, by non lawyers, of any such committee having, as one or more of its members, 'community representatives'; but if the criteria for appointment are, as I think, character, temperament, ability and experience, community representatives would be unlikely to know anything of the character or temperament of any possible candidates and they would not be competent to judge either their ability or relevant experience.

recognized by many, and assuming, as I do with some confidence, that they will continue. As I mentioned at the outset they are related: both are products of the information age and with it the emergence of more highly educated, sophisticated and questioning communities. Both, if fully understood and properly managed, will lead to fairer and more efficient civil justice systems.

But we cannot ensure that the public fully understands these trends, nor can we manage them properly, unless we recognize them for what they are and openly discuss them. And here, I believe, lies a problem. We are a conservative profession. We do not like change and we tend to resist it or ignore it when it is in fact occurring.

Convergence is already occurring. We must discuss among ourselves and with our colleagues from other systems how best that can be managed so as to select the best from each system for a fairer and more economical civil justice system.

Orality is declining. We should not bemoan this but welcome the greater reliability of evidence and efficiency of justice delivery which is also a consequence of the causes of that decline.

The public, led by elements in the media and among politicians, have passed from thinking that judges mechanically apply the law to facts as if it were a mathematical exercise, to thinking that we exercise broad choices in almost all of our decision making. Both views represent gross distortions of our role. Our concern must now be to correct the latter view whilst ensuring that idiosyncratic opinions are, as nearly as possible, eliminated from our judgments. And we should ensure, as best we can, that false perceptions of our role do not lead to the appointment of other than the very best qualified candidates.

My purpose today is to stimulate some discussion of these trends. Only by doing so can we hope to ensure the best possible result from them, not for ourselves of course, but for those who come to us seeking justice according to law.

Brisbane City Council v Warren Bolton Consulting Pty Ltd (Case No D2001-0047 WIPO)

Annelies Moens

A recent decision on a domain name dispute involving the complainant, Brisbane City Council (BCC) was handed down on 7 May 2001, by a sole WIPO arbitrator under the Uniform Domain Name Dispute Resolution Policy (Uniform Policy). The domain name in dispute was www.brisbanecity.com. The complaint was filed at the beginning of 2001 by BCC, a body corporate. The respondent, Warren Bolton Consulting Pty Ltd (WBC), is a company situated in Rockhampton. BCC did not receive an arbitral award in its favour. The decision impacts upon the policy surrounding protection of geographical place names as domain names. The decision can officially be found at arbiter.wipo.int/domains/decisions/html/2001/d2001-0047.html and ironically unofficially at www.brisbanecity.com.

BCC is a well-known city council in Australia and is also one of the largest councils in the world. Its assets are valued in excess of AU$14 billion. BCC also has extensive intellectual property protection over its assets. Of significance to the dispute, BCC owns 28 Australian registered trademarks with nine pending trademark applications (at the time of the decision). Four of its registered trademarks and trademark applications include the words 'Brisbane City'. Two of its registered trademarks, numbers 510495 and 510496 have disclaimers, which state that, 'Registration of this trademark shall give no right to the exclusive use of the ... words Brisbane City'. In its ordinary dealings, BCC uses the words 'Brisbane City' in conjunction with its registered Australian trademarks. BCC also has a corporate logo containing the words 'Brisbane City', which it has used extensively for more than 15 years.

WBC registered the domain name www.brisbanecity.com on 21 April 1999 and advertised it for sale at US$25,000 on www.greatdomains.com. Since WBC was registering in the .com domain name, it was not required to hold any trademarks for its chosen domain names. WBC has registered other domain names, such as perthcity.com, canberracity.com, hobartcity.com, brisbanelaw.com etc, with the intention (according to WBC) of using these sites to build a network of portals to service the capital cities of Australia. At the time of the decision, WBC had not implemented its plan to build such a portal network.

BCC contended that in accordance with paragraph 4(a) of the Uniform Policy:

(i) the disputed domain name was identical or confusingly similar to a trademark or service mark in which the complainant had rights; and

(ii) WBC had no rights or legitimate interests in respect of the domain name; and

(iii) the disputed domain name had been registered and was being used in bad faith

For BCC to have succeeded in the action the above three elements had to be found to exist.

Under (i), BCC contended that the disputed domain name was identical to its alleged unregistered trademark, Brisbane City and that it was confusingly similar to its registered trademarks, Brisbane City Works and its name Brisbane City Council. Under (ii), BCC contended that WBC's business had no connection with the words, 'Brisbane City'. Indeed WBC's business is in Rockhampton, 745km north of Brisbane, Australia. Under (iii), BCC contended that WBC registered the disputed domain name for the purposes of selling the name to a third party, along with all the other 90 or so domain names listed. WBC advertised these names for sale on www.ozdomainsales.com.

The arbitrator focused on WBC's argument that BCC had no trademark rights in respect of the words, 'Brisbane City', therefore BCC failed to satisfy paragraph 4(a)(i) of the Uniform Policy. BCC contended that the disputed domain name was identical to its alleged unregistered trademark, 'Brisbane City'. The arbitrator found that the alleged unregistered trademark was not a trademark to which the Uniform Policy applied. Under the Uniform Policy, an unregistered trademark is still within its scope, so long as it functions as a trademark. In other words, 'the unregistered mark must perform the function of distinguishing the goods or services of one person in trade from the goods or services of any other person in trade'. In the opinion of the arbitrator, the evidence did not show that the alleged unregistered trademark distinguished the goods or services of BCC, but rather that it was merely descriptive of a geographical location, ie: Brisbane City. This type of a conclusion very much depends on the facts of the case, because in some previous cases, geographic names have been found to constitute trademarks. This occurred in WIPO case D2001-0001 (portofhamina.com), where the Panel found that the mark had 'acquired distinctiveness and become established in the meaning of the Trademarks Act as a trademark/service mark relating to services originating from the City of Hamina/Port of Hamina. Consequently, Port of Hamina is a trademark/service mark to which the Complainant has rights'.

With respect to BCC's assertion that 'Brisbane City' was confusingly similar to its registered trademark 'Brisbane City Works', the arbitrator did not agree, since the registered trademark was not visually similar with the words 'Brisbane City'. BCC's trademark registration consisted of an image of a diamond indented by three triangles, with the words 'Brisbane City Works' around the diamond image.

In relation to BCC's assertion that 'Brisbane City' was confusingly similar to its name, Brisbane City Council, the arbitrator noted that the Uniform Policy, at this stage, does not apply to the name of the complainant, though this is under review. BCC, however, relied on its extensive use of its corporate logo with the words 'Brisbane City' to support its assertion. However, the arbitrator did not find that extensive use of its corporate logo, which could be considered a trademark at common law, extended to having obtained common law rights in respect of the words 'Brisbane City', since on the facts the words did not perform the function of a trademark. Since all three sections of paragraph 4(a) of the Uniform Policy had to be met, the arbitrator did not go on to consider whether WBC had rights or legitimate interests in respect of the domain name; and whether the disputed domain name was being used in bad faith.

It is likely that BCC would have satisfied 4(a)(ii) and (iii) of the Uniform Policy. Paragraph 4(c) of the Uniform Policy lists legitimate rights and interests, which WBC could have pointed to, if there was evidence, to counter BCC's assertion under 4(a)(ii) that WBC had no rights or legitimate interests in respect of the domain name. Paragraph 4(c) of the Uniform Policy states:

> (i) before any notice to you [the respondent] of the dispute, your use of, or demonstrable preparations to use, the domain name or a name corresponding to the domain name in connection with a bona fide offering of goods or services; or
>
> (ii) you (as an individual, business or other organisation) have been commonly known by the domain name, even if you have acquired no trademark or service mark rights; or
>
> (iii) you are making a legitimate non-commercial or fair use of the domain name, without intent for commercial gain to misleadingly divert consumers or to tarnish the trademark or service mark at issue.

WBC had been using the disputed domain name for less than a month and its business was in no way connected to Brisbane City. WBC is a consultancy company in local government located in Rockhampton. The evidence also revealed that WBC intended to sell the domain name, therefore it is unlikely they had legitimate rights or interests in the disputed domain name.

Paragraph 4(b) of the Uniform Policy lists factors, which tend to show that under 4(a)(iii) the disputed domain name had been registered and used in bad faith. These include, amongst others, 'circumstances indicating that you [the respondent] have registered or you have acquired the domain name primarily for the purpose of selling, renting or otherwise transferring the domain name registration to the complainant who is the owner of the trademark or service mark or to a competitor of that complainant, for valuable consideration in excess of your documented out-of-pocket costs directly related to the domain name'. Brisbanecity.com was listed for sale at $US 25,000, along with several other domain names, hence BCC would most likely have been able to prove 4(a)(iii).

There have been a small number of other recent Australian decisions involving disputed geographical domain names, including brisbane.com, which BCC also lost. This was a three-panel decision decided in favour of the respondent, Joyce Russ Advertising. The text of this decision was unavailable at the time of writing. Another recent Australian decision, this time decided in favour of the trademark holder, Daydream Island Resort Investments P/L (DIR Investments) was handed down on 12 January 2001. The domain name in dispute was daydreamisland.com. The respondent was Alessandro Sorbello. The decision was made under the Uniform Policy, but was submitted through eresolution and can be found at: www.eresolution.ca/services/dnd/decisions/0586.htm.

The complainant, DIR Investments had four registered Australian trademarks in respect of the name Daydream Island. The registration, as in the brisbanecity.com case also had a disclaimer, stating that the rights of the trademark registration did not extend to exclusive use of the words 'Daydream Island'. The arbitrator in this case did not think this was fatal to DIR Investments' case. The arbitrator found that DIR Investments had established common law trademark rights in the name 'Daydream Island Resort' and that the disputed domain name was confusingly similar to its registered and unregistered trademarks. Elements 4(ii) and 4(iii) were also found to have been satisfied in this case.

These cases show that domain name rights in geographical place names are subject to the facts of the case and their interpretation. However, a recent Interim Report of the Second WIPO Internet Domain Name Process of April 12, 2001 made recommendations with respect to geographical place names. Chapter 5 of the Interim Report entitled, 'Geographical Indications, Indications of Source and other Geographical Terms' (wipo2.wipo.int/process2/rfc/rfc3/report.html) discusses the protection of names of places with countries in the gTLDs. In that chapter it is recommended at paragraph 278 that 'the consideration of any measures to protect the names of places in the gTLDs, at this stage, should be restricted to the names of: (i) countries; and (ii) administratively recognized regions and municipalities within countries'. It also suggests at paragraph 283, a new possible cause of action framed in the same language of paragraph 4(a) of the Uniform Policy, to the effect that:

> The registration of a domain name shall be considered to be abusive and the competent national authorities shall be entitled to its cancellation or transfer when all of the following conditions are met:

(i) The domain name is identical or confusingly similar to the name of a country or of an administratively recognized region or municipality within a country; and

(ii) The registrant of the domain name has no rights or legitimate interests in respect of the domain name; and

(iii) The domain name has been registered and is used in bad faith.

Accordingly, in the future an administratively recognised region or municipality, such as BCC may be more successful in an action seeking transfer of a geographical place domain name from a respondent.

Addendum: on 3 September 2001, the Final Report of the Second WIPO Internet Domain Name Process was released. A decision was taken by the WIPO Member States at their meeting from 24 September to 3 October 2001, to subject the Final Report to a comprehensive analysis to the Standing Committee on the Law of Trademarks, Industrial Designs and Geographical Indications, which will meet in two Special Sessions for this purpose.

Homosexual Rights and the Free Movement of Persons in the European Union

Andrew Stumer

Introduction

The European Union[1] was created with the primary goal of promoting economic integration and removing barriers to free trade. However, in recent years there has been increasing pressure on the Union to take a more active role in advancing the social conditions of European citizens. The purpose of this paper is to examine the role of the European Union in the advancement of equality rights for lesbians and gay men. Part I of the paper examines the measures adopted by the institutions of the European Union for the advancement and protection of homosexual rights. Part II describes the domestic laws of the Member States in relation to decriminalization of homosexuality, prohibition of anti-homosexual discrimination in employment, and recognition of same-sex partnerships. Part III outlines the relevant jurisprudence of the European Court of Human Rights and demonstrates the connection between those decisions and European Union law. Part IV is a summary of the case law emanating from the European Court of Justice relating to the recognition of equality rights for homosexuals. It will be shown that by analysing homosexual rights under an economic framework, the European Court of Justice has the potential to promote those rights, unfettered by the moral arguments that have traditionally impeded homosexual equality.

Part I: European Union measures to protect homosexual rights

The population of the European Union is approximately 365 million people and, by some estimates, this includes 80 million lesbians, gays and bisexuals.[2] Thus, the unequal treatment of gay men and lesbians has the potential to limit

---

1 The Member States of the European Union are Austria, Belgium, Denmark, Finland, France, Germany, Greece, Ireland, Italy, Luxembourg, the Netherlands, Portugal, Spain, Sweden and the United Kingdom. The major treaties of the European Union are: European Coal and Steel Community (ECSC) Treaty (1951), European Atomic Energy Community (EAEC) Treaty (1958), European Economic Community (EEC) Treaty (1958), Treaty on European Union (TEU) (1992), Treaty of Amsterdam (1997). The EEC Treaty was renamed the European Community (EC) Treaty when the TEU came into force.

2 Peter Tatchell, *Europe in the Pink: Lesbian and Gay Equality in the New Europe*, 1992, London: Macmillan, 15.

the European Union's goals of full economic integration,[3] harmonization of social systems,[4] and close co-operation in employment, labour law, and working conditions.[5] In recognition of this the European Parliament has made a number of statements relating to the equal treatment of homosexuals. In 1984, the European Parliament made a statement deploring 'all forms of discrimination based on an individual's sexual tendencies' and asked Member States to take action to stop legal and social anti-homosexual discrimination.[6] In 1989, the European Parliament reiterated its support for equal treatment of homosexuals by proposing that the European Social Charter ensure the rights of all workers to equal treatment regardless of sexual orientation. Similarly, in 1994, a resolution was passed requesting Member States to enact legislation allowing homosexuals to have access to 'marriage or an equivalent legal framework.'[7] However, the European Commission and the Council of the European Union took no action to support these statements because, in the words of Commission President Jaques Delors, they had 'no powers to intervene in possible cases of discrimination by member states against sexual minorities'.[8]

This position has been altered by the most recent attempt to eliminate discrimination based on sexual orientation, contained in the Amsterdam Treaty of 1997. Article 13 of the Amsterdam Treaty states that:

> [T]he Council, acting unanimously on a proposal from the Commission and after consulting the European Parliament, may take appropriate action to combat discrimination based on sex, racial or ethnic origin, religion or belief, disability, age *or sexual orientation*. (Emphasis added.)[9]

This provision has immense significance because it is the first official action taken by the European Union to prohibit discrimination based on sexual orientation throughout all the Member States. All previous attempts to prevent discrimination have been contingent upon action by the legislatures of the Member States to enact their own provisions protecting homosexual rights.

---

3 Article 2 EC Treaty.

4 Article 136 EC Treaty (Article 117 EEC Treaty). Discussed in Kees Waaldjik, 'The Legal Situation in the Member States' in Andrew Clapham and Kees Waaldjik (eds), *Homosexuality: A European Community Issue: Essays on Lesbian and Gay Rights in European Law and Policy*, 1993, Boston: Martinus Nijhoff, 75.

5 Article 137 EC Treaty (Article 118 EEC Treaty). Discussed in Tatchell, *supra*, note 2, 55.

6 Laurence R Helfer, 'Lesbian and Gay Rights as Human Rights: Strategies for a United Europe' (1991) 32 Virginia Journal of International Law: 157 at 184.

7 Leslie Goransson, 'International Trends in Same-Sex Marriage' in Robert Cabaj and David Purcell, (eds), 1998, *On the Road to Same-Sex Marriage: A Supportive Guide to Psychological, Political and Legal Issues*, 1998, San Francisco: Jossey-Bass, 176.

8 Qtd in Tatchell, *supra*, note 2, 21. At the time, this statement was correct since there was no Treaty provision giving the Community 'competence to enact a global measure interdicting discrimination against lesbians and gay men.' Andrew Clapham and Joseph Weiler, 'Lesbians and Gay Men in the European Community Legal Order' in Clapham & Waaldijk, *supra*, note 31.

9 Article 13 EC Treaty (as amended by Treaty of Amsterdam).

However, Article 13 of the Amsterdam Treaty 'is only a framework for passing laws in the future; it does not constitute a current prohibition on discrimination based on sexual orientation'.[10] A directive drafted by the Council of the European Union to establish a general basis for equal treatment in employment and profession was circulated in 1999 but as yet has not been implemented.[11] The limitation on Article 13 is that, in order to implement prohibitions on anti-homosexual discrimination, the Council must act unanimously. This means that one Member State can act unilaterally to prevent the Council from passing provisions prohibiting discrimination. Given the hostility of some Member States to homosexual rights, the unanimity requirement could make it difficult to pass effective measures, or even to pass any measures at all.[12]

Part II: The status of homosexual rights in the Member States

Domestic legislation for the advancement or protection of homosexual rights can be divided into three categories: (a) decriminalization of homosexual acts; (b) prohibition of employment discrimination based on sexual orientation; and (c) recognition of same-sex partnerships.[13] In each of these areas, there is considerable diversity within the legal systems of the Member States.

(a) Decriminalization

Until the 1960s and 1970s, private homosexual acts between men were regarded as criminal in a number of Member States. Legislation specifically

10 Heather Hunt, 'Diversity and the European Union: Grant v SWT, The Treaty of Amsterdam, and the Free Movement of Persons' (1999) 27 Denver Journal of International Law and Policy: 633 at 651. See also Angela Broughton, 'International Employment' (1998) 32 International Lawyer: 303 at 305.

11 See Caroline Forder, 'European Models of Domestic Partnership Laws: the Field of Choice' (2000) 17 Canadian Journal of Family Law: 371 at 401.

12 For example, England has historically been hostile towards homosexual relationships. At present, Section 28 Local Government Act (1988) prohibits local authorities from intentionally promoting homosexuality as a 'pretended family relationship'. The Labour Government supports removal of that section. Section 11(c) Matrimonial Causes Act 1973 (UK) makes a marriage void if it is not respectively male and female. See Jorge Martin, 'English Polygamy Law and the Danish Registered Partnership Act: A Case for the Consistent Treatment of Foreign Polygamous Marriages and Danish Same-Sex Marriages in England' (1994) 27 Cornell International Law Journal: 419 at 428–30.

13 Same sex partnership should be distinguished from the more limited concept of cohabitation protection. Cohabitation protection regulates property rights between couples, whether they are same sex or opposite sex. In Canada, the concept derives from unjust enrichment, unconscionable conduct or reasonable expectation: *Rathwell v Rathwell* [1978] 2 Supreme Court Reports 436; *Peter v Beblow* [1993] 1 Supreme Court Reports 980. In some European countries the principle is recognized by statute: see Hungarian Civil Code, s 578/G; Swedish Cohabitees (Joint Home) Act 1987; Catalonian Stable Couples Act (Spain); Belgian Statutory Cohabitation Act of 29 October 1998 in force 1 January 2000: See Forder, *supra*, note 11, 375–84.

prohibiting male homosexuality was enacted in England and Germany as early as the 16th century. These statutes did not deal with homosexual acts between women and, in the same way, anti-homosexual legislation in most Member States never addressed this issue.[14] The first country to decriminalize homosexuality was France, where the Napoleonic Penal Code of 1810 was drafted without including the offence of homosexual activity.[15] The French influence extended into Belgium, Luxembourg, the Netherlands and some parts of Italy, where similar penal codes were adopted. During the 20th century, each of these countries introduced higher ages of consent for homosexual sex; the Netherlands in 1911, France in 1942, Belgium in 1965 and Luxembourg in 1971.[16]

Homosexual acts were decriminalized in Denmark in 1930, Sweden in 1944, Portugal in 1945 and Greece in 1950. At these times, Denmark, Sweden and Greece effected only a partial decriminalization because they enacted higher ages of consent for homosexual sex. In England, the process of law reform began with the Wolfenden Report, which recommended the decriminalization of private homosexual acts.[17] In response to this report, the British Parliament passed the Sexual Offences Act 1967, decriminalizing private homosexual acts, but setting the age of consent at 21 years.[18] The prohibition on homosexuality was lifted in East Germany in 1968, West Germany in 1969, Austria and Finland in 1971 and Scotland in 1980.[19] Austria, Greece and England still retain different ages of consent for homosexual and heterosexual intercourse, although there has been pressure for change since the decision of the European Commission of Human Rights in *Sutherland v United Kingdom*.[20]

(b) Anti-discrimination

In 1975 and 1976, the Council of the European Communities adopted Directives requiring Member States to enact legislation prohibiting employment discrimination on the basis of gender.[21] As a result, all fifteen Member States currently have equal opportunity legislation preventing sex

---

14 Kees Waaldjik, 'Civil Developments: Patterns of Reform in the Legal Position of Same Sex Partners in Europe' (2000) 17 Canadian Journal of Family Law: 62 at 66–67.

15 *Ibid*, 68.

16 *Ibid.*

17 *Report of the Committee on Homosexual Offences and Prostitution*, 1957 (Wolfenden Report): cited in Clarice B Rabinowitz, 'Sodomy Laws and the European Convention on Human Rights' (1995) 21 Brooklyn Journal of International Law: 425 at 431.

18 The Sexual Offences Act 1967 amended the Sexual Offences Act 1957. The decriminalization of homosexuality took effect in England and Wales, but not in Scotland and Northern Ireland.

19 Waaldjik, *supra*, note 14, 71.

20 *Sutherland v United Kingdom*, No 25186/94 (1997) 24 European Human Rights Reports 22. See *infra*, note 66, and accompanying text.

21 Council Directive 75/117; Council Directive 76/207.

discrimination. In 1987, Denmark introduced the first provisions prohibiting anti-homosexual discrimination in employment, when it amended its equal opportunity legislation to include sexual orientation as a prohibited ground of discrimination.[22] In a similar fashion, discrimination on the basis of sexual orientation was prohibited in Sweden in 1987, the Netherlands in 1992, Ireland in 1993, and Finland and Spain in 1995.[23] In addition, the Constitutions of the Netherlands and Finland prohibit discrimination on the basis of race, sex 'or any other ground whatsoever'. This could be interpreted as an implicit constitutional prohibition on anti-homosexual discrimination.[24] Other Member States do not have constitutional or legislative prohibitions on employment discrimination on the basis of sexual orientation.

(c) Same-sex partnerships

The first Member State to recognise same-sex partnerships in law was Denmark where, on 7 June 1989, the Danish Parliament passed a law allowing registered partnerships for two persons of the same-sex.[25] Public registration extends to same-sex couples all the legal rights enjoyed by married couples, with the exception of adoption, *in vitro* fertilization, artificial insemination and church weddings.[26] The Swedish Registered Partnership Act,[27] which came into effect in 1995, grants marriage rights to same-sex couples equivalent to the rights accorded to married heterosexual couples, but with the same limitations as in Denmark. In addition, Sweden recognises the relationships of unregistered same-sex couples, giving them the same rights as registered couples, except for inheritance.[28]

In Sweden, registered partnership is only available if at least one prospective partner is a Swedish national and resident.[29] A similar requirement applied in Denmark until July 1999 when amendments to the legislation came into force.[30] These amendments permit registration provided that one partner is a national either of Denmark, or of Sweden, Iceland or Norway, the other European countries that accommodate registered partnerships. In addition, two long-term residents, without relevant nationality,

22 Waaldjik, *supra*, note 14, 75.

23 *Ibid*, 76.

24 *Ibid*, 75–76.

25 Danish Registered Partnership Act No 372 of 7 June 1989 in force 1 October 1989: Cited in Forder, *supra*, note 10, 390; Hunt, *supra*, note 10, 648.

26 In 1997, the State Lutheran Church approved same-sex marriage in the church, but the ceremony is different to a heterosexual marriage: Goransson, *supra, note* 7, 173.

27 Swedish Registered Partnership Act of 23 June 1994 in force 1 January 1995: cited in Forder, *supra*, note 11, 390.

28 Hunt, *supra*, note 10, 648.

29 Forder, *supra*, note 11, 394.

30 Danish Registered Partnership Act No 372 of 7 June 1989, as substituted by Act No 360 of 2 June 1999 in force 1 July 1999: cited in Forder, *supra*, note 11, 395

are able to register a partnership if they can prove that they intend to continue living in Denmark after registration.[31] The reason for these restrictions is to prevent so-called 'partnership tourism' by non-nationals. The legitimacy of this justification has been called into question following the experience under the Registered Partnership Act, introduced by the Netherlands in 1998. Dutch law allows registration by anyone who is a Dutch national or who has a valid right of residence in the Netherlands.[32] In the first year that this Act was in force, only six percent of registrants were foreign, suggesting there is no market for 'partnership tourism'.[33]

In other Member States, there is currently no legislation that recognises same-sex partnerships. In France, a same-sex couple is permitted to enroll on a special register after undertaking to provide mutual material assistance and to be jointly liable for debts incurred for domestic needs.[34] This regime does not attempt to provide an institution equivalent to marriage, but rather it seeks to protect the economic solidarity of the couple. Belgium provides an even more limited scheme under the Statutory Cohabitation Act of 1998,[35] which amended the property rights provisions of the Belgian Civil Code. Couples that choose to come under the scheme are obliged to share the costs of cohabitation and one partner is prohibited from dealing with the joint home or household goods without the consent of the other.[36] A proposal to introduce registered partnership in Belgium lapsed, following elections in the summer of 1999.[37]

On 4 July 2000, a Bill was presented in the German Parliament proposing to introduce partnership laws.[38] In addition, a Finnish working group established by the Ministry of Justice reported in 1999 that registered partnership laws modeled on the Nordic example ought to be enacted.[39] In Spain and Italy, several cities have registers of civil partnership, but these registers do not accord rights to homosexual couples on a national level.[40] In the United Kingdom, far from recognizing same-sex partnerships, Section 11(c) of the Matrimonial Causes Act 1973 makes a marriage void if it is not 'respectively male and female'.

In conclusion, the domestic laws of the European Union Member States display considerable diversity in attitudes to homosexual rights. As will be

31 *Ibid*, 395.

32 Article 1:80a (1) and (2) of the Dutch Civil Code; cited in Forder, *supra*, note 11, 395.

33 Forder, *supra*, note 11, 396.

34 *Ibid*, 387.

35 Belgian Statutory Cohabitation Act of 29 October 1998 in force 1 January 2000: cited in Forder, *supra*, note 11, 383.

36 *Ibid*, 384.

37 *Ibid*, 390.

38 *Ibid*.

39 *Ibid*.

40 See Hunt, *supra*, note 10, 648.

discussed in Part IV, the lack of conformity within the European Union has the potential to affect the goals of economic integration and social harmonisation, particularly in relation to the free movement of persons.

Part III: Homosexual rights under the European Convention on Human Rights

The European Convention for the Protection of Human Rights and Fundamental Freedoms (ECHR) came into force on 3 September 1953 and since that time it has become the foundation of the world's most successful international human rights regime.[41] However, the ECHR is not a creature of the European Union, but rather was drafted and implemented by the Council of Europe, a body established in 1949 with the general aim of enhancing the cultural, social and political life of Europe, in the aftermath of World War II. Originally, the responsibility for adjudicating claims under the ECHR was shared by the European Commission of Human Rights and the European Court of Human Rights, but the functions of these two bodies have recently been consolidated into a new European Court of Human Rights, which began operations in November 1998.[42] Despite the fact that the ECHR is not part of the European Union system, it is nevertheless of great significance to the functioning of that system. All Member States have independently ratified the ECHR and it therefore represents a core component of the common fundamental values recognised throughout those States. By 1998, the European Court of Justice had referred to the ECHR in 79 separate decisions, beginning with the *Nold*[43] judgment in 1974.[44]

The most important Article of the ECHR in the context of homosexual rights is Article 8(1), which states that: 'Everyone has the right to respect for his privacy and family life, his home and his correspondence.'[45] The European

41 Brice Dickson (ed), *Human Rights and the European Convention*, 1997, London: Sweet & Maxwell, 1.

42 In 1994, Protocol No 11, which provided for the re-structuring of the system, was opened for signature. The new European Court of Human Rights began operations on 1 November 1998 and on 31 October 1999 the European Commission of Human Rights was abolished.

43 *Nold v Commission*, Case 4/73 [1974] European Court Reports 491 at 508.

44 See Elspeth Guild and Guillaume Lesieur, *The European Court of Justice on the European Convention on Human Rights*, 1998, Boston: Kluwer Law International.

45 Also of significance is Article 14 of the ECHR which states that: 'The enjoyment of the rights and freedoms set forth in this Convention shall be secured without discrimination on any ground such as sex, race, colour, language, religion, political or other opinion, national or social origin, association with a national minority, property, birth or other status.' It has been held that sexual orientation is also a prohibited ground of discrimination under Article 14: *Sutherland v United Kingdom*, No 25186/94 (1997) 24 European Human Rights Reports 22. However, more often, the Court has found it unnecessary to consider Article 14, having already reached its decision under Article 8: *Dudgeon v United Kingdom* (1981) 4 European Human Rights Reports 149; *Norris v Ireland* (1988) 13 European Human Rights Reports 186; *ADT v United Kingdom*, European Court of Human Rights, Decision of 31 July 2000, Hudoc Reference REF00001940, <http://hudoc.echr.coe.int>.

Court of Human Rights has held in several cases[46] that the criminalization of private homosexual conduct between consenting adults violates the right to privacy in Article 8 of the ECHR. While the opinions in these cases are undoubtedly important for the recognition of the self-determination and autonomy rights of lesbians and gay men, the scope and applicability of these rights is subject to limitations. These limitations are the result of the Court's interpretation of the second paragraph of Article 8 which permits infringements of the right to privacy that are 'necessary in a democratic society in the interests of national security... for the protection of wealth or morals, or for the protection of the rights and freedoms of others.'

The Court of Human Rights has held that, on issues raising questions of morality, State authorities are to be granted a wide 'margin of appreciation' in determining whether acts or conduct should be proscribed by law.[47] The margin of appreciation doctrine can be traced to the decision in *Greece v United Kingdom*,[48] in which the British Government sought to rely on Article 15 ECHR, which allows states to derogate from Convention provisions when a public emergency threatens the life of the nation. It was held that a 'Government should be able to exercise a certain measure of discretion' in formulating its response to the exigencies of a situation.[49] Since that decision, the doctrine has been extended beyond the confines of Article 15 and is now used to determine the extent of all rights protected by the Convention. In the *Belgian Linguistic* case,[50] it was concluded that: 'The Convention ... implies a just balance between the protection of the general interest of the community and the respect due to fundamental human rights while attaching particular importance to the latter.'[51] The margin of appreciation doctrine was applied to

46 *Dudgeon v United Kingdom* (1981) 4 European Human Rights Reports 149; *Norris v Ireland* (1988) 13 European Human Rights Reports 186; *Modinos v Cyprus* (1993) 16 European Human Rights Reports 485. In *ADT v United Kingdom*. European Court of Human Rights. Decision of 31 July 2000 Hudoc Reference REF00001940 <http://hudoc.echr.coe.int>, the Court found that criminalization of sexual acts between two or more men was in contravention of the right to privacy. Cf *Laskey, Jaggard and Brown v United Kingdom* (1997) 24 European Human Rights Reports 39, in which the prohibition of sado-masochism was found to be justified under Article 8(2). The United Nations Human Rights Committee has also held that the criminalization of homosexual intercourse violated Article 2 (equal protection) and Article 17 (privacy) of the International Covenant on Civil and Political Rights: *Toonen v Australia*. UN Human Rights Committee Case No 488/1992 of April 4 1994.

47 '[T]he margin of appreciation must be particularly broad where the protection of morals is at issue': *ADT v United Kingdom*. European Court of Human Rights. Decision of 31 July 2000. Hudoc Reference REF00001940, paragraph 27, http://hudoc.echr.coe.int.

48 *Greece v United Kingdom* (the *Cyprus* case) 2 Yearbook of the European Convention 174.

49 *Ibid*, 178. See also *Lawless v Ireland* (1961) 1 European Human Rights Reports 1; *Ireland v United Kingdom* (1978) 2 European Human Rights Reports 25.

50 *Case Relating to Certain Aspects of the Laws on the Use of Languages in Education in Belgium (No 2) (Merits)* (1967) 1 European Human Rights Reports 252.

51 *Ibid*, 282.

Article 8 in *Klass v Germany*,[52] in which it was held that surveillance measures that infringed privacy were justified for the protection of national security.[53]

In *Dudgeon v United Kingdom*,[54] the margin of appreciation doctrine was integral to the reasoning of the Court, which held that a Northern Ireland statute criminalizing consensual homosexual conduct was in contravention of the right to privacy in Article 8. The main issue for the Court was how wide a margin of appreciation should be accorded to the State authorities in a controversy that was considered to raise issues of morality. The Court began its analysis by recognising that 'some degree of regulation of male homosexual conduct, as indeed of other forms of sexual conduct, by means of the criminal law can be justified as 'necessary in a democratic society'.[55] The Court then considered whether the legislation in Northern Ireland was within the bounds of what might be considered necessary to protect particular sections of society taking into account 'the moral ethos of society as a whole'.[56] In this context, the Court observed that '[t]he moral climate in Northern Ireland in sexual matters, in particular as evidenced by the opposition to proposed legislative change, is one of the matters which the national authorities may legitimately take into account in exercising their discretion'.[57] Ultimately, the Court concluded that 'the moral attitudes towards lesbians and gay men in Northern Ireland ... cannot, without more, warrant interfering with the applicant's private life'.[58] This was because the statute went further than was necessary to protect the morals of society by criminalizing all male homosexual conduct, regardless of the age of the participants or the presence of consent. The Court applied the same reasoning and reached the same conclusion in *Norris v Ireland*.[59]

In both *Dudgeon* and *Norris*, the Court of Human Rights rejected the position that homosexuality was morally neutral, and thus found it necessary to review the impugned legislation within the morality exception to the right to

52 *Klass v Federal Republic of Germany* (1978) 2 European Human Rights Reports 214. See also *Buckley v United Kingdom* (1996) 23 European Human Rights Reports 101; *Laskey, Jaggard and Brown v United Kingdom* (1997) 24 European Human Rights Reports 39 at 48: 'The scope of the margin of appreciation is not identical in each case but will vary according to the context. Relevant factors include the nature of the Convention right in issue, its importance for the individual and the nature of the activities concerned.'

53 See generally Howard Charles Yourow, *The Margin of Appreciation Doctrine in the Dynamics of the European Human Rights Jurisprudence*, 1996, Boston: Martinus Nijhoff Publishers.

54 *Dudgeon v United Kingdom* (1981) 4 European Human Rights Reports 149.

55 *Ibid*, 163.

56 *Ibid*, 164.

57 *Ibid*, 166.

58 *Ibid*, 168.

59 *Norris v Ireland* (1988) 13 European Human Rights Reports 186.

privacy, contained in Article 8(2).[60] Although the Court ultimately concluded that the applicant's right to privacy was not outweighed by majoritarian moral values, the analysis adopted by the Court has had consequences for other claims alleging discrimination on the basis of sexual orientation. This is particularly evident in the history of litigation aimed at eliminating differential ages of consent for heterosexual and homosexual intercourse.

In *Johnson v United Kingdom*,[61] the petitioner challenged the British laws governing the age of consent, which at the time, was 21 for gay men and 16 for heterosexuals and lesbians. The Commission of Human Rights concluded that the difference in treatment between gay men and heterosexuals was based on 'an objective and reasonable justification in the criteria of social protection' and was necessitated by the 'specific social danger in the case of male homosexuality'.[62] The difference between the age of consent for gay men and the age of consent for lesbians was also found to be based on an 'objective and reasonable justification' which the Commission derived from a report of the Criminal Law Revision Committee of the British Parliament. The report found that sexual orientation tended to be determined earlier in women than in men and that, despite this, lesbian relationships arose later in life and 'adolescent girls did not seem especially attractive to older women ... there being greater emphasis in male homosexual culture on this age group'.[63] The Commission concluded that 'heterosexuality and lesbianism do not give rise to comparable social problems' and that an unequal age of consent was justified 'to protect the individual, particularly the young and vulnerable'.[64] As a result of this decision, and others to the same effect,[65] an unequal age of consent for gay men was regarded as acceptable under the ECHR for over 20 years. It was not until the 1997 judgment in *Sutherland v United Kingdom*[66] that the Commission overruled this decision, citing advancements in medical evidence relating to the age at which sexual orientation was determined.

The Commission has also been exceedingly deferential to the judgments of governments in other cases in which lesbians and gay men have challenged national laws and practices under the ECHR. In *X and Y v United Kingdom*,[67] the petitioners challenged the deportation from the United Kingdom of the

60 Article 8(2) departs from the traditional liberal view that majoritarian standards of morality are an insufficient rationale to support the imposition of legal obligations on individuals. See John Stuart Mill, *On Liberty*, 1985, Harmondsworth: Penguin .

61 *Johnson v United Kingdom*, No 10389/83 (1986) 47 European Commission of Human Rights: Decisions and Reports 72.

62 *Ibid*, 77.

63 *Ibid*.

64 *Ibid*, 78.

65 *X v Federal Republic of Germany*, No 5935/72 (1975) 3 European Commission of Human Rights: Decisions and Reports 46; *X v United Kingdom*, No 7215/75 (1978) 11 European Commission of Human Rights: Decisions and Reports 36.

66 *Sutherland v United Kingdom*, No 25186/94 (1997) 24 European Human Rights Reports 22.

67 *X and Y v United Kingdom* (1983) 32 European Commission of Human Rights: Decisions and Reports 220.

Malaysian gay partner of a British citizen. The Commission held that it was within the discretion of the British government not to recognise gay partnerships, and that consequently the four year relationship of the petitioners did not 'fall within the scope of the right to respect for family life ensured by Article 8'.[68] In 1999, the Court of Human Rights overruled earlier decisions by the Commission which permitted discrimination against lesbians and gay men in the military.[69] In *Lustig-Prean v United Kingdom*,[70] the investigation and dismissal of military officers after it was revealed that they were homosexual was held to be in contravention of the right to privacy. It was found that there was no 'pressing social need' to exclude homosexuals from the military and that there was no evidence that their presence would endanger national security by reducing morale. Despite the more liberal decisions of the Court in the last several years, the determination of the extent of homosexual equality has continued to be performed under a morality analysis. This framework provides a broad justification for national measures that infringe the rights of homosexual citizens.[71]

Part IV: Homosexual rights in the ECJ

The European Court of Justice (ECJ)[72] is the institution responsible for interpreting the treaties, regulations and directives of the European Union. In so doing, the Court has held that European Union law 'not only imposes obligations on individuals but is also intended to confer upon them rights which become part of their legal heritage'.[73] For the most part, these are economic rights associated with the creation of an integrated common market between Member States through the elimination of barriers to the free

68 *Ibid*, 221. See also *X v United Kingdom* (1989) 11 European Human Commission of Human Rights: Decisions and Reports 50 in which the Commission concluded that even though a lesbian couple was in a stable homosexual relationship attempts to deport one of them did not fall within the ambit of family protection under Article 8(1).

69 *B v United Kingdom*, No 9237/81 (1983) 34 European Commission of Human Rights: Decisions and Reports 68.

70 *Lustig Prean and Beckett v United Kingdom*. European Court of Human Rights. Decision of 27 September 1999. Hudoc Reference REF00001275, http://hudoc.echr.coe.int. See also *Smith and Grady v United Kingdom*. European Court of Human Rights. Decision of 22 October 1999. Hudoc Reference REF00001276 <http://hudoc.echr.coe.int>.

71 Carlos A Ball, 'The Making of a Transnational Capitalist Society: The Court of Justice, Social Policy and Individual Rights Under the European Community's Legal Order' (1996) 37 Harvard International Law Journal: 307 at 381.

72 For information on the structure, procedures and powers of the ECJ see Neville March Hunnings, *The European Courts*, 1996, London: Cartermill, 47–121.

73 *Van Gend en Loos v Nederlandse Administratie der Belastingen*, Case 26/62 [1968] European Court Reports 1, 12.

movement of goods,[74] persons,[75] services,[76] and capital.[77] References to social rights in the European Community (EC) Treaty are limited and have been interpreted narrowly by the ECJ. For example, Article 2 of the EC Treaty states that one of the goals of European integration is the promotion of 'a high level of employment and of social protection' and 'the raising of the standard of living and quality of life'.[78] However, in *Zaera v Instituto Nacional de la Seguridad*,[79] the Court, in contrast to its language in the context of economic rights, held that Article 2 does not have direct effect and 'cannot impose legal obligations on Member States or confer rights on individuals'.[80] In general, the EC Treaty is not concerned with social rights as a result of the widely held view that improved living standards and working conditions will flow automatically from the benefits of the common market.[81]

One exception to this rule is Article 141[82] which states that: 'Each Member State shall ensure that the principle of equal pay for male and female workers for equal work or work of equal value is applied.' In *Defrenne v Sabena*,[83] the ECJ heard a complaint by an airline steward who was paid less than her male counterparts for performing the same work. The Court noted that Article 141 had an economic goal in eliminating discrimination that would have the effect of distorting the common market, but also a social goal in promoting the constant improvement of the living and working conditions of European Union citizens.[84] The Court held that Article 141 had direct effect in prohibiting discrimination which could be 'identified solely with the aid of the criteria based on equal work and equal pay referred to by the article

---

74 Article 23 EC Treaty.

75 Article 39 EC Treaty.

76 Article 49 EC Treaty.

77 Article 56 EC Treaty.

78 Article 2 EC Treaty.

79 *Zaera v Instituto Nacional de la Seguridad*, Case 120/86 [1987] European Court Reports 3697.

80 *Ibid*, 3716. In *Zaera* the ECJ also considered the effect of Articles 117 and 118 (now Article 136, 137–40 of the EC Treaty), which mention social rights such as education, social security, working conditions and collective bargaining. It was held that these sections do not have direct effect. See also regarding Article 118, *Federal Republic of Germany & Others v Commission*, Joined Cases 281, 283, 285, 287/85 [1987] European Court Reports 3203.

81 '[T]he improved distribution and utilization of the workforce will result in a higher average income. The consequence will precisely be the accelerated raising of the standard of living.' *Zaera v Instituto Nacional de la Seguridad*, Case 120/86 [1987] European Court Reports 3697, 3709. See also Carl Nielsen and Alvin Szyszczak, *The Social Dimension of the European Union*, 3rd edn, 1997, Boston: Martinus Nijhoff, 19; Michael Shanks, 'The Social Policy of the European Communities' (1977) 14 Common Market Law Review: 375; Anthony Arnull, *The European Union and its Court of Justice*, 1999, Oxford: OUP, 459.

82 Previously, Article 119 EEC Treaty. See discussion in Noreen Burrows and Sacha Prechal, *Gender Discrimination of the European Community*, 1990, Brookfield: Dartmouth, 48–98.

83 *Defrenne v Société Anonyme Belge de Navigation Aerienne Sabena*, Case 43/75 [1976] European Court Reports 455.

84 *Ibid*, 459.

in question'.[85] The scope of Article 141 was broadened by Council Directive 76/207 (Equal Treatment Directive), which prohibited gender-based discrimination in relation to employment opportunity, vocational training, and promotion and working conditions.[86] Thus in *Marshall v Southampton*,[87] a female employee successfully made a claim of gender discrimination when she was dismissed at the age of 62 for the sole reason she had exceeded the retirement age for women, even though the retirement age for men was 65.[88]

The ECJ heralded a new brand of decision-making in *P v S and Cornwall County Council*,[89] when it held that Article 141 prohibits discrimination on the basis of gender reassignment. P, whose biological sex was originally male, was dismissed from his employment with the Council, after he informed his superiors that he intended to undertake gender reassignment surgery. P brought proceedings against the Council alleging the dismissal was the result of sex discrimination, contrary to the Equal Treatment Directive. This claim required the expansion of the Equal Treatment Directive, since P had not been dismissed because she belonged to one sex or the other but because she had changed her sex.[90] The Court began by emphasising that the right not to be discriminated against on the ground of gender was a fundamental human right which it had a duty to uphold. The Court stated that:

> [T]he scope of the directive cannot be confined simply to discrimination based on the fact that a person is of one or other sex. In view of its purpose and the nature of the rights which it seeks to safeguard, the scope of the directive is also such as to apply to discrimination arising, as in this case, from the gender reassignment of the person concerned ... To tolerate such discrimination would be tantamount, as regards such a person, to a failure to respect the dignity and freedom to which he or she is entitled, and which the Court has a duty to safeguard.[91]

The focus in this case on fundamental human rights represented a marked departure from the predominantly economic considerations previously applied

---

85 *Ibid*, 460. However, in relation to systemic gender discrimination based on the fact that women tend to be employed in lower paying industries, Article 141 did not have direct effect. See also *Worringham and Humphreys v Lloyds Bank*, Case 69/80 [1981] European Court Reports 767.

86 See also Council Directive 79/7 guaranteeing equal treatment in social security benefits; and Council Directive 86/378 guaranteeing equal treatment in occupational social security benefits.

87 *Marshall v Southampton and South-West Hampshire Area Health Authority*, Case 152/84 [1986] European Court Reports 723.

88 This may be contrasted with the decision before Directive 76/207 came into effect in *Defrenne v Societe Anonyme Belge de Navigation Aerienne (No 3)*, Case 149/77 [1978] European Court Reports, in which an airline steward could not rely on Article 141 to challenge a provision in her employment contract which terminated her employment when she reached the age of 40, even though no such provision was inserted in the contracts of male airline stewards.

89 *P v S and Cornwall County Council*, Case 13/94 [1996] European Court Reports 2143.

90 Arnull, *supra*, note 81, 483.

91 *P v S and Cornwall County Council*, Case 13/94 [1996] European Court Reports 2143 at 2165.

by the Court.[92] It is notable that the Court of Human Rights has not taken such a sensitive approach to transsexuality. In *Sheffield and Horsham v United Kingdom*,[93] the Court of Human Rights held that 'transsexualism raises complex legal, moral and social issues' and that a State authority is entitled to a 'margin of appreciation to defend its continuing refusal to recognize in law a transsexual's post-operative gender'.[94]

The liberal and expansive approach adopted in *P v S* was narrowed by the ECJ in the decision of *Grant v South-West Trains*.[95] At issue in that case was whether the prohibition of sex discrimination in Article 141 also includes discrimination on the ground of sexual orientation. Grant was a lesbian employed by a railway company. She applied for travel concessions on behalf of a female cohabitee with whom she had been involved in an intimate relationship for over two years. However, the regulations adopted by the railway company only permitted concessions for dependants, a legal spouse or a 'common law opposite sex spouse'. Grant's application for travel concessions on behalf of her female partner was rejected by the railway company and she commenced proceedings alleging gender-based discrimination contrary to Article 141.

The Court rejected the argument that the rules applied by the railway company constituted discrimination directly based on sex. The Court observed that 'travel concessions are refused to a male worker if he is living with a person of the same sex, just as they are refused to a female worker if she is living with a person of the same sex'.[96] Moreover, the Court found that no instrument of the European Union could be said to have elevated stable relationships between two persons of the same sex, to the same status as 'marriages or stable relationships outside marriage between persons of opposite sex'.[97] In an attempt to distinguish *P v S*, the Court stated that discrimination related to gender reassignment was a distinction on the ground of gender, whereas discrimination based on sexual orientation was not.[98] The Court pointed out further that the Treaty of Amsterdam granted power to the

92 Paul Barnard, '*P v S*: Kite Flying or a New Constitutional Approach', in Mark Dashwood and Robert O'Leary (eds), *The Principle of Equal Treatment in EC Law*, Boston: Martinus Nijhoff, 1997), 63.

93 *Sheffield and Horsham v United Kingdom* (1999) 27 European Human Rights Reports 163.

94 *Ibid*, 171. The Court of Human Rights was following its earlier decisions in *Rees v United Kingdom* (1986) 9 European Human Rights Reports 56; *Cossey v United Kingdom* (1990) 13 European Human Rights Reports 622; *X, Y and Z v United Kingdom* (1997) 24 European Human Rights Reports 143.

95 *Grant v South West Trains*, Case 249/96 [1998] European Court Reports 621. See discussion in Paul L Spackman '*Grant v South West Trains*: Equality for Same Sex Partners in the European Community' (1997) 12 American University Journal of International Law and Policy: 1063.

96 *Ibid*, 641.

97 *Ibid*, 643.

98 This of course was in contradiction to the terms of the decision in *P v S*, in which it was said that the prohibition of discrimination was not limited to whether a person was 'of one or other sex'. *Supra*, notes 89–92 and accompanying text.

Council to legislate against discrimination based on sexual orientation, which suggested an intention on the part of Member States that the matter be dealt with at the level of the Council, rather than by expansive interpretation of existing provisions. Therefore, the Court deferred to the Council to resolve the position that discrimination against transsexuals is prohibited but discrimination against homosexuals is not.[99]

Until such time as the Council agrees upon measures to prevent discrimination against homosexuals, there is an alternative approach by which the rights of lesbians and gay men might be protected. This approach would involve a return to one of the economic considerations with which the ECJ has traditionally concerned itself, specifically, the free movement of persons. The basic principles relating to the free movement of persons are contained in Articles 39–48 EC Treaty. The right to free movement entails, *inter alia*, the right to accept offers of employment,[100] the right to take up residence,[101] the right to payment of benefits,[102] the right to establish companies and firms to manage undertakings,[103] and the right to mutual recognition of qualifications.[104] Acting under the provisions of the EC Treaty, the Council has issued subordinate legislation implementing these rights.[105] The instruments enshrining the principle of the free movement of persons have direct effect and hence they are 'a fertile source of rights for individuals'.[106]

Employment discrimination based on sexual orientation interferes with the fluidity of the labour market by hindering the free movement of persons across national borders. To the extent that discrimination laws among Member States differ, there will be a disincentive for homosexual citizens of one Member State to move and find work in a Member State that permits discrimination against homosexuals.[107] The Treaties of the European Union promote the free movement of persons by prohibiting discrimination on the grounds of

99 This decision was followed by the English High Court in *R v Secretary of State for Defence ex p Perkins* [1999] 1 Family Law Reports 491 *per* Lightman J.

100 Article 39(3)(a) EC Treaty.

101 Article 39(3)(c) EC Treaty.

102 Article 42(b) EC Treaty.

103 Article 43 EC Treaty.

104 Article 47 EC Treaty.

105 See Directive 68/360 (rights of entry and residence); Regulation 1612/68 (access to and conditions of employment); Regulation 1251/70 (right to remain after ceasing employment).

106 Josephine Steiner and Lorna Woods, *Textbook on EC Law*, 6th edn, 1998, London: Blackstone Press, 271.

107 Ball, *supra*, note 71, 382. See also Henry G Schermers, 'Human Rights and Free Movement of Persons: The Role of the European Commission and Court of Human Rights' in Henry G Schermers, Cees Flinterman *et al* (eds), *Free Movement of Persons in Europe*, 1993, Boston: Martinus Nijhoff, 235–47.

nationality[108] and gender.[109] Although with respect to gender there is a distinct component of social protection, the underlying purpose has always been protection of economic freedoms in the common market. Indeed, the prohibition of sex discrimination in Article 141 was primarily a concession to France to allay its concerns that its more progressive social legislation would undermine its ability to compete on equal terms with the other Member States.[110]

Economic considerations have led the ECJ to conclude that other factors, not directly related to nationality or gender, should be recognised as impediments to the free movement of persons. Of particular relevance to lesbians and gay men is the decision of the Court in *Netherlands v Reed*.[111] The applicant in *Reed* was a British woman living in the Netherlands with her British common law partner who had a Dutch residency permit. The applicant was denied a residency permit because she and her partner were not married. The Court found that Dutch law was discriminatory because it permitted the common law foreign partners of Dutch citizens to remain in the country but not the partners of nationals of other Members States who had Dutch residency permits. The Court reasoned that this discrimination impeded the free movement of persons because the Netherlands had failed to offer 'social advantages' to nationals of other Member States that were provided to Dutch citizens.[112] It was stated that: '[T]he possibility for a migrant worker of obtaining permission for his unmarried companion to reside with him…can assist his integration in the host State and thus contribute to the achievement of freedom of movement for workers.'[113]

This reasoning ought to apply whether the migrant worker is heterosexual or homosexual. If the primary motivation is to induce freedom of movement across the borders of Member States by permitting individuals with residency permits to live with their foreign partners, the gender of the partner is not relevant. Those States that have domestic partnership laws, and therefore permit the foreign same-sex partners of their nationals to remain in the country, would have to offer the same treatment to same-sex partners of nationals from other Member States. This is particularly significant in relation

108 Article 12 EC Treaty. See also *Commission v Greece*, Case 305/87 [1989] European Court Reports 1461, 1476; *Marson and Jhanjan v Netherlands*, Joined Cases 35, 36/82 [1982] ECR 3723, 3736; *Walrave & Koch v Association Union Cycliste Internationale*, Case 36/74 [1974] European Court Reports 1405, 1417; *Reyners v Belgium*, Case 2/74 [1974] European Court Reports 631, 650.

109 Article 141; *supra*, notes 82–88 and accompanying text.

110 Lammy Breten, 'Prospects for a Social Policy of the European Community and its Impact on the Functioning of the European Social Charter', in Lammy Breten (ed), *The Future of European Social Policy*, 1991, London: Cartermill, 114; Sandra Fredman, 'European Community Discrimination Law: A Critique' (1992) 21 Industrial Law Journal: 119 at 130; Josephine Steiner & Lorna Woods, *Textbook on EC Law*, 6th edn, 1998, London: Blackstone Press, 266.

111 *Netherlands v Reed*, Case 59/85 [1986] European Court Reports 1283.

112 See Article 7(2) of Regulation 1612/68 which requires Member States to offer the social advantages provided to their own nationals to workers from other States.

113 *Netherlands v Reed*, Case 59/85 [1986] European Court Reports 1283, 1303.

to the nationality requirements in the partnerships laws of Sweden and Denmark. By preventing non-nationals from registering a partnership, Sweden and Denmark provide less favourable treatment, and consequently inhibit the right to free movement.[114]

Beyond the implications of the Reed decision, the principle of free movement of persons has the potential to prevent any discrimination against homosexuals that affects the capacity to take up residence and employment in another Member State. For example, the right to free movement of homosexual citizens in Denmark, Ireland, Finland, Spain, Sweden and the Netherlands is infringed because no other countries offer protection against employment discrimination based on sexual orientation.[115] As the number of Member States that prohibit such discrimination increases, the lack of corresponding legislation in other countries will inhibit the free movement of persons to those countries.

This economic argument available to the ECJ has an advantage over the approach adopted by the Court of Human Rights because it does not involve deference to the national concerns of the Member States. The ECJ grants only a limited 'margin of appreciation' to a Member State when a national measure interferes, directly or indirectly, with the free movement of persons. Hence, in *Cowan v Tresor Public*,[116] it was held that a criminal compensation scheme had to be extended to a tourist, despite France's contention that the scheme concerned 'a right which is a manifestation of national solidarity'.[117] Similarly, in *Commission v Italy*,[118] the Italian government was required to provide to migrant workers the benefits of a housing policy, which Italy argued was a crucial part of its national social policy.[119] Thus, by pursuing rights for lesbians and gay men through the economic rationale applied by the ECJ, there is no need to consider the moral interests of Member States in the manner engaged in by the Court of Human Rights.[120] Lesbian and gay litigants can therefore avoid participating in normative moral arguments, which are often dominated by the anti-homosexual sentiments prevalent in society.

---

114 Forder, *supra*, note 11, 396.

115 Hunt, *supra*, note 10, 633. See also *supra*, notes 13–14 and accompanying text.

116 *Cowan v Tresor Public*, Case 186/87 [1989] European Court Reports 195.

117 *Ibid*, 221.

118 *Commission v Italy*, Case 63/86 [1988] European Court Reports 29.

119 See also *Steinhouser v Biarritz*, Case 197/84 [1985] European Court Reports 1819. Cf *Ministère Public v Even*, Case 207/78 [1979] European Court Reports 2019. In this case, the Court upheld a Belgian law which granted early retirement benefits to Belgian war veterans, but not to veterans of other countries. The Court deferred to the national policy which was to give nationals an advantage because they suffered for their country. This decision may be explained on political grounds since extension of veterans' benefits to nationals of all Member States would have included veterans from Germany.

120 Hunt, *supra*, note 10, 655; Ball, *supra*, note 71, 385.

Conclusion

The most obvious direction from which Community-wide prohibition of discrimination on the ground of sexual orientation may be expected is the Council of the European Union under Article 13 of the Treaty of Amsterdam. However, given the controversial nature of homosexual rights it may be some time before the Council is able to reach the unanimity required to introduce regulatory measures. If unanimity in the Council is difficult to achieve then, *a fortiori*, it cannot be expected that the legislatures of Member States will spontaneously adopt standard laws relating to homosexual equality. Within the European Union system, this leaves the ECJ as the sole possibility, at least for the time being, that homosexual equality will be recognised. In *Grant v South-West Trains,* the ECJ declined to hold that discrimination on the basis of sexual orientation was included within Article 141 or the Equal Treatment Directive. Hence, the greatest potential for recognition of homosexual rights lies within the doctrine of the free movement of persons. By adopting a judgment in favour of homosexual rights in this context, the ECJ could enhance the equality rights of lesbians and gay men and, most importantly, eliminate from its considerations the moral arguments against homosexual rights.

German Constitutional Decisions in English Translation

John Trone[1]

1 Introduction

The decisions of the German Federal Constitutional Court have been the subject of surprisingly little attention in the English-speaking world.[2] However, in recent years the linguistic barriers to consulting this extensive body of constitutional law have been greatly reduced as a result of painstaking translation work. This article seeks to make that work more accessible to researchers.

The first part of this article is introductory. The second part discusses the use of Federal Constitutional Court decisions by foreign judges. The third part outlines the sources in which English translations of the Court's decisions may be found. The fourth part provides an introduction to the three appendices to this article. These appendices provide a catalogue of the translations (indexed by citation and popular name), together with a list of abbreviations used herein.

2 Citation of the Court by other national courts

While insufficiently utilised in the English speaking world, the Court's decisions have not gone entirely unnoticed by foreign courts. Certain decisions have been the subject of particular attention. The Court's abortion rulings are an obvious example.[3]

---

1 BA/LLB, PhD.

2 For general introductions to the Court, see David P Currie, *The Constitution of the Federal Republic of Germany*, 1994, Chicago: University of Chicago Press, 27–30; Donald P Kommers, *The Constitutional Jurisprudence of the Federal Republic of Germany,* 2nd edn, 1997, Durham: Duke University Press, 3–29 (hereafter Kommers).

3 Eg, *Borowski v Attorney-General for Canada* (1987) 39 DLR (4th) 731 at 747–48, affd [1989] 1 SCR 342; *R v Morgentaler* [1988] 1 SCR 30 at 46; *S v Makwanyane* 1995 (3) SA 391 at 513 (hereafter *Makwanyane*); *Christian Lawyers Assoc of SA v Minister of Health* 1998 (4) SA 1113 at 1125–26; *Planned Parenthood of Southeastern Pa v Casey* 505 US 833 at 945 (1992) (Rehnquist CJ, dissenting) (hereafter *Casey*).

English courts have referred favourably to the Court's sovereign immunity decisions.[4] Lord Diplock described the judgment in the *Philippine Embassy Bank Account* case[5] as 'wholly convincing' and 'comprehensive and closely reasoned'.[6] Similarly, Lord Wilberforce described the *Empire of Iran* case[7] as a 'leading case' of 'great clarity'.[8]

The South African Constitutional Court frequently cites German constitutional decisions,[9] often examining German rulings *in extenso*.[10] This frequent citation has arisen partly because of textual similarities between the two Constitutions[11] and partly because both Constitutions were adopted soon after each country emerged from dictatorship.[12]

The German Court's cases have received less attention elsewhere in the English-speaking world. Australian, Canadian, and United States courts have only very rarely cited its decisions.[13] Outside the English speaking world, the

---

4 Eg, *Trendtex Trading Corporation v Central Bank of Nigeria* [1977] QB 529 at 563, 566; *I Congreso del Partido* [1981] 1 All ER 1092 at 1102, 1106–07, revd [1983] 1 AC 244 at 263–64, 267, 276 (hereafter *I Congreso del Partido*); *Alcom Ltd v Republic of Colombia* [1984] AC 580 at 599 (hereafter *Alcom*). Decisions concerning other issues have also been cited by the House of Lords. See eg *R v Bow Street Stipendiary Magistrate, ex p Pinochet (No 3)* [2000] 1 AC 147 at 255–57; *MacFarlane v Tayside Health Board* [2000] 2 AC 59 at 80.

5 *Philippine Embassy Bank Account* case BVerfGE 46, 342 (1977).

6 *Alcom, supra* n 4, 599.

7 *Claim Against the Empire of Iran* Case BVerfGE 16, 27 (1963).

8 *I Congreso del Partido, supra* n 4, 263. The Canadian Federal Court of Appeal also praised the clarity of the German Constitutional Court's decision: *Lorac Transport Ltd v The 'Atra'* [1987] 1 FC 108 at 116. The *Empire of Iran* case has also been cited by the English Court of Appeal, the New Zealand Court of Appeal and the High Court of Zimbabwe. See *Kuwait Airways Corp v Iraqi Airways* [1995] 1 LRC 1 at 12–13, 19–20, 23, affd in part and revd in part [1995] 1 WLR 1147; *Governor of Pitcairn and Associated Islands v Sutton* [1995] 1 NZLR 426 at 436; *Barker McCormac (Pvt) Ltd v Government of Kenya* 1985 (4) SA 197 at 203–04.

9 Eg, *Nel v Le Roux* 1996 (3) SA 562 at 575; *Case v Minister of Safety and Security* 1996 (3) SA 617 at 651 n 115; *President of the Republic of South Africa v Hugo* 1997 (4) SA 1 at 16; *De Lange v Smuts* 1998 (3) SA 785 at 802–03 n 49, 808, 826 n 131; *Jooste v Score Supermarket Trading (Pty) Ltd* 1999 (2) SA 1 at 12 n 31; *National Coalition for Gay and Lesbian Equality v Minister of Home Affairs* 2000 (2) SA 1 at 37. Many Southern African courts have cited decisions of the Federal Constitutional Court. See eg *S v Tcoeib* [1997] 1 LRC 90 at 101 (SC Namibia); *United Parties v Minister of Justice, Legal and Parliamentary Affairs* [1998] 1 LRC 614 at 622–23 (SC Zimbabwe); *National Media Ltd v Bogoshi* 1998 (4) SA 1196 at 1210 (SCA); *City of Cape Town v AD Outpost Pty Ltd* 2000 (2) SA 733 at 746 (C).

10 Eg, *Makwanyane, supra* n 3, 406, 423, 438, 446, 447, 458–59, 470, 513; *Ferreira v Levin* 1996 (1) SA 984 at 1007–08, 1032-1035, 1089; *Bernstein v Bester* 1996 (2) SA 751 at 785–86 n 87, 793–95; *Du Plessis v De Klerk* 1996 (3) SA 850 at 898–904 (hereafter *Du Plessis*).

11 See *Makwanyane, supra* n 3, 446, 458, 470; *Du Plessis, supra* n 10, 903 & n 37.

12 *Du Plessis, supra* n 10, 898.

13 Australian examples include *Commonwealth v Tasmania* (1983) 158 CLR 1 at 166; *De L v Director-General NSW Department of Community Services* (1996) 187 CLR 640 at 684 n 137. United States examples include the *Casey* decision, *supra* n 3, and *United States v Then* 56 F 3d 464 at 468–69 (2nd Cir 1995). For Canadian examples, see *supra* n 3. An Irish example is *Murphy v Attorney General* [1982] IR 241 at 272–73, 284–85. For an example from Hong Kong, where English is used in many courts, see *HKSAR v Ng Kung Siu* (1999) 2 HKCFAR 442 at 466.

courts of continental European nations have often referred to German constitutional decisions.[14] So too has the European Court of Human Rights.[15]

3 Sources of English translations

Obviously, the comprehensive sources of the Federal Constitutional Court's decisions are in the German language. The most significant decisions are published in the official reports, *Entscheidungen des Bundesverfassungsgerichts*. Less significant cases generally appear in unofficial reporters such as *Neue Juristische Wochenschrift*.

The sources for English translations of these decisions are widely scattered. The most readily accessible source is Donald Kommers' very substantial casebook.[16] To improve readability and to avoid creating a book of inordinate length, Kommers rigorously edited the cases included. Hence this book contains extracts from the cases rather than full reports.

Of inestimable value are the two volumes of translations produced by the Court itself. The first volume contains decisions relating to international law and European Community law, while the second contains decisions concerning freedom of speech.[17]

The decisions are translated verbatim. The full citation of authority by the Court is always included, which is useful for tracking down other important cases. In several cases the depth of the Court's comparative legal scholarship is quite astonishing. Headnotes are also reproduced. Each volume contains a very detailed index.

---

14 Eg VfSlg 10029/1984, 10291/1984, 11402/1987, 11774/1988, 14390/1995, 14466/1996, 15094/1998, 15103/1998 (Austrian Constitutional Court); BGE (1976) 102 Ia 468 at 472-473, 480, (1978) 104 Ia 367 at 371, 65 ILR 417 at 421, (1980) 106 Ia 142 at 147-148, 62 ILR 228 at 233, (1983) 109 Ia 273 at 285, 288-292, 299-300, (1984) 110 II 255 at 260, 82 ILR 13 at 19, (1986) 112 Ia 161 at 162-163, (1987) 113 Ia 1 at 7, 11, (1998) 124 I 55 at 61-75 (Swiss Federal Court); *Republic of 'A' Embassy Bank Account* case (1986) 77 ILR 488 at 492-494 (Austrian Supreme Court); *Libyan Arab Socialist People's Jamahiriya v Rossbeton SRL* (1989) 87 ILR 63 at 66 (Italian Court of Cassation); *Nicolo* [1990] 1 CMLR 173 at 185 (French Conseil d'Etat); *Abbott v Republic of South Africa* (1992) 113 ILR 412 at 422, 424 (Spanish Constitutional Court); Portuguese Constitutional Court, Decision 510/98, 14 July 1998; Czech Republic Constitutional Court, Judgment Pl.US 19/93, 21 December 1993; Hungarian Constitutional Court, Decision 4/1997 (I.22) AB; Slovenian Constitutional Court, Decision U-I-304/94, 9 November 1995; Decision U-I-40/96, 3 April 1997; Opinion Rm-1/97, 5 June 1997.

15 Eg *Cossey v United Kingdom* (1990) 13 EHRR 622 at 647-648; *Borgers v Belgium* (1991) 15 EHRR 92 at 122 n 92; *Fischer v Austria* (1995) 20 EHRR 349 at 387 n 8; *Grigoriades v Greece* (1997) 27 EHRR 464 at 487. See also *Liberal Party v United Kingdom* (1980) 4 EHRR 106 at 123 (Commission).

16 Kommers, *supra* n 2. See the reviews by Horst Eidenmüller [1991] Cambridge Law Journal 168; Nigel Foster (1991) 12 Journal of Legal History 97; John Trone (1999) 4 International Trade and Business Law Annual 295.

17 See Bundesverfassungsgericht, *Decisions of the Bundesverfassungsgericht Vol 1: International Law and Law of the European Communities 1952–1989* (Baden-Baden: Nomos, 1992); *Vol 2: Freedom of Speech 1958–1995* (Baden-Baden: Nomos, 1998). See the review of the first volume by Ulrich R Haltern (1996) 7 European Journal of International Law 458.

Raymond Youngs has also written a general 'sourcebook' on German law. For each case the German text and English translation are displayed on opposite pages, facilitating comparison. These translations are essentially the full text of each decision, including headnotes.

The International Law Reports contain a wealth of translated cases. In early volumes, the decisions were sometimes translated in summary form, and important issues were often neglected. In more recent years, the cases are translated more fully, and even the pagination of the official reports is faithfully reproduced. Several comparative law casebooks also contain an impressive series of translations.[18]

4 The appendices

To better facilitate the use of this extensive body of translated case law, the appendices to this note offer a reasonably comprehensive catalogue of English translations of the Court's decisions. The first appendix is a key to abbreviations used herein. The second and third appendices are lists of translated cases: one by citation, the other by popular name.

It should be noted that German cases are not cited by the names of the parties but by their citations in the law reports. However, popular names have been coined for each case. The names used here are generally those used by Kommers, but alternative names are often given.

The citation of German decisions herein follows the German format, ie, reporter, volume number, page number. For the convenience of readers the year of each decision has also been included.

5 Conclusion

Comparative study of the decisions of the German Federal Constitutional Court could be greatly facilitated by the ready availability of English translations. However, use of these translations is hampered by the absence of any comprehensive indexing of their locations. This article has sought to fill this gap, and to provide an entrée to consultation of this important body of constitutional law.

18 See Walter F Murphy and Joseph Tanenhaus, *Comparative Constitutional Law: Cases and Commentaries*, 1977, New York: St Martin's Press, and Mauro Cappelletti and William Cohen, *Comparative Constitutional Law: Cases and Materials*, 1979, Indianapolis: Bobbs-Merrill. See the review by Donald Kommers, 'Comparative Constitutional Law: Casebooks for a Developing Discipline' (1982) 57 Notre Dame Lawyer 642.

Appendix 1: Abbreviations

Archive	German Law Archive, http://www.iuscomp.org/gla/
AVR	*Archiv des Völkerrechts.*
AWD	*Aussenwirtschaftsdienst des Betriebs-Beraters.*
Brinkhorst & Schermers	LJ Brinkhorst and HG Schermers, *Judicial Remedies in the European Communities: A Casebook*, 1969, Deventer: Kluwer.
BVerfGE	*Entscheidungen des Bundesverfassungsgerichts.*
Cappelletti & Cohen	Mauro Cappelletti and William Cohen, *Comparative Constitutional Law: Cases and Materials*, 1979, Indianapolis: Bobbs-Merrill.
CMLR	Common Market Law Reports.
CML Rev	Common Market Law Review.
Craig & de Búrca	Paul Craig and Gráinne de Búrca, *EC Law: Text, Cases and Materials*, 1995, Oxford: Clarendon Press.
Decisions 1	Federal Constitutional Court, *Decisions of the Bundesverfassungsgericht Vol 1: International Law and Law of the European Communities 1952–1989*, 1992, Baden-Baden: Nomos.
Decisions 2	Federal Constitutional Court, *Decisions of the Bundesverfassungsgericht Vol 2: Freedom of Speech 1958–1995*, 1998, Baden-Baden: Nomos.
ECC	European Commercial Cases.
EuGRZ	*Europaische Grundrechte Zeitschrift.*
HRCR	http://www.hrcr.org/safrica [Human and Constitutional Rights Resource Page at Columbia University, Bill of Rights Comparative Law Materials].
ILM	International Legal Materials.
I L Pr	International Litigation Procedure.
ILR	International Law Reports.
Jackson & Tushnet	Vicki C Jackson and Mark Tushnet, *Comparative Constitutional Law*, 1999, New York: Foundation Press.
Jann	Edmund C Jann (trans), *The Abortion Decision of February 25, 1975 of the Federal Constitutional Court, Federal Republic of Germany*, 1975, Washington: Library of Congress, Law Library.

Jones & Garby	Robert E Jones and John D Garby, 'West German Abortion Decision: A Contrast to *Roe v Wade* with Commentaries' (1976) 9 John Marshall Journal of Practice and Procedure 605.
JZ	*Juristen Zeitung*.
Karpen (1980)	Ulrich Karpen (ed), *Access to Higher Education and its Restrictions Under the Constitution: Decision of the Federal Constitutional Court of the Federal Republic of Germany*, 1980, München: Minerva-Publikation.
Karpen (1988)	Ulrich Karpen, *Access to Higher Education in the Federal Republic of Germany: With Texts from the Federal Higher Education Law and Cases*, 1988, Frankfurt am Main: Peter Lang.
Kommers (1st ed)	Donald P Kommers, *The Constitutional Jurisprudence of the Federal Republic of Germany,* 1st edn, 1989, Durham: Duke University Press.
Kommers (2nd ed)	Donald P Kommers, *The Constitutional Jurisprudence of the Federal Republic of Germany,* 2nd edn, 1997, Durham: Duke University Press.
Lane & Pollock	John C Lane and James K Pollock, *Source Materials on the Government and Politics of Germany*, 1964, Ann Arbor, Mich: Wahrs Pub Co.
Markesinis (1st ed)	BS Markesinis, *The German Law of Torts: A Comparative Introduction,* 1st edn, 1986, Oxford: Clarendon Press.
Markesinis (2nd ed)	BS Markesinis, *The German Law of Torts: A Comparative Introduction*, 2nd edn, 1990, Oxford: Clarendon Press.
Markesinis (3rd ed)	BS Markesinis, *The German Law of Torts: A Comparative Introduction,* 3rd edn, 1994, Oxford: Clarendon Press.
Materials	United Nations Legislative Series, *Materials on Jurisdictional Immunities of States and Their Property,* ST/LEG/SER B.20, 1982, New York: United Nations.
Murphy & Tanenhaus	Walter F Murphy and Joseph Tanenhaus, *Comparative Constitutional Law: Cases and Commentaries*, 1977, New York: St Martin's Press.
NJW	*Neue Juristische Wochenschrift*.

Notre Dame Int'l & Comp LJ	Notre Dame International and Comparative Law Journal.
Oppenheimer	Andrew Oppenheimer (ed), *The Relationship Between European Community Law and National Law: The Cases*, 1994, Cambridge: Cambridge University Press.
Pfeiffer and Strickert	Gerd Pfeiffer and Hans-Georg Strickert, *Outlawing the Communist Party: A Case History,* trans Wolfgang P von Schmertzing, 1957, New York, Bookmailer.
Schlesinger	Rudolf B Schlesinger, Hans W Baade, Mirjan R Damaska, Peter E Herzog, *Comparative Law: Cases-Text-Materials,* 5th edn, 1988, Mineola, NY: Foundation Press.
Schweitzer (1984)	Carl-Christoph Schweitzer, Detlev Karsten, Robert Spencer, R Taylor Cole, Donald Kommers, Anthony Nicholls (eds), *Politics and Government in the Federal Republic of Germany: Basic Documents*, 1984, Leamington Spa: Berg Publishers.
Schweitzer (1995)	Carl-Christoph Schweitzer, Detlev Karsten, Robert Spencer, R Taylor Cole, Donald Kommers, Anthony Nicholls (eds), *Politics and Government in Germany, 1944–1994 Basic Documents*, 1995, Providence, RI: Berghahn Books.
YB ECHR	*Yearbook of the European Convention on Human Rights*.
Youngs	Raymond Youngs, *Sourcebook on German Law*, 1994, London: Cavendish Publishing.

Appendix 2: Index by Popular Name

Abortion I Case	BVerfGE 39, 1 (1975)
Abortion II Case	BVerfGE 88, 203 (1993)
Act on Reparations for War Losses Case	BVerfGE 41, 126 (1976)
Aircraft Noise Control Case	BVerfGE 56, 54 (1981)
Alfons Lütticke GMBH	BVerfGE 31, 145 (1971)
Allied Property Damage Case	BVerfGE 27, 253 (1969)
All Germany Election Case	BVerfGE 82, 322 (1990)
Anachronistic Parade Case	BVerfGE 67, 213 (1984)
Apportionment Case II	BVerfGE 16, 130 (1963)
Arrested Admiral Case	BVerfGE 19, 342 (1965)
Assembly Dispersal Case	BVerfGE 84, 203 (1991)
Assessment of Aliens for War Taxation Case	BVerfGE 18, 441 (1965)
Association Prohibition Case	BVerfGE 80, 244 (1989)
Atomic Weapons Referenda I Case	BVerfGE 8, 104 (1958)
Auschwitz Lie Case	BVerfGE 90, 241 (1994)
Austrian Nationality Case	BVerfGE 4, 322 (1955)
'Baader-Meinhof' Group Terrorist Case	BVerfGE 46, 214 (1977)
Baden-Württemberg Private Broadcasting Case	BVerfGE 74, 297 (1987)
Basic East-West Treaty Case	BVerfGE 36, 1 (1973)
Basic Right to Marry Case	BVerfGE 31, 58 (1971)
Bavarian Party Case	BVerfGE 6, 84 (1957)
Bayer Pharmaceutical Case	BVerfGE 85, 1 (1991)
Berlin Wall Shootings Case	BVerfGE 95, 96 (1996)
Blinkfüer Case	BVerfGE 25, 256 (1969)
Blood Transfusion Case	BVerfGE 32, 98 (1971)
Böll Case	BVerfGE 54, 208 (1980)
Border Killings Case	BVerfGE 95, 96 (1996)
Bosnia Flight Exclusion Zone Case	BVerfGE 88, 173 (1993)
Broadcast Injunction Case	BVerfGE 80, 74 (1989)
Broadcasting in North Rhine-Westphalia Case	BVerfGE 83, 238 (1991)
Brokdorf Demonstration Case	BVerfGE 69, 315 (1985)
Brückman Case	27 March 1974, 2 BvR 38/74
Bundesrat Case	BVerfGE 37, 363 (1975)
Cable Penny Case	BVerfGE 90, 60 (1994)

Campaign Slur Case	BVerfGE 61, 1 (1982)
Census Act Case	BVerfGE 65, 1 (1983)
Chemical Weapons Deployment (Danger to Life) Case	BVerfGE 77, 170 (1987)
Chocolate Candy Case	BVerfGE 53, 135 (1980)
Church Construction Tax Case	BVerfGE 19, 206 (1965)
Civil Servant Loyalty Case	BVerfGE 39, 334 (1975)
Claim Against the Empire of Iran Case	BVerfGE 16, 27 (1963)
Classroom Crucifix II Case	BVerfGE 93, 1 (1995)
Codetermination Case	BVerfGE 50, 290 (1979)
Coerced Democrat Case	BVerfGE 82, 272 (1990)
Commercial Treaty Case	BVerfGE 1, 372 (1952)
Communist Party Case	BVerfGE 5, 85 (1956)
Concordat Case	BVerfGE 6, 309 (1957)
Critical Shareholder Case	BVerfGE 85, 1 (1991)
Cruise Missiles (Danger to Life) Case	BVerfGE 66, 39 (1983)
Cruise Missiles Deployment (German Approval) Case	BVerfGE 68, 1 (1984)
CSU-NPD Case	BVerfGE 61, 1 (1982)
DDR Citizenship Case	BVerfGE 77, 137 (1987)
Decision of 9 November 1955	BVerfGE 4, 331 (1955)
Decision of 20 March 1956	BVerfGE 4, 412 (1956)
Decision of 18 June 1957	BVerfGE 7, 53 (1957)
Decision of 16 December 1958	BVerfGE 9, 36 (1958)
Decision of 8 January 1959	BVerfGE 9, 89 (1959)
Decision of 22 January 1959	BVerfGE 9, 124 (1959)
Decision of 12 January 1960	BVerfGE 10, 264 (1960)
Decision of 24 July 1963	BVerfGE 17, 86 (1963)
Decision of 24 March 1964	BVerfGE 17, 294 (1964)
Decision of 1 February 1967	BVerfGE 21, 132 (1967)
Decision of 6 June 1967	BVerfGE 22, 83 (1967)
Demokrat Newspaper Case	BVerfGE 27, 88 (1969)
Detention on Remand Case	BVerfGE 19, 342 (1965)
Disparaging Question Case	BVerfGE 85, 23 (1991)
Divorce Records Case	BVerfGE 27, 344 (1970)
Eastern Treaties Constitutionality Case	BVerfGE 40, 141 (1975)

East German Politicians Trial Publicity Case I	BVerfGE 87, 331 (1992)
East German Politicians Trial Publicity Case II	BVerfGE 87, 334 (1992)
East-Treaties Constitutionality Case (Injunction)	BVerfGE 33, 195 (1972)
EEC Regulations Constitutionality Case	BVerfGE 22, 293 (1967)
Election Campaign Case	BVerfGE 61, 1 (1982)
Elfes Case	BVerfGE 6, 32 (1957)
Emergency Price Control Case	BVerfGE 8, 274 (1958)
Empire of Iran Case	BVerfGE 16, 27 (1963)
Enforcement of Soviet Zone Panel Judgment	BVerfGE 1, 332 (1952)
Engineers Case	BVerfGE 26, 246 (1969)
Entry of Aliens to Join Family Members Case	BVerfGE 76, 1 (1987)
Eppler Case	BVerfGE 54, 148 (1980)
Equalization of Burden Case	BVerfGE 2, 237 (1953)
Equalization of Burdens Taxation Case	BVerfGE 23, 288 (1968)
Equestrian Case	BVerfGE 80, 137 (1989)
Eurocontrol I	BVerfGE 58, 1 (1981)
Eurocontrol II	BVerfGE 59, 63 (1981)
European Convention on Human Rights Case	BVerfGE 10, 271 (1960)
European Defense Community Injunction Case	BVerfGE 1, 281 (1952)
European Elections Act, Re the	BVerfGE 51, 222 (1979)
Evangelical Church Case	BVerfGE 18, 385 (1965)
Extradition Following Conviction by Trial Conducted in Absentia in Italy	BVerfGE 63, 332 (1983)
Extradition (Germany) Case	BVerfGE 10, 136 (1959)
Extradition (Yugoslav Refugee in Germany) Case	BVerfGE 9, 174 (1959)
Failure to Observe Deadline in Asylum Proceedings Case	BVerfGE 60, 253 (1982)
FA Steinike und Weinlig v Bundesamt für Erführung und Forstwirtschaft	BVerfGE 52, 187 (1979)
Federal Postal Service Case	BVerfGE 80, 124 (1989)
Fifth Broadcasting Case	BVerfGE 74, 297 (1987)
Financial Agreement with the Netherlands Case	BVerfGE 16, 220 (1963)
Financial Subsidies Case	BVerfGE 39, 96 (1975)
First Television Case	BVerfGE 12, 205 (1961)
Flag Desecration Case	BVerfGE 81, 278 (1990)
Foreign Voters I Case	BVerfGE 83, 37 (1990)

Former Syrian Ambassador to the German Democratic Republic Case	BVerfGE 96, 68 (1997)
Fourth Broadcasting Case	BVerfGE 73, 118 (1986)
Framework Legislation Case	BVerfGE 4, 115 (1954)
Freelance Broadcasting Employees Case	BVerfGE 59, 231
German Assets in Switzerland Case	BVerfGE 6, 290 (1957)
German-Austrian Legal Cooperation Treaty Case	BVerfGE 63, 343 (1983)
German Civil Service Case	BVerfGE 3, 58 (1953)
German Constitutional Rights Case	BVerfGE 22, 293 (1967)
German-Czechoslovakian Treaty Case	BVerfGE 43, 203 (1977)
German French-Barley Case	BVerfGE 22, 134 (1967)
German Industrial Injuries Insurance, Re	BVerfGE 23, 112 (1967)
German Inter-Zonal Trade Case	BVerfGE 18, 353 (1965)
German National Anthem Case	BVerfGE 81, 298 (1990)
German-Portuguese Assets Case	16 October 1968, 1 BvR 118/62, 1 BvR 104/63
German-Swiss Double Taxation Agreement Case	BVerfGE 72, 200 (1986)
Germany-Poland Border Treaty Constitutionality Case	NJW 1992, 3222
Green Party Exclusion Case	BVerfGE 70, 324 (1986)
Groundwater Case	BVerfGE 58, 300 (1981)
Group University Case	BVerfGE 35, 79 (1973)
Hague Child Abduction Convention Case	10 October 1995, 2 BvR 982/95 & 2 BvR 983/85
Hamburg Flood Control Case	BVerfGE 24, 367 (1968)
Hess Case	BVerfGE 55, 349 (1980)
Historical Falsification Case	BVerfGE 90, 1 (1994)
Hoheneggelsen Case	BVerfGE 59, 216 (1982)
Holocaust Denial Case	BVerfGE 90, 241 (1994)
Homosexuality Case	BVerfGE 6, 389 (1957)
Honour Impairing Questions Case	BVerfGE 85, 23 (1991)
Housework Day Case	BVerfGE 52, 369 (1979)
Import of Dutch Barley, Re	AWD 1973, p 549
Individual Responsibility and Liability to Punishment for Killing Fugitives at the Inner-German Frontier	BVerfGE 95, 96 (1996)

Interdenominational School Case	BVerfGE 41, 29 (1975)
Internationale Handelsgesellschaft mbH v Einfuhr-und vorratsstelle für Gertreide und Futtermittel	BVerfGE 37, 271 (1974)
International Military Operations (German Participation) Case	BVerfGE 90, 286 (1994)
Intervention Buying, Re	BVerfGE 45, 142 (1977)
Investment Aid I Case	BVerfGE 4, 7 (1954)
Joint Income Tax Case	BVerfGE 6, 55 (1957)
Judicial Qualification Case	BVerfGE 34, 52 (1972)
Jurisdiction of Federal Constitutional Court over Berlin Case	BVerfGE 20, 257 (1966)
Jurisdiction over Yugoslav Military Mission (Germany) Case	BVerfGE 15, 25 (1962)
Kalkar I Case	BVerfGE 49, 89 (1978)
Kalkar II Case	BVerfGE 81, 310 (1990)
Kloppenberg	BVerfGE 75, 223 (1987)
Lebach Case	BVerfGE 35, 202 (1973)
Legal Aid Case	BVerfGE 78, 104 (1988)
Legislative Pay Case	BVerfGE 40, 296 (1975)
Leipzig Daily Newspaper Case	BVerfGE 27, 71 (1969)
Life Imprisonment Case	BVerfGE 45, 187 (1977)
Lock-out Case	BVerfGE 84, 212 (1991)
Lower Saxony Broadcasting Act, Re the	BVerfGE 73, 118 (1986)
Lüth Case	BVerfGE 7, 198 (1958)
Maastricht Case	BVerfGE 89, 155 (1993)
Mayen Absentee Ballot Case	BVerfGE 59, 119 (1981)
Mephisto Case	BVerfGE 30, 173 (1971)
Microcensus Case	BVerfGE 27, 1 (1969)
Mixed-Marriage Church Tax I Case	BVerfGE 19, 226 (1965)
Movie Boycott Case	BVerfGE 7, 198 (1958)
Mutlangen Demonstration Case	BVerfGE 73, 206 (1986)
Mutzenbacher Case	BVerfGE 83, 130 (1990)
Nachrücker Case	BVerfGE 7, 77 (1957)
National Anthem Case	BVerfGE 81, 298 (1990)
National Iranian Oil Company Revenues from Oil Sales Case	BVerfGE 64, 1 (1983)

Return Extradition Case	BVerfGE 29, 183 (1970)
Römerberg Speech Case	BVerfGE 54, 129 (1980)
Rudolf Hess Case	BVerfGE 55, 349 (1980)
Rumpelkammer Case	BVerfGE 24, 236 (1968)
Saar Territory Case	JZ 1955, 670
Salzburg Airport Case	BVerfGE 72, 66 (1986)
Schleswig-Holstein Investigative Committee Case	BVerfGE 49, 70 (1978)
Schleyer Kidnapping Case	BVerfGE 46, 160 (1977)
Schmid-Spiegel Case	BVerfGE 12, 113 (1961)
Schoolbook Case	BVerfGE 31, 229 (1971)
School Prayer Case	BVerfGE 52, 223 (1979)
Service of Punitive Damages Claims Case I	BVerfGE 91, 140 (1994)
Service of Punitive Damages Claims Case II	BVerfGE 91, 335 (1994)
Sex Education Case	BVerfGE 47, 46 (1977)
Short Work Week Case	BVerfGE 52, 369 (1979)
Single German Nationality (Teso) Case	BVerfGE 77, 137 (1987)
Sixth Broadcasting Case	BVerfGE 83, 238 (1991)
Socialist Reich Party Case	BVerfGE 2, 1 (1952)
Solange I	BVerfGE 37, 271 (1974)
Solange II	BVerfGE 73, 339 (1986)
Soldiers are Murderers Case	BVerfGE 93, 266 (1995)
Soraya Case	BVerfGE 34, 269 (1973)
Southwest State Case	BVerfGE 1, 14 (1951)
Spiegel Case	BVerfGE 20, 162 (1966)
Spinal Tap Case	BVerfGE 16, 194 (1963)
Statute of Saar Territory Case	BVerfGE 4, 157 (1955)
Stern-Strauss Case	BVerfGE 82, 272 (1990)
Strauß Caricature Case	BVerfGE 75, 369 (1987)
Street Theater Case	BVerfGE 67, 213 (1984)
Suspended Sentence Community Service Case	BVerfGE 83, 119 (1990)
Tax on Malt Barley, Re	BVerfGE 22, 134 (1967)
Televised News Reports, Re	BVerfGE 97, 228 (1998)
Television I Case	BVerfGE 12, 205 (1961)
Television III Case	BVerfGE 57, 295 (1981)
Television IV Case	BVerfGE 73, 118 (1986)
Television V Case	BVerfGE 74, 297 (1987)

Television VI Case	BVerfGE 83, 238 (1991)
Teso Case	BVerfGE 77, 137 (1987)
Third Broadcasting Case	BVerfGE 57, 295 (1981)
Third Television Case	BVerfGE 57, 295 (1981)
Tobacco Atheist Case	BVerfGE 12, 1 (1960)
Transsexual Case	BVerfGE 49, 286 (1979)
Truth for Germany Case	BVerfGE 90, 1 (1994)
Tucholsky I Case	NJW 1994, 2943
Tucholsky II Case	BVerfGE 93, 266 (1995)
Turkish National Detention on Remand Case	BVerfGE 30, 409 (1971)
Two Trustees in Bankruptcy, Constitutional Complaints of	BVerfGE 65, 182 (1983)
Unification Treaty Constitutional Case (Merits)	BVerfGE 84, 90 (1991)
Value Added Tax Exemption, Re	NJW 1988, 2173
Volga Artikel Case	BVerfGE 12, 113 (1961)
Volkswagen Denationalization Case	BVerfGE 12, 354 (1961)
Wallraff Case	BVerfGE 66, 116 (1984)
Wall Shootings Case	BVerfGE 95, 96 (1996)
West German Media Case	BVerfGE 14, 121 (1962)
Worker Participation, Re	BVerfGE 50, 290 (1979)
Working Hours Equality Case	BVerfGE 85, 191 (1992)
Wünsche Handelsgesellschaft, Re the Application of	BVerfGE 73, 339 (1986)
Wüppesahl Case	BVerfGE 80, 188 (1989)

Appendix 3: Index by Citation

Cases reported in BVerfGE

BVerfGE 6, 32 (1957)	Elfes Case, Kommers (1st edn) 324, Kommers (2nd edn) 315, Archive.
BVerfGE 6, 55 (1957)	Joint Income Tax Case, Kommers (1st edn) 493, Kommers (2nd edn) 495, Murphy & Tanenhaus 339.
BVerfGE 6, 84 (1957)	Bavarian Party Case, Murphy & Tanenhaus 578, Kommers (1st edn) 187.
BVerfGE 6, 290 (1957)	German Assets in Switzerland Case, 24 ILR 542, Decisions 1: 92.
BVerfGE 6, 309 (1957)	Concordat Case, Murphy & Tanenhaus 225, Kommers (1st edn) 91, Kommers (2nd edn) 80, 24 ILR 592, Decisions 1: 99, Schweitzer (1984) 146, Schweitzer (1995) 364, Brinkhorst & Schermers 143, Lane & Pollock 136, Jackson & Tushnet 831.
BVerfGE 6, 389 (1957)	Homosexuality Case, Murphy & Tanenhaus 35, 403; 2 YB ECHR 594.
BVerfGE 7, 53 (1957)	Decision of 18 June 1957, Cappelletti & Cohen 477.
BVerfGE 7, 77 (1957)	Nachrücker Case, Kommers (1st edn) 190.
BVerfGE 7, 198 (1958)	Lüth Case / Movie Boycott Case, Kommers (1st edn) 368, Kommers (2nd edn) 361, Murphy & Tanenhaus 528, Markesinis (2nd edn) 270, Markesinis (3rd edn) 352, Schweitzer (1984) 122, Schweitzer (1995) 307, Lane & Pollock 317, Decisions 2: 1, Youngs 431, Jackson & Tushnet 1403, Archive.
BVerfGE 7, 377 (1958)	Pharmacy Case, Kommers (1st edn) 285, Kommers (2nd edn) 274.
BVerfGE 8, 51 (1958)	Party Finance II Case, Kommers (1st edn) 202, Kommers (2nd edn) 201, Lane & Pollock 231.
BVerfGE 8, 104 (1958)	Atomic Weapons Referenda I Case, Kommers (1st edn) 86, Kommers (2nd edn) 76, Murphy & Tanenhaus 229.
BVerfGE 8, 274 (1958)	Emergency Price Control Case, Kommers (1st edn) 147, Kommers (2nd edn) 137.
BVerfGE 9, 36 (1958)	Decision of 16 December 1958, Cappelletti & Cohen 424.
BVerfGE 9, 89 (1959)	Decision of 8 January 1959, Cappelletti & Cohen 268.

BVerfGE 9, 124 (1959)	Decision of 22 January 1959, Cappelletti & Cohen 485.
BVerfGE 9, 174 (1959)	Extradition (Yugoslav Refugee in Germany) Case, 28 ILR 347.
BVerfGE 10, 136 (1959)	Extradition (Germany) Case, 28 ILR 319.
BVerfGE 10, 264 (1960)	Decision of 12 January 1960, Cappelletti & Cohen 221.
BVerfGE 10, 271 (1960)	European Convention on Human Rights Case, 3 YB ECHR 628.
BVerfGE 12, 1 (1960)	Tobacco Atheist Case, Murphy & Tanenhaus 466.
BVerfGE 12, 113 (1961)	Schmid-Spiegel Case / Volga Artikel Case, Kommers (1st edn) 377, Kommers (2nd edn) 369, Decisions 2: 21.
BVerfGE 12, 205 (1961)	Television I Case, Kommers (1st edn) 79, 404, Kommers (2nd edn) 69, 404, Murphy & Tanenhaus 212, Schweitzer (1984) 149, Schweitzer (1995) 367, Decisions 2: 31, Lane & Pollock 138, Jackson & Tushnet 827.
BVerfGE 12, 354 (1961)	Volkswagen Denationalization Case, Kommers (1st edn) 254, Kommers (2nd edn) 248, Murphy & Tanenhaus 280.
BVerfGE 14, 121 (1962)	West German Media Case, Kommers (1st edn) 218, Kommers (2nd edn) 215.
BVerfGE 15, 25 (1962)	Jurisdiction over Yugoslav Military Mission (Germany) Case, 38 ILR 162, Decisions 1: 137, Materials 272.
BVerfGE 16, 27 (1963)	Claim Against the Empire of Iran Case, 45 ILR 57, Decisions 1: 150, Materials 282.
BVerfGE 16, 130 (1963)	Apportionment Case II, Kommers (1st edn) 192, Kommers (2nd edn) 193.
BVerfGE 16, 194 (1963)	Spinal Tap Case, Kommers (1st edn) 344, Kommers (2nd edn) 333.
BVerfGE 16, 220 (1963)	Ratification of Financial Agreement with the Netherlands Case, 43 ILR 246.
BVerfGE 17, 86 (1963)	Decision of 24 July 1963, Cappelletti & Cohen 264.
BVerfGE 17, 294 (1964)	Decision of 24 March 1964, Cappelletti & Cohen 367.
BVerfGE 18, 353 (1965)	German Inter-Zonal Trade Case, 45 ILR 37.
BVerfGE 18, 385 (1965)	Evangelical Church Case, Kommers (1st edn) 487, Kommers (2nd edn) 491, Schweitzer (1984) 125, Schweitzer (1995) 311.

BVerfGE 27, 88 (1969)	Demokrat Newspaper Case, Decisions 2: 136.
BVerfGE 27, 104 (1969)	Publication Seizure Case, Decisions 2: 143.
BVerfGE 27, 253 (1969)	Allied Property Damage Case, Decisions 1: 206.
BVerfGE 27, 344 (1970)	Divorce Records Case, Kommers (1st edn) 337, Kommers (2nd edn) 327.
BVerfGE 29, 183 (1970)	Return Extradition Case, HRCR (Citizenship).
BVerfGE 30, 1 (1970)	Privacy of Communications Case / Klass Case, Murphy & Tanenhaus 659, Schweitzer (1984) 135, Schweitzer (1995) 319.
BVerfGE 30, 173 (1971)	Mephisto Case, Kommers (1st edn) 309, 426, Kommers (2nd edn) 301, 427, Murphy & Tanehaus 538, Markesinis (2nd edn) 277, Markesinis (3rd edn) 358, Decisions 2: 147, HRCR (Dignity), Archive.
BVerfGE 30, 409 (1971)	Turkish National Detention on Remand Case, 72 ILR 263.
BVerfGE 31, 58 (1971)	Basic Right to Marry Case, 72 ILR 294.
BVerfGE 31, 145 (1971)	Alfons Lütticke GMBH, 93 ILR 358, Decisions 1: 230, Oppenheimer 415.
BVerfGE 31, 229 (1971)	Schoolbook Case, Kommers (1st edn) 271, Kommers (2nd edn) 262.
BVerfGE 32, 98 (1971)	Blood Transfusion Case, Kommers (1st edn) 451, Kommers (2nd edn) 449.
BVerfGE 33, 23 (1972)	Religious Oath Case, Kommers (1st edn) 456, Kommers (2nd edn) 453.
BVerfGE 33, 195 (1972)	East-Treaties Constitutionality Case (Injunction), 73 ILR 691.
BVerfGE 33, 303 (1972)	Numerus Clausus I Case, Karpen (1980), Karpen (1988) 73, Kommers (1st edn) 295, Kommers (2nd edn) 282.
BVerfGE 34, 52 (1972)	Judicial Qualification Case, Kommers (1st edn) 157, Kommers (2nd edn) 145.
BVerfGE 34, 269 (1973)	Princess Soraya Case, Kommers (1st edn) 131, Kommers (2nd edn) 124, Schlesinger 627.
BVerfGE 35, 79 (1973)	Group University Case, Kommers (1st edn) 437, Kommers (2nd edn) 437.
BVerfGE 35, 202 (1973)	Lebach Case, Kommers (1st edn) 414, Kommers (2nd edn) 416, Markesinis (1st edn) 205, Markesinis (2nd edn) 308, Markesinis (3rd edn) 390, Archive.

BVerfGE 36, 1 (1973)	Basic East-West Treaty Case, 78 ILR 149, Murphy & Tanenhaus 232, Decisions 1: 244.
BVerfGE 36, 264 (1973)	Overburdening of Courts Case, HRCR (Life).
BVerfGE 37, 271 (1974)	Internationale Handelsgesellschaft mbH v Einfuhr- und vorratsstelle für Gertreide und Futtermittel / Solange I, 93 ILR 362, [1974] 2 CMLR 540, Cappelletti & Cohen 178, Decisions 1: 270, Oppenheimer 419, 12 CML Rev 303.
BVerfGE 37, 363 (1975)	Pension Insurance Amendment Case / Bundesrat Case, Kommers (1st edn) 108, Kommers (2nd edn) 98, Jackson & Tushnet 839.
BVerfGE 38, 128 (1974)	Polish Priest Compensation Case, 74 ILR 419.
BVerfGE 39, 1 (1975)	Abortion I Case, Kommers (1st edn) 348, Kommers (2nd edn) 336, Murphy & Tanenhaus 422, Cappelletti & Cohen 586, 18 YB ECHR 426, Jones & Garby, Jann passim, Schweitzer (1984) 127, Schweitzer (1995) 312, Jackson & Tushnet 115, HRCR (Life).
BVerfGE 39, 96 (1975)	Financial Subsidies Case, Kommers (1st edn) 102, Kommers (2nd edn) 93.
BVerfGE 39, 334 (1975)	Civil Servant Loyalty Case, Kommers (1st edn) 232, Kommers (2nd edn) 229, Schweitzer (1984) 131, Schweitzer (1995) 317.
BVerfGE 40, 141 (1975)	Eastern Treaties Constitutionality Case, 78 ILR 75, Decisions 1: 284.
BVerfGE 40, 296 (1975)	Legislative Pay Case, Kommers (1st edn) 142, Kommers (2nd edn) 133.
BVerfGE 41, 29 (1975)	Interdenominational School Case, Kommers (1st edn) 473, Kommers (2nd edn) 467.
BVerfGE 41, 126 (1976)	Act on Reparations for War Losses Case, Decisions 1: 309.
BVerfGE 42, 120 (1976)	Procedural Rights of Aliens Case, 74 ILR 412.
BVerfGE 43, 203 (1977)	German-Czechoslovakian Treaty Case, Decisions 1: 350, HRCR (Movement).
BVerfGE 44, 125 (1977)	Official Propaganda Case, Kommers (1st edn) 180, Kommers (2nd edn) 177.
BVerfGE 45, 142 (1977)	Re Intervention Buying, [1978] 2 CMLR 644.
BVerfGE 45, 187 (1977)	Life Imprisonment Case, Kommers (1st edn) 314, Kommers (2nd edn) 306, HRCR (Dignity).

BVerfGE 46, 160 (1977)	Schleyer Kidnapping Case, Kommers (1st edn) 362, Kommers (2nd edn) 356, HRCR (Life).
BVerfGE 46, 214 (1977)	'Baader-Meinhof' Group Terrorist Case, 74 ILR 493.
BVerfGE 46, 342 (1977)	Philippine Embassy Bank Account Case, 65 ILR 146, Materials 297, Decisions 1: 358.
BVerfGE 47, 46 (1977)	Sex Education Case, Kommers (1st edn) 498, Kommers (2nd edn) 500.
BVerfGE 47, 198 (1978)	Radical Groups Case, Kommers (1st edn) 240, Kommers (2nd edn) 224.
BVerfGE 49, 70 (1978)	Schleswig-Holstein Investigative Committee Case, Kommers (1st edn) 171, Kommers (2nd edn) 167.
BVerfGE 49, 89 (1978)	Kalkar I Case, Kommers (1st edn) 150, Kommers (2nd edn) 139, Archive.
BVerfGE 49, 286 (1979)	Transsexual Case, Kommers (1st edn) 341, Kommers (2nd edn) 330.
BVerfGE 50, 290 (1979)	Re Worker Participation / Codetermination Case, [1979] ECC 324, Kommers (1st edn) 278, Kommers (2nd edn) 267.
BVerfGE 51, 222 (1979)	Re the European Elections Act, [1980] 1 CMLR 497.
BVerfGE 52, 187 (1979)	Weinlig v Bundesamt fur Ernahrung und Forstwirtschaft, [1980] 2 CMLR 531.
BVerfGE 52, 223 (1979)	School Prayer Case, Kommers (1st edn) 466, Kommers (2nd edn) 461, Jackson & Tushnet 1169.
BVerfGE 52, 369 (1979)	Housework Day Case / Short Work Week Case, Youngs 129.
BVerfGE 53, 135 (1980)	Chocolate Candy Case, Kommers (1st edn) 292, Kommers (2nd edn) 279.
BVerfGE 54, 129 (1980)	Römerberg Speech Case, Decisions 2: 181.
BVerfGE 54, 148 (1980)	Eppler Case, Kommers (1st edn) 329, Kommers (2nd edn) 320.
BVerfGE 54, 208 (1980)	Böll Case, Kommers (1st edn) 419, Kommers (2nd edn) 420, Decisions 2: 189, Jackson & Tushnet 1409.
BVerfGE 55, 349 (1980)	Rudolf Hess Case, 90 ILR 386, Decisions 1: 391.
BVerfGE 56, 54 (1981)	Aircraft Noise Control Case, Kommers (1st edn) 137, Kommers (2nd edn) 128.
BVerfGE 57, 295 (1981)	Television III Case, Kommers (1st edn) 409, Kommers (2nd edn) 408, Decisions 2: 199.

BVerfGE 58, 1 (1981)	Eurocontrol I Case, Decisions 1: 399.
BVerfGE 58, 300 (1981)	Groundwater Case, Kommers (1st edn) 265, Kommers (2nd edn) 257.
BVerfGE 59, 63 (1981)	Eurocontrol II Case, Decisions 1: 417.
BVerfGE 59, 119 (1981)	Mayen Absentee Ballot Case, Kommers (1st edn) 197.
BVerfGE 59, 216 (1982)	Hoheneggelsen Case, Kommers (1st edn) 115, Kommers (2nd edn) 103.
BVerfGE 59, 231 (1982)	Freelance Broadcasting Employees Case, Decisions 2: 220.
BVerfGE 60, 253 (1982)	Failure to Observe Deadline in Asylum Proceedings Case, Decisions 1: 432.
BVerfGE 61, 1 (1982)	Campaign Slur Case / CSU-NPD Case / Election Campaign Case, Kommers (1st edn) 389, Kommers (2nd edn) 378, Decisions 2: 244.
BVerfGE 62, 1 (1983)	Parliamentary Dissolution Case, Kommers (1st edn) 125, Kommers (2nd edn) 118, Schweitzer (1984) 77, Schweitzer (1995) 270.
BVerfGE 63, 332 (1983)	Extradition Following Conviction by Trial Conducted in Absentia in Italy, Bundesverfassunsgericht 1: 450.
BVerfGE 63, 343 (1983)	German-Austrian Legal Cooperation Treaty Case, Decisions 1: 455.
BVerfGE 64, 1 (1983)	National Iranian Oil Company Revenues from Oil Sales Case, 65 ILR 215, 22 ILM 1279, Decisions 1: 479.
BVerfGE 65, 1 (1983)	Census Act Case, 5 HRLJ 94, Kommers (1st edn) 332, Kommers (2nd edn) 323.
BVerfGE 65, 182 (1983)	Constitutional Complaints of Two Trustees in Bankruptcy, Schlesinger 639.
BVerfGE 66, 39 (1983)	Cruise Missiles (Danger to Life) Case, 106 ILR 353, 2 Notre Dame Int'l & Comp LJ 193, Kommers (1st edn) 164, Kommers (2nd edn) 155, Decisions 1: 499.
BVerfGE 66, 116 (1984)	Wallraff Case, Decisions 2: 253.
BVerfGE 67, 213 (1984)	Street Theater Case / Anachronistic Parade Case, Kommers (1st edn) 431, Kommers (2nd edn) 431, Decisions 2: 272.
BVerfGE 68, 1 (1984)	Cruise Missiles Deployment (German Approval) Case, 106 ILR 364, Decisions 1: 511.

BVerfGE 69, 315 (1985)	Brokdorf Demonstration Case, Decisions 2: 284, HRCR (Assembly), Archive.
BVerfGE 70, 324 (1986)	Green Party Exclusion Case, Kommers (1st edn) 175, Kommers (2nd edn) 170.
BVerfGE 72, 66 (1986)	Salzburg Airport Case, Decisions 1: 550.
BVerfGE 72, 200 (1986)	German-Swiss Double Taxation Agreement Case, Decisions 1: 561.
BVerfGE 73, 118 (1986)	Re the Lower Saxony Broadcasting Act / Fourth Broadcasting Case, [1988] ECC 442, Decisions 2: 313.
BVerfGE 73, 206 (1986)	Mutlangen Demonstration Case, Decisions 2: 357.
BVerfGE 73, 339 (1986)	Re the Application of Wünsche Handelsgesellschaft/Solange II, 93 ILR 403, [1987] 3 CMLR 225, Decisions 1: 613, Oppenheimer 461.
BVerfGE 74, 163 (1987)	Pension Reform Case, HRCR (Equality).
BVerfGE 74, 297 (1987)	Fifth Broadcasting Case / Baden-Württemberg Private Broadcasting Case, Decisions 2: 386.
BVerfGE 74, 358 (1987)	Presumption of Innocence and the European Convention on Human Rights Case, Decisions 1: 634.
BVerfGE 75, 1 (1987)	Principle of 'Ne Bis Idem' Under International Law Case, Decisions 1: 644.
BVerfGE 75, 223 (1987)	Kloppenberg, [1988] 3 CMLR 1, 93 ILR 438, Oppenheimer 496.
BVerfGE 75, 369 (1987)	Strauß Caricature Case, Decisions 2: 420.
BVerfGE 76, 1 (1987)	Entry of Aliens to Join Family Members Case, Decisions 1: 662.
BVerfGE 77, 137 (1987)	Single German Nationality (Teso) Case / DDR Citizenship Case, 91 ILR 211, Decisions 1: 718, Schweitzer (1995) 323.
BVerfGE 77, 170 (1987)	Chemical Weapons Deployment (Danger to Life) Case, 106 ILR 389, Decisions 1: 738, HRCR (Life).
BVerfGE 78, 104 (1988)	Legal Aid Case, HRCR (Equality).
BVerfGE 80, 124 (1989)	Federal Postal Service Case, Decisions 2: 428.
BVerfGE 80, 137 (1989)	Equestrian Case, Archive.
BVerfGE 80, 188 (1989)	Wüppesahl Case, Kommers (2nd edn) 174.
BVerfGE 80, 244 (1989)	Association Prohibition Case, HRCR (Association).
BVerfGE 81, 278 (1990)	Flag Desecration Case, Decisions 2: 437.
BVerfGE 81, 298 (1990)	German National Anthem Case, Decisions 2: 450.

BVerfGE 81, 310 (1990)	Kalkar II Case, Kommers (2nd edn) 84.
BVerfGE 82, 1 (1990)	Nazi Symbols Case, Decisions 2: 458.
BVerfGE 82, 272 (1990)	Stern-Strauss Case / Coerced Democrat Case, Decisions 2: 463.
BVerfGE 82, 322 (1990)	National Unity Election Case / All Germany Election Case, Kommers (2nd edn) 187, Youngs 53, Archive.
BVerfGE 83, 37 (1990)	Foreign Voters I Case, Kommers (2nd edn) 197.
BVerfGE 83, 119 (1990)	Suspended Sentence Community Service Case, HRCR (Trade).
BVerfGE 83, 130 (1990)	Mutzenbacher Case, Decisions 2: 474.
BVerfGE 83, 238 (1991)	Sixth Broadcasting Case / Broadcasting in North Rhine-Westphalia Case, Decisions 2: 493.
BVerfGE 84, 90 (1991)	Unification Treaty Constitutional Case (Merits), 94 ILR 42.
BVerfGE 84, 203 (1991)	Assembly Dispersal Case, Decisions 2: 535.
BVerfGE 84, 212 (1991)	Lock-out Case, HRCR (Association).
BVerfGE 85, 1 (1991)	Critical Shareholder Case / Bayer Pharmaceutical Case, Decisions 2: 542.
BVerfGE 85, 23 (1991)	Disparaging Question Case / Honour Impairing Questions Case, Decisions 2: 559.
BVerfGE 85, 191 (1992)	Working Hours Equality Case / Nocturnal Employment Case, 98 ILR 190, Oppenheimer 520, Kommers (2nd edn) 291, HRCR (Equality), Archive.
BVerfGE 87, 331 (1992)	East German Politicians Trial Publicity Case I, Youngs 145.
BVerfGE 87, 334 (1992)	East German Politicians Trial Publicity Case II, Youngs 149.
BVerfGE 88, 173 (1993)	Bosnia Flight Exclusion Zone Case, Youngs 19.
BVerfGE 88, 203 (1993)	Abortion II Case, Kommers (2nd edn) 349, Schweitzer (1995) 314.
BVerfGE 89, 1 (1993)	Possessory Title Case, HRCR (Property).
BVerfGE 89, 155 (1993)	Maastricht Case, [1994] 1 CMLR 57, 98 ILR 196, 33 ILM 388, Oppenheimer 526, Kommers (2nd edn) 109, 182, 31 CML Rev 251, Craig & de Búrca 261.
BVerfGE 90, 1 (1994)	Historical Falsification Case / Truth for Germany Case, Decisions 2: 570.

BVerfGE 90, 60 (1994)	Cable Penny Case, Decisions 2: 587.
BVerfGE 90, 145 (1994)	Cannabis Case, Archive.
BVerfGE 90, 241 (1994)	Holocaust Denial Case / Auschwitz Lie Case, Kommers (2nd edn) 382, Decisions 2: 620.
BVerfGE 90, 255 (1994)	Prison Letter Surveillance Case, HRCR (Dignity).
BVerfGE 90, 286 (1994)	International Military Operations (German Participation) Case, 106 ILR 319.
BVerfGE 91, 140 (1994)	Service of Punitive Damages Claims Case I, 34 ILM 975.
BVerfGE 91, 335 (1994)	Service of Punitive Damages Claims Case II, 34 ILM 975, [1997] I L Pr 325, Jackson & Tushnet 1174.
BVerfGE 93, 1 (1995)	Classroom Crucifix II Case, 17 HRLJ 458, Kommers (2nd edn) 472, Decisions 2: 631.
BVerfGE 93, 266 (1995)	Tucholsky II Case / Soldiers are Murderers Case, 17 HRLJ 140, Decisions 2: 659.
BVerfGE 95, 96 (1996)	Individual Responsibility and Liability to Punishment for Killing Fugitives at the Inner-German Frontier / Border Killings Case, 18 HRLJ 65.
BVerfGE 96, 68 (1997)	Former Syrian Ambassador to the German Democratic Republic Case, 115 ILR 595.
BVerfGE 97, 228 (1998)	Re Televised News Reports, [1999] ECC 399.
BVerfGE 97, 391 (1998)	Abuse Accusation Case, Archive.
BVerfGE 101, 361 (1999)	Princess Caroline of Monaco Case, 10 BHRC 131.
BVerfGE 102, 147 (2000)	Banana Market Regulations Case, 21 HRLJ 251.

Decisions reported in other series, unreported decisions

AWD 1973, 549	Re Import of Dutch Barley, [1973] CMLR 785.
JZ 1955, 670	Rendition of Suspected Criminal (Saar Territory) Case, 22 ILR 512.
NJW 1988, 2173	Re Value Added Tax Exemption, [1989] 1 CMLR 113.
NJW 1990, 974	M GmbH and Others v Bundesregierung, [1990] 1 CMLR 570, 93 ILR 437.

NJW 1992, 3222	Germany-Poland Border Treaty Constitutionality Case, 108 ILR 656.
NJW 1994, 2943	Tucholsky I Case, Kommers (2nd edn) 388.
EuGRZ 1988, 109	Re Patented Feeding Stuffs, [1989] 2 CMLR 902.
16 October 1968, 1 BvR 118/62, 1 BvR 104/63	German-Portuguese Assets Case, 51 ILR 401.
27 March 1974, 2 BvR 38/74	Brückman Case, 17 YB ECHR 656.
10 October 1995, 2 BvR 982/95 & 2 BvR 983/85	Hague Child Abduction Convention Case, 35 ILM 529.
22 November 2001, 2 BvE 6/99	NATO Strategic Concept Case, http://www.bverfg.de

The Black Hole: Where are the Four Corners of the CISG?

Bruno Zeller

Introduction

Article 7 CISG stipulates that the Vienna Convention must be interpreted having regard to its international character and the need to promote uniformity in its application. It is well established in literature and case law that the 'international character' of the CISG demands that its terms and concepts be interpreted autonomously; that is 'in the context of the Convention itself and not by referring to the meaning, which might traditionally be attached to them within a particular domestic law.'[1] Courts are also expected to abandon the literal or grammatical approach in favor of a purposive one because, in interpreting the CISG, regard must be had to the 'underlying purposes and policies of individual provisions as well as of the Convention as a whole'.[2]

The application of the CISG is limited due to the fact that it was consciously drafted so as not to cover all aspects of a sale of goods. For example, Art 4 expressly excludes matters of 'validity' and other matters are simply left out of the sphere of application of the CISG. This paper examines whether terms such as 'validity' of contract are clear and definable within the four corners of the CISG or whether they have 'elastic' corners. If such 'elastic' corners are discovered do the rules contained in Art 7, mandating interpretation in accordance with 'international character' and 'general principles', assist in including matters within the CISG, which at first glance are excluded? In the application of Art 7, it is necessary to be mindful of the possible criticism that laws are being fabricated or invented, which are not within the mandate of Art 7 or the Convention as a whole.[3] The real question is where the boundary lies between interpretation and the making of law.

---

1 Bianca, CM and Bonell, MJ, *Commentary on the International Sales Law, The 1980 Vienna Sales Convention*, 1987, Milan: Giuffre, at 74.

2 *Ibid* at 73.

3 In the context of 'fabricating' laws it is interesting to note a Swiss decision of 10 October 1997 in the Cour de Justice Geneve, (*Filinter v Moulinages Poizat*, C/21501/1996) [http://cisgw3.law.pace.edu/cases/971010s1.html]. The question was whether the one-year limitation period under Article 210 of the Swiss Civil Code, overruled a two-year limitation period provided under the CISG. The court invoked Article 1(2) of the Swiss Civil Code, which allows a judge to lay down a law in cases of ambiguities, as though the judge were a legislator. The court extended the one-year period under Swiss law to two years and brought it in line with the CISG. By bringing Swiss Law into line with the CISG, the judge bypassed the application of Article 4.

Many commentators point to important gaps and ambiguities within the CISG, such as the uncertain status of good faith as a behavioral norm and the meaning of validity in Art 4.[4] Louis and Patrick Del Duca record that of 142 reported cases, 52 involved disputed issues of law, which had to be settled according to domestic provisions.[5]

Excessive reliance on domestic law would undermine the primary purpose of the CISG, which, simply stated, is to overcome the 'awesome relics from the dead past'[6] by creating a law which overcomes the serious obstacles for free trade created by municipal laws. Predictability of outcome and clear and simplified norms, the most important goals of any law, can only be achieved through uniformity of application at an international level as opposed to a national one. When properly applied, the CISG will overcome the danger posed by municipal law of a 'parachute drop into the darkness'.[7] Through the correct application of Art 7, the CISG has the ability to produce a jurisprudence that will achieve uniform and predictable outcomes.

This paper seeks solutions to some of the complex problems facing courts by using the interpretative tool provided by the Convention in Art 7. In other words it considers how far the influence of domestic law can be pushed back in favor of an international interpretation of the CISG.

International sales laws

Before considering the CISG, it is important to examine other international sales laws such as the UNIDROIT Principles of International Commercial Contracts (UNIDROIT Principles) and the Principles of European Contract Law (European Principles) to see how these principles can assist in filling gaps in the CISG. Both sets of Principles declare that they may be used as a tool in helping to interpret and fill gaps within other legal instruments such as the CISG.[8] The UNIDROIT Principles and the European Principles could potentially resolve many ambiguities and fill gaps within the CISG. However, a direct application of these laws would not be legitimate because in the absence of express provision by the parties, they would not be the governing

4 Ziegel, JS, 'The UNIDROIT Contract Principles, CISG and National Law' [http://cisg.law.pace.edu/cisg/biblio/ziegel2.html].

5 Del Duca, L and Del Duca P, 'Practice Under the Convention on International Sale of Goods (CISG): A Primer for Attorneys and International Traders (Part II)' (1996) 29 Uniform Commercial Code Law Journal: 99.

6 Rabel, E, 'The Hague Conference on the Unification of Sales Law' (1952) 1 American Journal of Comparative Law 58 at 61.

7 Diedrich, F, 'Maintaining Uniformity in International Uniform Law via Autonomous Interpretation: Software Contracts and the CISG' (1996) 8 Pace International Law Review: 303–38, at 305.

8 Preamble to the UNIDROIT Principles: 'They may be used to interpret or supplement international uniform law instruments.' Article 1:101(4) European Principles: 'These principles may provide a solution to the issue raised where the system or rules of law applicable do not do so.'

law of an international sales contract. Furthermore, direct application to fill gaps would contravene Art 7(2), which requires unsettled issues to be resolved by application of the 'general principles' of the CISG. The UNIDROIT Principles and the European Principles have the advantage that their provisions were constructed by relying on the CISG, which was already in operation. The other advantage was that the sponsors of the two Principles were not representatives of States but were eminent jurists not bound by political considerations. For that reason they tried to overcome the perceived shortcomings of the CISG and where possible built on its strengths.

Despite the fact that the European Principles or the UNIDROIT Principles would provide an attractive solution to an interpretative problem neither can be used unless the CISG does not supply an answer. It has been argued that functionally similar rules can be used to interpret the CISG, at least by analogy. Ziegel considered this possibility and stated:

> The post-CISG generation of lawyers may feel impatient with this fussy approach and may prefer to resolve ambiguities by going directly to the Principles. While I understand and sympathize ... it is nevertheless unacceptable.[9]

Scholars and judges alike have expressed similar views. For example, Meagher JA in *Kotsambasis v Singapore Airlines Ltd*[10] considered that:

> The interpretation of a particular phrase used in municipal law and the change over the years in that interpretation cannot guide an interpretation of the same phrase that might appear in an international agreement.[11]

There is a middle ground, which is to apply functionally similar principles to help in the interpretation and filling of gaps, provided that the intellectual process of reasoning is adopted and not the outcome of the process, which would amount to the direct application of a law external to the CISG. The UNIDROIT Principles and the European Principles have a distinct role to play in this regard. The interesting debate however, when we are testing the flexibility of the CISG, is whether to match provisions of the CISG with provisions of the European Principles and the UNIDROIT Principles. Such an approach is defendable, as we know that both alternative sets of sales law 'reflect a more rounded view of contractual principles'.[12] It is therefore conceivable that within the mandate of Art 7 an interpretation of the CISG can be 'stretched' to include reference to matters upon which the European Principles and the UNIDROIT Principles have managed to legislate. At the very least these international sales laws can assist in providing a possible direction for interpretation without falling into the trap of 'manufacturing' laws.

9 Ziegel, JS, *supra* note 4.

10 Matter No CA 40154/96 (13 August 1997) [http://austlii.edu.au] last update 27 Feb 1998.

11 Ziegel, JS, *supra* note 4.

12 Ziegel, JS, *supra* note 4.

Article 4: the validity issue

Article 4 CISG states:

> This Convention governs only the formation of the contract of sale and the rights and obligations of the seller and buyer arising from such a contract. In particular, except as otherwise expressly provided in this Convention, it is not concerned with:
>
> (a) the validity of the contract or of any of its provisions or of any usage;
>
> (b) the effect, which the contract may have on the property in the goods sold.

Article 4(b) has posed few problems and has been applied without difficulty. For example, the *Oberlandesgericht Koblenz*[13] ruled that retention of title clauses are outside the scope of the CISG, pursuant to Art 4(b), and must be ruled upon under domestic law. The issue that poses problems is the meaning of validity under Art 4(a).

A total elimination of domestic law from international sales contracts will never eventuate, as the drafters were not willing or able to develop a compromise when discussing general principles of contract law. The general principle of validity of contract is a prime example. Drobnig describes the reasons for the impasse by stating that: 'The difficulties in this area are due in part to the legal complexities and to divergent social policies, in part also to conceptual complications.'[14] Article 4 has been described as a 'contractual scheme [of] uncertain functional characteristics'.[15] This points to the exact problem and it is not surprising to see different views emerging in relation to the interpretation and function of Art 4.

Hartnell suggests that the validity question poses a danger to the development of a coherent jurisprudence of international trade by giving courts and tribunals wide discretion to determine when to apply domestic law.[16] This view is far too narrow and ignores the application of Art 7, which in effect sets the boundaries between issues within the CISG and those where the CISG permits the application of domestic law. It certainly can be argued that principles such as good faith are nebulous and incapable of definition. However, in the fullness of time the question will not be whether vague principles are capable of definition but rather the manner in which courts and tribunals will apply these principles. The jurisprudence of Art 7 to this point

---

13 Germany 16 January 1992, 5 U 534/91 [http://cisgw3.law.pace.edu/cases/920116g1.html].

14 Drobnig, U, in Sarcevic and Volken (eds), *International Sales of Goods*, 1986, Dubrovnik Lectures. Oceana Publishing, at 313.

15 Ferrari, F, 'Specific Topics of the CISG in the Light of Judicial Application and Scholarly Writing' (1995) 15 Journal of Law and Commerce: 1-126 [http://cisg.law.pace.edu/cisg/text/franco3.html].

16 Hartnell, HE, 'Rousing the Sleeping Dog: The Validity Exception to the Convention on Contracts for the International Sale of Goods, (1993) 18 Yale Journal of International Law: 1 at 3 [http://cisg.law.pace.edu/cisg/biblio/hartnell.html].

has shown that there is a remarkable similarity between decisions of different national jurisdictions when applying the CISG.[17]

There are about 100 decisions worldwide applying Art 4 and the majority deal with set-off, or agency and distribution agreements. At first glance it can certainly be argued that Art 4 allows a wide discretion, however, in practice Art 4 has been limited to very few scenarios. Agency and distribution agreements are a case in point. Tribunals and courts have recognized that distribution agreements or agency contracts are not covered by the CISG. In *Box Doccia Megius v Wilux International BV*,[18] the judge correctly decided that the Convention would be applicable 'if the dispute between the parties concerned the individual contracts of sale under the "frame agreement" [but would not be applicable to disputes] concerning the frame contract itself'.[19] The view expressed by the Dutch court is by no means isolated. The *Oberlandesgericht Düsseldorf*[20] amongst others reached the same conclusion.

The Court in *Helen Kaminski Pty Ltd v Marketing Australia Products Inc d/b/a Fiona Waterstreet Hats*[21] summed up the debate by stating:

> [The defendant] maintains that the Distributor agreement is merely a 'frame work agreement' and that such agreements are not covered by the CISG. The Distributor Agreement requires the [defendant] to purchase a minimum quantity of total goods, but does not identify the goods to be sold by type, date or price. In contrast, the CISG requires an enforceable contract to have definite terms regarding quantity and price.

In other words, frame agreements or agency are matters determined by domestic law whereas sales of goods are governed by the CISG. This point is clearly confirmed by the German *Bundesgerichtshof*,[22] which reached the correct conclusion that it did not matter whether a franchise agreement violated German or European antitrust laws. That was an issue for domestic law. The important point was that each supply contract had to be examined under the CISG in accordance with which the disputed contract was valid and the buyer was obliged to pay the seller.

In the European Principles, the classes of validity that fall outside the scope of the law are defined in Art 4:101 which states that, '[t]his chapter does not deal with invalidity arising from illegality, immorality or lack of

17 See *Tribunale di Vigevano*, 12 July 2000 (*Rheinland Versicherungen v Atlarex Srl*) [http://cisgw3.law.pace.edu/cases/000712i3.html]. In this Italian decision, no less than 42 cases were cited from different countries including the United States, Austria, Holland, France, Germany and Switzerland.

18 *Gerechtshof* Amsterdam 16 July 1992, 550/92SKG [http://cisgw3.law.pace.edu/cases/920716n1.html].

19 *Ibid.*

20 Germany, 11 July 1996, 6 U 152/95 [http://cisgw3.law.pace.edu/cases/960711g1.html].

21 United States District Court, Southern District of New York, 21 July 1997, M-47 (DLC) [http://cisgw3.law.pace.edu/cases/970721u1.html].

22 Germany 23 July, 1997, VIII ZR 134/96 [http://cisgw3.law.pace.edu/cases/970723g2.html].

capacity'.[23] The UNIDROIT Principles are nearly identical in this respect and also exclude questions of lack of capacity, lack of authority, immorality and illegality.[24] One could argue that the European Principles and UNIDROIT Principles are an improvement over the CISG as validity is clearly defined.

The question arising out of the above is whether the variables listed in the European Principles can be used to define validity within the CISG. When looking at Art 4 with the aid of Art 7, a tribunal or court could deal with the issue of validity in two ways. First, questions of validity could be excluded if they relate to illegality, immorality and capacity in the sense described by the European Principles. However, the better approach is that validity questions should only be excluded from the scope of the Convention if through the gap filling procedure a general principle is found to be lacking and hence recourse to domestic law is unavoidable.

Good faith and the international goals expressed in Art 7(1) demand that Art 4 be approached with a mind set that is conducive to uniformity of international laws. On the one hand, it is suggested that 'the drafting history of CISG, Art 4(a) demonstrates a clear concern for preserving the applicability of certain domestic laws'.[25] Parochial interests are undoubtedly present and were intended to be treated carefully by the drafters of the CISG. However to draw the line between application of the CISG or domestic law at a point where 'any provisions of the contract are inconsistent with the mandatory rules of the national law of the parties'[26] is certainly not correct. If that were so the interpretation of Art 4 could vary from one domestic system to another. As a result this view would be in direct conflict with the mandate of Art 7, namely uniformity of interpretation. Furthermore the CISG itself proceeds on the assumption that 'certain facts do not constitute a reason for nullifying a contract'.[27] An example within the CISG is Art 35(2)(a), which requires that goods be fit for their purpose. Any breach of this requirement will give the buyer the right to seek remedies such as avoidance of the contract due to a fundamental breach.

The suggestion could be made that conformity of goods is an issue of validity[28] and should be excluded from the Convention despite the fact that there are functionally equivalent solutions within the CISG. It is obvious that such a solution was not envisaged and must be rejected. Enderlein and Maskow believe that 'national law on validity will not apply when the CISG

23 Article 4:101 Principles of European Contract Law.

24 Article 3.1 UNIDROIT Principles.

25 Enderlein E and Maskow D, 'International Sales Law, United Nations Convention on Contracts for the International Sale of Goods', 1992, Oceana Publications, at 19.

26 Enderlein, E, in Dubrovnik Lectures, *supra* note 14, at 137.

27 Enderlein and Maskow, *supra* note 25, at 41.

28 This would be the case for example if the goods had perished at the time the contract was made. See Goods Act 1958 (Vic), s 11 and equivalent provisions in other Australian States.

provides a functionally adequate solution to the problem which has been settled nationally by questioning the validity of the contract'.[29] The broadest argument that can be mounted is that, if there is a general principle contained in the CISG having a counterpart in domestic law, the CISG would prevail in case of conflict therefore restricting the scope of Art 4.

It is 'fatal' for the CISG to remain static instead of evolving and moving with the needs of those for whom the CISG was written. At the same time it must be said that it is also inappropriate to 'invent' areas of concern within the CISG where they do not exist. In other words fabrication of law is not within the mandate of the CISG.

Nevertheless, Art 4 must be read in a different light than is envisaged by the drafting history of the CISG in any situation where the words of the CISG contradict the drafting history. Of importance is the directive that the Convention governs the 'rights and obligations of the seller and the buyer'[30] arising from a contract. Any matter falling within this phrase that is specifically provided for in the Convention is not excluded as a question of validity. The argument that Art 4(a) will determinatively exclude some issues that could be governed by the CISG[31] is false on two grounds. First, it places too much emphasis on the drafting history. The fact that a matter was a question of validity in 1980 is not necessarily conclusive in 2001 because circumstances change. The significance of this point cannot be overstated because there is no supra-national body or committee that can alter the Convention.

Second, as Honnold correctly points out the 'substance rather than the label' of the domestic rule of validity is relevant.[32] The Cour d'appel Paris[33] recognized this point and did not apply Art 4 to an issue dealing with the validity of standard terms and conditions, which were printed on the reverse side of an order. The court stated that: 'in the absence of an explicit reference on the front side of the buyer's form to the sales conditions indicated on the reverse side, the seller could not be deemed to have accepted those conditions.' Pursuant to Art 19(1) the document had to be interpreted as a counter offer that was rendered inapplicable due to lack of acceptance by the seller and so did not raise an issue of validity.

29 Enderlein and Maskow, *supra* note 25, at 41.

30 Article 4 CISG.

31 Hartnell, *supra* note 16, at 22.

32 Honnold, J, *Uniform Sales for International Sales*, 1991, Boston: Kluwer Law and Taxation Publishers, at 115 and 120–24.

33 13 December 1995, *Ste ISEA Industrie SpA/Companie d'Assurances Generali v Lu SA et al*, 95-018179 [http://cisgw3.law.pace.edu/cases/951213f1.html].

Conformity of goods as a question of validity

Article 4 CISG must be interpreted with the aid of Art 7. Article 4 does not purport to exclude validity in total since it uses the phrase: 'Except as otherwise expressly provided in this convention.' Article 7(2) expands the definition of 'expressly provided in this Convention' by allowing the use of general principles to settle matters governed by the Convention but not expressly settled in it. If the CISG governs matters but does not expressly settle those matters then general principles will aid in the construction and interpretation of these matters within the four corners of the CISG. Matters of validity are only excluded if they are not related to either the formation of contract or the rights and obligations of buyers and sellers. For example, the CISG treats the question of conformity of goods as a question of breach of contract rather than validity. This argument is supported by several decisions. In a Hungarian ruling[34] the court rejected the buyer's argument that the seller's claim as to lack of conformity must be settled according to the Hungarian Civil Code. The court held that the matter was covered by the CISG and hence applied Art 39. A German court came to the same conclusion holding that the 'application of the CISG precludes recourse to domestic law regarding mistake as to the quality of goods as the matter is exhaustively covered by the CISG.'[35] More telling is the opinion of an ICC arbitration ruling where the arbitrator found that: '[t]he Convention applies … also to the question whether or not a contract has been validly made [which] is apparent from the fact that the Convention contains a section entitled "Formation of Contract".'[36]

In sum, the Convention governs the formation of contracts and the rights and obligations of the seller and buyer arising from such a contract. This indicates that any breach of a contract or any direct contravention of any Articles within the Convention is covered by the CISG. Pursuant to Art 4(a) the Convention does not concern itself with questions of the validity of a contract or of its provisions or of any usage. However validity as such is not excluded, as the proviso does not extend to matters expressly provided for in the Convention. In simple terms and pursuant to Article 7(2), if a matter is governed by the CISG then, irrespective of its label, the CISG is applicable to the exclusion of domestic law. The ICC arbitral decision cited above indicates that matters of conformity of goods are to be dealt with by the Convention.

In domestic laws, validity is sometimes used synonymously with breach of contract, which is covered by the CISG. However, domestic law will only apply if the matter is not covered either expressly or by recourse to the gap filling provision of Art 7(2). Whether domestic law labels any matter as an

34 FB Budapest, July 1 1997 [http://cisgw3.law.pace.edu/cases/970701h2.html].

35 *Landgericht* Aachen, 14 May 1993, 43 O 136/92 [http://cisgw3.law.pace.edu/cases/930514g.1.html].

36 *ICC Arbitration* Case No 7399 of 1993 [http://cisgw3.law.pace.edu/cases/937399i1.html].

issue of validity of contract is of no consequence as far as validity pursuant to the CISG is concerned. To restate Professor Honnold, substance rather than the label is of consequence.[37] Validity as a general principle is not governed by the CISG but validity must be carefully distinguished from breaches of contracts or actions which will render a contract void. Validity in the context of Art 4 refers only to matters that go to the root of the contract making it void *ab initio*. This narrows the field considerably.

As Drobnig suggests, validity is one of the general principles of contract law and comes in three forms: the binding effect of contractual promises, defects of consent; and illegality and immorality.[38] In common law countries the binding effect of contractual promises depends on the existence of consideration.[39] This issue is expressly dealt with in the CISG under the provision on formation of contract and hence validity due to the lack of consideration is not to be settled in accordance with domestic law. The questions of consent, immorality and illegality are clearly not covered by the CISG and hence they are subject to domestic law.

In sum it can be seen that 'validity' is a misleading term and cannot be invoked merely because of a label. Article 4 alludes to the fact that issues which domestic law treats as issues of validity will not be excluded if they relate to formation of contract or the obligations of buyers and sellers arising out of a contract.

The jurisprudence of Article 4

To test the above conclusions we must return to the jurisprudence of Art 4. The distributorship issue has already been discussed above. Another area frequently in dispute is the question of set-off. A number of courts have explained their disallowance of set-offs by reference to Art 4. The *Oberlandesgericht* Stuttgart[40] as well as the *Amtsgericht* Frankfurt[41] noted that set-off was excluded due to Art 4. In addition, the *Oberlandesgericht* München[42] held that both set-off and restitution are excluded from the scope of the CISG by Art 4.

37 Honnold, *supra* note 32.

38 Drobnig, *supra* note 14, at 313.

39 *Ibid.*

40 Germany 21 August 1995, 5 U 195/94 [http://cisgw3.law.pace.edu/cases/950821g1.html].

41 Germany 31 January 1991, 32 C 1074/90-41 [http://cisgw3.law.pace.edu/cases/910131g1.html].

42 *Oberlandesgericht* München, 28 January 1998, 7 U 3771/97 [http://cisgw3.law.pace.edu/cases/980128g1.html].

(a) Set-off

In *PT Van den Heuvel v Santini Maglificio Sportivo de Santini P&C SAS*,[43] the court distinguished between two types of set-off. One concerned overcharging, and the other concerned damages. In relation to a set-off for overcharging the claim was allowed as neither party contested the value of the invoices. The court implied that the set-off was allowable because the claims were subject to the CISG.[44] Damages due to a breach of the contract were considered to be outside the scope of the CISG and hence to be covered by domestic laws pursuant to Art 7(2). However, in a later ICC Arbitration case[45] the arbitrator held that the buyer was allowed a set-off for damages suffered due to the seller's breach of the contract, pursuant to Art 74.

The Dutch court, unlike the ICC arbitrator, did not read Art 74 correctly. Article 74 allows for damages due to a breach of contract including loss of profit. Therefore, provided that the set-off pertains to damages due to breach of contract or loss of profits it will be within the scope of the CISG. A set-off due to other reasons, such as punitive damages not contained within the contract, is outside the scope of the Convention and in accordance with Art 7(2) recourse must be had to domestic law. Some courts have misinterpreted Art 4 as defining all those matters, which are not included in the CISG. However, this question must be solved pursuant to Art 7(2).

Careful attention must be given to set-off provisions if they are in breach of some domestic law, which could make them invalid. In such a case Art 4 could be used to implement domestic law. However in the cases described above the set-off was not a question of a breach of domestic laws and therefore Art 4 was misinterpreted.

A Swiss decision explains the issue well. The Court of Freiburg[46] noted that the only question at hand was the amount of set-off. The right of set-off was based on one party's General Terms and Conditions and the question was whether these terms formed part of the sales contract. The court correctly noted that the question was one of validity and pursuant to Art 4 was not governed by the CISG. Domestic law, in this case German law, had to be applied. Under German law the set-off was not excluded. The interesting part of the decision was the fact that in making its interpretation the court tried to solve the issue within the CISG. Article 8 was consulted and it was found that if the statement made by the parties in relation to set-off corresponded with the intent of the parties then the CISG was applicable. The Court stated that: 'If the interpretation of statements made by both parties does not lead to a

43 Netherlands 25 February 1993, 1992/182 [http://cisgw3.law.pace.edu/cases/930225n1.html].

44 The same decision was reached in *Oberlandesgericht* München, 9 July 1997, 7U 2070/97 [http://cisgw3.law.pace.edu/cases/970709g1.html].

45 1997, 8611/HV/JK [http://cisgw3.law.pace.edu/cases/978611i1.html].

46 *Kantonsgericht* Freiburg, 23 January 1998 [http://cisgw3.law.pace.edu/cases/980123s1.html].

congruent result, the intent of the parties has to be elicited in accordance with the principles of domestic law.'[47]

In conclusion, it can be said that rulings on set-off have produced the correct result but in some instances for the wrong reasons. Generally speaking set-offs, which are due to breaches of contract that are not covered by Art 74, have been recognized as being excluded by Art 4.

(b) Other issues

The above analysis illustrates that courts and tribunals confuse the application of Art 7(2) with the application of Art 4. Several other issues can be used to demonstrate this point. For the time being this examination is restricted to the burden of proof, currency payments and assumption of debt. The *Handelsgericht* Zürich[48] noted that the question concerning the burden of proof is not governed by the CISG. This determination has been repeated by the *Bezirksgericht der Saane*[49] and the *Tribunale d'appelo del Cantone del Ticino*.[50]

All three courts decided that the CISG does not determine the burden of proof however 'due to its underlying systematic structure, certain principles may be inferred'.[51] The three Swiss courts in the end came to the correct decision however they should have used Art 7(2) to determine the issue. Burden of proof as the courts correctly pointed out is not explicitly ruled upon within the CISG. However by applying Art 7(2) a gap is discoverable. The above courts expressed correctly that according to Art 35 the buyer must notify defects to the seller and therefore the burden of proof as to defects rests with the buyer. The *Bezirksgericht der Saane*[52] came to an interesting decision. It ruled that the burden of proof as to the means of transportation is not settled in the CISG. Through the application of Art 7(2) the court applied domestic law and as the buyer could not meet the burden of proof Art 32(2) was used. It declares that the choice of the mode of transportation is left to the seller. This decision nearly reflects a correct application of the CISG. The only flaw is the use of Art 4 in declaring that the burden of proof is not settled in the CISG. The court should have bypassed Art 4 and directly applied Art 7(2).

In contrast, a decision by the *Kantonsgericht Wallis*[53] exhibits an undesirable approach to the CISG. The ruling hinged upon the currency in which the purchase price had to be paid. Again Art 4 instead of Art 7(2) was

47 *Ibid.*

48 Switzerland 30 November 1998, HG 930634/O [http://cisgw3.law.pace.edu/cases/981130s1.html].

49 Switzerland 20 February 1997, T 171/95 [http://cisgw3.law.pace.edu/cases/970220s1.html].

50 Switzerland 15 January 1998, 12.97.00193 [http://cisgw3.law.pace.edu/cases/980115s1.html].

51 Drobnig, *supra* note 14.

52 *Supra* note 49.

53 Switzerland 30 June 1998, CI 98 9 [http://cisgw3.law.pace.edu/cases/980630s1.html].

applied. Rather than discovering a general principle under Art 54, which deals with the buyer's obligation to pay the price, the court applied Italian law, which incidentally led to the same conclusion as the CISG. This approach is incorrect because the court did not follow Art 7(2) and search for general principles to fill a gap.

(c) Concluding the argument

The above discussion has shown that the CISG cannot be applied Article by Article. Rather it has to be read in its entirety taking a holistic approach. Article 4 contains two important expressions: 'in particular' and 'except as otherwise expressly provided in this convention'. Ferrari in his commentary on OGH, April 24, 1997[54] came to the conclusion that the above expressions delineate the spheres of influence of the CISG and domestic law. This is also the goal of Art 7(2). However, priority must be given in any interpretation or question of delineation to Art 7(2).

This should not be taken as acceptance of the narrow view that Art 4 deals only with the issue of validity. Understood correctly, Art 4 has a much wider application as it assists courts and tribunals in a determination of the scope of the CISG. When a French court[55] had to deal with the question of privity of contract in an action by a sub-purchaser against the initial seller, the court directed its attention to Art 4. Pursuant to Art 4, the CISG only governs rights and obligations of the buyer and seller arising out of their contract. As there is no contract between a sub-purchaser and an initial seller, the CISG was not applicable. In *KSTP-FM,LLC v Specialized Communications, Inc and Adtronics Signs, Ltd*[56] the plaintiff alleged that in Minnesota the UCC expressly allows certain parties the right to sue for breach of implied conditions in the absence of contractual privity. The court relied on Art 4 and concluded, like the French court above, that the CISG is limited to rights under the contract between buyer and seller.

However, many courts have applied Art 4 within the domain of Art 7(2). The expression 'in particular' in Art 4(a) 'only serves to emphasise that, apart from matters listed in article 4(a) and (b), there are other matters not governed by the CISG'.[57] As an example Art 5 can be cited. It excludes product liability as far as personal injury is concerned. At the same time the other important expression – 'except as otherwise provided in this convention' – alerts us to the fact that not all matters in relation to validity are excluded. For example, Art 11 lays down the principle that contracts do not have to be evidenced in

---

54 Austria, *Oberster Gerichtshof*, 2 Ob 109/97 [http://cisgw3.law.pace.edu/cases/970424a3.html].

55 5 January 1999, *Cour de Cassation*, P 96-19.992 [http://cisgw3.law.pace.edu/cases/990105f1.html].

56 United States 9 March 1999, Minnesota District Court CT 98-013101 [http://cisgw3.law.pace.edu/cases/990309u1.html].

57 *Ibid.*

writing. Furthermore, courts have also held that validity issues such as conformity of goods are dealt with in Art 35.[58] Schlechtriem comments that:

> The uniformity reached by the Convention would be in grave danger if … national provisions could be applied [simply] because [their] application leads to invalidity or avoidance of a contract and thereby could be brought under article 4(a).[59]

It is quite obvious that the CISG does not intend for a matter to be brought under domestic laws when the matter is regulated by the Convention. Furthermore, if we examine the list of matters excluded from the CISG through Art 4 namely: statute of limitation, set-off, agency, distributorship and frame contracts, validity of penal clauses, assignment of receivables, assumption of debts, and others, it can be seen that these matters need not be treated as questions of validity.

For instance, agency and distributorship agreements would be excluded under Art 3(2), which states that the CISG does not apply to service contracts. This point can be illustrated by a decision of the Obergericht Luzern,[60] which interpreted Art 3(2) in a wide fashion. It noted that if elements other than those relating to the contract of sale were preponderant then the CISG would not apply.[61] The court specifically referred to exclusive distribution or franchise contracts but noted that a single sale of goods pursuant to the franchise agreement would be governed by the CISG.[62]

The solution as indicated above is that Art 7(2) must be consulted first and an examination of the CISG as a whole must be undertaken to determine if general principles can be divined. What then is the purpose of Art 4? It can be argued that Art 4 expressly draws a line in the sand where the CISG is not applicable. Validity of contract is excluded but the concept of validity requires definition and substance. By analogy to the UNIDROIT Principles and the European Principles, validity can be reduced to questions of illegality, immorality, or lack of capacity.

In conclusion it can be observed that courts have not generally used domestic law in preference to the CISG, with the proviso that a full understanding of the capacity of Art 7(2) has not been achieved. However, this does not undermine the fact that national courts are, by and large, interpreting the CISG in a uniform manner and that decisions have tended towards a converging jurisprudence of international sales law.

58 *Supra* notes 34, 35 and 36.

59 Schlechtriem,. P, 'Uniform Sales Law – The Experience with Uniform Sales Law in the Federal Republic of Germany' Juridisk Tidskrift (1991/92) 12–13

60 Switzerland 8 January 1997, 11 95 123/357 [http://cisgw3.law.pace.edu/cases/970108s1.html].

61 *Ibid.*

62 *Ibid.*

International Law as Domestic Law in the Philippines

John Trone[1]

1 Introduction

In the West, increasing attention is being given to the position of international law in Asian legal systems.[2] This article examines the position of treaties and customary international law in the domestic law of the Philippines, where the courts have produced a strong body of decisions relating to international law.

This article is divided into seven parts. The first part is this introduction. The second, third and fourth parts discuss the position of international law in domestic law. These parts deal with customary international law, treaties and executive agreements respectively. The fifth and sixth parts concern the resolution of conflicts between domestic law and international law. The types of domestic law dealt with by these parts are statutes and the Constitution respectively. The seventh part is the conclusion. Within each topic, the position under the Philippine Constitutions of 1935, 1973 and 1987 will be examined.

2 Customary international law as domestic law

Under each of the three Philippine Constitutions, customary international law has been applied directly as the law of the land. The 1935 Constitution provided that '[t]he Philippines ... adopts the generally accepted principles of international law as part of the law of the Nation'.[3] The Supreme Court held that if the principles embodied in a treaty represented 'generally accepted principles of international law' those principles would be part of the law of the nation though the Philippines was not a party to the Treaty.[4]

---

1 BA/LLB, PhD.

2 For recent discussions of the position of international law in particular Asian legal systems, see P Chandrasekhara Rao, *The Indian Constitution and International Law*, 1993, New Delhi: Taxmann; Tunku Sofia Jewa, *Public International Law: A Malaysian Perspective*, 1996, Kuala Lumpur: Pacifica Publications; Thio Li-Ann, 'The Impact of Internationalisation on Domestic Governance: Gender Egalitarianism and the Transformative Potential of CEDAW' (1997) 1 Singapore Journal of International and Comparative Law 278; Yuji Iwasawa, *International Law, Human Rights and Japanese Law: The Impact of International Law on Japanese Law*, 1998, Oxford: Clarendon Press.

3 Sec 3, Art II, 1935 Constitution.

4 *Kuroda v Jalandoni* 83 Phil 171 at 178 (1949) (hereafter *Kuroda*).

Under the 1973 Constitution the wording of this constitutional provision was slightly different from that in the 1935 charter.[5] International law now became part of the 'law of the land', rather than the 'law of the Nation'.[6] The Court held that foreign state immunity was one of the generally recognised principles of international law.[7]

On this matter the 1987 Constitution retained the same wording as the 1973 Constitution.[8] Interestingly, the Court has taken the view that even if such a provision had not been included in the Constitution, the generally accepted principles of international law would still have been part of Philippine law under the doctrine of incorporation.[9] The Court argued that under this doctrine, 'such principles are deemed incorporated in the law of every civilized state as a condition and consequence of its membership in the society of nations'.[10]

3 Treaties as domestic law

The constitutional provisions discussed above also adopted the nation's treaty commitments as part of domestic law. Under the 1935 Constitution, the Supreme Court confirmed that 'a treaty commitment voluntarily assumed by the Philippine Government ... has the force and effect of law'.[11]

On numerous occasions, the Supreme Court held that treaties were part of domestic law under the 1973 Constitution. The Court held that a treaty concerning employment at US bases[12] was part of Philippine domestic law and that its provisions formed part of contracts between Philippine nationals and the base authorities.[13] The Court also held that, given the principle of *pacta sunt servanda*, the Vienna Convention on Road Signs and Signals[14]

5 Sec 3, Art II, 1973 Constitution.

6 See Hector S De Leon, *Textbook on the Philippine Constitution*, 5th edn, 1997, Manila: Rex Book Store, 46 (hereafter De Leon).

7 *United States v Ruiz* 136 SCRA 487 at 490–91 (1985). For a discussion of the cases on foreign sovereign immunity, see Florentino P Feliciano, 'The Doctrine of Sovereign Immunity from Suit in a Developing and Liberalizing Economy: Philippine Experience and Case-Law' in Nisuke Ando (ed), *Japan and International Law: Past, Present and Future*, 1999, The Hague: Kluwer Law International, 173.

8 Sec 2, Art II, 1987 Constitution.

9 In the common law systems, compare *Trendtex Trading Corporation Ltd v Central Bank of Nigeria* [1977] QB 529; *Nulyarimma v Thompson* (1999) 96 FCR 153.

10 *United States v Guinto* 182 SCRA 644 at 653 (1990). See similarly *Holy See v Rosario* 238 SCRA 524 (1994); *Tañada v Angara* 272 SCRA 18 (1997) (hereafter *Tañada*).

11 *World Health Organization v Aquino* 48 SCRA 242 at 249 (1972). See also *Kuroda, supra* n 4, 178.

12 Agreement Relating to the Employment of Philippine Nationals in the United States Military Bases in the Philippines, Manila, 27 May 1968, 658 UNTS 347.

13 *Guerrero's Transport Services, Inc v Blaylock Transportation Services Employees Association-Kilusan* 71 SCRA 621 at 629 (1976).

14 Convention on Road Signs and Signals, Vienna, 8 November 1968, 1091 UNTS 3.

contained provisions that were generally accepted principles of international law.[15]

On the other hand, in one decision the Court appeared to limit the class of ratified treaties that became part of the law of the nation. The Court stated: 'To the extent that the ... Convention is a restatement of the generally accepted principles of international law, it should be a part of the law of the land.'[16] The Court's remarks appeared to suggest that treaties which did not restate generally accepted principles of international law might not be part of domestic law.

In interpreting the equivalent provision under the 1987 Constitution the Court has held that a treaty has the 'force and effect of law'.[17] For example, the Court has stated that the Warsaw Convention,[18] a treaty to which the Philippines is a party, 'is as much a part of Philippine law as the Civil Code, Code of Commerce and other municipal special laws'.[19]

Notably, in one decision the Court held that the right to return to one's country, guaranteed by the International Covenant on Civil and Political Rights,[20] was part of the law of the nation as a generally accepted principle of international law.[21] In another case, the opinion of a concurring judge indicated that the Convention on the Elimination of All Forms of Discrimination Against Women[22] has a similar status.[23]

4 Executive agreements as domestic law

Each of the three Constitutions was held to permit the making of various executive agreements. Executive agreements may be of several types: agreements entered into on the President's own authority (sole executive agreements) or agreements entered into by the President pursuant to statutory authorisation (Congressional-executive agreements).

15 *Agustin v Edu* 88 SCRA 195 at 213 (1979). See also *La Chemise Lacoste, SA v Fernandez* 129 SCRA 373 at 390 (1984).

16 *Reyes v Bagatsing* 125 SCRA 553 at 566 (1983) (hereafter *Reyes*).

17 See eg *Santos v Northwest Orient Airlines* 210 SCRA 256 (1992) (hereafter *Santos*); *Luna v Court of Appeals* 216 SCRA 107 (1992); *Cathay Pacific Airways Ltd v Court of Appeals* 219 SCRA 520 (1993); *Lasco v United Nations Revolving Fund for Natural Resources Exploration* 241 SCRA 681 (1995); *Ebro v National Labor Relations Commission*, GR No 110187, 4 September 1996.

18 International Convention for the Unification of Certain Rules Relating to International Carriage by Air, Warsaw, 12 October 1929, 137 LNTS 11.

19 *Philippine Airlines Inc v Court of Appeals*, GR No 119706, 14 March 1996. See also *Abbas v Commission on Elections* 179 SCRA 287 (1989) (hereafter *Abbas*).

20 International Covenant on Civil and Political Rights, New York, 19 December 1966, 999 UNTS 171 (hereafter ICCPR).

21 *Marcos v Manglapus* 177 SCRA 668 (1989).

22 Convention on the Elimination of All Forms of Discrimination Against Women, New York, 18 December 1979, 1249 UNTS 13.

23 *Marcos v Commission on Elections*, GR No 119976, 18 September 1995 *per* Romero J, concurring.

The 1935 Constitution conferred upon the President the power to make treaties, but subject to the concurrence of two-thirds of the Senate.[24] Nonetheless, in a 1959 decision the Supreme Court suggested that the executive could validly make certain types of international agreements without the concurrence of the Senate, but did not decide the issue.[25]

In a subsequent decision the Court argued that the concurrence of the Senate was required only for 'treaties' and not for 'executive agreements', which were a distinct category of international agreement under domestic law.[26] The Court gave some indication of the constitutional scope of each type of agreement:

> International agreements involving political issues or changes of national policy and those involving international arrangements of a permanent character usually take the form of treaties. But international agreements embodying *adjustments of detail* carrying out well-established national policies and traditions and those involving arrangements of a more or less temporary nature usually take the form of executive agreements.[27]

In another case the Court held that a sole executive agreement will be invalid if it is inconsistent with a prior statute.[28] The President cannot 'indirectly repeal' a statute by entering into a sole executive agreement.[29] This principle is a consequence of the separation of powers.[30]

It was noted that the Constitution expressly conferred jurisdiction upon the Court to determine the 'constitutionality or validity of any treaty'.[31] Here the Court evidently interpreted the word 'treaty' as including an executive agreement. The Court also saw significance in the Constitution's distinction between 'constitutionality' and 'validity', holding that it had jurisdiction to nullify an executive agreement both for unconstitutionality and for conflict with a statute.[32]

---

24 Sec 10(7), Art VII, 1935 Constitution.

25 *USAFFE Veterans Association v Treasurer of the Philippines* 105 Phil 1030 at 1038 (1959).

26 *Commissioner of Customs v Eastern Sea Trading* 113 Phil 333 at 355 (1961) (hereafter *Eastern Sea Trading*).

27 *Ibid*, 357, quoting Francis B Sayre, 'The Constitutionality of the Trade Agreements Act' (1939) 39 Columbia Law Review 751 at 755 (emphasis in original). In a later decision the Court dismissed as moot a lawsuit which argued that a sole executive agreement should have been submitted to the Senate for its concurrence: *Adolfo v Court of First Instance of Zambales* 34 SCRA 166 at 172 (1970).

28 United States courts have taken a similar view: *United States v Guy W Capps Inc* 204 F 2d 655 at 658 (4th Cir 1953), affd on other grounds 348 US 296 (1955); *Swearingen v United States* 565 F Supp 1019 at 1021 (D Colo 1983).

29 *Gonzales v Hechanova* 9 SCRA 230 at 242 (1963) (hereafter *Hechanova*).

30 *Ibid*, 243.

31 Sec 2, Art VIII, 1935 Constitution. Similar provisions appear in Sec 1, 5(2), Art X, 1973 Constitution and Sec 2, 5(2), Art VIII, 1987 Constitution.

32 *Hechanova, supra* n 29, 243.

Under the 1973 Constitution, most powers were concentrated in the President, and treaty-making was no exception to this pattern. The Constitution provided that no treaty would be valid unless a majority of the National Assembly had concurred in its making.[33] The National Assembly was a legislative body which was to be established at some future time. Until the Assembly was established its powers were to be exercised by an interim legislature,[34] which was never convened.

Moreover, the stipulations relating to the National Assembly were subject to other constitutional provisions.[35] For example, one provision stated that, notwithstanding the provisions requiring legislative concurrence, 'the President may enter into international treaties or agreements as the national welfare and interest may require'.[36]

In 1976, the Constitution was amended to provide for a different interim legislature.[37] This legislature was specifically prohibited from exercising the power to concur in the making of treaties.[38] The interim legislature was elected in 1978.

In 1981, the Constitution was amended again. The interim legislature was now given the power to concur in the making of treaties.[39] This provision was again subject to other constitutional provisions and the President retained a broad treaty-making power.[40]

The 1981 version of the Constitution continued to speak of a permanent legislature, to be created at some time in the future. When the legislature was created, no treaty would be valid and effective without its concurrence, but again this was subject to other constitutional provisions.[41] Hence this power would still be subject to the President's treaty-making power.[42]

---

33 Sec 14(1), Art VIII, 1973 Constitution.

34 Sec 1, Art XVII, 1973 Constitution.

35 Sec 14(1), Art VIII, 1973 Constitution.

36 Sec 15, Art XIV, 1973 Constitution. On this phrase see Antonio Orendain, *New Philippine Constitution and Government Annotated*, 1983, Manila: Merriam & Webster, 349.

37 Amendment 1, 1973 Constitution.

38 Amendment 2, 1973 Constitution. See *Occena v Commission on Elections* 95 SCRA 755 at 759 (1980).

39 Amended text of Amendment 2; Sec 14(1), Art VIII, read together with Sec 1, Art XVII, 1973 Constitution. See Sec 7, Batasan Resolution No 2, 27 February 1981.

40 Amended text of Sec 16, Art XIV, 1973 Constitution. See Sec 5, Batasan Resolution No 2, 27 February 1981.

41 1981 amended text of Sec 14(1), Art VIII, 1973 Constitution. See Sec 6, Batasan Resolution No 2, 27 February 1981.

42 Amended text of Sec 16, Art XIV, 1973 Constitution (renumbered by Batasan Resolution No 1, 5 February 1981). See Sec 5, Batasan Resolution No 2, 27 February 1981.

Apart from this express treaty-making power, under the martial law powers exercised between 1972 and 1981,[43] the President possessed the power to ratify treaties on his own authority. After the entry into force of the 1973 Constitution, he ratified several treaties on the basis of such authority.[44]

Under the 1973 Constitution, the President also possessed legislative power.[45] This power permitted the President to unilaterally implement a non-self-executing treaty provision by way of legislation. The Racial Discrimination Convention[46] had been approved by the Senate under the 1935 Constitution. However, Congress did not enact legislation implementing a non-self-executing provision of this treaty. Therefore, using the legislative powers conferred upon him by the 1973 Constitution the President implemented this provision with a criminal prohibition.[47]

Over a decade later, President Aquino established a Provisional Constitution,[48] which was to be in force while a new Constitution was being drafted. This Provisional Constitution retained the provision of the 1973 Constitution which empowered the President to make treaties without legislative approval.[49] The Constitution also 'superseded' the provision of the 1973 Constitution regarding legislative approval of treaties.[50] There was no rush of Presidential treaty-making during this period. However, two important human rights treaties were ratified: the International Covenant on Civil and Political Rights[51] and the Torture Convention.[52]

---

43 See Proclamation No 1081, Proclaiming a State of Martial Law in the Philippines, 21 September 1972, 68 Off Gaz 7624; General Order No 1, 22 September 1972; Proclamation No 2045, Proclaiming the Termination of the State of Martial Law throughout the Philippines, 17 January 1981, 77 Off Gaz 441.

44 Presidential Decree No 207, ratifying the 1968 Vienna Conventions of the United Nations on Road Traffic and Road Signs and Signals, respectively, 6 June 1973.

45 This power was initially derived from Sec 3(2), Art XVII, 1973 Constitution. See *Aquino, Jr v COMELEC* 62 SCRA 275 (1975). The power was later derived from Amendment 6, 1973 Constitution. See Joaquin G Bernas, *The Constitution of the Republic of the Philippines*, 1988, Manila: Rex Book Store, II: 70 (hereafter Bernas), citing *Legaspi v Minister of Finance* 115 SCRA 418 (1982).

46 International Convention on the Elimination of All Forms of Racial Discrimination, New York, 7 March 1966, 660 UNTS 195.

47 Presidential Decree No 966, declaring Violations of the International Convention on the Elimination of All Forms of Racial Discrimination to be Criminal Offenses and Providing Penalties therefor, 20 July 1976.

48 Proclamation No 3, declaring a national policy to implement the reforms mandated by the people, protecting their basic rights, adopting a Provisional Constitution, and providing for an orderly transition to a government under a new Constitution, 25 March 1986, 82 Off Gaz 1567.

49 Sec 2, Art I, Proclamation No 3; Sec 16, Art XIV, 1973 Constitution.

50 Sec 3, Art I, Proclamation No 3; Sec 14(1), Art VIII, 1973 Constitution.

51 ICCPR, *supra* n 20 (Ratification by the Philippines, 23 October 1986: 1438 UNTS 432).

52 Convention Against Torture and Other Cruel, Inhuman or Degrading Treatment or Punishment, New York, 10 December 1984, 1465 UNTS 85 (Accession for the Philippines, 18 June 1986: 1465 UNTS 113).

The Supreme Court has described the Senate's power of concurrence as 'a check on the executive power'.[53] Despite this, under the 1987 Constitution the President still possesses the power to enter into executive agreements. Justice Cruz remarked that this 'is a rather strange decision in the light of the general intention to limit the President's powers as a hedge against the resurgence of another dictatorship'.[54]

The 1987 Constitution provides that a 'treaty or international agreement'[55] must be approved by two thirds of the Senate to be valid.[56] However, several constitutional provisions refer to an 'executive agreement' as a concept distinct from a 'treaty' or 'international agreement'.[57] It is generally agreed that the terms 'treaty or international agreement' do not include an 'executive agreement'.[58]

There is relatively little authority regarding the constitutional limits of executive agreements under the present Constitution. However, soon after the 1987 Constitution came into force,[59] the Court upheld as valid an executive agreement[60] which had been entered into under the 1935 Constitution. The Court wrote: 'While treaties are required to be ratified by the Senate ... less formal types of international agreements may be entered into by the Chief Executive ... without the concurrence of the legislative body.'[61]

A Secretary of Justice legal opinion has adopted the Supreme Court's view of the boundaries of executive agreements and treaties under the 1935 Constitution.[62] The Constitutional Commission which drafted the present Constitution appears to have taken a similar view.[63]

---

53 *Tolentino v Secretary of Finance* 235 SCRA 630 (1994).

54 Isagani A Cruz, *Philippine Political Law*, 1987, Quezon City: Central Lawbook Publishing, 210–11 (hereafter Cruz).

55 The Vienna Convention on the Law of Treaties defines a 'treaty' as an agreement concluded between states. See Art 1(a), Vienna Convention on the Law of Treaties, Vienna, 23 May 1969, 1155 UNTS 331 at 333. A separate treaty deals with treaties entered into by international organisations: Vienna Convention on the Law of Treaties between States and International Organisations or between International Organisations, Vienna, 21 March 1986, 25 ILM 543. The term 'international agreement' was included in the Constitution to encompass agreements between states and international organisations as well as agreements between states: De Leon, *supra* n 6, 227–28.

56 Sec 21, Art VII, 1987 Constitution.

57 Sec 4(2), Art VIII; Sec 5(2)(a), Art VII, 1987 Constitution.

58 Bernas, *supra* n 45, II: 248; Cruz, *supra* n 54, 210; Raphael Perpetuo M Lotilla, 'Treaty-making Power' (1991) 1 Asian Yearbook of International Law 168 at 176 (hereafter Lotilla); De Leon, *supra* n 6, 228.

59 The 1987 Constitution came into force on 2 February 1987: *De Leon v Esguerra* 153 SCRA 602 at 605–08 (1987). The Court's decision was handed down on 27 February 1987.

60 Agreement between the Philippines and the World Health Organization on the Privileges, Immunities and Facilities to be Granted by the Government of the Philippines to the World Health Organization, Manila, 22 July 1951, 149 UNTS 197.

61 *Commissioner of Internal Revenue v Gotamco* 148 SCRA 36 at 39 (1987).

62 Opinion No 84 Series 1990, cited in Lotilla, *supra* n 58, 176. See *Eastern Sea Trading*, *supra* n 26.

63 See Bernas, *supra* n 45, II: 250.

The 1987 Constitution confers upon the Supreme Court the power to rule upon the 'constitutionality or validity of any treaty, international or executive agreement'.[64] The Court's express power to rule upon the 'validity' of an 'executive agreement' gives it clear authority to invalidate a sole executive agreement for inconsistency with a prior statute. There is thus no need to interpret the word 'treaty' as including an executive agreement, as the Court did under the 1935 Constitution.[65]

Only those international instruments which are part of a treaty or international agreement need be submitted for Senate concurrence. The treaty itself will require Senate concurrence, but the Final Act of the conference adopting the treaty will not.[66] Finally, it should be noted that the Constitution expressly requires Senate concurrence in any agreement providing for the stationing of foreign military bases.[67]

5 Conflict between statute and international law

Under the 1935 Constitution, treaty provisions were subject to 'amendment' by subsequent legislation.[68] Under the present Constitution the Court has adhered to this view. The Court has stated that treaties and statutes are 'in the same class' and that a treaty is subject to 'amendment' by the provisions of a subsequent law.[69]

The logical corollary of such a rule is that in the event of inconsistency a treaty would take precedence over a prior statute.[70] However, in a 1993 decision the Court appeared to suggest that, in a case of inconsistency, a prior statute will prevail over a subsequent treaty.[71] It is not clear from the decision whether the provisions of the statute concerned were enacted prior or subsequent to the treaty involved.[72] However, in a more recent decision the Court stated that whichever is the later in time will take precedence.[73]

The question of conflict between executive agreements and statutes will not be discussed here as it was dealt with in Section 4. As for the conflict

---

64 Sec 5(2)(a), Art VII, 1987 Constitution.

65 *Hechanova, supra* n 29, 243.

66 *Tañada, supra* n 10.

67 Sec 25, Art XVIII, 1987 Constitution. For commentary, see Bernas, *supra* n 45, II: 620-624; Ambrosio B Padilla, *The 1987 Constitution of the Republic of the Philippines with Comments and Cases* (Manila: np, 1990), III: 752–55.

68 *Ichong v Hernandez* 101 Phil 1155 at 1191 (1957), citing *United States v Thompson* 258 F 257 (ED Ark 1919).

69 *Abbas, supra* n 19.

70 This is the position in the United States: *Cook v United States* 288 US 102 at 118 (1933).

71 *Philip Morris Inc v Court of Appeals* 224 SCRA 576 (1993).

72 *Ibid.*

73 *Secretary of Justice v Lantion*, GR No 139465, 18 January 2000 (hereafter *Lantion*).

between customary international law and statute, there appears to be no judicial authority regarding the issue.

Finally, the Supreme Court has never examined a claim that a treaty provision was unconstitutional as violating *jus cogens*. However, in 1973 the Court suggested that the power to propose constitutional amendments under the 1935 Constitution[74] might not extend to amendments which were inconsistent with *jus cogens*.[75]

In another case the Court rejected an argument that where a treaty had 'lost its basis for approval', it had become unconstitutional. A specific act of rejection by the Philippine government would be necessary to deprive a treaty of force in domestic law. The Court indicated that the power to reject a treaty on the ground of *rebus sic stantibus* lies with the political branches of government.[76]

6 Conflict between the constitution and international law

The Philippine Constitution has always expressly conferred upon the Supreme Court the power to hold that a treaty is unconstitutional.[77] The 1935 Constitution provided that the Court could not be deprived of jurisdiction to decide upon the 'constitutionality ... of any treaty'.[78] The Court took the view that this grant of jurisdiction authorised it to declare that an executive agreement was unconstitutional,[79] evidently interpreting the word treaty to include an executive agreement.[80] The Court possessed such a power 'despite the eminently political character of the treaty-making power'.[81]

Under the 1973 Constitution the Supreme Court retained the power to invalidate a treaty on the ground that it was unconstitutional.[82] As was the case under the 1935 Constitution, the legislature could not deprive the court of this power.[83] In a 1983 decision, the Court examined the constitutionality of the Vienna Convention on Diplomatic Relations[84] as well as an Ordinance

74 Sec 1, Art XV, 1935 Constitution.

75 *Planas v Commission on Elections* 49 SCRA 105 at 126 (1973).

76 *Santos, supra* n 17.

77 So far as the practice of the political branches is concerned, the Philippines has sometimes invoked its Constitution in reservations lodged upon ratification of a treaty. See eg Reservations to the Convention on the Prevention and Punishment of the Crime of Genocide made upon ratification by the Philippines, 7 July 1950, 78 UNTS 314; Understanding to the United Nations Convention on the Law of the Sea made upon ratification, 8 May 1984, 1835 UNTS 86, 149–50, 164.

78 Sec 2, Art 8, 1935 Constitution.

79 *Hechanova, supra* n 29, 243.

80 *Ibid.*

81 *Gonzales v Commission on Elections* 21 SCRA 774 at 787 (1967).

82 Sec 5(2)(a), Art X, 1973 Constitution. For an unusual 'transitory provision', see Sec 12, Art XVII, 1973 Constitution; *Cadwallader v Abeleda* 98 SCRA 123 at 159 (1980).

83 Sec 1, Art X, 1973 Constitution.

84 Vienna Convention on Diplomatic Relations, Vienna, 18 April 1961, 500 UNTS 95.

implementing the treaty. The Court appears to have tested the Convention under the 'clear and present danger test' which it uses to determine the validity of laws impinging upon the freedoms of speech and assembly.[85] While it did not find it necessary to decide the issue, the Court displayed sympathy for the view that the application of the Ordinance in a particular factual circumstance might be challenged as unconstitutional.[86]

Two concurring opinions emphasised the supremacy of the Constitution over a treaty provision. One judge stated that if the Convention conflicted with constitutional prohibitions such as the Bill of Rights,[87] the Constitution would prevail.[88] Another judge argued that the government could not validly rely upon the implementing Ordinance where its operation would infringe a constitutional prohibition.[89]

Like its predecessors, the 1987 Constitution confers upon the Supreme Court the power to rule upon the constitutionality of any treaty or executive agreement.[90] The legislature may not deprive the Court of this power.[91] The Court has also held that treaties are to be accorded a presumption of validity.[92] In several recent cases the Court upheld treaties against constitutional challenge.

For example, in *Wright v Court of Appeals*[93] the Court rejected a challenge to the extradition treaty between the Philippines and Australia.[94] The petitioner argued that the treaty's retroactive operation infringed the constitutional prohibition against *ex post facto* laws.[95] The Court held that the treaty did not violate this prohibition.

In *Tañada v Angara*[96] the Supreme Court upheld the constitutionality of the Senate's concurrence in ratification of the World Trade Organization Agreement.[97] The petitioners argued that the Agreement infringed various provisions of the Constitution regarding 'economic nationalism' and that it impaired the exercise of legislative power by Congress.

---

85 *Reyes, supra* n 16, 566.

86 *Ibid*, 570.

87 Art IV, 1973 Constitution. Cp Art 3, 1935 Constitution; Art III, 1987 Constitution.

88 *Reyes, supra* n 16, 571.

89 *Ibid*, 576.

90 Sec 5(2)(a), Art VIII, 1987 Constitution.

91 Sec 2, Art VIII, 1987 Constitution.

92 *Santos, supra* n 17; *Tañada, supra* n 10. In *Re Garcia* 2 SCRA 984 at 986 (1961) the Court interpreted a treaty in accordance with constitutional requirements.

93 235 SCRA 341 (1994).

94 Treaty between Australia and the Philippines on Extradition, Manila, 7 March 1988, 1641 UNTS 331.

95 Sec 21, Art VI, 1987 Constitution.

96 *Tañada, supra* n 10.

97 Agreement Establishing the World Trade Organization, Marrakesh, 15 April 1994, 1867 UNTS 154.

In a unanimous decision, the Court held that the petition presented a justiciable controversy since it raised a serious allegation of constitutional invalidity. Nevertheless, on the merits, the Court rejected the challenge to the WTO Agreement. The 1987 Constitution required the Court to determine whether there had been 'a grave abuse of discretion amounting to lack or excess of jurisdiction' on the part of the Senate.[98] Therefore, the Court did not have to determine the wisdom or otherwise of trade liberalisation. The Court held that there was no 'cogent reason to impute grave abuse of discretion' to the Senate's concurrence to ratification.

So far as the provisions of the Constitution which promoted economic nationalism were concerned, the Court argued that 'the Constitution did not intend to pursue an isolationist policy'. The Court also held that the Constitution permitted the Philippines to voluntarily waive the exercise of a 'portion of sovereignty', noting that many treaties did precisely that.

In a recent decision the majority stated that '[t]his Court will not tolerate the least disregard of constitutional guarantees in the enforcement of a law or treaty'. A concurring opinion similarly emphasised that 'the rights of the accused guaranteed in our Constitution should take precedence over treaty rights claimed by a contracting state'.[99]

7 Conclusion

Under the Constitution of the Philippines international law has been accorded a privileged status. Treaties and customary international law are part of the law of the land. Executive agreements have also been accorded domestic legal status, within important limitations. The law regarding conflicts between a statute and international law is not yet clear. However, treaties and other international agreements are clearly subject to constitutional prohibitions.

98 Sec 1(2), Art VIII, 1987 Constitution.

99 *Lantion*, *supra* n 73.

The Practice of International Commercial Law in Queensland: a Survey

Gabriël Moens, Simon Fisher and Steve Williams

Introduction

Nelson[1] reported that the deregulation of international financial markets, and movements toward free trade, have resulted in a greater complexity and fluidity of international finance. International and domestic markets have become much more competitive, more entrepreneurial, and more efficiency-oriented. As a result, there is a greater demand for corporate lawyers as well as lawyers trained in international commercial law. There has been an increase in new uses and applications of law in international commercial transactions, as a wider range of legal strategies becomes available.[2]

According to Feurstein,[3] rapid developments in advanced technology, such as globally-based workgroups connected electronically, web browsers allowing lawyers to download documents from anywhere in the world for research, and automatic translation services, have greatly assisted firms to engage in international business. As a result, US law firms have added new specialties, employed more paralegals and associates, expanded into new areas of business, and have become more 'international', both in focus and through the opening of offices overseas.[4] In addition, the internationalisation of domestic law is also gaining momentum.[5]

The internationalisation of the Australian economy has dramatically increased the number of international transactions made by Australian firms, and has increased the demand for specialist legal services. The Australian government is increasingly engaged in international transactions at all levels, and public and private foreign entities are approaching Australian legal firms

---

1 Nelson, RL, 'The Future of the Legal Profession: The Futures of American Lawyers: A Demographic Profile of a Changing Profession in a Changing Society' (1994) 4 Case W Res Law Review: 345, 355–57.

2 Harper, T, 'Going Global – Big Law Firms Expand Overseas' American Bar Association Journal, September 1998: 68–72.

3 Feurstein, J, 'Advanced Technology Helps Firms go Global' (February 1999) National Law Journal.

4 Harper, T, 'Going Global – Big Law Firms Expand Overseas' American Bar Association Journal, September 1998: 68–72; Silver, C, 'Globalisation and the Market for Legal Services' (2000) 31 Law and Policy in International Business: 1093–1150.

5 Mason, A, *The Internationalisation of Domestic Law*, Centre for International and Public Law, Law Faculty, Australian National University, Law and Policy Paper No 4, 1996.

for assistance in their business in Australia. The process of internationalisation has been seen in Australia with large national firms opening offices overseas (eg, Blake Dawson Waldron; Corrs Chambers Westgarth; Mallesons Stephen Jaques; and Minter Ellison).

According to Fisher,[6] forces driving change in Australian legal practice are globalisation, the quest for seamless business transactions through harmonisation of laws and procedures, and a shift from product-based trade to knowledge-based trade. He noted[7] that Australian commercial legal work is becoming less constrained by borders, and that Australian lawyers need more than ever to be internationalist. He stated that it is no longer sufficient for lawyers to retain an insular mindset that takes no account of international legal developments and that Australian lawyers must be informed of these developments.

Responses to these pressures can be seen in the increasing importance of international trade and commercial law subjects in Australian law schools. A driving force for internationalisation in Australia is the signing of the United Nations Convention on Contracts for the International Sale of Goods (CISG) and its integration into the law of each state, as well as the promotion of the UNIDROIT Principles of International Commercial Contracts, which have a much wider application to international transactions than the CISG. Australian legal practitioners can use the UNIDROIT Principles for the formation of international commercial contracts and for the adjudication of disputes.

Other responses can be seen in the changing organisational structures of Australian and New Zealand law firms, which are becoming more managerial, more specialist and more international. These, to some extent, have mirrored the changes seen in Australian business – Australian firms are now more international, and have moved from manufacturing-based to services-based industries that are heavily involved in international transactions.[8] The past 10 years have seen the emergence of small, specialist firms working in niche markets and the rise of 'professional conglomerates' and multidisciplinary practices offering a wide range of services. The threat of overseas competitors entering the Australian market to engage in international legal practice is perceived as real.

Although there is much anecdotal evidence available on the internationalisation of Queensland law firms, and the practice of international commercial law, there has been little empirical systematic study of this

6 Fisher, S, 'Commercial Law in a Global Context – Current Influences and the Future for Australia', in Mugasha, A, (ed), *Commercial Law: Issues for the 21st Century*, 2001, Sydney, Prospect Media, at 115.

7 *Ibid*, 138.

8 Nelson, RL, 'The Future of the Legal Profession: The Futures of American Lawyers: A Demographic Profile of a Changing Profession in a Changing Society' (1994) 4 Case W Res Law Review: 345, 355–57.

activity. Janssen[9] noted that the use of the Internet to streamline work practices and to create cost efficiencies in Brisbane law firms is increasing, and that the use of the Internet was increasing the range of marketing strategies used by firms and the delivery of legal services. However, he did not investigate the use of the Internet as part of the process of internationalisation.[10] This article is a first step towards providing data that describes the practice of international commercial law in Queensland.

Research questions/hypotheses

The research had two main objectives. The first was to gather empirical information on the current state of international commercial law practice in Queensland. The second was linked to earlier research done by one of the authors suggesting that one of the reasons food exporters did not seek legal advice prior to exporting was that it was not readily available.

A series of hypotheses was suggested by the literature as well as by exploratory research with three Brisbane law firms (two small [less than 10 professional staff] and one large [10 or more]). The exploratory study was a personal interview with the partners of each firm, and was aimed at clarifying issues.

The hypotheses tested were as follows:

H1: Large firms will have more international involvement than small firms (larger firms were thought more likely to have international clients).

H2: 'Older' firms (those established for 10 or more years) will have more international involvement than 'new' firms (older firms were thought to have more time to develop expertise and contacts necessary for international legal business).

H3: Firms with staff trained in international law will have more international involvement than those without (firms engaging in international commercial law would be seeking staff with appropriate training).

H4: Firms with significant involvement in international commercial law will maintain reference materials in international commercial law (more involvement would mean more need for resource materials).

H5: Firms with significant involvement in international commercial law will keep up-to-date with developments in international commercial law (more involvement would mean more need for keeping up-to-date).

9 Janssen, A, 'A Decade of Change' Lawyers Weekly, 8 September 2000:14–15.

10 See Elliott, E, 'The Internet – A New World Without Frontiers' (1998) New Zealand Law Journal: 405–08.

H6: Generalist firms will be more likely to be involved in international commercial law than 'specialist' firms (generalist firms were thought to be more likely candidates for international work).

H7: Firms with a significant involvement in international commercial law will have more dealings with the CISG than firms with only a slight involvement (a greater involvement would be linked to more international contract work).

H8: Firms with a significant involvement in international commercial law will have more dealings with the UNIDROIT Principles than firms with only a slight involvement (greater involvement would be linked to more use of UNIDROIT Principles).

H9: Firms with a significant involvement in international commercial law will have a greater involvement in international dispute resolution than firms with only a slight involvement (greater involvement would be linked to more involvement in dispute resolution).

H10: Firms with significant involvement in international commercial law will make more use of INCOTERMS than firms with only a slight involvement (greater involvement would be linked to more use of INCOTERMS).

Method

The survey was conducted by mail in May/June 2000, and forms were sent to every law firm in Queensland on the TC Beirne School of Law mailing list. The survey questionnaire consisted of twelve questions pertaining to the firm's involvement in international commercial law and three questions on firm details such as the size of the firm, years in business, and areas of legal practice. Questions provided a series of choices for a 'tick the box' response as well as space for 'other' categories and additional comment. The survey was pre-tested before release with the three firms that participated in the exploratory study.

A follow-up survey reminder letter and another copy of the survey were sent out three weeks after the first mail-out.

Questions covered the following issues:

1 The extent to which the practice worked in the area of international commercial law.

2 The branches of international commercial law engaged in.

3 The extent to which the international commercial work related to the CISG.

4 The extent to which the international commercial work related to the UNIDROIT Principles.

5 The perceived advantages or disadvantages of international conventions to the practice of international commercial law.

6 The extent to which the firm was involved in international dispute resolution.

7 The extent to which the firm's international commercial work involved the use of international commercial terms (INCOTERMS).

8 Whether or not international commercial law specialists were employed on staff, and the extent of their training.

9 Whether or not the firm maintained a source library of materials on international commercial law.

10 How the firm kept up with developments in international commercial law.

Results of the Survey

A total of 245 firms responded, of which 243 replies were usable and analysed. Of these, 183 firms reported that international commercial law was no part of their practice. The distribution of these firms was as follows (Table 1):

Table 1: Distribution of firms reporting no involvement

New	78	Old	105
Small	168	Large	15
Specialist	139	Generalist	44

Of the 60 firms which reported that international commercial law was part of their practice to some extent, 4 firms reported a 'major' involvement in international commercial work; 24 reported 'minor' involvement, and 32 reported 'slight' involvement. The distribution was as follows (Table 2):

Table 2: Distribution of firms with some involvement

New	21	Old	39
Small	38	Large	22
Specialist	23	Generalist	37

Of the 4 firms reporting that international commercial law was a major part of their work, two were in the category of 'new, small, specialist'; one was 'old, small, generalist' and one was 'old, large, generalist'.

For the 24 firms reporting 'minor' involvement the distribution was as follows:

Table 3: Distribution of firms reporting minor involvement

New/Small/Specialist	4
New/Small/Generalist	3
Old/Small/Specialist	2
Old/Small/Generalist	4
New/Large/Specialist	0
New/Large/Generalist	1
Old/Large/Specialist	1
Old/Large/Generalist	9

Given the small sample size, the hypotheses were tested using a statistical test of simple proportions using Z scores (Reference). The critical value was set at the 5% level. All of the hypotheses were accepted.

H1: Large firms have more international involvement than small firms.
$Z = 6.26$

H2: Older firms have more international involvement than 'newer' firms.
$Z = 15.126$.

H3: Firms with staff trained in international law have more international involvement than those without.
$Z = 8.732$.

H4: Firms with significant involvement in international commercial law maintain reference materials.
$Z = 4.28$.

H5: Firms with significant involvement in international commercial law keep up to date with developments in international law.
$Z = 7.23$.

H6: 'Generalist' firms are more involved in international law than 'specialist' firms.
$Z = 5.6$.

H7: Firms with a significant involvement in international commercial law have more dealings with the CISG than firms with only a slight involvement.
$Z = 3.86$.

H8: Firms with a significant involvement in international commercial law have more dealings with the UNIDROIT Principles than firms with only a slight involvement.
$Z = 2.6$.

H9: Firms with a significant involvement in international commercial law have a greater involvement in international dispute resolution than those with only a slight involvement.
$Z = 3.71$.

H10: Firms with a significant involvement in international commercial law have a greater involvement in dispute resolution than those with only a slight involvement.
$Z = 3.71$.

While all hypotheses were accepted, interesting information is found in the detail. For example, of 60 firms expressing involvement in international commercial law practice, only 28 had some involvement with the CISG, and only 25 had any involvement with the UNIDROIT Principles. On the other hand, 40 firms did use INCOTERMS in their international work and 35 firms were involved in international dispute resolution. Fourteen out of the 60 firms had international law specialists on staff. Forty-six did not. Only 21 out of the 60 firms maintained reference materials, and only six of the 60 firms reported they were planning to employ staff with international commercial law training.

While 28 firms out of the 60 reported they had some training in international law, 10 reported they were trained 'on the job', six received training as part of their undergraduate degree, six as part of a higher degree, and six attended short specialist courses.

Forty-three firms reported that they kept up with international commercial law developments. The most important sources of information were (in order):

1 The Internet
2 University/Court libraries
3 Seminars/Discussions with overseas colleagues
4 Membership of International Legal Organisations
5 Consultants
6 Attendance at international legal conferences

With respect to international dispute resolution, most of the work involved enforcing contracts overseas, insolvency overseas, and cargo claims. Other dispute activities included sports arbitration, mergers and acquisitions, and trademarks.

With respect to the CISG, UNIDROIT Principles, and INCOTERMS, most respondents in contact with these conventions reported that they were very helpful to international commercial legal practice. The only disadvantage cited was that there is still a lack of knowledge of these conventions on the part of the general profession.

Discussion of results

The results of the survey show that while international commercial expertise is available in Queensland, it is limited. Only four firms out of 243 respondents reported that international commercial law was a major part of their work, and only 32 firms reported more than a slight involvement. 183 firms had no involvement at all. This suggests that the internationalisation of the commercial legal process reported elsewhere (eg, the USA,)[11] may be proceeding only slowly in Queensland, and that calls for greater internationalisation of Australian legal practice are not being heeded.

According to Silver,[12] the internationalisation of law firms in the USA generally passes through an evolutionary process where the firm will first expand into other states in order to obtain a 'national' identity rather than 'local', and then will add foreign offices to extend the 'national' identity to an international one. She noted, however, that some 'local' firms were able to by-pass the process and engaged directly in international practice. The results of the survey showed that nine 'new, small' firms were involved in international work, thus confirming this observation in Australia.

One of the outcomes of a Queensland exporter survey conducted earlier was that exporters did not find lawyers to be very helpful with respect to their international business transactions. Lawyers were consulted when setting up their companies, and sometimes for assistance with the drafting of contracts and the resolution of disputes, but the general feeling was that lawyers do not understand the business issues and problems of exporters. The idea of obtaining assistance from lawyers with respect to the development of appropriate market entry strategies, pricing strategies, and distribution strategies, and having a legal strategy at the core of overall corporate strategy was foreign to them, although it is recommended in most textbooks. There appears to be a substantial gap between theory and practice.

Fisher[13] suggests that one of the things businesses look for in their international trading is 'seamless business transactions'. Silver[14] noted that one of the reasons US firms were successful in the area of international commercial law was that they are able to offer international and domestic clients their expertise with sophisticated corporate and financial transactions, even where US law is not involved. They have developed a capacity to assist clients through the strategic use of law in business transactions, and a capacity

11 Silver, C, 'Globalisation and the Market for Legal Services' (2000) 31 Law and Policy in International Business: 1093–1150.

12 *Ibid.*

13 Fisher, S, 'Commercial Law in a Global Context – Current Influences and the Future for Australia' In Mugasha, A, (ed), *Commercial Law: Issues for the 21st Century*, 2001, Sydney, Prospect Media, 2001.

14 Silver, C, 'Globalisation and the Market for Legal Services' (2000) 31 Law and Policy in International Business: 1093–1150 at 1098.

to 'think outside the box' when assisting clients with a problem. She suggests that this is a unique feature of US legal practice, and that UK lawyers (and Australian lawyers, by implication) tend not to give this service.[15] She notes that UK lawyers see themselves as 'instructed' by the client as to their needs, whereas US lawyers never refer to their relationship with a client as 'instructed'. US law firms have 'deal experience' that they can offer to their clients. They can offer packaged solutions to trader needs and their experience helps them to respond to the timing demands of their clients. This gives them the ability to make business transactions appear seamless, and gives them a competitive advantage.

Fisher[16] noted that it is no longer appropriate for Australian lawyers just to handle the physical and tangible elements such as the instruction. Lawyers must look to the whole transaction and provide service inputs where they will produce an 'advantage'.

Conclusion

The survey gathered empirical data on the status of international commercial legal practice in Queensland. It was found that progress appears to be slow. The implications for the profession and for legal training in Queensland are that the survey provides an empirical base for further work, and also suggests pathways by which Queensland law firms may increasingly engage in international commercial law. For example, the finding that Queensland firms do not appear to offer US-style service to companies wishing to do business overseas is of interest. A similar finding has been reported in New Zealand, where Webb[17] found that there was a general resistance to the internationalisation of legal practice. He noted that most of the services provided by major law firms involved following client instructions, in contrast to the 'can do' US approach. While there is no doubt there is a trend among larger law firms to merge with accounting firms and other business service providers to provide a 'total service' package for clients,[18] the traditional UK attitude of being 'instructed' by clients persists. While Australian law schools have responded to perceived needs by providing elective subjects in international law, they are not generally providing the kind of practical training in the use of legal strategy and creative legal solutions that are taught

15 *Ibid*, 1096–97.

16 Fisher, S, 'Commercial Law in a Global Context – Current Influences and the Future for Australia', in Mugasha, A, (ed), *Commercial Law: Issues for the 21st Century*, 2001, Sydney, Prospect Media, 2001, at 119.

17 Webb, D, 'Restructuring the Professional Firm' (August 2000) New Zealand Law Journal: 287–88.

18 Warnecke, A (ed), *Legal Profiles – A Client's Guide to Australia's Leading Law Firms and their Practices*, 1999, Sydney, Profiles Publishing.

in US law schools. They are clearly doing their part, but much more can be done.

The profession can be active in the training process by ensuring that international law, and particularly commercial law, becomes a strongly recommended or even compulsory component of legal education. Fisher[19] suggests that the profession can also become more involved through greater participation in the international commercial law-making framework and active involvement in international legal bodies and the law formulation process. This is occurring to some extent but again much more can be done.

19 Fisher, S, 'Commercial Law in a Global Context – Current Influences and the Future for Australia', in Mugasha, A (ed), *Commercial Law: Issues for the 21st Century*, 2001, Sydney, Prospect Media.

Respecting Contractual Intentions: Balancing Consumer Expectations with the Sanctity of Contract in the Context of Standard Form Insurance Contracts

JR Tarr[1]

Common law judges in all jurisdictions have struggled to achieve a workable balance between providing appropriate consumer protection to signatories of standard form contracts while still retaining adequate respect for the sanctity of contract. The British judge, Steyn LJ, in his struggles with the competing implications legal formalism and legal functionalism would have for a beleaguered consumer enmeshed in a standard form contract, observed that:

> The theme that runs through our law of contract is that the reasonable expectations of honest men must be protected. It is not a rule or a principle of law. It is the objective which has been and still is the principal moulding force of our law of contract. It affords no license to a Judge to depart from binding precedent. On the other hand, if the *prima facie* solution to a problem runs counter to the reasonable expectations of honest men, this criterion sometimes requires a rigorous re-examination of the problem to ascertain whether the law does indeed compel demonstrable unfairness.[2]

Although these comments arose in relation to a banking dispute, it is perhaps in the insurance industry's use of contracts of adhesion that this 'battle front' appears most clearly defined and active.[3] Given the gross disparity in bargaining power often found in such contracts and the degree of complexity that exists as to the nature and effect of policy terms and exclusions, it is perhaps not surprising that a number of mechanisms and processes have been developed, or are emerging, that aim to reconcile parties' expectations with the language employed in these contracts. It is the purpose of this article to examine the means currently available to judges in this respect and, based on this analysis, to determine whether a significantly greater scope of contract (re)construction is likely to become the norm in most common law jurisdictions in the coming decades.

---

1 Senior Lecturer, TC Beirne School of Law, University of Queensland, BA (Wisc), JD (Cornell), LLM (Monash), PhD (UQ).

2 *First Energy (UK) Ltd v Hungarian International Bank Ltd* [1993] 2 Lloyd's Rep 194 (CA), at 196.

3 See, for example, leading British insurance expert M Clarke's observation in *The Law of Insurance Contracts*, 3rd edn, 1997, p 369, that in the United Kingdom the Insurance Ombudsman Bureau has chosen to approach these words as the 'guiding light'.

I Introduction: standard tools for judicial construction of party intentions

Traditionally, judges seeking to redress disadvantaged insureds have, short of invoking equity, been limited to construing ambiguities as they appear in the contract or to interpreting implied terms as part of an otherwise silent document. Accordingly, provided ambiguity or silence exists in a document, a policy-holder might prevail on the basis of the *contra proferentem* rule of contract construction or through judicial interpretation of implied terms such as business efficacy or the nature and commercial purpose of the policy. Theoretically under the traditional liberalist framework on which the last two centuries of contract law have been premised, if after careful scrutiny (and without the necessary grounds to satisfy equitable intervention), a document is such that it is neither ambiguous nor amenable to implied terms the situation would in fact be that described by Justice Steyn as one wherein the law 'compel[s] demonstrable unfairness.'

Judicial abhorrence of this result is not surprisingly such that cases wherein construction based on ambiguity or interpretation of implied terms have resulted in decisions which can best be described as straining readers' credulity. While in the short term this level of judicial activism undoubtedly has decided advantages for the prevailing policy holder, in the longer term it not only creates an impression of unprincipled judicial prejudice against the insurance industry but also produces confusion and uncertainty about the nature and extent of judicial control of contract terms. For these reasons, over the last forty years a number of United States and Canadian jurisdictions have formally abandoned the fiction that construction of contracts is limited only to clarification or elimination of ambiguity and have moved instead to explicitly recognising that in some circumstances, pro-insured decisions can be reached as a reflection of the justice system's duty to honour or protect the reasonable expectations of policy holders. Known as the doctrine of reasonable expectations, this doctrine, broadly stated, recognises that applicants, insureds, and intended beneficiaries may have an additional cause of action based on their reasonable expectations regarding the coverage afforded by insurance contracts even though a careful examination of the policy provisions indicates that such expectations are contrary to the expressed intention of the insurer. Whether this approach really does constitute a growing trend in judicial activism towards more aggressive intervention on behalf of insureds' rights on the grounds of construction of contractual terms, however, presupposes that this doctrine is genuinely more than an expanded version of already existing principles of construction and interpretation.

Contra proferentem

The *contra proferentem* rule[4] is the rule of construction most familiar and readily accepted in all jurisdictions. This rule has been described[5] as 'the main protection for the insured under the existing law' against his or her understandable ignorance of many insurance provisions. The rule is based on the principle that a person is responsible for ambiguities in his or her own expression and may not induce another into a contract on the supposition that the selected words may mean one thing, while at the same time hoping that a court which has to construe them will give them another meaning, more to his or her advantage.[6] As policies and other documentation such as cover notes and proposals are generally drafted by the insurers themselves, it is evident that these organisations are doubtlessly best placed to monitor and control the precision and clarity achieved in the material produced. When ambiguity issues arise out of such documentation, resolving such dilemmas in this manner seems the eminently more reasonable approach.[7] The same principle applies in reverse where, for example, the insured's broker proffers the policy or special terms to be added to a standard policy. Accordingly, the *contra proferentem* rule is a useful constructional device that may offer a means of protecting an insured, or indeed an insurer, in an individual case where the justice of the principle warrants it. Its principal limitations are that it may only be invoked for true ambiguity, and it may only be deployed in the process of litigation, though it must be considered by the parties' advisers. It does not serve to address the imbalance in information and understanding in a pre-contractual setting, but may be of assistance in the fair resolution of ambiguities in a post-contractual dispute.[8] To the extent that it operates, it is fair, which is its *raison d'être*; and insofar as it provides a remedy to whichever party may be unfairly disadvantaged, its application is also fair.

Implied terms: business efficacy and commercial purposes of policies

The business efficacy, nature and commercial purpose of the policy are further considerations that a court may take into account in reconciling an insured's

4 The full expression is *verba chartarum fortius accipiuntur contra proferentem*; that is, an ambiguous provision is construed most strongly against the person who selected the language: *Black's Law Dictionary*, 1979, 5th edn, p 296.

5 Australian Law Reform Commission, *Report on Insurance Contracts* (No 20, 1982), para 49.

6 *Anderson v Fitzgerald* (1853) 4 HLC 484, 510–11; Voet, *Commentarius ad Pandectas,* 18.1.27, in describing the Roman origins of the rule put the matter thus: 'Dubious pacts are to be construed against the party by whom they are imposed, as everyone must impute it to his own imprudence that he has not expressed himself more plainly.'

7 Compare U Procaccia, 'Readable Insurance Policies: Judicial regulation and Interpretation' (1979) 14 Israel LR 74 at 102. See also Liederman, 'Insurance Coverage Disputes in the United States: a Period of Uncertainty for the Insurer' (1986) LMCLQ 79, at 83–85.

8 Generally see the Australian Law Reform Commission Report on Insurance Contracts (No 20, 1982), para 49.

legitimate expectations with the actual policy delivered. As Vautier J observed in *Tru-Line Plumbers Ltd v CML Fire & General Insurance Co Ltd*[9] 'it is essential … to have regard to the nature of the policy in question and what it was intended to cover.' In this regard, the commercial purpose is an essential consideration.[10] A good illustration is afforded by *Alex Kay Pty Ltd v General Motors Acceptance Corporation and Hartord Fire Insurance Co.*[11] The insured, a car hire firm, effected an insurance policy which provided an indemnity in respect of losses sustained by the insured in the course of its operations, unless that loss arose from 'a breach of contract, agreement or obligation.' The insured claimed for losses sustained when a customer failed, in violation of the rental agreement, to return a car. The claim was resisted on the ground the loss arose from a breach of contract. Sholl J rejected this argument as undermining the commercial objective of the contract by noting that:

> This is a commercial contract. One of its professed objects is to indemnify the insured with respect to loss of, or damage to, one of its vehicles, which was … to the knowledge of the parties to be used in the insured's business of letting out cars for hire, and indeed a larger premium was attached on that account. From a commercial point of view, it would be the merest common sense for the insurer to assume that any hirer of one of their cars would be under a contractual obligation, express or implied, to return it in good order and condition, and not to damage or lose it by negligence.[12]

As a matter of business common sense and having regard to the nature of the policy and what it was intended to cover, he limited the operation of the clause to losses arising out of the insured's breach of contract with another party; for example, where the insured incurred liability through supplying a defective vehicle pursuant to a hire agreement.[13] Courts have further ruled that, as an insurance policy is a commercial document, fair and reasonable construction of a clause requires that it accord with sound commercial principles and good business sense.[14] Derrington and Ashton[15] state that practical business

9 Unreported, High Court, Auckland, New Zealand, 26 February 1982, M191/81.

10 See *Fraser v BN Furman (Productions) Ltd* [1967] 1 WLR 898; *Tru-Line Plumbers Ltd v CML Fire and General Insurance Co Ltd*, Unreported, High Court, Auckland, New Zealand, 26 February 1982, M191/81, p 7.

11 [1963] VR 458.

12 *Ibid*, at 462.

13 See also, *Cornish v Accident Insurance Co* (1889) 23 QBD 453; *Re Sun Alliance Insurance Ltd ex p Bonastre* [1974] Qld R 128; *State Government Insurance Commission v Steven Bros Pty Ltd* (1984) 58 ALJR 346, at 349; *Transport Industries Insurance Co Ltd v New South Wales Medical Defence Union Ltd* (1986) 4 ANZ Insurance Cases 60-736, at 74,410 *per* Kirby P, *Legal & General Insurance Co Ltd v Eather* (1986) 4 ANZ Insurance Cases 60-749; 6 NSWLR 390.

14 *MacGillivray and Parkington on Insurance Law*, 8th edn, 1988, p 439; *National Protector Fire Insurance Co Ltd v Nivert* [1913] AC 507, at 513; *Minucoe v London and Liverpool and Globe Insurance Co Ltd* (1925) 36 CLR 513; *MGICA Ltd v United City Merchants (Aust) Ltd* (1986) 4 ANZ Insurance Cases 60-937.

15 *The Law of Liability Insurance*, 1990, Butterworths, p 102.

considerations and common sense may be operative canons of construction in giving to an ill-drafted clause a meaning which the parties as sensible business people must have intended. For example, in *Boys v State Insurance General Manager*[16] the insurer rejected a claim that it argued breached a condition in the policy requiring notification of other insurance. The policy in question was an indemnity policy whereas the other policy covered the replacement cost of the house concerned. The Court in holding that no duty to give notice arose as it was not a case of double insurance (eg, different risks were covered), stated that conditions should be interpreted in a way which is reasonable and gives business efficacy.

II Towards the reasonable expectations of the parties: a new doctrine or the Emperor's new clothes?

These rules and approaches to construction, along with the obvious need to deliver a policy consistent with the terms indicated by the proposal,[17] are uncontroversial and retain traditional respect for sanctity of contract. The same cannot be said for the doctrine of reasonable expectations. This doctrine had its origins in the United States and more recently appears to be emerging in the United Kingdom and Canada. The context in which it arises is where the technical language in which a contract is couched is severely at odds with the understanding or expectations of the non-drafting party.[18] Associated primarily with standard form contracts or contracts of adhesion, this defensive doctrine is least controversially invoked in circumstances where the language of the document is such that, if literally applied, it produces a result largely devoid of value to the insured; for example, it defeats his or her 'reasonable expectation' of why the contract was entered into in the first place. This doctrine seems to reside uneasily between the *contra proferentem* rule of construction and the doctrine of unconscionability.[19]

Section 211 of the Restatement (Second) of Contracts in the United States sets forth the principles on which this doctrine rests by stating that an insured remains bound by a specific provision of a contract of adhesion when:

> (1) Except as stated in Subsection (3), where a party to an agreement signs or otherwise manifests assent to a writing and has reason to believe that like

16 [1980] 1 NZLR 87.

17 See, for example, *Steadfast Insurance Co Ltd v F & B Trading Co Ltd* (1971) 125 CLR 578, at 586; *Randell v Atlantica Insurance Co Ltd* (1985) 80 FLR 253; *Re Bradley and Essex and Suffolk Accident Indemnity Society* [1912] 1 KB 415, at 430; *Inn Cor International Ltd v American Home Assurance Co* (1947) 42 DLR (3d) 46.

18 R Jerry, 'Insurance, Contract, and the Doctrine of Reasonable Expectation' (1998) 5 Connecticut Law Journal 21, at 22, offers the following call to arms on the issues of interpretation of standard form insurance contracts when noting that his dialectic constitutes a battle for the heart and soul – not only of contract law, or insurance law – but of American jurisprudence generally.

19 See cases discussed below.

writings are regularly used to embody terms of agreement of the same type, he adopts the writing as an integrated agreement with respect to the terms included in the writing.

(2) Such a writing is interpreted wherever reasonable as treating alike all those similarly situated, without regard to their knowledge or understanding of the standard terms of the writing.

(3) Where the other party has reason to believe that the party manifesting such assent would not do so if he knew that the writing contained a particular term, the term is not part of the agreement.[20]

The drafters go on to offer the following comment on the interpretation of this provision:

> Although customers typically adhere to standardized agreements and are bound by them without even appearing to know the standard terms in detail, they are not bound to unknown terms which are beyond the range of reasonable expectations. A debtor who delivers a check to his creditor with the amount blank does not authorize the insertion of an infinite figure. Similarly, a party who adheres to the other party's standard terms does not assent to a term if the other party has reason to believe that the adhering party would not have accepted the agreement if he had known that the agreement contained the particular term. Such a belief or assumption may be shown by the prior negotiations or inferred from the circumstances. Reason to believe may be inferred from the fact that the term is bizarre or oppressive, from the fact that it eviscerates the non-standard terms explicitly agreed to, or from the fact that it eliminates the dominant purpose of the transaction. The inference is reinforced if the adhering party never had an opportunity to read the term, or if it is illegible or otherwise hidden from view.[21]

Unlike the *contra proferentem* rule the doctrine of reasonable expectations is not dependent upon the existence of an ambiguity in the contract. Rather, it is a legal concept that United States courts in ten jurisdictions have employed, in instances where no ambiguity was involved, to nullify certain provisions of standard form contracts of insurance that are found to be unfair to those who have no opportunity but to adhere to the agreement and would consequently, in the view of the courts, be deprived of the benefit of their bargain.

Formal recognition of reasonable expectations as a judicial principle of reasoning arose initially out of a two part Harvard Law Review article

---

20 The Restatement (Third) of Contracts is at this time currently being drafted amidst considerable academic speculation that these provisions will be extended to incorporate more accurately Keeton's original formulation of the principle (see R Keeton, 'Insurance Law Rights at Variance with Policy Provisions' (1970) 83 Harvard Law Review 961, and 1281) and/or may possibly be reformulated to include a separate provision for insurance contracts only. Movement is also afoot to revise section 2-206 of the Uniform Commercial Code in this direction. See White, 'Consumer Protection and the Uniform Commercial Code: Form Contracts Under Revised Article 2' (1997) 75 Washington University Law Quarterly 315.

21 Restatement (Second) of Contracts, s 211, cmt F(1981).

published in 1970 by Professor (now Judge) Keeton.[22] Advanced as a principle, Keeton argued that '[t]he objectively reasonable expectations of applicants and intended beneficiaries regarding the terms of insurance contracts will be honored even though painstaking study of the policy provisions would have negated those expectations'.[23]

Judicial use of this premise was first formally articulated in 1961 in *Kievit v Loyal Protective Life Insurance Co.*[24] The New Hampshire court, in granting coverage for the insured despite the presence of contrary language reasoned that '[w]hen members of the public purchase policies of insurance they are entitled to the broad measure of protection necessary to fulfil their reasonable expectations.' It then went on to conclude that given the clause at stake, it would, if literally interpreted render the policy 'of little value to a [man of 48] since disability or death resulting from accidental injury would in all probability be in some sense contributed by the infirmities of old age'. As is discussed below, similar reasoning was adopted by the House of Lords in the 1998 case of *Cook v Financial Ins Co.*[25]

It is evident, however, that this was not an entirely new approach in that Judge Learned Hand in *Gaunt v John Hancock Mutual Life Insurance Co* offered the foreshadowing comment that:

> An underwriter might so understand the phrase, when read in its context, [to start coverage at a later date] but the application was not to be submitted to underwriters; it was to go to persons utterly unacquainted with the niceties of life insurance, who would read it colloquially. It is the understanding of such persons that counts ... A man must indeed read what he signs, and he is charged, if he does not; but insurers who seek to impose upon words of common speech an esoteric significance intelligible only to their craft, must bear the burden of any resulting confusion.[26]

Judicial interpretation of the nature of this doctrine varies substantially. In its most conservative form, courts have invoked it as a rule of construction to resolve ambiguities – that is, the ambiguous phrase or term is to be construed in accordance with the insured's reasonable expectations which is the *contra proferentem* rule.[27] In contrast to this, however, the courts generally look to

22 R Keeton, 'Insurance Law Rights at Variance with Policy Provisions' (1970) 83 Harvard Law Review 961; Keeton, 'Insurance Law Rights at Variance with Policy Provisions: Part Two' (1970) 83 Harvard Law Review 1281.

23 Keeton, 'Insurance Law Rights at Variance with Policy Provisions' (1970) 83 Harvard Law Review 961, at 967.

24 34 NJ 475, 170 A 2d 22 (1961).

25 [1998] 1 WLR 1765.

26 *Gaunt v John Hancock Mutual Life Insurance Co*, 160 F 2d 599 (2d Cir), cert denied, 331 US 849 (1947), at p 1185–86.

27 See, for example, *Carly v Lumberman's Mutual Casualty Co*, 521 A 2d 1053 (Conn App Ct 1987); *Eli Lilly & Co v Home Ins Co*, 482 NE 2d 467 (Ind 1985); *Allstate Ins Co v Elwell*, 513 A 2d 269 (Me 1986); *Rodriguez v General Accident Ins Co*, 898 SW 2d 379 (Mo 1991) en banc; *Kracl v Aetna Cas & Sur Co*, 374 NW 2d 40 (Neb 1985); *National Union Fire Ins Co v Reno's Executive Air Inc*, 682 2d 1380 (Nev 1984); *Max True Plastering Co v United States Fidelity & Guar Co*, 912 P 2d 861 (Okla 1996).

the overall purpose of the contract, or the reasonable expectations the insured brings to the transaction, to identify phrases that may be ambiguous[28] in the context of what an average insured would believe them to be.[29] This contrasts with the *contra proferentem* rule in that it is not ambiguous words or phrases being sought to determine whether the language can support an alternative meaning – the language itself is clear. What is being sought is a clause or language that bestows a condition on the contract that the insured, if he or she had understood the language, would (presumably) not have entered the contract. That the standard adopted is that of the average insured is vital in Keeton's view as a higher standard could potentially penalise a policyholder who took the time to read and understand the document(s).[30]

In its most aggressive application the doctrine provides protection of reasonable expectations even in instances where express policy language to the contrary exists.[31] The Iowa Supreme Court's analysis in *C & J Fertilizer*

28 Australian and New Zealand Courts have similarly mirrored this reasoning in a number of cases. In *Legal & General Insurance Australia Ltd v Eather* (1986) 4 ANZ Insurance Cases 60-749; 6 NSWLR 390, the court was required to interpret the meaning of the words 'all reasonable precautions to avoid or minimise injury, loss or damage' in relation to the theft of jewellery. The court held that this phrase had to be read down to give effect to the commercial purpose of the contract. The insured was required to avoid recklessness, that is, to take such steps to protect the jewellery as were reasonable having regard to the dangers which he recognised. Kirby P, in particular, was of the opinion that the word 'all' must be read down to achieve this effect, thereby bringing in the objective of the contract to clarify this seemingly ambiguous word. It is submitted that within the facts of this case, the level of 'ambiguity' identified for reading down purposes would possibly fall more happily under the ambit of the reasonable expectations approach. See also *Tru-Line Plumbing Ltd v CML Fire & General Insurance Co Ltd*, unreported, High Court, Auckland, New Zealand, 26 February 1982, M191/81; *Fraser v BN Furman (Productions) Ltd* [1967] 1 WLR 898; *Alex Kay Pty Ltd v General Motors Acceptance Corp and Hartford Fire Insurance Co* [1963] VR 458; *Boys v State Insurance General Manager* [1980] 1 NZLR 87; *Re Etherington and Lancashire and Yorkshire Accident Insurance Co* [1909] 1 KB 591 (literal meaning of words must not be allowed to prevail where it would produce an unrealistic and generally unanticipated result).

29 A similar result has been achieved by at least one court using the rubric of implied warranty. See *C & J Fertilizer Inc v Allied Mut Ins Co*, 227 NW 2d 169 (Iowa 1975), at 178–79. In this case, the Iowa court in dealing with an insurance policy looked to the broad purpose of the whole contract and concluded that as the insurer is said to have impliedly warranted that the provisions within the contract are consistent with the broad purpose of the document, an implied warranty of fitness existed and had been breached. Implied warranties are, however, rarely applied to insurance contracts for privity purposes (as they potentially can give rise to unexpected third party rights of suit against the insurer) and for doctrinal purposes. In the latter instance, it is not clear whether an implied warranty arises in contract law, tort law or both. As the positioning of the claim affects both remedies and statutes of limitations, the jurisprudential implications are of significant complexity.

30 R Keeton, *Basic Text on Insurance Law*, 1971, section 6.3(b), at 351. Keeton goes on to advocate the more stringent corollary that 'If the enforcement of a policy provision would defeat the reasonable expectations of the great majority of policy holders to whose claims it is relevant, it will not be enforced even against those who know of its restrictive terms', id, at section 6.3(a).

31 See, for example, *Reliance Ins Co v Moessner*, 121 F 3d 895 (3rd Cir 1997); *State Farm Mut Auto Ins Co v Falness*, 29 F 3d 966 (9th Cir 1994); *Regional Bank of Colorado v St Paul Fire and Marine Ins Co*, 35 F 3d 494 (10th Cir 1994); *Bering Strait School Dist v RLI Ins Co*, 873 P 2d 1292 (Alaska 1994); *Darner Motor Sales, Inc v Universal Underwriters Ins Co*, 682 P 2d 388 (Ariz 1984); *Clark-Peterson Co v Independent Ins Assocs*, 492 NW 2d 675 (Iowa 1992); *Transamerica Ins Co v Royle*, 565 P 2d 820 (Mont 1983); *Atwood v Hartford Accident & Indem Co*, 365 A 2d 744 (NH 1976); *Sparks v St Paul Ins Co*, 495 A 2d 406 (NJ 1985); *West Virginia v Janicki*, 422 SE 2d 822 (W Va 1992).

Inc v Allied Mutual Insurance Co[32] is illustrative of this latter approach. In this case, a small businessman sought to claim for a burglary loss under his general storekeeper's policy of insurance. Although burglary losses were covered, the definitional section set forth the requisite that 'visible marks … or physical damage to, the exterior of the premises' be present. As the insured's premises appeared to have been entered through a un-marked plexiglass door, which was subsequently shown to be able to be forced open without leaving scratch marks, cover was refused. The Court, in upholding the insured's claim, looked to the doctrine of reasonable expectations in setting aside the specific definitional language of the policy. In reaching this conclusion, the court tried to reconstruct the expectation of the insured based on the bargain struck at the time he purchased the policy. The court noted the evidence of a conversation at the time of the inspection of the premises prior to the policy being issued where the insured was told that 'there had to be visible evidence of burglary'. This conversation, however, did not explicitly tell the insured that the evidence had to be visible marks or physical damage to the exterior of the building. From this the court concluded that the 'negotiation was for … the insurer's promise "to pay for loss by burglary" … so long as it was not an "inside job". But there was nothing relating to the negotiations [which would have led the insured] to reasonably anticipate … another exclusion denying coverage when, no matter how extensive the proof of a third-party burglary, no marks were left on the exterior of the premises.' In addition, the definition was not the common or legal definition of burglary. Under these circumstances, the court concluded that '[t]he most plaintiff might have reasonably anticipated was a policy requirement of visual evidence (abundant here) indicating the burglary was an "outside" not an "inside" job'.

Where individual courts will register on this continuum is further complicated by the absence of doctrinal refinement or identification of salient factors. One commentator argues that the doctrine is often invoked 'as a kind of 'mantra' to justify the desired outcome, but without the support of much explicit legal analysis'.[33] As a result, the doctrine may be viewed as an equitable process of judicial interpretation that considers the surrounding circumstances, public policy and fair treatment.

In summary, at this time, the majority of American courts have neither expressly adopted nor expressly rejected use of the doctrine of reasonable expectations.[34] Since its inception 30 years earlier, less than a quarter of States

32 227 NW 2d 169 (Iowa 1975).

33 See M Rahdert, 'Reasonable Expectations Reconsidered' (1986) 18 Connecticut Law Review 323 (1986), at 370.

34 See, for example, *Collins v Farmers' Inc Co*, 822 P 2d 1146, at 1162, noting 'this court has not explicitly adopted the doctrine of reasonable expectations, at least by name, in any of its forms. Neither has this court explicitly rejected it … At some point, this court will have to address this series of conflicting precedents in our cases which today's majority opinion simply ignores.' Unis, J dissenting.

in the US have clearly invoked this doctrine as a substantive rule of insurance law that permits courts to ignore unambiguous terms in standard form insurance contracts that would otherwise defeat the expectations of the insured. In part this seeming judicial reluctance may be attributable to confusion over the function of the doctrine, particularly with respect to that of the *contra proferentem* rule.

It is similarly arguable, however, that a number of courts are reluctant to embrace contract reformation for consumer protection purposes with perhaps the same zealousness that the consumer oriented judgments of the 1960s seemed to evidence. It would not be the first time in the United States' legal experience that a legal principle intended as a shield for weaker parties has been transformed into a sword for aggressive litigation purposes. Awareness of the Pandora's Box potential of this doctrine may therefore be implicit in what one commentator has described as the doctrine's 'failure to thrive'.[35]

Nevertheless there is emerging evidence that this doctrine is establishing itself in the United Kingdom and Canada. A search of Canadian precedent over the last decades reveals a significant body of precedent affording judicial recognition to the existence of the doctrine of reasonable expectations as being distinct from that of the *contra proferentem* rule.[36] In 1993, the Supreme Court of Canada's affirmation on this point in *Reid Crowther v Simcoe & Erie General Insurance Co*,[37] citing United States precedent, set out the now frequently invoked principle that:

> In each case the courts must examine the provisions of the particular policy at issue (and the surrounding circumstances) to determine if the events in question fall within the terms of the coverage of that particular policy. This is not to say that there are no principles governing this type of analysis. Far from it. In each case, the courts must interpret the provisions of the policy at issue in light of general principles of interpretation of insurance policies, including but not limited to:
>
> (1) the *contra proferentem* rule;

35 R Henderson, 'The Formulation of the Doctrine of Reasonable Expectations and the Influence of Forces Outside Insurance Law' (1998) 5 Connecticut Law Journal 69, at p 71.

36 See, for example, *Consolidated-Bathurst Export Ltd v Mutual Boiler and Machinery Insurance Co* [1980] 1 SCR 888; *Wigle v Allstate Insurance Co of Canada* (1984), 49 OR (2d) 101 (leave to appeal to SCC refused, [1985] 1 SCR); *Elite Builders Ltd v Maritime Life Assurance* (1985) BCD Civ 2114-01; *United Realty Ltd v Guardian Insurance Co of Canada* [1986] BCD Civ 1933-02; *Scott v Wawanesa Mutual Insurance Co* [1989] 1 SCR 1445; *Fletcher v Manitoba Public Insurance Co* [1990] 3 SCR; *Chilton v Co-operators General Insurance Co* (1997) 143 DLR 4th 647; *University of Saskatchewan v Firemans' Fund Insurance Co of Canada* [1998] 5 WWR 276 (Sask CA), at 289; *Kildonan Tree Service Ltd v Sovereign General Insurance Co* (1997) Man D Lexis 505; [1997] Man D 470.55.55.35-03; *Montigny v Montigny and the General Accident Assurance Company of Canada* (1999) ACWS 3d 468; *Brissette Estate v Westbury Life Insurance Co*; *Brissette Estate v Crown Life Insurance Co* [1992] 3 SCR 87; *Smith v Crown Life Insurance Co* (1999) ACWS 3d 423; *Tansey Estate v Mutual Life Assurance Co of Canada* (1999) BCD Civ 470.55.50.40-01; *Scalera v Oppenheim* (2000) SCC 24; Can Sup Ct Lexis 24.

37 [1993] 1 SCR 252.

(2) the principle that coverage provisions should be construed broadly and exclusion clauses narrowly; and

(3) the desirability, at least where the policy is ambiguous, of giving effect to the reasonable expectations of the parties.[38]

Consideration of the preponderance of cases generated on this basis indicates Canadian courts can best be described as following what is referred to above as the most 'conservative' application of this rule.

United Kingdom precedent is similarly gathering momentum in this respect. Although shying away from actual invocation of the doctrine by name, the House of Lords in *Cook v Financial Insurance Co*,[39] held that a self-employed builder's certificate of insurance for disability insurance taken out with the defendant, 'must be construed in the sense in which it would have been reasonably understood by him as the consumer.' Additionally, paralleling Keeton's directive that such a principle be invoked when 'painstaking' readings of policy materials are necessary to achieve clear understandings of the final result, United Kingdom courts have refused to give meaning to clauses inconspicuously printed in non-contractual written material[40] or 'tucked away at the end of the policy'.[41] Professor Malcolm Clarke,[42] in reviewing the mounting ground swell of precedent in this direction and reviewing Steyn LJ's comments regarding the protection of reasonable expectations of honest men set forth *First Energy (UK) Ltd v Hungarian International Bank Ltd*[43] concludes in his most recent text, that it may indeed 'now be the time to draw these strands together in England to form a rule of reasonable expectations applied to insurance contracts'.[44]

III Towards an overarching common law doctrine: the way forward?

It remains to be seen to what extent this doctrine will establish itself. Other more predictable strategies have been deployed by legislatures around the world to ensure that reasonable expectations are met and to protect insureds against unexpected exclusions or obligations. The most common strategy is to specify the standard terms and conditions that all insurers operating in a particular market must offer in their policies. This approach, that is used

38 [1993]1 SCR 252, at 269.

39 [1998] 1 WLR 1765, 1768 *per* Lord Lloyd, with Lord Steyn and Lord Hope in agreement.

40 *Stephen v International Sleeping-Car Co Ltd* (1903) 19 TLR 621.

41 *Woolfall & Rimmer Ltd v Moyle* [1942] 1 KB 66, 73. See also, Insurance Ombudsman, Annual Report 1990, paras 2.4, 2.6.

42 See *The Law of Insurance Contracts*, 1999, Looseleaf Edition, at 15-5B2.

43 [1993] 2 Lloyd's Rep 194, at 196.

44 *The Law of Insurance Contracts*, 1999, Looseleaf Edition, at 15-30.

extensively in areas of compulsory insurance such as workers' compensation and third party motor vehicle insurance, endeavours to deliver peace of mind that certain minimum terms and coverage are offered by the insurer. Where derogation from standard cover is permitted, this is usually only effective where clear notice is given.[45] A good example of this standard cover approach is afforded by the Insurance Contracts Act 1984 (Australia) where standard policies are prescribed in six areas of domestic insurance.[46] The combined effect of the Act and the Regulations is that where an insured makes a claim under a prescribed contract (that is, a contract to which the standard cover provisions apply) and that claim is in respect of a loss arising from an event prescribed in the Regulations, the insurer must pay the insured the minimum amount specified in the Regulations. The insurer cannot rely on the terms of the contract to deny liability or reduce the amount of liability below a certain prescribed minimum unless the insurer proves that before the contract was entered into, the insured was clearly informed in writing (whether by providing the insured with a document containing the provisions, or the relevant provisions, of the proposed contract, or otherwise).[47] Or, in the alternative, that the insured knew, or that a reasonable person in the circumstances could be expected to have known, that the insurer was liable only for the lesser amount or that the particular risk was not covered by the contract of insurance.[48] This standard cover approach is designed to simplify insurance for insureds and the intention is also to protect them against unexpected exclusions and obligations. Of course, this approach does have an anti-competitive effect in that insurers must compete on the basis of price, reputation and service in the absence of flexibility in product design.[49]

Mention should also be made of the position under German Law. Commentators[50] observe:

> Not only can a German judge achieve justice through the interpretation of the contract, but he also has another powerful statutory tool for the purpose. The Civil Code requires that obligations be performed according to standards of good faith.

45 See, for example, the Insurance Contracts Act 1984 (Australia), s 35.

46 See ss 34–37 of the Act and the Insurance Contracts Regulations 1985 (Australia), SR No 162 of 1985; as amended by SR No 444 of 1990. Standard cover is provided in respect of motor vehicle insurance (property damage), home buildings insurance, home contents insurance, sickness and accident insurance, consumer credit insurance, and travel insurance.

47 Insurance Contracts Act 1984 (Australia), s 35(2); as amended by the Statute Law (Miscellaneous Provisions) Act (No 1) 1985 (Australia), s 3. See D St L Kelly, 'Amendment to the Insurance Contracts Act 1984: Misuse of the Omnibus' Bill Procedure' (1987) 15 Australian Business Law Review 275 where it is pointed out that no real notice of derogation is achieved by simply providing the insured with a policy document.

48 *Idem.* Generally see JR Tarr, *Information Disclosure – Consumers, Insurers and the Insurance Contracting Process*, 2001, p 164.

49 See Australian Law Reform Commission, Report on Insurance Contracts (No 20, 1982), para 56.

50 Kimball and Pfennigstorf, 'Legislative and Judicial Controls of the Terms of Insurance Contracts: A Comparative Study of American and European Practice' (1964) 39 Indiana Law Journal 675; H Lucke, 'Good faith and contractual performance', in P Finn (ed), *Essays in Contract*, 1987, chapter 5.

> There seems to be an increasing tendency of German courts to use this provision as an indirect way to modify contractual stipulations they regard at unfair.[51]

The same potential exists in other jurisdictions. The duty of utmost good faith underpins the insurance relationship and while case law in this area is overwhelmingly concerned with the failure or alleged failure by the insured to disclose material information in a pre-contract setting, recent cases such as the House of Lords decision in *Banque Financière de la Cité SA v Westgate (UK) Insurance Co Ltd*[52] confirms the application of this duty to all contractual matters. Similarly the passage of legislation like the Insurance Contracts Act 1984 (Australia),[53] enshrining utmost good faith provisions in all insurance contracts to which the Act applies, gives Australian courts the opportunity to take a more interventionist and reconstructive role in relation to insurance contracts, their terms and conditions and the insured's reasonable expectations.[54] Particular mention should be made in this context to *Beverley v Tyndall Life Insurance Co Ltd*[55] where the Full Court of the Supreme Court of Western Australia decided that the insurer's duty of utmost good faith to an insured obliged it to follow rules of procedural fairness and to disclose to the insured all the material upon which the insurer intended to rely, in sufficient time to allow the insured to respond to any adverse material. The key issue in this case was the definition of 'disability' in an insurance contract and as this depended upon the insurer being satisfied that the insured was disabled, the insurer was in a very real sense acting as a judge in the insurer's own cause. This was, therefore, a particularly appropriate circumstance in which to apply the duty of utmost good faith.

Conclusions

In conclusion, reconciling contractual language with the 'spirit' of a given deal is effectively a *leitmotif* of 20th century contract jurisprudence. Aligning parties' expectations with the language employed in agreements is necessarily

51 Kimball and Pfennigstorf, *ibid*, at 724.

52 [1991] 2 AC 249. See, however, *Manifest Shipping Co Ltd v Uni-Polaris Shipping Co Ltd; The Sea Star* [2001] Lloyd's Rep 1 R where the continuing duty of utmost good faith was narrowly construed. Lord Hobhouse distinguished a lack of good faith which was material to the making of the contract itself (or some variation of it) and a lack of good faith during the performance of the contract. The remedy for the former was avoidance. The latter, because it derived from the contract, attracted only those remedies provided by the laws of contract. See Insurance Law Monthly, Volume 13, March 2001, p 6.

53 See ss 12–14.

54 See, for example, *Moss v Sun Alliance Australia Ltd* (1990) 6 ANZ Insurance Cases 60-967; *Gugliotti v Commercial Union Assurance Co of Australia* (1992) 7 ANZ Insurance Cases 61-104; *Australian Associated Motor Insurers Ltd v Ellis* (1990) 6 ANZ Insurance Cases 60-987; *Kelly v New Zealand Insurance Co Ltd* (1993) 7 ANZ Insurance Cases 61-197; *Ibrahim v Greater Pacific Life Insurance Co Ltd* (1996) 9 ANZ Insurance Cases 61-330; cf: *Re Zurich Australian Insurance Ltd* (1999) 10 ANZ Insurance Cases 61-429.

55 (1999) 10 ANZ Insurance Cases 61-453.

a difficult balance – both layers being capable of semantic ambiguity.[56] The tension between respecting the sanctity of contract – legal formalism – and that of recognising the ultimate objective of fairness and justice for individual plaintiffs – legal functionalism – is a recurrent theme in all jurisdictions. What emerges broadly from the examination of cases and discussions above is a growing willingness on the part of the courts in the United States, Canada and the United Kingdom to reconsider the relative weightings assigned, at least as regards standard form insurance contracts, to the interests of individual justice over the sanctity of contract. However, there is reluctance evident from the jurisprudential struggle in various jurisdictions in the United States with the doctrine of reasonable expectations. At one extreme the doctrine provides protection of reasonable expectations even in instances where express language to the contrary exists in the policy – at the other extreme is simply used as a rule of construction to resolve ambiguities.

The major problem with the development of a more interventionist approach to the reconstruction of contractual obligations based upon utmost good faith provisions is uncertainty. It was this factor of uncertainty that led the Australian Law Reform Commission[57] to reject a general power of review of contractual terms. General insurers were concerned that a general power of review would lead to great uncertainty and would further complicate the process of setting appropriate rates.[58] A broadly based application of the good faith provisions in the construction and modification of contractual provisions would engender as much uncertainty as a general power of review.

Finally, the major limitation upon such an approach and the reasonable expectations doctrine and with constructional devices such as the *contra proferentem* rule is that they can only be deployed in the context of litigation. The insured has to take the initiative and incur the expense and risk in an endeavour to cure what he or she perceives to be ambiguities or obligations not in accord with information provided or understandings reached in the pre-contract setting. Against this it may be said that a willingness by courts to modify contractual obligations on the basis of the statutory good faith provisions or in the context of reasonable expectations could encourage more careful drafting of policies and a greater level of caution when seeking to invoke their strict terms.[59]

56 M Clarke, *The Law of Insurance Contracts*, 3rd edn, 1997, p 363, nicely encapsulates this common jurisdictional dichotomy by observing that '[t]he concern of the philosopher or semanticist is with the truth of such language. The terms of contract ('Seller will deliver goods to Buyer at Seller's warehouse') may be similar in form to the law of science ('Ice will melt at 0 degrees Celsius'), but they are fundamentally different in significance. The language of a contract is not directed at describing experience but at controlling human behaviour ordinarily the behaviour of the contracting parties. The concern of a court is not with the truth of this language but with the expectations that it arouses in the parties.'

57 Report on Insurance Contracts (No 20, 1982), at para 51.

58 *Idem.*

59 See, for example, Kimball & Pfenningsdorf, 'Legislative and Judicial Control of the terms of Insurance Contracts: A Comparative Study of American and European Practice' (1964) 39 Indiana Law Journal 675.

China: Trade, Law and Human Rights

Alice ES Tay[1] *and Hamish Redd*[2]

> If the realities of life were to coincide perfectly with theory,
> social science would be superfluous.
> Out of the crooked timber of humanity
> nothing straight was ever made.
> [Kant as translated by Isaiah Berlin]

In November 2001, trade ministers from around the world will gather in Qatar for the Fourth World Trade Organisation (WTO) Ministerial Conference.[3] Qatar is an interesting choice for the venue of the Conference, its own legal system still controlled in an arbitrary and discretionary manner by the Amir,[4] although the implementation of codes of civil and commercial law signals a nascent commitment to the rule of law. Constituents of the trade ministers will watch with interest developments both inside the marbled walls of Doha's government buildings, and outside on the dusty streets. The pre-millennial angst that erupted onto the pavements of Seattle two years ago showed little sign of abating as the World Economic Forum met in Melbourne late last year, or in Davos and Quebec, and will very likely manifest itself again.

On 15 November 1999 the United States and China sealed their bilateral WTO deal, in the most significant development between those two countries since diplomatic relations, first informal and then formal, were established nearly three decades ago. On 19 May 2000, China and the European Union finally concluded an agreement, with Australia and China signing their agreement three days later. While China's long march towards WTO membership is not over yet (there is still work to do in Geneva to reach agreement on its accession protocol, and Japan has warned that China's latest imposition of special duties on imports of Japanese cars, mobile phones, and air conditioners could derail China's bid[5]) the major obstacles have been

---

1 Challis Professor of Jurisprudence, University of Sydney and President, Human Rights and Equal Opportunity Commission, Australia.

2 BA/LLB (Hons) (Melb) Solicitor of the Supreme Courts of the Australian Capital Territory and New South Wales, Human Rights & Equal Opportunity Commission.

3 The General Council of the WTO, on 8 February 2001, agreed that the Fourth WTO Ministerial Conference will be held in Doha, Qatar from 9–13 November 2001.

4 Amir Hamad bin Khalifa Al Thani (since 27 June 1995 when, as crown prince, he ousted his father, Amir Khalifa bin Hamad Al Thani, in a bloodless coup).

5 Stephen Lunn, 'Duty threat to Chinese WTO entry', The Australian, 20 June 2001, 8.

surmounted. China's Minister for Foreign Trade, Shi Guangsheng, told a seminar in Beijing at the end of February 2001, that the revisions required to make Chinese laws compliant with WTO rules would not be completed until late 2001. For the last two years or so, with mounting optimism, agreement has been repeatedly anticipated 'in the next few months'. Meanwhile, Mr Mike Moore (Director General of the WTO) told a conference in Washington that China's demand to be treated as a developing country with respect to trade rules on agricultural subsidies was also delaying the Mainland's accession.[6] It is now looking less likely that Mr Shi will join his international counterparts this November.

Regional elder statesman Lee Kuan Yew was reported as describing the accession as 'the single biggest economic and political decision China has made since 1949'[7] – it is a grand claim, and one which merits an examination of the nature of the WTO, and how it impacts upon, or interacts with human rights, and what effect this will have on Chinese society.

This paper will examine economic globalisation and the new global agenda, noting what role the WTO sees itself playing within this, and how its perceptions differ from perceptions external to the WTO. 'Civil society' will be introduced as an important partner to the WTO and other multinational organs in what is a joint effort at achieving the goals agreed for all humanity by the United Nations.

The second section of the paper looks at the human rights situation in China and the linking of trade negotiations to human rights dialogue by the US and approaches from other countries such as Australia. Structural problems in the Chinese legal system are highlighted with regard to the struggle for the rule of law and the enforcement of civil judgments. Recent legislative responses to growing domestic and international concerns in light of China's accession to the WTO and intensifying human rights dialogues are then canvassed, before we can return to Lee Kuan Yew's statement.

I Globalisation, the WTO and human rights

A Perceptions of globalisation inside and outside the WTO

In an illuminating linguistic shift, Mike Moore has twice during 2001 referred pejoratively to 'globalisation'. In Adelaide in February 2001 he referred to it

6 Michael Dwyer, 'China WTO Entry Delayed', Australian Financial Review, 27 February 2001, 7.

7 Quoted in The WTO: Challenges Ahead, speech delivered by Director General of the WTO Mike Moore, to the National Press Club, Canberra, 5 February 2001 http://www.wto.org/english/news_e/spmm_e/spmm52_e.htm.

as 'that terrible word'[8] while three days later it was 'that ugly word'.[9] This attitudinal change is symptomatic of the frustration building within the WTO, as it is blamed for everything from civil unrest to fragile markets collapsing. Regardless of their validity, in part the criticisms are misdirected at the WTO: the organisation's ominous title and the meetings around the globe invite high-profile focal points for anger not easily targeted at disparate level economic activities and other effects of globalisation in its infinite manifestations. The protests in Seattle and Melbourne should not only be viewed as directed against the organisations represented there, but at the very people who constitute those entities, and therefore as individuals who wield significant power both domestically and internationally. The people's outrage is based on fear and anxiety in the search by the protestors, as *Le Monde* saw it, 'for a new world order, one of an open world but of a world which isn't, under any circumstances, reduced to mere merchandise'.[10] Recognising this, Mike Moore now prefers to talk of 'opening up' rather than 'globalisation' because the latter term has lost political credibility.

The change is not confined to mere nomenclature either. In 1995, former Director General of the WTO, Renato Ruggiero, defined globalisation to mean 'a multiplicity of interlocking economic relationships among national economies' and 'a natural outgrowth of technological advances in communications and transport'.[11] It was an incredibly narrow definition that failed to encompass wider ramifications, and as such it was soon to disappear. By 1997, Ruggiero was speaking in much broader, and more sympathetic, terms:

> Our ability to move towards the construction of a truly global system for an increasing globalised economy stands as a powerful and encouraging symbol for those *seeking solutions to the many other issues which now spill across borders, jurisdictions, and cultures*. Whether we are talking about the environment, development, labour, human rights or other ethical values – in all these areas there are positive signs that the policy debate is moving beyond the sterile divisions and polarities of the past.[12]

In one of his last speeches as Director General, Ruggiero paved a particularly tricky path for his successor to tread: '[f]rom human rights, to climate change,

8 The Case for the 'Open Society' and the Role the WTO Plays, speech delivered by Mike Moore to the Australia-Israel Chamber of Commerce, Adelaide, 2 February 2001 http://www.wto.org/english/news_e/spmm_e/spmm51_e.htm.

9 Speech by Mike Moore, above n 7.

10 Editorial, *Le Monde,* Paris, 30 November 1999.

11 The Global Challenge: Opportunities and Choices in the Multilateral Trading System, the Fourteenth Paul-Henri Spaak Lecture delivered at Harvard, 16 October 1995 http://www.wto.org/english/news_e/sprr_e/harvar_e.htm.

12 A Shared Responsibility: Global Policy Coherence for our Global Age, speech by Renato Ruggiero to the Conference on 'Globalisation as a Challenge for German Business; export opportunities for small and medium-sized companies in the environmental field', 9 December 1997 http://www.wto.org/english/news_e/sprr_e/bonn_e.htm. Emphasis added.

to capital flows – our globalising world demands global solutions. And these solutions must increasingly be based on shared agreements and rules.'[13] Further, '[w]e can no longer treat human rights, the environment, development, trade, health, or finance as separate sectoral issues, to be addressed through separate policies and institutions'.[14] These are bold statements, and a coded invitation for the WTO to play its part 'in shared agreements and rules' in the new global agenda. The enunciation of a new global agenda that places states and non-state actors in a closer matrix with international problems is consistent with the trend away from statism, towards some form of liberal agenda[15] or 'social clause'. The scope of the new agenda is unclear: although confrontation of terrorism and the prevention of the threat of nuclear, chemical and biological weapons are clearly within it,[16] it is questionable whether the plight of a billion or so people living in poverty is.[17] Human rights, however glacially, appear to be moving somewhere towards the centre of this agenda. The implication is that, at a minimum, the WTO cannot implement agreements or policies that are inconsistent with human rights as understood at international law.

B The relationship between human rights and the WTO

> That which cannot be done directly cannot be done indirectly
> [a constitutional law principle]

The WTO's overriding purpose, its *raison d'être*, is to 'help trade flow as freely as possible – so long as there are no undesirable side-effects'.[18] That one billion or so people are still living in abject poverty and suffering cannot be attributed solely as an undesirable side-effect of the WTO, although it does reflect poorly on a global trade order that concentrates unimaginable wealth in a tiny percentage of the population. Increasing global trade has only meant an increasing gulf between the haves and the have nots, between sartorial splendour and the daily struggle to enjoy the right to live. An international system of trade governance since 1948 has separated trade from human rights concerns. Thus, despite the grotesque distribution of wealth across the globe that such a system has overseen, governments continue to separate these two areas, on the ground that their fusion 'would dilute the WTO's core business

13 Beyond the Multilateral Trading System, address to the 20th Seminar on International Security, Politics and Economics de l'Institut pour les Hautes Etudes Internationales, 12 April 1999 http://www.wto.org/english/news_e/sprr_e/ih_e.htm.

14 *Ibid.*

15 Karen Knop, 'Re/Statements: Feminism and State Sovereignty in International Law (1993) 3 Transnational and Contemporary Problems 293.

16 See Slaughter, 'The Real New World Order' (1997) 76 Foreign Affairs 183.

17 Philip Alston, 'The Myopia of the Handmaidens: International Lawyers and Globalisation' (1997) European Journal of International Law, 435.

18 WTO, *Trading into the Future*, 2nd edn revised April 1999, 4.

and weaken its authority and credibility in the eyes of significant members'.[19] It is a valid point. Developing countries are highly suspicious that introducing a social agenda into the WTO will have a negative effect on their hard-fought concessions from the Uruguay Round.

Fortunately for many of its current members, the observation – or lack thereof – of human rights is no hurdle to WTO membership. While the WTO mediates trade disputes and seeks to reduce trade barriers between countries, it does not have, and does not seek to have, any mandate on human rights: '[t]he WTO is not a world government, a global policeman, or an agent for corporate interests.'[20] As an organisation operating by consensus, a realistic approach indicates that a progressive social agenda will not be able to succeed in the WTO, or if it does, it will be an organisation with a greatly reduced membership.

1 The social clause debate

There has been spirited debate about the need for a 'social clause' in trade agreements made under the auspices of the WTO.[21] Support has been drawn from the US, the EU, as well as various trade union organizations, for guarantees already found in various International Labour Organisation (ILO) agreements. That the proposals rarely venture beyond workers' rights in the form of freedom of association, freedom from forced labour, non-discrimination in employment and child labour, is testament to the consensus amongst states that the WTO should not have jurisdiction over other human rights, or that labour rights are the only realistic inclusion for consensus. While the latter proposition can be debated, the former is on safer ground.

Some commentators have suggested that the WTO Constitution should be amended to include both customary and treaty-based human rights standards.[22] It is difficult to reconcile this approach with any genuine concern for the international advancement of human rights standards, and as such most multilateral efforts have not dared to suggest this tactic. As the Australian Government pushes strongly for a new round of trade negotiations, it recognises that a 'limited and realistic degree of ambition' is essential to its success. 'Other issues, such as labour standards and environment, require careful handling and any push for their inclusion could undermine confidence for an early launch, *particularly with developing countries*.'[23] The suggestion

19 Australian Department of Foreign Affairs and Trade, In the National Interest: Australia's Foreign and Trade Policy White Paper, Canberra, 1997, 44.

20 WTO. The WTO is not a World Government and no one has any intention of making it one, Moore tells NGOs, Press Release No 155, 29 November 1999.

21 For an overview of recent debate see Johanna Sutherland, 'International Trade and the GATT/WTO Social Clause: Broadening the Debate' 14 QUTLJ (1998), 83.

22 *Ibid*, 107.

23 Australian Department of Foreign Affairs and Trade, 'Australia – A Successful Global Economy', http://www.dfat.gov.au/trade/trade_bytes/global_eco.html. Emphasis added.

is not that labour standards and the environment are intrinsically inappropriate to an organ such as the WTO, but that they are inappropriate now. Another reiteration of customary and international human rights into yet another 'global' document will not bring universal human rights nearer materialisation – what is more realistic is mechanisms for enforcing a more practicable and limited set of human rights claims, like those of the ILO.

A ministerial declaration from the WTO on labour standards made after a meeting in Singapore in 1996 said as much:

> We renew our commitment to the observance of internationally recognized core labour standards. The International Labour Organisation (ILO) is the competent body to set and deal with these standards, and we affirm our support for its work in promoting them ... We reject the use of labour standards for protectionist purposes, and agree that the comparative advantage of countries, particularly low-wage developing countries, must in no way be put into question.[24]

Many developing nations have argued that efforts to bring labour standards into the arena of multilateral trade negotiations are little more than a smokescreen for protectionism. Whether this scepticism is valid or not is a secondary concern; the mere scepticism itself indicates that merely placing labour standards on the WTO agenda will halt further efforts at trade liberalisation.

States have not been nearly as mawkish when it comes to environmental issues. After all, parties to the WTO recognise, in accordance with the agreement they have signed, that the pursuit of wealth cannot be unbridled. The preamble to the *Agreement Establishing the WTO* notes that in the field of trade and economic endeavour, parties' relations must allow 'for the optimal use of the world's resources in accordance with the objective of sustainable development' and enable them to 'protect and preserve the environment and ... enhance the means for doing so in a manner *consistent with their respective needs and concerns at different levels of economic development*'.[25] While the WTO has no specific agreement dealing with the environment, at the end of the 1994 Uruguay Round, trade ministers decided to begin a comprehensive work programme on trade and environment in the WTO, and created the WTO Committee on Trade and Environment. The name is slightly misleading, as the committee's work is based on two important principles:

> (i) The WTO is only competent to deal with trade, so in environmental issues its only task is to study questions that arise when environmental policies have a significant impact upon trade. Other agencies that specialise in environmental issues are better qualified to intervene in national or international environmental policies/laws or standards.

24 WTO, *Trading into the Future*, above n 18, 48.

25 *Agreement Establishing the World Trade Organisation*, preamble. Available at http://www.wto.org/english/docs_e/legal_e/final_e.htm#GATT94 .

(ii) If the committee does identify problems, the solutions must continue to uphold the principles of the WTO trading system.[26]

By limiting itself in this way, the WTO has been careful not to turn its name into a misnomer: its core competency is international trade and it will only brush against issues incidental to it. Despite so-called 'green' provisions in the GATT and WTO agreements,[27] the committee has decided that the most effective way to deal with international environmental problems is through multilateral environmental agreements, that is, not by one country trying to unilaterally change another's environmental policies.[28] Such resistance to incorporating a broader agenda into the direct workings of the WTO is merely reflective of practicalities. Other mechanisms, organs and agreements exist to pursue non-trade goals, and their inclusion in the WTO would act as a stick jamming the cogs of trade liberalisation. The WTO must not, however, behave in a manner inconsistent with international human rights standards.

Human rights principles imply obligations. Obligations need enforcement, and enforcement mechanisms. The logic of increased human rights demand and recognition points to the need for strong, well-equipped, efficient state able and willing to carry out its responsibilities. Article 55 of the UN Charter notes, amongst other things, that the United Nations shall promote higher standards of living, solutions of international economic, social, health and related problems, and universal respect for, and observance of, human rights and fundamental freedoms for all. Under Art 56, '[a]ll members pledge themselves to take joint and separate action … for the achievement of the purpose set forth in Art 55'. That human rights are not placed fluorescently on the WTO agenda as an arbitrator of potential deals, does not deny that international human rights law provides a context in which all states conduct their relations, be they through the WTO or elsewhere. Neither WTO nor other social mechanisms stand in isolation, or at least no longer. 'We must reinforce the argument that human rights law has primacy over the trade law regime, that where there are competing interpretations of the WTO/GATT provisions, the interpretation that recognises this primacy should be adopted.'[29]

26 WTO, *Trading into the Future*, above n 18, 43.

27 See GATT, Article 20: policies affecting trade in goods for protecting human, animal or plant life or health are exempt from normal GATT disciplines under certain conditions; Technical Barriers to Trade and Sanitary and Phytosanitary Measures Agreement contains explicit recognition of environmental objectives; TRIPS Article 27 allows governments to refuse to issue patents that threaten human, animal or plant life or health, or risk serious damage to the environment; GATS Article 14 exempts policies affecting trade in services for protecting human, animal or plant life or health from normal GATS disciplines under certain conditions.

28 An illustration of which is the infamous *Dolphin-Tuna* case between the United States and Mexico and others.

29 Alice ES Tay, 'The New Century, Globalisation and Human Rights' 8 Asia Pacific Law Review 2 (2000), 139–52.

2 *An open and civil society*

Relieving the WTO of an unworkable social clause does not relieve it of obligations that should be shouldered by all international organisations. NGOs, governments and other international actors cannot afford to blindly pursue their goals without realising that their various hobbyhorses are essentially in the same race. In pursuing a world free of trade barriers, the WTO recognises that its hobbyhorse is international trade, but it must also realise that that horse cannot run blinkered to other goals being chased side-by-side: environment, human rights, stemming the spread of transnational disease etc. Human rights jurisprudence is sophisticated and mature enough to inform multi-national corporations, international organisations and governments of behaviour that is conducive to creating an open, and civilised society. Civil society has an important role to play in this process, one that has been perceived as a threat by traditional powers.

Barely had the fog settled from the pepper spray in Seattle before NGOs had been branded as isolationist, disruptive or anti-progress.[30] Yet through their advocacy and constant pressure on governments, NGOs have continued to set the pace in many areas of international concern, and their influence should not be underestimated. NGOs play a vital role in highlighting issues more conveniently swept under the carpet by governments, and force such governments to respond to NGO reports, through the domestic pressure that they create. The United Nations has recognised the importance of NGOs through the Millennium Forum that produced a series of recommendations in the form of a 'Forum Declaration', later placed directly on the agenda for world leaders by Kofi Annan at the Millennium Summit.[31] It is an example of how civil society has grown into a truly global phenomenon.

In July 2000, Kofi Annan brought together a group of leaders from business, international labour unions and NGOs in a Global Compact, challenging business to embrace and enact a set of core values in the area of labour standards, human rights and the environment.[32] Other institutions that help manage the world economy, like the Bretton Woods institutions, should be involved in WTO processes along with NGOs, recognising that international civil society can play a meaningful and constructive role in the responsible removal of trade barriers. There are two levels at which the WTO can interact with, and support, civil society. The first of these is at the international level.

30 The Secretary General, United Nations, Secretary-General, Addressing Participants at Millennium Forum, Calls for Intensified 'NGO Revolution', Press Release, No SG/SM/7411GA/9710, 22 May 2000 http://www.un.org/News/Press/docs/2000/20000522.sgsm7411.doc.html.

31 Secretary General, United Nations, Global Networks 'The Most Promising Partnerships of our Globalising Age', Secretary-General tells Fifty-third Annual DPI/NGO Conference', Press Release No SG/SM/7517/PI/1273, 28 August 2000. http://www.un.org/News/Press/docs/2000/20000828.sgsm7517.doc.html.

32 *Ibid.*

(a) International civil society

Although not a new concept, civil society in the contemporary world has fed upon the opportunities globalisation has afforded: speed and ease of communication, the intertwining of economies and issues common to all humanity. To this extent civil society stands uniquely broad-based, globalised and positive.[33] Seattle and Melbourne have demonstrated that the WTO must engage with civil society, and empower itself with it. The WTO cannot afford to stand against civil society, and vice versa.[34] NGOs of all description have been repulsed at the lack of transparency, at the meetings behind closed doors, at the ambiguous and curt media releases: the WTO must listen and respond appropriately. Mike Moore has suggested that, at last, it may be hearing the call: 'Protest and questioning is part of progress, that in fact is the basis of Karl Popper's proposals in his work the "Open Society and its Enemies". That is why freedom, both economic and political, returns superior results.'[35] There is a moral and democratic duty on states not only to commit itself to the alleged good of its citizenry but to do so with its informed consent and participation. Let us hope then, that Mr Moore is comfortable with the protesting and questioning of his own organisation, after all, his comments that '[t]hose who oppose and protest are not all bad or mad' suggest, at best, a level of condescension.[36]

One of the key complaints against the WTO has been the lack of transparency in the making of trade agreements. On 18 July 1996 the WTO's General Council agreed to make more information about WTO activities available publicly and decided that public information, including de-restricted WTO documents, would be accessible on-line.[37] It is claimed that the objective is to make more information available to the public, including NGOs – this should, in any case, be first and foremost the duty of states, almost a condition precedent of democratic states to make citizens' participation meaningful. History has revealed this to be a painfully inadequate step, and a complete misjudgement of the structural reform demanded by the people on the streets. NGOs and other important organs such as the ILO and UN Human rights agencies need to be granted observer status. Most important, however, would be the opportunity for civil society groups to have a meaningful and structured participation in the brokering of international trade agreements. To recall again the equine analogy, these are different horses, but on the same course. For an organisation that claims much credit for ensuring greater

33 Alice ES Tay, above n 29.

34 For more on the concept of civil society and its relationship with and against the state and bureaucracy, see Alice ES Tay, 'The Conceptual Evolution of Civil Society' Address to the Australia-China Joint Seminar on Civil Society, September 1999.

35 Above n 7.

36 Above n 20.

37 Above n 18, 65.

transparency in its members' societies, it is a nauseating irony that it cannot recognise its own opacity.

(b) Civil society in a domestic context

The second layer with which the WTO must interact and support civil society is at the domestic level. Domestic transparency of trade regulations and policies has been an integral objective of the WTO and the GATT before it. Governments are required to inform the WTO and fellow-members of specific measures, policies or laws through regular 'notifications'. In addition the WTO will conduct regular reviews of individual countries' trade policies. In this regard, the rule of law may be strengthened amongst member states, although as will be shown, this is by no means guaranteed. Nonetheless, the WTO's dispute process that provides for trade sanctions in severe breaches of the rules, engenders (in a trade arena at least) a commitment to predictability and transparency. The WTO in this sense helps encourage a strong state, and the theory is that a strong matrix of laws governing foreign investment and trade will be co-dependent on other areas of state and civil society: 'the State providing the stability, security and institutional guarantees, and civil society the specific quality and virtues, the psychological and ethical resources.'[38] It is incumbent on the WTO to both recognise this series of relationships, and actively encourage it, more so than it has done in the past.

These themes and caveats will now inform a fuller analysis of China's accession to the WTO, and its relationship to human rights. Will this event prove not only the economic, but also the political cataclysm that Lee Kuan Yew has boldly predicted?

II Human rights in China: challenges and opportunities in the new millennium

A Human rights in trade negotiations in China

The United States has been particularly loud on human rights in its trade negotiations with China. Until recently, China was subjected to a yearly scrutiny by Congress of its human rights record, before inevitably being granted Most Favoured Nation status once more. In its testimony before the House Committee on International Relations last year, Human Rights Watch provided a clarion warning:

> WTO membership in itself will not guarantee the rule of law, respect for workers rights, or meaningful political reform. Economic openness could be accompanied by tight restrictions on basic freedoms and a lack of governmental accountability. The Chinese government might seek to build the rule of law in the economic sphere while simultaneously continuing to pervert and undermine the rule of law elsewhere.

38 Alice ES Tay, above n 29.

> For example, Chinese authorities claim to be upholding the 'rule of law' by arresting and throwing in jail pro-democracy activists, and the nationwide crackdown on the Falun Gong movement has been cloaked in rhetoric about the 'rule of law'.[39]

Looking at Singapore it is fair to comment that economic liberalism does not guarantee political freedom, or guarantee against authoritarianism; and if Beijing's relations with the commercial and political communities of the Hong Kong Special Administrative Region is any indication, a wealthy but politically controlled environment might be cultivated on the Mainland as in the former colony of Hong Kong.

The US position linking human rights with trade is less about globalisation and the international rule of law, and more about domestic lobbying and pressure. After all, the US maintains tariffs on lamb imports that directly and adversely affect Australia, one of its closest allies. This is despite continuing rhetoric about trade liberalisation and posturing as the guardian of the new economic order – it has happened not because the US government necessarily wants to maintain these tariffs, but because domestic pressures ensure the US must protect its industries, and thereby its votes. By visibly linking human rights to trade negotiations when in all likelihood it would rather leave the two apart, the US government appeals to the American political imperialist sensibility, placating powerful blocks of votes, particularly in its southern states.

To demonstrate the point, out of the suite of indivisible human rights, the US-Sino dialogue seems to focus exclusively on dissidents, freedom of religion, and the right for Tibet to self-determine its governance. America's strong and powerful Christian right ensures that religious freedom issues remain on the US foreign policy agenda, while civil society actively lobbies on freedom of speech, an issue long close to America's heart. Less prominent on the US agenda have been economic rights, issues of arbitrary detention for non-dissidents, right to a fair trial, to due process, freedom of peaceful assembly, freedom of movement, discrimination against ethnic minorities, female infanticide and workers rights. All of these remain serious problems, as the US State Department recognises.[40]

While the pressure from the US has indeed been immense, other countries have been quietly pursuing a track-two diplomatic approach more amenable to Chinese sensibilities. Great Britain, France, Australia, Canada, Norway, Sweden, Brazil, and Japan, as well as the European Union (EU) all conduct human rights dialogues with the Chinese government. The US claims these dialogues have not produced improvements in the Chinese government's

39 'China's Accession to the WTO and Human Rights' Testimony before the House Committee on International Relations, Statement by Mike Jendrzejzyk, Washington Director, Asia Division, 10 May 2000 http://www.hrw.org/campaigns/china-99/china-testimony-051100.htm.

40 Bureau of Democracy, Human Rights and Labour, US Department of State, Country Report on Human Rights Practices – 2000: China, February 2001 http://www.state.gov./g/drl/rls/hrrpt/2000/eap/index.cfm?docid=684.

human rights practices, yet despite such protests in November last year the US and China agreed in principle to resume the bilateral dialogue that was suspended by China in 1999.[41] This is another example of the State Department and the Congress awkwardly straddling a schizophrenic foreign policy with China. The confrontation of wills of two nations, one incontestably huge and the other indisputably wealthy, can only be conducted on unequal and unresolvable, complex and incomparable, bases. Paradoxically, there is more opportunity for a meeting of minds where the huge confronts the small and modest.

The Australian-Chinese dialogue was initiated in August 1997, during which it was agreed to implement a cooperative program of human rights technical co-operation (HRTC), administered by the Human Rights and Equal Opportunity Commission and aimed at strengthening the administration, promotion and protection of human rights in China. While the program is designed to have immediate as well as long-term effects, important outcomes can be invisible to the untrained eye. It is misleading and inaccurate to conclude that these dialogues 'have not produced improvements' – such programs are not designed to get a knee-jerk reaction from the Chinese Communist Party (CCP). In the initial stages a building of a relationship of trust and confidence is required with cooperating organisations, and a commitment to an extended process of refinement. During the introductory stage of the HRTC (1997–99) Australian and Chinese parties explored the limits of what is likely to be productive in terms of the goals of the HRTC. Seminars, workshops and symposiums identified opportunities for fruitful cooperation during 1999/2000. In 2001 the program will concentrate on reaching and working within a third stage, involving the delivery of training focused on the areas identified and developed through the first two stages. These areas include: mass communication law and freedom of expression, scholarships for study in Australia of human rights issues, police ethics and accountability training, criminal procedure training, discussion of legal aid options, judicial training, and a workshop on domestic violence in minority regions.

Such activities play their part in imperceptibly changing the legal culture in China, as well as addressing more tangible structural issues. In this sense, the WTO and human rights dialogues share common objectives: both desire transparency, predictability and conformity with accepted international norms. As shall be demonstrated, both face similar structural hurdles on different legislative platforms.

41 *Ibid*, 34.

B Catching fish in clean water

In February 2001 Beijing was fluttering its eyelashes at International Olympic Organisation officials as seventeen delegates from around the globe descended for an official scrutinising visit. Rubbish had been cleared, trees planted, hawkers and beggars removed from the streets, and grass sprayed a pleasant green. Despite these best efforts at looking clean, revitalised and neo-millennial, a thick fog shrouded Beijing,[42] symbolising a continuing opacity that clouds so many activities in that city. In fact Pricewaterhouse Coopers recently proclaimed China the most opaque country in the world to do business, with the equivalent of 46% tax being levied on investments through corruption, arbitrariness and other structural quirks.[43] Both Indonesia and Russia outscored China in terms of corruption in government bureaucracy, but China had the highest level of opacity in its legal and regulatory structures. Commentators have been quick to point out that such apocalyptic figures are unlikely to deter the ever-growing number of foreign companies eager to set up operations in China as it prepares to enter the WTO.[44] In 2000, for instance, three firms – oil giants PetroChina and China Petroleum and Chemical Corp (Sinopec) and China's number two mobile company China Unicom – raised US$12 billion through overseas listings. More mega-listings are expected in 2001.[45] Further, Premier Zhu Rongji has been dangling the prospect of a free-trade zone with China's southern neighbours: it shall no doubt prove a tantalising topic of discussion when Shanghai hosts the Asia-Pacific Economic Cooperation summit in October 2001. Speaking at an investment forum in Hong Kong in November 2000, Zhu's colleague, vice-minister of foreign trade Long Yongtu, has also been hinting at reform: 'we have to create a new culture that even in clean waters, there will be fish.'[46] Yet despite all these flashes of apparent increased transparency in China, the reality is quite different. This is an enduring theme in the analysis of the Chinese legal system and one that will be touched on again.

1 Enforcing civil judgments

The problem of enforcement of civil judgements in China is flagged here to illustrate one area of law that will require significant reform to provide the transparency and predictability that the WTO requires of its members. The problems that impede the enforcement of civil judgements are both unique

---

42 Reuters, 'Thick fog shrouds Beijing amid Olympic Inspection', 22 February 2001 http://dailynews.muzi.com.

43 Pricewaterhouse Coopers, *The Opacity Index*, January 2001, http://www.opacityindex.com.

44 Michael Dwyer, 'China tops the world as the worst place to do business', Australian Financial Review, 14 February 2001, 11.

45 Paul Eckert (Reuters) 'For China, globalisation brings power, scrutiny', 20 December 2000.

46 'China vows new era of transparency with WTO entry', Lateline news 19 December 2000, http://dailynews.muzi.com.

and common to the whole of the Chinese legal system. Indeed, while certain civil legislation can be scrutinised for its inconsistencies, structural and ideological factors are marbled throughout the entire legal system, providing noticeable flashpoints in this area, and also the Criminal Law that will require our attention shortly. If China's accession to the WTO can overcome some of these factors, it may help create a cultural shift in Chinese legal logic, which in turn will affect the treatment of human rights, particularly under the Criminal Law.

The decision to reconstruct the Chinese legal system was made at the same time as the decision to undertake a process of economic reform and modernisation. Indeed, the 'modernisation' of the legal system, urged by Deng Xiao Ping as vital to the achievement of the Four Modernisations [of agriculture, industry, national defence and science and technology], soon came to be known as the Fifth Modernisation. As the legislative engines were slowly cranked up again after a long period of disuse, their first major outputs were to 'perfect' the economic legal system. Inevitably, the Chinese Government failed to adequately recognise that the move from a hierarchically administered economy to a market economy means more than reams of legislation: a completely new method of rule-making and enforcing is required.

Donald Clarke listed a range of factors, internal and external, that interact to create a real problem for the resolution of Chinese civil economic disputes,[47] not all of which need to be canvassed here. The enforcement of judgements referred to here are not Chinese-Foreign disputes, but Chinese-Chinese civil economic disputes, which of course directly affect an assessment of revenue potential by foreign entities considering investing in China. The essence of the problem is local protectionism (*difang baohuzhuyi*). Local governments rely on local enterprises for revenue and employment. Such governments, therefore, have no interest in funds being sucked from such enterprises by inconvenient judgments often made by a court in a neighbouring jurisdiction. In addition, a local political leader, who will exert his influence to protect the enterprise, may well run a local enterprise.[48] Most financial/administrative aspects of local courts (budgets, housing facilities) are controlled by local Party and government organs, and with no tenure to protect them, judges are particularly susceptible to Party influence. As local governments will protect local enterprises, and local courts are beholden to local governments, this equation ensures local courts are reluctant to rule against their 'own' local enterprises, or reluctant to enforce adverse judgments of a court in another jurisdiction. Consistent with this institutional pressure,

47 Donald C Clarke 'Power and Politics in the Chinese Court System: The Enforcement of Civil Judgments' (1996) 10 Columbia Journal of Asian Law 1, esp 35–61.

48 *Ibid*, 42.

'[t]he practice of execution shows that if court work is supported and assisted by local Party and government departments, execution work goes smoothly'.[49]

The absence of an adequate separation of powers has also affected the relationship between the people, other units and organs of justice: judges are appointed by and accountable to local governments. Banks have been known to ignore judicial orders with impunity, preventing the seizure or otherwise of defendants' funds. Clarke attributes this to the fact that the court is 'essentially just another bureaucracy, with no more power to tell banks what to do than the Post Office'.[50] Unlike Common Law courts, the Chinese judiciary has no general power of contempt to wield when it is ignored.

It is hoped that China's eventual accession to the WTO, along with increasing foreign investment, will strengthen the rule of law in China as the number of economic disputes rise. In the 20 year period since the reform of the legal system began a number of important steps towards stability and transparency have been made;[51] some of which will be scrutinised in Part II of this paper. Certainly pressure will be placed on the government to accelerate legal reform to keep pace with economic reform, for substance over form. Greater transparency in economic matters could support and increase demands and expectations from within China for more openness in other areas.

2 *Rule of law*

Of the four goals currently on the Secretary-General of the United Nations reform agenda, the international rule of law is placed as the second priority, behind international peace and security.[52] Of course the two concepts are artificially separated, as they are mutually dependent on each other. In China, as in many other developing countries, it has been a long struggle towards a rule of law, and it is worth taking a brief excursion to discover why.

Historically, Confucianism conspired with geo-social and geo-political factors to ferment a strong and resilient tradition of extra-judicial administration of justice.[53] Confucian ethics and political theory perceive state

49 Chen Youxi and Xue Chunbao, 'Zaocheng Fayuan Zhixing Nan De San Da Jiben Yinsu' Zhejian Fazhi Bao August 16 1990, 3 [trans: 'The Three Major Reasons why Courts Have Difficulty in Execution'] in Clarke, above n 47, 51.

50 Clarke, above n 47, 56.

51 Company Law 1993 (Zhonghua Renmin Gongheguo Gongsi Fa); Contract Law 1999 (Zhonghua Renmin Gongheguo Hetong Fa); Administrative Punishments Law 1996 (Zhonghua Renmin Gongheguo Xingzheng Chufa Fa); Administrative Litigation Law 1989 (Zhonghua Renmin Gongheguo Xingzheng Susong Fa); Civil Procedure Law 1991 (Zhonghua Renmin Gongheguo Minshi Susong Fa); Administrative Review Law 1999 (Zhonghua Renmin Gongheguo Xingzheng Fuyi Fa).

52 Palitha Kohona, Chief of UN Treaty Section, Office of Legal Affairs, 'The Advancement of the International Rule of Law – the role of the United Nations', speech delivered in Sydney, 20 February 2001.

53 Alice ES Tay, 'From Confucianism to the Socialist Market Economy: The Rule of Man vs The Rule of Law' in Alice ES Tay/Guenther Doeker-Mach (eds) *Asia-Pacific Handbook* Vol I: People's Republic of China, 84, 1998, Baden-Baden, Germany: Nomos.

imposed law (fa) as a human construct that is subservient to higher principles of propriety (li), an external force made necessary by human inadequacies. Confucianism thus relegates law to a secondary role in social control. In the Confucian conception of state and society, law was a terroristic and punitive tool welded by the state as a last resort against those who failed to respond to the moral exhortation of Confucian values and virtues. In time, through a process of 'Confucianisation', these coercive rules came to incorporate or have embedded within them, that broader philosophical and moral scheme concerning personal and social conduct. Punishments were increased or relaxed, applied, in accordance with status in society. The ideology of coercive but universalist law, written and knowable, severe, strictly equally applicable to all, was known as the School of Legalism (Fajia Zhuyi), a school that gained prominence during the Qin Dynasty (221–207 BC): In its original form, Legalism rose in opposition to society governed on a moral precept, and in an attempt to unify rival kingdoms into one nation.[54] A necessary corollary of this was the need for a bureaucratic fabric that provided order where the tendrils of Confucianism did not reach. Confucian virtues were achievable by and accessible to the literati, the educated; to the 'little people' who could not be reached by education and moral cultivation, the full force of the law would apply. Unlike the Confucianists, Legalists believed in the original malignity of human kind, and their emphasis, therefore, was not on moral persuasion to find virtue, but laws and punishments to prevent a state of chaos. Such legal positivism, however, was not to introduce any rule of law, and conception of individual rights, but something rather different. Shang Yang (sometimes referred to as Lord Yang), generally understood to be the founder of this school of thought, had proclaimed:

> A wise ruler must signify the rule by law … and act according to that law so that the country would expand, the army would be strong, and the ruler would be venerated. Rule by law is fundamental to governing.[55]

And so another enduring theme is introduced: rule by law. Law was an effective tool for controlling growing populations under Legalist jurisdiction. Although the Legalist School officially vanished with the end of the Qin Dynasty, today's leaders recall this totalistic technique well enough, revive and indeed revitalise it, for it is now also useful for them to control and unify their nation once more.

The remnants of continuing suspicion and reserve towards law can in part be traced to these dynastic times. Severe criminal punishments of the Tang Code were applied to the 'small people', creating no conditions for recourse to or conceptions of individual rights or protection from state authority. The

54 For a more thorough history of Legalism, see Bodde D and Morris C 'Basic Concepts of Chinese Law' in *Law in Imperial China: exemplified in 190 Ch'ing Dynasty Cases*, 1967, Harvard University Press.

55 Quoted in Bodde and Morris, above.

absence of protection, and the relentless brutality that the law represented, prevented individuation of guilt or liability, or a respect for the law being infused into Chinese legal logic. There was no separation of administration from law or criminal subject matter from civil, or any codes of procedure to administer justice.[56] It was a system that declared, not justice but punishment. It should be no surprise that the people turned their backs on these methods and evolved and maintained a method of dispute resolution described in current western legal parlance as 'alternative'. Briefly, during the period of Nationalist rule after 1911, codes were enacted, based largely on European models, in which an apparent attempt at the rule of law was made. Not unlike the Legalists, however, law was a tool for strengthening and unifying the nation, not the creating of juridical right and duty bearing individuals and units. Like the Qin Dynasty nearly 2,000 years earlier, Chiang Kai-shek and his legal reforms were to disappear. In the wake of Chiang who fled with his Six Codes to Taiwan, the Communist Party rose to power and promptly abolished all existing laws.[57]

Abolishing the Six Codes meant only a very rudimentary, experimental legal system was in place when the Chinese Communist Party (CCP) claimed power, so the Central Committee ordered that where the 'new laws of the people' did not exist, that judicial work should be carried out in accordance with the concept of 'revolutionary justice' and the programmes and policies of the Party.[58] This decree formalised the legal authority of Party policy directives that underpins the contemporary Chinese legal system: law is the mature form of policy, the programme of the party uttered in the words of power. The work of Stalinist jurist A Vishinsky further entrenched this proposition into the Chinese socialist-legal model. Vishinsky declared that in the socialist state, the Communist Party, as the guiding force of the people, the representative of the ruling proletariat, should enjoy absolute control over the creation of positive law by the organs of the state.[59] The Party would define the form and content of these laws to suit its evolving program of social and economic development. Thus, even in more contemporary times, it has been a struggle for law to gain an independent existence. International trade pressures may help this process, and also drag human rights observance with it. The increasing exposure to and growing awareness within China of foreign legal systems and international law, its signing and sometimes ratification of UN

56 Alice ES Tay, above n 53, 89.

57 'Directive Concerning the Abolition of the Nationalist Six Codes and the Establishment of Principles of Law in the Liberated Areas' issued by the Central Committee of the Chinese Communist Party (CCP), February 1949, in Zhonghua Renmin Gongheguo Falh Quanshu [trans: The Complete Laws of the PRC], Jilin Renmin, 1989.

58 See Perry Keller, 'Sources of Order in Chinese Law' 42 The American Journal of Comparative Law, 1995, 711, 719.

59 See Yu Xingzhong, 'Legal Pragmatism in the People's Republic of China' 3 Journal of Chinese Law 1980, 28, 36.

treaties and covenants, together with the real pressures of globalisation, have already prompted China to respond and quicken the reform of its legal system.

C Chinese legislative responses

Human rights breaches are often most dramatically located in the system of criminal justice. On 14 March 1997, the Fifth Session of the Eight National People's Congress substantially approved a new criminal law, and a new criminal procedural law, after a long process of discussion on the inadequacies of the previous 1979 laws. Western scholars have been quick to analyse the Chinese criminal justice system and expose its shortcomings – the criminal justice system is more visible and less complex than other areas of law, thereby providing greater accessibility to the interested observer.

1 Criminal Law 1997

It is unclear whether the overriding purpose of the new Criminal Law is to create greater order in a society increasingly plagued by waves of criminality, suppress political dissent, to tidy up a criminal code which had been amended and enormously added to almost the day after promulgation, or to meet some of the criticisms levelled at the 1979 Law. The reference to Marxism-Leninism and Mao Zedong Thought as the guiding ideology of criminal law has been removed from Art 1. Article 2, however, reminds us that '[t]he tasks of the PRC Criminal Law are to use punishment against all criminal acts to defend national security, the political power of the people's democratic dictatorship, and the socialist system'.[60] The Criminal Law, therefore, is necessary timber in socialist construction. The CCP, as the vanguard of the people's democratic dictatorship, is protected implicitly in this article, despite Art 4 that states '[e]very one is equal before the law in committing crime. No one is permitted to have privileges to transgress the law'. Significantly, the new provisions removed the old Art 90 that stated 'all acts endangering the PRC committed with the goal of overthrowing the political power of the dictatorship of the proletariat and the socialist system are crimes of counter-revolution'. Under Part I of the 1997 Criminal Law (the general provisions), Art 13 now expresses a similar prohibition, but in different language:

> All acts that endanger the sovereignty, territorial integrity, and security of the state; split the state; subvert the political power of the people's democratic dictatorship and overthrow the socialist system; undermine social and economic order; violate property owned by the state or property collectively owned by the labouring masses; violate citizens' privately owned property; infringe upon citizens' rights of the

60 Criminal Law of the People's Republic of China, adopted by the Second Session of the Fifth National People's Congress on 1 July 1979 and amended by the Fifth Session of the Eight National People's Congress on 14 March 1997. A translation of this is available at http://www.qis.net/chinalaw/lawtran1.htm.

> person, democratic rights, and other rights; and other acts that endanger society, are crimes if according to law they should be criminally punished. However, if the circumstances are clearly minor and the harm is not great, they are not to be deemed crimes.

It is not accidental that in this general list of crimes, issues of sovereignty, territorial integrity and political power are placed before economic order, state and collectively owned property, privately owned property, and finally rights of the person, democratic rights, and other rights. The specific provisions relating to crimes of endangering national security are listed in Arts 102–13 Part II Chapter I of the Law. These crimes include colluding or plotting to harm the motherland's sovereignty (Art 102); organising, plotting or acting (cl 1) or instigating (cl 2) to split the country or undermine national security (Art 103), organising, plotting or acting (cl 1) or instigating (cl 2) to subvert the political power of the state and overthrow the socialist system (Art 105). Offences under Art 102, and Art 103 (cl 1) can carry the death penalty when the circumstances 'are particularly vile'.[61] Local level governments interpret these sections in accordance with centralised policy directives.

Chapter III (Arts 140–231) of the Criminal Law is headed 'Crimes of Undermining the Order of Socialist Market Economy' and is responsible for a host of new crimes, reflecting the profound social and economic changes that China has experienced. Several provisions can attract the death penalty: producing fake medicine that causes death to another human (Art 141), smuggling of arms, nuclear materials, counterfeit currency, cultural relics, precious metals and rare animals (Art 151), and counterfeiting an especially large amount of money, or being the ringleader (Art 170). There is also a plethora of other crimes under this Chapter which impose a range of punishments ranging from fines to imprisonment, including corporate fraud, infringement of intellectual property rights and disrupting the market order.

In the Chinese socialist-legal history, there are 'loosening and tightening' (*fengsou*) of policy and 'political crackdowns' (*yanda*, literally 'hard strike') which will influence the enforcement and content of these provisions. Such 'extra-legal' considerations surround the statute and cast a shadow over what are otherwise reasonably promising reforms in the 1997 Criminal Procedure Law.

2 *Criminal Procedure Law 1997*

In 1996 the NPC adopted a 110-article decision revising the 1979 Criminal Procedure Law[62] (CPL) that came in effect on 1 January 1997. Of the 164

---

61 Article 113 reads 'When one commits the aforementioned crimes in this chapter that endanger national security – except those stipulated in the second clause of Article 103, and Articles 105, 107 and 109 – and has incurred particularly serious harms to the country and the people, and the circumstances are particularly vile, he may be sentenced to death.'

62 Decision of the National People's Congress on the Revision of the 'Criminal Procedure Law of the PRC' adopted 17 March 1996.

articles in the original law, 70 were eliminated, two altered and 63 new articles included. A greater awareness of international practice was an important stimulant to revise the CPL, just as a greater international awareness, and criticism of China's criminal law had their effect.[63] Though the 1954 State Constitution and Organic Law of the Courts of the same year had declared that 'the people's courts shall conduct adjudication independently and are subject only to the law' (Art 78, and Art 4 of the Organic Law) the 1982 Constitution provides that 'the people's courts shall, in accordance with the law, exercise judicial power independently and are not subject to interference by administrative organs, public organisations or individuals'.[64] The 1997 Law declared courts to be the only competent organs to judge and convict.[65] Other provisions made fundamental changes and improvements to the Chinese criminal justice process: judges must now determine on presentation of the indictment whether the indictment was sufficient, in which case the trial commences but if not, it is rejected, with the judge having no power to send it back for further investigation or direct its further investigation. The new Law requires the prosecution and defence to present evidence to the court, question and debate on the evidence and examine witnesses, with the judge taking an essentially passive 'umpire' role, concerning themselves mainly with the maintenance of court order and orderly debate, thus creating a better environment for a meaningful defence. After deliberation of the guilt of the defendant, the collegial panel (judge and assessors) must render a judgement and may request the president of the court to transfer the case to the judicial committee for discussion and decision only in difficult, major or complex cases – whereas in the past such cases were automatically discussed and decided by the judicial committee prior to the trial. Unfortunately, as has already been discussed, without an overhaul of the institutional structure of the Chinese justice system, including improvement of the quality of the judiciary and the legal profession, such provisions will remain as largely unenforceable as their constitutional counterparts have long been.[66]

In its analysis of the revisions, the US-based Lawyers for Human Rights Committee deciphered four areas particularly relevant to human rights: pre-trial detention, the right to counsel, prosecutorial determination of guilt and the trial process.[67] For brevity's sake, only the first two of these shall be discussed here, although this is enough to demonstrate a lack of total commitment to reform by the government. Pre-arrest detention had traditionally been a problem in China on the basis of people being detained for

63 Lawyers Committee for Human Rights, *Opening to Reform?*, 1996, New York, 10.

64 Criminal Procedure Law 1997 Art 5. The ambiguity of this provision has been quickly noticed and noted in both Chinese and Western legal analyses.

65 *Ibid*, Art 12.

66 Constitution of the PRC 1982 Art 126.

67 Lawyers Committee for Human Rights, 20.

'shelter and investigation' (*shourong shencha*), an administrative not criminal provision, because the arrest standard in the CPL 1979 was seen as too high. The revised CPL sought to address this by lowering the arrest standard[68] and also expanding the categories of people to whom the 'shelter and investigation' provisions had originally been directed towards, so such pre-arrest detentions would be governed by the criminal law, not administrative regulations (and thereby governed by the courts, not the police). In theory, it was a good move as it removed a 'legal' method for police to avoid prescribed time limits and procedural requirements contained in the CPL. Yet the revisions also slipped through an increase in the time of pre-arrest detention for this class of suspects from seven to 30 days, and granted an extra four days for the procuracy to decide whether to authorise the arrest.[69] Further, the original CPL allowed for a maximum three months detention of those suspected committing crimes punishable by 10 years or longer, while the revised version permits 10 months.[70]

Another response by China to growing international concern, and also awareness amongst its expanding legal profession, of deficiencies in its criminal procedure, was to reform provisions regarding a right to counsel. Like the amendments to pre-trial detention, however, the commitment of Chinese law-makers to meet international human rights standards is questionable. The new CPL provides suspects with a right to counsel from the moment case materials are transferred from investigating authorities to the procuracy to assess whether to proceed with prosecution, and also stipulates that suspects must be informed of that right within three days of the transfer.[71] There is no right of counsel, however, during the investigative phase when of course all manner of illegally-obtained evidence may prove fatal to the suspect, and the suspect may also be vulnerable to torture or other coercive measures. It is a deliberate tactic by the drafters, as Art 96 explains that suspects may have counsel during this stage, but there is no obligation to inform suspects of this 'right'. Acquiring competent counsel at such an early stage of pre-trial detention and investigation is certainly not part of the Chinese legal culture, and in the absence of positive measures to give substance to this right, it remains illusory to the suspects it *prima facie* seeks to protect.

3 Other legislation

While time and space do not permit a detailed discussion here, by way of completeness, it is important to note that China has also responded to the recognised need for a 'rule of law' environment with some other major pieces

68 Article 60.

69 Article 69.

70 Article 127.

71 Article 33.

of legislation in its continuing 'modernisation' of the legal system. The Administrative Litigation Law 1989 (ALL)[72] was introduced in response to a problem Deng Xiao Ping (and many others) had observed: 'For a long time we have lacked strict administrative regulations ... [and] clear stipulations regarding the competence of each organ and even each person; whatever the matter, more often than not there have been no regulations to follow.'[73] In other words legislation was required to restrain official abuse of power and corruption. The ALL provides a process of judicial review of 'concrete' administrative acts, but not 'abstract' and discretionary ones, the latter being one of the primary sources of administrative abuses and corruption.[74] This is particularly of concern in the criminal law, where although there has been an attempt to relocate notorious abuses into the criminal law, and therefore out of the administrative law (note the 'shelter and investigation' case discussed above) several problems remain in administrative (non-reviewable) discretion.[75] The ALL is accompanied by four other legislative outputs, that together form a suite of administrative review for the first time in China.[76] Although the absence of an independent and competent judiciary, as already noted, largely leaves the abuse of administrative power unbridled, the importance of this suite of legislation should not be underestimated. The process of reforming the legal system in China is only two decades old, and swims upstream against a current of hostility towards the law, and emphasis of individual subordination to greater authorities. Such legislative outputs are significant steps in a cultural shift that will lead to more substantive rights and remedies, along with continuing structural reform.

D Rhetoric versus reality

It would be premature, however, to conclude that the changes to the criminal and administrative law have led to alleviation of human rights abuses. Endemic inefficiency and corruption in the judiciary, and a questionable commitment to rectify these continue to cause grave concern. The Justice Ministry set a target of 150,000 lawyers, 30,000 notaries and 40,000 grass roots legal services centres by 2000, yet according to the All-China Lawyers

72 *Zhonghua Renmin Gongheguo Susong Fa*, promulgated 4 April 1989.

73 Deng Xiao Ping, *Dang he Guojia Lingdao Zhidu de Gaige* [trans: Reform of Party and Government Leadership] quoted in Susan Finder 'Like Throwing an Egg against a Stone? Administrative Litigation in the People's Republic of China' 3 Journal of Chinese Law 1 (1989), 1, 5.

74 See Alice ES Tay and Ghnther Doeker-Mach 'Twenty Years of Law-Making' in Alice ES Tay and Ghnther Doeker-Mach (eds), *Asia Pacific Handbook – PRC Legislation*, 2001, Baden-Baden, Germany: Nomos.

75 The reach of the Security Administration Punishment Regulations 1987, for example, is extremely broad.

76 Administrative Review Regulations 1990, State Compensation Act 1994, Administrative Penalties Law 1996, Administrative Review Act 1999. See fn 72, where a lengthy Introduction sets out the relations between these legislative acts and their functions.

Association, the country fell short of that goal.[77] Further, for the entire legal history of the People's Republic of China, until the last few years, neither prosecutors nor judges were required to have law degrees or legal experience; most of them were retired army officers and former public security personnel. Since the last few years, a genuine effort is being made to encourage law graduates to enter the judiciary (including a call by members of the Shanghai People's Congress) to increase judicial salary to make a judicial career an attractive alternative opening to law practice in lucrative commercial areas.

Senior officials acknowledge that torture and coerced confessions are chronic problems.[78] Electric shocks administered with cattle prods, prolonged periods of solitary confinement, beatings, and shackles remain favoured methods of torture by the security organs: the US State Department's latest report, drawing on information from various NGOs, lists a range of instances that occurred across provinces. The latest available official statistics indicate that 230,000 persons remain in re-education through labour camps (an administrative punishment, therefore out of the CPL's scope). While defendants can challenge their sentences under the ALL, inadequate legal counsel and short appeal times defeat the promise of the law in preventing or reversing arbitrary decisions.

Anecdotal evidence gathered by the US Government indicates that the implementation of the CPL 'remains uneven and far from complete, especially in politically sensitive cases'.[79] This is indicative of two paths that change must follow: it must cascade down the various levels of government and state and it must also spread outwards from Beijing into the provinces and penetrate traditional extra-legal handling of justice in rural areas. In April 2000, the Beijing newspaper Legal Daily published an article on torture that concluded that the practice was due to police officials not having adequate legal or human rights training and holding antiquated ideas about a presumption of guilt.[80]

III Conclusion

The 'Fifth Modernisation' is a continuing process for China. The last two decades have witnessed an extraordinary amount of legal reform judging by almost any standard. Human rights, like international trade, is a new concept not easily absorbed into China's legal culture, and incompatible with its legal and constitutional structures. It has been seen that human rights and international trade face similar challenges in China as they seek to effect their

77 US State Department, above n 40, 10.

78 *Ibid*, 4.

79 *Ibid*, 11.

80 *Ibid*, 12.

separate but related causes. In recognition of this NGOs and UN agencies require observer status at the WTO to ensure that a unified and complete approach to plans for higher living standards for all humanity be continuously promoted and developed.

China's accession to the WTO will provide significant impetus for further domestic reform of its legal system. Strengthening its judiciary and dismantling at least those features and aspects of the politico-legal apparatus at all levels that stand in direct opposition to legality will remain priorities for China as it responds to increased foreign investment and scrutiny. Reflecting on the changes China has experienced during the 20th century, the legal reforms already in place together with those on the horizon, may be fairly described as a 'legal revolution'. Senior Minister Lee Kuan Yew may be overstating the eventual accession when he proclaims it 'the single biggest economic and political decision China has made since 1949'. The accession is a natural medium-term consequence of the reforms enacted shortly after the death of Chairman Mao, as part of the 'economic revolution'. Should the WTO embrace the new global agenda and work in partnership with civil society and UN agencies, Lee Kuan Yew may well prove the soothsayer. The danger is that international trade will refract through the WTO divorced from greater social concerns: if this proves to be true, China may well follow in the footsteps of the country Mr Lee has created. The 'socialist' part of Deng Xiao Ping's 'socialist market economy [for which read state controlled and licensed market economy] will define the market economy, as Mr Lee's 'Asian values' has provided Singapore characteristics to the Singapore miracle.

The Willem C Vis International Commercial Arbitration Moot 2000–2001

Katherine Louise Brown, Mariel Brooke Dimsey, Martin Ehrenberg, Michael Robert Hodge, Radha Dawn Ivory, Jens Thomas John, Christopher Justin Peters, and Gabriël Adelin Moens

Introduction

The TC Beirne School of Law, The University of Queensland again participated in the prestigious Willem C Vis International Commercial Arbitration Moot held in Vienna, Austria between 5–12 April 2001. The Moot is named after Willem C Vis (1924–93) who was an expert in international commercial transactions and dispute settlement procedures. The University of Queensland was one of 94 law schools from 32 different countries invited to participate in the Moot. The team consisted of Kathryn Louise Brown, Mariel Brooke Dimsey, Martin Ehrenberg, Michael Robert Hodge, Radha Dawn Ivory, Jens Thomas John and Christopher Justin Peters. They were coached by Garrick Professor Gabriël A Moens. As in the past, the School's Willem C Vis team was generously sponsored by Corrs Chambers Westgarth, a leading law firm in Brisbane.

The Willem C Vis competition brings together students from diverse cultures through a common endeavour: the training of law leaders of tomorrow in principles of international commercial law and techniques of international commercial arbitration. The Moot is organised by the Institute of International Commercial Law at the Pace University School of Law, New York and is sponsored by various international commercial arbitration institutions, including UNCITRAL. The goals of the Moot are described in Volumes II and III of International Trade and Business Law Annual ((1996) 2 ITBLA 229; (1997) 3 ITBLA 277). It suffices for the purposes of this Introduction to emphasise that the competition stimulates the study of international commercial law, especially the United Nations Convention on Contracts for the international Sale of Goods, 1980 (CISG) and various arbitration rules. The Competition offers participants an opportunity to interpret these texts in the light of different legal systems and to develop an expertise in advocating a position before an arbitral panel composed of arbitrators from different legal systems.

The Moot Problem in the 2000–01 competition involved a controversy arising out of a hypothetical international sale of goods subject to the CISG and the Rules of Arbitration of the International Chamber of Commerce.

Kathryn Brown and Michael Hodge presented the arguments to panels consisting of three arbitrators. In the general rounds, they defeated the University of Kiel, Germany; the Federal University of Rio Grande do Sul, Brazil; Laval University, Quebec; and Pontificia Universidad Catolica Madre y Maestra, Dominican Republic. In the octo-finals, Queensland defeated the University of Rijeka, Croatia. Queensland met Harvard University in the quarter-finals. Following a hotly contested moot, Harvard University proceeded to the semi-finals. The University of Queensland was placed second in the general rounds with a score of 1096 points out of a maximum of 1200. Both Kathryn Brown and Michael Hodge won best oralist awards.

In addition, the students also received the 3rd prize for best Memorandum for the Respondent. Professor Nicholas Sellers assessed the team's Memorandum for the Respondent. He stated:

> This is a most impressive brief for the Respondent; it is splendidly researched and well argued. It meets all the arguments made by the Claimant ... and brings in many other arguments as well. It reveals a complete grasp of the legal principles involved in the case. The only general criticism that might be made ... is whether this brief is too good. It merits the highest score. The list of authorities is greater than the total contents of the law library to be found in certain Eastern European universities.

Professor Marlene Andrae, University of Potsdam, Germany, who assessed the Queensland Memorandum for the Claimant said in her report:

> The memorandum presents all issues on which the claimant should rely in a clear, logically structured way and is therefore comfortable to read and to understand. The memorandum does not discuss matters that were not necessary to the case for the claimant but reaches, instead, an interesting, analytical profundity. The relevant authorities ... have been excellently analysed. This holds true for the quantity of the references as well as for their internationalism.

In the next sections, the 2000–2001 Moot problem and its clarifications are reproduced. This is followed by the Memorandum for the Respondent, prepared by the team representing the University of Queensland. The problem, clarifications and the memorandum are useful resources in the teaching of the CISG, and of international commercial arbitration law. It also serves as a historical record of the Eighth Willem C Vis International Commercial Arbitration Moot 2000–2001.

The Moot Problem

EIGHTH ANNUAL WILLEM C VIS INTERNATIONAL COMMERCIAL ARBITRATION MOOT

Vienna, Austria
April 6 to 12, 2001

THE PROBLEM

Organized by:
Institute of International Commercial Law
Pace University School of Law
78 North Broadway
White Plains, NY 10603
USA

6 June 2000

Secretariat

ICC International Court of Arbitration

38, Cours Albert 1er

75008 Paris

France

Dear Sirs:

We represent Sports and More Sports, Inc. It is engaged in a dispute with the Vis Water Sports Co. The contract between the parties included an ICC arbitration clause.

I enclose five copies of the Request for Arbitration with its supporting exhibits. I also enclose US $2,500 as an advance payment on the administrative costs, as provided in Appendix III, article 1, of the ICC Arbitration Rules.

Sincerely,

(Signed)

Counsel for Sports and More Sports

Sports and More Sports, Inc
Claimant
v
Vis Water Sports Co
Respondent

REQUEST FOR ARBITRATION

I Parties

1 Sports and More Sports, Inc (hereafter referred to as 'Sports') is a corporation organized under the laws of Danubia. It has its principal office at 214 Commercial Ave, Oceanside, Danubia. The telephone number is 555-1212 and the fax number is 555-1214. Sports is the largest retail seller of athletic equipment of all types in the country of Danubia.

2 Vis Water Sports Co is a corporation organized under the laws of Equatoriana. It has its principal office at 395 Industrial Place, Capitol City, Equatoriana. The telephone number is 483-5800 and the fax number is 483-5810. Vis is a manufacturer of equipment for water sports.

II The Dispute

3 On 31 March 1999 Sports received in the mail an announcement from Vis Water Sports that they had opened a new web site on the Internet. The announcement invited the recipients to visit the site and gave the Uniform Resource Locater (URL). Mr Samuel Hirst, the Purchasing Manager of Sports, did so that day. The web site showed the line of goods available from Vis Water Sports along with prices. Many of the items available from Vis Water Sports were attractive and at reasonable prices. Vis Water Sports was a company known to Sports by reputation, although there had never been any previous dealings between them. Since Vis Water Sports equipment had not previously been marketed in Danubia, Sports considered that a significant order should be placed with it.

4 The web site was organized in such a way that it would have been possible to place an order from the site. However, since there had been no prior relationship between the two firms and to see whether better terms than were offered directly on the web site might be available, negotiations were commenced by an e-mail message from Sports to Vis Water Sports on 31 March 1999. (Claimant's Exhibit No 1.) After a short exchange of e-mails, a contract for the purchase of water sports equipment in the amount of list price $100,000 FOB Capitol City was entered into. (Claimant's Exhibits Nos 2-4.) There was a discount of 5 percent on the price to which was

added a further sum of $7,000 for transportation from Equatoriana to Danubia, for a total delivered price of $102,000.

5 The goods were delivered from Vis Water Sports on 19 May 1999. Sports saw immediately that they would sell well in Danubia and on 27 May 1999 Sports increased the size of its order by an additional list price of $500,000, which was accepted by Vis on 28 May 1999. (Claimant's Exhibits Nos 5 and 6.) After a discount of 8 percent and transportation costs of $26,000, Sports paid Vis a total of $483,000 for the second purchase. When the Vis Water Sports equipment was first put on sale in the various Sports stores throughout Danubia, a significant advertising campaign was undertaken. The Vis Water Sports slogan 'Like a fish in water' was prominently used.

6 On 20 September 1999 Sports received a letter from the Vis Fish Company stating that the trademark 'Vis' was registered in Danubia by them and that the registration covered all water-related goods. (Claimant's Exhibit No 7.) They claimed that Sports was violating their trademark by selling goods under the trademark 'Vis', by advertising the goods throughout Danubia under that name and by using the slogan 'like a fish in water'.

7 On 4 October 1999 Sports replied that it was not violating the trademark owned by the Vis Fish Company since it was inconceivable that anyone would confuse the athletic equipment Sports was selling under the name of 'Vis' with the fish products being sold by the Vis Fish Company. (Claimant's Exhibit No 8.)

8 On 15 October 1999 Sports received a further letter from the Vis Fish Company insisting that it stop selling Vis Water Sports equipment. Sports was threatened with legal action if it failed to do so. (Claimant's Exhibit No 9.) Legal counsel specializing in trademark and other intellectual property matters informed Sports that in their opinion Sports was not violating the Vis Fish Company trademark. However, they also told Sports that the Vis Fish Company had aggressively defended its trademark in the past. They went on to say that, even though Sports could expect to recover its legal fees once the Vis Fish Company claim had been dismissed, the litigation would not be easy and would cause a certain amount of disruption to Sport's business. (Claimant's Exhibit No 10.) In order to avoid the anticipated disruption to its business, Sports decided that it would be better to accede to the demands of the Vis Fish Company and withdraw the goods from the market.

9 On 3 November 1999 Sports wrote Vis Water Sports informing it of the claim by the Vis Fish Company and, since it was not possible to continue selling the Vis Water Sports equipment without risk of legal action against it, Vis Water Sports had violated its obligation under article 42 of the United Nations Convention on Contracts for the International Sale of Goods (CISG) to deliver goods free from any right or claim of a third party based on intellectual property. (Claimant's Exhibit No 12.) Sports went on

to say that it was avoiding the contract under article 49 of the CISG. Sports also referred to articles 81 to 84 of the CISG and stated that it would propose just how it would make restitution of the unsold Vis equipment and the amount of the price paid as soon as it had been able to gather the necessary information.

10 Since the Vis trademark was registered in Danubia for all water-related products, Vis Water Sports could not have been unaware of its existence when it sold the equipment to Sports.

11 Vis Water Sports replied on 10 November 1999 that it saw no basis for Sports to avoid the contract. As a result it refused to consider taking back the unsold water sports equipment or to refund any of the price that had been paid. (Claimant's Exhibit No 13.) Sports answered on 16 November 1999 that, if Vis Water Sports was able to clarify that sale of its equipment in Danubia would not lead to litigation arising out of claims of trademark infringement, Sports would reconsider its avoidance of the two contracts. (Claimant's Exhibit No 14.) Vis Water Sports has not done so.

12 Sports has withdrawn all of the unsold equipment from its stores and is currently storing it for the account of Vis Water Sports.

III Amount claimed

13 In accordance with article 81, CISG, avoidance of the contract releases both parties from their obligations under it, subject to any damages that may be due. Either party may claim restitution, in which case both parties are required to make restitution concurrently. Sports is prepared to deliver to Vis Water Sports the remaining unsold goods and the price paid for the goods that were sold in the normal course of business prior to the declaration of avoidance of the contract. Goods delivered under the contract in the amount of list price $200,000 were sold by Sports prior to the avoidance of the contract, ie, one-third of the contract amount of $600,000. Therefore, the amount due from Vis Water Sports is as follows:

Restitution	
Reimbursement of purchase price $600,000 list price	$552,000
Less purchase price of goods sold by Sports	184,000
Net restitution of purchase price	368,000
Damages	
Shipping costs of goods purchased	33,000
Advertising	35,000
General selling and administrative expenses allocated to goods sold	40,000
Storage and misc expenses after avoidance to date	4,000
Total amount claimed	$480,000

14 Sports claims for additional storage and other expenses from the date of submission of this Request for Arbitration until mutual restitution has been made.

15 Sports claims interest on the purchase price from the date paid by Sports to the date reimbursement of the price is made by Vis Water Sports as well as on the damages to the date paid by Vis Water Sports.

16 Sports claims for costs of arbitration, including legal costs, as provided in article 31 of the ICC Arbitration Rules.

IV Contract and Arbitration Agreement

17 The original contract was concluded by the exchange of e-mail messages between Mr Hirst and Mr Singer dated 5 and 6 April 1999. (Claimant's Exhibits Nos 3 and 4.) The contract included the Conditions of Purchase, attached to the e-mail message of 5 April 1999 from Mr Hirst to Mr Singer. (Claimant's Exhibit No 3.) The second contract was concluded by the exchange of e-mails of 27 and 28 May 1999. (Claimant's Exhibits Nos 5 and 6.) The Conditions of Purchase, which Vis Water Sports already had, were referred to in Mr Hirst's message. (Claimant's Exhibit No 5.)

18 Clause 14 of the Conditions of Purchase attached to Claimant's Exhibit No 3 was the International Chamber of Commerce standard arbitration clause with three additions:

> All disputes arising out of or in connection with the present contract shall be finally settled under the Rules of Arbitration of the International Chamber of Commerce by one or more arbitrators appointed in accordance with the said Rules. If the amount in dispute is more than $400,000, there shall be three arbitrators. The arbitration shall take place in Vindobona, Danubia. The language of the arbitration shall be English.

V Arbitrators

19 Since the amount claimed by Sports is more than $400,000, the arbitration clause provides that it should be settled by three arbitrators.

20 In accord with article 8(4) of the ICC Arbitration Rules, Sports nominates Dr xxxxx xxxxx to be one of the arbitrators. His address is (omitted).

VI Place of arbitration, applicable rules of law, language

21 The arbitration agreement provides that the place of arbitration should be Vindobona, Danubia. The arbitration agreement also provides that the language of the arbitration should be English.

22 Both Danubia and Equatoriana are party to the United Nations Convention on Contracts for the International Sale of Goods. Accordingly, article 1(1)(a) of the Convention provides that it is applicable to the contract.

23 Both Danubia and Equatoriana are party to the Convention on the Recognition and Enforcement of Foreign Arbitral Awards. Danubia has adopted the UNCITRAL Model Law on International Commercial Arbitration.

Signed 6 June 2000

Attorneys for Sports and More Sports, Inc

Claimant's Exhibit No 1

E-mail
From: Samuel Hirst
Date: 31 March 1999
To: Vis Water Sports

Subject: Inquiry as to terms of purchase

I am the Purchasing Manager of Sports and More Sports, the largest retailer of sporting equipment in the country of Danubia.

We have recently received your announcement of the enlargement of your web site and have taken a look at it. I congratulate you on an attractive and easy to navigate site.

We are continuously looking for new and additional sources of supply. We note that the Vis line of water sports equipment has not previously been sold in Danubia. If you were able to offer us sufficiently attractive terms, we would be interested in considering taking it on.

Sincerely yours,

Samuel Hirst
Purchasing Manager
Sports and More Sports, Inc
214 Commercial Ave
Oceanside, Danubia
Tel 555-1212, fax 555-1214

Claimant's Exhibit No 2

E-mail
From: Jonathon Singer
Date: 2 April 1999
To: Samuel Hirst

Subject: Your inquiry as to terms of purchase

Attach: Price list

Thank you for your e-mail of 31 March 1999. We are well aware of the reputation of Sports and More Sports in Danubia as a respected and effective retailer of sporting goods.

You are correct in saying that the Vis line of water sports equipment has not previously been sold in Danubia. We have long desired to enter that market, but have not previously taken the steps necessary to do so. Your interest in our goods is, therefore, very welcome.

I am attaching to this message the list of goods available for export and the prices per item. You will note that these prices are FOB Capitol City. We will, of course, be willing to make transportation arrangements for your account. We would be willing to make a concession on the price of 5 percent for an order of $100,000 and 8 percent for an order of $500,000. Normally, shipment can be made within 30 days from the receipt of a firm order and a letter of credit for the invoice amount plus 10%. We can be more precise once we know the size of your order and the choice of goods that you have made.

Although it is our policy not to grant exclusive dealerships, we would make a limited exception if Sports and More Sports were to place an order for a minimum of $1,000,000. In that case we would be willing to commit not to sell to any other sporting goods dealer in Danubia for a period of one year.

You will find our general conditions of sale on our web site [URL omitted].

I look forward to hearing from you.

Sincerely yours,

Jonathon Singer
Sales Manager
Vis Water Sports Co
395 Industrial Place
Capitol City, Equatoriana
Tel 483-5800, fax 483-5810

Claimant's Exhibit No 3

E-mail
From: Samuel Hirst
Date: 5 April 1999
To: Jonathon Singer

Subject: Purchase order

Attach: Purchase order No 6839; Conditions of purchase. (Not reproduced except for arbitration clause in Conditions of Purchase set out in Request for Arbitration.)

Dear Mr Singer:

We have reviewed your e-mail and the attached price list. We find your offer attractive and we wish to make a moderate sized first order so as to be able to evaluate the market for the Vis brand of water sports equipment in Danubia. I am attaching to this message our purchase order No 6839. You will notice that the total order is for list price $100,000. With the 5 percent discount, our purchase total will be $95,000.

We would ask you to let us know the firm shipping dates that we can expect. We would indeed ask you to arrange the shipping. As soon as you have an estimate of the shipping costs, we will establish the letter of credit that you asked for.

We look forward to a long and profitable relationship with Vis Water Sports.

For your reference I have attached our General Conditions of Purchase, which are part of our purchase order.

Sincerely yours,

Samuel Hirst
Purchasing Manager
Sports and More Sports, Inc
214 Commercial Ave
Oceanside, Danubia
Tel 555-1212, fax 555-1214

Claimant's Exhibit No 4

E-mail
From: Jonathon Singer
Date: 6 April 1999
To: Samuel Hirst

Subject: Your inquiry as to terms of purchase

Attach: *Pro forma* invoice (Not reproduced)

Thank you for your purchase order. We will be able to ship by 5 May 1999. The *pro forma* invoice that is attached includes $7,000 for shipping and insurance, for a total of $102,000. We would, therefore, request you to establish a letter of credit for $112,200.

I should like to remind you that our General Conditions of Sale, which we include in all sales contracts, are available at [URL omitted]. I suggest that you take a look at them.

If you have any questions about your order or about any of the Vis Water Sports equipment, please feel free to ask.

Sincerely yours,
Jonathon Singer
Sales Manager
Vis Water Sports Co
395 Industrial Place
Capitol City, Equatoriana
Tel: 483-5800, fax: 483-5810

Claimant's Exhibit No 5

E-mail
From: Samuel Hirst
Date: 27 May 1999
To: Jonathon Singer

Subject: Purchase order

Attach: Purchase order No 6910

Dear Mr Singer:

The first shipment of equipment from Vis Water Sports Inc has arrived and we are delighted with them. Therefore, we would like to make our initial purchase larger than anticipated. I am attaching our purchase order No 6910 for additional goods totaling list price $500,000. Since you already have a copy of our General Conditions of Purchase, I need not attach them to this order. As before, we will establish a letter of credit. Please inform me of shipping dates.

Sincerely yours,

Samuel Hirst

Purchasing Manager
Sports and More Sports, Inc
214 Commercial Ave
Oceanside, Danubia
Tel 555-1212, fax 555-1214

Claimant's Exhibit No 6

E-mail
From: Jonathon Singer
Date: 28 May 1999
To: Samuel Hirst

Subject: Your inquiry as to terms of purchase

I hereby acknowledge receipt of your purchase order No 6910. Since you have re-ordered so quickly, even before you have had the opportunity to see how the Vis Water Sports equipment will sell, for purposes of establishing the appropriate discount, we have treated your two purchase orders as one purchase. That means you will effectively receive the 8 percent discount on your PO 6839 rather than the 5 percent discount previously calculated. Although our *pro forma* invoice will be sent separately, I will set out our calculation below.

PO 6839	$100,000
PO 6910	500,000
Sub-total	600,000
Discount 8%	48,000
	552,000
Shipping 6839	7,000
Shipping 6910	26,000
Total	$585,000
Paid on 6839	102,000
Due	$483,000

Therefore, the total is $483,000, including transport and insurance of $26,000 on the current shipment. You can expect the goods to be shipped by 20 June 1999.

Sincerely yours,

Jonathon Singer
Sales Manager
Vis Water Sports Co
395 Industrial Place
Capitol City, Equatoriana
Tel 483-5800, fax 483-5810

Claimant's Exhibit No 7

Vis Fish Company
14 Water Street
Port City, Danubia
20 September 1999

Sports and More Sports, Inc
214 Commercial Ave
Oceanside

Dear Sirs:

Your recent advertisements in all the major newspapers in Danubia that feature Vis Water Sports equipment and that use the slogan 'like a fish in water' have come to our attention.

We should like you to know that 'Vis' is registered in Danubia as a trademark covering all water-related products and it belongs to the Vis Fish Company. Your advertisement and sale of goods bearing the name 'Vis' are, therefore, in violation of our trademark. The violation is particularly egregious because of the slogan associated with the Vis Water Sports equipment 'like a fish in water'. It evokes an obvious association between the use of the equipment and the fish that we sell under our trademark Vis, which means fish in the Dutch language.

We would ask you to promptly withdraw all advertisements that use our trademark 'Vis' and to stop selling any goods under that name.

We would ask you to respond to this letter and to tell us the measures you have taken to be sure that you are no longer violating our rights to the 'Vis' trademark.

Sincerely,

Kurt Streng
Managing Director

Claimant's Exhibit No 8

Sports and More Sports, Inc
214 Commercial Ave
Oceanside, Danubia
4 October 1999

Mr Kurt Streng
Managing Director
Vis Fish Company
14 Water Street
Port City

Dear Mr Streng:

I refer to your letter dated 20 September 1999 in which you claim that Sports and More Sports, Inc is violating your registered trademark 'Vis' by advertising and selling equipment in Danubia under the trademark 'Vis Water Sports'.

I must reject your demand that Sports and More Sports cease advertising and selling equipment under the 'Vis Water Sports' brand. There is no likelihood that anyone would confuse athletic equipment, even that used for water sports, with the fish and fish products that I now understand are sold by your company. The markets and the nature of the products are simply too different.

May I suggest, however, that there might be possibilities for joint promotion of the Vis name. I would be pleased to be in contact with Vis Water Sports, Co to inquire whether they might be interested. If you find this to be of interest, please let me know.

Sincerely,

Thomas Kent

President

Claimant's Exhibit No 9

Vis Fish Company
14 Water Street
Port City, Danubia
15 October 1999

Mr Thomas Kent, President
Sports and More Sports, Inc
214 Commercial Ave
Oceanside

Dear Mr Kent:

I was sorely disappointed in your letter dated 4 October 1999 in which you refused to cease advertising and selling water sports equipment under the brand name 'Vis Water Sports'.

There is no doubt that under the law of Danubia Sports and More Sports, Inc is in violation of our registered trademark 'Vis'. In spite of your denial that there could be any confusion between the water sports equipment that you are selling and the fish and fish products that we sell under the 'Vis' trademark, you suggested the possibilities of joint promotion of the 'Vis' name.

If Sports and More Sports, Inc does not cease advertising and selling goods under any name that incorporates our registered trademark 'Vis' within one week from receipt of this letter, we shall be forced to take legal action. I trust that such an unpleasant step will not be necessary.

Sincerely,

Kurt Streng
Managing Director

Claimant's Exhibit No 10

Howard & Heward
Advocates at the Court
28 October 1999

Mr Thomas Kent, President
Sports and More Sports, Inc
214 Commercial Ave.
Oceanside

Dear Mr Kent:

You have informed us that Sports and More Sports, Inc has recently begun to purchase from the Vis Water Sports Co of Equatoriana athletic equipment that carries the Vis Water Sports name. You have purchased this equipment for the purpose of sale in Danubia. You have also furnished a copy of correspondence with the Vis Fish Company in which that company has claimed to have registered the 'Vis' trademark in Danubia and in which that company has claimed that advertisement and sale of 'Vis Water Sports' equipment would be a violation of their trademark. The Vis Fish Company has threatened legal action if Sports and More Sports were not to cease selling 'Vis Water Sports' equipment in Danubia. You have asked us whether the claim of the Vis Fish Company is well founded.

We have verified that the Vis Fish Company has registered the 'Vis' name as a trademark. The registration claims the name for all water-related products. Nevertheless, from a search of the applicable registries it appears that the Vis Fish Company engages only in the business of selling fish, other water-related food products and their derivatives. There is no indication that the Vis Fish Company engages in any commercial activities that are in any way related to athletics or recreation.

In our opinion the claim of the Vis Fish Company to trade mark infringement is unfounded. We are of the opinion that any legal action that they might bring would eventually be dismissed. We must caution you, however, that the Vis Fish Company has aggressively defended its trademark in the past. The fact that they have registered the trademark for all water-related products is likely to mean that the litigation will not be easy. You could expect that even though, once successful, you could recover your legal costs from them, the litigation would cause a certain amount of disruption to your business.

If we can be of any further service to you in this matter, please feel free to contact me.

Sincerely,

Thomas Howard

Claimant's Exhibit No 11

Sports and More Sports, Inc
214 Commercial Ave
Oceanside, Danubia

3 November 1999

Mr Kurt Streng
Managing Director
Vis Fish Company
14 Water Street
Port City

Dear Mr Streng:

We are sorry that you have not accepted our suggestion that we might work together to promote the 'Vis' brands for both your fish and fish products and the Vis Water Sports brand equipment. Although the two types of goods are so different that we continue to insist that there would be no confusion in the minds of consumers, we do believe that an effective promotion could be made.

However, since you have rejected out suggestion and have stated that you would institute legal action if we were not to cease advertising and selling the Vis Water Sports brand equipment, we have decided to rely on the other brands of water sports equipment that we have been selling successfully for the past several years.

Sincerely,

Thomas Kent

President

Claimant's Exhibit No 12

Sports and More Sports, Inc
214 Commercial Ave
Oceanside, Danubia

3 November 1999

Mr Jonathon Singer
Sales Manager
Vis Water Sports Co
395 Industrial Place
Capitol City, Equatoriana

Dear Mr Singer:

This letter is to notify you that Vis Water Sports has violated its obligation under article 42 United Nations Convention on Contracts for the International Sale of Goods (CISG) to deliver goods free from any right or claim of a third party based on intellectual property. Therefore, Sports and More Sports, Inc is hereby avoiding the contract for the purchase of water sports equipment from the Vis Water Sports Co entered into by your e-mail acceptance of our purchase orders No 6839 and 6910 as provided in article 49 CISG. We look forward to mutual restitution being made as provided in articles 82 to 84 of the Convention.

The trademark 'Vis' has been registered in Danubia by the Vis Fish Company for all water-related products. By letters of 20 September 1999 and 15 October 1999 the Vis Fish Company has claimed that the advertising and selling of goods bearing the name Vis Water Sports in Danubia would violate their trademark and they have threatened legal action if we continued to do so. Legal counsel has advised us that, although in their opinion the claim of trade mark infringement would eventually be dismissed, the legal action would take a significant period of time and would be disruptive to our business. We are not in a position to contest any legal action that they might take in regard to what is, after all, your brand. Since we cannot continue to sell the Vis Water Sports equipment without the serious threat of legal action, we are withdrawing all the goods bearing the Vis Water Sports name from our stores and avoiding the contract.

I should like to assure you that this action on our part is in no way a reflection on your goods, with which we are quite satisfied and which have been well received by our clientele. If you are able to reach an understanding with the Vis Fish Company permitting the sale of your goods in Danubia, we would be pleased to consider placing further orders in the future.

As soon as we have been able to ascertain the amount of your goods that remain unsold and the additional costs that we have been forced to undertake in regard to your goods, we shall be in further communication with you about the means of mutual restitution. Until you give us instructions as to what we should do with the goods, we will store them in our warehouses for your account. Let me express my disappointment at this turn of events.

Sincerely,

Thomas Kent
President

Claimant's Exhibit No 13

Vis Water Sports Co
395 Industrial Place
Capitol City, Equatoriana

10 November 1999

Mr Thomas Kent, President
Sports and More Sports, Inc
214 Commercial Ave
Oceanside

Dear Mr Kent:

I hereby acknowledge receipt of your letter of 3 November 1999.

Vis Water Sports Co does not accept your purported avoidance of the contracts entered into between our two companies on the basis of your purchase orders Nos 6839 and 6910.

As you yourself have indicated, even though the Vis Fish Company may have registered the trademark 'Vis' for all water-related products, their business is fish and similar products. Vis Water Sports equipment certainly does not violate that trademark. If you were to search the Internet you would find any number of companies in different countries and different lines of business that use the trademark 'Vis', of which the Vis Fish Company is just one. We are obviously not all in violation of one another's trademark. Since the claim of the Vis Fish Company is manifestly unfounded, we see no basis for you to avoid the contract between us.

We will, of course, do all in our power to aid you in your defense against the assertion of trademark infringement. If, at the conclusion of any litigation that might take place, you were not able to recover your legal costs from the Vis Fish Company, we would stand ready to reimburse you for such reasonable costs as you had incurred.

We are sorry that this matter has occurred, but we are sure that it will soon be resolved. We look forward to a long and profitable relationship with you.

Sincerely,

Mr Jonathon Singer
Sales Manager
Vis Water Sports Co
395 Industrial Place
Capitol City, Equatoriana

Claimant's Exhibit No 14

Sports and More Sports, Inc
214 Commercial Ave
Oceanside, Danubia

16 November 1999

Mr Jonathon Singer
Sales Manager
Vis Water Sports Co
395 Industrial Place
Capitol City, Equatoriana

Dear Mr Singer:

I understand your reaction to our letter of 3 November 1999 by which we have avoided the contracts entered into between us. We at Sports and More Sports are also disappointed not to be able to continue selling the Vis Water Sports equipment.

We also appreciate your offer to give whatever help is in the power of the Vis Water Sports Co in a defense we might undertake against the claim of trademark infringement, including a guarantee of our 'reasonable' legal costs in the matter. Your offer, however, shows that you misunderstand the fundamental basis of our decision to avoid the contract. We are in the business of selling athletic equipment at retail. We are not in the business of defending against claims of trademark infringement. Any litigation brought by the Vis Fish Company would be disruptive to our business to some degree. While we appreciate the quality of the Vis Water Sports equipment, it is not unique. We are able to sell similar equipment from other suppliers to our customers without facing the threat of trademark infringement.

If you are able to clarify that sale of your equipment in Danubia will not lead to litigation arising out of claims of trademark infringement, we would be more than happy to consider rescinding our avoidance of the contracts and to making further purchases in the future. In the meantime, however, we must insist that we have avoided the contracts that we entered into with you. As a result, I again ask you to give instructions as to what should be done with the goods that have not yet been sold. As soon as possible we will send to you a detailed accounting of the amounts due between us so as to be able to effect the mutual restitution.

Sincerely,

Thomas Kent
President

International Court of Arbitration
Cour internationale d'arbitrage

Letter to Claimant acknowledging receipt of the Request for Arbitration

Address ***

By fax *** & Mail

Our Ref: 410/HGN/EP

Case N°: Moot No 8 9 June 2000

Dear *******,

We wish to acknowledge receipt of 5 copies of your Request for Arbitration dated 6 June 2000 and 5 copies of its exhibits submitted by you in the dispute between:

Sports and More Sports, Inc

– and –

Vis Water Sports Co

This Request for Arbitration was received by us on 9 June 2000 and has been assigned the following reference: Moot No 8.

The Counsel in the Secretariat of the ICC International Court of Arbitration who is in charge of the file is:

*** (direct dial number 33 1 49 53 ** **)

The Assistant-Counsel are:

*** (direct dial number 33 1 49 53 ** **)

*** (direct dial number 33 1 49 53 ** **)

The Secretaries are:

*** (direct dial number 33 1 49 53 ** **)

*** (direct dial number 33 1 49 53 ** **)

Mr/Ms *** will soon write to you concerning the notification of the Request for Arbitration and other relevant information.

Thank you for your payment of the non-refundable advance on administrative expenses of US$ 2 500.

Sincerely yours,

Horacio A Grigera Naón
Secretary General
ICC International Court of Arbitration

Encl: – 1998 ICC Rules of Arbitration
– International Court of Arbitration Brochure

International Court of Arbitration
Cour internationale d'arbitrage

Letter notifying Request for Arbitration to Respondent 9 June 2000

Moot No 8

Sports and More Sports, Inc (Danubia) v/ Vis Water Sports Co (Equatoriana)

Counsel in charge of the file: ***
(Direct dial: 33 1 49 53 ** **)
(Direct fax: 33 1 49 53 ** **)

Mr ***
Vis Water Sports Co
395 Industrial Place
Capitol City, Equatoriana
Fax: ******

Dear Mr ***,

The Secretariat hereby notifies you that it has received a Request for Arbitration (the 'Request') from Sports and More Sports, Inc represented by *** in which you have been named as Respondent.

This Request has been filed under reference Moot No 8. Please state the complete reference in all future correspondence.

We enclose a copy of the Request along with its exhibits, which was received today.

Pursuant to Article 5(1) of the ICC Rules of Arbitration (the 'Rules'), you are required to submit your Answer to the Request (the 'Answer') within 30 days from the day following the date of receipt of this letter. Please send the Secretariat 5 copies of your Answer.

In accordance with Article 5(2) of the Rules, Respondent may apply to the Secretariat for an extension of the time for the filing of its Answer, provided the application for such an extension contains Respondent's comments concerning the number of arbitrators and their choice and, where appropriate, the nomination of an arbitrator. In any event, the ICC International Court of Arbitration (the 'Court') has the power, pursuant to Article 6(3) of the Rules, to set the procedure in motion in the absence of an Answer on your part.

.../...

Moot No 8

Page 2

Constitution of the Arbitral Tribunal

The arbitration clause to which reference has been made provides for a three-member Arbitral Tribunal and Claimant has nominated Dr *** as an arbitrator. The Secretariat will invite Dr *** to complete a Declaration of Acceptance and Statement of Independence, copies of which will be forwarded to the parties in due course

In compliance with Article 8(4) of the Rules, you are hereby requested to nominate an arbitrator within 30 days of receipt of the present letter, failing which such appointment shall be made by the Court.

In this regard, please note that Article 7(1) of the Rules provides that every arbitrator must be and remain independent of the parties involved in the arbitration. Accordingly, you must confirm that any arbitrator nominated by you is independent. In addition, the Secretariat will invite any such prospective arbitrator to complete a Declaration of Acceptance and Statement of Independence.

Please also be advised that pursuant to Article 8(4) of the Rules, the third arbitrator, who will act as Chairman of the Arbitral Tribunal, shall be appointed by the Court unless the parties have agreed upon another procedure.

If you foresee being represented by counsel in this matter, please inform the Secretariat of the name and address of such counsel.

For any information about this file, please do not hesitate to contact:

- the undersigned, ***, Counsel. . . . .(extension ***)
- ***, Assistant Counsel . . . . (extension ***)
- ***, Assistant Counsel . . . . (extension ***)
- ***, Secretary . . . . (extension ***)
- ***, Secretary . . . . (extension ***)

Finally, while maintaining strict neutrality, the Secretariat is at the disposal of the parties with regard to any information they may require concerning the application of the Rules.

Yours sincerely,

***

Counsel

Secretariat of the ICC International Court of Arbitration

Encl: – Request for Arbitration with Exhibits
– 1998 version of the ICC Rules of Arbitration
– International Court of Arbitration Brochure
– Copy of the Secretariat's letter of today to Claimant

cc: Claimant

International Court of Arbitration
Cour internationale d'arbitrage

Letter informing Claimant of the notification of Request to Respondent

9 June 2000

Moot No 8

Sports and More Sports, Inc (Danubia) v/ Vis Water Sports Co (Equatoriana)

Counsel in charge of the file: *** (Direct dial: 33 1 49 53 ** **) (Direct fax: 33 1 49 53 ** **)

Mr ***
Address ***
Fax: ******

Dear Mr ***,

Further to the Secretary General's letter to you of today, we gratefully acknowledge receipt of your payment of US$ 2,500. We confirm that your Request for Arbitration (the 'Request') has been assigned the reference *****/***. Please state the complete reference in all future correspondence.

We are sending a copy of your Request to Respondent and asking it to respond in accordance with the requirements of Article 5 of the ICC Rules of Arbitration (the 'Rules').

Constitution of the Arbitral Tribunal

The Secretariat notes that in accordance with the arbitration clause referred to in the Request, which provides for a three-member Arbitral Tribunal, you have nominated Dr *** as an arbitrator.

In this regard, please be advised that Article 7(1) of the Rules provides that every arbitrator must be and remain independent of the parties involved in the arbitration. Accordingly, please confirm to us that Dr *** is independent. In addition, the Secretariat will invite the prospective arbitrator to complete a Declaration of Acceptance and Statement of Independence, copies of which will be forwarded to the parties in due course.

Please also note that pursuant to Article 8(4) of the Rules, the third arbitrator, who will act as Chairman of the Arbitral Tribunal shall be appointed by the Court unless the parties have agreed upon another procedure.

.../...

Moot No 8

Page 2

Provisional Advance

Please note that in accordance with Article 30(1) of the Rules and Article 1(2) of Appendix III, the Secretary General has fixed a provisional advance of US$ 18,000 to be paid by Claimant to cover the costs of the arbitration until the Terms of Reference have been drawn up. This provisional advance must be paid before the file can be transmitted to the Arbitral Tribunal once constituted. Said advance has been fixed by reference to the information presently in the possession of the Secretariat, and on the basis of an amount in dispute quantified at US$ 480,000 and taking into account that there shall be three arbitrators.

You are thus invited to pay US$ 15,500 (ie, US$ 18,000 less US$ 2,500) already paid) within 30 days from the day following the date of receipt of this letter, by bank check in favor of the International Chamber of Commerce or by transfer to our account N° *** at Bank ***.

Please include the reference Moot No 8 on your payment for its prompt and accurate crediting.

Finally, while maintaining strict neutrality, the Secretariat is at the disposal of the parties with regard to any information they may require concerning the application of the Rules.

Yours sincerely,

***

Counsel
Secretariat of the ICC International Court of Arbitration

Encl: – Copy of the Secretariat's letter of today to Respondent
– Copy of the Secretariat's letter of today to Dr *** (arbitrator proposed)

International Court of Arbitration
Cour internationale d'arbitrage

Letter to the arbitrator proposed by Claimant 9 June 2000

Moot No 8

Sports and More Sports, Inc (Danubia) v/ Vis Water Sports Co (Equatoriana)

Dear Dr ***,

We are pleased to inform you that you have been nominated by Claimant for confirmation as arbitrator in the above-referenced case. We are writing to inquire whether you accept this nomination.

Please note, in particular, that under Article 7(1) of the ICC Rules of Arbitration (the 'Rules'), every arbitrator must be and remain independent of the parties involved in the arbitration. Accordingly, you must complete and return the enclosed Declaration of Acceptance and Statement of Independence. We will also be required to provide the parties and the Court with a copy of your curriculum vitae (a blank form copy of which is enclosed).

Please also note that the Rules contain strict time-limits for the conduct of the arbitral proceedings (see Articles 18(2) and 24(1)). Prior to accepting your appointment, you should therefore be satisfied, to the extent reasonably possible, that you will be in a position to devote the time and effort necessary to conduct the arbitration in accordance with the requirements of the Rules. In this connection, your attention is also drawn to Article 7(5) of the Rules.

Furthermore, we wish to emphasize that the arbitral mission demands of the arbitrator the utmost respect for the confidential nature of the proceedings.

With regard to remuneration, we urge you to familiarize yourself with the relevant provisions of the Rules and the scale of arbitrator's fees contained in Appendix III thereto. Please note, in particular, that the arbitrator's fees are fixed exclusively by the Court and that separate fee arrangements between the parties and the arbitrators are not permitted. Arbitral fees are moreover fixed only at the end of the proceedings, although advances and reimbursement of expenses may be granted upon the completion of concrete steps in the arbitration.

.../...

Moot No 8

Page 2

In determining the level of the arbitrator's fees, the Court considers the factors set forth in Article 2(2) of Appendix III to the Rules. We must emphasize in this regard that your usual hourly rate or the usual systems of remuneration in your profession in your country are not taken into consideration by the Court in determining fees.

When the Arbitral Tribunal is composed of three members, unless the arbitrators inform us in writing that they have agreed to a different allocation, the Court normally fixes the fees of the arbitrators so that the Chairman receives 40% of the total fees and each coarbitrator receives 30%. However, the Court may decide upon a different allocation based on the circumstances of the case.

In order that the constitution of the Arbitral Tribunal in this case not be delayed, we would appreciate it if you would inform us within 10 days from the day following the date of receipt of the present letter whether you accept your nomination. If so, you should also ensure that we have received within that period the documents requested above.

For your information, the counsel of the parties in this matter are:

– for the Claimant: Sports and More Sports, Inc

  ***

– for the Respondent: Vis Water Sports Co

  ***

Should you have any questions with regard to the above, please do not hesitate to contact:

– the undersigned, **, Counsel. . . . . . .(direct dial number 33 1 49 53 ** **)
– ***, Assistant Counsel . . . . (direct dial number 33 1 49 53 ** **)
– ***, Assistant Counsel . . . . (direct dial number 33 1 49 53 ** **)
– ***, Secretary. . . . . (direct dial number 33 1 49 53 ** **)
– ***, Secretary. . . . . (direct dial number 33 1 49 53 ** **)

Yours sincerely,

***

*/Counsel

Secretariat of the ICC International Court of Arbitration

Encl: 1998 version of the ICC Rules of Arbitration

Blank Declaration of Acceptance and Statement of Independence

Blank curriculum vitae

cc: parties

ICC, International Court of Arbitration

Case: Moot No 8

Sports and More Sports, Inc

Claimant

v

Vis Water Sports Co

Respondent

ANSWER TO THE REQUEST FOR ARBITRATION

I Name and address of Respondent

1 Vis Water Sports Co, the Respondent, is a corporation organized under the laws of Equatoriana. It has its principal office at 395 Industrial Place, Capitol City, Equatoriana. The telephone number is 483-5800 and the fax number is 483-5810. Vis is a manufacturer of equipment for water sports.

II Nature of the Dispute

2 Vis Water Sports accepts the statements of Sports and More Sports, Inc as to the circumstances under which the contract for the sale of water sports equipment from Vis Water Sports to Sports and More Sports pursuant to the purchase orders nos 6839 and 6910 took place. (Request paras 3–5, Claimant's Exhibits Nos 1–6.)

3 Vis Water Sports does not dispute that the Vis Fish Company had registered the 'Vis' trademark in Danubia in connection with its fish business and that it had asserted that Sports and More Sports was infringing the 'Vis' trademark by advertising and selling Vis Water Sports equipment. (Claimant's Exhibits Nos 7 and 9.) Vis Water Sports agrees with Sports and More Sports, as set out in its letter of 4 October 1999 to the Vis Fish Company (Claimant's Exhibit No 8), and more particularly in the letter of 28 October 1999 from the law firm of Howard and Heward to Sports and More Sports (Claimant's Exhibit No 10) that 'the claim of the Vis Fish Company to trade mark infringement is unfounded.'

4 As a result, Vis Water Sports denies that it has breached its obligations under article 42, United Nations Convention on Contracts for the International Sale of Goods. The water sports equipment that it sold to Sports and More Sports under the Vis Water Sports trademark were free from any right or claim of a third person.

5 Furthermore, even if it is the case that the Vis Fish Company had registered the trademark 'Vis' for all water-related products, that by itself would not be sufficient to establish that Vis Water Sports knew or should

have known that the Vis Fish Company would attempt to assert a claim in regard to athletic equipment, a field in which they have never engaged. A search of the Internet will show that the name 'Vis' is used by many companies in many different fields of business. They are not all infringing each other's trade mark, so long as the businesses are separate and there is no confusion between them.

6 Sports and More Sports first became aware that the Vis Fish Company was attempting to assert a trademark infringement claim when Sports received the letter from the Vis Fish Company dated 20 September 1999. (Claimant's Exhibit No 7.) It first notified Vis Water Sports about this assertion of trademark infringement six weeks later in its letter of 3 November 1999. The primary purpose of that letter was not, however, to inform Vis Water Sports about the assertion of trademark infringement, but to assert that it was avoiding the contract of sale between it and Vis Water Sports. (Claimant's Exhibit No 12.) The notification to Vis Water Sports of the assertion of trademark infringement was not made within a reasonable time. Therefore, Sports and More Sports is not permitted to rely upon it.

7 Sports and More Sports asserted that it had avoided the contract under article 49, United Nations Convention on Contracts for the International Sale of Goods. In order to avoid the contract, it would be necessary for there to have been a fundamental breach of contract on the part of Vis Water Sports. Even if one takes the assertions of Sports and More Sports at face value, they do not amount to fundamental breach of the contract. Therefore, the asserted avoidance of the contract by the letter of 3 November 1999 (Claimant's Exhibit No 12) did not occur.

III Comments on the Relief Sought

8 Sports and More Sports has claimed relief on the basis of articles 81 to 84, United Nations Convention on Contracts for the International Sale of Goods. Since there was no effective avoidance of the contract, no relief under those provisions is due.

9 On the assumption that the avoidance was proper, Sports and More Sports has claimed as damages the general selling and administrative costs of the goods sold by it prior to its asserted avoidance of the contract. Since they refer to these costs as 'allocated' costs, it appears that they are applying to this contract the average of their general selling and administrative costs. The damages they would have a right to claim would be the additional costs incurred by them in regard to the goods purchased from Vis Water Sports, and not an allocated share of costs that would include their general overhead.

10 If Sports and More Sports had the right to avoid the contract, and they had sold goods in the normal course of business, they would have to account

for the benefit they had derived from the goods. Article 84 United Nations Convention on Contracts for the International Sale of Goods. Since they state that they have sold goods to the extent of one-third of that which they purchased from Vis Water Sports, their delivered cost including transportation and freight would be $211,000. The normal retail mark-up on Vis Water Sports products is 70 percent of delivered purchase cost. Therefore, an estimated gross profit on the sales by Sports and More Sports of $147,700 is claimed as an off-set on their claim.

11 Vis Water Sports claims from Sports and More Sports the costs of arbitration, including legal costs as provided in the ICC Arbitration Rules, article 31.

IV Lack of arbitration clause

12 Vis Water Sports contests the jurisdiction of the arbitral tribunal for lack of agreement on an arbitration clause. We acknowledge that the clause set out in the Request for Arbitration, paragraph 18, appears as clause 14 of the Sports and More Sports General Conditions of Purchase. We also acknowledge that a copy of the General Conditions were attached to the e-mail message of 5 April 1999 from Mr Hirst to Mr Singer by which Sports and More Sports transmitted to Vis Water Sports its purchase order No 6839. Therefore, we acknowledge that there is a prima facie arbitration clause and we do not request the ICC Court to reject the Request for Arbitration as provided in the ICC Arbitration Rules, article 6(2). We do request the arbitral tribunal that is to be established to decide that the arbitration clause in Sports and More Sports General Conditions of Purchase was not agreed to by Vis Water Sports and is not applicable to the dispute.

13 The reply from Mr Singer of Vis Water Sports to Mr Hirst of Sports and More Sports acknowledging the purchase order dated 6 April 1999 stated: 'I should like to remind you that our General Conditions of Sale, which we include in all sales contracts, are available at [URL omitted]. I suggest that you take a look at them.' (Claimant's Exhibit No 4.) These words are a clear statement that any contract of sale concluded by Vis Water Sports must include those General Conditions. The General Conditions of Sale that were on the web site referred to included a forum selection clause in its clause 23. This forum selection clause provided:

> Any dispute in regard to or arising out of this contract shall be submitted to the Commercial Court in Capitol City, Equatoriana.

14 According to article 19 of the United Nations Convention on Contracts for the International Sale of Goods, when the reply to an offer contains an additional or different term relating to the settlement of disputes, the reply constitutes a rejection of the offer and constitutes a counter-offer.

Therefore, the effective offer in the contract was made by Vis Water Sports and contained its forum selection clause calling for disputes to be settled in the Commercial Court in Capitol City, Equatoriana.

15 Both parties treated the two shipments as a single contract or, at least, as two closely related contracts. Therefore, the forum selection clause agreed upon by the parties in regard to the shipment requested by purchase order no 6839 also was applicable to the shipment requested by purchase order no 6910.

V Arbitrators

16 The arbitration clause in the General Conditions of Purchase clause 14 calls for an arbitral tribunal of three for any dispute of more than $400,000. While a dispute of that size does not merit a tribunal of three and only increases the costs, we do not dispute it.

17 We nominate as one of the members of the tribunal Ms Xxxx xxxx. Her address is (omitted).

VI Place of arbitration, rules of law and language

18 The arbitration clause provides that the place of arbitration will be Vindobona, Danubia and the language of the arbitration will be English. We do not contest either.

19 We also have no comments to make on the rules of law applicable to the dispute as set out in the Request for Arbitration, paragraphs 20 and 21.

Signed 10 July 2000

Attorneys for Vis Water Sports

International Court of Arbitration
Cour internationale d'arbitrage

Letter to the parties notifying Respondent's Answer 13 July 2000

Moot No 8

Sports and More Sports, Inc (Danubia) v/ Vis Water Sports Co (Equatoriana)

Counsel in charge of the file: *** (Direct dial: 33 1 49 53 ** **) (Direct fax: 33 1 49 53 ** **)

Mr ***

Address ***

Fax: ******

Mr ***

Address ***

Fax: ******

Dear Madams/Sirs,

The Secretariat hereby acknowledges receipt of Respondent's Answer dated 10 July 2000.

In accordance with Article 5(4) of the Rules, a copy of said Answer is enclosed for Claimant's information.

We note that Respondent shall be represented in this matter by *** of *** in Equatoriana. Accordingly, all future correspondence addressed to Respondent shall henceforth be sent solely to ***.

Constitution of the Arbitral Tribunal

The Secretariat notes that in accordance with the arbitration clause referred to in the Request, which provides for a three-member Arbitral Tribunal, you have nominated Ms *** as an arbitrator. By separate letter of today, we are sending Ms *** the necessary forms to be completed before his/her confirmation as an arbitrator.

Article 6(2) of the Rules

We note that Respondent has set forth jurisdictional objections, indicating that the arbitration clause in the General Conditions of Purchase did not become part of the contract between the parties. Claimant is hereby invited to provide its comments on Respondent's jurisdictional objections by 20 July 2000. Thereafter, the Court will be invited to examine the setting in motion of this matter, in accordance with Article 6(2) of the Rules.

…/…

Moot No 8

Page 2

Provisional advance

As the provisional advance has been fully paid, in accordance with Article 13 of the Rules, the file shall be transmitted to the Arbitral Tribunal once fully constituted.

Yours sincerely,

***

/*Counsel
Secretariat of the ICC International Court of Arbitration

Encl: (for Claimant) copy of Respondent's Answer

19 July 2000

Secretariat of the ICC International Court of Arbitration
38, Cours Albert 1er
75008 Paris, France

Re: Moot No 8

Sports and More Sports, Inc v Vis Water Sports Co

Dear ****,

I refer to your letter of 13 July 2000 notifying to me the Respondent's answer in the above referenced case. You have indicated that Claimant, Sports and More Sports, Inc should provide its comments on Respondent's jurisdictional objections by 20 July 2000.

As is noted in the Request for Arbitration, paragraphs 17 and 18, the Claimant's General Conditions of Purchase were attached the e-mail message sent by Mr Hirst of Sports and More Sports, Inc to Mr Singer of Vis Water Sports Co dated 5 April 1999. (Claimant's Exhibit No 3.) The message stated that the General Conditions of Purchase were part of the purchase order No 6839. When it came time to send the e-mail message conveying purchase order No 6910, it was obvious that Vis Water Sports Co already had the General Conditions of Purchase, so they were not attached. However, the body of the e-mail message referred to them, clearly indicating that they were part of that purchase order as well.

The ICC Arbitration Clause was clause 14 of those General Conditions of Purchase, which part of both contracts of purchase.

The Respondent claims that its General Conditions of Sale, which contain the forum selection clause providing for litigation in the Commercial Court in Capitol City, Equatoriana, superseded the General Conditions of Purchase. However, while the e-mail message of 6 April 1999 from Mr Singer to Mr Hirst accepting our purchase order No 6839 stated that they included those

General Conditions of Sale in all their sales contracts, there were no words in that message to state that they were including the General Conditions of Sale in this contract. (Claimant's Exhibit No 4.)

Moreover, even if one were to find that their General Conditions of Sale were applicable to the first contract, they would not be applicable to the second contract formed by the exchange of messages on 27 and 28 May 1999. (Claimant's Exhibits Nos 5 and 6.) They were not even mentioned by Vis Water Sports Inc, much less made a part of the contract.

Consequently, Sports and More Sports, Inc would request the Court, and subsequently the Arbitral Tribunal, to find that the Arbitral Tribunal has jurisdiction in this dispute.

Sincerely,

(Signed)

Counsel for Sports and More Sports, Inc

International Court of Arbitration
Cour internationale d'arbitrage

Letter to the parties notifying the Court's decisions 26 July 2000

Moot No 8

Sports and More Sports, Inc (Danubia) v/ Vis Water Sports Co (Equatoriana)

Counsel in charge of the file: *** (Direct dial: 33 1 49 53 ** **) (Direct fax: 33 1 49 53 ** **) (Direct fax: 33 1 49 53 ** **)

Mr ***

Address ***

Fax: ******

Mr ***

Address ***

Fax: ******

Dear Madams/Sirs,

Please be advised that the International Court of Arbitration, at its session of 26 July 2000, took the following decisions in this matter. The Court:

1 decided that this matter shall proceed in accordance with Article 6(2) of the ICC Rules;

2 took the necessary steps for the appointment of the Chairman of the Arbitral Tribunal;

3 fixed the advance on costs at US$ 80,000, subject to later readjustments.

Pursuant to Articles 30(2) of the Rules and Article 1(4) of Appendix III, the advance on costs is fixed to cover the fees of the Arbitral Tribunal, the out-of-pocket expenses, if any, and the ICC administrative expenses. In the present matter, the advance on costs has been fixed on the basis of the information available to the Court to date, and is based on an amount in dispute quantified at US$ 480,000 and taking into account that there shall be a three-member Arbitral Tribunal.

Depending on the evolution of the matter, the Court may readjust the advance on costs at a later date.

In conformity with Article 30(3) of the Rules, the parties shall be invited to pay within 30 days from the day following the date of transmission of the file to the Arbitral Tribunal, the advance on costs in the following manner:

.../...

Moot No 8

Page 2

– Claimant: US$ 22 000 (US $ 40 000 less US$ 18 000 already paid)
– Respondent: US$ 40 000

We remind the parties that as the provisional advance has been fully paid, in accordance with Article 13 of the Rules, the file shall be transmitted to the Arbitral Tribunal once fully constituted.

Yours sincerely,

/*

/*Counsel
Secretariat of the ICC International Court of Arbitration

cc: Coarbitrators

International Court of Arbitration
Cour internationale d'arbitrage

Letter to the Arbitral Tribunal for transmission of the file 9 August 2000

Moot No 8

Sports and More Sports, Inc (Danubia) v/ Vis Water Sports Co (Equatoriana)

Counsel in charge of the file: *** (Direct dial: 33 1 49 53 ** **) (Direct fax: 33 1 49 53 ** **)

Mr ***

Address ***

Fax: ******

Mr ***

Address ***

Fax: ******

Mr ***

Address ***

Fax: ******

Dear Madams/Sirs,

In accordance with Article 13 of the ICC Rules, the Secretariat herewith forwards to you the file in the above-referenced case. The file consists of the documents on the attached list. [Not attached.]

The Secretariat takes this opportunity to draw your attention to the following points:

I Constitution of the Arbitral Tribunal

On 9 August 2000, the Court appointed *** as Chairman of the Arbitral Tribunal upon proposal of the Mediterraneo National Committee.

On 20 July 2000, the Secretary General, pursuant to Article 9(2) of the Rules, confirmed Dr *** as coarbitrator upon the proposal of Claimant and Ms *** as coarbitrator upon the proposal of Respondent.

II Names and addresses of the parties to the proceedings

- Claimant:

  Sports and More Sports, Inc

  Represented by: ***
- Respondent:

  Vis Water Sports Co

  Represented by: ***

III Place of arbitration

Vindobona (Danubia) is the place of arbitration.

IV Financial status of the file

Based on the information in the Secretariat's possession, the Secretary General fixed the provisional advance at US$ 18,000, which is intended to cover the costs of this arbitration until the Terms of Reference have been drawn up, in accordance with Article 30(1).

The provisional advance has been fully paid by Claimant.

The Court, at its session of 26 July 2000, fixed the advance on costs at US$ 80,000, subject to later readjustments. To date, the advance on costs has been paid by the parties in the following manner:

- Claimant: US$ 18,000
- Respondent: ———

As indicated in Article 30(2) of the Rules and Article 1(4) of Appendix III, the advance on costs covers the fees of the Arbitral Tribunal, the reimbursable expenses and the ICC administrative expenses.

Depending on the evolution of the matter, the Court may readjust the advance on costs at a later date.

The amount in dispute is presently quantified at US$ 480,000.

The Secretariat encourages the Arbitral Tribunal to state the amount in dispute in the Terms of Reference as precisely as possible. Furthermore, during the course of the proceedings, the Arbitral Tribunal should inform the Secretariat of any change in the amount in dispute in order to permit the Court to consider whether any adjustment of the advance on costs is appropriate.

V Procedure

Your first task is to establish the Terms of Reference and the provisional timetable, in accordance with Article 18 of the Rules. In this regard, we draw your attention to the time-limit of two months within which the Terms of Reference must be transmitted to the Court.

The Court attaches particular importance to the rapid resolution of arbitrations conducted under its Rules. You should therefore make every effort to finalize the Terms of Reference within the period provided for in the Rules. Although extensions of time may be granted by the Court, avoidable delay in the completion of the Terms of Reference may be taken into account by the Court in fixing the arbitrators' fees (see Article 2(2) of Appendix III). Moreover, Article 12(2) of the Rules provides that an arbitrator shall be replaced when the Court decides that he is not fulfilling his functions within the prescribed time-limits.

You are also advised that:

(i) when drawing up the Terms of Reference, or as soon as possible thereafter, the Arbitral Tribunal, after having consulted with the parties, shall establish in a separate document a provisional timetable that it intends to follow for the conduct of the arbitration and communicate it to the Court and the parties (see Article 18(4) of the Rules);

(ii) pursuant to Article 24(1) of the Rules, the time-limit within which the Arbitral Tribunal must render its final Award is six months, running from the date of the last signature of the Terms of Reference, or in case of application of Article 18(3) of the Rules, from the date of the Secretariat's notification to the Arbitral Tribunal of the Court's approval of the Terms of Reference;

(iii) although the Rules permit this time-limit to be extended by the Court if necessary, we would like to emphasize the importance of conducting the arbitration proceedings as rapidly as may be reasonably possible in the circumstances; and

(iv) when the Arbitral Tribunal shall have declared the proceedings closed according to Article 22(1) of the Rules, it should indicate to the Secretariat an approximate date by which the draft Award shall be submitted to the Court for approval (see Article 22(2) of the Rules).

VI Payment of fees and reimbursement of expenses

When the Arbitral Tribunal is composed of three members, unless the arbitrators inform us in writing that they have agreed to a different allocation, the Court normally fixes the fees of the arbitrators so that the Chairman receives 40% of the total fees and each coarbitrator receives 30%. However, the Court may decide upon a different allocation based on the circumstances of the case.

Please find enclosed a note concerning the reimbursement of arbitrators' expenses.

We also draw your attention to Article 2(9) of Appendix III of the Rules, which states that the amounts paid to the arbitrators do not include any possible value-added taxes (VAT), and that the recovery of any such taxes payable by the arbitrators in respect of their fees is a matter solely between the arbitrators and the parties.

VII Correspondence

The parties should henceforth correspond directly with the Arbitral Tribunal and send copies of their correspondence to the other party and to the Secretariat. The Arbitral Tribunal is invited to send a copy of all its correspondence with the parties to the Secretariat.

VIII Article 6(2) of the Rules

At its session of 26 July 2000 the Court, being *prima facie* satisfied that an arbitration agreement under the Rules may exist, decided that this arbitration shall proceed. This decision being administrative in nature, the Arbitral Tribunal must still decide on its own jurisdiction pursuant to Article 6(2) of the Rules.

Yours sincerely,

/***

/*Counsel
Secretariat of the ICC International Court of Arbitration

Encl: – Copy of the Secretariat's letter of today to the parties
– List of Documents and documents mentioned therein
– Note regarding Personal and Arbitral Tribunal Expenses
– Curriculum vitae of your fellow arbitrators

cc: parties

ICC, International Court of Arbitration

Sports and More Sports, Inc
Claimant
v
Vis Water Sports Co
Respondent

TERMS OF REFERENCE

1 These Terms of Reference are prepared pursuant to ICC Arbitration Rules, Article 18.

I Parties

2 Sports and More Sports, Inc (hereafter referred to as 'Sports') is a corporation organized under the laws of Danubia. It has its principal office at 214 Commercial Ave, Oceanside, Danubia. The telephone number is 555-1212, the fax number is 555-1214 and e-mail sports@sportsandmoresports.da. Sports is the largest retail seller of athletic equipment of all types in the country of Danubia.

3 Vis Water Sports Co is a corporation organized under the laws of Equatoriana. It has its principal office at 395 Industrial Place, Capitol City, Equatoriana. The telephone number is 483-5800, the fax number is 483-5810 and e-mail info@watersports.com.eq. Vis is a manufacturer of equipment for water sports.

II Claims of the Parties

Jurisdiction

4 Vis Water Sports contests the jurisdiction of the Arbitral Tribunal. It acknowledges that there was a standard ICC arbitration clause (with three additions) in the General Conditions of Purchase attached to the e-mail message dated 5 April 1999 conveying purchase order No 6839. (Claimant's Exhibit No 3.) However, it claims that the message from Mr Singer dated 6 April 1999 in reply operated as a rejection of the offer from Sports and More Sports and constituted a counter-offer by Vis Water Sports. In particular, it claims that its General Conditions of Sale, to which Mr Singer referred and gave the URL, contained a forum selection clause selecting the Commercial Court in Capitol City, Equatoriana as the forum for any dispute settlement. (Claimant's Exhibit No 4.)

5 Vis Water Sports claims that its forum selection clause relates to both shipments of goods, the shipment pursuant to purchase order No 6839 and that pursuant to purchase order No 6910.

6 Sports and More Sports relies on the arbitration clause in its General Conditions of Purchase attached to its e-mail message of 5 April 1999 conveying purchase order No 6839. (Claimant's Exhibit No 3.) Although they were not attached to the e-mail message of 27 May 1999 conveying purchase order No 6910 'Since you already have a copy of our General Conditions of Purchase', Sports and More Sports claims that the arbitration clause applies to that shipment as well. (Claimant's Exhibit No 5.)

Article 42, United Nations Convention on Contracts for the International Sale of Goods

7 Sports and More Sports claims that Vis Water Sports failed to deliver goods that were free from the claim of a third party based on intellectual property, as required by article 42, United Nations Convention on Contracts for the International Sale of Goods. It cites in this respect the letters from Vis Fish Company dated 20 September 1999 and 15 October 1999 in which it is claimed that the advertising for sale and the selling of goods in Danubia bearing the Vis Water Sports name infringed on their registered trademark 'Vis'.

8 Vis Water Sports disputes that it has delivered goods that were not free from a right or claim of a third party based on intellectual property. There is agreement between the parties that the assertions of the Vis Fish Company of trademark infringement are unlikely to be upheld in litigation in Danubia. The parties disagree whether the threat of litigation by a third party for trademark infringement, even though the claimed infringement is not likely to be upheld, is sufficient to invoke article 42.

9 There is no claim that Vis Water Sports had ever heard of the Vis Fish Company prior to the letter from Sports and More Sports dated 3 November 1999. (Claimant's Exhibit No 12.) They disagree whether Vis Water Sports 'could not have been unaware' of the fact that the Vis Fish Company had registered in Danubia the trademark 'Vis' for all water-related goods and that this might lead to a claim of trademark infringement.

Article 43, United Nations Convention on Contracts for the International Sale of Goods

10 Sports and More Sports first learned of the assertion of trademark infringement by the Vis Fish Company when it received the letter from them dated 20 September 1999. (Claimant's Exhibit No 7.) It did not notify Vis Water Sports of the assertion of trademark infringement until it sent its letter to them avoiding the contract. That letter was dated 3 November 1999, approximately six weeks later. (Claimant's Exhibit No 12.) Vis Water Sports claims that that was more than the reasonable time allowed under article 43 and that as a result Sports and More Sports has lost any right it may have had under article 42.

Article 49, United Nations Convention on Contracts for the International Sale of Goods

11 Sports and More Sports claims to have avoided the contract or contracts between it and Vis Water Sports by its letter of 3 November 1999 in accord with article 49, United Nations Convention on Contracts for the International Sale of Goods. (Claimant's Exhibit No 12.) Vis Water Sports contests that there was an effective avoidance of the contract on two grounds. The first is that Sports and More Sports cannot rely on any alleged failure by Vis Water Sports under article 42 for the reasons given above. The second is that, even if there was a failure to deliver goods free from the claim of a third person based on intellectual property, there was no fundamental breach of contract as required by article 49.

Articles 82–84, United Nations Convention on Contracts for the International Sale of Goods

12 Sports and More Sports claims for mutual restitution and damages pursuant to articles 82 to 84, United Nations Convention on Contracts for the International Sale of Goods. The total monetary claim as presently constituted is for $480,000. Sports and More Sports also asks for additional damages that will accrue from the date of its Request for Arbitration until mutual restitution is made. It also asks for interest on the purchase price to be reimbursed and for costs of arbitration.

13 Vis Water Sports does not contest the right of Sports and More Sports to claim restitution, if it is found to have had a right to avoid the contract. However, it claims the right to receive the benefit that Vis Water Sports had from all goods delivered under the contract of which Sports and More Sports is unable to make restitution. It understands that to mean that Sports and More Sports must pay to Vis Water Sports the difference between the cost to it of the goods it sold at retail and the retail price it received. Vis Water Sports states that the average retail markup on its goods is 70 percent of the delivered cost of the goods. It calculates the benefit to which it would be entitled to be $147,700.

14 Vis Water Sports disagrees with the method of determining the general selling and administrative expenses that would constitute part of the damages claimed by Sports and More Sports. It asserts that Sports and More Sports can claim only those expenses that were additional to those that would have been incurred even without the Vis Water Sports goods, ie, that Sports and More Sports cannot claim for an allocated share of the average of their general selling and administrative costs. Allocation of average costs would lead to the reimbursement of expenditures that were not caused by the contract with Vis Water Sports or its avoidance, claims Vis Water Sports.

15 Sports and More Sports claims for interest on the purchase price from the date paid by Sports to the date reimbursement of the price is made by Vis Water Sports as well as on the damages to the date paid by Vis Water Sports. Vis Water Sports has made no comments on this claim.

16 Both Sports and More Sports and Vis Water Sports claim for the costs of arbitration, including the legal costs.

III Names and Addresses of the Arbitrators

17 XXX, Chairman

(Address omitted)

Dr XXX

(Address omitted)

Ms XXX

(Address omitted)

IV Place of Arbitration, Language, Procedural Rules

18 The parties have agreed that the place of arbitration shall be Vindobona, Danubia. The arbitration shall be conducted in English.

19 The parties have agreed that, pursuant to ICC Arbitration Rules, Article 15, the Arbitral Tribunal shall have the power to decide on the rules of procedure to be followed where the ICC Arbitration Rules themselves are silent. The parties have agreed that the Arbitral Tribunal should consult the IBA Rules on the Taking of Evidence in International Commercial Arbitration currently in force for guidance.

(Signed_________)

Counsel for Claimant, Sports and More Sports, Inc

(Signed_________)

Counsel for Respondent, Vis Water Sports Co

(Signed_________)

Member of the Tribunal

(Signed_________)

Member of the Tribunal

(Signed_________)

President of the Tribunal

6 October 2000

ICC, International Court of Arbitration

Sports and More Sports, Inc
Claimant
v
Vis Water Sports Co
Respondent

PROVISIONAL TIMETABLE

At the joint request of the Parties, they and the Arbitral Tribunal have agreed on the following provisional timetable for the first stages of the arbitration. The Parties and the Tribunal are fully conscious that this will not allow a final Award to be rendered within six months of the signing of the Terms of Reference, as called for by ICC Arbitration Rules, Article 24.

Requests for clarification are due	27 October 2000
Answers to requests for clarification will be distributed	3 November 2000
Submission of Memorandum for Claimant	4 December 2000
Submission of Memorandum for Respondent	12 February 2001
Oral argument on legal issues	7 –12 April 2001

The Parties have agreed to meet the evening of 6 April 2001 prior to the commencement of oral argument for a general introduction to one another. They are also aware of the festivities organized the evening of 5 April 2001 by the Moot Alumni Association and have agreed to attempt to be present.

Moot No 8

Sports and More Sports, Inc
Claimant
v
Vis Water Sports Co
Respondent

Procedural Order No 1

The Provisional Timetable for this arbitration attached to the Terms of Reference provided that Requests for Clarification of the file would be submitted by 27 October 2000 and that the Answers to those Requests would be distributed by 3 November 2000. The following Requests have been submitted and the Answers immediately follow them.
Counsel
Secretariat of the ICC International Court of Arbitration
31 October 2000

Legal Rules

1 Have either Danubia or Equatoriana made any reservations to the United Nations Convention on Contracts for the International Sale of Goods?

No.

2 Have either Danubia or Equatoriana adopted any law pertaining to electronic commerce?

Both have adopted the UNCITRAL Model Law on Electronic Commerce. It is available from the UNCITRAL web site, http://www.uncitral.org/.

3 Is either Danubia or Equatoriana a member of the European Union?

No.

Trademark

4 Are Danubia and Equatoriana parties to any convention regarding trademarks as intellectual property?

Danubia and Equatoriana are both parties to the following conventions that relate to trade marks:

Paris Convention for the Protection of Industrial Property

Madrid Agreement Concerning the International Registration of Marks

Protocol Relating to the Madrid Agreement Concerning the International Registration of Marks

Nice Agreement Concerning the International Classification of Goods and Services for the Purposes of the Registration of Marks

Trademark Law Treaty

Agreement on Trade-Related Aspects of Intellectual Property Rights (TRIPS)

All of the agreements with the exception of TRIPS are available on the web site of the World Intellectual Property Organization http://www.wipo.int/. TRIPS is Annex 1C to the Uruguay Round Final Act and is administered by and to be found on the web site of the World Trade Organization http://www.wto.org/.

5 What is the nature of the law regarding trademarks in Danubia?

The relevant provision, article 23 of the Trademark Law, provides:

The owner of a registered trademark shall have the exclusive right to prevent all third parties not having the owner's consent from using in the course of trade identical or similar signs for goods or services which are identical or similar to those in respect of which the trademark is registered where such use would result in a likelihood of confusion.

6 Does registration give notice to all of the existence of the trademark?

The relevant provision is article 23 of the Trademark Law quoted above. There is nothing in the statute or any of the known decisions applying the law that uses the word 'notice'. However, there have been successful infringement actions against parties who did not actually know of the trademark that they had infringed.

7 In which classes of the Nice Agreement Concerning the International Classification of Goods and Services for the Purposes of the Registration of Marks has the Vis Fish Company trademark been registered?

The trademark has been registered in classes 22, 28 and 29. At the present time the Vis Fish Company sells only edible fish and other seafood products under the Vis trademark. They are in class 29. Until January 1996 it also sold under the Vis trademark sports fishing equipment, which is in class 28, and fishing nets, which are in class 22.

Class 22 Ropes, string, nets tents, awnings, tarpaulins, tarpaulins, sails, sacks. Padding and stuffing materials (hair, kapok, feathers, seaweed, etc), raw fibrous textile materials.

Class 28 Games and playthings; gymnastic and sporting articles not included in other classes; decorations for Christmas trees.

Class 29 Meat, fish, poultry and game; meat extracts; preserved, dried and cooked fruits and vegetables; jellies, jams, fruit sauces; eggs, milk and milk products; edible oils and fats.

8 Does Danubia permit broad trademarks even though the owner is using it in only a restricted way?

Under the law of Danubia it was permissible to use the term 'all water related products' in the trademark application so long as the categories were indicated in which the trademark was being used. When renewing the trademark, the owner has to certify as to the categories in which the trademark is continuing to be used. The trademark does not lapse as to products for which it is not being used until the expiration of the registration. The owner of the trademark could bring an action for trademark infringement during the period of registration in regard to products which had carried the trademark if it could show that it intended to use the mark in connection with the product during the remaining period of registration.

9 Is there a public register in which the name 'Vis' for the Vis Fish Company was registered?

Yes. All registered trademarks are in a registry that can be consulted freely by the public. The registry is not on the Internet. Registry searches are normally undertaken by lawyers or other professional specialists, especially for clients outside of the capital city where it is located. Registrations are also published in a journal.

10 When did the Vis Fish Company register its trademark and for how long is it valid?

The trademark was first registered on 25 September 1972. A registration is valid for ten years and can be renewed for an additional period of ten years. The last renewal was in 1992.

11 Does the trademark law of Danubia permit a court to prohibit the sale of the product allegedly infringing a trademark pending final resolution of the claim?

Yes, it is possible, but rarely ordered by the court.

12 When did Sports and More Sports make its inquiry at the offices of Howard & Heward?

21 October 1999.

13 When did Sports and More Sports cease selling the Vis Water Sports equipment?

3 November 1999, the same day on which it sent the letters set out in Claimant's Exhibits Nos 11 and 12.

14 What was the nature of the earlier case in which the Vis Fish Company had aggressively defended its trademark?

No cases have gone to trial. There have been two cases in which an infringement action was begun but the defendant company agreed to stop using the name 'Vis' prior to any decision by the court. In one case the goods concerned were stuffing material made from seaweed and in the other playground equipment. There is no public information as to why the two companies decided to stop using the name 'Vis'.

15 Did Vis Fish Company take legal action against Sports and More Sports within one week after its threat of legal action?

No.

16 Is the Vis Fish Company a well-known company?

It is well known throughout Danubia for its fish and related food products. It does not conduct business outside of Danubia.

17 Does the word 'Vis' have any significance in Danubia other than as it may be associated with the products of particular companies?

No, in Danubia the word in itself has no association with fish or any geographical or other association. The word is known as a name only through the promotion of the Vis Fish Company and more recently of the Vis Water Sports equipment by Sports and More Sports.

18 Did Sports and More Sports know of the Vis Fish Company?

Since the company was well known in Danubia for its fish and other water-related products, the relevant personnel in Sports and More Sports were aware of it.

19 Did Vis Water Sports know of the Vis Fish Company prior to 31 March 1999?

They had no actual knowledge of its existence.

20 Did Vis Water Sports conduct an Internet search under the word 'Vis' before selling their goods to Sports and More Sports?

No, but they would not have found the Vis Fish Company if they had since at that time the Vis Fish Company did not have a web site.

21 Did Vis Water Sports perform a trademark search in Danubia before they contracted with Sports and More Sports?

No. If they had they would easily have found the registration.

22 Who created the slogan 'like a fish in water'?

It is the slogan used by Vis Water Sports Company to advertise its products. It encourages retailers selling its products to advertise using the slogan. It is not registered in any country.

23 Was the name 'Vis' removable from the goods without damaging the equipment?

No.

24 Is the name Vis Water Sports registered as a trademark?

It is registered in Equatoriana and in several other countries where the equipment is sold. It is not registered in Danubia.

25 Is the name Vis Water Sports a well known name?

It is well known in Equatoriana. It began to export only in 1995 and to date sells in only seven other countries. In those countries it is reasonably well known. It is not well known in other countries, but it is known to firms like Sports and More Sports that are in the trade. It was not well known in Danubia until Sports and More Sports began to advertise and sell the products, and even now it is only somewhat better known.

26 Could Sports and More Sports have asked Vis Water Sports to conduct the trademark infringement litigation on behalf of Sports and More Sports?

Under the procedural law of Danubia Sports and More Sports could not have required Vis Water Sports to participate in the litigation. The most it could have done was request Vis Water Sports to aid Sports and More Sports in the litigation and to pay for it.

27 What did Vis Water Sports mean when it offered to pay 'reasonable' legal costs of Sports and More Sports should those costs not be recoverable from Vis Fish Company?

See United Nations Convention on Contracts for the International Sale of Goods, Article 8. Remember that Vis Water Sports and Sports and More Sports are from different countries where the system and amount of lawyers' fees may be quite different. It should not be assumed that either knew the practice in the other country for determining the level of compensation for a lawyer's services.

28 What is standard practice in Danubia for dealing with goods subject to a claim of trademark infringement?

There is no standard practice. It depends on the circumstances of the individual case.

29 Has Vis Water Sports taken any steps to contact Vis Fish Company or vice versa?

No.

30 When did Sports and More Sports withdraw the Vis Water Sports equipment from sale?

On 3 November 1999, the same day on which it sent the letters to the Vis Fish Company and to Vis Water Sports Company (Claimant's Exhibits Nos 11 and 12).

Communications

31 How long did it take for the various communications to arrive at their destination?

E-mail messages arrived essentially instantaneously. Domestic letters arrived on the second business day. International letters arrived on the third business day.

Contract of Sale

32 Was it normal practice for Vis Water Sports or Sports and More Sports to contract by exchange of e-mails?

It had not been several years ago, but both companies were beginning to do so.

33 Can a binding legal contract be concluded by e-mail in Equatoriana or Danubia?

The relevant text is the United Nations Convention on Contracts for the International Sale of Goods.

34 What is the location of the servers that Vis Water Sports and Sports and More Sports used for their e-mail correspondence?

The Internet Service Providers and their servers were located in Equatoriana and Danubia respectively.

35 Neither the Conditions of Sale nor the Conditions of Purchase are reproduced. Do they contain any provisions that might be relevant to the dispute?

In both sets of General Conditions the only provision that might be relevant to the case is the dispute settlement provision, ie, clause 14 of the Conditions of Purchase quoted in paragraph 18 of the Request for Arbitration and clause 23 of the General Conditions of Sale quoted in paragraph 13 of the Answer to the Request for Arbitration. Specifically, neither set of General Conditions provided that the General Conditions would prevail in case of conflict or that no contract could be entered into unless the other party accepted all of the terms of the General Conditions and neither provided for a choice of law.

In both cases the arbitration clause and the choice of forum clause were reasonably conspicuous. In both cases the General Conditions were in English.

36 Were the Sports and More Sports' Conditions of Purchase in the same e-mail attachment as Purchase Order No 6839 (Claimant's Exhibit No 3)?

There were two separate attachments to the e-mail message. One contained the purchase order and the other contained the General Conditions of Purchase. Vis Water Sports opened both attachments.

37 Were the Vis Water Sports General Conditions of Sale easily available?

The web page on which it was possible to see what goods were offered for sale and the list price contained a link to the General Conditions of Sale. It was easy to open the link. It was not necessary to do so in order to place an order from the web site and obviously it was not necessary to do so if placing an order by e-mail. The links in the e-mails from Jonathon Singer, Sales Manager, Vis Water Sports Company, dated 2 April 1999 and 6 April

1999 (Claimant's Exhibits Nos 2 and 4) went directly to the General Conditions.

38 Is it correct, as stated in the e-mail of 6 April 1999 (Claimant's Exhibit No 4), that Vis Water Sports includes its General Conditions of Sale in all its sales contracts?

Yes, as to first contracts with a customer. Of course, as in this case, the buyer may send his General Conditions as well. When a purchaser becomes a regular customer a negotiated contract is often concluded.

39 Are forum selection clauses valid in Equatoriana and Danubia?

Yes, with certain restrictions, none of which are relevant in this case.

40 Was Vis Water Sports aware of the discrepancy between the dispute resolution clauses contained in each party's General Conditions?

As so often happens, neither party read the other party's General Conditions. As experienced businesses, both were aware as a general matter that the general conditions of their trading partners, and especially those from another country, were never identical to their own in one respect or another.

41 Was the Vis Water Sports web site only for business-to-business purposes or could consumers also order from it?

The site was only for business-to-business sales. Vis Water Sports does not sell directly to consumers.

42 Does Vis Water Sports sell to other business by means other than the Internet?

Yes. The web site is relatively new and most of its business is still conducted by mail, fax and the telephone.

43 Did Vis Water Sports send its advertisement that first told Sports and More Sports about the web site to any other retailers in Danubia?

Yes, but no others responded to it.

44 Does Vis Water Sports normally combine multiple orders into one order solely for the purpose of providing a discount?

It has done so before, especially with a new customer. Once the customer is established a discount is usually given on the basis of the yearly total sales.

Goods Sold

45 Were the $200,000 worth of goods sold from the first delivery, from the second delivery or some from both?

$50,000 worth of the goods were from the first delivery and $150,000 were from the second delivery.

46 What kinds of water sports equipment were purchased?

There were surfboards, wind surfboards, water skis, scuba diving equipment, water slides for installation by a pool and other items of similar nature. There was no fishing equipment of any type.

Letter of Credit and payment mechanisms

47 Why was the letter of credit mentioned in Claimant's Exhibit No 4 required to be for $112,200 when the *pro forma* invoice showed the total price to be $102,000?

It is normal business practice for the letter of credit to be for an amount 10 percent higher than the *pro forma* invoice. It is not unusual that there are additional charges to those set out in the *pro forma* invoice for which the buyer will be responsible. An easy example is in a contract for the sale of a commodity, eg, wheat. The contract price will usually be measured by a quantity of volume, weight or the like. It is often impossible to load an exact amount. Therefore, the letter of credit is larger than the anticipated payment to be able to cover any extra amounts or charges.

48 Did Sports and More Sports pay for the two shipments by one payment or by two?

Sports and More Sports made two separate payments. The first for $102,000 was paid through the letter of credit. The second for $483,000 was also paid through a letter of credit, not otherwise mentioned in the record. The bills of exchange drawn under the letters of credit were paid by the opening bank, and the account of Sports and More Sports was charged, on 10 May 1999 and 25 June 1999 respectively.

Expenses-Damages

49 Did the sale of Vis Water Sports goods increase the general selling and administrative costs for Sports and More Sports?

There are no specific additional expenses associated with the purchase or sale of the Vis Water Sports goods that could be isolated other than the cost of the letters of credit. They totaled $620. The $40,000 of general selling and administrative costs allocated to the Vis Water Sports goods sold was calculated by dividing the total amount of such costs by the total sales and applying that percentage to the amount of Vis Water Sports goods sold. The advertising of the Vis Water Sports equipment was in general newspaper advertisements for the stores and did not constitute expenses that would not otherwise have been incurred. Of course, if the Visa Water Sports Goods had not been advertised, other goods would have been advertised in their place.

50 What was the amount paid to Howard & Heward for its legal opinion in regard to the claim of trademark infringement?

It was paid $2,000.

51 Is the statement in paragraph 10 of the Answer that the normal retail mark-up on Vis Water Sports products is 70 percent of delivered purchase cost accurate?

Yes, the statement is accurate. At this stage of the proceedings, only Sports and More Sports knows if the mark-up it took was at this rate or at some other. If it were to become relevant, it would have to come out in any evidentiary proceedings that would take place subsequently. However, for the purposes of this case, you may assume that Sports and More Sports did take a 70 percent mark-up on the goods sold and would in all probability have taken a 70 percent mark-up on the remaining goods were it not for the claim by Vis Fish Company.

52 Did the unsold goods stored by Sports and More Sports decline in value while being stored? Were they seasonal goods?

No, the goods were not seasonal and they did not decline in value while being stored.

53 In what currency was the purchase price expressed and in what currency have the claimed damages been expressed?

Everything is expressed in US dollars. There is no dispute about the exchange rate of the Danubian currency into dollars.

54 What is the prevailing rate of interest in Danubia and Equatoriana?

In the following table the commercial and interbank rates are for US dollars.

* Equatoriana

  7% Short term commercial lending rate

  4% Official discount rate

  6% Legal rate on unpaid judgments

* London

  6% Short term commercial lending rate

  6.7% Interbank rate (LIBOR)

* Danubia

  5% Short term commercial lending rate

  3% Official discount rate

  4% Legal rate unpaid judgments

55 What is the amount of the legal fees paid to the counsel for Sports and More Sports and for Vis Water Sports?

The amount will be known and assessed by the Arbitral Tribunal under ICC Arbitration Rules, Article 31 at the conclusion of the arbitration.

56 Did Sports and More Sports ever sell outside of Danubia?

No.

57 Would it be possible for Sports and More Sports to sell the Vis Water Sports equipment in another country?

It may be possible. However, since it has never done so, it would not have any easy way to find a buyer and it has no experience in selling either at wholesale or for export.

58 Was the Vis Water Sports line of equipment well-known in Danubia prior to the advertising campaign conducted by Sports and More Sports?

No. As indicated in Claimant's Exhibit No 1 the Vis Water Sports line of equipment had not been previously sold in Danubia.

59 Did Sports and More Sports suffer a loss in total sales by virtue of not selling the entire amount of Vis Water Sports equipment that had been purchased?

Perhaps, but it would be difficult to substantiate. As noted in the letter of 16 November 1999 to Vis Water Sports (Claimant's Exhibit No 14), they are able to sell similar equipment from other suppliers.

60 Can new claims or counterclaims be made?

The question is governed by the ICC Arbitration Rules.

The University of Queensland Memorandum for Respondent

LIST OF ABBREVIATIONS

§	Paragraph
2nd Cir	Second Circuit
9th Cir	Ninth Circuit
AAA	American Arbitration Association
AAA International Arbitration Rules	American Arbitration Association International Arbitration Rules, 1 September 2000
All ER	All England Reports
Arbitration Act 1996 (UK)	Arbitration Act 1996 (United Kingdom)
BGB	*Bürgerliches Gesetzbuch* (Germany)
BIP	*Bundesgesetz für das Internationale Privatrecht* (Switzerland)
Brussels Convention	Convention on the Jurisdiction and Enforcement of Judgements in Civil and Commercial Matters, Brussels
CCPA	Court of Customs and Patent Appeals
CISG	United Nations Convention on Contracts for the International Sale of Goods, Vienna, 11 April 1980
Co	Company
E-Comm Model Law	UNCITRAL Model Law on Electronic Commerce, 1996
ECJ	European Court of Justice
ECR	Reports of Cases before the Court of Justice and the Court of First Instance
Ed	Editor
Eds	Editors
F.2d	Federal Reporter. Second Series
F.Supp	Federal Supplement
HGB (Austria)	*Handelsgesetzbuch* (Austria)
HGB (Germany)	*Handelsgesetzbuch* (Germany)
ICC	International Chamber of Commerce
ICC Court	The International Court of Arbitration

ICC Rules	Rules of Arbitration of the International Chamber of Commerce, 1 January 1998
Inc	Incorporated
Lanham Act	Lanham (Trademark) Act, 15 United States Code
LCIA Rules	London Court of International Arbitration Rules, 1 January 1998
Lloyd's Rep	Lloyd's Reports
MarkenG	*Markengesetz* (Germany)
Model Law	UNCITRAL Model Law on International Commercial Arbitration, 21 June 1985
New York Convention	Convention on the Recognition and Enforcement of Foreign Arbitral Awards, New York, 10 June 1958
Nice Agreement	Nice Agreement Concerning the International Classification of Goods and Services for the Purposes of Registration of Marks, Nice, 15 June 1957
No	Number
Nos	Numbers
SDNY	Southern District of New York
SPORTS	Sports and More Sports, Inc
TRIPS	Agreement on Trade-Related Aspects of Intellectual Property, Marrakesh, 15 April 1994
UCC	Uniform Commercial Code (United States of America)
ULIS	Uniform Law on the International Sale of Goods
UNCITRAL Arbitration Rules	UNCITRAL Arbitration Rules, 15 December 1976
UNIDROIT	International Institute for the Unification of Private Law
UNIDROIT Principles	UNIDROIT Principles of International Commercial Contracts, Rome, 1994
URL	Uniform Resource Locator

	United States Supreme Court Reports
US Dist	United States District Court
USA	United States of America
v	Versus
VIS FISH COMPANY	Vis Fish Company
VIS WATER SPORTS	Vis Water Sports Co
ZPO	*Zivilprozeßordnung* (Germany)

AUTHORITIES CITED

Alpa, G — *Contratto e impresa.* 1996, Europe: CEDAM, [Cited as Alpa]

Andersen, C — 'Reasonable Time in Article 39(1) of the CISG – Is Article 39(1) Truly a Uniform Provision?' (1998) Review of the Convention on Contracts for the International Sale of Goods: 63–176. [Cited as Andersen]

Audit, B — *La vente internationale de marchandises. Convention des Nations-Unies du 11 avril 1980.* Paris: LGDJ, 1990. [Cited as Audit]

Baron, G — 'Do the UNIDROIT Principles of International Commercial Contracts form a new *lex mercatoria*?' (1998)URL: http://www.cisg.law.pace.edu/cisg/biblio/baron.html [Cited as Baron]

Beldarrain, T — 'The Delivery of Goods Not Free from Third-Party Rights or Claims' presentation at XXXVI UIA Congress (Berlin: 26 August 1992). [Cited as Beldarrain]

Benicke, C — '*Zur Vertragsaufhebung nach UN-Kaufrecht bei Lieferung mangelhafter Ware*' (1997) *Praxis des Internationalen Privat – und Verfahrensrechts*: 326–31. [Cited as Benicke]

Berger, K — *The Creeping Codification of the* Lex Mercatoria. 1999, The Hague: Kluwer. [Cited as Berger (1999)]

Berger, K — '*Das neue deutsche Schiedsverfahrensrecht*' (1998) *Deutsche Zeitschrift für Wirtschaftsrecht*: 45–55 [Cited as Berger (1998)]

Bianca, C and Bonell, M (eds) — Commentary on the International Sales Law: The 1980 Vienna Sales Convention. Milan: Dott A Giuffrè Editore, 1987. [Cited as Bianca & Bonell]

Black, H	*Black's Law Dictionary*. St Paul: West Publishing Co, 1990. [Cited as Black]
Board of Governors of the Federal Reserve System	*The Federal Reserve System – Purposes and Functions*. Washington DC: Board of Governors of the Federal Reserve System, 1994. URL: http://www.federalreserve.gov/pf/pdf/frspurp.pdf [Cited as Federal Reserve]
Böckstiegel, K	'The Role of Party Autonomy in International Arbitration' (1997) Dispute Resolution Journal: 24–30. [Cited as Böckstiegel (1997)]
Böckstiegel, K	'The Relevance of National Arbitration Law for Arbitration under the UNCITRAL Rules' (1984) 1 Journal of International Arbitration: 223–36. [Cited as Böckstiegel (1984)]
Bonell, M	*An International Restatement of Contract Law: The UNIDROIT Principles of International Commercial Contracts*. 2nd edn, 1984, New York: Transnational Juris. [Cited as Bonell]
Bonell, M & Bonelli, F	*La vendita internazionale*. Milan: *Quaderni di Giurisprudenza Commerciale*, 1981. [Cited as Bonell & Bonelli]
Born, G	*International Arbitration and Forum Selection Agreement*, 1999, The Hague: Kluwer. [Cited as Born]
Brandner, G	'Admissibility of Analogy in Gap-filling under the CISG' (1999) URL: http://www.cisg.law.pace.edu/cisg/biblio/brandner.html [Cited as Brandner]
Broches, A	*Commentary on the UNCITRAL Model Law on International Commercial Arbitration*, 1999, Deventer: Kluwer. [Cited as Broches]
Bühring-Uhle, C	*Arbitration and Mediation in International Business*, 1996, The Hague: Kluwer. [Cited as Bühring-Uhle]
Carbonneau, T	Lex Mercatoria *and Arbitration. A Discussion of the New Law Merchant*, 1990, New York: Transnational Juris. [Cited as Carbonneau]
Center for Transnational Law (ed)	*Understanding Transnational Commercial Arbitration*, 2000, Münster: Quadis. [Cited as CENTRAL]
Coe, J	*International Commercial Arbitration: American Principles and Practice in a Global Context*, 1997, New York: Transnational Juris, 1997. [Cited as Coe]

Corney, G — 'Obligations and Remedies Under the 1980 Vienna Sales Convention' (1993) 23 Queensland Law Society Journal: 37–58. [Cited as Corney]

Corterier, A — 'A New Approach to Solving the Interest Rate Problem of Art 78 CISG' (2000) 5 International Trade and Business Law Annual: 33–42. [Cited as Corterier]

Craig, W, Park, W and Paulsson, J — *Annotated Guide to the 1998 ICC Arbitration Rules*, 1998, New York: Oceana. [Cited as Craig, Park & Paulsson]

Darkey, J — 'A US Court's Interpretation of Damage Provisions under the UN Convention on Contracts for the International Sale of Goods: A Preliminary Step towards an International Jurisprudence of CISG or a Missed Opportunity?' (1995) 15 Journal of Law and Commerce: 139–52. [Cited as Darkey]

Derains, Y and Schwartz, E — A Guide to the New ICC Rules of Arbitration. The Hague: Kluwer, 1998. [Cited as Derains & Schwartz]

Dodge, W — 'Teaching the CISG in Contracts' (2000) 50 Journal of Legal Education: 72–94. [Cited as Dodge]

Drobnig, U — 'Standard Forms and General Conditions in International Trade: Dutch, German and Uniform Law.' (1983) Hague-Zagreb Essays 4: 117–34. [Cited as Drobnig]

Enderlein, F and Maskow, D — International Sales Law, 1992, New York: Oceana. [Cited as Enderlein & Maskow]

Farnsworth, E — *Contracts*. 2nd edn, 1990, Boston: Little, Brown. [Cited as Farnsworth (1990)]

Farnsworth, E — 'Damages and Specific Relief' (1979) 27 American Journal of Comparative Law: 247–53. [Cited as Farnsworth (1979)]

Ferrari, F — 'CISG Case Law on the Rate of Interest on Sums in Arrears' (1999) Revue de Droit des Affaires Internationales: 86–93. [Cited as Ferrari (1999)]

Ferrari, F — 'General Principles and International Uniform Commercial Law Conventions: A Study of the 1980 Vienna Sales Convention and the 1988 Unidroit Conventions' (1997) Uniform Law Review: 451–73. [Cited as Ferrari (1997)]

Ferrari, F — 'Specific Topics of the CISG in the Light of Judicial Application and Scholarly Writing: The Examination and Notification in Case of Non-Conformity of Goods' (1995) 15 Journal of Law and Commerce: 1–126. [Cited as Ferrari (1995)]

Ferrari, F — 'Uniform Interpretation of the 1980 Uniform Sales Law' (1994) 24 Georgia Journal of International and Comparative Law: 183–228. [Cited as Ferrari (1994)]

Flechtner, H — 'Transcript of a Workshop on the Sales Convention: Leading CISG scholars discuss Contract Formation, Validity, Excuse for Hardship, Avoidance, Nachfrist, Contract Interpretation, Parol Evidence, Analogical Application, and much more' (1999) 18 Journal of Law and Commerce: 191–258. [Cited as Flechtner]

Fox, H — 'States and the Undertaking to Arbitrate' (1998) 37 International and Comparative Law Quarterly: 1–29. [Cited as Fox]

Gabriel, H — 'A Primer on the United Nations Convention on the International Sale of Goods: From the Perspective of the Uniform Commercial Code' (1997) 7 Indiana International and Comparative Law Review: 279–310. [Cited as Gabriel (1997)]

Gabriel, H — *Practitioner's Guide to the Convention on Contracts for the International Sale of Goods (CISG) and the Uniform Commercial Code (UCC)*, 1994, New York: Oceana. [Cited as Gabriel (1994)]

Gaillard, E and Savage, J (eds) — *Fouchard, Gaillard, Goldman on International Commercial Arbitration*, 1999, The Hague: Kluwer. [Cited as Gaillard & Savage]

Galston, N and Smit, H (eds) — *International Sales: The United Nations Convention on Contracts for the International Sale of Goods*, 1984, New York: Matthew Bender. [Cited as Galston & Smit]

Garro, A — 'Reconciliation of Legal Traditions in the U.N. Convention on Contracts for the International Sale of Goods' (1989) 23 International Lawyer: 443–83. [Cited as Garro]

Ghestin, C — '*Les obligations du vendeur selon la Convention de Vienne du 11 avril 1980 sur les contrats de vente internationale de marchandises*' (1988) 13 Revue de droit des affaires internationales: 5–26. [Cited as Ghestin]

Gotanda, J	'Awarding Interest in International Arbitration' (1996) 90 American Journal of International Law: 40-63. [Cited as Gotanda]
Graf von Bernstorff, C	'*Ausgewählte Rechtsprobleme im Electronic Commerce*' (2000) Recht der Internationalen Wirtschaft: 14-20. [Cited as Graf von Bernstorff]
Hill, J	*The Law Relating to International Commercial Disputes*. 2nd edn, 1998, London: LLP Reference Publishing. [Cited as Hill]
Hoellering, M	'International Arbitration under US Law and AAA Rules' (1995) Dispute Resolution Journal: 25–36. [Cited as Hoellering]
Holthausen, R	'*Die wesentliche Vertragsverletzung des Verkäufers nach Art 25 UN-Kaufrecht*' (1990) Recht der Internationalen Wirtschaft: 101–07. [Cited as Holthausen]
Holtzmann, H and Neuhaus, J	*A Guide to the UNCITRAL Model Law on International Commercial Arbitration: Legislative History and Commentary*, 1991, The Hague: Kluwer. [Cited as Holtzmann & Neuhaus]
Honnold, J	*Uniform Law for International Sales Under the 1980 United Nations Convention*. 3rd edn, 1999, Deventer: Kluwer. [Cited as Honnold]
Honsell, H	'*Die Rolle des CISG in der Schweiz (I) / Das Einheitliche UN-Kaufrecht (CISG) aus schweizerischer Sicht (II)*' (2000) URL: http://www.cisg.ru/20_Jahre/honsell6.html [Cited as Honsell (2000)]
Honsell, H (ed)	*Kommentar zum UN-Kaufrecht*, 1997, Zürich: Springer. [Cited as Honsell (1997)]
Huleatt-James, M and Gould, N	*International Commercial Arbitration: A Handbook*. 2nd edition, 1999, London: LLP Reference Publishing. [Cited as Huleatt-James & Gould]
Karollus, M	'*Anmerkung zu BGH: VIII ZR 51/95 of 3.4.96*' (1997) Juristen Zeitung: 38–39. [Cited as Karollus (1997)]
Karollus, M	'Judicial Interpretation and Application of the CISG in Germany 1988-1994' (1995) Cornell Review of the Convention on Contracts for the International Sale of Goods: 51–94. [Cited as Karollus (1995)]

Kastely, A — 'Unification and Community: A Rhetorical Analysis of the United Nations Sales Convention' (1988) 8 Northwestern Journal of International Law and Business: 574–622. [Cited as Kastely]

Kazimierska, A — 'The Remedy of Avoidance under the Vienna Convention on the International Sale of Goods' (1999). URL: http://www.cisg.law.pace.edu/cisg/biblio/kazimierska.html [Cited as Kazimierska]

Keily, T — 'Good Faith and the Vienna Convention on Contracts for the International Sale of Goods (CISG)' (1999) 3 Vindobona Journal of International Law and Arbitration: 15–40. [Cited as Keily]

Kizery, K — 'Minding the Gap; determining interest rates under the UN Convention for the International Sale of Goods' (1998) 65 University of Chicago Law Review: 1279–306. [Cited as Kizery]

Klein, J — 'Good Faith in International Transactions' (1993) 15 Liverpool Law Review: 115–41. [Cited as Klein]

Knoll, M — 'A Primer on Prejudgement Interest' (1996) 75 Texas Law Review: 293–374. [Cited as Knoll]

Koch, R — 'The Concept of Fundamental Breach of Contract under the United Nations Convention on Contracts for the International Sale of Goods (CISG)' (1998) Review of the Convention on Contracts for the International Sale of Goods (CISG): 177–354. [Cited as Koch (1998)]

Koch, R — '*Zu den Voraussetzungen der Vertragsaufhebung wegen einer wesentlichen Vertragsverletzung*' (1996) Recht der Internationalen Wirtschaft: 687–88. [Cited as Koch (1996)]

Koch, R — '*Zur Bestimmung des Begriffs der wesentlichen Vertragsverletzung im UN-Kaufrecht im Falle der Lieferung nicht vertragsgemäßer Ware*' (1995) Recht der Internationalen Wirtschaft: 98-100. [Cited as Koch (1995)]

Koneru, P — 'The International Interpretation of the UN Convention on Contracts for the International Sale of Goods: An Approach Based on General Principles' (1997) 6 Minnesota Journal of Global Trade: 105–52. [Cited as Koneru]

Kritzer, A — *International Contract Manual: Guide to Practical Applications of the United Nations Convention on Contracts for the International Sale of Goods*, 1994, Deventer: Kluwer. [Cited as Kritzer]

Kroppholler, J — *Europäisches Zivilprozeßrecht. Kommentar zu EuGVÜ und Luganer Übereinkommen*. 6th edn, 1998, Heidelberg: Recht und Wirtschaft. [Cited as Kroppholler]

Law Commission of New Zealand — *The United Nations Convention on Contracts for the International Sale of Goods: New Zealand's Proposed Acceptance*, 1992, Wellington: Law Commission of New Zealand. [Cited as Law Commission of New Zealand]

Lillich, R and Brower, C (eds) — *International Arbitration in the 21st Century: Towards 'Judicialisation' and Uniformity?* 1992, New York: Transnational Juris. [Cited as Lillich & Brower]

Lindacher, W, Pfaff, D, Roth, G, Schlosser, P and Wieser, E (eds) — *Festschrift für Walther J. Habscheid zum 65. Geburtstag 6. April 1989*. 1989, Bielefeld: Verlag Ernst und Werner Gieseking. [Cited as Lindacher]

Lionnet, K — 'Should the Procedural Law Applicable to International Arbitration be Denationalised or Unified?' (1991) 8 Journal of International Arbitration: 5–16. [Cited as Lionnet]

Lookofsky, J — *Transnational Litigation and Commercial Arbitration: A Comparative Analysis of American, European and International Law*, 1992, Copenhagen: Transnational Juris. [Cited as Lookofsky]

Lorenz, A — 'Fundamental Breach under the CISG' (1998) URL: http://www.cisg.law.pace.edu/cisg/biblio/lorenz.html [Cited as Lorenz (1998)]

Lorenz, W — '*Konsensprobleme bei international-schuldrechtlichen Distanzverträgen*' (1960) 159 Archiv für Civilistische Praxis: 193–235. [Cited as Lorenz (1960)]

Magnus, U — 'General Principles of UN-Sales Law' (1997) 3 International Trade and Business Law Annual: 33–56. [Cited as Magnus (1997)]

Magnus, U	'*Die allgemeinen Grundsätze im UN-Kaufrecht*' (1995) 59 Rabels Zeitschrift für ausländisches und internationales Privatrecht: 469–94. [Cited as Magnus (1995)]
Mankowski, P	'*Das Internet im Internationalen Vertrags- und Deliktsrecht*' (1999) Rabels Zeitschrift für ausländisches und internationales Privatrecht: 203–94. [Cited as Mankowski]
McConnaughy, P	'The Risks and Virtues of Lawlessness: A Second Look at International Commercial Arbitration' (1999) 93 Northwestern University Law Review: 453–523. [Cited as McConnaughy]
Mezger, E	'*Anmerkung zu Oberlandesgericht Hamburg: 14 U 76/77 vom 22.9.1978*' (1979) Recht der Internationalen Wirtschaft: 486–93. [Cited as Mezger]
Moloney, G and Robinson, N (eds)	The Brussels Convention on Jurisdiction and Enforcement of Foreign Judgements: Papers and Precedents from the Joint Conference with the Union des Avocats Européens held in Cork, September 1989. URL: http://www.maths.tcd.ie/pub/IrishLaw/table.htm [Cited as Moloney & Robinson]
Murray, J	'An Essay on the Formation of Contracts and Related Matters under the United Nations Convention on Contracts for the International Sale of Goods' (1988) 8 Journal of Law and Commerce: 11–51. [Cited as Murray]
Musger, G	*Die wesentliche Vertragsverletzung – Probleme des Art. 25 WKR und Parallelen im österreichischen Recht*. 1989, Saarbrücken: Europa-Institut. [Cited as Musger]
Neumayer, K and Ming, C	*Convention de Vienne sur les contrats de vente internationale de marchandises – Commentaire*. 1993, Lausanne: CEDIDAC. [Cited as Neumayer & Ming]
Nörenberg, H	'*Internationale Verträge und Allgemeine Geschäftsbedingungen*' (1978) 31 Neue Juristische Wochenschrift: 1082–87. [Cited as Nörenberg]
Park, W	'The Arbitrability *Dicta* in *First Options v Kaplan*: What Sort of *Kompetenz-Kompetenz* Has Crossed the Atlantic?' (1996) 11(10) Mealey's International Arbitration Reports: 1–12. [Cited as Park]

Perales Viscasillas, M — 'Battle of the Forms under the 1980 United Nations Convention on Contracts for the International Sale of Goods: A Comparison with Section 2-207 UCC and the UNIDROIT Principles' (1998) 10 Pace International Law Review: 97–155. [Cited as Perales Viscasillas (1998)]

Perales Viscasillas, M — 'Recent Developments Relating to CISG: Contract Conclusion Under CISG' (1997) 16 Journal of Law and Commerce: 315–43. [Cited as Perales Viscasillas (1997)]

Perales Viscasillas, M — 'UNIDROIT Principles of International Commercial Contracts: Sphere of Application and General Provisions' (1996) 13 Arizona Journal of International and Comparative Law: 381–441. [Cited as Perales Viscasillas (1996)]

Pierani, M — '*La Battle of Forms e la Formazione del Vincolo nel Diritto dei Contratti Internazionali*' (1997) URL: http://www.jus.unitn.it/cardozo/review/contract/pierani-1997/indice.htm [Cited as Pierani]

Piltz, B — '*Neue Entwicklungen im UN-Kaufrecht*' (2000) Neue Juristische Wochenschrift: 553–60. [Cited as Piltz (2000)]

Piltz, B — '*Anmerkung zu Bundesgerichtshof: VIII ZR 51/95 of 3.4.96*' (1996) Europäische Zeitschrift zum Wirtschaftsrecht: 448. [Cited as Piltz (1996)]

Piltz, B — *Internationales Kaufrecht, Das UN-Kaufrecht* (*Wiener Übereinkommen von 1980*). München: Praxisorientierte Darstellung, 1993. [Cited as Piltz (1993)]

Plantard, J — '*Un nouveau droit uniforme de la vente internationale: La Convention des Nations Unies du 11 avril 1980*' (1988) Journal de Droit Internationale: 311–67. [Cited as Plantard]

Povrzenic, N — 'Interpretation and Gap-Filling Under the United Nations Convention on Contracts for the International Sale of Goods' (1997) URL: http://www.cisg.law.pace.edu/cisg/biblio/alpha15.html [Cited as Povrzenic]

Poznanski, B — 'The Nature and Extent of Arbitration Powers in International Commercial Arbitration' (1987) 4 Journal of International Arbitration: 71–108. [Cited as Poznanski]

Rauda, C and Etier, G — 'Warranty for Intellectual Property Rights in the International Sale of Goods' (2000) 4 Vindobona Journal of International Commercial Law and Arbitration: 30–61. [Cited as Rauda & Etier]

Redfern, A and Hunter, M — *Law and Practice of International Commercial Arbitration*, 3rd edn, 1999, London: Sweet & Maxwell. [Cited as Redfern & Hunter]

Rogers, R and Launders, R — 'Separability – The Indestructible Arbitration Clause' (1994) 10 Arbitration International: 77–90. [Cited as Rogers & Launders]

Rosen, J — 'Arbitration Under Private International Law: The Doctrines of Separability and *Compétence de la Compétence*' (1994) 17 Fordham International Law Journal: 599–666. [Cited as Rosen]

Rosenberg, M — 'The Vienna Convention: Uniformity in Interpretation for Gap-Filling – An Analysis and Application' (1992) 20 Australian Business Law Review: 442–60. [Cited as Rosenberg]

Rosett, A — 'A Critical Reflection on the United Nations Convention on Contracts for the International Sale of Goods' (1984) 45 Ohio State Law Journal: 265–305. [Cited as Rosett]

Roßmeier, D — '*Schadensersatz und Zinsen nach UN Kaufrecht – Art 74 bis 78 CISG*' (2000) Recht der Internationalen Wirtschaft: 407–15. [Cited as Roßmeier]

Rothschild, A — 'Prejudgement Interest: Survey and Suggestion' (1982) 77 Northwestern University Law Review: 192–222. [Cited as Rothschild]

Rubino-Sammartano, M — International Arbitration Law, 1990, Boston: Kluwer. [Cited as Rubino-Sammartano]

Sanders, P — Quo Vadis *Arbitration?* 1999, The Hague: Kluwer. [Cited as Sanders (1999)]

Sanders, (ed) — *UNCITRAL's Project for Model Law on International Commercial Arbitration*, 1984, London: Kluwer. [Cited as Sanders (1984)]

Schlechtriem, P (ed) — *Kommentar zum Einheitlichen UN-Kaufrecht*. München: CH Beck'sche Verlagsbüchhandlüng, 2000. [Cited as Schlechtriem (2000)]

Schlechtriem, P (ed) — Commentary on the UN Convention on the International Sale of Goods (CISG), 1998, Oxford: Clarendon Press, [Cited as Schlechtriem (1998)]

Schlechtriem, P — '*Wesentlicher Vertragsbruch durch Lieferung gezuckerten Weins*' (1997) Praxis des Internationalen Privat- und Verfahrensrecht: 132. [Cited as Schlechtriem (1997)]

Schlechtriem, P — '*Kurzkommentar zu Bundesgerichtshof: VIII ZR 51/95 of 3.4.1996*' (1996) Entscheidungen zum Wirtschaftsrecht: 597–98. [Cited as Schlechtriem (1996)]

Schlechtriem, P — 'Uniform Sales Law – The Experience with Uniform Sales Law in the Federal Republic of Germany' (1991/92) 3 Juridisk Tidskrift (Stockholm): 1–28. [Cited as Schlechtriem (1991/92)]

Schlechtriem, P (ed) — *Einheitliches Kaufrecht und nationales Obligationenrecht*, 1987, Baden-Baden: Nomos Verlagsgesellschaft. [Cited as Schlechtriem (1987)]

Schlechtriem, P — *Commentary on the UN Convention on the International Sale of Goods (CISG)*, 1986, Oxford: Clarendon Press. [Cited as Schlechtriem (1986)]

Schlosser, P — '*Schiedsklauseln in Allgemeinen Geschäftsbedingungen – Entscheidung des Züricher Handelsgerichts vom 25 August 1992 mit Anmerkung*' (1994) Zeitschrift für Europäisches Privatrecht: 682–93. [Cited as Schlosser]

Schmidt, M — '*Kann Schweigen auf eine Gerichtsstandklausel in AGB einen Gerichtsstand nach Art 17 EuGVÜ/LuganoÜ begründen*' (1992) Recht der Internationalen Wirtschaft: 173–79. [Cited as Schmidt]

Schmidt-Kessel, M — '*Vertragsaufhebung nach UN-Kaufrecht*' (1996) Recht der Internationalen Wirtschaft: 60–65. [Cited as Schmidt-Kessel]

Schmitthoff, C — *International Commercial Arbitration*, 1974, New York: Oceana. [Cited as Schmitthoff]

Schneider, E — 'Measuring Damages Under the CISG: Article 74 of the United Nations Convention on Contracts for the International Sale of Goods' (1997) 9 Pace International Law Review: 223–37. [Cited as Schneider]

Schwerha, J	'Warranties against Infringement in the Sale of Goods: A Comparison of UCC § 2-312(3) and Article 42 of the UN Convention on Contracts for the International Sale of Goods' (1995) 16 Michigan Journal of International Law: 441–83. [Cited as Schwerha]
Shinn, A	'Liabilities Under Article 42 of the UN Convention on Contracts for the International Sale of Goods' (1993) 2 Minnesota Journal of Global Trade: 115–42. [Cited as Shinn]
Speidel, R	'Buyer's Remedies of Rejection and Cancellation under the UCC and the Convention' (1993) 6 Journal of Contemporary Law: 131. [Cited as Speidel]
Stipanowich, T	'Arbitration and the Multi-Party Dispute: The Search for Workable Solutions' (1987) 72 Iowa Law Review: 473–528. [Cited as Stipanowich]
Stoffel, W	'Ein neues Recht des internationalen Warenkaufes in der Schweiz' (1990) 86 Schweizerische Juristen-Zeitung: 169–79. [URL: http://www.cisg.ru/20_Jahre/stoffel.html] [Cited as Stoffel]
Sutton, J	'Measuring Damages Under the United Nations Convention on the International Sale of Goods' (1989) 50 Ohio State Law Journal: 737–52. [Cited as Sutton]
Thiele, C	'Interest on Damages and Rate of Interest Under Article 78 of the UN Convention on Contracts for the International Sale of Goods' (1998) 2 Vindobona Journal of International Commercial Law and Arbitration: 3–35. [Cited as Thiele]
Toope, S	Mixed International Arbitration, 1990, Cambridge: Grotius. [Cited as Toope]
UNCITRAL	*III Yearbook*. New York: United Nations, 1972. [Cited as III YB]
UNCITRAL	*IX Yearbook*. New York: United Nations, 1978 [Cited as IX YB]
UNCITRAL	*Official Records: Documents of the Conference and Summary Records of the Plenary Meetings and of the Meetings of the Main Committees*, 1981, New York: United Nations. [Cited as Official Records]

van Alstine, M — 'Dynamic Treaty Interpretation' (1998) 146 University of Pennsylvania Law Review: 687–793. [Cited as van Alstine]

van den Berg, A — *The New York Convention of 1958: Towards a Uniform Judicial Interpretation*, 1981, Antwerp: Kluwer, 1981. [Cited as van den Berg]

Vergne, F — 'The "Battle of the Forms" Under the 1980 United Nations Convention on Contracts for the International Sale of Goods' (1985) 33 American Journal of Comparative Law: 233–58. [Cited as Vergne]

Vida, A — '*Garantie du vendeur et propriété industrielle: les "vices juridiques" dans la vente internationale de marchandises (convention de Vienne)*' (1994) Revue trimestrielle de droit commercial et de droit économique: 21–36. [Cited as Vida]

von Mehren, A — 'The "Battle of the Forms": A Comparative View' (1990) 38 American Journal of Comparative Law: 265–98. [Cited as von Mehren]

Wackenhuth, M — '*Die Schriftform für Schiedsvereinbarungen nach dem UN-Übereinkommen und Allgemeine Geschäftsbedingungen*' (1986) Zeitschrift für Zivilprozess: 445–67. [Cited as Wackenhuth]

Zhang, X — *Die Rechtsmängelhaftung des Verkäufers nach UN-Kaufrecht*, U. Novotny-Starnberg (Thesis 1994). [Cited as Zhang]

Zoccolillo, A — 'Determination of the Interest Rate under the 1980 United Nations Convention on Contracts for the International Sale of Goods: General Principles vs. National Law' (1997) 1 Vindobona Journal of International Commercial Law and Arbitration: 3–43. [Cited as Zoccolillo]

CASES CITED

Amtsgericht Augsburg: 11 C 4004/95 of 29 January 1996. URL: http://cisgw3.law.pace.edu/cases/960129g1.html

Amtsgericht Kehl: 3 C 925/93 of 6 October 1995. URL: http://cisgw3.law.pace.edu/cases/951006g1.html

Amtsgericht Riedlingen: 2 C 395/93 of 21 October 1994. URL: http://cisgw3.law.pace.edu/cases/941021g1.html

Bobbie Brooks, Inc v Lanificio Walter Banci SaS Corte di Appello di Firenze of 8 October 1977. Noted in (1979) IV Yearbook of Commercial Arbitration: 200.

Bundesgerichtshof: I ZR 143/98 of 21 September 2000. URL: http://www.grur.de/Seiten/Aufbau/Frame.html

Bundesgerichtshof: I ZR 223/97 of 13 January 2000. URL: http://www.grur.de/Seiten/Aufbau/Frame.html

Bundesgerichtshof: I ZR 136/97 of 3 November 1999. URL: http://www.grur.de/Seiten/Aufbau/Frame.html

Bundesgerichtsof: VIII ZR 51/95 of 3 April 1996. URL: http://cisgw3.law.pace.edu/cases/960403g1.html

Bundesgerichtshof: VIII ZR 159/94 of 8 March 1995. URL: http://cisgw3.law.pace.edu/cases/950308g3.html

Bundesgerichtshof: VIII ZR 185/92 of 9 March 1994. Noted in (1994) Recht der Internationalen Wirtschaft: 508–10.

Butler Machine Tool Co Ltd v Ex-Cell-O-Co Ltd. [1979] 1 All England Reports 965.

Calzaturificio Moreo Junior Srl v SPR LU Philmar Diff Tribunal Commercial de Bruxelles: R.G. 1.205/93 of 5 October 1994. URL: http://cisgw3.law.pace.edu/cases/941005b1.html

Channel Island Ferries Ltd. v Cenargo Navigation Ltd [1994] 2 Lloyd's Reports 161.

David L. Threlkeld & Co v Metallgesellschaft Ltd 923 Federal Reporter. Second Series 245 (2nd Circuit, 1991).

The Dreyfus Fund, Inc v Royal Bank of Canada 525 Federal Supplement 1108 (Southern District of New York, 1981).

Enterprise Alain Veyron v Société E Ambrosio. Cour d'appel de Grenoble: 93/1613 of 26 April 1995. URL: http://cisgw3.law.pace.edu/cases/950426f1.html

Estasis Salotti di Colzani Aimo et Gianmario Colzani v Rüwa Polstereimaschinen GmbH (1976) Reports of Cases before the Court of Justice and the Court of First Instance 1831.

Estée Lauder Cosmetics GmbH & Co OHG v Lancaster Group GmbH (2000) Reports of Cases before the Court of Justice and the Court of First Instance 6.

Fallini Stefano & Co S.N.C. v Foodik BV. Arrondissementsrechtbank Roermond: 900336 of 19 December 1991. URL: http://cisgw3.law.pace.edu/cases/911219n1.html

Federated Food, Inc v Fort Howard Paper Co 554 Federal Reporter. Second Series 1098 (Court of Customs and Patent Appeals, 1976).

Filanto SpA v Chilewich International Corp. 789 Federal Supplement 1229 (District Court, Southern District of New York, 1992).

Frey, Milota, Seitelberger and Vesely v F. Cuccaro e Figli Corte di Appello di Napoli of 13 December 1974. Noted in (1976) I Yearbook of Commercial Arbitration: 193.

Gruppo IMAR SpA v Protech Horst Arrondissementsrechtbank Roermond: 920159 of 6 May 1993. URL: http://cisgw3.law.pace.edu/cases/930506n1.html

Handelsgericht Zürich: HG 940513 of 10 July 1996. URL: http://cisgw3.law.pace.edu/cases/960710s1.html

Handelsgericht Zürich: HG 920670 of 26 April 1995. URL: http://cisgw3.law.pace.edu/cases/950426s1.html

Hungarian Chamber of Commerce and Industry, Court of Arbitration Award of 5 December 1995. URL: http://cisgw3.law.pace.edu/cases/951205h1.html

ICC Arbitration Case No 7531 of 1994. URL: http://cisgw3.law.pace.edu/cases/947531i1.html

ICC Arbitration Case No 6653 of 1993. URL: http://cisgw3.law.pace.edu/cases/936653i1.html

ICC Arbitration Case No. 7585 of 1992. URL: http://cisgw3.law.pace.edu/cases/927585i1.html

ICC Arbitration Case No. 3344 of 1981. Noted in (1982) Journal de Droit International: 978–87.

ICC Arbitration Case No. 2103 of 1972. Noted in (1974) Revue de Droit International: 902–04.

Internationales Schiedsgericht der Bundeskammer der gewerblichen Wirtschaft: SCH-4318 of 15 June 1994. URL: http://cisgw3.law.pace.edu/cases/940615a4.html

Internationales Schiedsgericht der Bundeskammer der gewerblichen Wirtschaft: SCH-4366 of 15 June 1994. URL: http://cisgw3.law.pace.edu/cases/940615a3.html

Kahn Lucas Lancaster, Inc v Lark International Ltd 956 Federal Supplement 1131 (Southern District of New York, 1997).

Landgericht Berlin: 99 O 123/92 of 30 September 1992. URL: http://cisgw3.aw.pace.edu/cases/920930g1.html

Landgericht Berlin: 99 O 29/93 of 16 September 1992. URL: http://cisgw3.law.pace.edu/cases/920916g1.html

Landgericht Düsseldorf: 31 O 231/94 of 23 June 1994. URL: http://cisgw3.law.pace.edu/cases/940623g1.html

Landgericht Hamburg: 5 O 543/88 of 26 September 1990. URL: http://www.jura.uni-freiburg.de/ipr1/cisg/urteile/text/21.htm

Landgericht Heilbronn: 3 KfH 653/93 of 15 September 1997. URL: http://www.jura.uni-freiburg.de/ipr1/cisg/urteile/text/562.htm

Landgericht Kassel: 11 O 4185/95 of 15 February 1996. URL: http://cisgw3.law.pace.edu/cases/960215g1.html

Landgericht Köln: 86 O 119/93 of 11 November 1992. URL: http://cisgw3.law.pace.edu/cases/931111g1.html

Landgericht Landshut: 54 O 644/94 of 5 April 1995. URL: http://cisgw3.law.pace.edu/cases/950405g1.html

Landgericht Mönchengladbach: 7 O 80/91 of 22 May 1992. URL: http://cisgw3.law.pace.edu/cases/920522g1.html

Landgericht Oldenburg: 12 O 3010 of 6 July 1994. URL: http://cisgw3.law.pace.edu/cases/940706g2.html

M. Caiato Roger v La Société française de factoring international factor France 'SFF' (SA). Cour d'appel de Grenoble: 93/4126 of 13 September 1995. URL: http://cisgw3.law.pace.edu/cases/950913f1.html

Melody BV v Loffredo, hodn Olympic. Gerechtshof's-Hertogenbosch: 856/91 of 26 February 1992. URL: http://cisgw3.law.pace.edu/cases/920226n1.html

Obergericht Kanton Luzern: 11 95 123/357 of 8 January 1997. URL: http://cisgw3.law.pace.edu/cases/970108s1.html

Oberlandesgericht Braunschweig: 2 U 27/99 of 28 October 1999. URL: http://cisgw3.law.pace.edu/cases/991028g1.html

Oberlandesgericht Düsseldorf: 17 U 136/92 of 12 March 1993. URL: http://cisgw3.law.pace.edu/cases/930312g1.html

Oberlandesgericht Düsseldorf: 17 U 82/92 of 8 January 1993. URL: http://cisgw3.law.pace.edu/cases/930108g1.html

Oberlandesgericht Frankfurt: 5 U 209/94 of 23 May 1995. URL: http://cisgw3.law.pace.edu/cases/950523g1.html

Oberlandesgericht Frankfurt: 5 U 15/93 of 18 January 1994. URL: http://cisgw3.law.pace.edu/cases/940118g1.html

Oberlandesgericht Hamburg: 14 U 76/77 of 22 September 1978. Noted in (1979) Recht der Internationalen Wirtschaft: 482–86.

Oberlandesgericht Innsbruck: 4 R 161/94 of 1 July 1994. URL: http://cisgw3.law.pace.edu/cases/940701a3.html

Oberlandesgericht Karlsruhe: 1 U 280/96 of 25 June 1997. URL: http://www.jura.uni-freiburg.de/ipr1/cisg/urteile/text/263.htm

Oberlandesgericht Koblenz: 2 U 580/96 of 11 September 1998. URL: http://cisgw3.law.pace.edu/cases/980911g1.html

Oberlandesgericht Koblenz: 2 U 31/96 of 31 January 1997. URL: http://cisgw3.law.pace.edu/cases/970131g1.html

Oberlandesgericht Köln: 18 U 121/96 of 21 August 1997. URL: http://cisgw3.law.pace.edu/cases/970821g1.html

Oberlandesgericht Köln: 27 U 58/96 of 8 January 1997. URL: http://cisgw3.law.pace.edu/cases/970108g1.html

Oberlandesgericht Köln: 22 U 202/93 of 22 February 1994. URL: http://www.jura.uni-freiburg.de/ipr1/cisg/urteile/text/127.htm

Oberlandesgericht München: 7 U 5460/94 of 8 March 1995. URL: http://cisgw3.law.pace.edu/cases/950308g1.html

Oberlandesgericht München: 7 U 1720/94 of 8 February 1995. URL: http://www.jura.uni-freiburg.de/ipr1/cisg/urteile/text/143.htm

Oberlandesgericht Oldenburg: 11 U 64/94 of 1 February 1995. URL: http://cisgw3.law.pace.edu/cases/950201g1.html

Oberlandesgericht Saarbrücken: 1 U 69/92 of 13 January 1993. URL: http://cisgw3.law.pace.edu/cases/930113g1.html

Oberlandesgericht Stuttgart: 5 U 195/94 of 21 August 1995. URL: http://cisgw3.law.pace.edu/cases/950821g1.html

Oberlandesgericht Zweibrücken: 8 U 46/97 of 31 March 1998. URL: http://cisgw3.law.pace.edu/cases/980331g1.html

Oberster Gerichtshof: 10 Ob 518/95 of 6 February 1996. URL: http://cisgw3.law.pace.edu/cases/960206a3.html

Partenreederei ms Tilly Russ and Ernest Russ v NV Haven- & Vervoerbedrijf Nova and NV Goeminne Hout (1984) Reports of Cases before the Court of Justice and the Court of First Instance 2417.

Powell Duffryn plc v Wolfgang Petereit (1992–93) Reports of Cases before the Court of Justice and the Court of First Instance I-1745.

Schluß-Schiedspruch der Handelskammer Hamburg of 21 June 1996. Noted in (1996) Recht der Internationalen Wirtschaft: 771–74.

Schweizerisches Bundesgericht: 4C.179/1998/odi of 28 October 1998. URL: http://www.cisg.law.pace.edu/cisg/wais/db/cases2/981028s1.html

Scarves by Vera, Inc v Todo Imports, Ltd 544 Federal Reporter. Second Series 1167 (2nd Circuit, 1976).

Schiedsgericht Hamburger Freundschaftliche Arbitrage of 29 December 1998. URL: http://cisgw3.law.pace.edu/cases/981229g1.html

Sociedad Cooperativa Epis-Centre v La Palentina, SA Tribunal Supremo: 3587/1996 of 17 February 1998. URL: http://cisgw3.law.pace.edu/cases/980217s5.html

Société Les Verreries de Saint Gobain, SA v Martinswerk GmbH. Cour de Cassation: J 96-11.984 of 16 July 1998. URL: http://cisgw3.law.pace.edu/cases/980716f1.html

Société Thyssen Stahlunion GmbH v Société Maaden General Foreign Trade Organisation for Metal and Building Materials. Cour d'appel de Paris of 6 April 1995. URL: http://cisgw3.law.pace.edu/cases/950406f1.html

Sport D'Hiver di Genevieve Culet v Ets Louyes et Fils Tribunale di Cuneo: 45/96 of 31 January 1996. URL: http://cisgw3.law.pace.edu/cases/960131i3.html

The Sports Authority, Inc v Prime Hospitality Corp 877 Federal Supplement 124 (United States District Court, 1995).

Sté ISEA Industrie SpA/Compagnie d'Assurances Generali v Lu SA et al. Cour d'appel de Paris: 95-018179 of 13 December 1995. URL: http://cisgw3.law.pace.edu/cases/951213f1.html

Three Valleys Municipal Water District v EF Hutton & Co 925 Federal Reporter. Second Series 1136 (9th Circuit, 1991).

United Steelworkers of America v Warrior & Gulf Navigation Co 363 United States Supreme Court Reports 574 (1960).

Volt Information Services v Board of Trustees of Leland Stanford Junior University. 489 United States Supreme Court Reports 468 (1989).

William Company v Chu Kong Agency Co Ltd and Guangzhou Ocean Shipping Company. Noted in (1993) Hong Kong Law Digest: B7.

Wonderfil SRL v NV Depraetere Industries. Rechtbank van Koophandel Kortrijk: 4143/96 of 6 October 1997. URL: http://cisgw3.law.pace.edu/cases/971006b1.html

LIST OF LEGAL AUTHORITIES

Agreement on Trade-Related Aspects of Intellectual Property, Marrakesh, 15 April 1994 [TRIPS].

American Arbitration Association International Arbitration Rules, 1 September 2000 [AAA International Arbitration Rules].

Arbitration Act (United Kingdom), 1996 [Arbitration Act 1996 (UK)].

Bundesgesetz für das Internationale Privatrecht (Switzerland) [BIP].

Bürgerliches Gesetzbuch (Germany) [BGB].

Code Civil (France).

Codice Civile (Italy).

Convention on the Jurisdiction and Enforcement of Judgements in Civil and Commercial Matters, Brussels, 27 September 1968 [Brussels Convention].

Convention on the Recognition and Enforcement of Foreign Arbitral Awards, New York, 10 June 1958 [New York Convention].

Handelsgesetzbuch (Austria) [HGB (Austria)].

Handelsgesetzbuch (Germany) [HGB (Germany)].

Lanham (Trademark) Act, 15 United States Code [Lanham Act].

London Court of International Arbitration Rules, 1 January 1998 [LCIA Rules].

Markengesetz (Germany) [MarkenG].

Nice Agreement Concerning the International Classification of Goods and Services for the Purposes of the Registration of Marks, Nice, 15 June 1957 [Nice Agreement].

Rules of Arbitration of the International Chamber of Commerce, 1 January 1998 [ICC Rules].

Schweizerisches Obligationenrecht (Switzerland).

UNCITRAL Arbitration Rules, 15 December 1976 [UNCITRAL Arbitration Rules].

UNCITRAL Model Law on Electronic Commerce, 1996 [E-Comm Model Law].

UNCITRAL Model Law on International Commercial Arbitration, 21 June 1985 [Model Law].

UNIDROIT Principles of International Commercial Contracts, Rome, 1994 [UNIDROIT Principles].

Uniform Commercial Code (United States of America) [UCC].

Uniform Law on the International Sale of Goods, The Hague, 2–22 April 1964 [ULIS].

United Nations Convention on Contracts for the International Sale of Goods, Vienna, 11 April 1980 [CISG].

Zivilprozeßordnung (Germany) [ZPO].

STATEMENT OF PURPOSE

The Respondent, Vis Water Sports Company (VIS WATER SPORTS), has prepared this Memorandum in compliance with the Arbitral Tribunal's Terms of Reference issued on 6 October 2000.

It is argued that:

- The Arbitral Tribunal has no jurisdiction because no arbitration agreement exists between VIS WATER SPORTS and the Claimant, Sports and More Sports, Inc (SPORTS);
- VIS WATER SPORTS did not breach its obligation under Article 42 CISG and is exempt from liability under Article 43 CISG;
- SPORTS wrongfully avoided the contract with VIS WATER SPORTS;
- VIS WATER SPORTS is only liable to make net restitution of $220,300 and is not liable to pay damages;
- VIS WATER SPORTS is only liable to pay interest at a rate of 3%; and that
- SPORTS should bear the costs of arbitration and VIS WATER SPORTS' legal costs.

In relation to each of these six issues, VIS WATER SPORTS summarises the arguments made by SPORTS in the Memorandum for the Claimant prepared by Universidade Federal do Rio Grande do Sul. These summaries are italicised. Where VIS WATER SPORTS refers to an issue which is not addressed in the Memorandum for the Claimant, the heading pertaining to that issue is followed by [NEW ARGUMENT].

1 THE ARBITRAL TRIBUNAL HAS NO JURISDICTION BECAUSE NO ARBITRATION AGREEMENT EXISTS BETWEEN *VIS WATER SPORTS* AND *SPORTS*

SPORTS argues that the correspondence between SPORTS and VIS WATER SPORTS constituted a 'battle of the forms' which resulted in a binding and enforceable arbitration agreement (Memorandum for the Claimant, Universidade Federal do Rio Grande do Sul, 7–9).

Pursuant to Article 6(2) Rules of Arbitration of the International Chamber of Commerce (ICC Rules), 'any decision as to the jurisdiction of the Arbitral Tribunal shall be taken by the Arbitral Tribunal itself'.[1] Therefore, the Arbitral Tribunal is authorised to determine the existence and validity of an arbitration agreement between VIS WATER SPORTS and SPORTS.[2]

1.1 NO ARBITRATION AGREEMENT EXISTS BETWEEN *VIS WATER SPORTS* AND *SPORTS*

An arbitration agreement may exist in the form of a clause in a contract.[3] The existence of an arbitration agreement in this form is 'governed by the same law, or rules of law, as the other provisions of the contract'.[4] Article 1(1)(a) United Nations Convention on Contracts for the International Sale of Goods (CISG) provides that 'This Convention applies to contracts of sale of goods between parties whose places of business are in different states ... when the States are Contracting States.' VIS WATER SPORTS and SPORTS contracted

---

1 Article 6(2) ICC Rules states that the Arbitral Tribunal shall only take such a decision if the ICC Court 'is *prima facie* satisfied that an arbitration agreement under the [ICC] Rules may exist'. However, on 26 July 2000, the ICC Court notified the parties that this threshold had been satisfied, and that the current arbitration should proceed.

2 This is a reflection of the general principle in international arbitration, usually referred to as 'competence-competence', that an arbitral tribunal is competent to rule on its own jurisdiction. Berger in CENTRAL, 28; Bucher in Lillich & Brower, 34; Bühring-Uhle, 62; Coe, 57–59; Craig, Park & Paulsson, 59; Derains & Schwartz, 99–102; Gaillard & Savage, 395–401; Holtzmann & Neuhaus, 478–87; Huleatt-James & Gould, 67; Park, 7; Redfern & Hunter, 264–67; Rosen, 608; Rubino-Sammartano, 329–30; van den Berg, 312; Art 15(1) AAA International Arbitration Rules; s 30 Arbitration Act 1996 (UK); Art 186 VII 1 BIP; Art 23(1) LCIA Rules; Art 16(1) Model Law; Art 21(2) UNCITRAL Arbitration Rules; § 1040 I ZPO.

3 Berger in CENTRAL, 12; Born, 37; Gaillard & Savage, 222; Huleatt-James & Gould, 31; Redfern & Hunter, 4; Schmitthoff in Schmitthoff, 46; Art 7(1) Model Law. SPORTS has specifically claimed that the arbitration agreement exists in this form, rather than in the form of a separate agreement. Request for Arbitration, Nos 17 & 18.

4 Redfern & Hunter, 157. See also Coe, 133–34; Holtzmann & Neuhaus, 259–60; Huleatt-James & Gould, 36; Lorenz (1960), 217; Mezger, 493; Piltz (2000), 556; *David L Threlkeld & Co v Metallgesellschaft Ltd* 923 F.2d 245 (2nd Cir 1991), 249-50; *Filanto, SpA v Chilewich International Corp* 789 F.Supp. 1229 (SDNY 1992), 1237; *Kahn Lucas Lancaster, Inc v Lark International Ltd.* 956 F.Supp. 1131 (SDNY 1997); *Oberlandesgericht* Braunschweig: 2 U 27/99 of 28 October 1999; *Oberlandesgericht* Hamburg: 14 U 76/77 of 22 September 1978.

for the sale of sporting goods[5] and have their places of business in Equatoriana and Danubia respectively,[6] both of which are 'Contracting States' within the meaning of Article 1(1)(a) CISG.[7] Therefore, the existence of an arbitration agreement, in the form of a clause in a contract between VIS WATER SPORTS and SPORTS, is governed by the CISG.[8]

The contractual relationship between VIS WATER SPORTS and SPORTS was based on e-mail correspondence between the two companies. SPORTS sent VIS WATER SPORTS two separate purchase orders,[9] each of which was acknowledged by VIS WATER SPORTS.[10] However, no arbitration agreement was concluded by either of these two exchanges of e-mail messages.

(a) VIS WATER SPORTS and SPORTS did not conclude an arbitration agreement in respect of the first purchase order (No 6839)

SPORTS' e-mail of 5 April 1999 included its first purchase order (No 6839), and its General Conditions of Purchase (which contained an arbitration clause).[11] This e-mail constituted an offer in accordance with Article 14(1) CISG.[12] VIS WATER SPORTS' Sales Manager, Mr Singer, replied to this offer by e-mail on 6 April 1999, and referred to VIS WATER SPORTS' General Conditions of Sale (which contained a forum selection clause).[13]

5 Procedural Order No 1, Clarification No 46.

6 Terms of Reference, Nos 2 & 3.

7 Request for Arbitration, No 22.

8 SPORTS also applies the CISG in determining the existence of an arbitration agreement. Memorandum for the Claimant, Universidade Federal do Rio Grande do Sul, 8–9.

9 SPORTS' first purchase order (No 6839) was attached to its e-mail of 5 April 1999. Claimant's Exhibit No 3. SPORTS' second purchase order (No 6910) was attached to its e-mail of 27 May 1999. Claimant's Exhibit No 5.

10 SPORTS' first purchase order (No 6839) was acknowledged in VIS WATER SPORTS' e-mail of 6 April 1999. Claimant's Exhibit No 4. SPORTS' second purchase order (No 6910) was acknowledged in VIS WATER SPORTS' e-mail of 28 May 1999. Claimant's Exhibit No 6.

11 Claimant's Exhibit No 3. The arbitration clause was Clause 14 of SPORTS' General Conditions of Purchase. It was the ICC standard arbitration clause with three additions: 'All disputes arising out of or in connection with the present contract shall be finally settled under the [ICC Rules] by one or more arbitrators appointed in accordance with the said Rules. If the amount in dispute is more than $400,000, there shall be three arbitrators. The arbitration shall take place in Vindobona, Danubia. The language of the arbitration shall be English.' Request for Arbitration, No 18.

12 Article 14(1) CISG states that 'A proposal for concluding a contract addressed to one or more specific persons constitutes an offer if it is sufficiently definite and indicates the intention of the offeror to be bound in case of acceptance. A proposal is sufficiently definite if it indicates the goods and expressly or implicitly fixes or makes provision for determining the quantity and the price'. SPORTS' first purchase order (No 6839) of 5 April 1999 was 'sufficiently definite' within the meaning of Art 14(1) CISG because it specified the quantity of goods, and fixed the list price of $100,000. Claimant's Exhibit No 3.

13 Claimant's Exhibit No 4. The forum selection clause was Clause 23 of VIS WATER SPORTS' General Conditions of Sale. It stated that 'Any dispute in regard to or arising out of this contract shall be submitted to the Commercial Court in Capitol City, Equatoriana'. Answer to the Request for Arbitration, No 13.

Such an exchange of general conditions is commonly referred to as a 'battle of the forms'.[14]

The CISG resolves the 'battle of the forms' under Article 19 CISG.[15] According to Article 19 CISG, a reply to an offer which purports to be an acceptance but which contains additional or different terms relating to the settlement of disputes constitutes a counter-offer.[16] A determination of whether Mr Singer's e-mail of 6 April 1999[17] contained different terms relating to the settlement of disputes, must be made by the application of Article 8 CISG.[18]

Article 8(1) CISG provides that 'statements made by and other conduct of a party are to be interpreted according to his intent where the other party knew or could not have been unaware what that intent was'. However, the subjective approach of Article 8(1) CISG requires proof of the actual intent of the parties.[19] Where there is insufficient evidence of the parties' subjective intent, Article 8(2) CISG provides that 'statements made by and other conduct of a party are to be interpreted according to the understanding that a reasonable

14 Dodge, 82–85; Drobnig, 124; Enderlein & Maskow, 99; Farnsworth in Bianca & Bonell, 178; Farnsworth (1990), 157; Gabriel (1994), 60; Gabriel (1997), 283-285; Honnold, 183; Karollus (1995), 61; Perales Viscasillas (1997), 337; Perales Viscasillas (1998), 103; Pierani; Schlechtriem in Schlechtriem (1998), 143–45; Schlechtriem in Schlechtriem (2000), 223; Schnyder & Straub in Honsell (1997), 197; Vergne, 234; *Butler Machine Tool Co Ltd v Ex-Cell-O-Co Ltd* [1979] 1 All ER 965, 966.

15 The 'battle of the forms' is exhaustively regulated by the CISG. Perales Viscasillas (1997), 340; Société Les Verreries de Saint Gobain, SA v Martinswerk GmbH Cour de Cassation: J 96-11.984 of 16 July 1998; *Sté ISEA Industrie SpA/Compagnie d'Assurances Generali v Lu SA et al.* Cour d'appel de Paris: 95-018179 of 13 December 1995. Indeed, a proposal at the Diplomatic Conference in Vienna to add a new Art 17 to the CISG to regulate the 'battle of the forms' was expressly rejected because the 'battle of the forms' was already comprehensively governed by the existing Draft Convention. Perales Viscasillas (1997), 341; First Committee Deliberations in Official Records, 288–89. In general, the CISG resolves the 'battle of the forms' in favour of the party that makes the last transmission of its general conditions. This approach is commonly referred to as the 'last shot' approach. Enderlein & Maskow, 99; Farnsworth (1990), 159–60; Honnold, 191; Schlechtriem in Schlechtriem (1998), 143–44; Schlechtriem in Schlechtriem (2000), 223; Schnyder & Straub in Honsell (1997), 197; von Mehren, 272–76.

16 Art 19(1) CISG provides that: 'A reply to an offer which purports to be an acceptance but which contains additions, limitations or other modifications is a rejection of the offer and constitutes a counter-offer.' Art 19(2) CISG provides that a statement does not constitute a counter-offer unless it 'materially' alters the terms of the offer. Art 19(3) CISG defines a material alteration to include 'Additional or different terms relating … to … the settlement of disputes'.

17 Claimant's Exhibit No 4.

18 According to Enderlein & Maskow, 61, 'Art 8 [CISG] governs the interpretation of statements and the otherwise legally relevant conduct of the parties'. See also Farnsworth in Bianca & Bonell, 97-98; Honnold, 61; Schlechtriem in Schlechtriem (1998), 113; Secretariat Commentary in Official Records, 18; *Landgericht* Heilbronn: 3 KfH 653/93 of 15 September 1997; *Oberlandesgericht* Zweibrücken: 8 U 46/97 of 31 March 1998; *Oberster Gerichtshof*: 10 Ob 518/95 of 6 February 1996. Indeed, a proposal in the Working Party that the incorporation of an offeror's general conditions should be expressly regulated was rejected on the ground that the existing Draft Convention already contained rules interpreting the content of the contract. IX YB, 81. Consequently, recourse to domestic law by the application of choice of law rules is excluded in this context. Drobnig, 125; Secretariat Commentary in Official Records, 261.

19 Enderlein & Maskow, 63; Farnsworth in Bianca & Bonell, 98; Honnold, 118; Schlechtriem (1986), 39.

person of the same kind as the other party would have had in the same circumstances.'[20] Consequently, even if SPORTS maintains that it could not have been aware of VIS WATER SPORTS' intent, the understanding of a reasonable person in SPORTS' position is the applicable standard in interpreting Mr Singer's e-mail of 6 April 1999.[21]

Mr Singer used the words: 'I should like to remind you that our General Conditions of Sale, which *we include in all sales contracts*, are available at [URL omitted]. I suggest that you take a look at them [emphasis added].'[22] Considering the explicit language used by VIS WATER SPORTS, a reasonable person in SPORTS' position must have understood that VIS WATER SPORTS intended any contract formed with SPORTS to include VIS WATER SPORTS' General Conditions of Sale. Since VIS WATER SPORTS' General Conditions of Sale included a forum selection clause, VIS WATER SPORTS' reply to SPORTS' offer contained a different term relating to the settlement of disputes. Therefore, according to Article 19 CISG, VIS WATER SPORTS' e-mail of 6 April 1999 constituted a counter-offer to incorporate VIS WATER SPORTS' General Conditions of Sale into the contract with SPORTS.[23]

SPORTS argues that it never accepted VIS WATER SPORTS' counter-offer.[24] However, according to Article 18(1) CISG 'a statement made by or other conduct of the offeree indicating assent [emphasis added]' to a counter-offer[25] is an acceptance of that counter-offer.[26] SPORTS' act of opening a letter of credit[27] was 'conduct ... indicating assent' to VIS WATER SPORTS'

---

20 In practice, Art 8(2) CISG is applied more commonly than Art 8(1) CISG. Honnold, 118, states that: 'because of the practical barriers to proving identity between the intent of the two parties (particularly when they are involved in a controversy) most problems of interpretation will be governed by [Art 8(2) CISG].' Similarly, Farnsworth in Bianca & Bonell, 99, states that: 'the test of actual intent contained in [Art 8(1) CISG] will not often be applied in practice.' See also Junge in Schlechtriem (2000), 143; Murray, VI; *M Caiato Roger v La Société Française de factoring international factor France 'SFF' (SA)*. Cour d'appel de Grenoble: 93/4126 of 13 September 1995.

21 Schlechtriem (1986), 39–40; Secretariat Commentary in Official Records, 261; *Oberlandesgericht* Saarbrücken: 1 U 69/92 of 13 January 1993.

22 Claimant's Exhibit No 4.

23 SPORTS acknowledges this. Memorandum for the Claimant, Universidade Federal do Rio Grande do Sul, 8.

24 Memorandum for the Claimant, Universidade Federal do Rio Grande do Sul, 8.

25 The same CISG provisions in respect of what constitutes acceptance apply to both offers and counter-offers. Enderlein & Maskow, 98; Karollus (1995), 61; Schlechtriem in Schlechtriem (1998), 142; Handelsgericht Zürich: HG 940513 of 10 July 1996; *Sociedad Cooperativa Epis-Centre v La Palentina, SA* Tribunal Supremo: 3587/1996 of 17 February 1998.

26 Enderlein & Maskow, 92; Farnsworth in Bianca & Bonell, 167; Honnold, 173; Murray, IV C; Schlechtriem in Schlechtriem (1998), 129; Secretariat Commentary in Official Records, 23; *Oberlandesgericht* München: 7 U 5460/94 of 8 March 1995.

27 'The [bill] of exchange drawn under the [letter] of credit [was] paid by the opening bank, and the account of Sports and More Sports was charged, on 10 May 1999.' Procedural Order No 1, Clarification No 48. The letter of credit was necessarily opened prior to the date upon which it was drawn.

counter-offer within the meaning of Article 18(1) CISG.[28] This terminated the 'battle of the forms'[29] and concluded a contract for the delivery of the goods specified in SPORTS' first purchase order (No 6839). This contract incorporated VIS WATER SPORTS' General Conditions of Sale, including the forum selection clause, and did not incorporate an arbitration clause. Consequently, VIS WATER SPORTS and SPORTS did not conclude an arbitration agreement in respect of the first purchase order (No 6839).

(b) VIS WATER SPORTS and SPORTS did not conclude an arbitration agreement in respect of the second purchase order (No 6910)

SPORTS maintains that its second purchase order (No 6910) of 27 May 1999 formed part of the original 'battle of the forms' between VIS WATER SPORTS and SPORTS.[30] However, the 'battle of the forms' was terminated when SPORTS accepted VIS WATER SPORTS' counter-offer by opening the first letter of credit.[31] Consequently, SPORTS' second purchase order (No 6910) operated as either an offer to modify the existing contract,[32] or a separate offer to contract. In either case, the same provisions of the CISG apply to determine the terms of the offer.[33]

(i) SPORTS' General Conditions of Purchase were not terms of the offer contained in its second purchase order (No 6910)

In his e-mail to VIS WATER SPORTS of 27 May 1999, which included SPORTS' second purchase order (No 6910), Mr Hirst, Purchasing Manager of SPORTS, stated that: 'Since [VIS WATER SPORTS] already have a copy of our General Conditions of Purchase, I need not attach them to this order.'[34] Under Articles 8(1) and 8(2) CISG, a party's statement will only incorporate general conditions into a contract where those general conditions are 'a part of the offer from the point of view of the offeree.'[35] Therefore, the offeror's

28 Opening a letter of credit constitutes 'other conduct' within the meaning of Art 18(1) CISG. Enderlein & Maskow, 92; Farnsworth in Bianca & Bonell, 166; Schlechtriem in Schlechtriem (1998), 129; Schlechtriem in Schlechtriem (2000), 206–07; Vergne, 241; *Enterprise Alain Veyron v Société E Ambrosio*. Cour d'appel de Grenoble: 93/1613 of 26 April 1995; *Handelsgericht* Zürich: HG 940513 of 10 July 1996; *Oberlandesgericht* Frankfurt: 5 U 209/94 of 23 May 1995; *Oberster Gerichtshof*: 10 Ob 518/95 of 6 February 1996.

29 A 'battle of the forms' is concluded when one party accepts a counter-offer through conduct. Honnold, 190. This favours the party who, in the 'battle of the forms' fires the last shot. Enderlein & Maskow, 99.

30 Memorandum for the Claimant, Universidade Federal do Rio Grande do Sul, 8–9.

31 See 1.1(a) and specifically footnote 29.

32 Art 29(1) CISG specifically envisages that: 'A contract may be modified … by the mere agreement of the parties.'

33 Enderlein & Maskow, 123; Karollus (1995), 66; Schlechtriem (1991/92), 19; Schlechtriem in Schlechtriem (1998), 211; Schmidt-Kessel, 61; *Landgericht* Hamburg: 5 O 543/88 of 26 September 1990; *Oberlandesgericht* Köln: 22 U 202/93 of 22 February 1994.

34 Claimant's Exhibit No 5.

35 *Oberster Gerichtshof:* 10 Ob 518/95 of 6 February 1996. See also Schlechtriem in Schlechtriem (1998), 113.

language must be unequivocal to ensure that the offeree understands the general conditions to be part of the offer.[36] Furthermore, Article 8(3) CISG requires that, in determining the understanding of the offeree, 'due consideration is to be given to all relevant circumstances of the case including the negotiations, any practices which the parties have established between themselves, usages and any subsequent conduct of the parties'.

In their previous negotiations, both VIS WATER SPORTS and SPORTS evinced an intention to include their respective general conditions in the contract. In his e-mail of 5 April 1999, Mr Hirst, Purchasing Manager of SPORTS, stated that: 'For your reference I have attached our General Conditions of Purchase, which are part of our purchase order.'[37] In its reply of 6 April 1999, VIS WATER SPORTS stated that 'our General Conditions of Sale, which we include in all sales contracts, are available at [URL omitted].'[38] The phrases 'are part of' and 'include in' refer unequivocally to the incorporation of general conditions into the purchase order and contract respectively. In contrast, Mr Hirst's statement, in his e-mail of 27 May 1999, 'Since you already have a copy of our General Conditions of Purchase, I need not attach them to this order,'[39] failed to express any intention to incorporate SPORTS' general conditions into the contract. In light of the explicit language used to incorporate general terms in the parties' first contract, Mr Hirst's statement in SPORTS' second purchase order (No 6910) was ambiguous. VIS WATER SPORTS could not have understood,[40] nor would a reasonable person in the position of VIS WATER SPORTS have understood,[41] that SPORTS intended its statement to constitute an offer to incorporate its General Conditions of Purchase into a contract. Therefore, SPORTS' General Conditions of Purchase were not terms of SPORTS' offer contained in its second purchase order (No 6910).

---

36 In *Sté ISEA Industrie SpA/Compagnie d'Assurances Generali v Lu SA et al.* Cour d'appel de Paris: 95-018179 of 13 December 1995, the Court held that in the absence of an explicit reference, the buyer could not be deemed to have accepted the conditions. See also *Wonderfil SRL v NV Depraetere Industries. Rechtbank van Koophandel Kortrijk*: 4143/96 of 6 October 1997. Honnold, 191, stresses the need to avoid ambiguous language by stipulating that: 'The generally accepted principle [is] that doubt is to be resolved against the person who created the ambiguity.' This principle is similar to the *contra proferentum* rule, articulated in Art 4.6 UNIDROIT Principles, which states that: 'If contract terms supplied by one party are unclear, an interpretation against that party is preferred.' Schlechtriem in Schlechtriem (1998), 113, states that: 'the need to take into account the understanding which a reasonable offeree of the same kind as the recipient of the offer would have in the same circumstances may … prevent … unclear standard clauses … from being within the understanding of the recipient.'

37 Claimant's Exhibit No 3.

38 Claimant's Exhibit No 4.

39 Claimant's Exhibit No 5.

40 Art 8(1) CISG states that: 'For the purposes of this Convention statements made by and other conduct of a party are to be interpreted according to his intent where the other party knew or could not have been unaware what that intent was.'

41 Art 8(2) CISG states that: 'If the preceding paragraph is not applicable, statements made by and other conduct of a party are to be interpreted according to the understanding that a reasonable person of the same kind as the other party would have had in the same circumstances.'

(ii) The contract concluded between VIS WATER SPORTS and SPORTS with respect to SPORTS' second purchase order (No 6910) did not contain an arbitration clause

SPORTS' second purchase order (No 6910) was acknowledged by VIS WATER SPORTS in its e-mail of 28 May 1999,[42] thereby concluding a contract.[43] However, regardless of whether SPORTS' second purchase order (No 6910) was an offer to modify the existing contract, or operated as a separate offer to contract, SPORTS' General Conditions of Purchase (including the arbitration clause) were not a part of the offer contained in that purchase order.[44] Consequently, the arbitration clause contained in SPORTS' General Conditions of Purchase was never incorporated into the contract between VIS WATER SPORTS and SPORTS with respect to the second purchase order (No 6910). Therefore, no arbitration agreement exists between VIS WATER SPORTS and SPORTS.

1.2 THE ALLEGED ARBITRATION AGREEMENT DOES NOT SATISFY THE 'IN WRITING' REQUIREMENT OF ARTicle 7(2) MODEL LAW [NEW ARGUMENT]

(a) The Arbitration Agreement must satisfy Article 7(2) Model Law

Both Equatoriana and Danubia are parties to the Convention on the Recognition and Enforcement of Foreign Arbitral Awards (New York Convention).[45] Article V(I)(a) New York Convention envisages that the recognition and enforcement of an arbitral award may be refused by domestic courts if the arbitration agreement does not comply with the law of the seat of arbitration.[46] The seat of arbitration is Danubia,[47] which has adopted the UNCITRAL Model Law on International Commercial Arbitration (Model Law).[48] Therefore, for the purposes of enforcement, it is necessary that the arbitration agreement complies with the Model Law, and in particular, the mandatory provisions of the Model Law.[49] Article 7(2) Model Law is consistently identified by commentators as a mandatory provision.[50]

42 Claimant's Exhibit No 6.

43 Art 18(1) CISG provides that 'A statement made by ... the offeree indicating assent to an offer is an acceptance.' Mr Singer, Sales Manager of VIS WATER SPORTS, in his e-mail of 28 May 1999 stated that: 'I hereby acknowledge receipt of your purchase order No 6910.' Claimant's Exhibit No 6.

44 See 1.1(b)(i).

45 Request for Arbitration, No 23.

46 Huleatt-James & Gould, 17; Poznanski, 87.

47 Terms of Reference, No 18.

48 Request for Arbitration, No 23.

49 Böckstiegel (1984), 225; Böckstiegel (1997), 25; Coe, 52; Fox, 1; Hill, 663; Hoellering, 25; Huleatt-James & Gould, 17; Lionnet, 7; Lookofsky, 563; McConnaughy, 455; Redfern & Hunter, 81; van den Berg, 34–40.

50 Coe, 128; Holtzmann & Neuhaus, 260; Huleatt-James & Gould, 31; Redfern & Hunter, 133–34; Szurski in Sanders (1984), 59.

Consequently, to be enforceable, any alleged arbitration agreement between VIS WATER SPORTS and SPORTS must comply with Article 7(2) Model Law.

(b) The exchange of e-mails between VIS WATER SPORTS and SPORTS does not satisfy the 'in writing' requirement of Art 7(2) Model Law

Article 7(2) Model Law provides that:

> The arbitration agreement shall be in writing. An agreement is in writing if it is contained in a document signed by the parties or in an exchange of letters, telex, telegrams or other means of telecommunication which provide a record of the agreement, or in an exchange of statements of claim and defence in which the existence of an agreement is alleged by one party and not denied by another. The reference in a contract to a document containing an arbitration clause constitutes an arbitration agreement provided that the contract is in writing and the reference is such as to make that clause part of the contract.

Statements made by e-mail may constitute written statements for the purposes of Article 7(2) Model Law.[51] However, Article 7(2) Model Law was drafted with the objective of excluding oral or tacit acceptance of an arbitration agreement or an alleged acceptance that did not reflect the fully informed consent of a party.[52] This reflects the basic principle of international arbitration law that the jurisdiction of an arbitral tribunal is derived exclusively from the consent of the parties.[53] Consequently, Article 7(2) Model Law is

---

51 Berger (1998), 49; Holtzmann & Neuhaus, 263; Mankowski, 215. See also Arts 2(a), 5 & 6 E-Comm Model Law; Graf von Bernstorff, 19.

52 Broches, 41; Holtzmann & Neuhaus, 260; van den Berg, 171; *Frey, Milota, Seitelberger and Vesely v F Cuccaro e Figli*. Corte di Appello di Napoli of 13 December 1974. Moreover, in the drafting of Art II(2) New York Convention, from which Art 7(2) Model Law derives, a proposal by the Dutch Delegation that a 'confirmation in writing by one of the parties [which is kept] without contestation by the other party' be considered an arbitration agreement, was rejected. van den Berg, 196.

53 Broches, 38; Coe, 55; Hill, 597; Lindacher in Lindacher, 168; Lorenz (1960), 196–97; Poznanski, 71; Redfern & Hunter, 271; Rogers & Launders, 77; Schlosser, 684; Stipanowich, 476–77; Toope, 9; van den Berg, 173, 210; Wackenhuth, 453–54; *Three Valleys Municipal Water District v EF Hutton & Co* 925 F.2d 1136 (9th Cir 1991), 1142; *United Steelworkers of America v Warrior & Gulf Navigation Co* 363 US 574 (1960), 582; *Volt Information Services v Board of Trustees of Leland Stanford Junior University* 489 US 468 (1989), 477. This conclusion is reinforced by Art 17 Brussels Convention, which requires the consent of the parties to abrogate from the general rules of jurisdiction. Schmidt, 175. The ECJ has held that in order to satisfy Art 17 Brussels Convention, it must be satisfied first, that the clause conferring the jurisdiction upon the court was in fact the subject of a consensus between the parties and second, that this consensus is clearly and precisely demonstrated. *Estasis Salotti di Colzani Aimo et Gianmario Colzani v Rüwa Polstereimaschinen GmbH* (1976) ECR 1831, 1841; *Partenreederei ms Tilly Russ and Ernest Russ v NV Haven- & Vervoerbedrijf Nova and NV Goeminne Hout* (1984) ECR 2417, 2432; *Powell Duffryn plc v Wolfgang Petereit* (1992–93) ECR I-1745, I-1776. In order to guarantee compliance, the ECJ also established in those decisions that the requirements of Art 17 Brussels Convention must be interpreted narrowly. See also Kropholler, 244; Moloney in Moloney & Robinson, 7; Nörenberg, 1084; *Bundesgerichtshof:* VIII ZR 185/92 of 9 March 1994; *Oberlandesgericht* Köln: 27 U 58/96 of 8 January 1997. Decisions relating to Art 17 Brussels Convention may be used to interpret Art II(2) New York Convention. Mankowski, 218; Schlosser, 690; van den Berg, 210; Wackenhuth, 454. Accordingly, such decisions are also relevant in interpreting Art 7(2) Model Law.

only satisfied where each party has declared 'in writing' its consent to arbitration.[54]

(i) *The exchange of e-mails in respect of the first purchase order (No 6839) does not satisfy the 'in writing' requirement of Art 7(2) Model Law*

Although SPORTS' first purchase order (No 6839) referred to its attached General Conditions of Purchase (which contained an arbitration clause),[55] VIS WATER SPORTS' reply expressly referred to its own General Conditions of Sale (which included a forum selection clause).[56] Where each party sends its own general conditions, van den Berg emphasises that 'if the arbitral clauses in both confirmations conflict with each other, there is no acceptance in writing for either clause, and Article II(2) New York Convention is not met in this case.'[57] Article 7(2) Model Law is derived from Article II(2) New York Convention,[58] and thus, the two provisions must be interpreted consistently.[59] Therefore, an exchange of inconsistent dispute resolution clauses does not constitute an 'agreement in writing' under Article 7(2) Model Law. Since VIS WATER SPORTS' forum selection clause is inconsistent with SPORTS' arbitration clause, there is no written evidence of each party's consent to arbitration as required by Article 7(2) Model Law.

(ii) *The exchange of e-mails in respect of the second purchase order (No 6910) does not satisfy the 'in writing' requirement of Art 7(2) Model Law*

SPORTS' purchase orders (Nos 6839 and 6910) both referred to SPORTS' General Conditions of Purchase which included the arbitration clause.[60] VIS WATER SPORTS, in its e-mail replying to SPORTS' second purchase order (No 6910),[61] referred to both purchase orders (Nos 6839 and 6910) but was silent with respect to SPORTS' General Conditions of Purchase. Silence,

---

54 Holtzmann & Neuhaus, 260.

55 Claimant's Exhibit No 3; Request for Arbitration, No 18.

56 Claimant's Exhibit No 4.

57 van den Berg, 206.

58 Holtzmann & Neuhaus, 260. Art II(2) New York Convention states that: 'The term 'agreement in writing' shall include an arbitral clause in a contract or an arbitration agreement, signed by the parties or contained in an exchange of letters or telegrams.' Art II(2) New York Convention requires that the addressee gives a written acceptance of the order together with the arbitration agreement contained therein. *Internationales Schiedsgericht der Bundeskammer der gewerblichen Wirtschaft:* SCH-4366 of 15 June 1994.

59 Gaillard & Savage, 370, 376–77; Holtzmann & Neuhaus, 260–63; Sanders (1999), 101.

60 Claimant's Exhibits Nos 3 & 5.

61 Claimant's Exhibit No 6.

without more, does not satisfy the 'in writing' requirement of Article 7(2) Model Law.[62]

In addition, Redfern and Hunter state that, when ascertaining whether a party has consented to arbitration, 'it is permissible to take extraneous evidence into account'.[63] In the parties' previous dealings, VIS WATER SPORTS had rejected SPORTS' General Conditions of Purchase, including the arbitration clause.[64] Taking into account this previous rejection, VIS WATER SPORTS' silence with regard to SPORTS' General Conditions of Purchase cannot be interpreted as signifying VIS WATER SPORTS' consent to arbitration. Since there is no written evidence of VIS WATER SPORTS' consent to arbitration, the mandatory 'in writing' requirement of Article 7(2) Model Law is not fulfilled. Therefore, any alleged arbitration agreement between VIS WATER SPORTS and SPORTS is unenforceable.

2 VIS WATER SPORTS DID NOT BREACH ITS OBLIGATION UNDER ART 42 CISG AND IS EXEMPT FROM LIABILITY UNDER ART 43 CISG

SPORTS argues that:

1 *VIS WATER SPORTS breached its obligation under Article 42(1) CISG (Memorandum for the Claimant, Universidade Federal do Rio Grande do Sul, 9–15); and*

62 Holtzmann & Neuhaus, 264, state that 'the written consent of each party is the *sine qua non* of the writing requirement.' See also Nienaber in CENTRAL, 111; *Frey, Milota, Seitelberger and Vesely v F Cuccaro e Figli*. Corte di Appello di Napoli of 13 December 1974. Only two cases have decided that mere reference in subsequent correspondence between the contracting parties to a document containing an arbitration clause satisfies the 'in writing' requirement of Art 7(2) Model Law. *William Company v Chu Kong Agency Co Ltd. and Guangzhou Ocean Shipping Company* (decided under Art 7(2) Model Law); *Bobbie Brooks Inc v Lanificio Walter Banci SaS*. Corte di Appello di Firenze of 8 October 1977 (decided under Art II(2) New York Convention). In each case, where one party proposed an arbitration clause, the other party specifically accepted the documents containing the arbitration clause but remained silent with respect to the incorporation of the clause into the contract. It appears from these cases that, in order to satisfy the 'in writing' requirement of Art 7(2) Model Law, the other party's silence with respect to arbitration itself must indicate that party's consent to arbitration as a method of dispute resolution between the parties. In *Bobbie Brooks Inc v Lanificio Walter Banci SaS*. Corte di Appello di Firenze of 8 October 1977, invoices sent by the seller specifically referred to the identification numbers of three purchase orders which all provided for arbitration. Although these orders were unsigned, the Court held that the mere reference to the identification numbers of the purchase orders constituted an exchange of documents within the meaning of Art II(2) New York Convention, and thus formed a formally valid agreement to arbitrate. However, the facts of the present dispute can be contrasted with the findings in these cases, because VIS WATER SPORTS was not silent, but rather expressly rejected the incorporation of SPORTS' General Conditions of Purchase.

63 Redfern & Hunter, 143.

64 In his e-mail to SPORTS of 6 April 1999, Mr Singer, Sales Manager of VIS WATER SPORTS, expressly stated that: 'I should like to remind you that our General Conditions of Sale, which we include in all sales contracts, are available at [URL omitted]. I suggest that you take a look at them.' Claimant's Exhibit No 4. Clause 23 of those general conditions was a forum selection clause. Answer to Request for Arbitration, No 13.

2 *VIS WATER SPORTS is not exempt from liability under Article 43(1) CISG (Memorandum for the Claimant, Universidade Federal do Rio Grande do Sul, 15–20).*

2.1 VIS WATER SPORTS DID NOT BREACH ITS OBLIGATION UNDER ART 42(1) CISG

Should the Arbitral Tribunal assume jurisdiction, VIS WATER SPORTS argues that it fulfilled its obligation under Article 42(1) CISG to deliver goods free from third party rights or claims. Article 42(1) CISG provides:

> The seller must deliver goods which are free from any right or claim of a third party based on industrial property or other intellectual property, of which at the time of the conclusion of the contract the seller knew or could not have been unaware, provided that the right or claim is based on industrial property or other intellectual property
>
> (a) under the law of the State where the goods will be resold or otherwise used, if it was contemplated by the parties at the time of the conclusion of the contract that the goods would be resold or otherwise used in that State.

(a) VIS FISH COMPANY's assertion of trademark infringement did not constitute a 'right' or a 'claim' within the meaning of Art 42(1) CISG

In its letter to SPORTS of 20 September 1999, VIS FISH COMPANY alleged that 'Your advertisement and sale of goods bearing the name 'Vis' are ... in violation of our trademark.'[65] SPORTS argues that VIS FISH COMPANY's trademark constitutes a 'right' under Article 42(1) CISG.[66] However, a third party's assertion of trademark infringement will only constitute a 'right' within the meaning of Article 42 CISG if that assertion would be upheld under the law of the country in which it is made.[67] Additionally, an assertion of trademark infringement will constitute a 'claim' under Article 42(1) CISG only where there is 'a minimum of seriousness' to the assertion.[68] This 'minimum of seriousness' standard requires that the assertion has some legal

---

65 Claimant's Exhibit No 7.

66 Memorandum for the Claimant, Universidade Federal do Rio Grande do Sul, 9.

67 According to the Secretariat Commentary in Official Records, 36, 'If the third party's claim is valid ... the third party has a right in or to the goods [emphasis added]'. See also Black, 1324; Magnus in Honsell (1997), 444; Schwenzer in Schlechtriem (2000), 426.

68 Piltz (1993), 86. See also Schwenzer in Schlechtriem (2000), 429, 438; Zhang, 86. Additionally, Schlechtriem (1986), 72, states that: 'Not every frivolous or even vexatious claim would be sufficient, but rather only substantiated claims.' The deliberations of the Working Group reveal concern that the word 'claim' without further qualification 'might lead to abuse by the buyer in that he might hold the seller responsible for any third party's claim, however frivolous or vexatious.' III YB, 90. Any other interpretation would lead to the seller being liable even for claims which only aim at damaging the buyer or which are made in bad faith. Schwerha, 457, states that: 'one should read into this provision [Art 42(1) CISG] that such claims should be made in good faith.'

merit.[69] SPORTS' legal representatives, Howard & Heward, have concluded that VIS FISH COMPANY's allegation 'would ... be dismissed' under the law of Danubia.[70] Moreover, both VIS WATER SPORTS and SPORTS agree that VIS FISH COMPANY's assertion of trademark infringement is without legal basis.[71] Since there is no legal merit to VIS FISH COMPANY's assertion of trademark infringement, it does not constitute a 'right' or a 'claim' within the meaning of Article 42(1) CISG.

(b) VIS WATER SPORTS did not know, and could not have been aware, of VIS FISH COMPANY's claim at the time of the conclusion of the contract

The seller's liability under Article 42(1) CISG for a third party 'right or claim' is limited to circumstances where the seller 'knew or could not have been unaware' of that 'right or claim.'

(i) VIS WATER SPORTS was under no legal obligation to research potential claims, and therefore could not have been aware of any 'right or claim' of VIS FISH COMPANY

SPORTS argues that the phrase 'could not have been unaware' in Article 42(1) CISG imposes a duty on the seller to research potential third party intellectual property claims.[72] However, the phrase 'could not have been unaware' must be read consistently with the language of the CISG as a whole.[73] The CISG specifically refers to two different standards of knowledge: 'could not have been unaware' and 'ought to have known.'[74] Honnold contrasts the two standards, and concludes that 'ought to have known' imposes a duty to research, whereas 'could not have been unaware' does not require research.[75] Consequently, the standard 'could not have been

69 Schwerha, 457, states that: 'Otherwise, a party could easily claim breach by convincing another party to make a claim on the goods, even though such claim was meritless.'

70 In his advice to SPORTS of 28 October 1999, Howard & Heward stated that: 'In our opinion the claim of the Vis Fish Company to trademark infringement is unfounded. We are of the opinion that any legal action that they might bring would eventually be dismissed.' Claimant's Exhibit No 10.

71 In his letter of 4 October 1999 to VIS FISH COMPANY, Mr Kent, President of SPORTS, stated that: 'There is no likelihood that anyone would confuse athletic equipment ... with the fish and fish products that I now understand are sold by your company.' Claimant's Exhibit No 8. In his letter of 10 November 1999 to Mr Kent, President of SPORTS, Mr Singer, Sales Manager of VIS WATER SPORTS, stated that: 'As you yourself have indicated, even though the Vis Fish Company may have registered the trademark 'Vis' for all water-related products, their business is fish and similar products. Vis Water Sports equipment certainly does not violate that trademark.' Claimant's Exhibit No 13. See also Claimant's Exhibit No 10.

72 Memorandum for the Claimant, Universidade Federal do Rio Grande do Sul, 12.

73 Honnold, 270; Koch (1998), 193; Law Commission of New Zealand, 40.

74 Arts 8(1), 35(3) and 40 CISG use the phrase 'could not have been unaware'. Arts 2(a), 9(2), 38(3), 49(2)(b)(i), 68, 74 and 79(4) CISG use the phrase 'ought to have known'.

75 Honnold, 295, states that ''Could not have been unaware' seems to set a standard close to actual knowledge, in contrast to 'ought to have known' which can imply a duty to inquire. This acts as a limitation on the seller's responsibility.' Similarly, the Law Commission of New Zealand, 40, states that: '"Could not have been unaware" appears to be close to actual knowledge. It can be contrasted with "ought to have known" or "discovered" which is used in several other provisions of the Convention ... While the latter formula appears to impose a duty to investigate, the former may not.'

unaware,' in the context of Article 42(1) CISG, does not impose a duty on the seller to research potential claims. Rather, this phrase establishes that the delivery of goods subject to a third party claim constitutes a breach of the seller's obligations if the seller possessed information that must have alerted it to the potential claim.[76]

VIS WATER SPORTS possessed no information that would have alerted it to VIS FISH COMPANY's potential claim. VIS WATER SPORTS was not aware of the existence of VIS FISH COMPANY.[77] VIS FISH COMPANY was not listed on the Internet[78] and had marketed its products solely in Danubia,[79] a country in which VIS WATER SPORTS had not previously sold its goods.[80] Indeed, VIS WATER SPORTS had never attempted to enter the Danubian market.[81] Consequently, VIS WATER SPORTS could not have been aware of VIS FISH COMPANY's potential trademark infringement claim.

(ii) Even if a legal obligation to research potential claims exists, VIS WATER SPORTS could not have been aware of any 'right or claim' by VIS FISH COMPANY

Even if the phrase 'could not have been unaware' in Article 42(1) CISG imposes an obligation on the seller to research potential claims, the seller is not liable for a claim which would not have been revealed by such research.[82] Shinn agrees that 'there is nothing … that suggests that the phrase ['could not have been unaware'] places an affirmative obligation on the seller to research for information that is not readily discoverable in the circumstances'.[83] If VIS WATER SPORTS had conducted research in Danubia[84] it would not have discovered VIS FISH COMPANY's potential claim.

VIS FISH COMPANY's trademark infringement claim is based on the argument that the use of the 'Vis' name in conjunction with the slogan 'like a fish in water' in relation to VIS WATER SPORTS' sporting goods could result in confusion with VIS FISH COMPANY's fish products.[85] However, any

76 This reasoning was adopted by the ICC representative in the Pre-Conference Proposals where he emphasised that it was not correct to assume that a seller could be aware of an intellectual property right or claim merely because it is published on a register. Pre-Conference Proposals in Official Records, 399. See also Honnold, 295; Shinn, 124.

77 Procedural Order No 1, Clarification No 19.

78 Procedural Order No 1, Clarification No 20.

79 Procedural Order No 1, Clarification No 16.

80 Claimant's Exhibit No 1; Procedural Order No 1, Clarification No 58.

81 Claimant's Exhibit No 2.

82 Enderlein & Maskow, 168; Schwerha, 450; Shinn, 127–28. Schwenzer in Schlechtriem (1998), 337, states that: 'Unfounded claims will … only exceptionally result in the seller's liability, because the seller will often lack the knowledge required by Art 42(1) CISG at the time of the conclusion of the contract.' See also Schwenzer in Schlechtriem (2000), 438.

83 Shinn, 126.

84 Any duty to research would be confined to the country of resale as contemplated by the parties. Date-Bah in Bianca & Bonell, 320; Enderlein & Maskow, 169; Schwenzer in Schlechtriem (1998), 338–39.

85 Claimant's Exhibit No 7.

research of the Danubian trademark register conducted by VIS WATER SPORTS would have revealed that VIS FISH COMPANY only engages in the business of selling fish, other water-related food products and their derivatives.[86] Additionally, there was no indication on the register that VIS FISH COMPANY engaged in any commercial activities related to athletics or recreation.[87] In contrast, the only products marketed in Danubia under the name 'Vis Water Sports' are surfboards, wind surfboards, water skis, scuba diving equipment and water slides.[88] Since the types of products marketed by the two companies are so divergent, VIS WATER SPORTS could not have been aware that VIS FISH COMPANY would allege that its fish products could be confused with VIS WATER SPORTS' sporting equipment.[89] Therefore, even if an obligation to research potential third party claims exists under Article 42(1) CISG, VIS WATER SPORTS could not have been aware of VIS FISH COMPANY's 'right or claim'.

2.2 VIS WATER SPORTS IS EXEMPT FROM LIABILITY UNDER ART 42(2)(a) CISG [NEW ARGUMENT]

Even if the Tribunal determines that VIS WATER SPORTS breached Article 42(1) CISG, it is exempted from liability under Article 42(2)(a) CISG. Article 42(2)(a) CISG states that: 'The obligation of the seller [under Article 42(1) CISG] … does not extend to cases where … at the time of the conclusion of

---

86 Claimant's Exhibit No 10.

87 Claimant's Exhibit No 10. Danubian Trademark Law provides that the owner of a dormant trademark may only maintain an action for trademark infringement if it can show that it intends to use the trademark in the relevant class during the remaining period of registration. Procedural Order No 1, Clarification No 8. VIS FISH COMPANY has a registered trademark under Class 28 Nice Agreement in relation to sporting products. Procedural Order No 1. Clarification No 7. However, in fact, VIS FISH COMPANY has not marketed any goods under Class 28 Nice Agreement since January 1996. Procedural Order No 1, Clarification No 7.

88 Procedural Order No 1, Clarification No 46.

89 Art 23 Danubian Trademark Law provides that 'The owner of a registered trademark shall have the exclusive right to prevent all third parties not having the owner's consent from using in the course of trade identical or similar signs for goods or services which are identical or similar to those in respect of which the trademark is registered where such use would result in a likelihood of confusion [emphasis added].' Procedural Order No 1, Clarification No 5. Art 23 Danubian Trademark Law is similar to § 1114 Lanham Act (USA), which provides that: 'Any person who … use[s] in commerce any ... registered mark in connection with the sale ... of any goods or services on or in connection with which such use is likely to cause confusion shall be liable in a civil action [emphasis added].' Art 23 Danubian Trademark Law is also similar to § 14 II 2 MarkenG (Germany). In interpreting the phrase 'likely to cause confusion', courts in the USA have considered two factors: first, the similarity between the marks, and second, the similarity between the goods. *Federated Food, Inc v Fort Howard Paper Co* 554 F 2d 1098 (CCPA 1976). Courts in Germany have also considered these factors. *Bundesgerichtshof*: I ZR 143/98 of 21 September 2000; *Bundesgerichtshof*: I ZR 136/97 of 3 November 1999. In both jurisdictions, it is the average consumer's perception that is determinative as to whether a similarity exists. *Bundesgerichtshof*: I ZR 223/97 of 13 January 2000; *The Dreyfus Fund, Inc v Royal Bank of Canada*. 525 F.Supp. 1108 (SDNY 1981), 1119–20; *Scarves by Vera, Inc v Todo Imports, Ltd* 544 F 2d 1167 (2nd Cir 1976), 1174–75; *The Sports Authority, Inc v Prime Hospitality Corp* 877 F Supp 124 (US Dist 1995), 129. See also *Estée Lauder Cosmetics GmbH & Co OHG v Lancaster Group GmbH* (2000) ECR 6, 8. An average consumer would not have perceived any similarity between VIS WATER SPORTS' sporting equipment and VIS FISH COMPANY's fish products.

the contract the buyer knew or could not have been unaware of the right or claim.'

A buyer may not ignore well-known or obvious intellectual property rights or claims.[90] SPORTS could not have been unaware of the existence of VIS FISH COMPANY's claim. VIS FISH COMPANY is a successful and well known business in Danubia[91] and SPORTS actually knew that VIS FISH COMPANY was a seller of 'fish and other water-related products [emphasis added]'.[92] These factors must have indicated to SPORTS that VIS FISH COMPANY might make an assertion of trademark infringement in respect of the 'Vis' trademark. In such a case, the buyer is under a duty to research the possibility of a claim.[93] If SPORTS had researched VIS FISH COMPANY's intellectual property rights, it would have discovered that VIS FISH COMPANY had an extensive history of aggressively defending its trademark[94] against products significantly different to its own goods.[95] As such, SPORTS 'could not have been unaware' of VIS FISH COMPANY's potential trademark infringement claim.

It is immaterial that research may have led SPORTS to conclude that VIS FISH COMPANY's claim would have been unsuccessful. According to Kritzer, 'Under Article 42(2)(a) [CISG], where the buyer has knowledge of a right, but based on an opinion of counsel or prior relevant activity of the proprietor of the right, believes the right to be invalid, unenforceable or historically unenforced, the Convention exempts the seller from an obligation if such right is raised or asserted'.[96] Therefore, since SPORTS 'could not have been unaware' of VIS FISH COMPANY's claim within the meaning of Article 42(2)(a) CISG, VIS WATER SPORTS is exempt from any liability under Article 42(1) CISG.

---

90 Rauda & Etier, 57; Shinn, 127–28; Vida, 30–31. According to Rauda & Etier, 56, this precludes a buyer from practising an 'ostrich's policy' by ignoring the existence of intellectual property rights. See also Enderlein & Maskow, 170; Schwenzer in Schlechtriem (1998), 340; Schwenzer in Schlechtriem (2000), 441; Vida, 30.

91 Procedural Order No 1, Clarification No 16.

92 Procedural Order No 1, Clarification No 18.

93 Schwenzer in Schlechtriem (1998), 340; Schwenzer in Schlechtriem (2000), 441. This requirement is particularly relevant if the country in which the goods are to be sold is the buyer's place of business, because the buyer potentially has unique knowledge of local intellectual property rights. Shinn, 125; Vida, 30–31. SPORTS was in a better position to undertake research in relation to any right of VIS FISH COMPANY. SPORTS is based in Capitol City, Danubia, where there is easy public access to the Danubian trademark register. Procedural Order No 1, Clarification No 9; Request for Arbitration, No 1. In contrast, since the Danubian trademark register is not on the Internet, VIS WATER SPORTS could only have accessed the register through a Danubian lawyer or other professional specialist. Procedural Order No 1, Clarification No 9.

94 Claimant's Exhibit No 10.

95 VIS FISH COMPANY had previously defended its trademark against first, a company which manufactured stuffing material made from seaweed, and second, against a company which manufactured playground equipment. Procedural Order No 1, Clarification No 14.

96 Kritzer, 358.

2.3 VIS WATER SPORTS IS EXEMPT FROM LIABILITY UNDER ART 43(1) CISG

Even if the Arbitral Tribunal determines that VIS WATER SPORTS breached its obligation under Article 42(1)(a) CISG, it is exempt from liability under Article 43(1) CISG. Article 43(1) CISG states that:

> The buyer loses the right to rely on the provisions of article 41 or article 42 if he does not give notice to the seller specifying the nature of the right or claim of the third party within a reasonable time after he has become aware or ought to have become aware of the right or claim.

Although SPORTS' notice of 3 November 1999[97] adequately specified the nature of VIS FISH COMPANY's right or claim,[98] SPORTS failed to fulfil its obligation under Article 43(1) CISG to give notice within a 'reasonable time'.

(a) *SPORTS gave notice of VIS FISH COMPANY's claim 45 days after it became aware of the claim*

SPORTS argues that it became aware of VIS FISH COMPANY's claim on 28 October 1999, when SPORTS was advised of VIS FISH COMPANY's litigious reputation by its legal representatives, Howard & Heward.[99] However, SPORTS received actual notice of the claim from VIS FISH COMPANY on 20 September 1999 when VIS FISH COMPANY stated that 'Your advertisement and sale of goods bearing the name 'Vis' are in violation of our trademark.'[100] Therefore, SPORTS became aware of VIS FISH COMPANY's claim on 20 September 1999. Forty-five days elapsed before SPORTS gave VIS WATER SPORTS notice of the claim on 3 November 1999.[101]

(b) *SPORTS' notice was not given within a 'reasonable time'*

The interpretation of the phrase 'reasonable time' under Article 43(1) CISG is influenced heavily by the interpretation of the same phrase in Article 39(1)

---

97 Claimant's Exhibit No 12.

98 According to Schwerha, 468, adequate specification of the right or claim includes reference to 'the parties making the claim, the grounds for the claim … and the goods against which the claim is made'. See also Enderlein & Maskow, 171; Schwenzer in Schlechtriem (1998), 345. In its letter to VIS WATER SPORTS of 3 November 1999, SPORTS stated that 'The trademark 'Vis' has been registered in Danubia by the Vis Fish Company for all water-related products. By letters of 20 September 1999 and 15 October 1999 the Vis Fish Company has claimed that the advertising and selling of goods bearing the name Vis Water Sports in Danubia would violate their trademark and they have threatened legal action if we continued to do so.' Claimant's Exhibit No 12.

99 Claimant's Exhibit No 10; Memorandum for the Claimant, Universidade Federal do Rio Grande do Sul, 17. SPORTS does not propose an argument in respect of when it 'ought to have become aware' of the claim.

100 Claimant's Exhibit No 7.

101 Claimant's Exhibit No 12.

CISG.[102] In the context of Article 39(1) CISG, courts and arbitral tribunals have consistently held that a period of more than eight days is not a 'reasonable time' under Article 39(1) CISG.[103] On this basis, a 'reasonable time' under Article 39(1) CISG has been interpreted as a period of approximately eight days.[104] This position derives support from Article 39(1) Uniform Law on the International Sale of Goods (ULIS), the predecessor to Article 39(1) CISG,[105] and is reflected in the domestic statutory laws of many countries.[106] Applying this eight day limit, SPORTS' notice to VIS WATER SPORTS was not within a 'reasonable time'.

Where 'reasonable time' has been interpreted as exceeding a period of eight days, commentators and courts have stipulated that one month is the

---

102 Art 39(1) CISG states that: 'The buyer loses the right to rely on a lack of conformity of the goods if he does not give notice to the seller specifying the nature of the lack of conformity within a reasonable time after he has discovered it or ought to have discovered it.' Beldarrain, 10, states that: 'the notice requirement under Art 43(1) [CISG] is similar to the provisions contained in Art 39(1) [CISG].' See also Enderlein & Maskow, 170–71; Gabriel (1994), 127; Honnold, 298; Schwenzer in Schlechtriem (1998), 344; Schwenzer in Schlechtriem (2000), 446; First Committee Deliberations in Official Records, 326; Secretariat Commentary in Official Records, 426; Sono in Bianca & Bonell, 322.

103 *Amtsgericht* Augsburg: 11 C 4004/95 of 29 January 1996; *Amtsgericht* Kehl: 3 C 925/93 of 6 October 1995; *Amtsgericht* Riedlingen: 2 C 395/93 of 21 October 1994; *Bundesgerichtshof:* VIII ZR 159/94 of 8 March 1995; *Calzaturificio Moreo Juniro Srl v SPR LU Philmar Diff.* Tribunal Commercial de Bruxelles: RG 1.205/93 of 5 October 1994; *Fallini Stefano & Co SNC v Foodik BV. Arrondissementsrechtbank* Roermond: 900366 of 19 December 1991; *Gruppo IMAR SpA v Protech Horst. Arrondissementsrechtbank Roermond*: 920159 of 6 May 1993; *Handelsgericht* Zürich: HG 920670 of 26 April 1995; Hungarian Chamber of Commerce and Industry, Court of Arbitration Award of 5 December 1995; *Landgericht* Berlin: 99 O 29/93 of 16 September 1992; *Landgericht* Berlin: 99 O 123/92 of 30 September 1992; *Landgericht* Düsseldorf: 31 O 231/94 of 23 June 1994; *Landgericht* Köln: 86 O 119/93 of 11 November 1992; *Landgericht* Mönchengladbach: 7 O 80/91 of 22 May 1992; *Oberlandesgericht* Düsseldorf: 17 U 82/92 of 8 January 1993; *Oberlandesgericht* Düsseldorf: 17 U 136/92 of 12 March 1993; *Oberlandesgericht* Innsbruck: 4 R 161/94 of 1 July 1994; *Oberlandesgericht* Karlsruhe: 1 U 280/96 of 25 June 1997; *Oberlandesgericht* München: 7 U 3758/94 of 8 February 1995; *Oberlandesgericht* Saarbrücken: 1 U 69/92 of 13 January 1993; *Sport D'Hiver di Genevieve Culet v Ets Louyes et Fils*: Tribunale di Cuneo: 45/96 of 31 January 1996.

104 Magnus in Honsell (1997), 432; Piltz (2000), 558. Similarly, according to Enderlein & Maskow, 159, 'the reasonable time is in any case a short period … reasonable, in many cases, will mean giving notice immediately'. *Landgericht* Landshut: 54 O 644/94 of 5 April 1995; *Oberlandesgericht* Karlsruhe: 1 U 280/96 of 25 June 1997; *Oberlandesgericht* Koblenz: 2 U 580/96 of 11 September 1998; *Oberlandesgericht* München: 7 U 3758/94 of 8 February 1995.

105 Art 39(1) ULIS states that: 'The buyer shall lose the right to rely on a lack of conformity of the goods if he has not given the seller notice thereof *promptly* after he discovered the lack of conformity or ought to have discovered it [emphasis added].' Some commentators have interpreted the change in wording from 'promptly' to 'within a reasonable time' to indicate that the word 'promptly' was too strict. However, Enderlein & Maskow, 159, state that 'the reasonable time is in any case … like [Art 39(1) ULIS]'. Therefore, it is possible to use the word 'promptly' as analogous to the phrase 'reasonable time'. Similarly, Andersen, 92, states that 'the change in wording of Art 39(1) [CISG] would not seem overly significant'.

106 Pursuant to Art 1495(1) Codice Civile (Italy), there exists a duty to notify of non-conformity strictly within eight days. Pursuant to s 377 HGB (Germany) and s 377 HGB (Austria), notice must be given '*unverzüglich*' ('without delay'). Art 1648 Code Civil (France) has been interpreted as allowing a buyer four months to give timely notice of non-conformity. However, this merely reflects the wording of Art 1648 Code Civil (France), which requires a buyer to give notice of non-conformity '*dans un bref delai*' ('with a brief delay'). Andersen, 135; Ghestin, 12–14.

absolute limit of the 'reasonable time' period.[107] According to Andersen, 'in reported practice, there has been no evidence of any factors which have been pronounced as extending [the period of one month]'.[108] Therefore, even extending 'reasonable time' to its absolute limit, SPORTS' notice to VIS WATER SPORTS, 45 days after it became aware of the purported breach of contract, was not given within a 'reasonable time'.

SPORTS argues that the 'reasonable time' period in Article 43(1) CISG may be extended in certain circumstances.[109] However, even if a period of one month is a flexible starting point, rather than the absolute limit of 'reasonable time', there are no special circumstances in the present dispute that would justify an extension of the 'reasonable time' period beyond one month. SPORTS' assertion that it required additional time to attempt to resolve the dispute directly with VIS FISH COMPANY[110] is unfounded given that it waited two weeks before responding to VIS FISH COMPANY's initial notice of the trademark infringement claim.[111] Furthermore, any argument by SPORTS that additional time was required in order to seek legal advice is countered by the fact that, after receiving notice of VIS FISH COMPANY's claim on 20 September 1999,[112] SPORTS waited 31 days before approaching its legal representatives, Howard & Heward.[113]

Indeed, the circumstances of the present case indicate that a period of less than one month should be applied. According to Sono, 'where the buyer is

107 Andersen, 97; Schwenzer in Schlechtriem (1998), 315; Schwenzer in Schlechtriem (2000), 416; *Amtsgericht* Augsburg: 11 C 4004/95 of 29 January 1996; *Bundesgerichtshof:* VIII ZR 159/94 of 8 March 1995; *M Caiato Roger v La Société française de factoring international factor France 'SFF'* (SA). Cour d'appel de Grenoble: 93/4126 of 13 September 1995; *Obergericht* Kanton Luzern: 11 95 123/357 of 8 January 1997; *Oberlandesgericht* Köln: 18 U 121/96 of 21 August 1997; *Oberlandesgericht* Stuttgart: 5 U 195/94 of 21 August 1995. Indeed, a large number of courts and arbitral tribunals have held that a period of more than one month is not a 'reasonable time' under Art 39(1) CISG. *Amtsgericht* Augsburg: 11 C 4004/95 of 29 January 1996; *Amtsgericht* Kehl: 3 C 925/93 of 6 October 1995; *Bundesgerichtshof*: VIII ZR 159/94 of 8 March 1995; *Calzaturificio Moreo Juniro Srl v SPR LU Philmar Diff.* Tribunal Commercial de Bruxelles: RG 1.205/93 of 5 October 1994; *Fallini Stefano & Co SNC v Foodik BV Arrondissementsrechtbank* Roermond: 900366 of 19 December 1991; *Gruppo IMAR SpA v Protech Horst. Arrondissementsrechtbank* Roermond: 920159 of 6 May 1993; *Handelsgericht* Zürich: HG 920670 of 26 April 1995; Hungarian Chamber of Commerce and Industry, Court of Arbitration Award of 5 December 1995; *Landgericht* Berlin: 99 O 29/93 of 16 September 1992; *Landgericht* Berlin: 99 O 123/92 of 30 September 1992; *Landgericht* Düsseldorf: 31 O 231/94 of 23 June 1994; *Oberlandesgericht* München: 7 U 3758/94 of 8 February 1995; *Oberlandesgericht* Saarbrücken: 1 U 69/92 of 13 January 1993.

108 Andersen, 157.

109 Memorandum for the Claimant, Universidade Federal do Rio Grande do Sul, 19–21.

110 Memorandum for the Claimant, Universidade Federal do Rio Grande do Sul, 16.

111 Mr Streng, Managing Director of VIS FISH COMPANY, in his letter of 20 September 1999, notified SPORTS of VIS FISH COMPANY's assertion of trademark infringement. Claimant's Exhibit No 7. SPORTS replied to this letter two weeks later, on 4 October 1999. Claimant's Exhibit No 8.

112 Claimant's Exhibit No 7.

113 SPORTS wrote to its legal representatives, Howard & Heward, on 21 October 1999. Procedural Order No 1, Clarification No 12.

rejecting the goods [rather than claiming damages], a prompt communication to the seller is important'.[114] This provides the seller with an opportunity to redispose of the rejected goods.[115] In notifying VIS WATER SPORTS of its breach of Article 42 CISG, SPORTS purported to reject the goods.[116] Therefore, notice should have been given promptly. SPORTS' notice to VIS WATER SPORTS,[117] after a delay of 45 days, was outside even the most liberal interpretation of 'reasonable time' under Article 43(1) CISG. Consequently, VIS WATER SPORTS is exempted from any liability under Article 42(1) CISG.

3 SPORTS WRONGFULLY AVOIDED THE CONTRACT WITH VIS WATER SPORTS

SPORTS argues that it validly avoided the contract. SPORTS asserts that VIS WATER SPORTS' breach was fundamental on the grounds that:

1. *VIS WATER SPORTS' breach resulted in a detriment which substantially deprived SPORTS of what it was entitled to expect under the contract (Memorandum for the Claimant, Universidade Federal do Rio Grande do Sul, 21–24); and*
2. *VIS WATER SPORTS could have foreseen the detriment resulting from its alleged breach (Memorandum for the Claimant, Universidade Federal do Rio Grande do Sul, 21–24).*

Should the Arbitral Tribunal determine that VIS WATER SPORTS breached its contract with SPORTS, SPORTS wrongfully avoided that contract by its letter of 3 November 1999.[118] Article 49(1)(a) CISG provides that: 'The buyer may declare the contract avoided ... if the failure by the seller to perform any of his obligations … amounts to a fundamental breach of contract.' Article 25 CISG defines fundamental breach:

> A breach of contract committed by one of the parties is fundamental if it results in such detriment to the other party as substantially to deprive him of what he is

---

114 Sono in Bianca & Bonell, 309. See also Andersen, 98; Ferrari (1995), 109–10; Schwenzer in Schlechtriem (1998), 315.

115 Sono in Bianca & Bonell, 309; *Landgericht* Kassel: 11 O 4185/95 of 15 February 1996. This conclusion is also consistent with Art 7(1) CISG, which states that: 'In the interpretation of this Convention, regard is to be had to … the observance of good faith in international trade.' It would be contrary to the principle of good faith to allow a buyer to delay unreasonably in informing the seller of non-conformity.

116 Claimant's Exhibit No 12.

117 Claimant's Exhibit No 12.

118 In his letter to Mr Singer, Sales Manager of VIS WATER SPORTS, of 3 November 1999, Mr Kent, President of SPORTS stated that: 'Sports and More Sports, Inc is hereby avoiding the contract for the purchase of water sports equipment from the Vis Water Sports Co entered into by your e-mail acceptance of our purchase orders No 6839 and 6910 as provided in Art 49 CISG.' Claimant's Exhibit No 12.

entitled to expect under the contract, unless the party in breach did not foresee and a reasonable person of the same kind in the same circumstances would not have foreseen such a result.

3.1 VIS WATER SPORTS' BREACH DID NOT RESULT IN A DETRIMENT WHICH SUBSTANTIALLY DEPRIVED SPORTS OF WHAT IT WAS ENTITLED TO EXPECT UNDER THE CONTRACT

Pursuant to Article 25 CISG, a fundamental breach only exists if a party's breach of contract results in 'such detriment to the other party as substantially to deprive him of what he is entitled to expect under the contract'. SPORTS argues that 'by receiving goods, which were not free from a third [party's] claim based on intellectual property rights, [SPORTS] was deprived of what it was entitled to expect under the contract'.[119] However, the delivery of goods subject to a third party claim does not automatically constitute a 'fundamental breach' under Article 25 CISG.[120] The *Oberlandesgericht* Frankfurt has recognised that 'it is possible that there is no fundamental breach in cases in which the buyer eventually can make some use of the defective goods'.[121] Similarly, Schlechtriem states that if a defect in title 'does not directly and immediately impair the buyer's freedom of action ... damages for the buyer may be an adequate remedy'.[122] Therefore, in order to establish a fundamental breach of contract, SPORTS must demonstrate that VIS WATER SPORTS' breach directly and immediately impaired SPORTS' use of the goods.

SPORTS removed VIS WATER SPORTS' goods from the Danubian market on 3 November 1999,[123] and was therefore unable to use VIS WATER SPORTS' goods as envisaged under the contract.[124] However, the existence of VIS FISH COMPANY's claim neither legally obliged SPORTS to cease selling those goods, nor justified that course of action. Consequently, SPORTS' ability to resell VIS WATER SPORTS' goods was not impeded by VIS WATER SPORTS' delivery of goods subject to the third party claim. Rather, SPORTS' use of VIS WATER SPORTS' goods was impaired only because it voluntarily decided to cease selling.

---

119 Memorandum for the Claimant, Universidade Federal do Rio Grande do Sul, 22.

120 Enderlein & Maskow, 115; Koch (1998), 332; Schlechtriem in Schlechtriem (1998), 183.

121 *Oberlandesgericht* Frankfurt: 5 U 15/93 of 18 January 1994 [translated from German]. See also *Bundesgerichtsof*: VIII ZR 51/95 of 3 April 1996; Huber in Schlechtriem (2000), 499, 538; Karollus (1997), 38; Koch (1996), 687; Piltz (1996), 448; Schlechtriem (1996), 597–98; Schlechtriem (1997), 132.

122 Schlechtriem in Schlechtriem (1998), 183.

123 Procedural Order No 1, Clarification No 13.

124 SPORTS is the largest retail seller of athletic equipment in Danubia. Request for Arbitration, No 1. Therefore, SPORTS had an expectation that it would be able to resell VIS WATER SPORTS' goods in Danubia.

(a) *SPORTS was under no legal obligation to remove VIS WATER SPORTS' goods from the market*

In the absence of a court order to remove any infringing goods from the market, there was no legal imperative to cease selling VIS WATER SPORTS' products. On 3 November 1999, when SPORTS purported to avoid the contract, VIS FISH COMPANY had not initiated any legal action against SPORTS.[125] Even if VIS FISH COMPANY had subsequently instituted legal action, it is unlikely that a Danubian court would have required SPORTS to remove VIS WATER SPORTS' goods from the market.[126] Additionally, SPORTS had received advice from its legal representatives, Howard & Heward, that 'any legal action that [VIS FISH COMPANY] might bring would eventually be dismissed'.[127] On this basis, at the conclusion of any litigation, SPORTS would have been authorised to continue selling VIS WATER SPORTS' goods. Therefore, SPORTS was under no legal obligation to remove VIS WATER SPORTS' goods from the market.

(b) *There was no legal justification for SPORTS' decision to remove VIS WATER SPORTS' goods from the market*

Article 25 CISG reflects the general principle of international commercial law, *favor contractus*.[128] Under this principle, parties to a contract have an obligation to preserve, where possible, the contract and prevent its premature avoidance.[129] Hence, avoidance for 'fundamental breach' within the meaning of Article 25 CISG 'should only be allowed as a last resort in response to a breach so serious that the non-breaching party would have lost his interest in performing the contract'.[130] VIS WATER SPORTS' delivery of goods subject to VIS FISH COMPANY's claim did not deprive SPORTS of its interest in performing the contract. According to SPORTS' own legal representatives, Howard & Heward, VIS FISH COMPANY's claim of trademark infringement

125 Claimant's Exhibit No 12; Procedural Order No 1, Clarification No 15.

126 While Danubian courts have the power to prohibit the sale of a product allegedly infringing a trademark, pending final resolution of the claim, such an order is rarely made. Procedural Order No 1, Clarification No 11.

127 Claimant's Exhibit No 10.

128 Enderlein & Maskow, 112; Magnus (1997), 45. The principle of favor contractus is common in international trade law and is also an essential element of the UNIDROIT principles. Alpa, 317–18; Baron, III 1 a; Berger (1999), 162–63; Bonell, 129–35.

129 Audit, 51; Bonell, 81; Bonell in Bianca & Bonell, 81; Brandner, II A 2; Ferrari in Schlechtriem (2000), 153; Ferrari (1994), 223; Ferrari (1997), 464; Honnold in Schlechtriem (1987), 140; Karollus in Honsell (1997), 261; Kazimierska, III E 1; Kritzer, 416; Melis in Honsell (1997), 91; Plantard, 333; Povrzenic, 4 B; Rosenberg, 452; Will in Bianca & Bonell, 206; *Bundesgerichtshof*: VIII ZR 51/95 of 3 April 1996.

130 *Bundesgerichtshof*: VIII ZR 51/95 of 3 April 1996 [translated from German]. See also Benicke, 329; Brandner, II A 2; Enderlein & Maskow, 112; Holthausen, 102; Honnold, 206–07; Honsell (2000), V 3, V 5 a; Karollus (1997), 38; Karollus in Honsell (1997), 263–64; Koch (1998), 245; Magnus (1995), 483; Schlechtriem (1996), 597–98; Schlechtriem in Schlechtriem (1998), 174; Schlechtriem in Schlechtriem (2000), 259–60; Sono in Flechtner, 210–11; Stoffel, C 3; Will in Bianca & Bonell, 206, 211; Schweizerisches *Bundesgericht*: 4C.179/1998/odi of 28 October 1998.

would not have been upheld under Danubian Law.[131] Therefore, the solution most conducive to the continuing existence of the contract between VIS WATER SPORTS and SPORTS, was for SPORTS to continue selling the goods and defend itself against the litigation. Additionally, any costs incurred by SPORTS as a result of the litigation would have been easily recoverable from VIS WATER SPORTS in a claim for damages.[132]

Moreover, under the CISG, the contracting parties have an obligation to act in good faith.[133] The principle of good faith requires the non-defaulting party to mitigate its loss in the event of a breach of contract.[134] This obligation is breached where the contract is avoided unnecessarily because avoidance of a contract for the international sale of goods generally results in very high additional costs for both parties to the contract.[135] This is particularly the case 'when rescission follows delivery, [as] the goods will have to be stored and then disposed of, generally at great expense and loss'.[136] By electing to remove the goods from the market, avoid the contract, and store the goods pending restitution, SPORTS failed to recover its purchase price and shipping costs and incurred substantial storage and other miscellaneous costs.[137] In contrast, if SPORTS had upheld the contract and continued retailing VIS WATER SPORTS' products, VIS WATER SPORTS would have supported

131 Claimant's Exhibit No 10.

132 Art 45(1) CISG provides that: 'If the seller fails to perform any of his obligations under the contract or this Convention, the buyer may … claim damages as provided in Arts 74 to 77 [CISG].' Art 74 CISG provides that: 'Damages for breach of contract by one party consist of a sum equal to the loss, including loss of profit, suffered by the other party as a consequence of the breach.' Loss under Art 74 CISG would include detriments flowing from a breach of Art 42 CISG. Enderlein & Maskow, 166; Honnold, 289. If SPORTS was found to have wilfully infringed VIS FISH COMPANY's trademark, and financial penalties were imposed under Art 61 TRIPS, VIS WATER SPORTS would also have been liable in damages for those financial penalties.

133 Art 7(1) CISG states that 'In the interpretation of this Convention, regard is to be had to its international character and to the need to promote uniformity in its application and the observance of good faith in international trade.' Although good faith is expressed as an interpretative tool, Art 7(1) also imposes an obligation on the contracting parties to act in good faith. Enderlein & Maskow, 56–57; Kastely, 619–20; Keily, 36–39; Klein, 122; Koneru, 139–40; ICC Arbitration Case No 7331 of 1994; *Melody BV v Loffredo, hodn Olympic. Gerechtshof*'s-Hertogenbosch: 856/91 of 26 February 1992.

134 Stoll in Schlechtriem (2000), 737, states that: 'The duty to mitigate loss is … an expression of the principle of good faith [translated from German].' See also Bonell in Bianca & Bonell, 85; Magnus in Honsell (1997), 974; Magnus (1997), 45–46. Specifically, Art 77 CISG requires a non-breaching party to 'take such measures as are reasonable in the circumstances to mitigate the loss … resulting from the breach.' The duty to mitigate loss also constitutes a usage in international commerce. *ICC Arbitration* Case No 2103 of 1972; ICC Arbitration Case No 3344 of 1981. The general duty to mitigate losses is also recognised in Art 7.4.8 UNIDROIT Principles, which states that 'the non-performing party is not liable for harm suffered by the aggrieved party to the extent that the harm could have been reduced by the latter party's taking reasonable steps.' Bonelli in Bonell & Bonelli, 315–16. Moreover, the duty to mitigate will be breached where there has been an anticipatory breach. Secretariat Commentary in Official Records, 61.

135 Benicke, 329; Honnold, 206; Karollus (1997), 38; Lorenz (1998), II C.

136 Audit in Carbonneau, 150. See also Honnold, 206.

137 Request for Arbitration, No 13.

SPORTS throughout any litigation against VIS FISH COMPANY,[138] and would have been liable for any damages incurred by SPORTS as a result of the continued retail of the goods.[139] Thus, SPORTS' removal of VIS WATER SPORTS' goods from the market was a breach of its obligation under the principle of *favor contractus*, and of its obligation to mitigate its loss under the principle of good faith.

SPORTS was under no legal obligation to remove VIS WATER SPORTS' goods from the Danubian market. Nor was there any legal justification for its decision to take that action. SPORTS was only impeded in its use of VIS WATER SPORTS' goods by its own voluntary decision to cease selling those goods.[140] As such, any breach by VIS WATER SPORTS of Article 42 CISG did not result in 'such a detriment to the other party as substantially to deprive him of what he is entitled to expect under the contract' within the meaning of Article 25 CISG.

3.2 ANY DETRIMENT WAS NOT FORESEEN BY VIS WATER SPORTS AND WAS NOT FORESEEABLE BY A REASONABLE PERSON IN VIS WATER SPORTS' POSITION

Under Article 25 CISG, a party will not have fundamentally breached a contract where '[it] did not foresee and a reasonable person of the same kind in the same circumstances would not have foreseen such a result'. Even if SPORTS did suffer a detriment that substantially deprived it of what it was entitled to expect under the contract, that detriment was neither foreseen by VIS WATER SPORTS nor foreseeable by a reasonable person in VIS WATER SPORTS' position.

VIS WATER SPORTS had no knowledge of VIS FISH COMPANY prior to 31 March 1999[141] and was unaware of the possibility that VIS FISH COMPANY would make an assertion of trademark infringement.[142] Consequently, VIS WATER SPORTS did not foresee the potential detriment associated with VIS FISH COMPANY's intellectual property claim.

---

138 Claimant's Exhibit No 13. Note that a breach will only substantially deprive the non-breaching party of what it was entitled to expect under the contract where the breach cannot be adequately compensated in damages. Honnold, 206; Koch (1998), 351; Schlechtriem in Schlechtriem (1998), 183; Schlechtriem in Schlechtriem (2000), 266–67. Benicke, 329, states that 'The relation between performance and counter-performance however is not substantially disturbed when the buyer can dispose of the goods in a reasonable way and receives compensation in damages or a reduction of the price for the detriment suffered because of the failure to receive a delivery complying with the contract [translated from German].' See also Koch (1995), 98; Koch (1998), 221; *Landgericht* Oldenburg: 12 O 3010 of 6 July 1994; *Oberlandesgericht* Frankfurt: 5 U 15/93 of 18 January 1994; *Oberlandesgericht* Oldenburg: 11 U 64/94 1 February 1995.

139 See footnote 132.

140 Claimant's Exhibit No 12.

141 Procedural Order No 1, Clarification No 19.

142 See 2.1(b).

Furthermore, SPORTS' alleged detriment was not foreseeable by a reasonable person within the meaning of Article 25 CISG. According to Will, a reasonable person is a 'hypothetical merchant … engaged in the same line of trade, exercising the same function' as the party in breach.[143] SPORTS was neither under a legal obligation, nor justified in its decision, to remove VIS WATER SPORTS' goods from the market.[144] Consequently, a reasonable merchant in the position of VIS WATER SPORTS could not have foreseen that SPORTS would take that course of action. Since SPORTS' alleged detriment was neither foreseen nor foreseeable, VIS WATER SPORTS did not fundamentally breach the contract.

3.3 IN LIGHT OF VIS WATER SPORTS' OFFER TO CURE, THERE WAS NO FUNDAMENTAL BREACH OF CONTRACT [NEW ARGUMENT]

In determining the existence of a fundamental breach, 'regard must be had not only to the gravity of the breach, but also to the willingness of the seller to cure the defect'.[145] Consequently, even if the Arbitral Tribunal finds that VIS WATER SPORTS' purported breach of contract resulted in a detriment to SPORTS within the meaning of Article 25 CISG, VIS WATER SPORTS' breach was not fundamental because it made an offer to cure in accordance with Article 48(1) CISG. Article 48(1) CISG provides that:

> Subject to article 49, the seller may, even after the date for delivery, remedy at his own expense any failure to perform his obligations, if he can do so without unreasonable delay and without causing the buyer unreasonable inconvenience or uncertainty of reimbursement by the seller of expenses advanced by the buyer.

(a) An offer to cure is relevant in determining whether VIS WATER SPORTS' breach is fundamental

Although the buyer's right to avoid the contract will often prevail over the seller's right to offer to cure,[146] Will emphasises that 'the seller's right to cure should be protected if … where cure is feasible, the buyer hastily declares the

143 Will in Bianca & Bonell, 219. See also Lorenz (1998), III B; Schlechtriem in Schlechtriem (1998), 179. The point in time at which the detriment must be foreseeable is the time of the conclusion of the contract. Enderlein & Maskow, 116; Holthausen, 105; Koch (1998), 321; Schlechtriem in Schlechtriem (1998), 180; Schlechtriem in Schlechtriem (2000), 263. This conclusion is reinforced by the fact that Art 10 ULIS (the predecessor to Art 25 CISG) expressly stated that foreseeability was to be determined 'at the time of the conclusion of the contract'. Will in Bianca & Bonell, 220.

144 See 3.1.

145 *Oberlandesgericht* Koblenz: 2 U 31/96 of 31 January 1997 [translated from German].

146 This interpretation is apparent from the wording of Art 48(1) CISG, which is expressed to be 'subject to Art 49 [CISG]'.

contract avoided before the seller has an opportunity to cure the defect'.[147] Any other interpretation 'puts the seller at the buyer's mercy and allows the buyer to speculate without observing his duty to mitigate losses'.[148] This would render the seller's right to cure 'futile'.[149] Consequently, where a serious offer to cure is foreseeable, whether a breach is fundamental must be determined in light of the seller's offer to cure.[150]

SPORTS foresaw the possibility that VIS WATER SPORTS would make a serious offer to cure. It was aware that there was no basis for VIS FISH COMPANY's claim.[151] This was confirmed by SPORTS' legal representatives, Howard & Heward, who advised SPORTS that 'the claim of the Vis Fish Company … is unfounded'.[152] Moreover, SPORTS specifically contemplated the possibility that VIS WATER SPORTS was able to cure the purported breach. In his letter to VIS WATER SPORTS of 3 November 1999, Mr Kent, President of SPORTS, stated that: 'If you are able to reach an understanding with the Vis Fish Company permitting the sale of your goods in Danubia, we would be pleased to consider placing further orders in the future.'[153] This statement indicates that SPORTS foresaw a possible offer to cure from VIS WATER SPORTS. Therefore, whether VIS WATER SPORTS' breach was fundamental must be determined in light of its offer to cure.

(b) VIS WATER SPORTS' proposed cure satisfied the requirements of Art 48(1) CISG

Where the seller's proposed cure satisfies the requirements of Article 48(1) CISG, there will be no fundamental breach.[154] Article 48(1) CISG provides that a cure must be 'without *unreasonable delay* and without causing the

147 Will in Bianca & Bonell, 349. Gabriel (1994), 139, refers to § 2-508 UCC in stating that: 'both the CISG and the UCC protect the seller's right to cure from surprise rejection by the buyer.' Schlechtriem in Schlechtriem (1998), 183, states that: 'there is initially no fundamental breach of contract in cases in which it can be expected of the seller to … remove a defect in title within a time which is reasonable.' Ziegel in Galston & Smit, 9–23, argues that: 'Conceivably, a tribunal could find that the injured party was acting in 'bad faith' if he precipitously exercised his right of avoidance for the very purpose of denying the breaching party an opportunity to cure.'

148 Will in Bianca & Bonell, 349.

149 Honnold, 210.

150 Honnold, 210. It is clear from the Secretariat Commentary in Official Records, 41, that 'in some cases the fact that the seller is able and willing to remedy the non-conformity of the goods without inconvenience to the buyer may mean that there would be no fundamental breach unless the seller failed to remedy the non-conformity within an appropriate period of time.' This conclusion is reinforced by the general principle of favor contractus which underlies the CISG. See footnote 129. This principle suggests that a contract should not be avoided where there remains a possibility to keep the contract on foot through an offer to cure. Kazimierska, III F 1; Speidel, 138.

151 In his letter to VIS FISH COMPANY of 4 October 1999, Mr Kent, President of SPORTS, stated that: 'There is no likelihood that anyone would confuse athletic equipment, even that used for water sports, with the fish and fish products that I now understand are sold by your company. The markets and the nature of the products are simply too different.' Claimant's Exhibit No 8.

152 Claimant's Exhibit No 10.

153 Claimant's Exhibit No 12.

154 Honnold, 210.

buyer *unreasonable inconvenience* or *uncertainty of reimbursement* by the seller of expenses advanced by the buyer [emphasis added]'. In its letter to SPORTS of 10 November 1999, VIS WATER SPORTS stated that 'We will ... do all in our power to aid you in your defense against the assertion of trademark infringement. If, at the conclusion of any litigation that might take place, you were not able to recover your legal costs from the Vis Fish Company, we would stand ready to reimburse you for such reasonable costs as you had incurred.'[155] This proposed cure satisfies the three requirements of Article 48(1) CISG.

First, if VIS FISH COMPANY commenced litigation, VIS WATER SPORTS' offer to 'do all in [its] power to aid in [SPORTS'] defense against the assertion of trademark infringement'[156] would have been effective without 'unreasonable delay'. Second, the offer to cure would not have caused 'unreasonable inconvenience' to SPORTS. The phrase 'unreasonable inconvenience' refers to effects of the cure, and not to effects of the breach.[157] Although SPORTS might have suffered some disruption to business,[158] that disruption was an effect of VIS WATER SPORTS' purported breach under Article 42(1) CISG and not an effect of VIS WATER SPORTS' proposed cure. Therefore, any alleged 'disruption to business' would not have constituted an 'unreasonable inconvenience' under Article 48(1) CISG. Furthermore, Kritzer states that: 'Article 48(1) [CISG] recognises that the buyer may have to incur certain expenses in order for the seller to remedy his failure to perform. This in itself does not give the buyer a reason to refuse to allow the seller to remedy his failure to perform.'[159] Consequently, although SPORTS may have incurred legal costs if VIS FISH COMPANY had commenced litigation, these costs would not have been an 'unreasonable inconvenience' within the meaning of Article 48(1) CISG. In any case, VIS WATER SPORTS expressly stated its willingness to reimburse SPORTS for any such costs.[160] Third, the offer to cure did not cause any 'uncertainty of reimbursement.' According to Will, the phrase 'uncertainty of reimbursement' is concerned with 'any serious doubt as to the ability or ... willingness of the seller to reimburse expenditures when due'.[161] VIS WATER SPORTS is an

155 Claimant's Exhibit No 13.

156 Claimant's Exhibit No 13.

157 Secretariat Commentary in Official Records, 430. Huber in Schlechtriem (2000), 522, and Schnyder & Straub in Honsell (1997), 541, refer to examples where, as a consequence of the subsequent performance, the buyer is subject to an unreasonable inconvenience. A similar principle is found in § 634 II BGB. Schlechtriem in Flechtner, 251–52.

158 Claimant's Exhibit No 12.

159 Kritzer, 405. See also Enderlein & Maskow, 187; Huber in Schlechtriem (1998), 406.

160 VIS WATER SPORTS stated that: 'we would stand ready to reimburse you for such reasonable costs as you had incurred.' Claimant's Exhibit No 13.

161 Will in Bianca Bonell, 353. See also Huber in Schlechtriem (1998), 406, who states that: 'if there is *a well-founded doubt as to the seller's willingness or ability to reimburse the costs* ... the seller has a right to cure ... only if he provides security for those costs [emphasis added]'. By implication, in any situation where no well-founded doubt exists, there exists no 'uncertainty of reimbursement.'

established company,[162] and it demonstrated its unequivocal intention to reimburse SPORTS when it stated that 'we would stand ready to reimburse you for such reasonable costs as you had incurred'.[163] Therefore, VIS WATER SPORTS' proposed cure satisfied the requirements of Article 48(1) CISG. In light of VIS WATER SPORTS' offer to cure, there was no fundamental breach.[164]

4 VIS WATER SPORTS IS ONLY LIABLE TO MAKE NET RESTITUTION OF $220,300 AND IS NOT LIABLE TO PAY DAMAGES

SPORTS argues that:

1 *VIS WATER SPORTS is liable to make restitution and is not entitled to the profits derived from the sale of the goods (Memorandum for the Claimant, Universidade Federal do Rio Grande do Sul, 24–26); and*

2 *VIS WATER SPORTS is liable to pay damages (Memorandum for the Claimant, Universidade Federal do Rio Grande do Sul, 26).*

4.1 VIS WATER SPORTS IS ONLY LIABLE TO MAKE NET RESTITUTION OF $220,300

If the Arbitral Tribunal determines that SPORTS validly avoided the contract pursuant to Article 49(1)(a) CISG, SPORTS' claim for restitution of $368,000 in respect of the unsold goods must be set off against VIS WATER SPORTS' entitlement to the $147,700 profit that SPORTS earned on the goods sold. Therefore, VIS WATER SPORTS is only liable to make net restitution of $220,300.

(a) VIS WATER SPORTS is liable to make restitution of $368,000 in respect of the unsold goods

According to Article 81(2) CISG, avoidance of the contract entitles 'a party who has performed the contract either wholly or in part [to] claim restitution

162 VIS WATER SPORTS is well-known in Equatoriana. It has exported goods since 1995, and has therefore existed for a period of at least five years. Procedural Order No 1, Clarification No 25.

163 Claimant's Exhibit No 13.

164 In order to avoid the contract, SPORTS was also required to comply with Arts 26 and 49(2)(b)(i) CISG. Art 26 CISG states that: 'a declaration of avoidance is effective only if made by notice to the other party.' SPORTS' notice of avoidance of 3 November 1999 satisfied the form requirements of Art 26 CISG. Art 49(2)(b)(i) CISG states that: 'in cases where the seller has delivered the goods, the buyer loses the right to declare the contract avoided unless he does so … in respect of any breach other than late delivery, within a reasonable time … after he knew or ought to have known of the breach.' SPORTS gave notice of avoidance within the same period as it gave notice of VIS FISH COMPANY's claim under Art 43(1) CISG. Assuming that the Arbitral Tribunal has already found that notice under Art 43(1) CISG was made within a 'reasonable time' (without which finding the Arbitral Tribunal would not consider the issue of avoidance), notice under Art 49(2)(b)(i) CISG was also given within a reasonable time.

from the other party of whatever the first party has supplied or paid under the contract.' Therefore, if the Arbitral Tribunal determines that SPORTS validly avoided the contract, VIS WATER SPORTS is liable to make restitution of $368,000[165] to SPORTS in exchange for the return of the two-thirds of the goods that remain unsold.

(b) SPORTS is liable to make restitution of the $147,700 profit on the goods sold

SPORTS is unable to make restitution of the one-third of the goods that have already been sold.[166] Where it is impossible for a buyer to make restitution of part of the goods, Article 84(2)(b) CISG provides that: 'The buyer must account to the seller for all benefits which he has derived from the goods.' Schlechtriem states that 'Article 84 [CISG] obligates the parties to return all benefits of possession (profits and advantages of use)'.[167] Therefore, SPORTS is liable to make restitution of the $147,700 profit[168] that it earned on the resale of VIS WATER SPORTS' goods.

SPORTS claims that: 'It wouldn't be fair to … reward … the seller who breaches the contract.'[169] However, the purpose of Article 84(2) CISG is to facilitate an equalisation of benefits, not to punish a party for its breach.[170] According to the Secretariat Commentary, 'It is irrelevant which party's failure gave rise to the avoidance of the contract or who demanded restitution

165 SPORTS paid a total of $552,000 (exclusive of shipping costs) for all the goods purchased from VIS WATER SPORTS, excluding shipping costs. Claimant's Exhibit No 6. One-third of those goods were sold by VIS WATER SPORTS. Request for Arbitration, No 13. Therefore, the value of the unsold goods is two-thirds of $552,000, which equals $368,000.

166 Request for Arbitration, No 13. However, this does not preclude the parties from undertaking restitution. Although Art 82(1) CISG states that: 'The buyer loses the right to declare the contract avoided … if it is impossible for him to make restitution of the goods substantially in the condition in which he received them,' Art 82(2)(c) CISG states that Art 82(1) CISG does not apply where the 'goods or part of the goods have been sold in the normal course of business'. Leser in Schlechtriem (1998), 636; Leser & Hornung in Schlechtriem (2000), 814.

167 Schlechtriem (1986), 107. See also Honnold, 517; Leser in Schlechtriem (1998), 662; Leser & Hornung in Schlechtriem (2000), 827; Neumayer & Ming, 557–58; Tallon in Bianca & Bonell, 612; *Oberlandesgericht* Oldenburg: 11 U 64/94 of 1 February 1995. In fact, SPORTS relied on *Oberlandesgericht* Oldenburg: 11 U 64/94 of 1 February 1995 to argue that Art 84(2)(b) CISG does not require the buyer to account to the seller for the profits derived from the sale of the goods. Memorandum for the Claimant, Universidade Federal do Rio Grande do Sul, 26. However, the Court only denied the seller's claim for profits because it was not clear that the buyer would receive any benefit from its customers.

168 The normal retail mark-up on VIS WATER SPORTS products is 70 percent of the delivered purchase cost. The delivered purchase cost of the goods sold was $211,000. Therefore, VIS WATER SPORTS estimates that the profit earned by SPORTS on the goods sold was 70 percent of $211,000, which equals $147,700. Answer to the Request for Arbitration, No 10; Procedural Order No 1, Clarification No 51.

169 Memorandum for the Claimant, Universidade Federal do Rio Grande do Sul, 25.

170 Tallon in Bianca & Bonell, 611, states that: 'The restitution is not designed to penalize the buyer; it aims at restoring the former state of things, ie, that which existed prior to the conclusion of the contract.'

[emphasis added].'[171] Therefore, SPORTS is liable to make restitution of its profit of $147,700. Consequently, VIS WATER SPORTS' liability to make restitution of $368,000 must be reduced by $147,700,[172] leaving it with a net liability of $220,300.[173]

4.2 VIS WATER SPORTS IS NOT LIABLE TO PAY DAMAGES

Pursuant to Article 74 CISG,[174] SPORTS claims that VIS WATER SPORTS is liable to pay liquidated damages of $112,000 plus unliquidated damages.[175] This amount comprises damages for advertising expenses ($35,000), shipping costs ($11,000 attributable to the goods sold, and $22,000 attributable to the unsold goods), storage and miscellaneous expenses (liquidated damages[176] of $4,000 prior to the claim, plus unliquidated damages[177]), and allocated general selling and administrative expenses ($40,000).[178] None of these claims for damages can be supported at law.

(a) VIS WATER SPORTS is not liable to pay damages for advertising expenses of $35,000, or for shipping costs of $11,000

Under Article 74 CISG, a party is only liable to pay damages if the other party suffers a 'loss'. SPORTS' advertising expenses of $35,000 are attributable to 'general newspaper advertisements for [SPORTS'] stores and did not constitute expenses that would not otherwise have been incurred'.[179] As such, the advertising expenses cannot be classified as a 'loss' within the meaning of Article 74 CISG. SPORTS' stores derived the benefit of increased market exposure, regardless of the availability of specific VIS WATER SPORTS

171 Secretariat Commentary in Official Records, 58. See also Enderlein & Maskow, 349; Gabriel (1994), 256–57; Leser in Schlechtriem (1998), 656.

172 Art 81(2) CISG states that: 'if both parties are bound to make restitution, they must do so concurrently.' Enderlein & Maskow, 344; Honnold, 507; Leser in Schlechtriem (1998), 641; Magnus (1997), 47; Tallon in Bianca & Bonell, 605. Therefore, although the CISG does not expressly provide a right of set-off, according to Leser in Schlechtriem (1998), 641, it is possible to imply such a right of into Art 81 CISG because the 'set-off of monetary claims under a contract of sale is a direct extension of the principle of concurrent restitution'. See also Magnus (1997), 47.

173 $368,000 - $147,700 = $220,300.

174 Art 74 CISG states that: 'Damages for breach of contract by one party consist of a sum equal to the loss ... suffered by the other party as a consequence of the breach. Such damages may not exceed the loss which the party in breach foresaw or ought to have foreseen at the time of the conclusion of the contract, in the light of the facts and matters of which he then knew of ought to have known, as a possible consequence of the breach of contract.'

175 Request for Arbitration, No 13.

176 A liquidated claim exists if the amount 'is fixed, has been agreed upon, or is capable of ascertainment by mathematical computation or operation of law'. Black, 930.

177 An unliquidated claim exists if the amount of damages has not been finally determined. Black, 1537.

178 Request for Arbitration, No 13.

179 Procedural Order No 1, Clarification No 49.

products.[180] Consequently, VIS WATER SPORTS is not liable for SPORTS' advertising expenses.

Similarly, SPORTS' shipping costs attributable to the goods sold ($11,000[181]) do not constitute a 'loss' within the meaning of Article 74 CISG. The shipping costs were incorporated into SPORTS' purchase price,[182] and were fully recovered through the sale of the goods. This remains true even if SPORTS is liable to make restitution of its profit on the goods sold, because SPORTS' profit excluded shipping costs.[183] Thus, VIS WATER SPORTS is not liable to pay damages in respect of the shipping costs attributable to the goods sold.

(b) VIS WATER SPORTS is not liable to pay damages for allocated general selling and administrative expenses of $40,000

Article 74 CISG also provides that a party is only liable to pay damages if the loss is suffered as a '*consequence* of the breach [emphasis added]'. Although SPORTS did incur general selling and administrative expenses, it is unable to identify any 'specific additional expenses associated with the purchase or sale of the Vis Water Sports' goods that could be isolated other than the cost of the letters of credit.'[184] The absence of a causal nexus between the expenses and the sale of VIS WATER SPORTS' goods dictates that no loss was suffered by SPORTS as a 'consequence of [VIS WATER SPORTS'] breach'. Therefore, VIS WATER SPORTS is not liable to pay damages in respect of the allocated general selling and administrative expenses.[185]

180 This conclusion is reinforced by the principle that 'the liability to pay damages ... must not result in a profit for the promisee'. Stoll in Schlechtriem (1998), 566. This principle is reflected in the absence of a clause providing for punitive damages in the CISG. Farnsworth (1979), 248; Roßmeier, 408; Schönle in Honsell (1997), 934; Sutton, 744. If VIS WATER SPORTS was liable to pay damages for the advertising expenses, SPORTS would effectively derive a profit, because it would derive a windfall from the free increased market exposure.

181 SPORTS incurred shipping costs totalling $33,000. SPORTS paid $7,000 in shipping costs on 10 May 1999, and a further $26,000 in shipping costs on 25 June, 1999. Claimant's Exhibits Nos 4 & 6; Procedural Order No 1, Clarification No 45. SPORTS sold one-third of the goods delivered. Request for Arbitration, No 13. Therefore, the shipping costs attributable to the goods sold equal $11,000 (one-third of $33,000).

182 Claimant's Exhibit No 6.

183 Profit is defined as 'the gross proceeds of a business transaction less the costs of the transaction'. Black, 1211. Therefore, SPORTS' profit derived from the sale of VIS WATER SPORTS' goods is calculated by deducting the shipping costs and other costs associated with the transaction from the resale price of the goods. Since SPORTS is only liable to make restitution of the profits derived from the resale of VIS WATER SPORTS' goods, SPORTS will retain the proceeds of sale covering its costs, including the shipping costs. This interpretation is reinforced by the method adopted for calculating SPORTS' profit, being 70% of delivered purchase cost. Answer to the Request for Arbitration, No 10; Procedural Order No 1, Clarification No 51. This definition of profit indicates that costs of delivery must have been incorporated in the cost, rather than the profit, associated with the transaction.

184 Procedural Order No 1, Clarification No 49.

185 Although SPORTS may claim the cost of the letters of credit ($620), it would have to amend its claim to do so. Art 19 ICC Rules states that: 'After the Terms of Reference have been signed or approved by the [ICC] Court, no party shall make new claims or counterclaims which fall outside the limits of the Terms of Reference unless it has been authorised to do so by the Arbitral ... [cont]

(c) *VIS WATER SPORTS is not liable to pay damages for shipping costs of $22,000, liquidated damages for storage and miscellaneous expenses of $4,000, or unliquidated damages for storage and miscellaneous expenses*

Article 77 CISG states that:

> A party who relies on a breach of contract must take such measures as are reasonable in the circumstances to mitigate the loss … resulting from the breach. If he fails to take such measures, the party in breach may claim a reduction in the damages in the amount by which the loss should have been mitigated.

According to Article 77 CISG, a buyer may not claim damages in respect of losses which would have been avoided had it taken 'such measures as are reasonable in the circumstances to mitigate the loss'.[186] VIS FISH COMPANY's claim is unfounded.[187] Consequently, SPORTS had no reason to remove VIS WATER SPORTS' goods from the market.[188] If SPORTS had continued to sell the goods, it would have fully recovered the shipping costs of $22,000[189] attributable to the unsold goods and avoided any storage and miscellaneous expenses associated with removing the goods from the shelves. Therefore, because SPORTS breached its obligation to mitigate losses under Article 77 CISG, VIS WATER SPORTS is not liable to pay damages for shipping costs attributable to the unsold goods, nor is it liable to pay damages for storage and miscellaneous expenses.[190]

---

185 [cont] Tribunal, which shall consider the nature of such new claims or counterclaims, the stage of the arbitration and other relevant circumstances.' Art 19 ICC Rules would also restrict the ability of SPORTS to bring any other additional claim, such as for the costs associated with the legal opinion delivered by SPORTS' legal representatives, Howard & Heward, or for lost profits.

186 Ghestin, 26; Magnus in Honsell (1997), 974; Roßmeier, 411; Tallon in Bianca & Bonell, 605; Secretariat Commentary in Official Records, 57; *Oberlandesgericht* Köln: 18 U 121/97 of 21 August 1997.

187 SPORTS' legal representatives, Howard & Heward, stated that: 'In our opinion the claim of the Vis Fish Company to trademark infringement is unfounded.' Claimant's Exhibit No 10.

188 See 3.1.

189 SPORTS incurred shipping costs totalling $33,000. SPORTS paid $7,000 in shipping costs on 10 May 1999, and a further $26,000 in shipping costs on 25 June, 1999. Claimant's Exhibits Nos 4 & 6; Procedural Order No 1, Clarification No 45. SPORTS sold one-third of the goods delivered. Request for Arbitration, No 13. Therefore, the shipping costs attributable to the goods remaining unsold equal $22,000 (two-thirds of $33,000).

190 Art 86(1) CISG provides that a buyer 'must take such steps to preserve [the goods it intends to reject] as are reasonable in the circumstances. He is entitled to retain them until he has been reimbursed his reasonable expenses by the seller'. However, SPORTS has made no claim pursuant to Art 86 CISG, and to do so would require an amendment of its claim under Art 19 ICC Rules.

5 VIS WATER SPORTS IS ONLY LIABLE TO PAY INTEREST AT A RATE OF 3%

SPORTS argues that VIS WATER SPORTS is liable to pay interest on the purchase price and on the damages (Memorandum for the Claimant, Universidade Federal do Rio Grande do Sul, 26).

5.1 VIS WATER SPORTS IS ONLY LIABLE TO PAY INTEREST ON THE NET PRICE

According to Article 84(1) CISG, 'If the seller is bound to refund the price, he must also pay interest on it'. If the Arbitral Tribunal determines that VIS WATER SPORTS is liable to make restitution of $220,300, VIS WATER SPORTS is also liable to pay interest on that net price.[191] Interest is to be paid from the date on which the price was paid,[192] which in this case occurred in two instalments. In relation to the 10 May 1999 instalment,[193] VIS WATER SPORTS is liable to make net restitution of $12,075.[194] In relation to the 25 June 1999 instalment,[195] VIS WATER SPORTS is liable to make net restitution of $208,225.[196] Therefore, VIS WATER SPORTS is liable to pay interest on $12,075 from 10 May 1999, and on $208,225 from 25 June 1999.

---

191 Pursuant to Art 84(1) CISG, SPORTS is entitled to interest on the price of $368,000. However, SPORTS is also liable to pay $147,700 to VIS WATER SPORTS. This constitutes a 'sum in arrears', and pursuant to Art 78 CISG, VIS WATER SPORTS is therefore entitled to interest on that sum in arrears. Therefore, because interest is payable on both sums, it is appropriate to offset SPORTS' entitlement to $368,000 by VIS WATER SPORTS' entitlement to $147,700 for the purposes of calculating the net amount in respect of which VIS WATER SPORTS is liable to pay interest.

192 Enderlein & Maskow, 349; Leser in Schlechtriem (1998), 659; Leser & Hornung in Schlechtriem (2000), 821; Magnus (1997), 51; Neumayer & Ming, 555–56; Weber in Honsell (1997), 1024; Secretariat Commentary in Official Records, 58; ICC Arbitration Case No 6653 of 1993; ICC Arbitration Case No 7531 of 1994; ICC Arbitration Case No 7585 of 1992; Schiedsgericht Hamburger Freundschaftliche Arbitrage of 29 December 1998; *Société Thyssen Stahlunion GmbH v Société Maaden General Foreign Trade Organisation for Metal and Building Materials. Cour d'appel de Paris* of 6 April 1995.

193 Procedural Order No 1, Clarification No 48.

194 SPORTS paid a first instalment of $95,000 ($102,000 less shipping costs of $7,000). Claimant's Exhibit No 4. SPORTS sold goods from that delivery valued at $46,000 (list price of $50,000 less a discount of 8%). Procedural Order No 1, Clarification No 45. Therefore, the value of the unsold goods is $95,000 – $46,000 = $49,000. However, SPORTS earned a profit on the goods sold of 70% of the delivered purchase cost. Answer to the Request for Arbitration, No 10; Procedural Order No 1, Clarification No 51. The goods sold had a delivered purchase cost of $52,750 (list price of $50,000 plus one-twelfth of the total shipping costs ie $33,000 ∏ 12 = $2,750). The profit on the goods sold was therefore 70% of $52,750 = $36,925. Therefore, VIS WATER SPORTS' net liability in relation to the first instalment is $49,000 - $36,925 = $12,075.

195 Procedural Order No 1, Clarification No 48.

196 SPORTS paid a second instalment of $457,000 ($483,000 less shipping costs of $26,000). Claimant's Exhibit No 6. SPORTS sold goods from that delivery valued at $138,000 (list price of $150,000 less a discount of 8%). Procedural Order No 1, Clarification No 45. Therefore, the value of the unsold goods is $457,000 - $138,000 = $319,000. However, SPORTS earned a profit on the goods sold of 70% of the delivered purchase cost. Answer to the Request for Arbitration, No 10; Procedural Order No 1, Clarification No 51. The goods sold had a delivered purchase cost of ... [cont]

5.2 VIS WATER SPORTS IS LIABLE TO PAY INTEREST ON ANY LIQUIDATED DAMAGES, BUT IS ONLY LIABLE TO PAY INTEREST ON ANY UNLIQUIDATED DAMAGES FROM THE DATE ON WHICH THEY BECOME LIQUIDATED

If the Arbitral Tribunal determines that VIS WATER SPORTS is liable to pay damages, Article 78 CISG provides that 'If a party fails to pay the price or any other sum that is in arrears, the other party is entitled to interest on it.' Liquidated damages are a 'sum in arrears' on which interest is payable from the date of the breach.[197] However, unliquidated damages are not a 'sum in arrears' until they become liquidated on the date of judgment.[198] According to Enderlein and Maskow, '[unliquidated claims] become due when they have been liquidated vis à vis the other party'.[199] Therefore, although interest is payable on the liquidated damages from the date of the breach, no interest is payable on the unliquidated storage and miscellaneous expenses until the date of the judgement.

5.3 THE APPLICABLE RATE OF INTEREST IS 3% [NEW ARGUMENT]

Neither Article 84(1) CISG nor Article 78 CISG specify the applicable rate of interest.[200] This issue must therefore be determined according to the mechanism provided in Article 7(2) CISG.[201] Article 7(2) CISG states that: 'Questions concerning matters governed by this Convention which are not

---

196 [cont] $158,250 (list price of $150,000 plus one-quarter of the total shipping costs ie $33,000 ÷ 4 = $8,250). The profit on the goods sold was therefore 70% of $158,250 = $110,775. Therefore, VIS WATER SPORTS' net liability in relation to the first instalment is $319,000 - $110,775 = $208,225.

197 Darkey, 148; Enderlein & Maskow, 313–14; Honnold, 468–69; Nicholas in Bianca & Bonell, 571; Schneider, 230; Sutton, 750; Thiele, 7.

198 According to Nicholas in Bianca & Bonell, 571, 'the word 'sum' suggests a liquidated sum'. This conclusion is reinforced by the fact that Art 83 ULIS only entitled the seller to interest on the price, a liquidated sum. Schneider, 230. The unequivocal nature of this conclusion indicates that there is no need to refer to Art 7(1) CISG to interpret Art 78 CISG. Art 7(1) CISG states that: 'In the interpretation of this Convention, regard is to be had to its international character and to the need to promote uniformity in its application.' However, even if Art 7(1) CISG is used to interpret Art 78 CISG, the same conclusion is reached. In France, Switzerland, Germany and Italy, the injured party is only entitled to interest on a certain sum of money. § 288 BGB (Germany); Art 1153 *Code Civil* (France); Art 1224 *Codice Civile* (Italy); Art 104 *Schweizerisches Obligationenrecht* (Switzerland). See also Gotanda, 42. It is also a general common law rule that interest is payable only on liquidated damages. Knoll, 298; Rothschild, 196.

199 Enderlein & Maskow, 314.

200 In relation to this issue, Art 78 CISG and Art 84(1) CISG may be considered together. Honnold, 516–17; Sutton, 751; Tallon in Bianca & Bonell, 611–12.

201 Corney, 56; Corterier, 39; Darkey, 150; Honnold, 467–68; Kizery, 1293; Koneru, 125; Perales Viscasillas (1996), 405; Rosett, 298–99; Roßmeier, 413; Thiele, 26; van Alstine, 766; Zoccolillo, 38, 42; *Internationales Schiedsgericht der Bundeskammer der gewerblichen Wirtschaft:* SCH-4318 of 15 June 1994; *Internationales Schiedsgericht der Bundeskammer der gewerblichen Wirtschaft:* SCH-4366 of 15 June 1994.

expressly settled in it are to be settled in conformity with the general principles on which it is based.'[202]

The general principle underlying the interest provisions of the CISG is the principle of full compensation.[203] This principle requires that the injured party should be fully compensated for its potential need to borrow funds in its own country.[204] The best approximation of the injured party's borrowing costs is the official discount rate in the country of its principal place of business.[205] Thus, because SPORTS is the injured party, it is entitled to interest at the official discount rate in the country of its principal place of business, Danubia, which is 3%.[206]

---

202 Art 7(2) CISG only permits reference to the rules of private international law in the absence of general principles. Accordingly, Zoccolillo, 28-29, states that it is clear from the text of Art 7(2) CISG that: 'the principles on which [the CISG] is based have priority over any reference to … private international law.' See also Corterier, 34; Darkey, 150; Ferrari (1999), 88; Garro, 1155; Koneru, 106; Rosett, 299; Thiele, 23. Indeed, a proposal by the United Kingdom delegation that domestic law should govern interest rates was clearly rejected. Action by First Committee in Official Records, 137–38. Therefore, any attempt to determine the applicable rate of interest primarily by reference to private international law is incorrect. Corterier, 34; Kizery, 1284; Koneru, 125; Thiele, 26; Zoccolillo, 38. This conclusion is consistent with Art 7(1) CISG, which states that 'In the interpretation of this Convention, regard is to be had to its international character and to the need to promote uniformity in its application.' Honnold, 468; Kizery, 1282; Perales Viscasillas (1996), 405; Thiele, 25–26; van Alstine, 766; Zoccolillo, 41–42.

203 Darkey, 150; Honnold, 467, 516; Kizery, 1294; Koneru, 125–26; Roßmeier, 412; Thiele, 31; van Alstine, 766; Zoccolillo, 30; *Internationales Schiedsgericht der Bundeskammer der gewerblichen Wirtschaft*: SCH-4318 of 15 June 1994.

204 van Alstine, 766; *Internationales Schiedsgericht der Bundeskammer der gewerblichen Wirtschaft*: SCH-4318 of 15 June 1994; *Internationales Schiedsgericht der Bundeskammer der gewerblichen Wirtschaft*: SCH-4366 of 15 June 1994. This conclusion is supported by reference to the history of the drafting of Art 78 CISG. Art 58 of the Working Group's Draft Convention in 1976 entitled the seller to interest at a rate applicable in the country of the seller's principal place of business. By analogy, it is appropriate to interpret Art 78 CISG, which entitles any injured party to interest, as providing for interest at a rate applicable in the country of the injured party's principal place of business. Darkey, 149; Nicolas in Bianca & Bonell, 570; Sutton, 749–50. Similarly, Art 81(1) ULIS stated that: 'where the seller is under an obligation to refund the price he shall also be liable for the interest thereon … as from the date of payment,' and Art 83 ULIS stipulates that the rate of interest is a 'rate … in the country where he [the seller] has his place of business'. By analogy, it is appropriate to interpret Art 78 CISG, which entitles any injured party to interest, as providing for interest at a rate applicable in the country of the injured party's place of business. Schneider, 230.

205 In the United States, the discount rate is defined by the Federal Reserve, 5, as 'the interest rate charged commercial banks and other depository institutions when they borrow reserves from a regional Federal Reserve bank'. As a rate of interest set by a country's central bank, the discount rate is therefore reflective of borrowing costs in the country. There is considerable support for using a discount rate or a rate derived directly from the discount rate. According to Art 83 ULIS, the applicable rate of interest was 'a rate equal to the official discount rate in the country where he [the seller] has his place of business or, if he has no place of business, his habitual residence, plus 1%'. Nicolas in Bianca Bonell, 569; Schneider, 230. Additionally, the domestic laws of some countries provide for interest to be paid at a rate derived from the discount rate. In Great Britain, the statutory rate of interest is the relevant discount rate plus 1%. In Switzerland, Art 104 *Schweizerisches Obligationenrecht* provides that the statutory rate of interest is a usual bank discount rate. Eberstein & Bacher in Schlechtriem (1998), 598–99.

206 Procedural Order No 1, Clarification No 54.

6 SPORTS SHOULD BEAR THE COSTS OF ARBITRATION AND VIS WATER SPORTS' LEGAL COSTS

SPORTS argues that VIS WATER SPORTS should bear the costs of arbitration (Memorandum for the Claimant, Universidade Federal do Rio Grande do Sul, 27).

The allocation of costs is a procedural matter to be determined by reference to the ICC Rules.[207] Article 31(1) ICC Rules states that: 'The costs of the arbitration shall include the fees and expenses of the arbitrators and the ICC administrative costs fixed by the court … and the reasonable legal and other costs incurred by the parties for the arbitration.' According to Article 31(3) ICC Rules, 'The final Award shall fix the costs of the arbitration and decide which of the parties shall bear them or in what proportion they shall be borne by the parties'. It is a general principle of international commercial arbitration that costs are borne by the unsuccessful party.[208] Accordingly, a decision by the Arbitral Tribunal in favour of VIS WATER SPORTS should be followed by a decision that SPORTS bears the costs of arbitration and VIS WATER SPORTS' legal costs.

VIS WATER SPORTS commends the arguments presented in this Memorandum to this Arbitral Tribunal's discretion to achieve a just and fair resolution of this dispute.

---

207 Clause 14 of SPORTS' General Conditions of Purchase was the ICC standard arbitration clause with three additions. Request for Arbitration, No 18. VIS WATER SPORTS acknowledges that the ICC Rules govern the current proceedings. Answer to the Request for Arbitration, No 11.

208 Berger in CENTRAL, 35; Derains & Schwartz, 342; Gaillard & Savage, 686; Redfern & Hunter, 407; s 61(2) Arbitration Act 1996 (UK); Art 28(4) LCIA Rules; Art 40 UNCITRAL Arbitration Rules; *Channel Island Ferries Ltd v Cenargo Navigation Ltd* [1994] 2 Lloyd's Rep 161; *ICC Arbitration* Case No 7585 of 1992; *Schluß-Schiedspruch der Handelskammer* Hamburg of 21 June 1996.

INTERNATIONAL MARITIME LAW ARBITRATION MOOT

Dr Sarah C Derrington, Moot Director[1]

BRISBANE, AUSTRALIA, 1 JULY–6 JULY 2000

A JOINT VENTURE OF THE CENTRE FOR MARITIME LAW AND THE AUSTRALIAN INSTITUTE OF FOREIGN AND COMPARATIVE LAW WITHIN THE TC BEIRNE SCHOOL OF LAW AT THE UNIVERSITY OF QUEENSLAND AUSTRALIA

The TC Beirne School of Law hosted this exciting new competition in July 2000. The venue for the competition alternates between Brisbane, Singapore and Hong Kong.

In its inaugural year, the competition attracted teams from the University of Hong Kong, the National University of Singapore, the University of Technology Sydney, the Queensland University of Technology, Marquette University, Milwaukee and the University of Queensland.

The competition attracted sponsorship from Wallanius Wilhelmsen Line, the Australian Shipping Federation, McCullough Robertson, MacDonnells, the Maritime Law Association of Australia and New Zealand and the Bar Association of Queensland.

The moot problem in 2000 involved a commercial shipping dispute about the carriage of goods by sea and was decided by an arbitral panel according to the LMAA Terms (1997). The competition stimulates and encourages the study of the commercial and practical aspects of maritime law and trains students in the procedural skills required to undertake international commercial arbitrations.

The final of the competition was judged by Justice Richard Cooper of the Federal Court of Australia, Mr Sandy Thompson SC and Professor Tony Tarr. The standard of the competition was exceptional but ultimately the National University of Singapore was victorious over the University of Hong Kong in the final. The award for best individual mooter went to Miss Puja Kupai of the University of Hong Kong.

---

1 Barrister-at-Law; Senior Lecturer in Law, TC Beirne School of Law.

The two teams which made it through to the final were also the successful teams in the written component of the competition. The National University of Singapore won the award for the Best Memorandum for the Claimant and the University of Hong Kong won the award for the Best Memorandum for the Respondent. These two excellent submissions are reproduced below.

Maritime Law Moot: Memorandum for the Claimant (National University Of Singapore)

*Jane A Banlihan, Lee Jwee Nguan, Vinod Sabanmi,
Lee Ker Sheng and Loh Wai Yue*

Statement of Facts

The Dispute

This dispute arises out of a contract of carriage evidenced by a bill of lading dated 1 May 1998 between Quickship Pte Ltd (Quickship), the carrier, and Jaguar Manufacturers, the shipper. Under the bill of lading, Quickship was to deliver 200 Jaguar cars from Europa to Pacifica. After delivery of the cars, it was found that 164 of them had black spots or blots to the bonnets, turrets and boots.

The legal dispute is between Millennium Automobiles Pty Ltd (Millennium) and Quickship. Millennium brings this action as endorsee, lawful holder of the bill of lading, or merchant as defined under the bill of lading. It claims the cost of repairs to the paintwork of the Jaguars, which amounts to E 820 000.

The Claimant

The Claimant, Millennium Automobiles Pty Ltd (Millennium), is a distributor of prestigious motor vehicles. It is a wholly-owned subsidiary of Jaguar Importers Ltd (JagImps), which is an importer of prestigious motor vehicles. Both companies are incorporated and carrying on business in the State of Pacifica.

The Respondent

The Respondent, Quickship, is a carrier of goods by sea. It is incorporated and carrying on business in the State of Europa. It had time-chartered the vessel, 'MV JASMINE', from her owners, Antwerp Line.

Facts Relating to the Merits of the Case

The Bill of Lading

A clean 'to order' bill of lading was issued by Quickship and dated 1 May 1998.

Under this bill of lading, Quickship was to carry a consignment of 200 Jaguar automobiles aboard 'MV JASMINE' from Port Seeweg, Europa to Port Idyllic, Pacifica. The bill of lading also indicates that the carrier had received the cargo from the shipper, Jaguar Manufactures, in apparent good order and condition.

On 25 April 1998, prior to the issue of the bill of lading, Quickship agreed with Jaguar Manufacturers that 'MV JASMINE' would take the shortest customary route for commercial shipments between Europa and Pacifica. Quickship also indicated that JagImps would take delivery of the cargo at Pacifica on the 13 June 1998.

The Delivery

However, the cars did not arrive on the 13 June 1998.

The vessel deviated to Marseilles during the voyage. According to Quickship, this was in response to a distress call, and also to load additional supplies for the crew.

The vessel finally arrived at Port Idyllic on 15 June 1998. On the same day, Millennium received a letter from JagImps authorising them to take delivery of the goods. An original copy of the bill of lading was attached to this letter. With this copy of the bill of lading, Millennium immediately took delivery of the Jaguar cars.

The Damage

These cars were coated with wax at the time of delivery. After stripping the cars of the wax, Millennium discovered that there was damage to 164 of the 200 Jaguar cars. The paintwork of the cars' bonnets, turrets and boots had black spots and blots on them.

Millennium sent a notice of damage to Quickship on 21 July 1998, slightly more than a month after the delivery of the Jaguar cars. In that notice, Millennium acknowledged that this notice was given after the three day limit under Clause 25 of the bill of lading and explained that this was because the damage was not apparent at the time of delivery due to the wax coatings on the cars.

The Surveyor's Report

Millennium employed a marine surveying firm to discover the cause of the damage to the cargo.

On 3, 6 and 10 November 1998, Mr Raines, a marine surveyor and Managing Director of the MSC Group, conducted a cargo survey of the damaged cars at three different locations. He stated that the re-spraying of the cars would cost E 5 000 per vehicle, amounting to E 820 000 in total.

Mr Raines was unable to survey the vessel as she was on charter between various ports. However, he managed to interview a deckhand, Mr Kavanagh. The deckhand gave evidence that on the night of 1 May 1998, after the loading of the cargo was completed, he had scrubbed the top deck of the ship with a pungent solution. As it was a special solution, he had to wear rubber gloves. This scrubbing was done in preparation for the Master's wedding on deck of the ship, on the evening of 2 May 1998, before the ship set sail for Pacifica. Mr Raines believes that this is an acid-based solution.

In his report, Mr Raines submitted that there were 2 possible causes of damage to the cars. The damage was caused either by the leaking of the acid or chemicals from the deck of the vessel onto the car deck during the scrubbing, or by industrial fallout (acid rain) at the load port.

Facts Relating to the Agreement to Arbitrate

The arbitration proceedings

On 15 June 1999, Millennium sent a facsimile to Quickship informing them that Millennium would be forced to consider commencing arbitration proceedings against Quickship unless Quickship indicated by return facsimile that they were prepared to bear the cost of repainting the Jaguars.

Receiving no reply, Millennium wrote to Quickship on 16 June 1999, informing them that they had appointed Mr R Salter to arbitrate the dispute. Millennium required Quickship to appoint an arbitrator within 14 calendar days, failing which Mr Salter would be the sole arbitrator.

Quickship replied on 1 July 1999, appointing Mrs Wilhelmina James QC as their arbitrator. They asserted that they had previously written a letter on 28 July 1998 disclaiming liability. Quickship further stated that they denied that Millennium was the owner of the Jaguars and argued that the claim was time-barred. In view of their objections, they asserted that they had appointed Mrs James to protect their interests.

The parties have agreed that the Arbitration will be held in Englandia, which has enacted the UNCITRAL Model Law on International Commercial Arbitration. The proceedings are to be held in accordance with the London

Maritime Arbitrators' Association Terms. All states involved are parties to the New York Convention on the Recognition and Enforcement of Foreign Arbitral Awards.

Clause 2 of the bill of lading states that the governing law of the contract is the law of Europa, unless otherwise provided within that same document. Clause 27 (Clause Paramount) incorporates the Hague Rules, the Hague-Visby Rules or the Hamburg Rules, or other similar national legislation as may apply mandatorily by virtue of origin or destination of bills of lading. It also states that any term in the bill of lading repugnant to such legislation shall be void to that extent. Pacifica has adopted the Hamburg Rules while Europa has adopted the Hague-Visby Rules.

Questions Presented

1 Whether the arbitral tribunal has jurisdiction to hear this dispute.

2 Whether Quickship has breached its obligations to Millennium under the contract of carriage by causing damage to the cargo.

3 Whether Quickship is liable to Millennium for the damage caused to the cargo.

Arguments and Authorities

I The arbitral tribunal has jurisdiction to hear this dispute

A The governing law of the contract of carriage supports Millennium's case

1 The contract of carriage is governed by the law of Europa and subject to the Hamburg Rules

In construing the law governing a contract, the intention of the parties is of importance.[1] This accords with the principle of freedom of choice. As long as the choice of law by the parties is *bona fide*, legal and not contrary to public policy, it will be upheld.[2]

The contract of carriage is subject to the Hamburg Rules, as this must have been the intention of the parties.

Clause 2 of the bill of lading states that 'the contract ... shall be governed by the law of Europa except as may be otherwise provided herein'.

1 Rome Convention (1980), Art 3.

2 *Vita Food Products Inc v Unus Shipping Co Ltd* [1939] AC 277 [hereinafter *Vita Food*].

Clause 27 of the same bill of lading provides that it is 'subject to the provisions of the Hague Rules, the Hague-Visby Rules or the Hamburg Rules, as applicable, or any such other national legislation as may mandatorily apply by virtue of origin or destination of the bill of lading … If any term of this bill of lading be repugnant to said applicable legislation to any extent, such term shall be void to that extent, but no further'.

Clause 27 also states that 'nothing herein contained shall be deemed a surrender by the carrier of any of its rights or immunities or an increase of any of its responsibilities or liabilities under said legislation'.

Clause 2 and clause 27 read together indicate that the parties intended the law of Europa to apply, subject to mandatory legislation in Europa (the origin of the bill of lading) and Pacifica (the destination of the bill of lading).

The difficulty lies in the fact that Europa has enacted the Hague-Visby Rules, while Pacifica has enacted the Hamburg Rules.[3] These statutes have the 'force of law' in their respective countries, and are therefore mandatory statutes in their own jurisdictions.[4] The Hamburg Rules apply when Pacifica is the port of discharge[5] or when the bill of lading is issued in Pacifica.[6] The Hague-Visby Rules apply when the bill of lading is issued in Europa or when the carriage is from a port in Europa.[7] Therefore, the Hamburg Rules and the Hague-Visby Rules are mandatory statutes applicable to this bill of lading. Clause 27 leaves open the door to the applicability of such statutes that may apply by virtue of origin or destination of the bill of lading.

The Hamburg Rules apply a higher set of package and kilo limitations[8] than the Hague-Visby Rules. They also provide more time to file suit in case of dispute[9] and more time to inspect delivered cargo.[10] Further, the Hamburg Rules do not provide for excepted perils as in the Hague-Visby Rules.[11] Therefore, the Hamburg Rules are less favourable to Quickship.

Article 23, R 1 of the Hamburg Rules states that: '[A]ny stipulation in a contract of carriage … is void to the extent that it derogates, directly or indirectly, from the provisions of this Convention.' As such, if the parties intended to choose the Hague-Visby Rules instead of the Hamburg Rules, it would have been an evasion of their liabilities and responsibilities under the Hamburg Rules. This evasion is not allowed under the Hamburg Rules. It

3 Adoption of the Hague-Visby Rules Act (Europa) 1978, No 121 of 1978, s 4; Adoption of the Hamburg Rules Act (Pacifica) 1999, No 34 of 1991, s 4.

4 *The Hollandia* [1983] AC 565 [hereinafter *The Hollandia*].

5 Hamburg Rules, Art 2, R 1(b).

6 Hamburg Rules, Art 2, R 1(d).

7 Hague-Visby Rules, Art X.

8 Hague-Visby Rules, Art IV, R 5, compared with the Hamburg Rules, Art 6, R 1.

9 Hague-Visby Rules, Art III, R 6, compared with the Hamburg Rules, Art 20, R 1.

10 Hague-Visby Rules, Art III, R 6, compared with the Hamburg Rules, Art 19, R 2.

11 Hague-Visby Rules, Art IV, R 2.

would also mean that this is not a *bona fide* choice of law[12] and would therefore be invalid.[13]

Clause 27 specifically states that the clause should not be construed as an increase of its liabilities and responsibilities. However, this clause is found in Quickship's own standard form contract;[14] it must have envisaged that the mandatory statutes might increase its responsibilities and liabilities. By wording clause 27 as such, Quickship is attempting to evade the additional responsibilities and liabilities imposed by the mandatory statutes. This is an evasion of its responsibilities and liabilities.[15] This would mean that there is no *bona fide* choice of law.[16]

Therefore, to give full effect to clause 27 and clause 2 of the bill of lading, it must be that the parties intended the law of Europa to apply, together with the Hamburg Rules.

2 Even if the Hague-Visby Rules apply, the carrier has increased its liabilities to those applicable under the Hamburg Rules

Even if the Hague-Visby Rules apply to the contract of carriage, the parties must have intended that the carrier's liabilities and responsibilities are increased to those applicable under the Hamburg Rules.

According to clause 2 of the bill of lading, the governing law of the contract is the law of Europa. The parties to the bill of lading are incorporated and carrying on business in Europa. The Hague-Visby Rules are already mandatory in Europa and the parties would have known this. Therefore, clause 27 would be superfluous unless the parties have attached a greater significance to it.

Therefore, the parties must have intended that although the laws of Europa and the Hague-Visby Rules apply,[17] the carriers' liabilities and responsibilities are increased to those in the Hamburg Rules (the mandatory legislation of the destination port of the bill of lading).

This is allowed under Article V of the Hague-Visby Rules, which states: '[A] carrier shall be at liberty to surrender in whole or in part all or any rights

---

12 JJ Fawcett, 'Evasion of law and mandatory rules in private international law' (1990) 49 Cambridge LJ 44 [hereinafter Evasion of Law]; JG Castel, *Canadian Conflict of Laws*, 1994, Toronto: Butterworths, at 555 [hereinafter *Canadian Conflict*]; W Tetley, *International Conflict of Laws: Common, Civil and Maritime*, 1994, Montreal: International Shipping Publications, at 141 [hereinafter *International Conflict*].

13 *Vita Food, supra* note 2.

14 This is a reasonable inference from the facts, as the bill of lading carried Quickship's letterhead.

15 Evasion of Law; *Canadian Conflict*; *International Conflict, supra* note 12.

16 *Vita Food, supra* note 2.

17 In interpreting the Hague-Visby Rules, the tribunal should note that commonwealth cases are highly persuasive, even in civil law jurisdictions. There is insufficient case law interpreting the Rules in civil law jurisdictions and cases from common law jurisdictions should be referred to. Moreover, commonwealth jurisdictions have given the regime a purposive and uniform interpretation. See *The Hollandia, supra* note 4 at 572.

an immunities or to increase his responsibilities and obligations under these Rules, provided such surrender or increase shall be embodied in the bill of lading issued to the shipper.'

This surrender or increase of its responsibilities and liabilities is evident in clause 27 of the bill of lading, and is allowed by the Hague-Visby Rules. Therefore, the proper construction of clause 2 and clause 27, read together, is that the law of Europa and the Hague-Visby Rules apply to the contract of carriage, but the parties have intended that the carrier increase its liabilities and responsibilities to those in the Hamburg Rules.

For the purposes of this dispute, it must be that Quickship has agreed to increase the package and kilo limitations,[18] the time limitation to file a suit[19] and the time given to inspect delivered cargo[20] to those applicable in the Hamburg Rules. Quickship has also agreed to surrender the carrier's rights to the excepted perils[21] in the Hague-Visby Rules.

3 In any case, the claimant will show that Quickship is liable to Millennium under the Hague-Visby regime

Even if this tribunal holds that only the Hague-Visby Rules apply, Millennium will show that Quickship has breached its obligations to Millennium.

B Quickship and Millennium are proper parties to the suit

1 The law of Englandia determines whether the parties have locus standi *in this dispute*

The law determining whether a person can be made a party to litigation or arbitration is the law of the seat of the arbitration.[22] It is not necessary that the person must also be a proper party according to the proper law of the contract.[23]

Therefore, the law of Englandia governs whether a party has *locus standi* to appear before the arbitral tribunal.

2 Quickship is a proper respondent as it is the carrier under the contract of carriage

Quickship contracted with the shipper, Jaguar Manufacturers, to perform the contract of carriage.

Article 1, R 1 of the Hamburg Rules states that: '"[C]arrier" means any person by whom or in whose name a contract of carriage of goods by sea has

18 Hague-Visby Rules, Art IV, R 5, compared with the Hamburg Rules, Art 6, R 1.

19 Hague-Visby Rules, Art III, R 6, compared with the Hamburg Rules, Art 20, R 1.

20 Hague-Visby Rules, Art III, R 6, compared with the Hamburg Rules, Art 19, R 2.

21 Hague-Visby Rules, Art IV, R 2.

22 L Collins, ed, *Dicey & Morris: The Conflict of Laws*, vol 1, 12th edn, 1993, London: Sweet & Maxwell, at 172 [hereinafter Dicey & Morris].

23 *Hartmann v Konig* (1933) 50 TLR 114 [hereinafter *Hartmann*].

been concluded with a shipper.' Quickship concluded the contract of carriage in its name with a shipper, Jaguar Manufacturers. It is therefore a carrier as defined by the Hamburg Rules.

Even if the contract of carriage is governed by the Hague-Visby Rules, Quickship is still a carrier as defined by the Rules. Article 1(a) of the Hague-Visby Rules provides that: '"[C]arrier" includes the owner or the charterer who enters into a contract of carriage with a shipper.' Quickship is the charterer of 'MV JASMINE' and has entered into a contract of carriage with a shipper. It is therefore a carrier under the Hague-Visby Rules.

Both the Hamburg Rules[24] and the Hague-Visby Rules[25] place responsibilities, duties and obligations on the carrier, who cannot contract out of these obligations and responsibilities.[26] Therefore Quickship is a proper party to this arbitration.

3 *Millennium is a proper claimant and is entitled to bring arbitration proceedings against Quickship*

(a) Millennium is the lawful holder of the bill of lading

Millennium is the proper claimant in this dispute because it is the lawful holder of the bill of lading.

On the face of the bill of lading, the goods were consigned 'to order'. Thus, the carrier must deliver the goods to order of any person specified by the shipper, Jaguar Manufacturers.

Section 5(2)(b) of the Carriage of Goods by Sea Act (Englandia) 1992[27] states that a holder of the bill of lading is:

> [A] person with possession of the bill … by the delivery of the bill …

Since Jaguar Importers gave possession of the bill of lading to Millennium to enable it to collect the goods at Port Idyllic, Millennium is a lawful holder of the bill of lading.[28]

Section 2(1) of the Carriage of Goods by Sea Act (Englandia) 1992[29] states that: '[A] person who becomes the lawful holder of a bill of lading … shall … have transferred and vested in him all rights of suit under the contract of carriage as if he had been a party to that contract.'

---

24 Hamburg Rules, Part II.

25 Hague-Visby Rules, Art III.

26 Hamburg Rules, Art 23, R 1; Hague-Visby Rules, Art III, R 8.

27 Carriage of Goods by Sea Act (Englandia) 1992, s 5(2)(b). Clarification No 6. Englandia has identical laws to those in force in the United Kingdom at the time when the dispute arose.

28 Correspondence from Jaguar Importers to Millennium, dated 15 June 1998. Delivery of the bill of lading to Millennium is a reasonable inference from the facts, since Millennium managed to collect the goods.

29 Carriage of Goods by Sea Act (Englandia) 1992, s 2(1).

Since Millennium is a lawful holder of the bill of lading, it has the right of suit under the contract of carriage.[30] It is therefore a proper claimant in these proceedings.

(b) Millennium is the 'merchant' under the bill of lading

Furthermore, Millennium is entitled to sue under the contract of carriage as it is a 'merchant' as defined in the contract. In clause 1(b) of the bill of lading, a merchant is defined as including 'receiver of the Goods and the holder of this bill of lading'. Since Millennium is the receiver of the goods[31] and a lawful holder of the bill of lading,[32] it is the 'merchant' as defined by clause 1(b).

When the bill of lading defines the parties to the contract, the party named as 'merchant' is entitled to bring suit under the contract of carriage.[33] Thus, Millennium is entitled to bring this dispute before this tribunal and is a proper party to the suit.

C Millennium has the right to bring this dispute before the tribunal

1 The arbitration agreement has its own governing law

The arbitration agreement is a separate contract apart from the contract of carriage.[34] This is so even if the agreement is a clause encapsulated in the bill of lading or the charterparty.[35]

Thus, the arbitration agreement has its own governing law. This law is that chosen by the parties to govern the arbitration agreement.[36] In the absence of such a choice, the contract is governed by the law that has the closest and most real connection to the arbitration agreement.[37]

In our subsequent arguments, we will show that there was an arbitration agreement in clause 45 of the charterparty. Millennium seeks to invoke this clause to bring the arbitration before this tribunal. In the alternative, we will show that an ad hoc arbitration agreement exists between Quickship and Millennium, evidenced by the correspondence between the parties.

In the first case, the arbitration agreement is governed by the law of Europa and the Hamburg Rules. There is no choice of law governing the

30 *Mirabit v Ottoman Bank* (1897) 3 Ex D 173 [hereinafter *Mirabit*]; FMB Reynolds, 'Carriage of Goods by Sea Act 1992' [1993] Lloyd's Mar & Comm LQ 436.

31 Correspondence between Jaguar Importers and Millennium dated 15 June 1998; Correspondence between Millennium and Quickship dated 21 July 1998.

32 Discussion of this *supra*, at 446.

33 The *Elbe Maru* [1978] 1 Lloyd's Rep 206 at 210 [hereinafter *The Elbe Maru*]; *The Venezuela* [1980] 1 Lloyd's Rep 393 at 396 [hereinafter *The Venezuela*].

34 Sir MJ Mustill and SC Boyd, *Commercial Arbitration*, 2nd edn, 1989, London: Butterworths, at 6 [hereinafter *Commercial Arbitration*].

35 *Heyman v Darwins Ltd* [1942] AC 356 [hereinafter *Heyman*].

36 *Commercial Arbitration, supra* note 34 at 62; C Ambrose & K Maxwell, *London Maritime Arbitration*, 1996, London: LLP, at 39 [hereinafter *London Maritime Arbitration*].

37 *Commercial Arbitration, supra* note 34 at 63.

arbitration agreement in this case. The proper law is therefore the law with the closest and most real connection with the arbitration agreement. There is a presumption that this law follows the proper law of the underlying contract of carriage.[38] It is our position that the contract of carriage is governed by the law of Europa and subject to the Hamburg Rules.[39] Thus, the arbitration agreement is also governed by the same law.

However, if an ad hoc arbitration agreement exists, the agreement is governed by the law of Englandia. The ad hoc arbitration agreement is not attached to an underlying contract of carriage. In such a case, there would be a presumption in favour of the seat of arbitration.[40] Thus, the governing law of the arbitration agreement is the law of Englandia.

2 *Millennium is entitled to invoke arbitration pursuant to clause 45 of the charterparty*

(a) The Hamburg Rules give Millennium the right to invoke arbitration pursuant to clause 45 of the charterparty

The arbitration agreement, evidenced by clause 45 of the charterparty, is governed by the Hamburg Rules.[41]

Article 22, R 2 of the Hamburg Rules states:

> Where a charterparty contains a provision that disputes arising thereunder shall be referred to arbitration and a bill of lading issued pursuant to the charterparty does not contain a special annotation providing that such provision shall be binding upon the holder of the bill of lading, the carrier may not invoke such provision as against a holder having acquired the bill of lading in good faith.

This means that a carrier, such as Quickship, cannot enforce such a clause against a lawful holder of the bill of lading, such as Millennium.[42] However, this does not preclude a lawful holder of the bill of lading from relying on the arbitration clause.[43]

The intention of Article 22, R 2 is to prevent the carrier from relying on an exception clause to the detriment of the holder of the bill of lading. Only the

---

38 *Commercial Arbitration, supra* note 34 at 63; *Hamlyn & Co v Talisker Distillery* [1894] AC 202 [hereinafter *Hamlyn & Co*]; *National Gypsum Co Inc v Northern Sales Ltd* [1963] 2 Lloyd's Rep 499 [hereinafter *National Gypsum*]; *Cia Maritime Zorroza SA v Sesostris SAE* [1984] 1 Lloyd's Rep 652 [hereinafter *Cia Maritime*].

39 Discussion of this *supra,* at 439.

40 *Compagnie Tunisienne de Navigation SA v Cie de Armement Maritime SA* [1971] AC 572 [hereinafter *Compagnie Tunisienne*]; *Deutsche Schachtbau und Tiefbohrgesellschaft mbH v Ras Al Khaiman National Oil Corporation* [1987] 2 Lloyd's Rep 246 [hereinafter *DST*]; *Dallal v Bank Mellat* [1986] QB 441 [hereinafter *Dallal*].

41 Discussion of this *supra,* at 447.

42 Discussion of this *supra,* at 446.

43 This is by application of the doctrine of *expressio unius personae rel rei, est exclusio alterius* (the express mention of one thing is the exclusion of another).

carrier has notice of the clause, and forcing the lawful holder of the bill of lading to be bound by the clause is inequitable.

However, in the present case, Millennium already has notice of the clause.[44] It would make sense to allow Millennium, the lawful holder of the bill of lading, to rely on a clause that is beneficial to it.

Clause 45 of the charterparty is such a clause. It states: 'Any dispute arising out of this Bill of Lading shall be referred to arbitration in Englandia in accordance with the UNCITRAL Model Law on International Commercial Arbitration …'

Therefore, Millennium is entitled to invoke arbitration under clause 45 of the charterparty, even though it is not incorporated into the bill of lading.

(b) If the Hague-Visby Rules govern the arbitration agreement, it is equitable to allow Millennium to rely on clause 45 of the charterparty.

The carrier is not allowed to rely on the arbitration clause in a charterparty unless the clause has been incorporated by express reference in the bill of lading.[45] However, in this case, it is the lawful holder of the bill of lading, Millennium, that has elected to rely on the arbitration clause in the charterparty. It is our case that where the lawful holder of the bill of lading seeks to rely on the clause, the requirement of incorporation is irrelevant.

Quickship intended to refer all disputes arising from the bill of lading to arbitration. This is evident from clause 45 of the charterparty.

Clause 45 states that: '[A]ny disputes arising out of this bill of lading shall be referred to arbitration in Englandia …' The use of words 'arising out of this bill of lading' shows that the clause was drafted with a holder of the bill of lading in mind.[46] This shows the intention to allow third parties, such as a holder of the bill of lading, to bring arbitral proceedings in reliance of the clause.[47]

Further, the use of the phrase 'this bill of lading' shows that the charterparty was concluded with the bill of lading in mind. The charterparty between Antwerp Line and Quickship was concluded for the purpose of hiring the 'MV JASMINE' to carry the Jaguars to Pacifica. Therefore, the specific reference in clause 45 to 'this bill of lading' shows Quickship's intention to arbitrate all disputes arising from the bill of lading.

In addition, Millennium had constructive notice of the charterparty, including clause 45.[48] Millennium conducted its business, knowing that

---

44 Clarification Nos 5 and 12.

45 *The Annefield* [1971] 1 Lloyd's Rep 252 [hereinafter *The Annefield*].

46 W Tetley, *Marine Cargo Claims*, 3rd edn, 1994, Montreal: International Shipping Publications, at 606 [hereinafter *Marine Cargo Claims*].

47 *The Northumbria* [1869] Lloyd's Rep 3 [hereinafter *The Northumbria*].

48 Clarification Nos 5 and 12.

disputes arising out of the bill of lading would be submitted to arbitration, pursuant to the clause 45.

Since Millennium knew of the arbitration agreement, to insist on the requirement of incorporation would be to 'close one's eyes to the realities of the case and to the plaintiff's knowledge'.[49] It is equitable to allow Millennium to rely on clause 45 of the charterparty to seek arbitration to resolve the dispute.

3 In the alternative, there is a valid ad hoc arbitration agreement between Quickship and Millennium

Even if the arbitration is not commenced pursuant to clause 45 of the charterparty, there was an ad hoc arbitration agreement between the parties. This agreement is evidenced by the correspondence between the parties from 15 June 1999 to 1 July 1999.

An arbitration agreement need not be found in the contract of carriage. Article 7 of the UNCITRAL Model Law on Commercial Arbitration[50] states:

> (1) ... An arbitration agreement may be in the form of an arbitration clause in a contract or in the form of a separate agreement.
>
> (2) The arbitration agreement shall be in writing. An agreement is in writing if it is contained in ... an exchange of letters, telex, telegrams or other means of communications which provide a record of the agreement ...

Millennium made an offer to arbitrate the dispute in its facsimile to Quickship dated 15 June 1999. Quickship accepted this offer by appointing its arbitrator on 1 July 1999. This exchange of written communications amounts to an agreement to arbitrate.

The terms of this express agreement are sufficiently clear and show the parties' consensual intention to arbitrate the matter.[51] The terms of the arbitral proceedings were certain and detailed. Both parties expended significant effort in adhering to the terms of the agreement, even going so far as to appoint their arbitrators and to prepare statements of claims and defence.

As such, there is a valid ad hoc arbitration agreement between the parties.

49 *The Merak* [1964] 2 Lloyd's Rep 527 [hereinafter *The Merak*].

50 UNCITRAL Model Law on Commercial Arbitration, Art 7. Rule 2.2 of the Competition Rules states that Englandia has adopted the UNCITRAL Model Law on Commercial Arbitration.

51 The *Almare Prima* [1989] 2 Lloyd's Rep 376 [hereinafter *The Almare Prima*]; *Semco Salvage & Marine Pte Ltd v Owners of and Other Persons Interested in the Ship or Vessel MV Benja Bhum* [1994] 1 SLR 88 [hereinafter *The Benja Bhum*]; *Westminster Chemicals and Produce Ltd v Eicholz and Loeser* [1954] 1 Lloyd's Rep 99 [hereinafter *Westminster Chemicals*]. In these cases, this step taken by the parties indicated their intention to enter into an arbitration agreement.

4 Quickship has acknowledged by its conduct that an arbitration agreement exists between Quickship and Millennium

In any event, Quickship has not challenged the jurisdiction of the tribunal. Therefore, it cannot deny that an arbitration agreement exists between the parties.

Millennium commenced arbitration proceedings on 15 June 1999. Quickship, in its reply dated 1 July 1999, did not reserve the right to object to the existence of an arbitration agreement between the parties. In that facsimile, Quickship instead indicated three issues to be decided by the tribunal:

(i) Whether Millennium was the owner of the Jaguars;

(ii) Whether Quickship was responsible for the damage to the vehicles;

(iii) Whether the claim was time-barred.

Therefore, it only reserved its rights with regards to the merits of the claim. Although Quickship challenged the jurisdiction of the tribunal in its facsimile of 1 July 1999, this was only with regards to the improper giving of notice.

The challenge of jurisdiction on this ground is again highlighted in paragraphs 2 and 3 of its Statement of Defence. The paragraphs state:

> (2) [T]he Claimant failed to give notice required by clause 25 of the bill of lading ... the Claimant's claim is therefore absolutely barred.
>
> (3) [T]he Claimant has failed to give appropriate notice of the arbitration and, in the premises, the Tribunal is not seised of the matter.

It is settled law that failure to give appropriate notice of the arbitration does not affect the jurisdiction of the tribunal.[52] Such failure to give appropriate notice of the arbitration only affects the procedural exercise of the tribunal's jurisdiction.[53]

Quickship appointed its arbitrator, Mrs Wilhelmina James QC, in their facsimile of 1 July 1999. It also filed their Statement of Defence on 17 January 2000. By taking these positive steps to progress the arbitration without objection, Quickship manifested its intention that the arbitrators should determine these claims.[54]

Since Quickship has agreed to arbitrate the dispute and has acted to arbitrate the dispute, it must not be allowed to 'play fast and loose with the arbitral process'.[55] Therefore, Quickship should be estopped from denying the existence of the arbitration agreement between the parties.

---

52 *London Maritime Arbitration, supra* note 36 at 53.

53 *Leif Hoegh & Co A/S v Petrolsea Inc* [1992] 1 Lloyd's Rep 45 [hereinafter *The World Era*].

54 *The Almare Prima, supra* note 51.

55 *London Maritime Arbitration, supra* note 36 at 54; *Commercial Arbitration, supra* note 34 at 108.

D *Millennium commenced arbitration within the relevant time limits*

1 ***Millennium commenced arbitration within the two-year time limit in the Hamburg Rules***

Article 20, R 1 of the Hamburg Rules states:

> Any action relating to carriage of goods under this Convention is time-barred if judicial or arbitral proceedings have not been instituted within a period of two years.

According to Article 20, R 2 of the Hamburg Rules, '[T]he limitation period commences on the day which the carrier has delivered the goods …'. Therefore, the Hamburg Rules require the parties to commence any arbitral proceedings within two years from the date when the goods were delivered.

Quickship might argue that Article 20, R 1 does not apply since there is an express time limitation clauses for bringing of suit in the bill of lading and the charterparty.

Clause 25(2) of the bill of lading provides that: '[T]he Carrier shall be discharged from all liability whatsoever in respect of the Goods unless suit is brought within one year after delivery of the Goods or the date when the Goods should have been delivered.'

Clause 45 of the charterparty states that: '[A] party wishing to refer a dispute to arbitration shall make its claim in writing and appoint its arbitrator within one year after the delivery of the goods … and where this provision is not complied with the claim shall be deemed waived and absolutely barred …'

The Hamburg Rules allow the parties to bring suit within two years from the date of delivery. These clauses in the charterparty and bill of lading seek allow a party to bring suit only within one year from the date of delivery. As such, they attempt to reduce the carrier's liability to a level lower than that allowed under the Hamburg Rules. Such a contractual evasion of the Rules is not allowed under Article 23, R 1 of the Hamburg Rules.[56] Therefore, these two contractual clauses are void to this extent.

Quickship delivered the goods to Millennium in Pacifica on 15 June 1998. Millennium wrote a letter to Quickship on 15 June 1999, making clear its intentions to commence the arbitral process. Therefore, Millennium's claim is not time-barred as it has commenced arbitration proceedings within the time limit allowed under the Hamburg Rules.

---

56 Discussion of this *supra*, at 443.

2 *Millennium commenced arbitration within the one-year time limit in the Hague-Visby Rules.*

Even if the tribunal holds that the Hague-Visby regime applies in the circumstances, Millennium has commenced arbitration within the one-year limitation period specified by these Rules.

Article III, R 6 of the Hague-Visby Rules stipulates:

> [T]he Carrier and the ship shall in any event be discharged from all liability whatsoever in respect of the goods, unless suit is brought within one year of their delivery ... This period may, however, be extended if the parties so agree after the cause of action has risen.

It is settled law that that as long as the date of commencement of arbitration proceedings falls within the time limitation period, Millennium is not barred from bringing the suit.[57]

According to Article 21 of the UNCITRAL Model Law on Commercial Arbitration, the date of commencement of arbitration proceedings is the date on 'which a request for that dispute to be referred to arbitration is received by the respondent'.

On the facts, Millennium sent out a request for arbitration in its facsimile dated 15 June 1999. In its letter, it stated: 'Further to our previous correspondence in this matter we now must inform you that, unless you indicate by return facsimile that you are prepared to meet the costs of repainting the Jaguars, which amount to E 82000 (*sic*), we will be forced to consider commencing arbitration proceedings.'

This is evidence of Millennium's intention to bring the dispute to arbitration if Quickship continued to refuse to pay the costs of repainting the Jaguars. This is a valid notice commencing arbitration proceedings.[58] Therefore, arbitration proceedings were commenced on 15 June 1999.

The cargo was delivered on 15 June 1998. The commencement of arbitration proceedings took place on 15 June 1999. Therefore, arbitration proceedings commenced within one year from the date of delivery, as stipulated by Article III, R 6 of the Hague-Visby Rules. Thus, the claim is not time-barred under the Hague-Visby Rules.

---

57 *The World Era, supra* note 53.

58 *Nea Agrex SA v Baltic Shipping Co Ltd* [1976] 2 Lloyd's Rep 47 [hereinafter *The Aghios Lazarus*]; *Charles M Willie & Co (Shipping) Ltd v Ocean Laser Shipping Ltd & Anor* [1999] 1 Lloyd's Rep 225 [hereinafter *The Smaro*]; *Allianz Versicherungs-Aktiengesellschaft & Ors v Fortuna Co Inc* [1999] 1 Lloyd's Rep 497 at 503 [hereinafter *The Baltic Universal*].

II Quickship breached its obligations to Millennium under the contract of carriage by causing damage to the cargo

A The leakage of the chemicals from the top deck of the ship to the car deck caused the damage to the paintwork of the cars

Millennium claims for costs of repairs to the damaged paintwork of the Jaguar cars delivered by Quickship.

On 20 November 1998, Mr Ron Raines, a marine surveyor, issued a damaged cargo survey report after inspecting the cargo and interviewing a deck hand of 'MV JASMINE'.

He noted that after the loading of the cargo onto 'MV JASMINE' was completed on 1 May 1998, the deck hand scrubbed the top deck of the ship with a special acidic solution. This was in preparation for the Captain's wedding on the evening of 2 May 1998.

Mr Raines suggests two possible causes of damage. Firstly, the acidic solution used to scrub the top deck might have leaked onto the car deck, damaging the paintwork of the Jaguars. Secondly, the damage might be due to acid rain at the port of lading.

The VIN of the damaged cars are JAGS97001 to JAGS97100 and JAGS97137 to JAGS97200. Only the paintwork of cars with VIN JAGS97101 to JAGS97136 are not damaged. This is indicated in Attachment 1 of the surveyor's report.

Millennium submits that the cause of the damage cannot be acid rain. Acid rain would have damaged the paintwork of all 200 cars. It is not conceivable that the middle batch of Jaguar motor cars was not affected by the acid rain. Moreover, there is no evidence that there had been acid rain at Port Seeweg in Europa on the day when the vessel loaded and sailed for Pacifica.

The damage was caused by the leaking of the acidic solution onto the car deck. This leaking probably occurred due to open hatches on the top deck while the scrubbing was carried out. Alternatively, the acidic solution leaked through the top deck onto the main deck.

B Quickship breached its obligations towards Millennium as it failed to take 'all measures reasonably required to avoid damage' to the cargo under the Hamburg Rules

Quickship has breached its obligations as a carrier under Article 5, R 1 of the Hamburg Rules. Article 5, R 1 states:

> The carrier is liable for loss resulting from loss of or damage to the goods, as well as from delay in delivery, if the occurrence which caused the loss, damage or delay took place while the goods were in his charge as defined in Article 4, unless the carrier proves that he, his servants or agents took all measures that could reasonably be required to avoid the occurrence and its consequences.

Liability under this Article is established if two elements are shown. Firstly, the claimant must show that the damage occurred when the goods were in the carrier's charge. Once it is shown, the carrier must then show that it took all reasonable measures to prevent the damage.

Millennium submits that the goods were damaged while they were in Quickship's charge. When Quickship received the consignment of cars for shipment, it represented on the bill of lading that the goods were received in 'apparent good order and condition'.[59] Quickship cannot deny this representation vis à vis Millennium, a third party who acted in reliance on that description of the goods.[60]

Article 16, R 3(b) of the Hamburg Rules states:

> Except for particulars in respect of which and to the extent to which a reservation permitted under para 1 of this Article has been entered, ... proof to the contrary by the carrier is not admissible if the bill of lading has been transferred to a third party ... who in good faith has acted in reliance on the description of the goods therein.

Article 16, R 1 allows the carrier to 'insert in the bill of lading a reservation specifying ... grounds of suspicion or the absence of reasonable means of checking' the 'quality of goods' taken over.

Millennium acknowledges that the damage to the paint work of the cars was not visible because of the protective wax coating. Therefore, Quickship would not have been able to ascertain the condition of paintwork at Port Seeweg. However, Quickship had an obligation under Article 16, R 1 of the Hamburg Rules to indicate in the bill of lading that they had 'no reasonable means of checking' the 'quality of the goods' received.[61] Quickship did not do this. Thus, they are now estopped from denying that the goods were indeed in good condition.

The cargo was found to be defective upon arrival at Port Idyllic, Pacifica.[62] 164 of the 200 Jaguar cars delivered had defective paintwork. It is thus established that the goods were damaged while in the carrier's charge.

Quickship, therefore, must show that they had taken 'all measures that could reasonably be required to avoid its occurrence'. There is no evidence indicating that Quickship fulfilled this obligation. On the contrary, the evidence suggests that the master and crew showed disregard for the safety of the cargo by scrubbing the main deck with a strong acidic solution. They did so despite knowing that there were cars stowed on the deck immediately below and that leakage to the car deck would probably cause damage to the cargo.

---

59 Cover page of the Bill of Lading.

60 Hamburg Rules, Art 16, R 3(b).

61 Hamburg Rules, Art 16, R 1.

62 Facsimile from Millennium to Quickship dated 21 July 1998.

Therefore, Quickship has breached its obligations as a carrier under Article 5, R 1 of the Hamburg Rules. Since this breach caused damage to the paintwork of the cars,[63] Quickship must be held liable for losses suffered by Millennium.

C Quickship breached its obligations towards Millennium as a under the Hague-Visby Rules

1 Quickship did not 'properly and carefully keep' and 'care for' the cargo

Even if the Hague-Visby Rules apply, Quickship has failed to keep and care for the cargo 'properly and carefully'. This is a breach of Article III, R 2 of the Hague-Visby Rules.

That Article provides that: '[S]ubject to the provisions of Article IV, the carrier shall properly and carefully load, handle, stow, carry, keep, care for, and discharge the goods carried.'

Under this Article, Millennium need only establish that the cargo was damaged while they were in Quickship's charge. Once this is established, Quickship is *prima facie* in breach of the Article.[64]

On the facts, Quickship received the cargo on board and noted in the bill of lading that the goods were received in 'apparent good order and condition'.

Article III, R 3 of the Hague-Visby Rules provides that a carrier is not bound to make any representations on the bill of lading which he has no reasonable means of checking.[65] Thus, Quickship had an obligation to disclose in the bill of lading that it had not been able to verify that the cars were shipped in apparent good order and condition as regards the paint work. By failing to do so, Quickship is estopped from denying otherwise vis à vis a Millennium, a third party acting in good faith.[66]

When the cars arrived in Pacifica, they were found to have damaged paintwork. The logical conclusion is that the cars were damaged while in Quickship's custody.

---

63 Discussion of this *supra,* at 454–55.

64 *Albacora SRL v Westcott & Laurence Line Ltd* [1966] 2 Lloyd's Rep 53 [hereinafter *Albacora*]; *Colonial Sugar Refining Co Ltd v British India Steam Navigation Co Ltd* (1931) 32 SR (NSW) 245; 49 WN 55 (NSW Sup Ct) [hereinafter *Colonial Sugar*]; *Yeo Choon Nyoh v Ocean Steamship Co Ltd* [1967] 2 MLJ 290 [hereinafter *Yeo Choon Nyoh*].

65 The position is similar to that under Hamburg Rules, Art 16, R 1. Discussion of this at 17. See also *Pendle & Rivet Ltd v Ellerman Lines* (1928) 33 Com Cas 70 [hereinafter *Pendle & Rivet*]; *AG of Ceylon v Scindia Steam Navigation Co Ltd* [1962] AC 60 [hereinafter *AG of Ceylon*].

66 Hague-Visby Rules, Art III, R 4. This was an amendment from the Hague Rules, added in 1978. See also *Associated Packaging Pty Ltd v Sankyo Kaiun Kabushiki Kaisha* (1983) 3 NSW LR 293 (NSW Sup Ct.) [hereinafter *Associated Packaging*].

Quickship is therefore *prima facie* in breach of Article III, R 2 of the Hague-Visby Rules.[67] There is no evidence showing otherwise.

Further, Millennium submits that Quickship failed to fulfil this obligation at all. The scrubbing of the main deck with the strong acidic solution was done in blatant disregard for the safety of the cargo. Thus, Quickship (or its agents) had failed to properly and carefully keep and care for the cargo while the goods were in its custody.

Quickship has breached its obligations as a carrier towards Millennium. This breach resulted in the damage caused to the cargo.[68]

2 *Quickship did not provide a cargoworthy ship for the voyage*

Further, Quickship is in breach of its obligation of due diligence to provide a cargoworthy ship under the Hague-Visby Rules.[69]

Article III, R 1(c) of the Hague-Visby Rules states that:

> The carrier shall be bound before and at the beginning of the voyage to exercise due diligence to … make the holds … and all other parts of the ship in which goods are carried, fit and safe for their reception, carriage and preservation.

The obligation to provide a cargoworthy ship subsists 'from at least the beginning of loading until the vessel starts its voyage'.[70]

On the facts, the cargo holds of 'MV JASMINE' were not fit for the preservation of the cars between 1 May 1998 (after commencement of loading) and 2 May 1998 (the date at which she set sail). Quickship was not duly diligent in ensuring that the vessel was cargoworthy. The deckhand had scrubbed the deck with the strong acid-based solution on the night of 1 May 1998, after loading had been completed, in preparation for the Master's wedding the following day.[71]

Thus, Quickship failed to exercise due diligence to ensure the cargoworthiness of the vessel. This act was tantamount to a total disregard for the need to ensure that the holds were cargoworthy.

On these grounds, Quickship is in breach of Article III, R 1(c) of the Hague-Visby Rules. This breach resulted in the loss suffered by Millennium.[72] Therefore, Quickship must compensate Millennium for these losses.

---

67 *Albacora, supra* note 64.

68 Discussion of this *supra,* at 454–55.

69 *Guan Bee Shipping & Co v Palembang Shipping Co Ltd* [1969] 1 MLJ 90 [hereinafter *Guan Bee Shipping*].

70 *Maxine Footwear Co Ltd v Canadian Government Merchant Marine Ltd* [1959] AC 589 at 603 [hereinafter *Maxine Footwear*].

71 Marine Surveyor's Report dated 20 November 1998.

72 Discussion of this *supra,* at 454–55.

III Quickship is liable to Millennium for the damage caused to the cargo

A *Millennium is entitled to claim for damages despite the date of notice of damage to the cargo*

1 ***The date of notice of damage to the cargo does not prejudice Millennium's claim under the Hamburg Rules***

Article 19, R 1 read with Article 19, R 2 of the Hamburg Rules states that 'where the loss or damage (of the goods) is not apparent', 'notice of loss or damage specifying the general nature of such loss or damage' should be 'given in writing by the consignee to the carrier' 'within fifteen consecutive days after the day when the goods were handed over to the consignee'. If this is not done, 'such handing over is *prima facie* evidence of the delivery by the carrier of the goods as described in the document of transport or, if no such document has been issued, in good condition.'

The claimant is given fifteen days to inspect the cargo. Non-compliance with this merely shifts the burden of proof to the claimant to show that the goods were not received in the condition stated in the bill of lading.

The goods arrived in Port Idyllic, Pacifica on 15 June 1998. On 21 July 1998, a notice was sent by Millennium to Quickship informing them of the damage to the cars' paintwork. It is acknowledged that the notice was sent out later than the fifteen days stated in the Hamburg Rules. However, Millennium has already shown that the goods were not received in 'apparent good order and condition', as stated in the bill of lading.[73] Thus, the late notice of damage to the cargo does not prejudice Millennium's claim.

Clause 25(1) of the bill of lading states that: '[U]nless notice of loss or damage be given in writing to the Carrier at the port of discharge or place of delivery before or at the time of delivery or, if the loss or damage be not apparent, within 3 days after delivery, the Goods shall be deemed to have been delivered as described in this Bill of Lading.'

However, clause 25(1) of the bill of lading is void as it derogates from the provisions of the Hamburg Rules.[74] Contrary to Article 19, R 1 of the Hamburg Rules, clause 25(1) reduces the time limitation allowed to inspect delivered cargo. Further, the clause states that upon failure to give notice within such the time period, there is an irrebuttable presumption that the goods were received in good condition. Therefore, clause 25(1) falls foul of Article 23, R 1 of the Hamburg Rules[75] and is void.

---

73 Discussion of this at 17.

74 Hamburg Rules, Art 23, R 1.

75 Discussion of this at 6.

2 Even if the Hague-Visby Rules apply, Millennium is not barred from claiming damages

Even if the Hague-Visby Rules apply, Millennium is not barred from claiming damages.

Article III, R 6 of the Hague-Visby Rules stipulates that:

> Unless notice of loss or damage and the general nature of such loss or damage be given in writing to the carrier or his agent at the port of discharge … if the loss or damage be not apparent, within three days, such removal shall be *prima facie* evidence of the delivery by the carrier of the goods as described in the bill of lading.

This Article merely creates a rebuttable presumption that the goods were delivered in the condition stated in the bill of lading if the notice of damage is late. The notice of damage to the cargo was sent later than the three days allowed in this case. However, Millennium has already shown that the goods were not received in the condition stated in the bill of lading.[76] Thus, the late notice of damage does not prejudice Millennium's claim.

Quickship cannot rely on clause 25(1) of the bill of lading, as that clause is also void under the Hague-Visby regime. Article III, R 8 of the Hague-Visby Rules states:

> Any clause, covenant, or agreement in a contract of carriage relieving the carrier or the ship from liability for loss or damage to, or in connection with, goods arising from negligence, fault, or failure in the duties and obligations provided in this article or lessening such liability otherwise than as provided in these Rules, shall be null and void and of no effect …

Clause 25(1) provides that a late notice of damages creates an irrebuttable presumption that the goods were received in the condition stated in the bill of lading. As clause 25(1) seeks to reduce the limits of liabilities as prescribed by the Hague-Visby Rules, it is repugnant to Article III, R 8 of the Rules, and is therefore void.[77]

B Quickship cannot rely on any clauses that exempt its liability towards Millennium

1 The Hamburg Rules do not allow Quickship to be exempted from liability

The Hamburg Rules are drafted in a manner that strips away the exception clauses that protected carriers under the Hague-Visby Rules.[78] Therefore,

---

76 Discussion of this at 17.

77 *The Hollandia* [1983] AC 565 [hereinafter *The Hollandia*]; *Shun Cheong Steam Navigation Co Ltd v Wo Fong Trading Co* [1979] 2 MLJ 254 [hereinafter *Shun Cheong Steam Navigation*]; *Pacific Electric Wire & Cable Co Ltd v Neptune Orient Lines Ltd* [1993] 3 SLR 60 [hereinafter *Neptune Orient Lines*]; *Unicoopjapan and Marubeni-Iida Co Ltd v Ion Shipping Co* [1971] 1 Lloyd's Rep 541 [hereinafter *The Ion*].

78 S Mankabady, ed, *The Hamburg Rules on the Carriage of Goods by Sea*, 1978, Leyden/Boston. Published for the British Institute of International and Comparative Law, London, by AW Sijthoff, at 139–40.

Quickship is not entitled to exempt itself from the breach of its obligations under the contract of carriage.

2 *Quickship cannot rely on the exemption clauses in the Hague-Visby Rules, even if these rules are applicable*

(a) Quickship has deviated unjustifiably to Marseilles during the voyage and therefore cannot rely on the exemption clauses in the Hague-Visby Rules

Even if the contract of carriage is governed by the Hague-Visby Rules, Quickship is barred from relying on all the exemption clauses available under the Hague-Visby Rules. This is because Quickship had deviated unjustifiably to Marseilles during the voyage in response to a purported distress call, as well as to load supplies for the crew.

'Deviation' is defined as 'a voluntary substitution of the contractual voyage'.[79] In our case, it is not possible to adduce extraneous evidence as to what the 'contractual voyage' is. This is because the bill of carriage is conclusive evidence of the contract of carriage as between Quickship and a third party, like Millennium.[80]

In such a situation, the courts have held that the 'contractual voyage' means the 'direct geographical route'.[81] Marseilles was not within the direct geographical route from Europa to Pacifica. Nor is it a customary port of call for vessels travelling between Europa and Pacifica.[82] Therefore, there has been a deviation by 'MV JASMINE' in this case.

Article IV, R 4 of the Rules states that: '[A]ny deviation in saving or attempting to save life or property at sea or any reasonable deviation shall not be deemed to be an infringement or breach of these Rules or of the contract of carriage, and the carrier shall not be liable for any loss or damage resulting therefrom.' Thus, deviation is justifiable if it is for the purposes of saving life or property[83] or any other reasonable purpose.

In this case, Quickship claims to have deviated to Marseilles in response to a distress call to save life and property. However, no evidence has been tendered to the tribunal concerning the distressed ship.

Even if the deviation was indeed to answer a distress call, this is rendered unjustifiable because the vessel called at Marseilles to 'load additional supplies for the crew'.[84] This is also not a 'reasonable deviation' under the

---

79 *Rio Tinto Co Ltd v Seed Shipping Co* (1926) 42 TLR 381 [hereinafter *Rio Tinto*]; *Verappa Chetty v Ventre* [1868] 1 Kyshe 174 at 178 [hereinafter *Verappa Chetty*].

80 *Leduc v Ward* [1888] 20 QB 475 [hereinafter *Leduc v Ward*].

81 *Reardon Smith Line Ltd v Black Sea and Baltic General Insurance Co Ltd* [1939] AC 562 at 584 [hereinafter *Reardon Smith*]; *Armoogum Chetty v Lee Cheng Tee* (1868) 1 Kyshe 181 [hereinafter *Armoogum Chetty*].

82 Clarification No 17.

83 *Scaramanga & Co v Stamp*, (1880) 5 CPD 295 [hereinafter *Scaramanga*].

84 Paragraph 4 of Quickship's Statement of Defence, dated 17 January 2000.

Hague-Visby Rules. The supplies were 'additional supplies for the crew' that were not crucial for the completion of the contractual voyage.[85]

Quickship may not rely on the 'Liberty to Deviate Clause' in the bill of lading,[86] to justify its deviation from the 'contractual voyage'. Such a clause is null and void as it is repugnant to Article III, R 8 of the Hague-Visby Rules. It seeks to allow a carrier to deviate from the contractual route without any liability. This is an attempt to evade the responsibilities under the Hague-Visby regime. Thus, Clause 6(2) of the bill of lading cannot stand in the face of Article III, R 8.[87]

An unjustifiable deviation is a fundamental breach of the contract.[88] When such a breach has been committed, the wrongdoer cannot rely on the exemption clauses in the contract, or any other exemption clauses applicable in the circumstances.[89] This breach would also displace the exemption clauses in Article IV, R 2 of the Hague-Visby Rules.[90]

Therefore, even if the Hague-Visby Rules are applicable, Quickship is not entitled to rely on the exception clauses contained in the Rules.

(b) Quickship failed to provide a cargoworthy ship for the voyage and therefore cannot rely on the exemption clauses in Article IV, R 2 of the Hague-Visby Rules

As Quickship failed to provide a cargoworthy ship, it is not entitled to rely on the Article IV, R 2 exceptions within the Hague-Visby Rules.

The obligation to provide a cargoworthy ship under Article III, R 1 of the Hague-Visby Rules does not begin with the words '[S]ubject to the provisions of Article IV'. This is in contrast to the obligation under Article III, R 2, which begins with the phrase '[S]ubject to the provisions of Article IV'. Therefore, once the carrier has breached the obligation to provide a cargoworthy ship, the Article IV exceptions do not apply. This is clear from the judgement of Lord Somervell in *Maxine Footwear*.[91]

---

85 This is distinguished from cases where deviation to load crucial supplies (eg. bunkers) were held to be 'reasonable deviation': *Reardon Smith, supra* note 81. See also *Thiess Brothers (Queensland) Pty. Ltd v Australian Steamships Pty Ltd* [1955] 1 LILR 459 (NSW Sup Ct) [hereinafter *Thiess Brothers*].

86 Clause 6(2) of the bill of lading.

87 Discussion is found *supra*, at 459.

88 *Photo Production Ltd v Securicor Transport Ltd* [1980] AC 827 at 845 [hereinafter *Photo Production*]. This is despite the decision of *Suisse Atlantique Société d'Armement Maritime SA v NV Rotterdamsche Kolen Centrale* [1967] 1 AC 361 at 433 [hereinafter *Suisse Atlantique*]. That case put the doctrine of fundamental breach to rest. However, the House of Lords in *Photo Production* explained that this doctrine still survives in carriage of goods by sea contracts. See also *F Kanematsu & Co Ltd v The 'SHAHZADA'* (1956) 96 CLR 477; 30 ALJ 478 (High Ct) [hereinafter *The Shahzada*].

89 *Hain Steamships Co Ltd v Tate and Lyle Ltd* (1936) 41 Com Cas 350 at 354 [hereinafter *Hain Steamships*].

90 *Stag Line Ltd v Foscolo Mango & Co Ltd* [1932] AC 328 at 347 [hereinafter *Stag Line*].

91 *Maxine Footwear, supra* note 70. See also *The Fiona* [1993] 1 Lloyd's Rep 257 [hereinafter *The Fiona*]; *The Commonwealth v Burns Philip & Co Ltd*, (1946) 46 SR (NSW) 307; 63 WN 211 (NSW Sup Ct) [hereinafter *The Commonwealth*].

In this case, Quickship has failed to provide a cargoworthy ship.[92] Therefore, it cannot rely on the exceptions contained within the Hague-Visby Rules.

(c) In any case, Quickship cannot fit into any of the specified immunities under Article IV, R 2 of the Hague-Visby Rules

Moreover, Quickship cannot rely on the Article IV, R 2 exceptions within the Hague-Visby Rules, as the specified immunities in the Rules do not apply to the facts.

Quickship might attempt to argue that it falls within the exceptions provided by Article IV, R 2(a), (d) and (m) of the Hague-Visby Rules.

Article IV, R 2(a), (d) and (m) provide that:

> Neither the carrier nor the ship shall be responsible for loss or damage arising or resulting from:
>
> (a) Act, neglect, or default of the master … or the servants of the carrier in the navigation or in the management of the ship.
>
> (d) Act of God.
>
> (m) … [A]ny other loss or damage arising from inherent defect, quality or vice of the goods.

Article IV, R 2(a) allows the carrier to be exempted from liability only if the neglect occurred in respect of the navigation or management of the ship. In the House of Lords case *Gosse Millard Ltd v Canadian Government Merchant Marine Ltd*.[93] the crew members' failure to pull tarpaulins over the hatches on the deck of the ship did not amount to negligence 'in the management of the ship'.[94] Similarly, the scrubbing of the deck with the acid-based solution by the deckhand on board the '*MV JASMINE*' was negligence in respect of keeping and caring for the cargo, and not negligence 'in the management of the ship'. Therefore, Quickship does not come under the Article IV, R 2(a) exception.

Quickship cannot exempt itself from liability by claiming that the damage was caused by acid rain, and therefore was an Act of God.[95] The evidence suggests that the damage was caused by the leakage of the acidic solution onto the car deck and not due to acid rain at Port Seeweg.[96]

Quickship also cannot prove that it is exempted under Article IV, R 2(m). Millennium has already shown that the goods were damaged while in

92 Discussion of this *supra,* at 457.

93 *Gosse Millard Ltd v Canadian Government Merchant Marine Ltd* [1929] AC 223 [hereinafter *Gosse Millard*].

94 See also *Caltex Refining Co Pty Ltd v BHP Transport Ltd* (1993) 34 NSWLR 29 (NSW Sup Ct) [hereinafter *Caltex Refining*].

95 Hague-Visby Rules, Art IV, R 2(d).

96 Discussion of this *supra,* at 454–55.

Quickship's custody.[97] Since there is no contrary evidence indicating that the damage to the goods was due to an inherent defect or quality, Quickship remains liable for the damage caused to the cargo.

The other exemptions found in Article IV, R 2 of the Hague-Visby Rules do not apply to this fact situation.

C Millennium is entitled to claim damages from Quickship

1 Millennium is entitled to claim damages under the Hamburg Rules

Millennium has shown that the tribunal has jurisdiction to hear this dispute.[98] Quickship breached its obligations as a carrier towards Millennium.[99] The damage to the goods was caused while they were in Quickship's charge.[100] There are no exemption clauses protecting Quickship from liability.[101] Therefore, Millennium is entitled to claim damages from Quickship.

Article 6, R 1(a) and Article 26, R 1 provide that the carrier will be liable for 835 SDR per package or unit, or 2.5 SDR per kilogram, whichever is higher.[102] Millennium therefore claims damages amounting to E 501 534.64.[103]

2 Due to the unjustifiable deviation to Marseilles during the voyage, Quickship cannot rely on the package and kilogram limitations in the Hague-Visby Rules

If the Hague-Visby Rules are applicable, Quickship must pay the full amount of damages to Millennium.

It cannot rely on the package and kilo limitations contained in the Hague-Visby Rules[104] to limit the damages payable to Millennium.

Quickship has breached its obligation not to deviate unjustifiably.[105] This not only precludes Quickship from relying on the exception clauses within the

97 Discussion of this *supra,* at 454–55.

98 Discussion of this *supra,* at 442–53.

99 Discussion of this *supra,* at 451–57.

100 Discussion of this *supra,* at 455.

101 Discussion of this *supra,* at 459–63.

102 Hamburg Rules, Art 6, R 1(a).

103 This is based on the per kilo limitation of the Hamburg Rules. Hamburg Rules, Art 26, R 1 states that the SDR amounts are to be converted into the national currency at the date of judgment or the date agreed upon by the parties. As the conversion rate at the date of judgment is unknown at this time, the figures are based on the IMF conversion rate as at 21 March 2000.

104 Hague-Visby Rules, Art IV, R 5.

105 Discussion of this *supra,* at 459–60.

Hague-Visby regime,[106] but also precludes it from relying on the package and kilo limitation therein.[107]

Therefore, Quickship is liable for the full amount of E 820 000 for breaching its obligations as carrier towards Millennium.

Prayer for Relief

For the above reasons, we request the tribunal to:

DECLARE that this tribunal has jurisdiction to hear this suit; and

ADJUDGE that Quickship has breached its obligations under the contract of carriage to Millennium by causing damage to the cargo.

ADJUDGE that there are no contractual or statutory clauses allowing Quickship to exempt or limit its liability towards Millennium.

AWARD damages of E 501 534.64 in favour of Millennium, with

(i) interest; and

(ii) costs.

---

106 Discussion of this *supra,* at 461. *Hain Steamships*, *supra* note 89.

107 *Stag Line*, *supra* note 90 at 340. The American courts have also adopted such an interpretation: *Spartus Corp v S/S Yafo*, 590 F 2d, 1979 AMC 2294 at 2300 (5 Cir 1979) [hereinafter *Spartus*]; *Encyclopaedia Britannica Inc v S/S Hong Kong Producer*, 422 F 2d 7, 1969 AMC 1741 (2 Cir 1969) [hereinafter *Encyclopaedia Britannica*]; *Electro-Tec Corp v Dart Atlantic*, 598 F Supp 929, 1985 AMC 1606 at 1610 (D Md 1984) [hereinafter *Electro-Tec Corp*]; *Seguros Banvenez v Oliver Drescher*, 761 F 2d 855, 1984 AMC 2168 (2 Cir 1985) [hereinafter *Seguros*]; *Gen Electric v Nancy Lykes*, 706 F 2d 80, 1983 AMC 1947 (2 Cir 1983) [hereinafter *Gen Electric*]; *Nemeth v General SS Corp Ltd*, 694 F 2d 609, 1983 AMC 885 at 889 (9 Cir 1982) [hereinafter *Nemeth*]; *Jones v The Flying Clipper*, 116 F Supp 386, 1954 AMC 259 (SDNY 1953) [hereinafter *The Flying Clipper*].

Maritime Law Moot: Memorandum for the Respondent (University of Hong Kong)

Jonathon Chang, Jennifer Cheung, Puja Kapai and Janice Wu

STATEMENT OF FACTS

Background to the Dispute

1 The claimant, Millennium, was at all material times a company incorporated and carrying on business in Pacifica as distributor of prestigious motor vehicles. It is a wholly owned subsidiary of Jaguar Importers Ltd (JagImps), an importer of prestigious motor vehicles.

2 The respondent, Quickship, was at all material times, incorporated and carrying on business as a carrier of goods by sea in Europa. It has time-chartered the vessel '*MV JASMINE*' from Antwerp Line.

The Dispute

3 The dispute arises out of a contract of carriage evidenced by a bill of lading dated 1 May issued at the Port Seeweg, Europa, between Quickship Pty Ltd (Quickship), the carrier, and Jaguar Manufacturers, the shipper. Under the bill of lading, Quickship was to deliver 200 Jaguar cars from Europa to Pacifica.

4 After the delivery of the cars, it was alleged that 164 of them had black spots or blots to the bonnets, turrets and boots. Millennium Automobiles Pty Ltd (Millennium) brought the dispute before the tribunal claiming to be the lawful holder or merchant or endorsee as defined under this bill of lading, claiming from Quickship, *inter alia*, the cost of repairs to the paintwork of the Jaguar cars which amounts to E 820 000.

5 The respondent denies Millennium's status as the endorsee of the bill of lading since the bill of lading, as a 'to order' bill, was never indorsed.

The Bill of Lading

6 A bill of lading was issued by Quickship and dated 1 May 1998, on which it was indicated that the goods were received in 'apparent good order and condition'.

7 Under this bill of lading Quickship was to carry a consignment of 200 Jaguar motor cars aboard '*MV JASMINE*' from Port Seeweg, Europa, to Port Idyllic, Pacifica.

8 It has been alleged by the claimant that there was an 'agreement' that Quickship would take the shortest customary route. The respondents says that there was only a communication from Quickship to Jaguar Manufacturers informing that the masters of '*MV JASMINE*' had received orders from Quickship to take the shortest customary route for commercial shipments between Europa and Pacifica. In the same correspondence Quickship also indicated that JagImps would take delivery of the cargo at Port Idyllic of Pacifica on 13 June 1998.

The Delivery

9 On 5 May 1998 '*MV JASMINE*' altered course in the Mediterranean Sea in response to a distress call and called at Marseilles where she remained for two days. During the stay in Marseilles, additional supplies for the crew were loaded.

10 The vessel arrived on 15 June 1998 at Port Idyllic. On the same day, Millennium received a letter from JagImps instructing it to take delivery of the cars. An original copy of the bill of lading was attached. Millennium took delivery of the cars.

The Damage

11 The cars were covered with protective wax coating at the time of loading at Port Seeweg, Europa, and at the time of discharge at Port Idyllic, Pacifica. After stripping off the wax, Millennium alleged damage to the paint work of 164 out of the 200 Jaguar cars, where black spots and blots were found on the cars' bonnets, turrets and boots.

12 Millennium sent a letter to Quickship on 21 July 1998. In that letter, Millennium acknowledged this notice was served out of time under clause 25 of the bill of lading and alleged it was because the damage was not apparent due to the wax coating.

The Surveyor's Report

13 Millennium employed a marine surveying firm, MSC Group, to discover the possible cause(s) of the damage to the cargo.

14 On 3, 6 and 10 November 1998, Mr Ronald Raines from the MSC conducted a cargo survey of the 164 damaged cars at 3 different locations. He was of the opinion that the re-spraying cost would amount to E 820 000 (E 5000 per vehicle).

15 Mr Raines did not inspect the vessel. However, he claimed to have interviewed an ex deck hand working on '*MV JASMINE*', Mr Kavanagh. The deckhand alleged that at the evening of 1 May 1998 after the loading was completed, he was ordered to scrub the upper deck of the ship in preparation of the master's wedding on the evening of 2 May 1998 before the vessel set sail for Pacifica. The cleaning solution bore a dreadful smell and he had to wear gloves during cleaning. Mr. Raines suggested that it might have been an acid-based solution.

16 In his report Mr Raines suggested two possible causes of damage to the cars: (1) leakage of acid / chemicals from the deck of the vessel during the scrubbing; or (2) industrial fallout (acid rain) at the port of loading.

The Arbitration Proceedings

17 On 15 June 1999, Millennium sent a facsimile to Quickship informing that Millennium would be forced to consider commencing arbitration proceedings against Quickship unless Quickship indicated by return facsimile that they were prepared to bear the cost of repainting.

18 Millennium wrote to Quickship on 16 June 1999 informing Quickship that they had appointed Mr R Salter to arbitrate the dispute. In the same letter, Millennium requested Quickship to appoint an arbitrator within 14 calendar days, failing which Mr Salter would be the sole arbitrator.

19 The respondent replied on 1 July 1999, denying the validity of Millennium's purported appointment but nonetheless appointed Mrs Wilhelmina James QC as their arbitrator only for protecting their interest. Quickship also drew Millennium's attention to the letter received by Millennium dated 28 July 1998 disclaiming liability, denying Millennium as the owners of the Jaguars and raising the fact that the claim was in any event time barred.

20 There is no arbitration clause in the disputed bill of lading. There is only an arbitration clause (clause 45) in the time charterparty between Antwerp Line (the shipowner) and Quickship. Millennium only had constructive notice of the whole time charterparty, but not the particular arbitration clause.

21 The arbitration clause in the charterparty states that the arbitration will be held in Englandia, which has enacted the UNCITRAL Model Law on International Commercial Arbitration. The claimant's claim that 'the parties have agreed that the arbitration be held in Englandia' is misleading as the agreement is between the shipowner and the charterer, but not the parties in the present proceeding. The proceedings are to be held in accordance with the London Maritime Arbitrators' Association (LMAA) Terms. All states involved are parties to the New York Convention on the Recognition and Enforcement of Foreign Arbitral Awards.

22 Clause 2 of the bill of lading states that the governing law of the contract is the law of Europa, except as may be provided otherwise in the bill of lading. Clause 27 of the bill of lading states that the bill of lading is subject to the Hague Rules, the Hague-Visby Rules, the Hamburg Rules or other similar national legislation as may mandatorily apply by virtue of origin or destination of the bill of lading. Any term of the bill which is repugnant to the applicable legislation is void to that extent. Pacifica has adopted the Hamburg Rules while Europa has adopted the Hague-Visby Rules.

23 Both states are members of the International Monetary Fund. The membership of International Monetary Fund is relevant to the issue of calculation of damages.

QUESTIONS PRESENTED

(1) Whether the arbitral tribunal has jurisdiction to hear the dispute.

(2) What is the proper law governing the contract of carriage.

(3) Whether Quickship has breached its obligation to Millennium under the contract of carriage.

(4) Whether Quickship is liable to Millennium for the damage caused to the cargo.

ARGUMENTS AND AUTHORITIES

I The Arbital Tribunal has no Jurisdiction to hear this Dispute

A The governing law of the arbitration proceeding is the law of Englandia

1 An arbitral tribunal has jurisdiction to hear the dispute only when there is an agreement to arbitrate. Before we decide whether or not there is any such agreement, the first issue is what is the law to be applied in deciding whether there is such an agreement.

2 It is submitted that the governing law of any arbitration proceedings between the parties, whether invoked by clause 45 of the charterparty or by virtue of an ad hoc agreement to arbitrate, is the law of Englandia.

3 Clause 45 of the charterparty expressly states that any arbitration will be conducted in accordance with the LMAA terms, Article 6 of which provides that the law applicable to the arbitration agreement is English Law unless there is any agreement to the contrary. As there is no

agreement to the contrary, the governing law of the arbitration proceedings is the law of Englandia.[1]

4 Even if it is found that the arbitration was commenced pursuant to an ad hoc agreement, the governing law of the arbitration proceedings will still be the law of Englandia. The general rule is that in the absence of agreement as to the choice of law in this respect, the law of the country in which the arbitration is held should be the governing law of the proceedings[2] and hence, this would be Englandia.

B The tribunal has no jurisdiction to hear the case because there is no arbitration agreement between the parties

(1) Millennium cannot invoke clause 45 of the charterparty

5 In general, arbitration between two parties can only be conducted if there is a valid arbitration agreement between them. This could either be by way of an express arbitration agreement or an ad hoc agreement to arbitrate.

6 Millennium sought to rely on clause 45 of the charterparty between Quickship and the shipowner to commence arbitration.[3] However, the terms of the charterparty only bind Quickship and the shipowner, and such terms have no effect on the bill of lading unless the whole charterparty or any specific clauses have been expressly incorporated into the bill of lading. In this respect, there are three conditions to be noted:

(a) a merely general reference to the charterparty will not suffice;

(b) the words of incorporation must describe the charterparty clause sought to be incorporated;[4] and

(c) the incorporation must be consistent with the rest of the bill of lading.[5]

7 In the present case, first, there is no evidence of such incorporating clause in the bill of lading, whether express or implied. Second, the constructive notice of the charterparty by Millennium arising from common usage and knowledge of industry does not amount to incorporating the arbitration clause.[6] Thus, Millennium cannot rely on the arbitration clause (clause 45) of the charterparty in order to commence arbitration.

---

1 Since Englandia has laws identical to those of England: Procedural Order No 1 para 6. The necessary implication is that English decisions and statutes are applicable in such proceedings.

2 L Collins (ed), *Dicey & Morris: The Conflict of Laws*, 1993, London: Sweet & Maxwell, at 574.

3 Clarifications Procedural Order No 1, para 7.

4 *The Varenna* [1984] QB 599, where the court held that 'all conditions and exceptions of the charterparty' do not adequately incorporate the arbitration clause.

5 *Hamilton & Co v Mackie & Sons* (1889) 5 TLR 677, where it was stated that the conditions of the charterparty which were inconsistent with the bill of lading must be disregarded.

6 See note 4 above, judicial decisions show that the court requires some specific reference to the arbitration clause before giving effect to the incorporation clause.

(2) *There was no valid ad hoc agreement to arbitrate between Millennium and Quickship*

8 Quickship has never agreed to settle the dispute between itself and Millennium by arbitration. Throughout the series of correspondences, Quickship has maintained that the appointment of the arbitrator on its behalf was to protect self-interest. Arbitration proceeding has indeed been initiated by Millennium, and it would be most natural for Quickship to appoint its own arbitrator to represent it before the tribunal rather than relying on the sole arbitrator appointed by Millennium. A respondent in an arbitration proceeding may challenge the jurisdiction of the tribunal but nevertheless continue to take part in the reference,[7] and such participation cannot be taken to mean an agreement to arbitrate.

9 Millennium contends[8] that in a facsimile dated 1 July 1999 Quickship indicated three issues to be 'decided by the tribunal', and thereby waived its right to object to the existence of an arbitration agreement and only reserved its rights with regards to the merits of the claim. The mere reference to the areas of dispute does not amount in any way whatsoever to an agreement to arbitrate. Furthermore neither does such a reference amount to acknowledgement of the fact that such a process has been initiated with approval.[9]

10 Millennium also contends that in its Defence, Quickship only challenged the improper serving of notice and therefore, had impliedly agreed to the jurisdiction of the tribunal to hear the case.[10] Paragraph 3 of the Defence contains no implied inference that Quickship has agreed that there is or should or can be an arbitration agreement. It merely seeks to establish the fact that even if there may be any such agreement (if the tribunal were to give the claimants the benefit of the doubt), they are barred from bringing such proceedings due to their delay.

11 In any event, Quickship's position towards the lack of jurisdiction of the tribunal to hear the dispute has always been clear and unequivocal. In the last sentence of that paragraph in the Defence where it has expressly been stated that the arbitral tribunal 'is not seized of the issue'. Quickship has never acknowledged by conduct that an arbitration agreement does exist between itself and Millennium.

---

7 Guest, AG, *Chitty on Contracts*, 27th edn, 1994, London: Sweet & Maxwell, at 724.

8 Page 17 of the claimant's written memorandum.

9 See note 7 above.

10 *Ibid.*

C *The putative proper law of the bill of lading is the law of Europa and therefore the Hague-Visby Rules apply. In such case Millennium is time-barred from claiming damages against Quickship*

12 Even if we agree with Millennium's proposition that the proper law of the contract should apply as the governing law of the arbitral proceeding pursuant to an ad hoc agreement, such law would be the law of Europa and therefore, the Hague-Visby Rules[11] should apply to govern the contract. Quickship's case is that even if there was an arbitration agreement, there would be insufficient notice given on 15 June 1999. The alleged sufficient notice given on 16 June 1999 was time-barred under the Hague-Visby Rules and clause 25 of the bill of lading.

13 The issue is whether the letter dated 15 June 1999 amount to a sufficient notice given by Millennium to commence arbitration. In The Agios Lazaros,[12] it was held that an arbitration shall only commence when one party to the arbitration serves on the other party or parties a notice expressly or by implication, requiring the other party to appoint his arbitrator.[13]

14 We submit that the first letter from Millennium dated 15 June 1999 was an insufficient notice to commence arbitration. That letter merely sought repayment from Quickship and was in effect a threat to consider the commencement of arbitration proceedings if repayment was not made. It cannot be inferred from this letter that there was any request to appoint an arbitrator and hence sufficient notice.

15 On the other hand, in the letter dated 16 June 1999 Millennium did purport to request the appointment of an arbitrator by Quickship. However, such commencement of arbitration was time-barred in view of its having missed the last date for making such a request under the Hague-Visby Rules, which provide a limitation period of one year.[14] Although the rules do permit for an extension of this limitation period, this is subject to an agreement between the parties to this effect. Given that there was no such agreement, the limitation period to commence such proceedings has not been extended, and hence, Millennium stand time-barred from claiming damages against Quickship.

---

11 Discussed in the next section of this memorandum substantiating the claim that the proper law of the contract is the law of Europa and Hague-Visby Rules.

12 [1976] 2 Lloyd's Rep 47 at 51.

13 For example if he simply says 'I require the difference to be submitted to arbitration in accordance with our agreement', that is sufficient to commence the arbitration because it is by implication a request to the other appoint his arbitrator.

14 Article III, Rule 6.

16 Due to their delay in invoking such proceedings, if Millennium could validly invoke them at all,[15] their notice to invoke proceedings is inappropriate because it is time-barred under clause 25(2) of the bill of lading.[16] The time limitation had already lapsed by the time the parties had served any notice of the commencement of arbitration proceedings and therefore Quickship was discharged from all liability arising thereof.

D Even if the Hamburg Rules apply Millennium is still barred from invoking clause 45 of the charterparty to initiate arbitration proceeding

17 Art 22 R2 of the Hamburg Rules states that the carrier cannot enforce the arbitration clause against the holder of the bill of lading if there is no special annotation in the bill of lading providing that such a provision should be binding. However, the rules are silent on the scenario where it is the holder of the bill of lading and not the carrier who relies on the clause to initiate the arbitration proceedings.

18 Millennium contends that is equitable for them to rely on Clause 45 of the charterparty because they have notice of such clause.[17] Thus, Art 22 R2 does not bind the holder of the bill of lading since a literal interpretation of this article only bars the carrier from invoking an arbitration clause which is not expressly annotated in the bill of lading.

19 It is submitted that Millennium's contention does not bring their case any further. Literally, Art 22 R2 of the Hamburg Rules only permits arbitration to be commenced by the holder of the bill of lading, and Millennium still has to show that there is a valid agreement to arbitrate between itself and Quickship. The requirement of 'special annotation' under this article reinforces the importance of an agreement to arbitrate: if there is indeed an arbitration clause which is intended to bind the holder of the bill of lading the carrier must note it expressly or else it could not be invoked. In essence it helps to ascertain whether there is any valid arbitration agreement through 'special annotation', and since such annotation was absent in our case the necessary implication is that there is no pre-existing agreement to arbitrate should any dispute arise.

20 In any case, since there is no arbitration agreement, neither by way of clause 45 of the charterparty,[18] nor by an ad hoc agreement,[19] the tribunal has no jurisdiction to hear the dispute even if Art 22 R2 of the Hamburg Rules is of any assistance.

---

15 *Aries Tanker Corporation v Total Transport Ltd* [1977] 1 All ER 398 (HL), where it was held that such expiration of time worked to extinguish the plaintiff's claim altogether.

16 Such limitation is identical to Art III R.6 of the Hague-Visby Rules.

17 Page 14 of the claimant's written memorandum.

18 Discussion at paras 5, 6, 7 *supra*.

19 See paras 8–11 above.

21 It is further submitted that such a narrow interpretation is flawed on two grounds. Firstly, Millennium did not have knowledge of this particular arbitration clause since its knowledge arose purely out of 'common usage and knowledge of the industry',[20] which enabled them to have constructive notice of the existence of the whole charterparty.[21] In other words, Millennium has knowledge, at most, of the possibility of such a clause being in existence. The corollary of Millennium's submission is that if a carrier could establish constructive notice on the part of the holder of the bill of lading (for it could be argued that this could possibly supersede a 'special annotation'), the arbitration proceedings could be commenced regardless of the special annotation requirement in Art 22 R2 of the Hamburg Rules. Such an inference from Millennium's narrow interpretation does not reconcile with the importance of having an agreement to arbitrate and could not be the intention behind the drafting of this rule.

22 Secondly, it would be absurd for there to be a difference between the carrier and the holder in respect of initiating arbitration pursuant to a clause not specially annotated into the bill of lading. The essence of Art 22 R2 is to render arbitration clause not incorporated into the bill of lading inoperative regardless of who seeks to commence the arbitration.

II The Governing Law of the Contract

23 Quickship submits that the proper law of the contract of carriage is the express choice of law, in the absence of *mala fide* intention.

A The express choice of law clause states that the applicable law is the law of Europa and therefore the Hague-Visby Rules should apply

24 Millennium concedes that the law of Europa is applicable to the contract as clause 2 of the bill of lading provides an express choice of the law of Europa as the governing law of the contract '... except as may be otherwise provided herein'. This has to be read in conjunction with clause 27 of the bill of lading which reads the terms of the bill of lading as '... subject to the provisions of the Hague Rules, the Hague-Visby Rules or the Hamburg Rules, as applicable, or such other similar national legislation as may mandatorily apply by virtue of origin or destination of the bill of lading ... If any term of this bill of lading may be repugnant to the said applicable legislation to any extent, such term shall be void to that extent, but no further'.

---

20 Clarification Procedural Order No 1, para 12.

21 *Ibid.*

25 Although both the Hague-Visby Rules and the Hamburg Rules are applicable to the contract on its face,[22] clause 27 uses the word 'or' which is disjunctive in nature. When applied to the construction of such a clause it means that the Hamburg Rules and the Hague-Visby Rules are not required to be applied at the same time. Naturally, the parties when determining which law is to govern their contract, will have been aware that one or more of these international conventions are applicable in that respective jurisdiction. Therefore, when choosing the law of that country to apply (evidenced by clause 2 of the present bill), they would have impliedly agreed to the application of the standards stipulated by the convention to which that country is a party. In the case of Europa, Hague-Visby Rules are adopted,[23] and therefore this is the applicable standard and none other.

26 It could not have been the intention of the parties to require the application of ALL possible international standards that have been drafted so far under these respective conventions. It is more likely that the parties, when drafting the contract, were using a standard clause which listed out the usual conventions that were normally applied depending on which country's law was chosen to govern the contract. Therefore, the most natural construction of this clause in conjunction with clause 2 is the application of the Hague-Visby Rules.

B The choice of law is bona fide *and should not be superseded*

27 Millennium contends that Quickship's choice of Europa as the governing law amounts to derogation of its liabilities under the Hamburg Rules because the Hague-Visby Rules which are applicable under the law of Europa allow for a lower standard of responsibilities. Therefore, they allege that this is not a *bona fide* choice of law[24] and therefore the choice should not be given effect.[25]

28 As the heading of Art 23 of the Hamburg Rules itself indicates,[26] the Hamburg Rules and the provisions regarding non-derogation as to certain responsibilities are aimed at striking out contractual provisions, and not the lower standards as may be applicable under other international conventions or national legislation governing the contract at the same time.[27] Therefore, the application of Hague-Visby Rules to the bill of lading could not amount to a 'derogation of liabilities' as envisaged by the Hamburg

22 Art 2 R1(e) of the Hamburg Rules, and Art X (c) of the Hague-Visby Rules.

23 Adoption of the Hague-Visby Rules Act (Europa) 1978, No 121 of 1978.

24 Page 7 of the claimant's written memorandum, *supra,* at 443.

25 *Vita Food Products Inc v Unus Shipping Co Ltd* [1939] AC 277.

26 'Contractual Stipulations'.

27 The Hague-Visby Rules are applicable both as national legislation (Adoption of the Hague-Visby Rules Act (Europa) 1978, No 121 of 1978: Procedural Order No 1 para 5) and as applicable international convention (since the port of loading is in a contracting state: Art X R(b)).

Rules since Art 23 does not (and cannot) have the effect of governing/overriding the appropriateness of the provisions of the Hague-Visby Rules.

29 Moreover, such an allegation cannot stand in light of the reality that there are many contracts which are necessarily governed by more than one set of laws, whether by way of international conventions or national legislation. Choosing the law which is favourable to the party relying on it[28] could not in itself be an implication of *mala fide* choice of law as this would be tantamount to stating that all choice of law clauses applying such favourable legislation/conventions be void.

30 Such an intention behind that choice is even harder to discern where there is no clear evidence of *mala fide* except, as the claimants allege, the fact that the law chosen favours one party more than the other. One cannot draw such an adverse inference from such an innocent choice or a choice made due to reasons of business efficacy. To deem such options *mala fide* cannot have been the rationale behind the doctrine of *bona fide* choice of law.

31 This is especially the case in view of the fact that there are so many nations today which are still parties to the Hague-Visby Rules rather than the Hamburg Rules. Millennium's suggestion almost amounts to an open attack on all such countries who are signatories to the Hague-Visby Rules and threatens to rob them of their freedom to choose to apply these. The burden on Millennium to show that any such nation who is a party to the Hague-Visby Rules should be estopped from relying on them and instead, should be subject to the application of the Hamburg Rules (merely because the latter stipulate a higher standard) is a very onerous one. If the court should uphold their argument, it would fly in the face of the freedom to contract.

32 In advancing such an argument, Millennium is itself guilty of that which it accuses Quickship Millennium itself has chosen a law which is most favourable to it (as they concede[29] that the Hamburg Rules are less favourable to the carrier). Thus it may similarly be advanced on our behalf that Millennium's urges to the arbitral tribunal to adopt the Hamburg Rules should be denied on this very ground for such a choice of law is *mala fide*.

33 Moreover, Millennium's argument, supporting their allegation of *mala fide* choice of law, based on Quickship's choice of a law applying a lower standard of responsibility in some respects (thereby being more to it) and therefore, amounting to an 'evasion of liability', is an argument tendered under the Hamburg Rules. In effect, Millennium is using the Hamburg Rules as a yardstick to judge what is a *bona fide* choice of law (and to

28 This practice is similar to choosing a *forum conveniens*.

29 Page 7 of the claimant's written memorandum, *supra*, at 443.

support their contention that Hamburg Rules apply). In the inherent circularity of its argument it naturally concludes that choosing the Hamburg Rules is the only *bona fide* choice of law as it sets a higher standard for carrier's responsibilities and obligations.

34 The fact that a choice is made in bad faith is evidenced by a lack of connection between the agreement and the law chosen. Conversely, in the situation where the agreement has a real connection with the law chosen, this is good evidence of a lack of evasive intent by the parties.[30] In the present case various contractual nexus could be established between Europa and the bill of lading (it being the place where both the supplier and the carrier of the goods carry business, and the port of loading of the cargo), and it is different from a case of clear *mala fide* where a party, upon discovering that a provision was either unfavourable or void under the proper law, tries to evade its consequences by claiming that the provision was subject to another legal system.

35 Millennium argues,[31] firstly that the Hamburg Rules should apply. In the alternative, it argues that the Hague-Visby Rules only apply where the Hamburg Rules are silent. Its final contention is that if the Hague-Visby Rules apply, then where they stipulate a standard lower than the Hamburg Rules in terms of carrier's liability the Hamburg Rules come into play. It is unimaginable that the parties intended for such uncertainty to prevail in terms of the governing law especially in view of the fact that there is clearly an express choice of law clause in the contract itself. It would be inequitable for the tribunal to ignore this express choice and enter into such legal gymnastics as invited to do so by Millennium in order to discern which rules should apply in what scenario. Such an interpretation by the tribunal would clearly contradict the intention of the parties as evidenced by the contract and it would undermine notions of business efficacy and certainty.

36 In conclusion, at its very best, Millennium's argument as to the applicability of the Hamburg Rules can only amount to this in the present case: for areas which are covered by both conventions (Hague-Visby Rules and the Hamburg Rules), the Hague-Visby Rules are the proper law to govern the contract by virtue of the express choice of law under clause 2 of the bill of lading. Where the Hague-Visby Rules are silent, the Hamburg Rules will come into application in respect of those specific areas only. Thus, in effect, in the present case, the application of the Hamburg Rules is subject to the application of the Hague-Visby Rules. Such an interpretation is also consistent with Art 23 of the Hamburg Rules which states that only

30 *Nike Informatic Systems Ltd v Avac Systems Ltd* (1979) 105 DLR (3d) 455; *Greenshields Inc v Johnston* (1981) 119 DLR (3d) 714, (1981) 131 DLR (3d) 234; *Bank of Montreal v Snoxell* (1983) 143 DLR (3d) 349.

31 Pages 6–9 of the claimant's written memorandum, *supra*, at 442–45.

those contractual stipulations (as opposed to the whole contract) which derogate from the Hamburg Rules are null and void.

III Breach of Obligations to Millennium – damage to cargo

37 Whether Quickship has breached its obligations to Millennium depends on the following issues:

- Whether the cars were damaged in Quickship's possession (issue of damage);
- Whether Quickship has provided a cargoworthy vessel in accordance with Art III, R1 of the Hague-Visby Rules (issue of cargoworthiness);
- Whether Quickship has exercised proper care according to Art III, R2 of the Hague-Visby Rules (issue of proper care);
- If Quickship failed to exercise proper care, whether Quickship would be entitled to rely on the exemptions in Art IV (issue of exemption);
- Whether Quickship has unjustifiably deviated from the route, with the result that exemptions cannot be relied upon (issue of deviation);
- Whether Quickship is liable if Hamburg Rules were to be applicable.

A The cars were not damaged in Quickship's charge

38 Paragraph 10 of Millennium's Statement of Claim unequivocally alleges that the damage to the cars occurred whilst they were in the charge of Quickship, and such allegation was based on the contention that leakage of chemicals from the top deck of the ship caused the damage to the paintwork.[32] However, there is no categorical evidence to this effect.

39 Only two inferences could be drawn from the surveyor's report. Mr. Ronald Raines, the marine surveyor, had interviewed one John Kavanagh, an ex-deck hand on board of '*MV JASMINE*'. Mr. Kavanagh revealed that after loading was completed on the evening of 1 May 1998, he was told by the master to scrub the top deck of the vessel (above the deck where the cars were placed) with a solution 'with a dreadful smell' in preparation for his wedding. The surveyor concluded that there were two possible causes of damage: (1) Industrial fallout (acid rain) at the port of loading; (2) Leaking acid/chemicals from the deck during the preparation of the master's wedding. The report does not conclude which was the more likely cause.

40 It is doubtful whether much weight should be attached to the report. The surveyor had not inspected the vessel or the cleaning solution himself and his conclusion was based largely on an interview with an ex deck hand on

32 *Ibid*; *supra*, at 454.

board the vessel. Without inspecting whether there were any cracks in the vessel's deck, or whether the solution had the potential to cause damage of this kind, it is doubtful, if not impossible that the surveyor could logically have concluded on the evidence available to him, that the solution could possibly have leaked and further that this leakage could have caused the damage.

41 Moreover, if the damage were indeed caused on board as alleged, the damage would have been quite apparent at the time of delivery. The protective wax coating would have melted in those spots where the solution had actually dripped (resulting in the black spots and blots) and this would have been visible to the naked eye. Given that the damage was apparent only after the removal of the wax coating (as Millennium concedes[33]), it is strong indication that the damage was indeed one which was not caused during transit either at the loading port (acid rain) or during the voyage (leakage of solution), and was more likely to have existed prior to Quickship's taking charge of the cargo. Therefore, Quickship should not be held liable for such damages whether the Hague-Visby or Hamburg Rules apply.

42 Millennium has failed to discharge its burden on a balance of probabilities that the goods were damaged whilst in Quickship's charge. The poor evidential value of the surveyor's report and Millennium's dependence on the protective wax coating as a reason why such defects were not discoverable by them upon delivery, all make it more likely than not that the damage had already been done prior to the cargo's arrival at the port of loading.

B Quickship is not liable under the Hague-Visby Rules

(1) Quickship is not liable under Art III, R1(c)

(a) Millennium has failed to prove that the vessel was uncargoworthy

43 Quickship denies Millennium's allegation on p 25 of the written memorandum that Quickship is in breach of Art III, R1(c) of the Hague-Visby Rules by its failure to exercise due diligence in ensuring that the vessel was cargoworthy.

44 According to *The Good Friend*,[34] the burden of proof under Art III R1 rests on the claimant (ie, Millennium) to establish that (1) '*MV JASMINE*' was uncargoworthy before and at the beginning of the voyage, and (2) the damage was occasioned from such uncargoworthiness.[35] It is only after

33 Page 2 of the claimant's written memorandum (statement of facts), *supra,* at 440–41; and p 22 of the same, *supra,* at 455.

34 *Empresa Cubana Importada de Alimentos 'Alimport' v Iasmos Shipping Co SA (The Good Friend)* [1984] 2 Lloyd's Rep 586 (QBD).

35 *Paterson Steamships Ltd v Canadian Cooperative Wheat Producers Ltd* [1934] AC 538; *Kish v Taylor* [1912] AC 604.

Millennium had discharged its burden that the burden would then shift to Quickship to show that it had exercised due diligence in providing a cargoworthy ship.[36]

45 Cargoworthiness has been defined as 'being reasonably fit to receive and carry the cargo and deliver it at the specified destination'.[37] Quickship has already submitted that it is important to exercise caution when relying on the surveyor's report, and that it was more likely than not that the goods were damaged before they came into Quickship's charge.[38] There being no evidence advanced to show uncargoworthiness and existence of cracks in the deck or the leakage of the acid, Millennium has failed to establish that the '*MV JASMINE*' was uncargoworthy before and at the beginning of the voyage, and that the damage had occasioned from such uncargoworthiness.

(b) Quickship has exercised due diligence to provide a cargoworthy ship

46 Even if Millennium has discharged its burden of establishing the vessel is uncargoworthy, Quickship has, in any event, exercised due diligence to make the ship cargoworthy before and at the beginning of the voyage.

47 The standard of due diligence is similar to the common law duty of care,[39] and thus, the carrier is only liable for damage which is reasonably foreseeable.

48 'Due diligence' has been defined as 'not merely a praiseworthy or sincere, though unsuccessful effort, but such an intelligent and efficient attempt as shall make it so seaworthy as far as diligence can serve'.[40] This standard depends on the knowledge available to the person who is being judged and the circumstances of the case. Thus, the standard is a 'genuine, competent and reasonable effort of the carrier to fulfil the prerequisites of Article III R1'.[41] What constitutes due diligence will always require consideration of the particular facts of the case.

49 There are two possible causes suggested by the surveyor. As to the possibility of acid rain being the cause, it is submitted that such an industrial fallout does affect the carrier's duty to provide a cargoworthy ship. The fact that Quickship did not act to prevent the effects acid rain on

---

36 *Maxine Footwear Co Ltd and Ano v Canadian Government Merchant Marine Ltd* [1959] 2 All ER 740 (PC).

37 *The Good Friend* at 592.

38 Discussion at paras 38–42 above.

39 *Riverstone Meat Co Pty Ltd v Lancashire Shipping Co Ltd, The Muncaster Castle* [1961] 1 All ER 495 at 527 (HL).

40 *Grain Growers Export Co v Canada Steamship Lines Ltd* (1918) 43 OLR 330.

41 John Richardson, *A Guide to the Hague and Hague-Visby Rules*, 3rd edn, 1994, Lloyd's of London Press at 37.

the cars is not relevant to the issue of cargoworthiness of the vessel,[42] but the issue of proper care.

50 In terms of the second possible cause (leakage of the solution), there was no circumstances to put Quickship under notice to question the cargoworthiness of the vessel before and at the beginning of the voyage.[43] Thus in terms of efforts which could be reasonably required of it, Quickship had already exercised due diligence to provide a cargoworthy vessel. Even if a higher standard of due diligence was required, it is unlikely that such cracks would have been discovered even with the exercise of this greater degree of due diligence so as to enable leakage to be envisaged as a 'likelihood or real possibility'.[44]

51 Moreover, the scrubbing (and subsequent leakage, if any) only occurred because the master was having a wedding on board which was not a part of or ancillary to preparing a cargoworthy vessel for the purposes of the voyage to Pacifica. Quickship should not be held to have failed in its duty to exercise due diligence in making the vessel seaworthy given the occurrence of such an unforeseeable event which did not fall within the scope of the master's duties. Such acts are solely the personal responsibility of the master as they were not in the contemplation of the carrier as part of the master's duties.

52 This is not to say that one can be reckless in the carrying out of any activities on the upper deck. But at the same time, it certainly does not mean that there is a heavier burden placed on the carrier to ensure and see to it that all possible causes of damage are alleviated in every conceivable way. To the extent that Quickship had a duty to ensure the ship was fit, it did so. The fact that such a mishap resulted from its unawareness of the possibility of cracks or other means of leakage to the lower deck does not mean that it failed in its duty to exercise due diligence, especially given the fact that the scrubbing does not formed part of an activity in the course of making the vessel cargoworthy for the purposes of the voyage. Even a higher standard of due diligence would have been insufficient to discover this chain of events. Although the act of scrubbing itself it foreseeable, the use of unusual solution causing the damage is unforeseeable which is then outside the scope of due diligence. In addition, the purposes for which the act was performed rendered it unconnected to the voyage and thus, brought it outside the responsibility of Quickship.

---

42 The issue of cargoworthiness focuses on the vessel itself which should not be affected by external factors such as acid rain.

43 Unlike the case of *The Toledo* [1995] 1 Lloyd's Rep 40 and *The Danica Brown* [1995] 2 Lloyd's Rep 264, where the carrier was put on notice of possible defects but nevertheless chose to ignore them.

44 *The Toledo, ibid.*

(2) Quickship has no liability under Art III R2

53 Quickship denies Millennium's allegation that Quickship is in breach of Art III, R2 of the Hague-Visby Rules by failing to 'properly and carefully keep' and 'care for' the cargo.[45] Quickship contends that (i) it is not in breach of Art III R2, and that even if it is, (ii) Quickship is exempted from liability as it falls within the exceptions under Art IV.

(a) There was no breach of obligation to 'properly and carefully load, handle, stow, carry, keep, care for, and discharge the goods carried'

54 Millennium has failed to establish that Quickship is prima facie in breach of the Article as it has not shown that the cargo was damaged while it was in Quickship's charge as alleged in p 24 of their memorandum.[46]

55 Under Art III, R3 of the Hague-Visby Rules, Quickship is not bound to make any representation on the bill of lading, which it has no reasonable means of checking. This provision is different from the obligation under Art 16, R 1 of the Hamburg Rules, where a reservation is required in the event that there is no reasonable means of checking the condition of the goods.[47] Therefore, even though the goods were marked to be in 'apparent good order and condition' on the bill of lading, Quickship is not estopped from contending the goods were actually defected upon receipt.

56 In any case, Quickship has complied with its duty to 'properly and carefully load, handle, stow, carry, keep, care for, and discharge the goods carried'. In *Albacora*,[48] the court defined 'properly' as 'adopting a system which was sound in light of all knowledge which a carrier had or ought to have about the nature of goods'. There was no evidence to suggest the deck which Quickship used to place the cars was in any way 'unsound'. No system of loading would be foolproof as against such the unforeseeable event of leakage of acid so as to be able to guard against it. Unless there are circumstances which put the carrier on notice to look for possible cracks or other factors which increase the possibility of leakage,[49] the carrier does not bear a higher burden than that reasonably required of him under the rules to properly keep and care for the cargo. It cannot be held that merely because Quickship failed to account for one possibility that was highly unlikely[50] that it failed to properly care for and keep the cargo.

---

45 Page 23 of the claimant's written memorandum; *supra,* at 456.

46 Discussion at paras 38–42 above.

47 Or else there will be a presumption that the condition of the goods when received were in conformity with the description of them in the bill of lading.

48 *Albacora SRL v Westcott & Laurance Line Ltd* [1966] 2 Lloyd's Rep 53 (HL).

49 *The Toledo*, at n 42.

50 In *Pyrene Co Ltd v Scindia Steam Navigation Co Ltd* [1954] 2 All ER 153 at 163, Lord Devlin stated that the extent to which the carrier has to take care while loading the cargo and in keeping it depends on the nature of the cargo and the practice of the port and the trade. The rules were not meant to impose universal rigidity.

(b) Quickship is exempted from liability under the Art IV exceptions

57 Even if Quickship has breach Art III, R2 it is still entitled to rely on exceptions under Art IV. Quickship herein relies on exceptions (a), (m), and (q).

58 Art IV, R 2(a), (m), and (q) provide that:

> [n]either the carrier nor the ship shall be responsible for loss or damage arising or resulting from:
>
> (a) Act, neglect, or default of the master… or the servants of the carrier in the navigation or in the management of the ship.
>
> (m) … any other loss or damage arising from inherent defect, quality or vice of goods.
>
> (q) any other cause arising without the actual fault or privity of the carrier or without the fault or negligence of the agents or servants of the carrier.

59 Quickship is entitled to rely on exception in Art IV, R2(a). Should the damage be caused by the leakage of acid due to the scrubbing, because the scrubbing was done 'in the management of the ship'[51] and the master was negligent in doing so, the carrier is not liable. The act of scrubbing 'affects the vessel herself' as it relates to the cleaning of the interior of the vessel itself, which would be done regardless of whether or not there is cargo on board. Thus, Millennium's contention[52] that this act was done with a view to keeping and caring for the cargo but not in the management of the ship is flawed.

60 If it is found that the scrubbing did not fall within the 'management of the ship', the act was still not done for the purpose of keeping or caring for the cargo, as it was clearly done with a view to ensuring 'spotlessness' of the deck for the wedding. Moreover, it was only the upper deck that was cleaned and thus, the hold below where the cars were stowed cannot have been thought likely to be affected and neither was it intended that it should be.

61 Quickship is also entitled to rely on Art. IV, R2(m) which exempts liability for damage arising from inherent defect. Quickship argues that the defects in the goods were already there prior to its taking charge of them upon receipt. It was only that these defects were undetectable due to the wax coating.[53] This is an inherent defect in the cargo,[54] which exempts Quickship from liability under the article.

---

51 *Goose Millard Ltd v Canadian Government Merchant Marine Ltd* [1929] AC 233 (HL); *International Packers London Ltd v Ocean Steam Ship Co Ltd* [1955] 2 Lloyd's Rep 218 (QBD).

52 Page 32 of the claimant's written memorandum; *supra*, at 462.

53 Discussion on this at paras 38–42, *supra*.

54 *FW Berk & Co Ltd v Style* [1955] 3 All ER 625; *The Polar* [1993] 2 Lloyd's Rep 478.

62 Alternatively, Quickship can rely on Art IV, R2(q) which excludes liability for damage resulting from no actual fault of the carrier and no negligence on the servants. Firstly, since the master is the agent of the shipowner but not the carrier, the acts of his servants fall within the scope of R2(q). Secondly, the leakage of acid (if this be deemed the cause), was not caused by Quickship's fault or negligence. The standard of care expected of them is not so high as to expect them to ensure that any possibility of leakage of acid while scrubbing the deck onto the lower deck should be absolutely eliminated. The surveyor's report identifying that the damage was in the form of 'spots' or 'blots' indicates that the area damaged is not so great as to take the form of large patches, thus it is unlikely that leakage could be from large holes or cracks in the upper deck floor. As such leakage is generally unforeseeable and could not be anticipated by the reasonable man, Quickship should be exempted from liability under Art IV, R2(q) and not be held negligent.[55]

(c) Deviation does not bar Quickship from relying on the exceptions under Article IV of the Hague-Visby Rules

63 Deviation no longer amounts to a fundamental breach going to the root of the contract. As long as the deviation can be shown to have occurred for a justifiable reason,[56] the carrier will not be held to have breached a fundamental term of the contract.[57] The fact that the vessel had deviated because she responded to a distress call is certainly 'justifiable' deviation because the law is careful that it should not punish those who strive to help others or else they would be reluctant to assist those in need for fear of having to pay for the 'breach' of their contract for deviation. This practice has been termed the 'unwritten law of the sea'.[58]

64 It is also of significance that the parties in the present case actually made an allowance for deviation[59] in the written contract.[60] Hence, Millennium is estopped from alleging that Quickship has been in breach of its

55 *Leesh River Tea Co Ltd v British India Steam Navigation Co Ltd* [1967] 2 QB 250 (CA), a case in which this exception was successfully invoked, sets out some of the criteria which are applied to determine whether or not this exception can avail the carrier of liability.

56 Not purely business enhancement reasons which would be of sole benefit to the carrier, although the courts have been known to accept such deviation as justifiable

57 John Richardson, see note 41 above at 53–55.

58 *Ibid* at 53.

59 *Renton v Palmyra Trading Corporation* [1956] 3 All ER 957 at 963 where it was held that despite such a wide clause allowing for deviation, the clause requires a sensible construction whereby the party intending to rely on it must show that the deviation occurred due to one of the exigencies probably in the contemplation of the parties when drafting such a clause, as opposed to granting the party an open license to breach the terms of the contract.

60 Clause 6(1) of the bill of lading states that the carrier has absolute discretion to decide the route of the carriage of goods, whether the route is the direct, advertised, or customary route. Clause 6(2) states that the carrier has liberty to stay in any port in or out of the direct, advertised or customary route.

obligations under the contract, and even more so from denying the carriers their entitlement to rely on the exception clauses under the Rules. This proposition holds even greater weight in light of the fact that the deviation was in no way unwarranted or for self-serving purposes but rather, it was a response to a distress call. This was probably one of the emergencies or 'permitted reasons' for deviation envisaged by the wide deviation clause in the contract. Therefore, as Millennium is unable to show that the deviation was unjustifiable or that there was a fundamental breach of contract, Quickship is entitled to rely on the exception clauses available to it under the Rules.

C Quickship is not liable under the Hamburg Rules

65 Liability of the carrier for damage to the goods attaches, as the claimant contends, if the claimant proves the damage was caused by an occurrence which took place when the goods are in the carrier's charge. The respondent then has to prove that all reasonable measures to avoid the occurrence have been taken.[61]

(1) The claimant cannot prove that damage was caused when the goods were in Quickship's charge

(a) Millennium's failure to give notice of damage to the cargo within the time limit gives rise to a presumption in favour of Quickship

66 Where the damage to the goods was not apparent, Millennium was required under Art 19 to give notice of damage in writing to Quickship within fifteen days after the goods passed to the consignee. The goods were received on 15 June 1998 but notice was only given on 21 July 1998. Therefore, Millennium failed to serve notice within the time limit.

67 Non-compliance with this requirement gives rise to a *prima facie* presumption that the goods are delivered in the condition as described in the bill of lading, ie, in apparent good condition and order. Millennium is under the burden to prove to the contrary. Failure to do so renders Millennium's allegation that the goods were damaged when in Quickship's charge unsubstantiated as a *prima facie* case and hence, no liability attaches to the carrier under the Hamburg Rules. Since the surveyor's report suggested both acid rain and the leakage of the acid due to scrubbing as possible causes (neither of which is more likely than the other), it is submitted that Millennium cannot prove on a balance of probabilities, that the goods were more likely to have been damaged while in Quickship's charge.

68 Millennium seeks to rely on Art 16 R3 to rebut the presumption that the goods were received in apparent good condition arising by virtue of Art 19

61 Art 5, R1.

in the event of failure to give notice as to damaged condition of goods. They draw support from Quickship's failure to insert the required reservation, and on this basis form their case that Art 16 R3(b) gives rise to a presumption that the goods were received in good condition and therefore the presumption that the goods were delivered in good condition under Art 19 could no longer stand because such duty to notify is necessarily extinguished once a claimant relies on the bill of lading as an endorsement as to the condition of the goods. This clearly highlights the apparent conflict between Art 16 and Art 19 for the reliance by both parties on these Articles have given rise to two different and conflicting presumptions. The question is which of these presumptions should stand and do they work together to reduce or put the parties to notice as to the performance of their respective duties or are they independent of each other in their operation.

69 If Millennium's argument is accepted, it would in mean that the Art 16 presumption prevails over the Art 19 presumption and the necessary implication is that whenever the carrier fails to insert a reservation as required by Art 16, the consignee will automatically be exempted from the duty to inspect the goods and send a notice of damage as required under Art 19. This would be an unnatural interpretation of the two provisions and it is unlikely that such a construction was intended as it would have further-reaching consequences than was contemplated by the rules or the parties at the Hamburg Conference. Art 16 must be read independently from Art 19 as both Articles impose separate duties on the respective parties, both are required to comply with the Article which requires such compliance before the Article applies to them and can avail them of liability or come to their assistance. It is not an excuse to say that since there was no reservation made by the carrier that this entitled that the consignee to determine that there was no longer a need to fulfil their end of the bargain to check the goods as required. This interpretation makes the obligation of the consignee to check the condition of the goods upon delivery conditional on the compliance by the carrier of its duty to insert a reservation clause if required. The drafters could not have intended such a consequence where the duty is a partial one only arising in the event of fulfilment of obligations by third parties. The law usually imposes a more certain and independent standard and thus, it is maintained that the presumptions under the two Articles do not affect each other and each come into operation under their own respective qualifications depending on whether or not the parties seeking to rely on the Articles have complied with their obligations, and as such amounts to evidence against the party who fails to comply.

(b) Millennium cannot rely on Art 16 R3(b) because it is not a 'third party' to the bill of lading

70 The damage to the paintwork of the cars was not visible because of the wax coating. However, Millennium relies heavily on Art 16 R1 to show that Quickship had an obligation to insert in the bill of lading a reservation to clarify that Quickship had no reasonable means of checking the quality or condition of the goods as received. Failure to do this gives rise to a presumption that the condition of the goods was *prima facie* in conformity with the description on the bill of lading (ie, in 'apparent good condition and order'), and Quickship is precluded from adducing proof to the contrary under Art 16 R3(b).

71 The fact that the goods are deemed to have been received in apparent good condition and order at the port of loading by operation of Art 16 R3(b) and that the damage to the cars was discovered after their arrival at the port of discharge, coincide to produce the conclusion that the cars were damaged in Quickship's charge. However, evidence of Millennium's inability to discover the damage sooner due to the protective wax coating which prevented the damage from being 'apparent', the 'apparent good condition' of the goods prior to their being handed over to Millennium or as received at the port of loading, serve to be inconclusive towards determining the actual condition of the goods or even their likely condition.

72 Furthermore, the claimant's interpretation of Art 16 R3 is ill-founded. The rule only precludes a carrier from adducing evidence to the contrary vis à vis a third party. A typical example is where the bill of lading is a contract made between A (carrier) and B (original endorsee) but B subsequently passes the bill of lading to C for consideration. A is precluded from adducing evidence to prove anything contrary to the description of the goods as described in the bill of lading when C seeks to recover damages from A because C should be allowed to rely on such description as to the condition of the goods in the bill of lading. A third party pays consideration and acquires the goods in good faith and so should be entitled to rely on the endorsement by the carrier that the goods are in conformity with the representation and it should not bear any burden to check the goods upon receipt.

73 Quickship contends that Millennium is not a third party to the bill of lading. Although it was not a party to the original contract between Quickship and JagImps to transport the cars, the evidence that JagImps and Millennium were unsure whether JagImps or its subsidiary, Millennium should be handling the transaction,[62] Millennium's being instructed to take delivery on behalf of JagImps and the fact that Millennium is a wholly owned subsidiary of JagImps all point towards the

62 Letter dated 15 June 1998 from JagImps to Millennium.

conclusion that JagImps and Millennium are inseparable. They are one and the same. Moreover, Millennium has done nothing in reliance of the description of the goods in the bill of lading (ie, paid no consideration for the document as title to the goods, etc as a 'third party' envisaged by the Article was expected to have done) and, therefore they do not qualify as a third party in order for the operation of Article 16 R3(b) and hence, it does not come into play to assist them. This is because the two requirements in order for the section to be applicable are that firstly, there must be a third party and secondly, such third party must have acted in reliance on such description.

(2) Quickship has taken all reasonable measures to avoid the occurrence which caused the damage and its consequences

74 Even if the tribunal decides against Quickship on the *prima facie* evidence of goods received in apparent good condition, Quickship has still complied with the duty placed on it under Art 5 which requires all reasonable measures to have been taken to avoid the occurrence which caused the damage or its consequences. Millennium must first show that the damage was indeed caused by the leakage of the chemical used to scrub the upper deck, and it is submitted that Millennium has failed to discharge such burden.[63]

75 Even if the tribunal held otherwise, since the occurrence of the leakage was unforeseeable (or replacing this standard with the objective standard of reasonable foreseeability), it is inconceivable that the argument that the mere use of an acidic solution would necessarily result in this kind of damage should stand. Millennium has repeatedly emphasized the mere fact of having this solution on board was tantamount to putting the carriers on guard as to the foreseeability of the likelihood of leakage, and hence to condemn them for their failure to take reasonable measures to avoid such leakage. It is submitted that this would be too high a burden to place on the carriers to be able to foresee all such possibilities. The requirement under the Hamburg Rules is one of reasonableness, therefore, Quickship has not been negligent in any respect and it has taken all measures that could reasonably be expected of them to avoid any such the occurrence and its consequences.

IV Quantification of damages

76 Quickship is not liable at all because the burden placed on the claimants cannot be discharged in view of the lack of evidence to support any of their contentions.

63 Discussion on this at paras 38–42, *supra*.

77 In light of the weakness of the surveyor's report or any of the other evidence, there is no probably cause that can be established as falling within the carrier's responsibility, and in such event, it is appropriate that the damages be apportioned because the cause or effective cause are unascertainable.[64]

78 Even if the tribunal decides that Millennium is entitled to claim damages from Quickship, Millennium is nevertheless not entitled to recover the cost of repainting the car (ie, E 840 000) in full under both the Hamburg and the Hague-Visby regimes, as pleaded in the Statement of Claim.

A Limitation of damages under the Hague-Visby Rules

79 It is submitted that Millennium defaulted in concluding (at p 33)[65] that Quickship cannot rely on the package and kilo limitations[66] because of unjustifiable deviation. Quickship was only precluded from relying on such limitation unless it is proved that '... the damage resulted from an act or omission of the carrier done with the intent to cause damage, or recklessly and with knowledge that damage would probably result'.[67] In other words, even if Millennium could establish unjustified deviation[68] on Quickship's part, it is of no consequence itself unless it is proved to have been intentional or reckless, with knowledge of consequences and that there were damaging consequences flowing from the deviation. There is no evidence suggesting any of this in the present action.

80 Therefore under the limitation Millennium is only entitled to claim 2 SDR[69] of gross weight of the goods lost or damaged, ie, an amount of E 421 174.1.[70]

B Limitation of Damages under the Hamburg Rules

81 As submitted by Millennium, Art 6 R1(a) and Art 26 R1 provide that the carrier will only be liable for 2.5 SDR per kilogram of gross weight of the goods lost or damaged, ie, an amount of E 526 467.64.

82 Therefore in either case, Millennium is not entitled to claim the full amount of E 840 000 for the repainting cost of the damaged cars.

---

64 *The Anneliesse, Arietta S Livanos (Owners) v Anneliese (Owners)* [1970] 1 Lloyd's Rep 355 (CA).

65 *Supra,* at 463–64.

66 Art IV R5(a).

67 Art IV R5(e).

68 Discussion on 'deviation' at para 63, *supra.*

69 Standard Drawing Rights (SDRs), as defined by the International Monetary Fund: Art IV R5(d) of the Hague-Visby Rules. The rate is 1 SDR to E 1.45421 (as at 22 May 2000).

70 2 SDR x 164 (no of damaged cars) x 883 (weight of each car).

PRAYER FOR RELIEF

For the above reasons, we request the tribunal to:

DECLARE that the Tribunal has no jurisdiction to hear the matter; and

DECLARE that Millennium's claim is barred; alternatively

DECLARE that Quickship is not liable to Millennium in the amount claimed (ie, E 820 000), or at all.

Review Article

William Crane

PERSPECTIVES ON THE PRECAUTIONARY PRINCIPLE

by R Harding and E Fisher (eds)

Federation Press, Sydney, 1999, 319pp
ISBN 1 86287 318 6

Many, outside the immediate areas of planning and environment law, may not yet be familiar with this concept. As a general rule planning lawyers have tended to view it with a fair degree of cynicism whilst environmental lawyers have been rather more enthusiastic. However, since it is becoming increasingly impossible to be a planning lawyer without a knowledge of environmental law even the planners are having to come to terms with the concept. Towards the end of this work which comprises 17 essays on various aspects of the principle the following definition is provided: 'When an activity raises threats to human health or the environment, precautionary measures should be taken even if some cause and effect relationships are not fully established scientifically. In this context the proponent of an activity, rather than the public should bear the burden of proof' (at pp 306–07). This is but one of many attempts to define the principle which have taken place in most developed jurisdictions. It has been adopted by the European Union in their Compendium of Spatial Planning, in the United States (though with some difficulty and not with the degree of particularly of other countries), in every Australian jurisdiction and is reiterated constantly in submissions at international conferences such as the 1992 Declaration of the UN Conference on Environment and Development. For comparison the Queensland Integrated Planning Act (1997) defines the principle as follows: '… if there are threats of serious or irreversible environmental damage, careful evaluation must be made to avoid wherever practicable serious or irreversible environmental damage including, if appropriate, assessing risk weighted consequences of various option.'

Perhaps the principle could be shortened even further to: 'If in doubt, don't'? There are a number of concerns that have been expressed as to the applicability of the principle that should be mentioned as a framework against which this collection of essays should be considered. First, since almost all economic activity such as manufacturing, mining and even some pastoral activity involve an application for development permission to some statutory authority this principle must now be taken into serious consideration in assessing the aggregate risk of a project. Secondly, the onus of proof is placed on the developer not the state which has raised questions as to the equity of the principle, thirdly, since international commerce is increasingly able to relocate and to minimize capital cost by the use of so-called Nike contracts amongst other mechanisms, a very strict regulatory regime in one jurisdiction may threaten the viability of a project in that jurisdiction resulting in the loss of the project to less bureaucratic countries and fourthly, it is in the nature of scientific knowledge to be equivocal. Scientists constantly disagree. In fact it is in this manner that scientific knowledge advances.

The precautionary principle resides in the interstice between the 'general' (as a statement of principle) and the 'specific' (in the sense of an application to build a fertilizer plant). In many instances these issues will need to be dealt with by a judiciary that may need an almost dialectical perspective to adjudicate the issues and this, in itself, could only be accomplished if the court were to operate on a precursor principle viz, that environmental issues may be able to be *managed*. For the principle not to become illusory over time the requirement is currently for content not further statements of principle. Clearly the editors and publisher have chosen the correct time to provide a much-needed overview of this contentious topic.

In their introduction Harding and Fisher successfully summarise the cardinal points around which the current international debate is centred. They provide a, thankfully short, history of the origins of the principle and an interesting treatment of the relationship between 'risk' and 'precaution'. They are prepared to concede, which is the appropriate response at this time, that there is no clear exposition of the 'threshold test'. Does it mean 'a reasonable risk', 'the mere possibility of risk' or is it simply a political issue and one which should be taken out of the realms of science and the legal system. Though I believe the risks which would attend extending unappealable executive discretion into an area with major economic, social and environmental consequences are rather too parlous to even consider it remains an interesting proposition though not necessarily one which the editors would support.

Both authors gave a commendable amount of space to the countervailing (if not iconoclastic) opinions of other writers such as Brunton who has described the Precautionary Principle as 'the greatest risk of all', as well as acknowledging the genuine concern being expressed by some under-developed nations, and some developed nations in South East Asia that the principle represents a grave threat to technological innovation and ultimately to their access to global markets. Ultimately the authors had to confront the essential question as to whether the Precautionary Principle can make a valid contribution to a sustainable global future. They gave a balanced, and in the opinion of this reviewer, a correct assessment viz a cautious and conditional 'yes'.

The book contains 17 separate articles which; taken together, represent an almost complete overview of the principle. These articles will be taken in turn.

(1) 'The precautionary principle: core meaning, constitutional framework and procedures for implementation' (*James Cameron*)

Cameron covers a wide ground in his article that is written from an obvious statist context. While accepting the now traditional view that the onus of proof in these matters should rest on the applicant rather than the state he believes the principle (through its incorporation *inter alia* in the Maastricht Treaty, 1992) has now become a norm of international law and should be incorporated also as a norm within domestic constitutions. He does however concede that neither proposition is accepted by Birnie and Boyle, *International Environmental Law* (Oxford University Press). He is firmly of the opinion that lack of scientific certainty should not delay the implementation of regulatory mechanisms. However, while he acknowledges that all human activity has environmental effects he leaves the crucial issue of 'threshold' effects to 'interested parties' (p 43). This does seem a rather vague conclusion on such a central issue. He accepts the principles of the Bamako Convention and is, accordingly, not a supporter of a 'permissible emissions approach'. It follows, though he does not mention the issue, that he is hardly likely to support 'tradable rights'.

(2) 'Will the precautionary principle affect environmental decision-making and impact assessment?' (*JP Whitehouse*)

Whitehouse initially provides a very interesting analysis of the precautionary principle as an expression of differing philosophical contexts. These he suggests are: (a) as a new philosophical ethos in itself, (b) as an overarching principle of legislation, (c) as a policy approach, not as an operational tool, (d) as a principle whose operation can only be limited to specific instances or substances or (e) as a genuine evaluative mechanism essential to environmental operational decision making. Again he believes the onus of proof should rest on applicants but is at least prepared to accept the 'balance of probabilities' as the appropriate standard. (Some writers have suggested that the criminal standard, 'beyond a reasonable doubt' should apply.)

(3) 'An industry perspective on the precautionary principle' (*J Segal*)

Segal, in common I suspect with quite a few lawyers and planners, has trouble with the principle in general. Specifically and speaking from an industry perspective he expresses difficulty in understanding how such a principle can fail to create a climate of uncertainty throughout large sections of industry and how it can be incorporated within the corporate processes of strategic business planning. At the very least, he suggests, detailed guidelines for its application are required. Most writers would concede however that we are a long way from that situation and indeed this book illustrates that, as yet, there is no agreement on a standard cognitive approach to the principle.

(4) 'The precautionary principle as a legal standard for public decision making' (*Elizabeth Fisher*)

Fisher has a number of criticisms of the approach taken by Australian courts to a principle which in most jurisdictions is entrenched in the relevant planning and environments Acts. These can be summarized as follows: (a) she believes that the principle involves rather more than a 'duty to be cautious' or as expressing a duty 'to use common sense'. (Both expressions have been used in recent decisions.) I fail to see the point of her argument here since both expressions come close to describing the underlying intent of the principle, (b) she believes the principle should be incorporated as a fundamental one within administrative law. My difficulty with this argument is that it should hardly matter where the principle is entrenched. Administrative law principles regularly make a transition into planning law with the *Wednesbury* test of reasonableness being a good example and there is no reason why the process should not occur in the opposite direction if required, and c) that the precautionary principle should be argued in court as part of a 'package of legal arguments' (p 96). I fail also to appreciate this point. To my knowledge when the principle is submitted to the court it is not submitted in isolation from other supporting legal argument.

(5) 'Factoring biodiversity conservation into decision-making processes' (*David Farrier*)

While viewing the gradual incorporation of the precautionary principle into legislation such as The Threatened Species Conservation Act, 1995 (NSW) as commendable he questions what he calls the 'development imperative' (p 115) of many of the administrative agencies and the courts and proposes a specialist environmental agency. The states however already possess such specialist agencies (such as the Environmental Protection Agency) and, as 'concurrence agencies' under the applicable planning legislation they have veto rights over any proposed development referred to them. He makes a good point nevertheless in stressing that the precautionary principle has nothing to say about the question of economic cost or who should ultimately bear those costs. He argues, I think appropriately, for a system of compensation should the state place reservations on the use of private land (p 120). In other words if the community is the beneficiary or future generations are deemed to be beneficiaries then the community as a whole should bear the cost. Interestingly, some Australian jurisdictions are proceeding in the opposite direction and are reducing the right to compensation.

(6) 'The application of precaution through economics' (*Harding and Fisher*)

The issue considered in this article is central to any rational implementation of the principle of precaution viz economics and the establishment of a balance between the costs to industry and the cost to the environment of damage. The two editors acknowledge (at p 123) that without proper consideration of these economic considerations the doctrine becomes merely an empty statement of principle. They note that the Rio Declaration in Article 15 requires such measures to be commensurate with the nature of individual national economies and for them to be 'cost effective'.

(7) 'The precautionary principle as a key element in ecologically sustainable development' (*MD Young*)

This article provides a most interesting analysis of the *economic* relationship between precaution, ESD, and another broad statement of principle 'inter-generational equity'.

Central to his argument is the traditional problem with any form of cost/benefit analysis that often results in the quite arbitrary choice of a discount rate to assess return on capital over extended time periods. When the same analysis is required to be applied to environmental damage, which may have long-term inter-generational effects, the problem is further compounded at two levels. How to assess the value in the reduction of 'natural capital' and what discount rate should be applied in such situations. Mechanisms are being developed to attempt this however and the writer supports Kula's work on a 'modified discount rate procedure' (Kula, E, *Economics of Natural Resources and the Environment*, 1992, Chapman and Hall).

(8) 'Economic concepts and the precautionary principle and the implementation of safe minimum standards' (*David James*)

Though he covers many of the points also raised by Young, James is prepared to make a case for 'tradable permits' as an economic mechanism to meet environmental objectives. It was refreshing to find some support for this procedure in an amongst so many articles which seem to consign the free market to irrelevance and adopt the classic statist approach that larger regulatory bodies, heavier penalties and strict enforcement are the only mechanisms that can deal with these issues. Personally I would have thought that the history of such bodies is hardly edifying and that if business and commerce, operating through free market mechanisms are effectively excluded from the process then precaution, ESD and other fundamental features of the new environmental law are unlikely ever to be effectively implemented.

(9) 'Ignorance, sustainability, and the precautionary principle: towards an analytical framework' (*Steven Dovers and John Handmer*)

In this article the authors properly describe precaution as a composite of several value-laden notions and loose qualitative descriptors. Its efficacy as an operational tool they consider to be highly doubtful. They describe and criticise the traditional approaches (at p 180) such as quantitative risk assessment, the familiar cost/benefit analyses and the imposition of safe minimum standard preferring 'an analytical framework for ignorance auditing'. The nature and content of this process is given in considerable detail in an appendix (at p 188). Unfortunately the mechanism appears to be so detailed, requiring as it does a complex intellectual interplay between science and social science that one must wonder whether any court would have the time or inclination to come to grips with it.

(10) 'Risk management, reality and the precautionary principle: coping with decisions' (*Gavin McDonell*)

McDonell, in a thought provoking approach, sets out initially to identify the various cognitive states that are applicable to the management of environmental issues. These, in his opinion, reflect the inevitable contingencies of life and are 'a state of risk', 'a state of uncertainty', 'a state of ignorance' and a 'state of indeterminacy'. Rittel and Webber (*Policy Sciences*, 1973) discuss the same issue and describing the underlying issues as 'wicked problems'. McDonell is concerned, justifiably, with the quality and reliability of scientific evidence given in court and proposes that the precautionary principle should incorporate some process for testing scientific reliability. Understandably he leaves that issue for the future. In my opinion, at least some of the difficulties could be alleviated if the courts could directly appoint their own independent experts and not have to rely solely on the suitably compliant evidence tended by the competing parties.

(11) 'Is cleaner production the answer to the precautionary principle?' (*Brian Robinson*)

Robinson makes two points in succinct fashion. Firstly, that cleaner production is an achievable goal and that engineering solutions are often available to substantially reduce or even eliminate waste. He provides a number of examples where such solutions have been successful.

(12) 'The precautionary principle, science and policy' (*Malcolm MacGavin*)

The author draws upon his experiences with The North West European Policy on contaminants in the marine environment and on the basis of this experience, doubts the efficacy of mechanisms other than the establishment of safe minimum standards together with constant monitoring to ensure those standards are met. He believes that we a such a long way from understanding the environmental consequences of any action and that absolute certainty or even integrated and systematic knowledge may be impossible to achieve; a proposition which David Hume would have agreed with in the 18th century. In common with Brian Robinson he sees, as a central mechanism, the establishment of clean production techniques that would be required to cover the 'entire life cycle of the product' (at p 225). MacGavin manages well to supply content to a debate that, without a practical framework, can quickly become arcane or indeed irrelevant. His concluding sentence in his penultimate paragraph (at p 235) is worth quoting: '... monitoring should concentrate simply on assessing whether the reduction targets that are now being set are actually being met. Once this is done, science will be relieved of the impossible and damaging burden of trying to determine ecological effects.' One suspects the courts would be similarly relieved.

(13) 'Chemical assessment and the precautionary principle' (*W Pearse and H Wright*)

Since environmental damage occasioned by the use of chemicals is well known, the inclusion of this article is appropriate. Although developed economies already have in place extensive and intensive assessment procedures the authors correctly point out that the problem of 'threshold' levels always remains. They are quite positive about the regulatory regime currently in place in Australia and are prepared, refreshingly, to concede that many adverse side effects can be effectively managed.

(14) 'Precautionary principles require changes in thinking about and planning environmental sampling' (*AJ Underwood*)

The article explores the consequences of precaution in relation to sampling, experiment and analysis as well as discussing the possibility of error in the interpretation of statistical data. It is a specialist paper and will be of interest to those readers with at least some background in statistics.

(15) 'Top down, ground up or inside out? Community practice and the precautionary principle' (*Valerie Brown*)

The author laments the lack of progress in the Australian states towards the implementation of precautionary strategies. As evidence she cites the fact that the Daintree World Heritage Area in far north Queensland still has no management plan. She could also have pointed out that the new Integrated Planning Act (Qld) still contains no expressed reference to regional planning (beyond the right of local authorities to set up 'Regional Planning Committees') though planning at this level is central to many Inter-governmental agreements. She notes a phenomenon that many of us in the field have commented on privately viz, that the real commitment to precaution and other principles is evident at the local level, in local authorities and from community action groups. At the same time progress at the Commonwealth and State level seems almost intolerably slow given the scale of the task nationwide.

(16) 'The politics of the precautionary principle' (*Tim O'Riordan*)

Instead of dealing with the ultimately ineluctable issue of *politico sensu largo* or 'politics in the large sense', the author chose to discuss the politics of the precautionary principle which I found disappointing because politics, as the 'art of the possible', will always remain the final arbiter of most of the issues referred to in this collection. An article on the political dynamics involved would have been appropriate and added further to the value of this collection.

(17) 'The precautionary principle: towards a deliberative, transdisciplinary problem solving process' (*Fisher and Harding*)

In this, the final article, the editors set out to consider the type of decision-making processes which are relevant to precaution. In summary they propose a 'deliberative' process (presumably in preference to an adversarial one) and provide reasons why such an approach should be adopted. Their second recommendation is that the entire approach should cross lines of discipline and, indeed, this particular suggestion is difficult to argue against. One of the continually expressed criticisms of various Environmental Protection Agencies for example is that they insufficiently incorporate ideas from other disciplines. Ultimately the editors ground both propositions in democratic theory and the idea of the public interest though without apparently being aware of the reservations expressed by James Buchanan (*The Calculus of Consent* 1999, Liberty Fund, Indianapolis) concerning the use of such illusory terms. I do have concern about the editor's final suggestions. How long, for example, will such a process take for completion, could such a process merely add to the compounding of grievances, would such a process ultimately come under the influence of community elites and where in the total scheme do equally valuable concepts such as efficiency and equity come into play?

Summary

'*Perspective on the Precautionary Principle*' sets out to both explain and assess precaution as one of the dominant statements of general principle now applicable by statute in most planning and environment jurisdictions. Though I would have liked to have seen a thorough analysis of what I consider to be the essential role of the corporate and financial sectors and the potential of free market mechanisms rather than the traditional reliance on 'big government', the book succeeds exceptionally well. It will appeal to lawyers struggling to come to terms with statements of general principle, to planners, to many working in disparate areas of social science and increasingly, I believe, to economists and accountants who will have to rather quickly come to terms with this principle at a corporate policy and strategic planning level.

Federation Press and the editors are to be congratulated for this excellent and comprehensive work. It provides the first integrated approach to this important principle and should form part of the libraries of all the groups mentioned above.

Book Review 1

Lianze Ma

CHINESE LAW SERIES

by Luo Wei

Volume 1: The 1997 Criminal Code of the People's Republic of China
William S Hein & Co, Inc, Buffalo, New York, 1998
ISBN 1 57588 398 8

Volume 2: The 1999 Contract Law of the People's Republic of China
William S Hein & Co, Inc, Buffalo, New York, 1999
ISBN 1 57588 490 9

Volume 3: The Amended Criminal Procedure Law and the Criminal Court Rules of the People's Republic of China
William S Hein & Co, Inc, Buffalo, New York, 2000
ISBN 1 57588 491 7

Volume 4: Guide to China Copyright Law Studies
William S Hein & Co, Inc, Buffalo, New York, 2000
ISBN 1 57588 629 4

China's impending entry into the World Trade Organisation makes it more important than ever to understand the Chinese legal system. As an effort to bring its legal system into harmony with international standards, China has recently amended the Criminal Code, the Criminal Procedure Law and the Contract Law.

The *Chinese Law Series* (vols 1, 2 and 3) provide the full text of the newly amended legislation together with the English translation. What should be noted is that these volumes include not only the legislation itself, but also related interpretations and implementing provisions which, in practice, play a critical role in practice.

All of the three volumes follow a similar structure:

- Introduction, including writer's comments on significant changes;
- English translations of legislation, implementing rules and interpretations; and
- Chinese texts of legislation, implementing rules and interpretations.

The Chapter of Introduction in each volume is most useful, in which the learned editor (Mr Luo) has examines the legislative history and any significant changes of the particular legislation in question.

Volume 1 of the *Chinese Law Series* focuses upon major amendments to the Criminal Code which are discussed in the Introduction such as the abolition of the Analogical Approach which enables a person to be convicted for an act in the light of the most analogous article under the special provisions of the present law, even though such an act is not specifically prescribed as a crime under the present law (Art 79 of 1979 Code). Instead Art 3 of 1997 Code states that a person shall not be convicted for an act unless it is deemed a crime by explicit stipulations. This is a considerable development to protect citizen's legal rights and freedom. There is also a change from 'crimes of counterrevolution' to 'crimes of endangering state security'. The old definition of 'counterrevolution' of 'overthrowing the regime of the proletarian dictatorship and the socialist system' has been abandoned. Under the 1997 Code such conducts will be punished under the crime of 'crime of endangering state security'. There has also been the introduction of new provisions and offences, such as computer fraud (Art 285), security fraud (Arts 194–97), and racial hatred (Art 249).

Volume 2 of the *Chinese Law Series* examines significant changes in the 1996 Criminal Procedure Law. Important developments that are examined include the adoption of 'no conviction without court trial'. Article 12 states 'no one shall be found guilty without a court judgment'. Although this adoption does represent a significant development towards the 'rule of law', it does not, in Mr Luo's opinion; mean that the Chinese Criminal Justice System has adopted the Anglo-American principle of the 'presumption of innocence'. There is the provision of more effective protection to criminal suspects by enhancing the attorney's involvement in a case. There is also the abolition of 'custody for investigation' under which police are allowed to detain criminal suspects for investigation without obtaining an arrest warrant. In addition, Mr Luo has also examined enforcement problems and expressed his concerns about the actual implementation of the measures.

Volume 3 of the *Chinese Law Series* examines the new Contract Law. As Mr Luo has pointed out that the most notable new feature is the incorporation of Western principles such as equality, fairness, honesty and faithfulness, which has brought China's contract law closer to its western counterparts. Emphasis must be placed on the implementing rules and interpretations that are more specific and practical.

Thanks to Mr Luo's training in both Chinese law and American law, the English translations in the *Chinese Law Series* are accurate and sometimes beautiful.

Volume 4 of the *Chinese Law Series* by Professor Robert Haibin Hu examines Chinese copyright law. Chapter 1 examines the 1990 copyright law. Chapter 2 contains useful resources for the copyright researcher. Chapter 3 examines Sino-US negotiations for copyright protection. Chapter 4 gives some useful references for keeping up with developments in copyright law. As laws change quickly, some useful web site addresses are included in this chapter.

The *Chinese Law Series* provide a comprehensive, accurate and also very timely texts of Chinese legislation. It is strongly recommended that law students, scholars, legal practitioners and business men should not miss them when studying Chinese laws and doing business with China. They are an indispensable part of any modern law library.

Book Review 2

Jasmine A Sommer

PRIVITY OF CONTRACT

Edited by Robert Merkin

Lloyd's of London Press, London, 2000
ISBN 1 85978 598 0

Robert Merkin's book opens with Viscount Haldane's remark 'that only a person who is a party to a contract can sue on it'. Since they give no consideration, historically, third parties are not a party to the contract and are, therefore, barred from recovery. In contract, consideration moves from the promisee who, in behalf of the third party, may chart the unhappy course between the Scylla and Charybdis of specific performance and estoppel. Merkin analyses how Great Britain's Contracts (Rights of Third Parties) Act, 1999, cuts through this third party conundrum by abrogating the Doctrine of Privity.

Merkin's Appendices include the Act itself, the Law Commission Report No 242, 1996, and the Law Commission Consultation Paper No 121, 1991. The latter examines international third party rights legislation (pp 309–19) and accommodates inter-jurisdictional comparison; for example, the similarities between the Queensland legislation and Roman-Dutch law in South Africa. Britain's 1999 Act draws on the strengths of these jurisdictions but is by no means a panacea. It has not, for example, overridden arcane aspects of the Married Women's Property Act, 1882. Nevertheless, the Act impacts commercial interests fundamentally. Merkin explores its effect on shipping and construction contracts, insurance and professional negligence.

Trusts, agency, joint promisees, assignments, subrogation, covenants, bankers' documentary credits and statutory exceptions to privity preface examination of third party immunity and imposition of burdens. Merkin then discusses themes from the Law Commission Report correlated with the 1999 Act: the promisee's right to enforce a term are juxtaposed with defences available to the promisor; exceptions to the Act, namely, areas in which 'A third party will have no right of enforceability' (pp 133–42) are discussed interactively with arbitration proceedings.

The effect of the 1999 Act is far reaching. For example, it protects rights of third parties to insurance contracts against the right of the maker to vary or revoke the terms (p 245). However, although it enables parties to replicate the advantages of collateral warranties, warrantors are perplexed as to their assignability (p 202).

The Bill for the 1999 Act was introduced to the House of Lords by Lord Irvine of Lairg, who referenced Lord Steyn: 'there is no … reason why the law should deny effectiveness to a contract for the benefit of a third party where that is the expressed intention of the parties' (p 464). Merkin's volume defines how the 1999 Act achieves that objective and its pitfalls. It also shows how the Act will apply in the commercial, insurance, banking and shipping industries. The book is also useful in those jurisdictions that have not reformed the law, as there is a very full survey of the doctrine of privity of contract.

Book Review 3

Oanh Tran

DOMESTIC STRUCTURES AND INTERNATIONAL TRADE: THE UNFAIR TRADE INSTRUMENTS OF THE UNITED STATES AND THE EUROPEAN UNION

by Candido Tomas Garcia Molyneux

Hart Publishing, Oxford and Portland, Oregon, 2001
ISBN 1 85978 598 0

This monograph explores the concept of globalisation and argues that the domestic structures of individual states strongly affects the development of international trade policy, and thus of globalisation. In doing so, the author analyses the domestic structures, social, political and economic, of the United States and the European Union to ascertain the elements that influence their trade policymaking. He then discusses a few of their more recent international trade agreements in the light of such structures.

The book is divided into a few parts, and those parts into chapters. The introduction (Chapter 1) deals with the theoretical grounding upon which the author bases his later arguments. He discusses the constraints of a state's actions pursuant to the international sphere. Such constraints are convincingly argued as being a polemic between the pursuit of defined goals and the reality of a state's domestic structures, most particularly its process of decision-making. Thus, the constitution and history of a state are seen as shackling its ability to act powerfully in the international fora. This polemic is expressed in the Unfair Trade Instruments of the United States and the European Union.

In the first part (Chapters 2 and 3), the author analyses the United States domestic structure and its reflection in the Unfair Trade Agreements, focusing particularly on the Uruguay Round Agreement on Research and Development Subsidies. The author strongly rejected an ahistorical approach to analysing domestic structures. His exposition on the workings of the United States government, the inefficiency of the separation of powers doctrine in relation to implementation of international agreements, the plurality and extreme liberalisation of the United States' domestic economy are well researched and very useful. He also controversially conceives the United States' trade policy as weak and inefficient due to its maintenance of the ideal of free trade, the problem of a schismatic Congress and a policy of ad hoc protectionism resulting in the inability to form coherent long term international trade policy and thereby retain its world hegemony. This same argument is supported by his analysis of the Uruguay Round Agreement on Research and Development Subsidies. The subsequent 'scaling down' of its broadened effects due to the threat that such an agreement was perceived to have on United States' domestic industries was shown to be indicative of the negative effects of powerful groups within Congress.

In the second part (Chapters 4 and 5), the author analyses the European Union's domestic structure, highlighting its diverse and fractious nature. The difficulty in forming a single coherent trade policy is argued as greater for the European Union as it attempts to balance the interests of all its different members. The problems particularly highlighted by the author are the apparent conservative and inert approach to international policy and the inability of the European Union to exert influence due to its 'soft approach'. The author assesses France and Germany in particular. He analyses their domestic structures, their self-assertion in the European Union and the consequent effects on the European Economic Community's policies. He argues that the fractious nature of the European Union leads to the development and adoption of 'second best policies' and the consequent failure to implement the aims of its member states.

As with the United States, the author uses specific examples of unfair trade instruments to support and strengthen his theoretical arguments. The Common Commercial Policy, which the European Union developed, is shown to be inefficient and often ineffective in implementing the goals of the European Economic Community. Furthermore, he shows that the interplay of power struggles and the uncertainty of problem solving mechanisms continue to undermine the efficiency of the European Economic Community. The author analyses the Audio Tapes in Cassettes Panel, thereby including in his analysis of states, Japan's domestic structures and international actions. This highlighted the problems that different market and domestic structures cause to international trade consensus. Finally, he analyses the Trade Barriers Regulations. The author conceives the regulations as an expression of the European Union's internal problems. He argues that its narrow scope and the effect of its strict commitment to adhere to international trade laws means that the European Union is unable to be an influential actor on the rules of international trade.

In his conclusion, the author reiterates his argument – that the domestic markets, constitutional arrangements and socio-political issues of a state shackles its own power in the international sphere. Furthermore, he argues that globalisation is unable to eliminate the structural differences between states and hence the 'thin Anglo-Saxon homogeneity' of both the international system and the European Union. The US has previously imposed its own market system and rules onto the international system and will probably continue to do so. The author argues that the present decision making process of the European Union means that it cannot impose its own rules onto the international trade system, nor affect new arenas of international trade, such as intellectual property.

This book is impressively and thoroughly argued and the author succeeds in convincing of his convictions regarding the problems of globalisation and a state's inability to deal with the same. Although his analysis is most impressive, the analysis would be strengthened had he suggested an alternative to the present situation that would create the efficient world stage that he envisages in his writing. However, overall this book and the arguments made are significant and a worthwhile addition to the literature.

Book Review 4

Peter McDermott

INTERNATIONAL TRUSTS:
TRUSTS IN PRIME JURISDICTIONS

Edited by Alon Kaplan

Kluwer Law International, The Hague, London, Boston, 2000
ISBN 90 411 9815 6

MODERN INTERNATIONAL DEVELOPMENTS IN TRUST LAW

Edited by David Hayton

Kluwer Law International, The Hague, London, Boston, 1999
ISBN 90 411 9706 0

In many respects both *Trusts in Prime Jurisdictions* and *Modern International Developments in Trust Law* are complementary works that are essential references to understand the use of trusts in the modern globalised economy. The first text looks at the use of trusts in 15 countries where trusts are used. Trusts are used for a variety of reasons such as asset protection, forced heirship issues and for tax and estate planning. Trusts are also used for other specific purposes. Both Trusts in Prime Jurisdictions and Modern International Developments in Trust Law contain a revision of Professor Hayton's Amakasu lecture on 'The Use of Trusts in the Commercial Context'. In Trusts in Prime Jurisdictions Douglas James has written an interesting chapter that focuses upon the use of UK trusts for holding works of art and chattels. In most Western economies trusts will also be the vehicle for holding pension funds.

Trusts in Prime Jurisdictions contains a number of interesting essays that focus on taxation. The book contains examines the taxation of trusts in the United Kingdom, the United States of America, Canada and Australia. Of great interest is the essay by Citron on the UK tax treatment of offshore trusts. The book also most adequately deals with trusts in the classic 'tax havens' as there are essays on the Bahamas, the British Virgin Islands, the Cayman Islands and Guernsey. Because of the use of trusts in tax minimisation the chapter by Richard Hay also refers to OECD initiatives in this field. Professor

David Hayton in his *Modern International Developments in Trust Law* concludes that offshore trusts 'are going to have a tough time in the twenty-first century'.

Modern International Developments in Trust Law focuses on the fundamental structural issues concerning trusts such as issues of confidentiality and enforcement rights by beneficiaries. A number of chapters examine the topical issue of law reform of the legislation that governs trustees. Professor David Hayton has written an interesting essay on the modernisation of the Trustee Act 1925 (Eng) as well as looking at modern trust law reform in the United Kingdom. These contributions are helpful for anybody desiring to appreciate the context for the passage of the Trustee Act 2000. The essay by Professor Donovan Waters QC focuses on the revision of trustee legislation in the United Kingdom.

Kluwer Law International has again done the legal profession a great service by the publication of these useful texts that should be in the library of every law school and certainly every trusts lawyer. These works would assist any reader to gain an understanding of the modern use of trusts.

Book Review 5

Peter McDermott

SCHMITTHOFF'S EXPORT TRADE, THE LAW AND PRACTICE OF INTERNATIONAL TRADE

by Leo D'Arcy, Carole Murray and Barbara Cleave

10th edition, London: Sweet & Maxwell, 2000
ISBN 0 421 54680 8

The last edition of this work was published in 1990 when the late Professor Clive Schmitthoff passed away. Although the book has been reprinted in 1995 important developments in international trade have necessitated the publication of this edition. For this purpose the work has been kept up-to-date under a new editorial team of an academic and practicing barristers. The book has monitored important developments in international trade law; some of those developments will be mentioned in this review.

There have been a number of reasons why the work had to be revised. One reason why a new edition of *Schmitthoff* was clearly warranted was the introduction of new measures for the finance of exports. The 1993 version of the Uniform Customs and Practice for Documentary Credits, the 1995 revised Uniform Rules for Collections and the 1992 Uniform Rules for Demand Guarantees are fully discussed in this edition of *Schmitthoff.* Since the last edition there have been a number of changes to international dispute resolution law. The Contracts (Applicable Law) Act 1990 which incorporates the Rome Convention as well as the Arbitration Act 1996 and the Brussels and Lugano Conventions are dealt with in this edition.

The new chapter on electronic commerce deals with the Electronic Commerce Act 2000 which facilitates electronic communication. Another matter of note in this edition is the new approach to the duty of disclosure in contracts of marine insurance. In *Pan Atlantic Insurance Co Ltd v Pine Top Insurance Co Ltd* [1994] 2 Lloyd's Rep 427 it was held that the insurer was entitled to avoid the contract if the non-disclosure induced the making of the contract. Recent cases in which *Pan Atlantic* has been applied in cases of a material misrepresentation are highlighted in this edition.

This reviewer still reads with some nostalgia the passages in *Schmitthoff* that deal with bills of lading. It was by such research that the book became such an authoritative work in relation to international trade law. Modern developments relating to the carriage of goods by air or sea are discussed.

Schmitthoff should continue to be consulted as a first point of reference by anybody who desires to gain an appreciation of international trade law.

Book Review 6

Alan Davidson

ELECTRONIC COMMERCE AND THE LAW

by Jay Forder and Patrick Quirk

John Wiley and Sons, Brisbane, Australia
ISBN 0 471 34164 9

International traders have embraced electronic commerce with fervour, extracting efficiencies, streamlining practices and realising opportunities. Electronic Commerce courses and even specialist degrees have emerged as a result of considerable demand. The law has tended to respond to the electronic revolution rather than lead. Queensland academics Jay Forder and Patrick Quirk and a team of specialist chapter writers have produced a splendid text in response to this revolution.

The text is clearly designed for the substantial student commercial law market. The stated aim is to 'provide a resource for all students in e-commerce whether they have a business information technology or legal background'. As such the authors have assumed readers possess no prior knowledge of the legal system or the internet. Both legal and computer jargon is avoided. As a result the use of case law is minimal and case analysis is sparing. Absent is a case index and a legislation index.

The first two chapters contain introductory material dealing with the internet, the Australian legal system, national and international frameworks. Because these chapters are by different authors there is a slight duplication dealing with the Australian legal system.

Substantive topics include introductory business and commercial issues such as contractual issues relating to electronic commerce and the important matters of security, authentication and digital signatures. Other topics include privacy and the securities industry.

Forder and Quirk have drawn on specialists for the authorship of chapters dealing with electronic payments systems, cyberbanking, taxation issues, intellectual property issues, in particular trade marks and domain names, consumer protection and on-line gambling. The style of the writing of these chapters naturally varies, however, the overall approach by including graphics, text boxes, extracts and figures has been standardised. This approach reflects the demand by business schools that demonstrate a preference for the cataloguing of topics and concepts in standardised layouts. The inserts are eye catching, relevant and informative. However, occasionally their inclusion interrupts the logical flow of ideas.

Because the book is designed to be a text for students studying electronic commerce law, each chapter commences with specified 'Learning Outcomes', which both summarise the content and outline the underlying purpose of each chapter. In a similar vein every chapter concludes with a summary, a series of discussion questions, a list of further reading material and a case study. As such tertiary course co-ordinators will find ready made tutorial questions, problems and the foundations for assignments.

The substantive issues are dealt with comprehensively within the context of a student's text on legal foundations in electronic commerce. The thirteen chapters are thorough and will fit neatly into appropriate tertiary education courses. The text includes a convenient glossary and a list of useful websites.

Two final minor concerns remain. First, the very nature of electronic commerce law is that legislation and new case law emerges literally daily. There are several aspects of the book that were out of date by the time it could be printed. For example the text refers to the New South Wales and Victorian versions of the federal Electronic Transactions Act 1999 but could not mention all that every other state and territory had passed similar legislation by the time the book was in fact released. Again this is not the fault of the authors. Last, and probably least, the decision to publish all text, figures and graphics in a purple ink has troubled a number of readers prompting several comments to this writer.

Electronic Commerce and the Law fills a gap that has been growing as quickly as the implementation of electronic commerce practices in business and industry. It is to be welcomed by industry players, electronic business parties and lawyers alike for addressing and meeting issues in the regulation in electronic commerce. For the professional lawyer, the text provides an excellent introduction to the important electronic commerce notions and to the emerging legal regulation.

Book Notice

LUMB AND MOENS' THE CONSTITUTION OF THE COMMONWEALTH OF AUSTRALIA ANNOTATED

by Gabriël Moens and John Trone

Sydney, Australia: Butterworths, 2001
ISBN 0 409 31442 0

It is welcome to have a new edition of this well known work. This book deals with all of the important constitutional developments that concern commerce such as the *Ha* case concerning an excise duty. The work should be consulted as a first reference point by anybody interested in Australian constitutional law.